(Continue

Dictionary of Literary Biography® • Volume One Hundred Fifty-Six

British Short-Fiction Writers, 1880–1914: The Romantic Tradition

British Short-Fiction Writers, 1880–1914: The Romantic Tradition

Edited by
William F. Naufftus
Winthrop University

A Bruccoli Clark Layman Book
Gale Research Inc.
Detroit, Washington, D.C., London

Printed in the United States of America

Published simultaneously in the United Kingdom
by Gale Research International Limited
(An affiliated company of Gale Research Inc.)

The paper used in this publication meets the minimum requirements
of American National Standard for Information Sciences–Permanence
Paper for Printed Library Materials, ANSI Z39.48-1984. ∞ ™

Library of Congress Cataloging-in-Publication Data

British short-fiction writers, 1880–1914: the romantic tradition / edited by William F. Naufftus.
    p. cm. – (Dictionary of literary biography; v. 156)
"A Bruccoli Clark Layman book."
Includes bibliographical references and index.
ISBN 0-8103-5717-8 (alk. paper)
    1. Short stories, English – Bio-bibliography. 2. Authors, English – 19th century – Biography –
Dictionaries. 3. Authors, English – 20th century – Biography – Dictionaries. 4. English fiction – 19th
century – Bio-bibliography. 5. English fiction – 20th century – Bio-bibliography. 6. English fiction –
19th century – Dictionaries. 7. English fiction – 20th century – Dictionaries. 8. Short stories, English –
Dictionaries. 9. Romanticism – Great Britain – Bio-bibliography. 10. Romanticism – Great Britain –
Dictionaries. I. Naufftus, William F. II. Series.
PR829.B744 1995
823'.010908 – dc20   95–22179
[B]   CIP

10 9 8 7 6 5 4 3 2 1

In memory of my parents, Franklin Alexander Naufftus
and Daisy Katherine Naufftus

Contents

Plan of the Series

. . . Almost the most prodigious asset of a country, and perhaps its most precious possession, is its native literary product — when that product is fine and noble and enduring.

Mark Twain*

The advisory board, the editors, and the publisher of the *Dictionary of Literary Biography* are joined in endorsing Mark Twain's declaration. The literature of a nation provides an inexhaustible resource of permanent worth. We intend to make literature and its creators better understood and more accessible to students and the reading public, while satisfying the standards of teachers and scholars.

To meet these requirements, *literary biography* has been construed in terms of the author's achievement. The most important thing about a writer is his writing. Accordingly, the entries in *DLB* are career biographies, tracing the development of the author's canon and the evolution of his reputation.

The purpose of *DLB* is not only to provide reliable information in a convenient format but also to place the figures in the larger perspective of literary history and to offer appraisals of their accomplishments by qualified scholars.

The publication plan for *DLB* resulted from two years of preparation. The project was proposed to Bruccoli Clark by Frederick C. Ruffner, president of the Gale Research Company, in November 1975. After specimen entries were prepared and typeset, an advisory board was formed to refine the entry format and develop the series rationale. In meetings held during 1976, the publisher, series editors, and advisory board approved the scheme for a comprehensive biographical dictionary of persons who contributed to North American literature. Editorial work on the first volume began in January 1977, and it was published in 1978. In order to make *DLB* more than a reference tool and to compile volumes that individually have claim to status as literary history, it was decided to organize vol-

umes by topic, period, or genre. Each of these free-standing volumes provides a biographical-bibliographical guide and overview for a particular area of literature. We are convinced that this organization — as opposed to a single alphabet method — constitutes a valuable innovation in the presentation of reference material. The volume plan necessarily requires many decisions for the placement and treatment of authors who might properly be included in two or three volumes. In some instances a major figure will be included in separate volumes, but with different entries emphasizing the aspect of his career appropriate to each volume. Ernest Hemingway, for example, is represented in *American Writers in Paris, 1920–1939* by an entry focusing on his expatriate apprenticeship; he is also in *American Novelists, 1910–1945* with an entry surveying his entire career. Each volume includes a cumulative index of the subject authors and articles. Comprehensive indexes to the entire series are planned.

With volume ten in 1982 it was decided to enlarge the scope of *DLB*. By the end of 1986 twenty-one volumes treating British literature had been published, and volumes for Commonwealth and Modern European literature were in progress. The series has been further augmented by the *DLB Yearbooks* (since 1981) which update published entries and add new entries to keep the *DLB* current with contemporary activity. There have also been *DLB Documentary Series* volumes which provide biographical and critical source materials for figures whose work is judged to have particular interest for students. One of these companion volumes is entirely devoted to Tennessee Williams.

We define literature as the *intellectual commerce of a nation:* not merely as belles lettres but as that ample and complex process by which ideas are generated, shaped, and transmitted. *DLB* entries are not limited to "creative writers" but extend to other figures who in their time and in their way influenced the mind of a people. Thus the series encompasses historians, journalists, publishers, and screenwriters. By this means readers of *DLB* may be aided to perceive literature not as cult scripture in the keeping of intellectual high

From an unpublished section of Mark Twain's autobiography, copyright by the Mark Twain Company

priests but firmly positioned at the center of a nation's life.

DLB includes the major writers appropriate to each volume and those standing in the ranks immediately behind them. Scholarly and critical counsel has been sought in deciding which minor figures to include and how full their entries should be. Wherever possible, useful references are made to figures who do not warrant separate entries.

Each *DLB* volume has a volume editor responsible for planning the volume, selecting the figures for inclusion, and assigning the entries. Volume editors are also responsible for preparing, where appropriate, appendices surveying the major periodicals and literary and intellectual movements for their volumes, as well as lists of further readings. Work on the series as a whole is coordinated at the Bruccoli Clark Layman editorial center in Columbia, South Carolina, where the editorial staff is responsible for accuracy of the published volumes.

One feature that distinguishes *DLB* is the illustration policy – its concern with the iconography of literature. Just as an author is influenced by his surroundings, so is the reader's understanding of the author enhanced by a knowledge of his environment. Therefore *DLB* volumes include not only drawings, paintings, and photographs of authors, often depicting them at various stages in their careers, but also illustrations of their families and places where they lived. Title pages are regularly reproduced in facsimile along with dust jackets for modern authors. The dust jackets are a special feature of *DLB* because they often document better than anything else the way in which an author's work was perceived in its own time. Specimens of the writers' manuscripts are included when feasible.

Samuel Johnson rightly decreed that "The chief glory of every people arises from its authors." The purpose of the *Dictionary of Literary Biography* is to compile literary history in the surest way available to us – by accurate and comprehensive treatment of the lives and work of those who contributed to it.

The *DLB* Advisory Board

Introduction

The period 1880–1914 has an emphatic conclusion with the beginning of World War I but a less obvious beginning. A whole world perished in the carnage and squalor of the trenches in World War I, and almost every thinking person in England realized that nothing would ever be the same again. However, 1880 also marks the approximate end of one age and the beginning of another. The deaths of George Eliot in 1880, of Thomas Carlyle and Benjamin Disraeli in 1881, and of Anthony Trollope in 1882 removed four well-known figures of Victorian letters. The triumph of Gladstonian Liberalism in the 1880 election set the stage for the final establishment of democracy and the founding of the modern welfare state. The British conquest of Egypt in 1882 showed that even Liberals could not resist the urge to expand the empire, and the founding of the Society for Psychic Research in the same year showed that the Victorian religious crisis had reached its final stage. If one looks behind these isolated events at the political, social, and intellectual life of the period as a whole, three trends seem most significant: the political and social reforms largely sponsored by the Liberal Party, the New Imperialism primarily championed by the Conservatives, and the advance of science and technology combined with secularism and materialism. All of these developments influenced the short fiction produced in these years. The same reformist zeal that animated the Liberal Party produced a large body of fiction dealing with the ills of society. The New Imperialism of the Conservatives was similarly reflected in the large number of stories celebrating, or at least set in, the expanding empire. Science and secularism inspired both the positive literary tribute of science fiction and a negative reaction most obviously seen in the enormous popularity of ghost stories.

In politics, the era began with the defeat of Disraeli's Conservatives by William Gladstone and the Liberals in 1880, followed shortly by Disraeli's death the next year, making way for Robert Cecil, third Marquis of Salisbury's leadership of the Conservative Party. The two great political parties each governed Britain for approximately seventeen of the thirty-four years of this period, but it both began and ended with Liberal governments passing a series of reform bills designed to reduce economic inequality and redistribute political power. Gladstone's second ministry (1880–1885) passed the first Employers Liability Act in 1880, followed by the Irish Land Act, which limited rents, in 1881; the Married Woman's Property Act in 1882; the Franchise Act, which extended universal male suffrage to rural districts, in 1884; and in 1885 the Redistribution Act, which substituted election districts of equal population for the ancient boroughs and counties. His brief third ministry (1886) and his fourth ministry (1892–1895) split the Liberal Party in unsuccessful efforts to pass Irish Home Rule bills, leading to a decade of Conservative governments from 1895 to 1905.

But when the Liberals returned to office in 1905, first under Sir Henry Campbell-Bannerman and then Herbert Asquith, the parade of reform bills resumed. Some were meant to benefit the poor and the working classes, beginning with the Trade Disputes Act, protecting labor unions from lawsuits, in 1906 and proceeding to the Old Age Pension Law (1909), the National Insurance Act (1911), and the Minimum Wage Law (1912). Two other reforms, designed to redistribute political power, provoked crises. The Parliament Act of 1911, which eliminated the veto power of the House of Lords, was only accepted by the Lords after the king expressed his willingness to create enough new Liberal peers to guarantee passage. The final passage of the Irish Home Rule Bill in 1914 caused a British Army mutiny at Curragh near Dublin and threatened civil war in Ulster until the outbreak of World War I caused the government to postpone action on Home Rule.

Throughout the period, militant workers, Irish nationalists, and suffragettes encouraged Liberal reforms by demonstrating that they deemed the concessions already made insufficient. Workers rioted in Trafalgar Square in 1887, formed the Miner's Federation of Great Britain in 1888, carried out the London dock strike of 1889, created the Independent Labor Party in 1893, and staged a series of strikes in 1911 and 1912 – most notably those of railway workers and coal miners. Various groups of Irish nationalists murdered Lord Frederick Cavendish in Phoenix Park in Dublin in 1882, set off dynamite explosions in London in 1885, continually agitated in the House of Commons for Home Rule, and ultimately staged the Easter Rebellion in Dublin in 1916. The one important group that did not win notable concessions from the government was the women's suffrage movement, and the last years before World War I were marked by the increasingly violent protests of the Women's Social and Political Union under the leadership of Emmeline Pankhurst. Suffragettes attacked the Houses of Parliament in 1909, hurling stones through windows and battling police. After the Liberal Conciliation Bill failed to pass in 1910, they went on hunger strikes in jail, smashed shop windows, and set fire to mailboxes. Finally, on 4 June 1913, Emily Davison threw herself in front of the king's racehorse on Derby Day at the Epsom Racecourse and died of injuries a few days later.

Liberal reforms were, among other things, attempts to maintain social and political stability in the face of chronic threats of violence from within the British Isles. The Conservative Party, on the other hand, was primarily interested in military and economic threats from outside, and its answer was imperial expansion. The British Empire had existed for hundreds of years, and most of it was already in place by 1880. But the empire had never been an important literary topic or had much popular appeal during most of this period. As late as 1840 Thomas Babington Macaulay had complained in his essay on Robert Clive, the great empire-builder in eighteenth-century India, about the average Englishman's ignorance of and indifference to the epic of British India. This situation was changing rapidly by 1880. Disraeli's Royal Titles Act (1876) gave Queen Victoria the romantic title of Empress of India, and British heroics in the 1877 Zulu War and the Second Afghan War (1878-1881) were well advertised and eagerly discussed at home. The strength of the imperial impulse, however, could only be properly appreciated when in 1882 Gladstone, a foe of imperial expansion, felt forced to intervene in Egypt, sending an army to occupy Cairo and beginning a chapter in British imperialism that did not completely end until the Suez crisis of 1956. He refused to annex Sudan as well, with the result that the popular British general Charles "Chinese" Gordon was killed in 1885 when Khartoum fell to Moslem rebels under Muhammad Ahmad, the "Mahdi." Public outrage at the abandonment of

General Gordon was one of several factors that brought down Gladstone's second ministry, giving Lord Salisbury and the Conservatives six months in office in 1885-1886.

This first Salisbury ministry lasted just long enough to preside over the Third Burmese War and the addition of Upper Burma to the empire. His second ministry (1886-1892) and his third (1895-1902), followed by another Conservative government under Arthur Balfour (1902-1905), accomplished much more. The parade of new colonies, protectorates, condominiums, and other forms of imperial possession was the Tory equivalent of the Liberal Party's steady stream of reform legislation. Shortly after Salisbury began his second ministry, Anglo-French condominium was declared in the New Hebrides, followed by acquisition – through treaty, conquest, or both – of Sarawak and North Borneo (1888); Uganda (1890); British Samoa (1891); Kenya (1895); the Sudan (1896-1898); Tonga (1900); Ashantiland (1901); and Northern Nigeria (1903).

Liberal support for reform legislation forced the Tories to come up with some reforms of their own, while Conservative enthusiasm for the empire made it all but impossible for the Liberals not to be imperialists too. Salisbury's first government passed the Ashbourne Act of 1885 to help Irish tenant farmers purchase the land they worked, and Balfour began his Conservative ministry with the Education Act of 1902, which brought all secondary education under state control. Similarly, Gladstone's reluctant occupation of Egypt in 1882 was followed by his establishment of British Somaliland and British New Guinea in 1884. In addition, the development of the "white" empire continued under both parties, with Australia becoming the second self-governing dominion, after Canada, under the Tories in 1901 and New Zealand (1907) and South Africa (1908) achieving Dominion status when Liberals governed Britain.

The New Imperialism was an international phenomenon, with England competing in a scramble for colonies with France, Germany, Russia, Italy, Japan, and the United States. But while its primary focus was to position Great Britain advantageously for competition with other countries, it also had domestic political value. With its romantic appeal to Britons of all classes, the empire was as much a source of national unity as was Liberal social reform legislation. Welsh coal miners, Irish tenant farmers, London dockworkers, and voteless women throughout the British Isles could all feel pride in being part of the greatest empire in the history of the world. Those who required more egalitarian societies could always emigrate to Australia, Canada, or some other part of the empire.

The increasing secularization of British life was not caused by government bills and acts, but its advance can to a certain extent be traced by such legislation. In 1880 the professed atheist Thomas Bradlaugh was elected to Parliament and, after being rejected by the House of Commons several times, was finally allowed to take his seat in 1886, thus ending the connection between religious profession and Parliament and completing the process begun by the abolition of the Test Act (1828), Catholic Emancipation (1829), and the removal of Jewish disabilities (1858). Parliamentary acts also disestablished the Anglican Church of Ireland (1869), removed religious exclusions of non-Anglican students and faculty at Oxford and Cambridge (1871), and disestablished Anglicanism in Wales (1914). These assaults on the Established Church were often supported by devout Christians in other denominations, but they were also supported by the religiously skeptical and indifferent and at least coincided with a general decline in religious faith and observance throughout Britain. The word *agnostic* was first coined by Thomas Henry Huxley in 1869 and in 1876 appeared in the title of Leslie Stephen's *An Agnostic's Apology*. The spread of doubts even to the strongholds of Anglicanism was demonstrated when several Oxford Anglo-Catholic scholars published *Lux Mundi* (1889), a collection of essays arguing for the need for Christians to accept the findings of modern Biblical criticism. Similarly, Arthur Balfour, the future prime minister, decided that even religious faith was best defended by doubt, and his *A Defence of Philosophic Doubt* (1879) argued for faith by suggesting doubts about the reality of the material world. The fact that so many Protestant English Liberals would side against Irish Protestants on the Home Rule question was simply one more indication of the secularization of British public life.

This process of secularization was accompanied and to some extent assisted by dramatic advances in science and technology. Recent historians of British imperial decline have often looked to this period for the ultimate sources of the collapse of British power after 1945, but the average English citizen of the time was probably more impressed by the enormous progress of technology than by the fact that most of the discoveries were originating abroad. From the United States, in the years immediately before 1880, had come the telephone (1876), the development of hydroelectric power and

the phonograph (1877), the dynamo (1878), and the electric light bulb (1879). Motion pictures were invented by Thomas Edison in 1887, and the film and kinetoscope that enabled them to be projected in theaters were invented by George Eastman by 1889. Other American developments included the linotype (1895), the straight-line printing press (1889), the airplane (1903), and the mass-produced automobile (1909). In Germany the first electric trolley car was developed by Werner Siemens in 1879, the internal combustion engine by Gottlieb Daimler in 1886, the heavy oil engine by Rudolf Diesel in 1895, the gyroscope by Ludwig Obry in 1896, and the airship by Graf Ferdinand von Zeppelin in 1898, with passenger service available by 1910. The major Italian contribution was Guglielmo Marconi's wireless telegraph (1895), while the French concentrated on military innovations, developing the first successful submarine (1885), smokeless gunpowder (1886), and rapid-fire artillery (1897). Faced with such formidable competition, British technology was respectable but no longer the leader, producing the steam turbine, the pneumatic rubber tire, and the Maxim machine gun (all between 1880 and 1884), as well as the first modern battleship, HMS *Dreadnought,* in 1906.

Advances in medicine and physics were often more theoretical than practical in this period, but they increased the prestige of the natural sciences and of the rationalism and materialism often associated with them. While cures or even preventive drugs sometimes had to wait, this period saw the discoveries of the germs responsible for typhoid and malaria (1880), tuberculosis (1882), diphtheria (1883), cholera (1884), and bubonic plague (1894). More immediately useful medical advances included Louis Pasteur's vaccinations for rabies (1881) and hydrophobia (1885) and Emil von Behring's diphtheria serum (1894). Important steps toward prevention came when it was established that plague was transmitted by fleas from rats (1894), malaria and yellow fever by mosquitoes (1900), and typhoid by lice (1913). The only comparable achievement of British medicine was Sir Frederick Hopkins's discovery of vitamins in 1906. Similarly, though Ernest Rutherford and Frederick Soddy made important advances in physics, this field was dominated by German and French scientists, including Wilhelm Roentgen, Max Planck, Albert Einstein, and Marie and Pierre Curie.

Both the form and the content of British fiction showed the influence of these political, social, and intellectual trends, with changes in fictional form being the most dramatic. With the deaths of

Eliot and Trollope, British letters lost the last great practitioners of the Victorian realistic three-decker novel. Shorter novels were already becoming common by 1880, and the old three-volume format disappeared almost completely after Mudie's and W. H. Smith's circulating libraries announced in 1894 that they would no longer purchase them. As the novels became shorter, so did the short fiction. British short fiction throughout most of the nineteenth century was dominated by what Wendell Harris has called the "sophisticated tale": a rather loosely structured shorter version of the three-decker novel. These short fictions – Charles Dickens's "A Christmas Carol" (1843) is the best known today – have, as Harris points out, "a kind of richness of character, situation, or narrative style possible only in more leisurely storytelling"; but their strengths and weaknesses are different from those of the modern short story. Harris sees George Meredith, Henry James, and Thomas Hardy all carrying this form into the late nineteenth century, but the modern short story, with its tight structure and characteristic unity of effect, became dominant in Britain during these years. Its first appearance is usually said to be Robert Louis Stevenson's "A Lodging for the Night" (1877). A decade later Rudyard Kipling began his career as a writer of short stories – generally much shorter than Stevenson's – and in 1891 Arthur Conan Doyle's phenomenally popular *The Adventures of Sherlock Holmes* began to appear in the *Strand*. It is worth noting that the first appearance of Holmes in the novel *A Study in Scarlet* (1887) had caused little excitement. It was the short stories, which began appearing almost four years later, that made Holmes (and Doyle) famous. By 1893 the young H. G. Wells announced in an essay on "The Future of Literature" in the *Pall Mall Gazette* that the future demanded "a spray of short stories instead of a Niagara of narrative, in which respect Mr. Rudyard Kipling is in advance of his age." By 1900 even James was having difficulty placing long tales because magazine editors wanted stories to be under five thousand words rather than the fifteen thousand to thirty thousand that he preferred.

The importance of magazines illustrates the way fiction was affected by both the Liberal reform legislation and the technological developments of the age. One Liberal social reform was the 1880 act making elementary education compulsory for children between the ages of seven and ten, thus furthering developments begun with the Elementary Education Act of 1870. These and later reforms produced an enormous new class of readers who were literate but not very prosperous, erudite, or bookish. They generally wanted their reading to be inexpensive, intellectually accessible to those whose formal educations were modest, and capable of completion in the relatively short amounts of time that they could devote to their leisure activities. Short stories and novellas serialized or printed whole in mass-circulation magazines could answer all of these needs. Furthermore, the development of the linotype and other inventions mechanizing the process of printing meant that illustrated magazines and newspapers could be produced more rapidly and less expensively than even a few years earlier.

Thus the *Strand,* which began publication in January 1891, sold for sixpence and soon had a circulation of 500,000. It focused on short stories and was the most popular magazine in England, but it had several competitors. Three writers included in this volume were themselves editors, for several years each, of prominent monthly magazines in which they published their own work: Mary Elizabeth Braddon of *Belgravia,* Charlotte Riddell of *St. James Magazine,* and Frank Harris of the *Fortnightly Review.* Other popular magazines that carried short fiction included *Black and White, Cassell's,* the *Cornhill Magazine, Macmillan's Magazine,* and *Temple Bar.* In the 1850s William Morris had edited and contributed to *The Oxford and Cambridge Magazine,* but this privately published and short-lived Pre-Raphaelite journal had little in common with the later mass-circulation monthlies. It does, however, bear comparison – in its aesthetic orientation, its specialized audience, and its short career – to later "decadent" periodicals such as the *Yellow Book* and the *Savoy.* Few volumes of short fiction were published in these years without prior periodical publication, usually in monthly magazines.

The themes, settings, and purposes of British short fiction during this period varied enormously; but the stories can be loosely categorized as realistic or romantic. The realists are the subject of *DLB 135: British Short-Fiction Writers, 1880–1914: The Realist Tradition,* but a brief summary is appropriate here. These writers often shared the concerns of social reformers in the Liberal and Labor parties. The cause of reform legislation was powerfully assisted by realistic fiction, which hauntingly presented the abuses of Victorian and Edwardian society, though some of the reforms were not brought about until later. The editor of the *Dictionary of Literary Biography* volume on realistic short-fiction writers from 1880 to 1914, William B. Thesing, finds that their social criticism focuses on three topics: the problems of marriage as an institution, the sufferings of the poor and the working class, and the problems created by women's changing legal, social, and economic status. Important writers of realistic short fiction in this period include Arnold Bennett, Hubert Crackenthorpe, Ella D'Arcy, George Gissing, W. W. Jacobs, George Moore, Arthur Morrison, Barry Pain, and Eden Phillpotts.

Despite their considerable merits, these were not the most popular writers of short fiction in this period – in part at least because their chosen topics were not likely to provide the favorite reading of the newly literate masses. Lower-middle-class clerks or shopgirls did not need to read about slums from which they may recently have escaped and to which bad health or bad luck could again consign them quickly. Neither were unhappy marriages or mistreated women likely to be their leisure reading of choice. Such readers – and the many middle-class readers who joined them in buying the monthly magazines – would be much more likely to find their sustenance in Anthony Hope's stories about high society, Kipling's tales of India, Wells's scientific adventures, Doyle's detective mysteries, or Algernon Blackwood's ghost stories – all of which are clearly more romantic than realistic.

Romantic is a notoriously slippery term to define, but examples of romanticism are not difficult to recognize. Many different romantic traits can be seen in British short fiction between 1880 and 1914: sentimentalism and aestheticism, fantasy and the supernatural, mystery and adventure, love of the historical past and enthusiasm for the geographically remote. Two basic impulses are, however, dominant: the reassertion of the spiritual and the appeal of the exotic. In *The Last Romantics* (1947) Graham Hough memorably summarized the cause of the first of these forms of romanticism: "In spite of the real probity and sobriety of public life, national ideals were becoming more and more material: in spite of a prevailing and genuine devoutness, spontaneous and imaginative religious experience was harder than ever to come by: in spite of material progress, the world was getting steadily uglier." Neither the material squalor of the actual industrial city nor the future material prosperity sought in different ways by industrialists and social reformers seemed attractive to readers or writers who regretted the disappearance of God. The short fiction of this period provides little in the way of Christian apologetics but a great deal in presumably compensatory spiritualism and supernaturalism.

The first short stories to register this protest against materialism constitute what Wendell Harris

has called "aesthetic fiction." Beginning with a single story by Dante Gabriel Rossetti and a series of stories by Morris in the 1850s, these stories often, says Harris, "present a theory of art or simply pay homage to an artist." As the tradition continued, however, in Stevenson's "A Lodging for the Night" and Pater's *Imaginary Portraits* (1887) and later in the works of Oscar Wilde, John Addington Symonds, Bernard Capes, and Vernon Lee (Violet Paget), aestheticism is less the subject matter than the way the subject is treated. In Harris's words this treatment is "a special kind of impressionism: an attempt to render the writer's intense impression not of the actual world he has experienced but of a past age, a type of mind, or a point of view with which he cannot have had direct or full contact." A related development was the attempt to revive various sorts of paganism – as seen in some of Pater's stories and in some of the writers from the Celtic regions of the British Isles. The Welshman Arthur Machen's early work "The Great God Pan" (1894) is one such effort; others include William Butler Yeats's stories of early Ireland and some of the Highland Scots stories of William Sharp (Fiona Macleod). H. Rider Haggard's tales of ancient Egyptians reincarnated and Lord Dunsany's fantasies represent yet other forms of neopaganism.

The most common reaction against materialism was the ghost story, which in this period enjoyed its golden age. The English ghost story had already reached an impressive standard in the generation before 1880 with the work of Bulwer-Lytton, Wilkie Collins, Amelia Edwards, Rhoda Broughton, and especially Joseph Sheridan Le Fanu. But a glance through any standard anthology of ghost stories will show that the period between 1880 and 1914 saw the great flowering of the form, including the work of quite a few writers who were primarily realists and are consequently not included in this volume, including E. F. Benson, Pain, Louisa Molesworth, Saki, D'Arcy, and Jacobs. As Michael Cox and R. A. Gilbert suggest in their introduction to *Victorian Ghost Stories: An Oxford Anthology* (1991), this was an age when even realists could feel the appeal of ghost stories: "With the shadow of change falling across virtually every area of life and thought, the receding past became a focus for anxiety, and in literature the ghost story offered a way of anchoring the past to an unsettled present by operating in a continuum of life and death."

Charlotte Riddell is the oldest writer included here; she was born in 1834 and had her greatest success as a novelist with *George Geith of Fen Court* in 1864, but six of her seven short-story collections were published after 1880, including *Weird Tales* (1882), the one that is now most admired. Algernon Blackwood and Lord Dunsany are the most recently deceased, dying in 1951 and 1957 respectively. However, they were both already successful writers by 1914, each having published several well-received short-story collections by that date. Blackwood, like M. R. James and Bernard Capes, was primarily known as a writer of ghost stories, but for most writers of this period the ghost story was just one of several genres. Stevenson and Kipling, for example, wrote stories of the supernatural throughout their careers. Barrie and Baring-Gould are best known for local-color stories of a frequently comic nature, about Scotland and Dartmoor respectively, but each of them produced fine ghost tales that can stand as their best works of short fiction. Mary Elizabeth Braddon, Vernon Lee, and Charlotte Riddell were important women writers who produced important ghost stories. Another woman, Amy Levy, wrote occasional stories involving visions of the departed and shared with poet and short-story writer Edward Thomas an obsession with death. Finally, Oscar Wilde and Richard Middleton subverted the form by writing comic ghost stories.

There is sometimes only a thin line dividing the ghost story of this period from the science fiction. One of the events that defines the period is the founding in 1882 of the Society for Psychical Research, which brought together a strange assortment of philosophers, spiritualists, psychologists, and physicists for the scientific study of occult phenomena. Indeed, while the technology by which the hero of Wells's *The Time Machine* (1895) moves from one era to another may be clothed in "scientific" language rather than ancient spells or curses, the results were closer to the occult than to anything that scientists could actually accomplish in 1895. Wells knew all this perfectly well: "It occurred to me," he later wrote of his early scientific romances, "that instead of the usual interview with the devil or a magician, an ingenious use of scientific patter might with advantage be substituted." The adventures of Doyle's Professor Challenger in *The Lost World* (1912) were equally far from actual scientific research, as was the science fiction occasionally produced by John Buchan and more often by William Hope Hodgson and Machen.

The reassertion of the spiritual is one of the two major strains of romanticism at work in the writers covered in this volume; the other is the appeal of the exotic. These two trends are, of course, allied in several ways. One of the many reasons for the development of the New Imperialism was the

work of Christian missionaries, who often concluded that the wilds of Africa or the South Pacific were less frustrating than the skepticism and religious indifference that had become so common in Britain. Also, in Britain writers often concentrated on rural areas that are presented as being more devout – or at least more superstitious – than the industrial cities or their suburbs. So Edward Thomas wrote about Wales; Sir Arthur Quiller-Couch about Cornwall; and Sabine Baring-Gould about the Dartmoor region of Devonshire. John Watson (Ian Maclaren) and Sir James Barrie wrote comic-sentimental "kailyard" stories about small Scottish towns dominated by the Kirk, while Fiona Macleod, Yeats, and sometimes Neil Munro presented the Celtic superstitions and folklore of Ireland and the Scottish Highlands.

Stevenson set a few stories in medieval and modern France, and Stanley Weyman set many in the French Renaissance, but the primary Continental location for short fiction was Italy. Some writers, such as Vernon Lee and Ouida (Marie Louise de la Ramée), lived there; Marie Corelli invented an Italian name for herself, and Frederick Rolfe claimed the Italian title of Baron Corvo. Vernon Lee, Ouida, Corelli, and Rolfe all used Italian sources and settings for their stories, as did Maurice Henry Hewlett.

Blackwood and Buchan set stories in Canada, and Frank Harris began his career as a short-story writer with tales of the American West. Canada was a venerable part of the empire, but most imperial fiction was set in the tropical areas, where expansion was still in progress in the late nineteenth century. Haggard's novel *King Solomon's Mines* (1885) first demonstrated the enormous appeal of imperial adventure stories, but short fiction was not far behind, beginning at least with Kipling's *Plain Tales from the Hills* (1888). Kipling continued to write short fiction about India and was joined by Alice Perrin and Flora Annie Steele. Haggard added short fiction about Africa as well as more novels, and more memorable short fiction about Africa was produced by Olive Schreiner and Joseph Conrad. The South Pacific was the last home of Stevenson and the setting for most of his late short fiction, and the Malaysian Archipelago was a recurring fictional setting for Conrad.

One interesting amalgam of the exotic and the spiritual is what Patrick Brantlinger, in *Rule of Darkness* (1988), has labeled "Imperial Gothic": stories dealing with the supernatural and the barbarous in remote parts of the empire. Many of these works are novels, but Imperial Gothic short stories are also common. Blackwood's "The Wendigo" (1910), for example, is a supernatural story from the Canadian backwoods, and Wells's "Pollock and the Porroh Man" (1895) tells of an Englishman placed under an effective curse by an African witch doctor. Several of Perrin's Anglo-Indians encounter ghosts, and Kipling's "The Phantom Rickshaw" (1888) and "The Mark of the Beast" (1890) are well-known examples of Imperial Gothic tales with Indian settings. The latter story's mocking Englishman, who desecrates a Hindu temple and suffers a strange bite that turns him into a sort of werewolf, demonstrates what Brantlinger sees as the anxiety behind this genre. "Imperialism and occultism both functioned as ersatz religions, but their fusion in imperial Gothic . . . [also] expresses anxieties about the ease with which civilization can revert to barbarism or savagery." So the supernatural werewolf in "The Mark of the Beast" is related to the natural savagery of Kurtz in Conrad's "Heart of Darkness" (1899), and both are related to Stevenson's Edward Hyde and the subterranean Morlocks in Wells's *The Time Machine*. The anxieties expressed in this fiction were soon amply justified by the actual savageries of the World War, which brings the period to a close.

Today, after many years of neglect, the short fiction of 1880 to 1914 is undergoing a revival of interest within the academy and with part of the general reading public. Broadly popular paperback series such as Everyman's Library, Penguin Classics, and Oxford World Classics now include in their lists much more British short fiction from this period than they once did. While these titles are usually those by major writers such as Kipling, Doyle, Stevenson, Conrad, Wilde, and Wells, the relatively minor writers also appear in anthologies of detective stories, ghost stories, or Victorian short stories. Within the academy, cultural historians, postcolonial literary critics, and interdisciplinary feminist scholars are rediscovering once-popular authors of short fiction and reexamining figures who were never quite forgotten. Yet copies of many volumes are extremely difficult to locate, and discovering either the location of manuscripts or even basic biographical information on many writers can be similarly challenging. There is consequently still a lot of work to be done before we have a comprehensive understanding of the most popular literary genre in Britain during the period when she reached her imperial zenith and made the transition to social democracy. It is hoped that this volume will be useful to those interested in that project.

– *William F. Naufftus*

Acknowledgments

This book was produced by Bruccoli Clark Layman, Inc. Karen L. Rood is senior editor for the *Dictionary of Literary Biography* series. Darren Harris-Fain was the in-house editor.

Production coordinator is James W. Hipp. Photography editor is Bruce Andrew Bowlin. Photographic copy work was performed by Joseph M. Bruccoli. Layout and graphics supervisor is Penney L. Haughton. Copyediting supervisor is Laurel M. Gladden. Typesetting supervisor is Kathleen M. Flanagan. Systems manager is George F. Dodge. Julie E. Frick is editorial associate. The production staff includes Phyllis A. Avant, Ann M. Cheschi, Melody W. Clegg, Patricia Coate, Denise Edwards, Joyce Fowler, Stephanie C. Hatchell, Jyll Johnston, Rebecca Mayo, Margaret Meriwether, Kathy Lawler Merlette, Jeff Miller, Pamela D. Norton, Susan Orr, Delores Plastow, Laura S. Pleicones, Jessica Rogers, Emily R. Sharpe, William L. Thomas Jr., Allison Trussell, Jonathan B. Watterson, and Jane M. J. Williamson.

Walter W. Ross and Robert S. McConnell did library research. They were assisted by the following librarians at the Thomas Cooper Library of the University of South Carolina: Linda Holderfield and the interlibrary-loan staff; reference-department head Virginia Weathers; reference librarians Marilee Birchfield, Stefanie Buck, Cathy Eckman, Rebecca Feind, Jill Holman, Karen Joseph, Jean Rhyne, Kwamine Washington, and Connie Widney; circulation-department head Caroline Taylor; and acquisitions-searching supervisor David Haggard.

The editor of a collection of essays incurs a great many debts. William B. Thesing, Patrick Scott, and John Greenfield have all made suggestions that have been helpful in planning this volume. The contributors, some from Britain and Canada, as well as many within the United States – from Arizona to Massachusetts and from Minnesota to Florida – have, of course, created the book. Particular gratitude is owed to those contributors who persevered despite the difficulty of finding the books they needed and to the many who have made useful suggestions concerning illustrations. Zachary Maddox, Susan Silverman, and Robert Gorman of the Dacus Library at Winthrop University have all been helpful in many ways, as have my colleagues Debra C. Boyd, Gloria G. Jones, and William A. Sullivan.

British Short-Fiction Writers, 1880–1914: The Romantic Tradition

Dictionary of Literary Biography

Sabine Baring-Gould

(28 January 1834 – 2 January 1924)

Max Keith Sutton
University of Kansas

BOOKS: *An Account of an English Camp Near Bayonne* (Cambridge, 1851);

The Chorister, a Tale of King's College Chapel in the Civil Wars (Cambridge: Meadows, 1856);

The Path of the Just: Tales of Holy Men and Children (London: Masters, 1857);

Iceland: Its Scenes and Sagas (London: Smith, Elder, 1863);

The Book of Were-Wolves: Being an Account of a Terrible Superstition (London: Smith, Elder, 1865);

Post-Mediaeval Preachers: Some Account of the Most Celebrated Preachers of the Fifteenth, Sixteenth, and Seventeenth Centuries; with Outlines of Their Sermons and Specimens of Their Style (London: Rivingtons, 1865);

Curious Myths of the Middle Ages (London, Oxford & Cambridge: Rivingtons, 1866; revised and enlarged, 1868);

Curious Myths of the Middle Ages, Second Series (London, Oxford & Cambridge: Rivingtons, 1868);

Through Flood and Flame, 3 volumes (London: Bentley, 1868);

The Silver Store: Collected from Mediaeval Christian and Jewish Mines (London: Longmans, 1868; revised edition, London: Skeffington, 1887);

Curiosities of Olden Times (London: Hayes, 1869; New York: Pott & Amery, 1869; revised and enlarged edition, Edinburgh: Grant, 1896);

The Golden Gate: A Complete Manual of Instructions, Devotions, and Preparations, 3 volumes (London: Simpkin, Marshall, 1869, 1870; revised edition, London: Skeffington, 1896);

The Origin and Development of Religious Belief, 2 volumes (London, Oxford & Cambridge: Rivingtons, 1869, 1870; New York: Appleton, 1871);

Sabine Baring-Gould

In Exitu Israel: An Historical Novel of the French Revolution, 2 volumes (London: Macmillan, 1870);

Organization: A Sermon Preached at St. Michael's Church, Wakefield (London: Hays, 1870);

Legends of Old Testament Characters, from the Talmud and Other Sources (London & New York: Macmillan, 1871); republished as *Legends of the Patriarchs and Prophets and Other Old Testament Characters from Various Sources* (New York: Holt & Williams, 1872);

One Hundred Sermon Sketches for Extempore Preachers (London: Masters, 1871);

The Lives of the Saints, 17 volumes (London: Hodges, 1872–1889); revised edition, 16 volumes (London: Nimmo, 1897, 1898); revised edition, 16 volumes (Edinburgh: Grant, 1914);

Protestant or Catholic? A Lecture (London: Hays, 1872);

Secular v. Religious Education: A Sermon (London: Hodges, 1872);

Village Conferences on the Creed (London: Masters, 1873);

How to Save Fuel (London: Chapman & Hall, 1874);

The Lost and Hostile Gospels: An Essay on the Toledoth Jeschu, and the Petrine and Pauline Gospels of the First Three Centuries of Which Fragments Remain (London: Williams & Norgate, 1874);

Yorkshire Oddities, Incidents, and Strange Events, 2 volumes (London: Hodges, 1874);

Some Modern Difficulties: Nine Lectures (London: Skeffington, 1875);

Village Preaching for a Year, 3 volumes (London: Skeffington, 1875, 1876); Second Series, 2 volumes (London: Skeffington, 1884);

Some Remarks upon "Two Recent Memoirs of R. S. Hawker, Late Vicar of Morwenstow," by Baring-Gould and F. G. Lee (London: Privately printed, 1876);

The Vicar of Morwenstow: A Life of Robert S. Hawker (London: King, 1876; New York: Whittaker, 1876; revised edition, London: King, 1876; revised edition, London: King, 1876; revised edition, London: Methuen, 1899);

The Mystery of Suffering: Six Lectures (London: Skeffington, 1877);

Germany, Present and Past, 2 volumes (London: Kegan Paul, 1879; New York: Holt, 1882);

Sermons to Children (London: Skeffington, 1879);

Mehalah: A Story of the Salt Marshes, 3 volumes (London: Smith, Elder, 1880; New York: Lovell, 1889);

The Preacher's Pocket: A Packet of Sermons (London: Skeffington, 1880);

Village Preaching for Saints' Days (London: Skeffington, 1881);

The Village Pulpit: A Complete Course of Sixty-Six Short Sermons, or Full Sermon Outlines for Each Sunday, and Some Chief Holy Days of the Christian Year, 2 volumes (London: Skeffington, 1881, 1887);

Germany (London: Sampson Low, 1883);

John Herring: A West of England Romance, 3 volumes (London: Smith, Elder, 1883; New York: Lovell, 1889);

Church Songs, First Series (London: Skeffington, 1884); Second Series (London: Skeffington, 1884);

The Seven Last Words: A Course of Sermons (London: Skeffington, 1884);

The Birth of Jesus: Eight Discourses for Advent, Christmas and Epiphany (London: Skeffington, 1885);

The Nativity (London, 1885);

Our Parish Church: Twenty Addresses to Children on Great Truths of the Christian Faith (London: Skeffington, 1885);

The Passion of Jesus: Seven Discourses for Lent, First Series (London: Skeffington, 1885); Second Series (London: Skeffington, 1886); Third Series (London: Skeffington, 1887);

Court Royal: A Story of Cross Currents, 3 volumes (London: Smith, Elder, 1886; New York: Munro, 1886);

Germany, by Baring-Gould and Arthur Gilman (London: Unwin, 1886; revised edition, London: Unwin, 1905);

Golden Feather (London: Christian Knowledge Society, 1886);

Nazareth and Capernaum: Ten Lectures on the Beginning of Our Lord's Ministry (London: Skeffington, 1886);

The Trials of Jesus: Seven Discourses for Lent (London: Skeffington, 1886);

The Gaverocks: A Tale of the Cornish Coast, 3 volumes (London: Smith, Elder, 1887; Philadelphia: Lippincott, 1888);

Little Tu'penny (London: Ward & Downey, 1887; New York: Munro, 1887);

Red Spider, 2 volumes (London: Chatto & Windus, 1887; New York: Lovell, 1888);

The Way of Sorrows: Seven Discourses for Lent (London: Skeffington, 1887);

The Death and Resurrection of Jesus: Ten Lectures for Holy Week and Easter (London: Skeffington, 1888);

Eve: A Novel, 2 volumes (London: Chatto & Windus, 1888; New York: Munro, 1888);

Our Inheritance: An Account of the Eucharistic Service in the First Three Centuries (London: Skeffington, 1888);

Richard Cable the Lightshipman, 3 volumes (London: Smith, Elder, 1888; Philadelphia: Lippincott, 1888);

Historic Oddities and Strange Events, First Series (London: Methuen, 1889); Second Series (London: Methuen, 1891);

The Pennycomequicks, 3 volumes (London: Blackett, 1889; New York: Lovell, 1889);

Arminell: A Social Romance, 3 volumes (London: Methuen, 1890; New York: Lovell, 1890);

Conscience and Sin: Daily Meditations for Lent (London: Skeffington, 1890);

Grettir the Outlaw: A Story of Iceland (London: Blackie, 1890; New York: Scibner & Welford, 1890);

Jacquetta and Other Stories (London: Methuen, 1890);

My Prague Pig and Other Stories for Children (London: Skeffington, 1890);

Old Country Life (London: Methuen, 1890);

The Church in Germany (London: Wells Gardner, 1891);

In Troubadour-Land: A Ramble in Provence and Languedoc (London: W. H. Allen, 1891);

Margery of Quether, and Other Stories (London: Methuen, 1891; New York: Lovell, 1892);

Urith: A Tale of Dartmoor, 3 volumes (London: Methuen, 1891; New York: United States Book Company, 1891);

In the Roar of the Sea: A Tale of the Cornish Coast, 3 volumes (London: Methuen, 1892; New York: Lovell, Coryell, 1892);

Strange Survivals: Some Chapters in the History of Man (London: Methuen, 1892);

Through All the Changing Scenes of Life (London: Christian Knowledge Society, 1892);

The Tragedy of the Caesars: A Study of the Characters of the Caesars of the Julian and Claudian Houses, 2 volumes (London: Methuen, 1892; New York: Scribners, 1907);

Wagner's Parsifal at Baireuth (London: Skeffington, 1892);

Cheap Jack Zita, 3 volumes (London: Methuen, 1893; New York: Tait, 1894);

The Icelander's Sword, or the Story of Oraefa-Dal (London: Methuen, 1893);

Mrs. Curgenven of Curgenven, 3 volumes (London: Methuen, 1893; New York: Lovell, Coryell, 1893);

A Book of Fairy Tales Retold by S. Baring-Gould (London: Methuen, 1894);

The Deserts of Southern France: An Introduction to the Limestone and Chalk Plateaux of Ancient Aquitaine, 2 volumes (London: Methuen, 1894; New York: Dodd, Mead, 1894);

Kitty Alone: A Story of Three Fires, 3 volumes (London: Methuen, 1894; New York: Dodd, Mead, 1894);

The Queen of Love, 3 volumes (London: Methuen, 1894; Philadelphia: Lippincott, 1894);

English Minstrelsie: A National Monument of English Song, 8 volumes (Edinburgh, 1895–1896);

Evening Communions: A Letter to the Lord Bishop of Exeter (Oxford: Mowbray, 1895);

Noem: A Story of Rock-Dwellers (London: Methuen, 1895; New York: Appleton, 1895);

The Broom Squire (London: Methuen, 1896; New York: Stokes, 1896);

Dartmoor Idylls (London: Methuen, 1896);

Bladys of the Stewponey (London: Methuen, 1897; New York: Stokes, 1898);

Guavas the Tinner (London: Methuen, 1897);

The Life of Napoleon Bonaparte (London: Methuen, 1897; abridged edition, London: Methuen, 1908);

Perpetua: A Story of Nimes in A.D. 213 (London: Isbister, 1897; New York: Dutton, 1897);

A Study of St. Paul, His Character and Opinions (London: Isbister, 1897);

An Armory of the Western Counties, Devon and Cornwall, by Baring-Gould and Robert William Twigge (Exeter: Commin, 1898);

Domitia (London: Methuen, 1898; New York: Stokes, 1898);

An Old English Home and Its Dependencies (London: Methuen, 1898);

Romances of the West Country, edited by William Henry Kearley Wright (Plymouth, U.K.: Doidge, 1898);

The Sunday Round: Plain Village Sermons for the Sundays of the Christian Year, 4 volumes (London: Skeffington, 1898, 1899);

A Book of the West, Being an Introduction to Devon and Cornwall, 2 volumes (London: Methuen, 1899);

The Crock of Gold (London: Methuen, 1899);

Furze Bloom: Tales of the Western Moors (London: Methuen, 1899);

Pabo the Priest (London: Methuen, 1899; New York: Stokes, 1899);

The Present Crisis: A Letter to the Bishop of Exeter (London: Skeffington, 1899);

A Book of Dartmoor (London: Methuen, 1900);

In a Quiet Village (London: Isbister, 1900);

Winefred: A Story of the Chalk Cliffs (London: Methuen, 1900; Boston: Pages, 1900);

Virgin Saints and Martyrs (London: Hutchinson, 1900; New York: Crowell, 1901);

The Frobishers: A Story of the Staffordshire Potteries (London: Methuen, 1901);

Royal Georgie (London: Methuen, 1901);

A Book of Brittany (London: Methuen, 1901);

Brittany (London: Methuen, 1902);

A Coronation Souvenir (London: Skeffington, 1902);

Miss Quillet (London: Methuen, 1902);

Nebo the Nailer (London: Cassell, 1902);

The Manor House in Lew Trenchard, West Devon, where Baring-Gould served as pastor and wrote stories about West Country life

Amazing Adventures (London: Skeffington, 1903);

A Book of North Wales (London: Methuen, 1903);

Chris of All Sorts (London: Methuen, 1903);

A Book of Ghosts (London: Methuen, 1904; New York: Putnam, 1904);

In Dewisland (London: Methuen, 1904);

Siegfried: A Romance Founded on Wagner's Operas, "Rheingold," "Siegfried," and "Gotterdammerung" (London: Dean, 1904; Boston: Page, 1905);

A Book of South Wales (London: Methuen, 1905);

A Book of the Riviera (London: Methuen, 1905; New York: Brentano, 1924; revised edition, London: Methuen, 1928);

A Memorial of Horatio Lord Nelson (London: Skeffington, 1905);

Monsieur Pichelmere, and Other Stories (London: Digby, Long, 1905);

A Book of the Rhine from Cleve to Mainz (London: Methuen, 1906; New York: Macmillan, 1906);

A Book of the Cevennes (London: Long, 1907);

A Book of the Pyrenees (London: Methuen, 1907; New York: Dutton, 1907);

Devon (London: Methuen, 1907);

The Lives of the British Saints: The Saints of Wales and Cornwall and Such Irish Saints as Have Dedications in Britain, 4 volumes, by Baring-Gould and John Fisher (London: Cymmrodorian Society, 1907–1913);

The Restitution of All Things; or, "The Hope That Is Set Before Us" (London: Skeffington, 1907);

The Baring-Gould Continuous Reader, edited by G. H. Rose (London: Methuen, 1908; revised, 1908);

Devonshire Characters and Strange Events (London: John Lane, 1908);

Cornish Characters and Strange Events (London: John Lane, 1909);

A History of Sarawak under Its Two White Rajahs (Sir James Brooke and Sir Charles Anthoni Johnson Brooke): 1839–1908, by Baring-Gould and C. A. Bampfylde (London: Sotheran, 1909);

Cornwall (Cambridge: Cambridge University Press, 1910);

Family Names and Their Story (London: Seeley, 1910);

Cliff Castles and Cave Dwellings of Europe (London: Seeley, 1911; Philadelphia: Lippincott, 1911);

A Coronation Souvenir (London: Skeffington, 1911);

The Land of Teck and Its Neighborhood (London & New York: John Lane, 1911);

Two Sermons for the Coronation of King George V, by Baring-Gould and Canon Duncan (London: Skeffington, 1911);

Sheepstor (Plymouth, U.K.: Hoyten & Cole, 1912);

A Book of Folk-Lore (London & Glasgow: Collins' Clear-Type Press, 1913);

The Church Revival: Thoughts Thereon and Reminiscences (London: Methuen, 1914);

Thoughts from S. Baring-Gould, edited by H. B. Elliott (London: Holden & Hardingham, 1917);

The Evangelical Revival (London: Methuen, 1920);

Early Reminiscences, 1834–1864 (London: John Lane, 1923);

My Few Last Words (London: Skeffington, 1924);

Further Reminiscences, 1864–1894 (London: John Lane, 1925).

OTHER: William Henderson, *Notes on the Folk Lore of the Northern Counties of England,* appendix by Baring-Gould (London: Folk Lore Society, 1866);

"On the Revival of Religious Confraternities" and "Origin of the Schools of Thought in the English Church," in *The Church and the World,* edited by Orby Shipley (London: Longmans, Green, Reader & Dyer, 1866), pp. 93–112;

Hanna Olava Winsnes, *Norwegian Stories: or, Evenings at Oakwood,* preface by Baring-Gould (London, 1868);

Cecilia Anne Jones, *Footprints of Our Fathers,* preface by Baring-Gould (London, 1876);

Wilhelmine von Hillern, *Ernestine, a Novel,* translated by Baring-Gould (London: De La Rue, 1879);

"Gottlob's Picture," in *Please Tell Me a Tale: A Collection of Short Stories for Children* (London: Skeffington, 1886), pp. 61–75;

"Wow Wow," in *Just One More Tale,* edited by Baring-Gould and C. M. Yonge (London: Skeffington, 1886), pp. 138–152;

John Ashton, *The Legendary History of the Cross,* preface by Baring-Gould (London: Unwin, 1887);

"The Cats' Tree" and "The Schnabelweid Plot, or, the Christmas Pudding," in *Jack Frost's Little Prisoners: A Collection of Stories for Children* (London: Skeffington, 1887), pp. 42–57, 133–144;

Sophia Francis Anne Caulfield, *The Lives of the Apostles,* introduction by Baring-Gould (London: Hatchards, 1887);

John Bickley Hughes, *Deans Rural,* introduction by Baring-Gould (London: Skeffington, 1889);

Songs and Ballads of the West, 4 volumes, edited by Baring-Gould and H. Fleetwood Sheppard (London: Methuen, 1890);

"Colour in Composition," in *On the Art of Writing Fiction* (London: Wells Gardner, 1894), pp. 35–46;

A Book of Nursery Songs and Rhymes, edited by Baring-Gould (London: Methuen, 1895; Chicago: McClurg, 1907);

J. L. C. Grimm and W. C. Grimm, *Fairy Tales from Grimm,* introduction by Baring-Gould (London: Wells, Gardner, 1895);

A Garland of Country Song: English Folk Songs with Their Traditional Melodies, edited by Baring-Gould and Sheppard (London: Methuen, 1895);

Old English Fairy Tales, edited by Baring-Gould (London: Methuen, 1895; Chicago: Way & Williams, 1895);

"Daddy Tregellos," in *Under One Cover,* by Baring-Gould and others (London: Skeffington, 1898);

Preston King, *Bath Waters,* with a historical sketch by Baring-Gould (Bristol: Arrowsmith, 1901);

Songs of the West: Folk Songs of Devon and Cornwall, edited by Baring-Gould, Sheppard, and F. W. Bussell (London: Methuen, 1905);

English Folk Songs for Schools, edited by Baring-Gould and Cecil J. Sharp (London: Curwen, 1906);

Saint Francis De Sales, edited by Baring-Gould (London: Library of the Soul, 1907);

James Matcham Gatrill, *Echoes: Some Words Pertaining to the Kingdom of God,* preface by Baring-Gould (London: Skeffington, 1912).

SELECTED PERIODICAL PUBLICATIONS – UNCOLLECTED: "Tommy," *Blackwood's Magazine,* 136 (August 1884): 213–230;

"The Last Words of Joseph Barrable," *Blackwood's Magazine,* 136 (October 1884): 501–520;

"Alexander Nesbitt, Ex-Schoolmaster," *Blackwood's Magazine,* 136 (November 1884): 632–645;

"The Deadleigh Sweep," *Cornhill Magazine,* new series 6 (March 1886): 297–313;

"A False Step," *Cornhill Magazine,* new series 9 (August–September 1887): 189–213, 271–296;

"Early Christian Greek Romances," *Contemporary Review,* 30 (October 1887): 858–876;

"What Is a Gentleman?," *Cornhill Magazine,* new series 9 (November 1887): 552–560;

"An Error Righted," *Cornhill Magazine,* third series 9 (December 1900): 740–753;

"The New Rich: Their Influence in Country Life,"
Times (London), 7 August 1922, p. 9; 14 August 1922, p. 13.

Of the many books by Sabine Baring-Gould, only six are collections of short fiction, not counting his volumes of fairy tales and other stories for children. He wrote far more novels (around thirty-five) and more than twenty guide books and accounts of his travels – to Iceland as a young man in 1861 and to parts of the Continent, where he spent most of his childhood. As a parson in Yorkshire he began bringing out his *Lives of the Saints* (1872–1889), which eventually ran to seventeen volumes. As a pioneer song collector and folklorist, he published more than twenty volumes, including the collection of West Country ballads that he considered his "principal achievement." He wrote biographies of such figures as Napoleon, historical studies of "Oddities and Strange Events," and two popular studies in comparative mythology, *Curious Myths of the Middle Ages* (1866, 1868), which reached thirty-five printings by 1914 and remained in print into the 1990s. In this mass of mostly forgotten publications, short stories form only a small segment. Yet in a broad sense, short narratives loom large in his writing, whether as free translations of sagas in his early book on Iceland or as legends gruesomely retold in *The Book of Were-Wolves: Being an Account of a Terrible Superstition* (1865), his most frequently read work today. Almost until his death in 1924, Baring-Gould continued to write anecdotes, stringing them together in the two volumes of reminiscences (1923, 1925) that provide the basis for any account of his life.

Born in Exeter on 28 January 1834, Baring-Gould grew up in circumstances that nurtured his various and eccentric interests. As the first son of Edward Baring-Gould, a former cavalry officer, he belonged to the landed gentry and would inherit the family estate, eventually becoming both squire and parson of Lew Trenchard in West Devon. From this vantage point near the edge of Dartmoor, he would write fiction of West Country life and find ample material for his studies in archaeology and folklore. But he did not have the advantage of growing up in one familiar place, as Thomas Hardy did in Dorset. His parents took him to the Continent, partly on account of his weak lungs but also because his father was a restless man who seldom stayed long in one spot.

Traveling by carriage across France to Switzerland and Italy and back north along the Rhine, the young Baring-Gould learned the importance of places. Believing that places could shape character, as a regional writer he would pay careful attention to setting. His leaning toward Catholicism began in boyhood as he noticed the contrast when passing from a Protestant to a Catholic canton in Switzerland: the one seemed gloomy, the other cheerful and beautiful, with painted chapels and wayside shrines, and he sensed a corresponding difference in the people. His travels also taught him to speak fluently in five languages by the time he was fifteen. At sixteen he organized the excavation of a Roman mosaic near Pau in the south of France. He received little formal schooling until he left for Clare Hall, Cambridge, in 1853. After taking his degree in 1857 he worked briefly among the poor in the East End of London and later taught school before his ordination in 1864. He then served as a curate at Horbury in Yorkshire, where he fell in love with Grace Taylor, a mill girl whom he married in 1868 after moving on to the rural Yorkshire parish of Dalton in 1867. He went next to East Mersea in Essex in 1872 before his return in 1881 to Devon as rector of Lew Trenchard, where he served until his death.

As a young schoolmaster and clergyman, Baring-Gould found himself drawn into the role of storyteller. While translating Icelandic sagas, he recited Grettir's adventures for the schoolboys at Hurstpierpoint in Sussex, and after evening lessons at Horbury the workers' children would sit on the skirts of the young curate's frock coat and force him to tell a story. Already at work on *The Book of Were-Wolves,* the curious young clergyman was drawn to the grotesque and uncanny. Describing himself in the preface to *Yorkshire Oddities, Incidents, and Strange Events* (1874) as an "inveterate" collector of "all kinds of odd and out-of-the-way information concerning men and manners," he used stories to keep alive past experiences of the preternatural. In *Early Reminiscences, 1834–1864* (1923) he notes the "triumph" of the scientific outlook in a world where people may observe bacteria but no longer see pixies. "Scientifically we have gained much. Imaginatively we have lost a great deal."

Yorkshire Oddities marks a major step in Baring-Gould's career as a reporter of strange events. Although at least one piece, "The Boggart of Wellen-Pot," was written as fiction, appearing first in *Once a Week* (March 1867), the stories are mainly non-fiction narratives; many include long extracts from earlier documents. The historical matter often sounds as bizarre as fantasy. The memoir of John Wroe (1782–1862) tells of a self-styled prophet who not only arranged for his baptism in a river before a reported thirty thousand spectators (many hostile) but also later had himself publicly circumcised. In

"James Naylor, the Quaker" the handsome, charismatic young visionary enters Bristol while women accompanied by their husbands shout, "Holy, holy, holy," as if he were riding into Jerusalem. Later, on trial under Oliver Cromwell's government, he fails to deny that he is the "everlasting Son of God" and has "his tongue bored through, and his forehead branded." In "Yorkshire Recusants" Baring-Gould reports the sufferings of Roman Catholic martyrs under Elizabeth I. His use of eyewitness accounts brings home the brutality of the officials and the faithfulness of the victims, especially in the case of Margaret Clitheroe, crushed to death under a weight of seven hundred or eight hundred pounds. Accounts of her martyrdom later inspired a poem by Gerard Manley Hopkins. Whether the focus on pain represents a cruel streak in Baring-Gould's nature, as James M. Barrie suggests, or merely reflects his view of the world as a "torture chamber," as he calls it in *The Mystery of Suffering: Six Lectures* (1877), *Yorkshire Oddities* is full of nightmarish and grotesque detail.

Baring-Gould moves closest to his subjects in humorous short sketches, such as "A Yorkshire Butcher" and "David Turton, Musician at Horbury," where the main characters do most of the talking. Their long speeches in dialect sound authentic, almost as if he had a tape recorder instead of a faulty memory that never could get anything word for word, as he confessed in his *Early Reminiscences, 1834–1864.* David Turton portrays himself through his own speech, even though the author never met the man (Turton died in 1846, long before Baring-Gould went to Horbury). Anticipating a story told by one of Hardy's rustics in *Tess of the d'Urbervilles* (1891), Baring-Gould reports the musician's words upon meeting an angry bull. Hardy's is the more artful, elaborate, and incredible version, with the bull in his novel smiling when the fiddler strikes up a jig and then kneeling for the Nativity hymn. In "David Turton, Musician at Horbury" when the bull bellows, the musician says to himself, "That was a double B nat'ral" and checks it by playing the note on his bass viol: "I thowt I were reet." The bull stops, and he continues with a piece by George Frideric Handel, at which the bull turns tail. The sketch ends with the old man's long report of his only visit to London, where he slips off to Saint Paul's to hear the music instead of going to chapel with his sister and her husband, who scold him afterward. "I said nowt; I just set and thowt o' what I'd heard, and I played it ower again on my in'ards."

With these nonfiction narratives and unplotted character sketches Baring-Gould quickly

Illustration by H. Furniss for Baring-Gould's "Margery of Quether," in the April–May 1884 issue of the Cornhill Magazine

achieved a modest distinction, but as a writer of novels and short stories in the conventional sense he was slow in getting started. He published three early attempts at fiction, the first an undergraduate novella, *The Chorister, a Tale of King's College Chapel in the Civil Wars* (1856), purportedly based on a historical document that in fact did not exist. His first novel, *Through Flood and Flame* (1868), includes a fictional version of his courtship of the Yorkshire mill girl whom he married in that year. *In Exitu Israel* (1870) is an intriguing historical novel of the French Revolution, but it met with no success, and he turned to other projects in the 1870s while attempting to care for his burgeoning family, which eventually included fourteen children after one died in infancy. His unpleasant stay in Essex inspired his best-known novel, *Mehalah: A Story of the Salt Marshes* (1880), and for the next two decades he was one of the most prolific fiction writers in England. His grand designs for Lew Trenchard – restoring the church, rebuilding the manor, building decent cottages for the workers – called for extra income, and he wrote rapidly for pay. After 1885 he often brought out two novels a year; some ran serially in such periodicals as the *Cornhill Magazine,* where his short fiction also began appearing. His major work in this genre came out in collections published in the 1890s, when the short story was well established as a popular literary form.

Unlike his novels, which sometimes went through several editions, none of these collections has ever been reprinted. Though some were praised by contemporary reviewers, his novellas and sketches generally lack the color and impact of his best novels and the sharp characterization of the nonfiction narratives in *Yorkshire Oddities.* He does best in his longer stories, which sometimes appeared serially in magazines and sometimes run as long as one hundred to two hundred pages. The greater length allows him to develop the setting and to show characters changing through ordeals that threaten their egoism and help them see themselves more nearly as they are. The three long narratives in *Jacquetta and Other Stories* (1890) each show women developing character through harsh testing. In "Jael," first published in the *English Illustrated Magazine* in October 1887, he returns to the Essex marshland setting of *Mehalah* and focuses once more on a fiery, headstrong heroine, named for the woman in Judges who drove a tent peg through a man's head. This Jael wants to punish her false lover, and she finds a way to destroy him and his bride by opening a railway bridge so that the locomotive in which they are riding will plunge into the water. Her last-minute change of heart and a mechanical failure that keeps the bridge from closing back again lead to her sacrificial death on the tracks to stop the engine.

The grimness of the plot, though not the occasional playfulness of the tone, matches the dreary marshland and the roughness of the secondary characters. Jael's father keeps wishing that the midwife had smothered her at birth, when her mother died, rather than leave him stuck with a "real live rampaging and roaring female baby." The midwife has only slightly finer sensibilities than the disreputable Sarah Gamp from Charles Dickens's *Martin Chuzzlewit* (1844), and Jael's suitor just wants her fifty sovereigns. He strikes her and refuses to marry her after she elopes with him to London without the money. Like *Mehalah,* the story illustrates Baring-Gould's belief that the land shapes the character of the people who have lived there for generations, so the setting, as he explains in his essay "Colour in Composition" (1894), is a primary concern in his fiction.

Baring-Gould describes the setting in almost travel-book detail in "Moth-Mullein," first published in the April 1889 *Cornhill Magazine,* here contrasting the hilly, wooded Kentish side of the Thames with the Essex side, the "flat, treeless, receiver-general of London sewage." Again the focus rests upon a headstrong and physically strong young woman. Hoping to catch some well-bred naturalist who comes moth-hunting in the woods, a forester's daughter scorns the suitors from her own social class, putting them through ordeals as if she were a princess in a fairy tale. Her own trials come when she overhears herself called a dragon and learns ex-

actly what the rejected men think of her. Instead of breaking down her pride, this unwelcome vision of herself only makes her more perverse, and she takes out her anger on the faithful little man who marries her. When he is mortally injured in an accident, the "shell" around her heart starts breaking as she heroically carries him toward home, but too late to save his life. She becomes a quiet and kindly young widow.

In the long title story from *Jacquetta and Other Stories* the heroine's ordeals generate changes not only in herself but also in the people around her. "Jacquetta," first published in the *English Illustrated Magazine* of December 1886–March 1887, is a miniature society novel set mainly on the Loire above Nantes. A nouveau riche English girl marries an impoverished French baron, suffers from the coldness of his domineering mother, and plans to run back to her parents before the village priest finds a way to save the marriage. Told from an objective and urbane point of view, the story has scenes of grotesque comedy, as when the young baron threatens to end his life if he cannot marry Jacquetta. After loading his pistol, he contemplates his face in the mirror. A shot brings his mother and aunt in panic to his room, where shattered glass reveals that he has carried out his threat, symbolically at least, by destroying his reflected self. The gesture works, and his mother relents, although she keeps trying to control her son after the wedding.

Of all Baring-Gould's short fiction, probably his best effort can be found in *Margery of Quether, and Other Stories* (1891). This volume includes a vivid, somewhat melodramatic story of rural Yorkshire, "Tom a' Tuddlams," which depicts intense marital discord followed by the wife's change of heart as she finally sees her "Real Self" on Christmas Eve during a folk ritual that would have intrigued Hardy, with its mirror, mistletoe, Yule candle, and prayers as a spell to call up a vision of the dead. The book also includes an unconventional, puzzling, and disturbing Devonshire tale, "At the Y," which offers the reader two or possibly three optional plots. A former soldier cannot make up his mind whether to forfeit his inheritance by marrying an Irish girl who comes to his farm with their baby. When she leaves the next day, he follows but stops at the Y, where the road forks. Going to the left, he abandons the girl and proposes to a rich farmer's daughter, only to be horsewhipped in public for letting the mother and child freeze to death on the moor. Again, however, he stands at the Y and this time chooses the other road, wedding the Irish girl, suffering a miserable marriage, and finally stabbing a man in jealousy. Once more he recovers, facing the Y, and now he chooses neither, returning home as if his Irish mistress and their child had never existed. The young man ends up, like the reader, wondering what really happened: "Did I go to the left, or to the right, or did I do neither?" At the end he says, "I'm always at the Y," like "some others in the world."

Margery of Quether, and Other Stories also includes two of Baring-Gould's infrequent experiments with point of view at a time when greater writers were refining this dimension of storytelling. By his own testimony, he read little fiction after Dickens (none by Hardy, he said), and he seems to have been ignorant of recent short stories by Robert Louis Stevenson, Rudyard Kipling, and Henry James. His typical narrative stance is either casually omniscient, with asides in the manner of Anthony Trollope, or limited to the persona of the inquisitive parson. But in this volume he tries letting the main characters write their own stories. "Wanted – A Reader" has two narrators, elderly London brothers, both bachelors, who fall in love with a young lady hired to read to them; each offers his version of events in his own diary. Entries for the same day are paired together for comic effect, with one brother leaving out embarrassing details that the other maliciously supplies. First published in *Gentleman's Magazine* in January 1886, this ingenious little piece deserves mention among the comic examples of Victorian fictional diaries, including George and Weedon Grossmith's *The Diary of a Nobody* (1892).

Unintentionally funny first-person narration also distinguishes what may be Baring-Gould's best short story, "Margery of Quether," first published in the *Cornhill Magazine* in April–May 1884. The narrator is a bluff young Devon farmer proud of his yeoman ancestry, his staunch conservatism in an age of "Gladstone-Chamberlain-Radical" disorder, his small estate on Blackdown in western Dartmoor, and his utter lack of that "delusive faculty," the imagination. He boasts of his plain straightforward style, which he thinks may offend current tastes, "vitiated by slipshod English and effeminacy of writing. Roast beef does not taste its best after Indian curry."

What he thinks about his style and his readers roughly parallels his views of himself and the opposite sex. Women, whom he considers "butchers" of male character, pose a threat to his plan to follow family tradition and remain single as long as possible. They are, he says, "impatient cattle." He believes that they go to church to capture husbands

and that young Margaret of Quether has stopped attending chapel and started climbing the steep slope up to Saint Michael's Church on Brentor for one simple reason: "I was there, aged three-and-twenty, was good-looking, and the sole owner of Foggaton."

Such a self-centered character is destined for an assault upon his masculine complacency. This begins when he goes to ring the bells at midnight on Christmas Eve in the little church on Brentor. First his pragmatic rationalism receives a jolt when he confronts the preternatural; then the self-assurance about his youth and good looks undergoes a long and severe testing. In the dark bell tower something descending the rope gives him a new experience, which he goes to great lengths to avoid identifying as fear: "As far as I can recollect and analyse my sensations at the time, I should say that blank amazement prevailed, attended by a dominating desire to be outside the church and careering down the flank of the hill." When the cause of his uneasiness reaches the floor, the narrator sees by lantern light that it has "a human form" and is "the size of a three months' old baby." He notes its distinguishing features as if he were a naturalist trying to identify a new species: "In colour the object was brown, as if it had been steeped in peat water for a century, and in texture leathery. It scrambled, much as I have seen a bat scramble, out of the puddle on the pavement to the heap of broken timber, and worked its way with little brown hands and long claws up a rafter, and seated itself thereon." The shrunken little creature identifies herself as Margery of Quether. She claims that she lived more than two hundred years earlier, was jilted by one of the narrator's cautious ancestors, and prayed in her youth that she might never die, since she was "so joyous and fond of life and full of giddiness." She was also "mortal afraid of death" and still is, despite her current diminished and dried-up existence.

As she sits before the narrator, worrying about rats that might gnaw holes in her leathery skin, he draws near enough to see her eyelashes, which are "white like frost needles," and falls victim to one of his "worst faults – compassion." When he picks her up to take her home, she drives her one tooth through his coat and waistcoat, sinks in her nails like "knife-blades," and sticks as tight to him "as a tick on a dog." She then grows young and lovely while he grows old and feeble. Nonetheless, he becomes fond of her and denies that she sucked his blood, at least "not grossly in the manner of a leech," but somehow she feeds on his "life and health." By the time she becomes desirable, he has lost all desire and apparently forfeited his chance to

Baring-Gould in 1923, shortly before his death

carry on the family line. But when the current Margaret of Quether and her father intervene, threatening to burn Margery as a witch unless she gives up her claim on the narrator and restores his virility, he accepts a compromise. He will agree to marry the current Margaret despite her alarming youth, which might lead to many offspring. A glance in the mirror relieves him by showing that he has only been restored to late middle age: "I was grey-headed and on the turn down of life. That was an advantage." Perhaps he will keep the estate intact by fathering only one son after all. Despite his ordeals, the narrator has not changed; he stays comic and incorrigible.

This departure from Baring-Gould's usually detached point of view makes "Margery of Quether" interesting in style and tone as well as in theme and action. Because of the narrator, it may rank among the minor masterpieces of a popular subgenre, the tale of terror in which a person who must face the inexplicable typically starts out with a routine life and a rationalistic outlook. Point of view is the secret that a reviewer in the 9 April 1892 *Academy* understood when he called "Margery of Quether" an "exceedingly powerful but gruesome tale – perhaps

one of the ablest its voluminous author has written." "Admirably suited both to the imaginary narrator and to the subject," the reviewer wrote, the style itself becomes a way of revealing character. The fictive author stands at many removes from Baring-Gould's usual persona as parson and collector of things strange and curious. The matter-of-fact farmer does not seek oddities, and he only writes about this one to protect her from inquisitive tourists trekking over Dartmoor: "Now that they know her story, I trust they will give her a wide berth."

Baring-Gould's later attempts at writing conventional character studies suffer by comparison with "Margery of Quether" on the one hand and *Yorkshire Oddities* on the other. Told from the author's own perspective, *Dartmoor Idylls* (1896) is a series of sketches inspired by his tramps across the moor in search of the surviving "song men" who gave him and his partner, H. Fleetwood Sheppard, the words and melodies for their *Songs and Ballads of the West* (1890). Like "David Turton, Musician at Horbury" in *Yorkshire Oddities*, "Daniel Jacobs" portrays a rustic musician, apparently one whom the author knew personally. Yet the need to give the sketch some of the pathos and pictorial completeness expected of an idyll makes it seem less authentic than the rougher, less finished sketch of the Yorkshire musician. Literary self-consciousness obscures the subject: "I write of the man as though he were before me. I cannot do otherwise, so strongly has he impressed me." To round off the story, the narrator finds him at last in a ruined cottage, "dead, in a sitting posture, and beside him, fallen from his hand – the violin."

This strained tone does not pervade all the stories in *Dartmoor Idylls*. Some, such as "Snaily House," are mildly humorous, and one, "The Hammetts," borders on the cynical. It tells how a husband and wife finally salvage their marriage after thirty years of feuding have made them "perfect masters of hurting and incensing one another." They threaten to commit suicide; each tries and fails, but a resolution comes when the husband upbraids his wife for trying to hang herself with the rope he needs to lead a calf to the butcher. She then uses the rope to beat him into submission, and the story comes to a not quite unhappy ending: "So the latter end of their married career was better than its beginning or middle."

Two subsequent collections follow the pattern of *Dartmoor Idylls*. *Furze Bloom: Tales of the Western Moors* (1899) includes twelve short West Country sketches, and *In a Quiet Village* (1900) sustains Baring-Gould's rural theme, although some of the stories are set as far away from Dartmoor as Wales. *In a Quiet Village* almost achieves a subtle thematic unity by focusing upon characters who puzzle the narrator. Their lives present problems "for a casuist to solve." The first three stories raise the sort of questions that Hardy might ask, even though Baring-Gould is obviously less predisposed to accept a negative answer. In "Dan'l Combe" a village tailor works at night for thirty-five years on a secret project before proudly telling the vicar that he has completed a concordance to the Bible. The news that "the thing had already been done" crushes the man. Only on his deathbed does he construct a meaning for his years of apparently wasted labor. The Bible runs like blood in his veins, and this supports him as he lies dying.

More questions about the order of things arise in "Doble Drewe," the story of a plumber and housepainter with a passion for music. He saves his money to buy a piano but discovers that he cannot play it; he marries in hopes of having a child who will learn how, but no child is ever born to him. The parson narrating the story ponders the mystery of why God would create a man with such "high-strung musical faculties" and yet leave him "absolutely incapacitated by position and circumstances for making any use of his great gift. . . . Why was Doble given a faculty he could not use?" By faith he finally gets a hint of an answer after hearing how the man died; Doble has been swept up in heavenly music. The answer would not have satisfied Hardy, who might have preferred the sardonic ending of "Timothy Slouch." Unable to keep a job, a blundering, shiftless misfit eventually falls to his death from a rotten rafter. After the burial the rector notes that Slouch at last has found his place on (or in) earth, and the young farmer who marries Slouch's hardworking widow discovers the reason for his existence: "I do believe the work and mission of that fellow was just this – to make for me the very model and perfection of a farmer's wife, and then to break his neck." The young man's pious mother agrees, " 'Twere all ordained."

Commenting in his own person, Baring-Gould is only a mildly interesting observer of rural people. His stories come to life when his characters gain voices of their own, as the narrator does in "Margery of Quether." Then Baring-Gould reveals an imaginative gift that shines through his best work. The same gift allowed him to re-create rustic speech in *Yorkshire Oddities* and to write the inspired monologues of Elijah Rebow in *Mehalah* and of Mrs. Veale, the pink-eyed albino witch in *Red Spider*

(1887). At his best, the antiquarian folklorist, mythographer, theologian, parson, squire, and inveterate collector of oddities ceases to be the outside observer and enters the mental world of his characters. Then the reader not only can see their moors and marshlands, churches and cottages but also can hear them speaking in their own peculiar tongues.

Interview:
Frederick Dolman, "Novel-Writing and Novel-Reading: A Chat with the Rev. S. Baring-Gould," *Cassell's Family Magazine,* new series 1 (December 1894): 17–24.

Bibliography:
Samuel J. Rogal, "Sabine Baring-Gould (1834–1924): A Checklist," *Serif,* 9 (Summer 1972): 22–35.

Biographies:
William Purcell, *Onward Christian Soldier: A Life of Sabine Baring-Gould, Parson, Squire, Novelist, Antiquary, 1834–1924* (London: Longmans, Green, 1957);
Bickford H. D. Dickinson, *Sabine Baring-Gould: Squarson, Writer and Folklorist, 1834–1924* (Newton Abbot, U.K.: David & Charles, 1970).

References:
William Addison, *The English Country Parson* (London: Dent, 1947), pp. 204–214;
James M. Barrie, "Novels of Sabine Baring-Gould," *Contemporary Review,* 57 (February 1890): 206–226;
John Fowles, Introduction to Baring-Gould's *Mehalah: A Story of the Salt Marshes* (London: Chatto & Windus, 1969);
Harold Orel, Introduction to *Victorian Short Stories: An Anthology,* edited by Orel (London: Dent, 1987);
Orel, *The Victorian Short Story: Development and Triumph of a Literary Genre* (Cambridge: Cambridge University Press, 1986);
David Roberts, "If One Had to Pick the Strangest Victorian . . . ," *Smithsonian,* 24 (July 1993): 74–82.

Papers:
Most of Baring-Gould's papers were lost in a 1967 fire at Dunsland House. Surviving letters to the author's eldest daughter are cited by Bickford H. D. Dickinson in his biography. The Plymouth City Library holds the unexpurgated manuscript copy of the folk songs transcribed by Baring-Gould, H. Fleetwood Sheppard, and F. W. Bussell.

J. M. Barrie

(9 May 1860 – 19 June 1937)

Siobhan Craft Brownson
University of South Carolina

See also the Barrie entries in *DLB 10: Modern British Dramatists, 1900–1945* and *DLB 141: British Children's Writers, 1880–1914.*

BOOKS: *Better Dead* (London: Swan Sonnenschein, Lowrie, 1888; Chicago & New York: Rand, McNally, 1891);

Auld Licht Idylls (London: Hodder & Stoughton, 1888; New York: Macmillan, 1891);

When a Man's Single (London: Hodder & Stoughton, 1888; New York: Harper, 1889; first authorized American edition, New York: Scribners, 1896);

An Edinburgh Eleven: Pencil Portraits from College Life (London: British Weekly, 1889; New York: Lovell, Coryell, 1892);

A Window in Thrums (London: Hodder & Stoughton, 1889; New York: Cassell, 1892; first authorized American edition, New York: Scribners, 1897);

My Lady Nicotine (London: Hodder & Stoughton, 1890; New York: Rand, McNally, 1891; first authorized American edition, New York: Scribners, 1896);

Richard Savage, by Barrie and H. B. Marriott Watson (London: Privately printed, 1891);

The Little Minister (London: Cassell, 1891; New York: Lovell, 1891);

A Holiday in Bed and Other Stories (New York: John Knox, 1893);

An Auld Licht Manse and Other Sketches (New York: John Knox, 1893);

Jane Annie; or, The Good Conduct Prize, by Barrie and Arthur Conan Doyle (London: Chapell, 1893);

A Powerful Drug and Other Stories (New York: Ogilvie, 1893);

A Tillyloss Scandal (New York: Lovell, Coryell, 1893);

Two of Them (New York: Lovell, Coryell, 1893);

A Lady's Shoe (London: Chapman & Hall, 1894; New York: Brentano's, 1898);

J. M. Barrie

Life in a Country Manse (New York: Ogilvie, 1894);

Scotland's Lament: A Poem on the Death of Robert Louis Stevenson (London: Privately printed for T. J. Wise, 1895);

Sentimental Tommy (London: Cassell, 1896; New York: Scribners, 1896);

Margaret Ogilvy (New York: Scribners, 1896; London: Hodder & Stoughton, 1896);

Jess (Boston: Estes, 1898);

Allahakbarrie Book of Broadway Cricket (N.p.: Privately printed, 1899);

14

Tommy and Grizel (London: Cassell, 1900; New York: Scribners, 1900);

The Wedding Guest (New York: Scribners, 1900);

The Boy Castaways of Black Lake Island (N.p.: Privately printed, 1901);

The Little White Bird, or Adventures in Kensington Gardens (London: Hodder & Stoughton, 1902; New York: Scribners, 1902);

Peter Pan in Kensington Gardens (London: Hodder & Stoughton, 1906; New York: Scribners, 1906);

Walker London (London & New York: French, 1907);

George Meredith, 1909 (London: Constable, 1909; Portland, Maine: Mosher, 1909);

Peter and Wendy (London: Hodder & Stoughton, 1911; New York: Scribners, 1911); republished as *Peter Pan and Wendy* (London: Hodder & Stoughton, 1921; New York: Scribners, 1921); republished as *The Blampied Edition of Peter Pan* (New York: Scribners, 1940); republished as *Peter Pan* (London: Hodder & Stoughton, 1949; New York: Scribners, 1950);

Quality Street (London: Hodder & Stoughton, 1913; New York: Scribners, 1918);

The Admirable Crichton (London, New York & Toronto: Hodder & Stoughton, 1914);

Half Hours (New York: Scribners, 1914; London: Hodder & Stoughton, 1914);

Der Tag; A Play (London, New York & Toronto: Hodder & Stoughton, 1914); republished as *Der Tag; or, The Tragic Man* (New York: Scribners, 1914);

Charles Frohman: A Tribute (London: Privately printed by Clement Shorter, 1915);

Shakespeare's Legacy (London: Privately printed by Clement Shorter, 1916);

Echoes of the War (London, New York & Toronto: Hodder & Stoughton, 1918);

The Old Lady Shows Her Medals (London: Hodder & Stoughton, 1918; New York: Scribners, 1918);

What Every Woman Knows (London: Hodder & Stoughton, 1918; New York: Scribners, 1918);

Alice-Sit-by-the-Fire (London & New York: Hodder & Stoughton, 1919);

A Kiss for Cinderella (London: Hodder & Stoughton, 1920; New York: Scribners, 1921);

The Twelve-Pound Look (London: Hodder & Stoughton, 1921; New York: Scribners, 1921);

Courage (London: Hodder & Stoughton, 1922; New York: Scribners, 1922);

Dear Brutus (London: Hodder & Stoughton, 1922; New York: Scribners, 1922);

Mary Rose (London: Hodder & Stoughton, 1924; New York: Scribners, 1924);

The Author (Cincinnati: Privately printed, 1925);

Cricket (London: Privately printed by Clement Shorter, 1926);

Representative Plays, edited by William Lyon Phelps (New York: Scribners, 1926);

Peter Pan; or, The Boy Who Would Not Grow Up (London: Hodder & Stoughton, 1928; New York: Scribners, 1928);

The Plays of J. M. Barrie (London: Hodder & Stoughton, 1928; New York: Scribners, 1930; revised, 1942);

Shall We Join the Ladies? (New York: Scribners, 1928; London: Hodder & Stoughton, 1929);

The Works of J. M. Barrie, 16 volumes (New York: Scribners, 1929–1940);

Farewell, Miss Julie Logan (New York: Scribners, 1932; London: Hodder & Stoughton, 1932);

The Greenwood Hat (Edinburgh: Constable, 1937; New York: Scribners, 1938);

The Boy David (London: Davies, 1938; New York: Scribners, 1938);

M'Connachie and J. M. B. (London: Davies, 1938; New York: Scribners, 1939);

When Wendy Grew Up: An Afterthought (New York: Dutton, 1957);

Ibsen's Ghost; or, Toole Up-to-Date (London: Cecil Woolf, 1975).

PLAY PRODUCTIONS: *Bandelero, the Bandit,* Dumfries, Scotland, Dumfries Academy, 1877;

Richard Savage, by Barrie and H. B. Marriott Watson, London, Criterion Theatre, 16 April 1891;

Ibsen's Ghost; or, Toole Up-to-Date, London, Toole's Theatre, 29 May 1891;

Walker, London, London, Toole's Theatre, 25 February 1892;

Jane Annie; or, The Good Conduct Prize, by Barrie and Arthur Conan Doyle, with music by Ernest Ford, London, Savoy Theatre, 13 May 1893;

Becky Sharp, London, Terry's Theatre, 3 June 1893;

The Professor's Love Story, New York, Star Theatre, 13 December 1893;

The Little Minister, London, Haymarket Theatre, 13 July 1897;

A Platonic Friendship, London, Theatre Royal (Drury Lane), 17 March 1898;

The Wedding Guest, London, Garrick Theatre, 27 September 1900;

Quality Street, Toledo, Ohio, 14 October 1901;

The Admirable Crichton, London, Duke of York's Theatre, 4 November 1902;

Little Mary, London, Wyndham's Theatre, 24 September 1903;

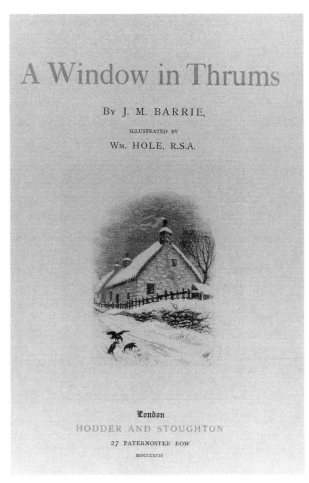

A Window in Thrums

By J. M. BARRIE,

ILLUSTRATED BY

Wm. HOLE, R.S.A.

London

HODDER AND STOUGHTON

27 PATERNOSTER ROW

MDCCCXCII

Title page for one of Barrie's books of stories about rural Scottish life (Special Collections, Thomas Cooper Library, University of South Carolina)

Peter Pan; or, The Boy Who Wouldn't Grow Up, London, Duke of York's Theatre, 27 December 1904;

Pantaloon; or, A Plea for an Ancient Family, with music by John Crook, London, Duke of York's Theatre, 5 April 1905;

Alice-Sit-by-the-Fire: A Page from a Daughter's Diary, London, Duke of York's Theatre, 5 April 1905;

Josephine, London, Comedy Theatre, 5 April 1906;

Punch: A Toy Tragedy, London, Comedy Theatre, 5 April 1906;

When Wendy Grew Up (An Afterthought), London, Duke of York's Theatre, 22 February 1908 (one performance);

What Every Woman Knows, London, Duke of York's Theatre, 3 September 1908;

Old Friends, London, Duke of York's Theatre, 1 March 1910;

The Twelve-Pound Look, London, Duke of York's Theatre, 1 March 1910;

A Slice of Life: An Advanced Drama, London, Duke of York's Theatre, 7 June 1910;

Rosalind, London, Duke of York's Theatre, 14 October 1912;

The Dramatists Get What They Want, London, Hippodrome, 23 December 1912;

The Adored One: A Legend of the Old Bailey, London, Duke of York's Theatre, 4 September 1913; Act I revised as *Seven Women,* London, New Theatre, 7 April 1917;

The Will, London, Duke of York's Theatre, 4 September 1913;

Half an Hour, New York, Lyceum Theatre, 25 September 1913;

Frank Tinney's Revue, London, Savoy Theatre, 3 July 1914;

Shakespeare's Legacy, Atlantic City, N. J., 8 October 1914;

The Duke of Christmas Daisies, Dumfries, Scotland, Dumfries Academy, 12 December 1914;

Der Tag; or, The Tragic Man, London, Coliseum, 21 December 1914;

The New Word, London, Duke of York's Theatre, 22 March 1915;

Rosy Rapture, the Pride of the Beauty Chorus, by Barrie, with lyrics by F. W. Mark, music by Hermann Darewski and Jerome D. Kern, London, Duke of York's Theatre, 22 March 1915;

The Fatal Typist, London, His Majesty's Theatre, 19 November 1915;

A Kiss for Cinderella, London, Wyndham's Theatre, 16 March 1916;

Irene Vanbrugh's Pantomime, London, Coliseum, 9 June 1916;

The Origin of Harlequin, with music by Herman Fincke, London, Palace Theatre, 16 February 1917;

Reconstructing the Crime, London, Palace Theatre, 16 February 1917;

The Old Lady Shows Her Medals, London, New Theatre, 7 April 1917;

Dear Brutus, London, Wyndham's Theatre, 17 October 1917;

La Politesse, London, Wyndham's Theatre, 28 June 1918;

A Well-Remembered Voice, London, Wyndham's Theatre, 28 June 1918;

The Truth About the Russian Dancers, London, Coliseum, 15 March 1920;

Mary Rose, London, Haymarket Theatre, 22 April 1920;

Shall We Join the Ladies?, London, Vanbrugh Theatre (Royal Academy of Dramatic Arts), 27 May 1921;

A Happy New Year, London, Little Theatre, 31 May 1922;

Barbara's Wedding, London, Savoy Theatre, 23 August 1927;

The Boy David, Edinburgh, King's Theatre, 21 November 1936.

MOTION PICTURES: *How Men Love,* script by Barrie, 1916;

The Real Thing at Last, script by Barrie, 1916.

OTHER: "A Word About Donkeys," in *Votiva Tabella: A Memorial Volume* (N.p.: Printed for Saint Andrew's University by Robert MacLehose, 1911), pp. 389–398;

"A Holiday in Bed," in *Princess Mary's Gift Book* (Toronto: Hodder & Stoughton, 1914), pp. 1–8;

Letter, *Commemoration of the Centenary of the Birth of James Russell Lowell* (New York: Scribners, 1919), pp. 29–31;

Daisy Ashford, *The Young Visitors, or Mr. Salteena's Plan,* preface by Barrie (London: Chatto & Windus, 1919);

David Donald, *The Conversation of Padan Aram,* foreword by Barrie (London: R. T. S., 1927);

"Brought Back from Elysium," in *Victorian Fiction: A Collection of Essays from the Period,* edited by Ira Bruce Nadel (New York & London: Garland, 1986), n.p.

J. M. Barrie wrote dozens of plays in his lifetime and is best known as the creator of Peter Pan, the boy who refused to grow up. However, he began his career as a journalist and during his early years as a writer composed some forty short stories; indeed, he ended his prose fiction career with what is arguably his best story. Though often viewed as the sentimental outpourings of a man who refused to grow up and of a writer who dodged the harsher realities of poverty and the severity of the church in his native Scotland, Barrie's short stories, which were well received in their time, provide a clear view of an accepted style of fiction common to late Victorian writing as well as a transition to the more distinctive fictional voices of James Joyce, Virginia Woolf, and D. H. Lawrence.

James Matthew Barrie was born on 9 May 1860 in Kirriemuir, Scotland, five hundred miles from London, to Margaret Ogilvy Barrie, daughter of an Auld Licht Kirk stonemason, and David Barrie, a weaver. He was their third son and the ninth of ten children. Kirriemuir, despite Barrie's later fictionalization of it as a small village, was a town of some four thousand inhabitants. Some biographers attribute much in his emotional development to a childhood event, which sent his emotionally devastated mother to her bed for the remainder of her life: in January 1867 Barrie's thirteen-year-old brother, David, was knocked down by an ice-skater, fractured his skull, and died. He recounts his attempt to take the place of this favorite son in his biography of his mother, *Margaret Ogilvy* (1896). Only seven years old, he told her, "Wait till I'm a man and you'll never have reason for greeting [weeping] again."

Barrie and his mother loved stories; they often read to each other, and she began to recall for him memories of her early life. These memories formed the basis of his early work in journalism and his two collections of short stories. At age twelve he regularly received a monthly penny magazine called *Sunshine.* One month the issue failed to arrive, and he decided to write his own stories to entertain his mother. He says in *Margaret Ogilvy* that after these early ventures in writing, "my mind was made up; there could be no hum-dreadful-drum profession for me; literature was my game." His first publication was a piece titled "Reckollections of a Skoolmaster" (1875) in a journal called *The Clown* begun by his friend Wellwood (Wedd) Anderson while they were at Dumfries Academy.

Barrie began his journalism career as an editorial writer for the *Nottingham Journal.* He worked on the paper from January 1883 to October 1884. In the fall of 1884 he submitted an article called "Auld Licht Idylls" to the *St. James's Gazette.* Frederick Greenwood, its editor and founder, retitled the piece "An Auld Licht Community" and published it on 17 November 1884. Barrie believed that he had finished with the subject and forwarded pieces on different topics. However, Greenwood rejected these articles, returning them with the famous note, "I like that Scotch thing. Any more of those?" Barrie's responses to this query are the foundation of his first two collections of stories and sketches, *Auld Licht Idylls* (1888) and *A Window in Thrums* (1889).

"That Scotch thing" was retitled "Thrums" and appears as the second story in *Auld Licht Idylls.* "Thrums," defined by John Kennedy in *Thrums and the Barrie Country* (1930) as "the fringe of threads left on the loom when the web is taken off," was the name Barrie gave the Kirriemuir of his mother's childhood. The kirk, the central force in the lives of the Thrums inhabitants, was the Auld Licht Kirk,

Mary Ansell Barrie, circa 1894

Barrie moved to London on 28 March 1885. William Robertson Nicoll, editor of the *British Weekly,* discovered his writing in 1887 after noticing an article by him in the *Edinburgh Evening Dispatch* and appreciating its restrained irreverence. Barrie began writing a regular column for the *British Weekly,* signing his articles Gavin Ogilvy, and continued to submit articles, sketches, and short stories to the *St. James's Gazette,* the *Scots Observer,* and the *Edinburgh Evening Dispatch,* among others. Biographers such as Denis Mackail and Janet Dunbar note that at this time Barrie had a strong desire to be married but that his social life was unsuccessful.

The evangelical firm of Hodder and Stoughton, publisher of the *British Weekly,* suggested to Barrie in 1888 that he collect some of his old articles in book form. He chose the Auld Licht stories and created a dominie (schoolmaster) narrator; *Auld Licht Idylls* was published in April 1888. The book reintroduced Thrums to the reading public as well as Barrie's version of Scottish ministers, weavers, and wives living in an Auld Licht Kirk community during the early part of the nineteenth century. Immediate critical reaction was enthusiastic, as typified by a review by William Wallace in the 26 May 1888 *Academy:* "[Barrie's] descriptive power, which is little if at all inferior to his humour, and, like it, has the saving grace of self-restraint, reminds one sometimes of Mr. Thomas Hardy." A generation later critics attempting to place Barrie's short stories within a body of Scottish literature found the humor of *Auld Licht Idylls* heavy-handed and the quaintness of his unusual Lowland rural folktales fantastic. In *Edinburgh Essays on Scots Literature* (1933) Angus Macdonald writes that Barrie, having "found that the taste for the day was for sentiment," responded accordingly. More-current critical studies of Barrie's short fiction do not dismiss his work yet are apt to find his sentimentality treacly rather than inspiring, his talent less a matter of literary skill than of measuring the popular culture. At any rate few compared Barrie's Thrums to Hardy's Wessex within twenty years after the publication of his first collected short fiction and sketches.

Though even Barrie's later detractors admired the quality of his prose and though Barrie was a skilled journalist, he displayed questionable abilities as a short-story writer. Readers might expect or hope for solid characterization, realistic dialogue, or integrated themes, or might respect individual style, but they usually demand a plot. Early reviews of *Auld Licht Idylls* often wavered between labeling the contents sketches or short stories. Indeed, few of the pieces qualify as short stories by most modern

founded in 1733 by those who seceded from the established Church of Scotland over the issue of a congregation's right to appoint its own minister. Some critics, such as Eric Anderson in "The Kailyard School Revisited" (1979), believe that Barrie takes some pains to show that Thrums does not represent a contemporary picture of late-nineteenth-century Scotland. However, Barrie's remark that "few Auld Licht communities [exist] in Scotland nowadays" is casual and was apparently missed by English and American readers who, enchanted with the strangeness of the church establishment and Scots dialogue, were quick to assume that they had gleaned an accurate portrayal of all Scottish people. Besides introducing the Thrums of dozens of subsequent stories and sketches and at least three novels, "Thrums" possesses many of the fictional qualities for which Barrie was later both lauded and dismissed – humor, stereotyping, Scots dialogue, realistic setting, mawkishness, and fantasy.

definitions. "The Schoolhouse," for example – written specifically to introduce the volume, establish the setting of Thrums, and acquaint readers with the narrator, the dominie of Glen Quharity (based on the Glen Clova of Barrie's youth) – relies on an extended brawl between a weasel and a water hen for the plot, complete with startling interior monologues by the animals, yet includes the occasional fine brief description, such as "[t]he crumbling gravestones keep cold vigil round the grey kirk." The setting Barrie creates foreshadows the "locked" glen atmosphere he masterfully achieves in his last short story, "Farewell, Miss Julie Logan."

"The Courting of T'nowhead's Bell," which Anderson calls "one of the best of Scottish short stories," recounts the competition between Sam'l Dickie and Sanders Elshioner for the hand of Bell McQuatty. The story seems to reach its climax at the church one Sunday when both men realize that Bell has stayed at home to care for her six-month-old sibling. Knowing that Bell will accept as a husband the first suitor who proposes, Sanders slips out of the church. Sam'l sees him, the race is on, and Sam'l reaches T'nowhead's farm first. But Barrie surprises the reader with Sanders's war of intimidation. Saying, "Weel, Sam'l, mairitch is a terrible responsibility an' no the thing to tak up withoot conseederation," Sanders adroitly manipulates Sam'l into relinquishing Bell and even makes Sam'l think it was his own idea. Not only does Barrie show his knack for moving the narrative ahead with dialogue, which makes up nearly half the story and presages his transition to drama in the early 1890s – in fact, the plot of "The Courting of T'nowhead's Bell" is a subplot in one of his first successful plays, *The Professor's Love Story* (1893) – his sense of the absurd has the power to amuse readers. The story easily appeals to readers more than a century later not only for its historical depiction of early-nineteenth-century Scottish traditions, customs, and language but for its mature portrayal of human sensibilities.

The nine months from April 1888 through January 1889 brought a flurry of publishing activity for Barrie. As a result of Greenwood's leaving the *St. James's Gazette,* Barrie began looking for another sympathetic editor and discovered one in William Ernest Henley, founder of the Edinburgh weekly the *Scots Observer.* Upon learning that Henley was a friend of George Meredith's, Barrie submitted a piece titled "The Lost Works of George Meredith" about a neglected essay and three short stories. Henley accepted the article, and Barrie became one of "Henley's young men," a group that included Hardy, Rudyard Kipling, H. G. Wells, and William Butler Yeats. In addition to writing for the *Scots Observer,* Barrie continued to contribute to the *St. James's Gazette,* the *British Weekly,* and the *Edinburgh Evening Dispatch.* In October 1888 Hodder and Stoughton published his novel *When a Man's Single,* which was based on his experiences as an editorial writer for the *Nottingham Journal.* In January 1889 Nicoll printed a collection of articles Barrie published between 15 July 1887 and 30 November 1888 titled *An Edinburgh Eleven: Pencil Portraits from College Life,* short studies of his professors at Edinburgh University.

In July 1889 Hodder and Stoughton published *A Window in Thrums,* a collection of short stories and sketches Barrie had written for various newspapers from 1887 to 1889 chiefly concerned with the family of Jess, Leeby, and Hendry McQumpha and what they see from the upper window in their house. *A Window in Thrums* follows the pattern of *Auld Licht Idylls* in three ways: the narrative device is the observant yet unobtrusive schoolmaster; the subject is Thrums and its inhabitants; and the pieces are uneven in their treatment of the short-story form. However, the two collections diverge in some important respects. For example, Barrie focuses on the McQumpha family not as a microcosm of Scottish village society, as Thrums as a whole was in *Auld Licht Idylls,* but as a singular shining ideal of love, devotion, and lasting support. In addition, for the first time Barrie incorporates a symbol, albeit an ironic one – the window at which Jess "sat for twenty years or more looking at the world as through a telescope." Jess uses the window to bring the details of life in Thrums into sharper focus while Barrie employs the window as a means of blurring and narrowing reality. Finally, *A Window in Thrums* can be said to possess true thematic unity. By concentrating on the McQumpha family's amusing and loving daily routines and by ending the book with the sad return of Jamie, who had abandoned this paradise for the big city of London and a woman, Barrie reveals his sense that happiness is illusory and easily spoiled by the passing of time and the acted-upon desire for assimilation into the adult world of work and sexual fulfillment and that, paradoxically, movement through life is what snatches life's richness away.

Critical reaction to the book was mixed and ranged from the glowing to the denunciatory. A similar combination of views is found in later criticism, which, while tending to lump *Auld Licht Idylls* and *A Window in Thrums* together, still manages to note differences between the two and even some maturing of Barrie's writing. Anderson finds that

*Barrie as chancellor of the University of Edinburgh and Prime
Minister Ramsay MacDonald, on whom he conferred an
honorary doctorate, 1932*

"the greatness of this minor masterpiece lies not in its humour and pathos, nor even in the brilliance of its dialogue and the spare prose of its descriptive passages, but in the sense of significance with which Barrie invests the humble life which he describes," while George Blake in *Barrie and the Kailyard School* (1951) sees the whole book as "sorry stuff in terms of life" and as "a debauch of sentimentality."

Some of the stories in *A Window in Thrums* illustrate one of Barrie's primary subjects, the mother/son dynamic. In these stories the mother figure maintains an iron grip on the son and uses emotional blackmail to an extreme degree. "The Tale of a Glove," in which Jess and Jamie struggle for possession of a lady's glove, is probably his best-known story because of Robert Louis Stevenson's response to it. In an often-quoted 5 December 1892 letter written from Samoa to Henry James, Stevenson comments, "But Barrie is a beauty, *The Little Minister*

and the *Window in Thrums,* eh? Stuff in that young man, but he must see and not be too funny. Genius in him, but there's a journalist at his elbow – there's the risk. Look what a page is the glove business in *Window!* Knocks a man flat; that's guts if you please." Some critics are similarly moved by the story, but others are harsher in their judgments of Jess's need to be the prevailing emotional force in her son's life. In spite of Stevenson's ardent praise of Barrie's genius, modern readers of "The Tale of a Glove," while admiring the quickly moving narrative and the skillfully rendered conflict between the two main characters, are apt to agree with critic Thomas Moult that Barrie lacks an awareness of the symbolic nature of the glove – that it represents not a son's betrayal of his mother but a mother's inability to accept her son's natural sexual maturity.

In 1891 Barrie wrote a novel called *The Little Minister,* which along with *Auld Licht Idylls* and *A Window in Thrums* placed him in what came to be known as the Kailyard School, a term first used by Henley when he titled an uncomplimentary article by J. H. Millar in the *New Review* of 1895 "Literature in the Kailyard." Barrie; S. R. Crockett, author of *The Stickit Minister* (1893) and *The Lilac Sunbonnet* (1894) and a Scottish Free Church minister; and John Watson, also a Free Church minister, who under the name Ian Maclaren wrote *Beside the Bonnie Brier Bush* (1894), were the primary laborers in the kailyard (cabbage patch). The term comes from a preface used by Maclaren for his book: "There grows a bonnie brier bush in our kailyard, / And white are the blossoms on't in our kailyard." Kailyard School writing is typified by an affected attitude toward the ministers, handloom weavers, and farmers who inhabit idealized Scottish rural communities in the early nineteenth century and by a celebration of their poor yet virtuous Christian lives and their never-ending respect for kirk, hearth, and family. Even detractors of the school recognize that Barrie was the most skilled of the three writers. He did not found the school – Herbert Paul's claim in "The Apotheosis of the Novel" (1897) to the contrary – but rather the school found and labeled him after Crockett and Maclaren planted the cabbage patch with imitations. Also, the editors of the newspapers for which Barrie wrote, particularly Nicoll, were at least partially responsible for molding the public taste for the strange, jolly pathos of the Scottish provincials. Scottish literary critics are the hardest on the Kailyard writers and deplore their unrealistic depictions of their fellow Scots on the scores of bad psychology, bad history, and bad art. Yet recent critics of Kailyard writing, such as Anderson and Thomas D. Knowles, find much to recommend in Barrie's short fiction and argue that to dismiss his work simply on the grounds that it has been placed in the Kailyard School is to oversimplify his intentions and ignore his talent.

Many more of Barrie's short stories can be found in unauthorized or pirated collections by American publishers eager to profit from his increasing popularity. Copyright laws did not protect British writers' work in the United States until 1896, the year Scribners was authorized to print Barrie's work. Upon hearing about the pirated collections, Barrie said, "I entirely disown them"; however, these editions quickly became valuable to collectors. *A Holiday in Bed and Other Stories* (1893), *An Auld Licht Manse and Other Sketches* (1893), and *A Tillyloss Scandal* (1893) best represent Barrie's work that was not collected in Great Britain. Two pieces that qualify as short stories from *A Holiday in Bed* illustrate his gift for humor. "A Powerful Drug," published in the 28 March 1888 *Edinburgh Evening Dispatch,* tells the story of Montgomery's belief in "cio-root" as the cure for headaches. He thinks he has overdosed one day, grows increasingly ill, and finds upon returning home that he forgot to take the offending medicine. "Thoughtful Boys Make Thoughtful Men," published in the 23 February 1889 *Edinburgh Evening Dispatch,* concerns a boy who receives the book in the story's title as a birthday present instead of the cake he expects. Terribly disappointed, he manages to sell the book to different boys, covering up his previous sales by "dropping hints that it was a deeply interesting story"; the irony is that the boy, in taking advantage of his friends, is clearly little edified by his gift. *A Tillyloss Scandal* includes the title story, first published in *Good Words* (January–February 1890), in which Barrie returns to Thrums and tells the story of how Tammas Haggart becomes a humorist. The story represents some of Barrie's strongest work in short fiction yet is almost never mentioned by literary critics, Scottish or otherwise. He here skillfully combines unencumbered prose, accessible Scots dialect, and a swiftly moving narrative in his most sustained work apart from "Farewell, Miss Julie Logan." Its lack of a unifying theme is notable but not bothersome, for the story serves to entertain and performs well on that score.

Barrie married Mary Ansell in 1894. His beloved sister, Jane Ann, and their mother died three days apart in 1895, an emotionally cataclysmic blow. Yet he completed the novel *Sentimental Tommy* and his mother's biography in 1896; he also set about dramatizing *The Little Minister.* The play

opened to appreciative reviews in 1897. He began a friendship with Hardy at about this time; the two men corresponded frequently, and Barrie was awed and thrilled to be associated with one whose work he so admired. Another novel, *Tommy and Grizel,* was published in 1900. At this point in his career Barrie was virtually finished with prose fiction and turned to drama. His most successful and best-remembered plays are *Quality Street* (1901), *The Admirable Crichton* (1902), *Peter Pan; or, The Boy Who Wouldn't Grow Up* (1904), *A Kiss for Cinderella* (1916), *Dear Brutus* (1917), and *Mary Rose* (1920). He also wrote many one-act plays and delivered dozens of speeches, which were posthumously collected in *M'Connachie and J. M. B.* (1938).

Barrie's last thirty years brought a steady stream of important honors. He was presented honorary degrees by Saint Andrews University, Scotland, in 1898; Edinburgh University in 1909; Oxford University in 1926; and Cambridge University in 1930. He was elected rector of Saint Andrews in 1919 and chancellor of Edinburgh in 1930; he succeeded Hardy as president of the Incorporated Society of Authors in 1928; a baronetcy was bestowed upon him by George V in 1913; and the Order of Merit was presented to him in 1922. Yet these were also years of substantial emotional hardship. His marriage ended in divorce in 1904, and nearly all of his siblings predeceased him, as did his literary friends Stevenson, Hardy, and Meredith. Barrie's last years were spent in poor health and loneliness despite a deep friendship with Lady Cynthia Asquith, who became his secretary. Nevertheless, he managed to go through his old stories and articles and compile *The Greenwood Hat* (1937). Denis Mackail in *Barrie: The Story of J. M. B.* (1941) suggests that his "delvings into the past had released something," setting "the secret processes to work," and that Barrie was once again motivated to write fiction.

The result was "Farewell, Miss Julie Logan," and the critics were almost unanimous in their approval. The review in the 28 December 1932 *Commonweal* represents the positive reaction, calling it "a marvel of construction, of characterization, deft humor, and amiable sentiment . . . with just that touch of fancifulness that distinguishes the highest artistic creation." Part of the story's appeal lies in its being a ghost story in the form of a diary kept by a young minister, Adam Yestreen, snowbound during his first winter in a Thrums-like village. On New Year's Eve – to Scots the Hogamany, a night when spirits walk the earth – Yestreen enters into a battle with Julie Logan, an ethereal beauty from the super-

Barrie in his apartment at Adelphi Terrace, London

natural world. They picnic in a small ruin, she challenges him to carry her across the burn (stream), they kiss, and in an oddly placed comic moment she declares, "I am a Papist," whereupon he drops her and is released from her spell. One of Barrie's surprise endings concludes the story when, twenty-five years later, Yestreen revisits the glen and confides to his friend, Dr. John, that after his experience, desperate to convince himself that the events of New Year's Eve were the product of his imagination, he had gone back to the glen and in the ruin found the picnic basket he and Julie Logan had shared.

Barrie creates, perhaps for the first time in his short-story career, an atmosphere rather than an attitude. The character of Adam Yestreen, a learned man open to new ideas and to a romantic approach to life, is fully realized, as is the voice of the narrative, knowing yet not sly. In addition, the supernatural element gives the piece an underpinning of intellectual suspense. Notably, Barrie finally achieves a thematic treatment of adult romantic love; Adam Yestreen's failure with a beautiful ghost parallels Barrie's own disappointing history with women.

Furthermore, Yestreen's willingness to traffic in the supernatural suggests that Barrie, at the end of his life, no longer feared the ambiguous and bewildering nature of existence. Many years after the publication of "Farewell, Miss Julie Logan," critics continue to find charm and skill in Barrie's last short story.

Barrie wrote one more play, *The Boy David* (1936), but was unable to attend the opening performance in Edinburgh because of his failing health. He died on 19 June 1937 at age seventy-seven and was buried next to his mother and his brother David in Kirriemuir.

Barrie seems to have emerged full-blown as a short-story writer. Greenwood, Nicoll, and Henley provided him with a formula, and he chose never to deviate far from it. The thematic content of his short fiction reveals characters who depend upon strict patterns in church, family, and work to deal with the stresses of daily living; his stories mirror their composer, who fiercely sought evidence that ignoring life's challenges could eradicate them. He saw himself as a writer rather than an artist. In fairness, his skill at creating dialogue, setting, mood, and humorous plots must be recognized. He simply had no interest in delving into the realities of the Industrial Revolution, which changed the lives of his fellow Scots, nor in exploring, for example, the effect of World War I upon his countrymen in England. While Stevenson, Meredith, Hardy, and Wells admired Barrie's work, it seems to have had no impact on their own writing. Barrie's major influence is seen only in the work of Crockett and Maclaren, who are usually mentioned only as examples of the usually deplored Kailyard School.

Apart from recent apologists for the Kailyard writers, Barrie's short fiction is currently rarely analyzed and even more rarely read by the general public. Nonetheless, Leonee Ormond's *J. M. Barrie* (1987) critically analyzes all of Barrie's work, including journalism, short and long fiction, and drama. Her treatment of the work rather than the man suggests a new willingness to discuss his writing apart from his life, his unfortunate classification as a Kailyard writer, and the easy dismissal of him as a sloppy sentimentalist. Despite his frequently facile treatment of his chosen subjects, some of his short fiction can withstand fairly rigorous examination and not be found lacking. A review of Barrie's stories can impress readers with his abilities in creating sturdy, if not elegant, dialogue, characters, and plots and can leave them with the sense that he left not only *Peter Pan* behind him but convincing evidence – in "The Courting of T'nowhead's Bell," "A Tillyloss Scandal," and "Farewell, Miss Julie Logan" – that his short fiction developed in important ways and deserves reexamination.

Letters:

The Letters of J. M. Barrie, edited by Viola Meynell (London: Davies, 1942; New York: Scribners, 1947).

Interview:

Alan Dale, "Peter Pan's Pater," *Cosmopolitan,* 52 (May 1912): 793-796.

Bibliographies:

Herbert Garland, *A Bibliography of the Writings of Sir James Matthew Barrie* (London: Bookman's Journal, 1928);

B. D. Cutler, *Sir James M. Barrie: A Bibliography, with Full Collations of the American Unauthorized Editions* (New York: Greenberg, 1931);

Carl Markgraf, *J. M. Barrie: An Annotated Secondary Bibliography* (Greensboro, N.C.: ELT Press, 1989).

Biographies:

J. A. Hammerton, *Barrie: The Story of a Genius* (London: Sampson Low, Marston, 1929);

James A. Roy, *James Matthew Barrie: An Appreciation* (New York: Scribners, 1938);

Denis Mackail, *Barrie: The Story of J.M.B.* (New York: Scribners, 1941);

Janet Dunbar, *J. M. Barrie: The Man Behind the Image* (Boston: Houghton Mifflin, 1970).

References:

Eric Anderson, "The Kailyard School Revisited," in *Nineteenth-Century Scottish Fiction: Critical Essays,* edited by Ian Campbell (New York: Barnes & Noble, 1979), pp. 130-147;

George Blake, *Barrie and the Kailyard School* (New York: Roy, 1951);

Alan N. Bold, "The Confines of the Kailyard: Barrie and Company," in his *Modern Scottish Literature* (New York: Longman, 1983), pp. 105-108;

David Craig, *Scottish Literature and the Scottish People 1680-1830* (London: Chatto & Windus, 1961);

Harry M. Geduld, *Sir James Barrie* (New York: Twayne, 1971);

Roger Lancelyn Green, Introduction to *J. M. Barrie's Plays and Stories,* edited by Green (London: Dent, 1962), pp. v-xii;

C. M. Grieve, *Contemporary Scottish Studies* (London: Parsons, 1926);

J. A. Hammerton, *J. M. Barrie and His Books* (London: Marshall, 1900);

Francis R. Hart, "The Liberals in the Kailyard," in his *The Scottish Novel from Smollett to Spark* (Cambridge, Mass.: Harvard University Press, 1978), pp. 126-130;

Tom Hubbard, "The Divided Scot: Scottish Fiction Between the 1880's and 1914," *Chapman,* 9 (Winter 1986-1987): 54-60;

Lynette Hunter, "J. M. Barrie: The Rejection of Fantasy," *Scottish Literary Journal,* 5 (May 1978): 39-52;

John Kennedy, *Thrums and the Barrie Country* (London: Heath Cranston, 1930);

Thomas D. Knowles, "Ideology, Art and Commerce: Aspects of Literary Sociology in the Late Victorian Kailyard," dissertation, Gothenberg University, 1983;

Angus Macdonald, "Modern Scots Novelists," in *Edinburgh Essays on Scots Literature* (Edinburgh: Oliver & Boyd, 1933), pp. 149-173;

William R. McGraw, "Barrie and the Critics," *Studies in Scottish Literature,* 1 (October 1963): 111–130;

J. H. Millar, "The Close of the Victorian Era: 1880–1901," in his *A Literary History of Scotland* (New York: Scribners, 1903), pp. 645–684;

Thomas Moult, *Barrie* (New York: Scribners, 1928);

Leonee Ormond, *J. M. Barrie* (Edinburgh: Scottish Academic Press, 1987);

J. B. Priestley, "Sir James Barrie," *London Mercury,* 10 (October 1924): 624–633;

J. M. Reid, Introduction to *Scottish Short Stories,* edited by Reid (London: Oxford University Press, 1963), pp. ix–xiii;

Gillian Shepherd, "The Kailyard," in *The Nineteenth Century,* edited by Douglas Gifford, volume 3 of *The History of Scottish Literature* (Aberdeen: Aberdeen University Press, 1988), pp. 309–320;

Brian M. Stableford, "J. M. Barrie," in *Supernatural Fiction Writers,* 2 volumes, edited by E. F. Bleiler (New York: Scribners, 1985), I: 405–410;

Robert Louis Stevenson, *The Letters of Robert Louis Stevenson,* volume 2, edited by Sidney Colvin (New York: Scribners, 1899);

Roderick Watson, *The Literature of Scotland* (New York: Schocken, 1985);

Harold Williams, *Modern English Writers: Being a Study of Imaginative Literature 1890–1914* (New York: Knopf, 1919).

Papers:
The Beinecke Library at Yale holds the largest collection of Barrie materials. Many of his early newspaper articles and stories can be found in the British Museum Library at Colindale. His university notebooks are contained in the archive of the National Library of Scotland, Edinburgh.

Algernon Blackwood

(14 March 1869 – 10 December 1951)

George M. Johnson
University College of the Cariboo

See also the Blackwood entry in *DLB 153: Late Victorian and Edwardian Novelists, First Series.*

BOOKS: *The Empty House and Other Ghost Stories* (London: Eveleigh Nash, 1906; New York: Vaughan, 1915);

The Listener and Other Stories (London: Eveleigh Nash, 1907; New York: Vaughan & Gomme, 1914);

John Silence: Physician Extraordinary (London: Eveleigh Nash, 1908; Boston: Luce, 1909);

Jimbo: A Fantasy (London & New York: Macmillan, 1909);

The Education of Uncle Paul (London: Macmillan, 1909; New York: Paget, 1909);

The Lost Valley and Other Stories (London: Eveleigh Nash, 1910; New York: Vaughan & Gomme, 1914);

The Human Chord (London: Macmillan, 1910; New York: Macmillan, 1911);

The Centaur (London: Macmillan, 1911; New York: Macmillan, 1912);

Pan's Garden: A Volume of Nature Stories (London & New York: Macmillan, 1912);

A Prisoner in Fairyland (The Book That 'Uncle Paul' Wrote) (London & New York: Macmillan, 1913);

Ten Minute Stories (London: Murray, 1914; New York: Dutton, 1914);

Incredible Adventures (London & New York: Macmillan, 1914);

The Extra Day (London & New York: Macmillan, 1915);

Julius Le Vallon: An Episode (London: Cassell, 1916; New York: Dutton, 1916);

The Wave: An Egyptian Aftermath (London: Macmillan, 1916; New York: Dutton, 1916);

Day and Night Stories (London: Cassell, 1917; New York: Dutton, 1917);

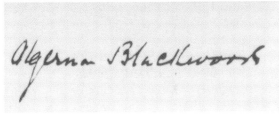

The Promise of Air (London: Macmillan, 1918; New York: Dutton, 1918);

Karma: A Reincarnation Play (London: Macmillan, 1918; New York: Dutton, 1918);

The Garden of Survival (London: Macmillan, 1918; New York: Dutton, 1918);

The Wolves of God, and Other Fey Stories (London: Cassell, 1921; New York: Dutton, 1921);

25

The Bright Messenger (London: Cassell, 1921; New York: Dutton, 1922);

Episodes Before Thirty (London: Cassell, 1923; New York: Dutton, 1924); revised as *Adventures Before Thirty* (London: Cape, 1934);

Tongues of Fire and Other Sketches (London: Jenkins, 1924); republished as *Tongues of Fire and Other Stories* (New York: Dutton, 1925);

Through the Crack (London: French, 1925);

Ancient Sorceries and Other Tales (London & Glasgow: Collins, 1927);

The Dance of Death and Other Tales (London: Jenkins, 1927; New York: Dial, 1928);

Sambo and Snitch (Oxford: Blackwell, 1927; New York: Appleton, 1927);

Mr. Cupboard (Oxford: Blackwell, 1928);

Dudley and Gilderoy: A Nonsense (London: Benn, 1929; New York: Dutton, 1929);

Strange Stories (London: Heinemann, 1929; New York: Arno, 1976);

Full Circle (London: Mathews & Marrot, 1929);

By Underground (Oxford: Blackwell, 1930);

Short Stories of To-Day and Yesterday (London: Harrap, 1930);

The Parrot and the- Cat (Oxford: Blackwell, 1931);

The Willows and Other Queer Tales (London & Glasgow: Collins, 1932);

The Italian Conjuror (Oxford: Blackwell, 1932);

Maria (of England) in the Rain (Oxford: Blackwell, 1933);

Sergeant Poppett and Policeman James (Oxford: Blackwell, 1934);

The Fruit Stoners: Being the Adventures of Maria among the Fruit Stoners (London: Grayson & Grayson, 1934; New York: Dutton, 1935);

The Fruit Stoners (Oxford: Blackwell, 1935);

Shocks (London: Grayson & Grayson, 1935; New York: Dutton, 1936);

How the Circus Came to Tea (Oxford: Blackwell, 1936);

The Tales of Algernon Blackwood (London: Secker, 1938; New York: Dutton, 1939);

The Adventures of Dudley and Gilderoy (New York: Dutton, 1941; London: Faber & Faber, 1941);

Selected Tales of Algernon Blackwood (Harmondsworth, U.K.: Penguin, 1942);

Selected Short Stories of Algernon Blackwood (New York: Armed Services Editions, 1945);

The Doll, and One Other (Sauk City, Wis.: Arkham House, 1946);

Tales of the Uncanny and Supernatural (London: Nevill, 1949; Secaucus, N.J.: Castle, 1974);

In the Realm of Terror (New York: Pantheon, 1957);

Selected Tales of Algernon Blackwood (London: Richards, 1964); republished as *Tales of Terror and the Unknown* (New York: Dutton, 1965);

Tales of the Mysterious and Macabre (London: Spring, 1967; Secaucus, N.J.: Castle, 1974);

Ancient Sorceries and Other Stories (Harmondsworth, U.K.: Penguin, 1968);

Best Ghost Stories of Algernon Blackwood (New York: Dover, 1973);

The Best Supernatural Tales of Algernon Blackwood (New York: Causeway, 1973);

Tales of Terror and Darkness (Feltham, U.K.: Spring, 1977);

Tales of the Supernatural (Woodbridge, U.K.: Boydell, 1983).

PLAY PRODUCTIONS: *The Starlight Express,* by Blackwood and Violet Pearn, London, Kingsway Theatre, 29 December 1915;

The Crossing, by Blackwood and Bertram Forsyth, London, Comedy Theatre, 29 September 1920;

Through the Crack, by Blackwood and Pearn, London, Everyman Theatre, 27 December 1920;

White Magic, by Blackwood and Forsyth, Toronto, Hart House Theatre, 21 November 1921;

The Halfway House, by Blackwood and Elaine Ainley, London, Victoria Palace, 5 December 1921;

Max Hensig, by Blackwood and Frederick Kinsey Peile, London, Gate Theatre Studio, 18 September 1929.

RADIO SCRIPTS: *Told in a Mountain Cabin,* script by Blackwood, BBC Home Service, 13 April 1942;

Running Wolf, script by Blackwood, BBC General Forces Programme, 12 October 1944;

It's About Time, script by Blackwood, BBC General Forces Programme, 26 February 1945;

In a Glass Darkly, script by Blackwood, BBC General Overseas Service, 23 July 1945;

The Secret Society, script by Blackwood, BBC Home Service, 22 October 1947.

SELECTED PERIODICAL PUBLICATIONS –
UNCOLLECTED: "A Mysterious House," *Belgravia,* 69 (July 1889): 98–107;

"The Story of Karl Ott," *Pall Mall Magazine,* 10 (October 1896): 189–200.

During a sixty-one-year career Algernon Blackwood wrote more stories and novels featuring psychic, mystical, and supernatural phenomena than any other contemporary. Many of his short stories are of high quality and particularly excel at evoking atmosphere, leading H. P. Lovecraft in 1927 to refer to Blackwood's work as "some of the finest spectral literature of this or any age." Scholar E. F. Bleiler confirms Blackwood's position as "the foremost British supernaturalist of the twentieth century." However, Blackwood has also been pigeonholed as a ghost-story writer and thus underrated, though he deals with a vast array of psychological and spiritual states in stories ranging from the psychologically realistic to those portraying nature as alive and potentially threatening to ones evoking mystical union with the divine. The variety of his fiction is matched only by the eclecticism of his sources and by the variety of his experiences. His adventuresome spirit appears to be in part a response to his upbringing, repressive even by late-Victorian standards and referred to by Blackwood in *Episodes Before Thirty* (1923) as both "sheltered to the point of ignorance" and "strange."

Algernon Henry Blackwood was born on 14 March 1869, the fourth of five children, in Shooter's Hill, Kent, to Stevenson Arthur "Beauty" Blackwood and Harriet Sydney Dobbs, both descended from aristocratic families. The couple became important in the evangelical movement, which exerted a profound influence on Blackwood's youth. He admired the "intense convictions" of his parents but feared their rigid belief system. A "dreamy" boy, as he described himself, he escaped from this narrow world by turning to nature. At Shortlands House near Beckenham, where he lived from age eleven, he would climb out the window at night, launch a boat on the garden pond, and imagine that supernatural beings observed him. His family also vacationed in remote areas of Britain. He would often accompany his father on long walks, though he never became as intimate with this sincere yet stern figure as he did with his mother. Of Celtic descent, she "read far deeper into things" than her husband, possessed an "old" soul, and, according to Blackwood, "always knew" her son's thoughts.

Like most English boys of his class, Blackwood was separated from his parents during his formal education. His schooling had an unsettling and even traumatic effect on him; he referred to the five schools he attended as "my horrible private schools." At one of these, in Kent in 1881, he was falsely accused by the "fiendish" evangelical headmaster of stealing a poetry book, an event that "haunted" him for years. He looked back "with disgust at the overstrict, semi-military discipline" at the

Moravian Brotherhood school in the German Black Forest, where he spent an unhappy eighteen months beginning in May 1885. Yet the remote setting of this school, which he claimed in *Episodes Before Thirty* was "haunted by elves and dwarfs and peopled by charming legends," also left a lasting impression, increasing his worship of nature. This passion for nature became the dominant influence in his life, bringing him "comfort, companionship, inspiration, [and] joy."

However, Blackwood's real education, his spiritual quest, did not truly begin until after he had left the Moravian school. In September 1886 his reading of Patanjali's *Yoga Aphorisms* prompted his conversion to Eastern wisdom, which was fueled by his father's disturbance at his son's new interest and by his further reading of works mentioned as subversive in G. H. Pember's evangelical book *Earth's Earliest Ages* (1876), given to him as a warning by his father. Foremost among these works was the Bhagavad Gita, considered by Blackwood "the profoundest world-scripture I have ever read." He also adopted the theosophy of Madame Blavatsky. Its claim that a spirit realm exists beyond the perception of the senses became a central preoccupation of his throughout the rest of his life. In 1938 he claimed, "My interest in psychic matters has always been the interest in questions of extended, or expanded consciousness." Even at age seventeen he cultivated this interest by reading about animal magnetism and hypnotism.

Blackwood continued his formal education in early 1887 at Bole in Switzerland. According to one friend, he was already telling ghost stories while on hikes. His future career, however, was still uncertain. Recognizing Algernon's love of nature, his father decided to see whether he would be interested in becoming a farmer, perhaps in Canada, which they visited together in 1887. After they crossed the country during ten weeks and visited a farm near Toronto, they decided that when Algernon was older he would return.

However, first Blackwood needed to learn more about agriculture; consequently, he attended Edinburgh University for a year from 1888 to 1889. More fascinated by lectures there on pathology than on farming, he soon encountered the first of several influential mentors. "Dr. H.," as he called him in *Episodes Before Thirty,* encouraged him to become a mental specialist, taught him hypnotism, and introduced him to spiritualism and séances. At several séances he claimed to have received prophecies, including one that he had been an Indian medicine man and needed to return to India "to work off cer-

Cover for Blackwood's first book, a collection of ghost stories and other supernatural tales (Courtesy of the Lilly Library, Indiana University)

be the most momentous of his life, since his character developed enormously and he met the men who would leave the most lasting impression on him. In his fiction he would repeatedly draw on his experiences in the wilds there.

Though his father had pulled strings at the Canadian Pacific Railway to ensure that he would prosper, Blackwood managed to ruin the opportunity by offending the key official. Left to his own devices, he worked without pay for a time in an insurance office and gave French, German, and violin lessons at night. Three months later he landed his first writing job, as editorial assistant on the *Methodist Magazine,* to which he contributed articles on Christmas in England and on travels in Europe. After admitting that he was a Buddhist, relations with the editor became less cordial. Fortunately for Blackwood, the editor, a Methodist preacher, did not discover that he was also involved in founding the Toronto branch of the Theosophical Society in February 1891. Blackwood voluntarily left the magazine once his capital of two thousand pounds arrived from England. He tried his hand at dairy farming and then at running a pub, failing at both.

On hearing of the latter venture his father, a temperance advocate, proclaimed, "Algie has gone to hell!," increasing Blackwood's guilt. His father died a year later, in 1893, and the two never had the chance to reconcile. However, the saloon experience also caused him to relish deeply his hours of relaxation away from work. He found release in nature, music, and a few friendships. With one friend, Johann Kay Pauw, he retreated to an island in Lake Rousseau, Ontario, in spring 1892, having sold his interest in the bar business. In the fall they decided to try their fortunes in New York City.

Blackwood's New York experience stripped away his illusions, shook his faith in others, and exposed him to unaccustomed hardships. He and Pauw were forced to live in a vermin-ridden boardinghouse on the East Side and to pawn their overcoats while searching for work. Though Blackwood had no desire to write, necessity drove him to apply at various magazines. Eventually, he landed a job as court reporter with the *Evening Sun* at the equivalent of three pounds a week. The reporting routine, he wrote in *Episodes Before Thirty,* introduced him to "vice, crime, horror, terror, and every kind of human degradation" and later provided the atmosphere for many of his tales. Abject poverty and an untreated wound eventually took their toll, and he succumbed to fever. He could not afford to pay the attending doctor, Otto Huebner, who became an-

tain painful Karma." Though he treated some of these experiences with skepticism, he soon supported another of the prophecies by composing his first short story, "A Mysterious House," while at the university. The tale, published in *Belgravia* in July 1889, contains elements of the conventional ghost story, including a haunted house, knives, blood, unaccountable movements and noises, and madness, but it focuses on developing the psychology of fear in the skeptical narrator, a focus that would become one of Blackwood's specialties. The revelation at the close that the events have occurred in a nightmare serves as commentary on the power of imagination.

After Blackwood left Edinburgh in the summer of 1889, better versed in matters of the spirit than the soil, he traveled in Switzerland before embarking for Toronto in April 1890. The nine adventurous years he spent in North America would

other mentor for Blackwood, and they shared thoughts about idealistic philosophy and literature as well as experiments with morphine. Blackwood experienced "an intensification of consciousness" while on the drug but managed to break the habit; Huebner died from his addiction less than a year later.

Blackwood's poverty was not eased until January 1893, when he had recuperated enough from illness to return to his *Sun* job. Apparently his sense of failure was so strong and he felt so estranged from his family that he considered it impossible to return to England. Also, his belief in karma convinced him that his unpleasant experiences were deserved, though this could be interpreted as a rationalization of an underlying passivity in his nature. Most important, Blackwood further developed his capacity to escape the horror of his circumstances through his imagination, stimulating it by devouring Percy Bysshe Shelley, Russian writers, his Eastern books, and books on psychology, as well as by daydreaming of natural places.

Blackwood found a receptive audience for the expression of his imagination in Angus Hamilton, a fellow Britisher employed by the *Sun*. According to Blackwood in *Episodes Before Thirty,* "He liked, above all to listen to weird stories I used to tell, strange, wild, improbable tales akin to ghost-stories." With characteristic humility he relates that he "found, to my surprise, that my listeners were enthralled" and that he had a "taste for spinning yarns." Hamilton would write out these stories that "poured forth endlessly," claiming that they would sell, though Blackwood had no impulse to do this himself. More than ten years later Hamilton took an active role in launching Blackwood's literary career, through which Blackwood claimed that he found his "liberty."

Meanwhile, Blackwood managed to escape the misery of New York by traveling to Ontario in 1893 and again in 1894 as a gold prospector. Though he did not find any gold, the experience seemed like "some legendary Golden Age" and provided inspiration for more than one wilderness tale, notably "The Wendigo" (1910). Lack of funds forced his return in October 1894 to New York, where he moved from odd job to odd job, including freelance journalism, acting, manufacturing, and selling cologne. When he discovered that his partner had stolen the cologne formula, Blackwood was nearly implicated.

During this period Blackwood met his most influential mentor, Alfred Hyman Louis, a Renaissance man in exile who had been the friend of

George Eliot, G. H. Lewes, Herbert Spencer, and Cardinal Manning before his fortunes and his mental health had declined. Louis's "upper-mind," to use Blackwood's term, was damaged, but Blackwood considered that his "under-mind" was whole and that he possessed otherworldly wisdom. Louis inspired Blackwood's story "The Old Man of Visions" (1907).

Blackwood's own fortunes began to improve when he signed on with *The New York Times* and sold a few short stories, including "The Story of Karl Ott" (1896), and then more dramatically when he became a millionaire banker's private secretary for two thousand dollars a year. This state of affairs lasted until one of Blackwood's sisters visited in late 1898, stirring a longing to return to England. Since he had bettered his position and had prospects to begin a dried-milk business in England, he felt he could return without shame. He arrived in Liverpool on 3 March 1899, eleven days before his thirtieth birthday.

Blackwood located at a boardinghouse in Chelsea after a search for rooms that would form the basis of "The Listener," written in 1899. He worked for his dried-milk company, but he also continued to travel extensively between 1900 and 1908. With Wilfred Wilson, who would become a friend for life, he made a six-week, twenty-four-hundred-mile voyage from the Danube's source to the Black Sea in a Canadian canoe. He described the expedition in several essays and transformed it into one of his most powerful tales, "The Willows" (1907). In the following year, 1901, he journeyed down the river again, likely with an archaeologist, Edwyn Bevan, and his wife, with both of whom he investigated haunted houses.

During these years Blackwood also became heavily involved in various orders of the Golden Dawn, organized in 1900 to study the occult and mysticism. More important, he became a professional writer, though characteristically he did not take an active role in gaining the notice of a publisher. Hamilton reappeared in Blackwood's life around 1905 and took a few dozen stories that Blackwood had in a cupboard. Blackwood completely forgot about the incident until he received a letter asking to publish them from Eveleigh Nash, the publisher to whom Hamilton had submitted the stories without his permission.

Blackwood's motivation for writing was undoubtedly complex, as suggested by his initial reaction to the proposal, as recorded in *Episodes Before Thirty:* "I never forget my shrinking fear at the idea of appearing in print, my desire to use another name, my feeling that I should have a book of my own published being too absurd to accept as true." He apparently feared the publicity partly because writing had become a solitary pleasure for him. He claimed, "It had been my habit and delight to spend my evenings composing yarns on my typewriter, finding more pleasure in this than in any dinner engagement, theatre or concert. Why this suddenly began I cannot say, but I guess at a venture that the accumulated horror of the years in New York was seeking expression." One suspects that he also found relief in exorcising the devils and fears engendered through his rigid upbringing, reshaping his childhood by projecting the demons within onto the natural world or into the ancient past.

Though Blackwood's stories vary enormously in theme, language, atmosphere, and length, some types recur throughout his canon. By far the most dominant are his nature tales. In all of these nature is a powerful living force, capable either of destruction or healing. Nature can also serve as a metaphor for or projection of the psyche. Another group of tales is more directly psychological, drawing on his extensive reading in psychopathology and psychiatry. These deal with various passions and preoccupations, notably dual personalities and obsession. A fairly distinct set of stories explores the then-popular idea of the invasion of personality. However, he develops his own twist, since the invading forces tend to be from the natural world rather than human. Many of his tales can more accurately be labeled psychic than psychological, since they treat phenomena not observable by the senses. These capture his fascination with psychic research, and they include prevision, thought transference, and survival of personality stories. The latter type, along with his reincarnation stories, reflects his Buddhist beliefs. Though he always excels at evoking atmosphere, some tales specifically focus on atmosphere, spirit of place, or mystical vision. A much smaller number of tales treats fantasies of escape from mundane reality. There are also a few thrillers, which realistically trace the pursuit or development of evil. Finally, he wrote a handful of ghost tales involving haunted houses – mostly near the beginning of his career, despite his continuing identification with this kind of tale.

Blackwood's techniques demonstrate great flexibility. He can capture the slang of New York in dialogue, describe nature with almost scientific precision, or soar lyrically in passages attempting to capture mystical experiences frequently considered beyond language. If he has a stylistic defect it is wordiness, though this mainly affects the series of fantasy novels he wrote from 1909 to 1921. His narrative viewpoint ranges from detached observers to skeptics forced to confront the existence of another realm to participants whose subconscious fantasies are deeply probed.

Many of these themes and techniques can be found in rather conventional form in Blackwood's first volume, *The Empty House and Other Ghost Stories* (1906), though he later veered away from convention. Most of the ten stories in the collection do not appear to have been published previously, though two had been placed in the *Pall Mall Magazine*. The collection features four variations on the haunted house ghost story and a protagonist, Jim Shorthouse, who appears in a handful of the stories. In the title story Shorthouse and his Aunt Julia hear the reenactment of a century-old murder of a servant by a jealous stableman, who then escapes the house in which the event occurred. "A Haunted Island," one of the two stories set in the Canadian wilderness, combines the haunted house scenario with a reincarnation theme. The narrator witnesses two Indians bringing a scalped white man with his own face downstairs from his cabin bedroom. The traumatic event either represents a hallucination or suggests that the narrator had such an experience in a previous life. Several other autobiographical stories show hallucinations and reenactments happening in boardinghouses, while one deals with an Edinburgh student's uncanny vision of an old friend who has recently died of starvation. All the reviews of the book were positive, including one by Hilaire Belloc, who used the volume to initiate a discussion of the English ghost story in the *Morning Post*.

Blackwood's success, dampened by the death of his mother in the spring of 1907, prompted him to produce a second collection, *The Listener and Other Stories* (1907), which was also warmly received. The title story, another haunted house tale, achieves greater intimacy and psychological insight than earlier ones by employing a diary form. The lonely narrator, a writer, becomes increasingly disturbed by various sensations occurring in his room, including a "fetid odour." Ironically, he is rescued from a potential invasion of his personality by a "crass materialist" friend named Chapter. "The Insanity of Jones (A Study in Reincarnation)" works with a metaphoric house in the protagonist's past. After Thorpe, a former coworker (now deceased), shows Jones that Jones was the victim of torture four hundred years ago, Jones kills the reincarnation of the torturer, the present manager in his insurance office. "Max Hensig: Bacteriologist and Murderer," another chilling tale of revenge, represents a departure for Blackwood, since it treats the horror of New York realistically and is autobiographical. In it a soulless German doctor attempts to poison a hardened reporter who has implied in his coverage of the doctor's trial that the doctor is guilty of poisoning his wife.

The most highly acclaimed and frequently reprinted story of *The Listener* is a nature tale, "The Willows." Blackwood vividly creates an isolated and then alarming atmosphere, as the narrator and a Swede canoe down the Danube between Vienna and Budapest. Nature is preternaturally alive, and the willows on the island where they camp seem threatening, especially after their equipment is tampered with. At the climax the river nearly claims a sacrifice of the hysterical Swede but instead victimizes a peasant, whose uncannily pockmarked body is carried away by the current as the narrative closes.

Blackwood achieved even greater notoriety and success with his third volume, *John Silence: Physician Extraordinary* (1908), partly because the publisher, Eveleigh Nash, promoted the book with the largest posters to appear on hoardings and horsecars that the English had ever seen. Nash had also suggested that Blackwood unify the stories with a central character, and at a dinner party the name John Silence was chosen. A condensation of a Hindu medical student Blackwood had befriended at Edinburgh and an unidentified member of the Order of the Golden Dawn, this psychic doctor treats difficult cases of spiritual affliction. His great knowledge, insight, and successful reputation for tracking down evil led the earliest reviewers to link him with Sherlock Holmes. However, Silence probably owes more to Joseph Sheridan Le Fanu's Dr. Hesselius because of the supernatural elements in the cases, including possession ("A Psychical Invasion," as in Le Fanu's "Green Tea"), sacrifice demanded by nature ("The Nemesis of Fire"), satanism ("Secret Worship"), lycanthropy ("The Camp of the Dog"), and reincarnation ("Ancient Sorceries"). In "Ancient Sorceries," perhaps the best in the volume, an English tourist almost partakes in a witch's sabbath with the catlike inhabitants of the French town where he had lived in an earlier life. Silence rescues the man and increases the ambiguity about the events by later claiming that "the entire affair took place subjectively in the man's own consciousness." Though a few critics find Silence's character problematic – including Edward Wagenknecht, who asserts that "Dr. Silence is both unconvincingly omniscient and unbelievably noble" – most would agree with Russell Letson Jr. in his assertion

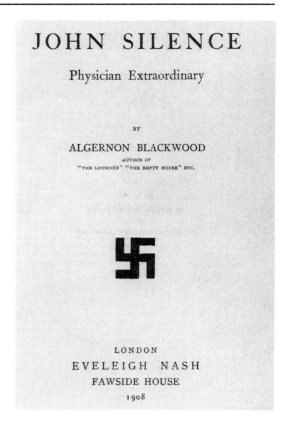

JOHN SILENCE

Physician Extraordinary

BY

ALGERNON BLACKWOOD

AUTHOR OF
"THE LISTENER" "THE EMPTY HOUSE" ETC.

LONDON
EVELEIGH NASH
FAWSIDE HOUSE
1908

Title page for Blackwood's third book, a collection of stories featuring a detective who investigates supernatural phenomena (Courtesy of the Lilly Library, Indiana University)

that "these five tales mark the blossoming of Blackwood's individuality in the supernatural field." Their popularity attests to the fact that they touched a nerve in a society suffering from spiritual malaise and searching out replacements for traditional religious figures and beliefs. These stories also influenced later psychic detective tales, including William Hope Hodgson's *Carnacki the Ghost Finder* (1913).

With the success of *John Silence* Blackwood was able to renounce the dried-milk business and to enjoy freedom at Bole in the Jura Mountains, where he lived and worked as a professional writer for the next six years. In that prolific period he published nine collections of short stories and novels, as well as many occasional pieces for papers such as *Country Life*. The first two works were novels about children: *Jimbo: A Fantasy* (1909), written before *The Empty House*, and *The Education of Uncle Paul* (1909), an autobiographical novel in which an uncle writes fantasies as "a safety-valve," which are then carried out by him and his nieces and nephews. The first collection of short stories of this period, *The Lost Valley and Other Stories* (1910), sets several stories in the Jura Mountains, notably the title story, and the volume typically treats psychic events that bring about radical changes in the protagonists. However, "The Wendigo," one of the best, deals with the concrete manifestation of the "Panic of the Wilderness" as a great moss-eating beast in the Canadian north. Joseph Defago, the guide on a hunting expedition, hears the call of the wild and disappears. After an unsuccessful search he reappears twice, once as "a ghastly caricature" who reveals that he has been with the Wendigo and a second time as a husk of his former self, having lost his mind, memory, and individuality.

Of Blackwood's next two novels, *The Human Chord* (1910) and *The Centaur* (1911), the latter, about a mystical journey to the Caucasus and within the protagonist's psyche, became his most highly acclaimed, impressing writers as diverse as Rainer Maria Rilke and James Stephens. He followed this favorite of his, based on a 1910 voyage to Greece, with an impressive collection of fifteen stories, *Pan's Garden: A Volume of Nature Stories* (1912). Nature is the most powerful presence here, and many of the protagonists, including Meiklejohn in "Special Delivery," are "peculiarly conscious of the presence of these forces of Nature — the irresistible powers that regenerate as easily as they destroy." In "Special Delivery" these forces act to protect Meiklejohn from a rock slide that destroys the part of the inn where he had been staying, but in other tales nature threatens humanity in order to protect itself, as in "The Temptations of the Clay," or takes possession of human beings, as in "The Transfer" and "The Man Whom the Trees Loved." Blackwood explored a new natural setting in the longest story, "Sand," the first of many essays and stories on the Egyptian desert. He was only able to complete the story after staying at Helouan, south of Cairo, from January to March 1912 with the Baron and Baroness de Knoop, the latter a soul mate to whom this volume as well as several others are dedicated. In "Sand" Lady Statham and Richard Vance invite the protagonist, Henriot, to observe a midnight ceremony to invoke the spirit of the Ka of Egypt. At the climax a vortex of sand swallows Statham, a victim of Vance's impure motives, who is sacrificed to the manifested Group-Soul. In the tale Statham claims that "knowledge is memory," and certainly memory is another powerful force in *Pan's Garden*. Several stories, including "The Attic," "The Return," and "Clairvoyance," involve the

transformation of memories of loved ones into visions providing comfort or heightened awareness.

The length and complexity of these visionary tales contrast dramatically with those contained in a volume Blackwood published early in 1914, the aptly titled *Ten Minute Stories*. Eighteen of the twenty-nine stories had appeared in the *Westminster Gazette*, which published more of his stories than any other periodical during his career. Most of the stories deal with various kinds of encounters — from superficial, realistic ones, as in "The Invitation," to those with the self in dreams ("Strange Disappearance of a Baronet"), to those involving the persistence of personality after death ("The Deferred Appointment") or thought transference ("You *May* Telephone From Here"). "Imagination," one of several featuring writers, is particularly interesting because of its autobiographical account of how an encounter with a beggar enabled Blackwood to overcome writer's block while working on *The Centaur*.

In the same year Blackwood published another collection, of five more-substantial stories called *Incredible Adventures*. The first, "The Regeneration of Lord Ernie," depicts a languid and empty English youth possessed by elemental energies during a worship ceremony of wild mountainmen of the Jura to which his tutor has taken him. Though Blackwood imbues these pagan rites with a mystical and supernatural quality, he increases the complexity of the event by suggesting a psychological outcome, reflecting Blackwood's early assimilation of Freudian principles: "Something had now awakened sex in [Ernie]. . . . [T]he will woke out of sleep, and all the currents of his system took aggressive form. For all energy, intellectual, emotional, or spiritual, is fundamentally one: it is primarily sexual." Another tale, "The Sacrifice," also involves a ceremony, here one that leads to renewal even though it has occurred entirely within the protagonist's head. The other adventures in the volume treat the persistent influence of powerful presences from the past on the present lives of the protagonists.

During World War I Blackwood continued to write prolifically, publishing five novels and one collection of stories and producing the first of several unsuccessful plays, while still managing to engage in incredible adventures of his own. Though refused for active service, he qualified as a translator and also wrote some propagandistic stories and essays. In the summer of 1916 he was about to set out for Serbia with a field ambulance corps when he was asked to operate as an undercover agent in Switzerland for British military intelligence. On one occasion he dispatched important information about the German U-boat campaign. According to his biographer, Mike Ashley, "Blackwood's exploits at this time read rather like a boy's adventure serial complete with code names, invisible ink and hair's-breadth escapes."

Only one of the stories in *Day and Night Stories* (1917), "Cain's Atonement," was inspired by the war, though several others of this type have not been collected. In it a Cain-like figure, Smith, sets self aside, enabling him to have a vision of an ancient debt owed to his cousin, Jones, before he dies in battle saving his relative. "A Desert Episode," "Transition," and "The Occupant of the Room" all show the survival of personality after death, while "The Tryst" portrays a lover's discovery of the irrevocable loss of his loved one just before he has returned after a fifteen-year absence. The final story in the collection – "A Victim of Higher Space," once again featuring John Silence – presents a twist on the telepathy theme, since Silence's client keeps slipping into the fourth dimension.

In the postwar period Blackwood regularly stayed at the estates of various friends, including Lady Essendon, Henry Ainley, and Baroness de Knoop. The baroness's house parties often included H. G. Wells, Noël Coward, and the mystic Pyotr Ouspenskii, under whom Blackwood studied throughout the 1920s. He became increasingly involved in the theater – acting, collaborating with various playwrights, and producing at least two popular successes, *The Crossing* and *Through The Crack* (both 1920). Though the volume of his prose writing correspondingly declined, he collaborated on one story collection, *The Wolves of God, and Other Fey Stories* (1921), with his friend Wilfred Wilson, who suggested some of the ideas. Most of the tales deal with the effects of wild animals on people or with animal instincts within people, and several of the best draw on experiences in the Canadian backwoods, including the title story as well as "Running Wolf" and "The Valley of the Beasts." All three portray the psychological and in some cases traumatic effects of encounters with legendary animals, specifically wolves and moose. "First Hate" and "Vengeance Is Mine" probe how the base instincts in humanity of hatred and revenge lead to murder and sacrifice; in the latter tale this theme is linked with "the essential principle" behind World War I. In "The Empty Sleeve" the violent desires of the violinist Hyman actually assume the shape of a cat, whose wounding is reproduced in the man himself.

Blackwood followed up this darker vision of humanity with a novel, *The Bright Messenger* (1921), and his autobiography, *Episodes Before Thirty,* before

collecting more stories. *Tongues of Fire and Other Sketches* (1924) focuses on uncanny connections between people, several occurring in moments out of time, notably in "Malahide and Forden," or in other dimensions of time, as in "The Pikestaffe Case." Many of the narratives are psychologically sophisticated; one of the most curious is "The Other Woman," in which an artist narrator asserts that an "inner woman," known as well as his own mother, has prevented him from carrying through early love affairs. It is tempting to read autobiographically his claim – "Alone of men the artist has within himself the perfect mate. He needs no other" – since Blackwood never married.

Though Blackwood felt that he had now said everything in him, he proceeded to develop yet another facet of his varied talent as a children's story writer. His most successful and highly acclaimed effort in this genre, *Dudley and Gilderoy: A Nonsense* (1929), humorously describes the London adventures of a renegade parrot and cat with human capabilities.

During the 1920s and 1930s Blackwood continued to travel extensively in Europe and returned briefly to New York in 1933. In 1934 the British Broadcasting Corporation persuaded him to embark on a broadcasting career. His success led to his appearance as a storyteller, in November 1936, on Britain's first television show, *Picture Page.* Though an exciting episode, it could not compare with the hike that Blackwood, now sixty-seven, had undertaken earlier in the year, from Austria to pre–civil war Spain, where he observed, according to Ashley, "rioting, arson, and murder."

Though Blackwood wrote the adult short stories collected in his next volume, *Shocks* (1935), from 1925 to 1935, these stories cohere remarkably well, since most explore the consequences of various types of shocks. As Mr. Adam in "The Land of the Green Ginger" claims, shocks "can bring out latent possibilities in the mind hitherto ignored." Loss of fortune prompts him to discover his writing talent, and in "Revenge" and "Shocks" (a realistic tale) a fortune or the threat of its loss also acts as the catalyst. In many of the tales, notably "Elsewhere and Otherwise" and "The Adventures of Tornado Smith," movements out of time into other dimensions, or the return to chronological time, provide the shocks. Others, such as "Full Circle" and "The Man Who Lived Backwards," show characters encountering earlier versions of themselves and illustrate the fluidity and simultaneity of time. His increasing fascination with time owes a great deal to his friendship with philosopher and aviator J. W.

Blackwood in 1949

Dunne, who read aloud to Blackwood his *An Experiment with Time,* an account of the serial nature of the universe, before its publication in 1927. Blackwood rounded out his collection, which did not entirely please him, with reincarnation tales, including one with a twist, "A Threefold Cord," and with two haunted house tales, "Dr. Feldman" and "Chemical."

In the late 1930s and through the 1940s Blackwood's literary production slowed to almost nothing. Ever seeking new experiences, he continued to travel until the outbreak of World War II. Refused service in espionage, he served as a fire watcher at his nephew's house in Hampstead until it suffered a direct hit during the Battle of Britain. Blackwood survived only because he and his nephew had gone to their bomb shelter to rescue some burning sausages just before the bomb struck. The shock of this event prompted him to move first to Devon and then to a friend's Sussex home, where he wrote several radio plays as well as three new short stories. Two of these, "The Doll" and "The Trod," were published by August Derleth's Arkham House in 1946. In "The Doll" a Hindustani wreaks revenge on a colonel by investing a doll with supernatural powers, though the real interest

in the tale lies in the religiously dogmatic governess's increasingly hysterical response to the doll. "The Trod" vividly describes the lure of a fairy path for Diana Travers, whose mother disappeared years before into the land of fairies. The ambiguous ending suggests that this is a tale of possession, since Diana's essence has gone elsewhere, even though the narrator manages to prevent her from physically running to her mother.

In 1947 Blackwood became increasingly involved in performing on radio and television and in short films. His regular *Saturday Night Story* spot on television made him a household name, and in 1949 he was made a Commander of the British Empire, one of his proudest moments. Following a Halloween broadcast in 1950, Blackwood suffered a slight stroke but had recovered enough by January 1951 to visit friends in Switzerland. The next Halloween broadcast, prerecorded on 13 October 1951, would be his last performance. His health deteriorated, and on 10 December he died of cerebral thrombosis and arteriosclerosis.

What is most striking about this prolific author is his openness to new ideas and experiences. Blackwood claimed in *Episodes Before Thirty* that he had "always taken ideas where [he] found them," and this quality is reflected in the variety of subjects that he explores, the variety in length of his printed work, and the variety of media in which he worked. The earliest reviewers realized that his work is not easily classified. However, subsequent critics have often restrictively viewed him as a genre writer of the ghost story, fantasy, or the supernatural, though most acknowledge his preeminence in these fields. E. F. Bleiler asserts:

> Historically Blackwood offered much to the development and continuity of the ghost story. He widened its subject matter greatly, and showed that the myriad rooms of the human mind were teeming with a strange, hidden life. He brought into the supernatural story the realms of philosophy, serious Oriental thought, modern psychology and new areas of magical lore. He demonstrated that the supernatural story did not have to be a revenge story nor a primitive justice drama, nor detritus of ancient wickedness, nor the crudities of the lower-level fiction of his day.

Blackwood deserves a wider hearing – if not for his poetic skills in evoking natural settings and atmosphere and for his probing the possibilities of expanded consciousness, then for his escape from the formulas of genre and for his brilliance as a storyteller.

Bibliographies:

John Robert Colombo, *Blackwood's Books* (Toronto: Hounslow Press, 1981);

Mike Ashley, *Algernon Blackwood: A Bio-Bibliography* (New York, Westport, Conn. & London: Greenwood Press, 1987).

Biography:

Mike Ashley, *Algernon Blackwood: A Bio-Bibliography* (New York, Westport, Conn. & London: Greenwood Press, 1987).

References:

Hilaire Belloc, Review of *John Silence: Physician Extraordinary, Morning Post* (17 September 1908): 2; reprinted in *Horror: One Hundred Best Books,* edited by Stephen Jones and Kim Newman (New York: Carroll & Graf, 1988), pp. 67–68;

E. F. Bleiler, Introduction, *Best Ghost Stories of Algernon Blackwood* (New York: Dover, 1973), pp. v–x;

Julia Briggs, *Night Visitors: The Rise and Fall of the English Ghost Story* (London: Faber & Faber, 1977);

Donald R. Burleson, "Algernon Blackwood's 'The Listener': A Hearing," *Studies in Weird Fiction,* 5 (Spring 1989): 15–19;

R. F. Fleissner, " 'No Ghosts Need Apply'? Or, The Adventure of the Empty House's Empty House," *Studies in Weird Fiction,* 6 (Fall 1989): 28–30;

Derek Hudson, "A Study of Algernon Blackwood," *Essays and Studies,* New Series, volume 14 (London: Murray, 1961), pp. 102–114; reprinted as "Algernon Blackwood" in his *Talks With Fuddy and Other Papers* (Fontwell, U.K.: Centaur Press, 1968), pp. 81–91;

S. T. Joshi, "Algernon Blackwood: The Expansion of Consciousness," in his *The Weird Tale: Arthur Machen, Lord Dunsany, Algernon Blackwood, M. R. James, Ambrose Bierce, H. P. Lovecraft* (Austin: University of Texas Press, 1990), pp. 87–132;

Russell Letson Jr., "The Approaches to Mystery: The Fantasies of Arthur Machen and Algernon Blackwood," dissertation, Southern Illinois University, August 1975;

H. P. Lovecraft, *Supernatural Horror in Literature* (New York: Abramson, 1945);

Peter Penzoldt, "Algernon Blackwood," in his *The Supernatural in Fiction* (London: Nevill, 1952), pp. 228–253;

Dorothy Scarborough, *The Supernatural in Modern English Fiction* (New York: Putnam, 1917);

Jack Sullivan, "The Visionary Ghost Story: Algernon Blackwood," in his *Elegant Nightmares: The English Ghost Story from Le Fanu to Blackwood* (Athens: Ohio University Press, 1978), pp. 112–129;

Edward Wagenknecht, "Algernon Blackwood," in his *Seven Masters of Supernatural Fiction* (New York: Greenwood Press, 1991), pp. 69–94.

Papers:

The main collection of Blackwood's manuscripts is at the BBC Written Archives at Caversham, Reading. Mike Ashley of Chatham, Kent, possesses the largest collection of Blackwood's letters, though the British Library also has a substantial collection. Other letters are scattered throughout archives in North America.

Mary Elizabeth Braddon

(4 October 1835 – 4 February 1915)

Cannon Schmitt
Grinnell College

See also the Braddon entries in *DLB 18: Victorian Novelists After 1885* and *DLB 70: British Mystery Writers, 1860–1919.*

BOOKS: *Three Times Dead* (London: W. M. Clark / Beverley: Empson, 1860); republished as *The Trail of the Serpent* (London: Ward, Lock & Tyler, 1861); republished as *Three Times Dead; or, The Secret of the Heath* (New York: Dick & Fitzgerald, 1864?);

Garibaldi, and Other Poems (London: Bosworth & Harrison, 1861);

The Lady Lisle (London: Ward, Lock & Tyler, 1862; New York: Dick & Fitzgerald, 1863?);

Lady Audley's Secret (3 volumes, London: Tinsley, 1862; 1 volume, New York: Dick & Fitzgerald, 1863);

Ralph the Bailiff and Other Stories (London: Ward, Lock & Tyler, 1862; enlarged edition, 1867);

The Captain of the Vulture (London: Ward, Lock & Tyler, 1863); republished as *Darrell Markham; or, The Captain of the Vulture,* bound with her *Lady Audley's Secret* (New York: Dick & Fitzgerald, 1863);

Aurora Floyd (3 volumes, London: Tinsley, 1863; 1 volume, New York: Harper, 1863);

Eleanor's Victory (3 volumes, London: Tinsley, 1863; 1 volume, New York: Harper, 1863);

John Marchmont's Legacy (3 volumes, London: Tinsley, 1863; 1 volume, New York: Harper, 1864);

Dudley Carleon; or, The Brother's Secret, and Other Tales (New York: Dick & Fitzgerald, 1864);

Henry Dunbar: The Story of an Outcast, 3 volumes (London: John Maxwell, 1864); republished as *Henry Dunbar; or, The Outcast,* 1 volume (New York: Dick & Fitzgerald, 186?);

The Doctor's Wife (3 volumes, London: John Maxwell, 1864; 1 volume, New York: Dick & Fitzgerald, 1864);

Mary Elizabeth Braddon, circa 1877

Only a Clod (3 volumes, London: John Maxwell, 1865; 1 volume, New York: Dick & Fitzgerald, 1865?);

Sir Jasper's Tenant (3 volumes, London: John Maxwell, 1865; 1 volume, New York: Dick & Fitzgerald, 1865?);

The Lady's Mile (3 volumes, London: Ward, Lock & Tyler, 1866; 1 volume, New York: Dick & Fitzgerald, 1876?);

What Is This Mystery? (New York: Hilton, 1866); republished as *The Black Band; or, The Mysteries of Midnight* (London: Vickers, 1877);

Circe, as Babington White, 2 volumes (London: Ward, Lock & Tyler, 1867); republished as *Circe; or, Three Acts in the Life of an Artist,* as Babington White, 1 volume (New York: Harper, 1867);

Rupert Godwin (3 volumes, London: Ward, Lock & Tyler, 1867; 1 volume, New York: Dick & Fitzgerald, 1867);

Birds of Prey (3 volumes, London: Ward, Lock & Tyler, 1867; 1 volume, New York: Harper, 1867);

Diavola (New York: Dick & Fitzgerald, 1867); republished as *Run to Earth* (London: Ward, Lock & Tyler, 1868);

Charlotte's Inheritance (3 volumes, London: Ward, Lock & Tyler, 1868; 1 volume, New York: Harper, 1868);

The White Phantom (New York: Williams, 1868);

Dead-Sea Fruit (3 volumes, London: Ward, Lock & Tyler, 1868; 1 volume, New York: Harper, 1868);

Bound to John Company; or, The Adventures and Misadventures of Robert Ainsleigh (New York: Harper, 1869); republished as *Robert Ainsleigh* (3 volumes, London: John Maxwell, 1872; 1 volume, Berlin: Asher / Philadelphia: Lippincott, 1872); republished as *Bound to John Company; or, Robert Ainsleigh* (New York: Munro, 1879);

The Octoroon; or, The Lily of Louisiana (New York: DeWitt, 1869);

The Factory Girl; or, All Is Not Gold That Glitters: A Romance of Real Life (New York: DeWitt, 1869?);

Oscar Bertrand (New York: DeWitt, 1869?);

Fenton's Quest (3 volumes, London: Ward, Lock & Tyler, 1871; 1 volume, New York: Harper, 1871);

The Lovels of Arden (3 volumes, London: John Maxwell, 1871; 1 volume, New York: Harper, 1872);

To the Bitter End (3 volumes, London: John Maxwell, 1872; 1 volume, New York: Harper, 1875);

Milly Darrell and Other Tales (3 volumes, London: John Maxwell, 1873; 1 volume, New York: Carleton, 1877); republished as *Meeting Her Fate* (New York: Carleton, 1881);

Strangers and Pilgrims (3 volumes, London: John Maxwell, 1873; 1 volume, New York: Harper, 1873);

Lucius Davoren; or, Publicans and Sinners, 3 volumes (London: John Maxwell, 1873); republished as *Publicans and Sinners; or, Lucius Davoren,* 1 volume (New York: Harper, 1874);

Taken at the Flood (3 volumes, London: John Maxwell, 1874; 1 volume, New York: Harper, 1874);

Lost for Love (3 volumes, London: Chatto & Windus, 1874; 1 volume, New York: Harper, 1875);

A Strange World (3 volumes, London: John Maxwell, 1875; 1 volume, New York: Harper, 1875);

Hostages to Fortune (3 volumes, London: John Maxwell, 1875; 1 volume, New York: Harper, 1875);

Dead Men's Shoes (3 volumes, London: John Maxwell, 1876; 1 volume, New York: Harper, 1876);

Joshua Haggard's Daughter (3 volumes, London: John Maxwell, 1876; 1 volume, New York: Harper, 1877);

Weavers and Weft, and Other Tales (3 volumes, London: John Maxwell, 1877; 1 volume, New York: Harper, 1877);

An Open Verdict (3 volumes, London: John Maxwell, 1878; 1 volume, New York: Harper, 1878);

Vixen (3 volumes, London: John & Robert Maxwell, 1879; 1 volume, New York: Harper, 1879);

The Cloven Foot (3 volumes, London: John & Robert Maxwell, 1879; 1 volume, New York: Harper, 1879);

The Missing Witness: An Original Drama in Four Acts (London: John & Robert Maxwell, 1880);

The Story of Barbara, 3 volumes (London: John & Robert Maxwell, 1880); republished as *Barbara; or, Splendid Misery,* 1 volume (New York: Harper, 1880); republished as *The Story of Barbara; Her Splendid Misery, and Her Gilded Cage* (London: Simpkin, Marshall, Hamilton, Kent, 1891);

Just as I Am (3 volumes, London: John & Robert Maxwell, 1880; 1 volume, New York: Harper, 1880); republished as *Just as I Am; or, A Living Lie* (New York: Munro, 1885);

Asphodel (3 volumes, London: John & Robert Maxwell, 1881; 1 volume, New York: Harper, 1881);

Dross; or, The Root of Evil: A Comedy in Four Acts (London: John & Robert Maxwell, 1882; New York: DeWitt, 188?);

Married Beneath Him: A Comedy in Four Acts (London: John & Robert Maxwell, 1882);

Marjorie Daw: A Household Idyl in Two Acts (London: John & Robert Maxwell, 1882); prepared for the American stage by Henry Llewellyn Williams (New York: DeWitt, 1885);

Mount Royal (3 volumes, London: John & Robert Maxwell, 1882; 1 volume, New York: Harper, 1882);

Flower and Weed: A Novel (London: John & Robert Maxwell, 1882 [as a volume of *The Mistletoe Bough*]; New York: Harper, 1882); enlarged as *Flower and Weed, and Other Tales* (London: John & Robert Maxwell, 1883);

The Golden Calf (London: John & Robert Maxwell, 1883; New York: Lovell, 1883);

Phantom Fortune (3 volumes, London: John & Robert Maxwell, 1883; 1 volume, New York: Harper, 1883);

Under the Red Flag (London: John & Robert Maxwell, 1883 [as a volume of *The Mistletoe Bough*]; New York: Harper, 1883); enlarged as *Under the Red Flag and Other Tales* (London: John & Robert Maxwell, 1886);

Ishmael (3 volumes, London: John & Robert Maxwell, 1884; 1 volume, New York: Harper, 1884); published as *An Ishmaelite* (Chicago: Belford, Clarke, 1884);

Cut by the County (New York: Harper, 1885; London: John & Robert Maxwell, 1886); enlarged as *One Thing Needful* (3 volumes, London: John & Robert Maxwell, 1886; 1 volume, New York: Harper, 1886); published as *One Thing Needful; or, The Penalty of Fate* (New York: Munro, 1886);

Wyllard's Weird (3 volumes, London: John & Robert Maxwell, 1885; 1 volume, New York: Harper, 1885);

The Good Hermione, as Aunt Belinda (London: John & Robert Maxwell, 1886);

Mohawks (3 volumes, London: John & Robert Maxwell, 1886; 1 volume, New York: Harper, 1886);

Like and Unlike (3 volumes, London: Blackett, 1887; 1 volume, New York: Munro, 1887);

The Fatal Three (3 volumes, London: Simpkin, Marshall, 1888; 1 volume, New York: Harper, 1888);

The Day Will Come (3 volumes, London: Simpkin, Marshall, 1889; 1 volume, New York: Harper, 1889);

One Life, One Love, 3 volumes (London: Simpkin, Marshall, Hamilton, Kent, 1890);

Gerard; or, The World, The Flesh, and the Devil, 3 volumes (London: Simpkin, Marshall, Hamilton, Kent, 1891); published as *The World, The Flesh, and the Devil,* 1 volume (New York: Lovell, 1891);

The Venetians (3 volumes, London: Simpkin, Marshall, Hamilton, Kent, 1892; 1 volume, New York: Harper, 1892);

All Along the River (3 volumes, London: Simpkin, Marshall, Hamilton, Kent, 1893; 1 volume, New York: Cassell, 1893);

The Christmas Hirelings (London: Simpkin, Marshall, Hamilton, Kent, 1894; New York: Harper, 1894);

Thou Art the Man, 3 volumes (London: Simpkin, Marshall, Hamilton, Kent, 1894);

Sons of Fire, 3 volumes (London: Simpkin, Marshall, Hamilton, Kent, 1895);

London Pride; or, When the World Was Younger (London: Simpkin, Marshall, Hamilton, Kent, 1896); published as *When the World Was Younger* (New York: Fenno, 1897);

Under Love's Rule (London: Simpkin, Marshall, Hamilton, Kent, 1897);

In High Places (London: Hutchinson, 1898);

Rough Justice (London: Simpkin, Marshall, Hamilton, Kent, 1898);

His Darling Sin (London: Simpkin, Marshall, Hamilton, Kent, 1899; New York: Harper, 1899);

The Infidel (London: Simpkin, Marshall, Hamilton, Kent, 1900; New York & London: Harper, 1900);

The Conflict (London: Simpkin, Marshall, Hamilton, Kent, 1903);

A Lost Eden (London: Hutchinson, 1904);

The Rose of Life (London: Hutchinson, 1905; New York: Brentano's, 1905);

The White House (London: Hurst & Blackett, 1906);

Dead Love Has Chains (London: Hurst & Blackett, 1907);

Her Convict (London: Hurst & Blackett, 1907);

During Her Majesty's Pleasure (London: Hurst & Blackett, 1908);

Our Adversary (London: Hutchinson, 1909);

Beyond These Voices (London: Hutchinson, 1910);

The Green Curtain (London: Hutchinson, 1911);

Miranda (London: Hutchinson, 1913);

Mary (London: Hutchinson, 1916).

PLAY PRODUCTIONS: *The Loves of Arcadia,* London, Strand Theatre, 12 March 1860;

Griselda; or, The Patient Wife, London, Princess's Theatre, 13 November 1873.

On 9 November 1865 the young Henry James published an essay in *The Nation* titled "Miss Braddon." The occasion was the runaway success of Mary Elizabeth Braddon's fifth novel, *Aurora Floyd* (1863). James placed *Aurora Floyd* and *Lady Audley's Secret* (1862), which established her fame nearly overnight, as "sensation novels." Such works, pioneered by Wilkie Collins but written by Braddon and others as well, constituted an innovation in the form of the Victorian novel. Critic Patrick Brantlinger describes this innovation as a combination of the verisimilitude and contemporary setting of domestic realism with the melodramatic plot structure of Gothic romance. As James puts it in his review, sensation novels "introduced into fiction those most mysterious of mysteries, the mysteries which are at our own doors." In addition to mixing realism and romance, these novels implicitly critique mid-Victorian society because they are peopled with characters who, though outwardly respectable, harbor a secret criminality. Braddon's lasting reputation is due chiefly to her work in the innovative, subversive, but ephemeral subgenre of sensational fiction. Sensation, though, comprises only part of her immense and various literary output.

The sheer volume of Braddon's writing is indicated by her biographer, Robert Lee Wolff, who notes that "from 1862 onward, a steady stream of novels poured from her pen, sometimes two or three a year. Her last, at least her eightieth, appeared posthumously in 1916." Variety is more difficult to quantify. Braddon, like many middle-class women writers of the period, turned to fiction as a means to make a living; she wrote for the market. Because of this, and because of the enduring marketability of sensation, many of her later novels merely repeat popular formulas from her fiction of the 1860s. Her own interests evolved, however, and other later works explore the possibilities of adapting French fiction to the demands of English sensibilities. The realism of Gustave Flaubert and Honoré de Balzac and, eventually, the naturalism of Emile Zola provided literary examples that she imitated with varying degrees of success.

Braddon's stories are in many ways like her novels. All her stories were written initially for periodical publication; many were later collected and issued in a three-volume format. Some of the earliest — lightweight pieces such as "Captain Thomas" and "My First Happy Christmas" — appeared in John Maxwell's periodical *The Welcome Guest.* Others were published in *Belgravia,* the magazine founded by Maxwell in 1866 that Braddon edited for ten years, and *The Mistletoe Bough,* a Christmas annual she edited from 1878 to 1887. Her short fiction also occasionally appeared in such journals as *Temple Bar,* edited by George Augustus Sala; Charles Dickens's *All the Year Round; The Pall Mall Magazine;* and the *Strand.* These stories — or "tales," as they are called on the title pages of the collections — range in quality from the throwaway to the compelling. Many retain an affinity with her early sensation novels, depending for interest upon crime among the wealthy and respectable. Several, however, are more conventional and rely upon the hackneyed plots and sentiment of much popular fic-

tion. Several bear the imprint of Braddon's varied and unusual experiences.

Braddon was born on 4 October 1835 to Henry and Fanny White Braddon. Her childhood, which she described in an unpublished memoir titled "Before the Knowledge of Evil," was remarkable mostly for the delinquency of her father, who provided little support for his wife and children. The family's straitened financial circumstances, and perhaps her own desire for fame, led Braddon to take up acting in 1857. This effort, which, she writes, "convulsed her family to the most distant cousin," was abandoned after three moderately successful years when she turned to writing fiction. Her short interlude on the stage served Braddon as an important source of material for stories, many of which borrow settings, themes, or plot devices from the world of provincial theater.

The transition from actress to writer was not easy. Braddon's earliest literary efforts, undertaken in the late 1850s and early 1860s, waver uncertainly between genres. *Three Times Dead* (1860), her first novel, is a weak amalgam of Charles Dickens and G. W. M. Reynolds. *Garibaldi, and Other Poems* (1861), an undistinguished book of verse on the war of Italian unification, was published to lukewarm reviews. But these early years also saw the appearance of the immensely successful *Lady Audley's Secret* and *Aurora Floyd,* as well as the short stories gathered in the first of six collections published in Braddon's lifetime, *Ralph the Bailiff and Other Stories* (1862).

Lady Audley's Secret, written under the influence of Collins's *The Woman in White* (1860), remains Braddon's best-known work. Of all the characteristic figures and themes of the sensation novel — bigamy, respectable criminals, murder, insanity, amateur detection — the most remarkable to appear in this novel is surely the attribution of criminality and sensuality to an Englishwoman, which outraged contemporary critics. Several recent critics, including Elaine Showalter, Winifred Hughes, and Thomas Boyle, have inferred from this response that Braddon's sensation novels posed a threat to Victorian social consensus, particularly to stereotypical gender roles. The many traits that her stories share with these novels suggest that the stories also had a certain subversive edge.

Ralph the Bailiff and Other Stories includes stories written during the composition of *Lady Audley's Secret.* The title story resembles the novel in its treatment of crime among the middle and upper classes. The upright gentleman farmer, Dudley Carleon, inherits Grey Farm upon the death of his older brother, Richard. From the time he possesses the

Braddon in the 1880s

farm, however, Dudley is followed by his bailiff, Ralph. It is revealed that Dudley, with the assistance of the bailiff, has poisoned his brother in order to collect money to pay off debts. He is then blackmailed into marrying Ralph's sister, by whom he has a child. Dudley takes advantage of a few weeks when Ralph is absent to remarry bigamously, this time to Jenny Trevor. On his return Ralph begins to poison Jenny gradually. She escapes on the night Dudley drowns himself in despair. Ralph and his sister emigrate to Australia and, unlike Lady Audley, become prosperous despite their crimes. Such a refusal to punish those who have done wrong distressed contemporary critics, who saw in sensation fiction a virtual enticement to crime.

Another characteristic common to *Lady Audley's Secret* and some of the stories in *Ralph the Bailiff* is a meticulous rendering of detail. James complains in "Miss Braddon" that her attention to her heroines' eyes and hair serves as a poor substitute for proper characterization. Ironically, her attention to the world of material objects anticipates James's own treatment of the bric-a-brac and objets d'art picked up by many of the characters in his works. Careful attention to contemporary material culture redeems otherwise forgettable stories in the collec-

tion, such as "Captain Thomas," about a man who mistakes his lover's cat, Captain Thomas, for his rival; "My Daughters," a complaint from a father about the trials of raising girls; and "My First Happy Christmas."

In *Ralph the Bailiff* there are several ghost stories, which at first appear to be distinct from the sensation novels. However, they parallel in interesting ways the emphasis in sensation fiction on the contemporary and the domestic. Michael Cox and R. A. Gilbert note that the Victorian love for ghost stories derived from their transitional historical position. Living in the wake of a "feudal and agrarian past" but before the outcome of industrialization and democratization was certain, "all that [the Victorians] knew was that a gulf was opening with the past." According to Cox and Gilbert, fictional ghosts functioned for Victorian readers as the representatives of a past that was at once comforting and frightening. If this is the case, it seems important that the ghosts in many of Braddon's stories are not long-dead figures from distant historical periods but personal ghosts. They are directly related to individual memory and guilt.

Though not exactly a ghost story, "The Mystery at Fernwood" mentions a historical ghost – a woman starved to death at Fernwood in the time of Henry VIII – who never appears. In the story the heroine unwittingly releases from imprisonment her fiancé's idiot brother, who promptly kills her fiancé. Despite the threat of past ages, the real danger, Braddon implies, is to be found in the immediate and familial realm. "The Scene Painter's Wife," "Eveline's Visitant," and "The Cold Embrace" all involve the return of ghosts whom the protagonists have known. The deep resonance of historical ghosts, who return from the distant past as if out of a psychological reservoir, is here collapsed into a feeling of guilt for crimes against a contemporary who returns after death to take revenge.

There are several possible explanations for Braddon's attraction to this type of ghost story. One of the most interesting has to do with her personal life. Many critics have noted parallels between her fiction and her life, which in many ways was just as sensational. In 1861 she began a relationship with publisher John Maxwell, living with him as his wife though they were not actually married until 1874. During the thirteen-year interim Maxwell's legal wife was an inmate in a Dublin asylum. This unusual family arrangement, which scandalized her in the eyes of her contemporaries, might have contributed to the harshness of the criticism her work received. Particularly in the 1860s, the attacks on her sensation fiction as immoral found additional impetus in her bigamous relationship to Maxwell.

This severe criticism, in addition to a heavy work schedule, led in 1868 to an emotional and physical collapse. Braddon quickly recovered and, despite social disapproval, went on to further success. The income from her prolific output contributed substantially to the support of a large family, which included for a time four of her own children with Maxwell as well as five of his children from his first marriage. (Of these nine children, only five survived into adulthood.) The lucrative profits from her fiction also provided part of the means with which, in 1866, the couple purchased Lichfield House, the mansion in Richmond, Surrey, where they lived for the rest of their lives.

Braddon's second collection of stories, *Milly Darrell and Other Tales* (1873), displays a concern with people, like her, who are recently wealthy – though through business pursuits rather than fiction. Stories such as "Old Rudderford Hall," "Hugh Damer's Last Leger," and "The Zoophyte's Revenge" deal with the nouveaux riches in plots that, like many of Jane Austen's novels, center on marriage between aristocrats or gentry and professional arrivistes. In "Old Rudderford Hall" the architec-

tural opposition between the distinguished mansion of the title and New Rudderford Hall, "the abode of commercial wealth," represents a similar social opposition between the inhabitants of the two structures. At first antipathetic to each other, the families of old and new wealth are reconciled by marriage in the end. "The Zoophyte's Revenge" tells essentially the same story, though the specifics are slightly altered. Called "the Zoophyte" due to his laziness, Reginald Ravenscroft, brother of the imperious Lady Talmash Brading, settles on marrying the daughter of a wealthy brewer. Lady Talmash forbids the connection because of her horror at being related to tradesmen. Reginald, by way of revenge against his sister, opens a butcher shop under his name. The humiliation she feels forces her to approve his proposed marriage, and the two families, as in "Old Rudderford Hall," learn to live with one another.

Milly Darrell and Other Tales also displays a new treatment of the sorts of passionate feelings described in Braddon's earlier novels. Stories with contemporary settings such as "A Good Hater" and "Colonel Benyon's Engagement," as well as historical tales such as "The Sins of the Fathers," detail the often harmful effects of strong feelings and thus deepen sensation into tragedy. Of these, "The Sins of the Fathers" is perhaps the most successful. Set during the Restoration, one of Braddon's favorite periods for historical fiction, the story chronicles Lord Deverill's marriage to Alice Treherne, the young daughter of one of his few friends. Suspicious of the sincerity of her love because of their difference in age, he watches her behavior closely. One night, discovering her with a young man disguised as a priest, he kills both, only to find that the man was her illegitimate half-brother. After ten years of aimless and mournful dissipation on the Continent, Deverill returns to England and confesses his crime. He dies in prison, a victim, like Alice and her brother, of the "the sins of the fathers" in the form of unfettered passion.

"The Dreaded Guest," one of the most interesting stories in the collection, cleverly retells Mary Shelley's *Frankenstein* (1818). One night in December, Dr. Prestwitch, a struggling physician with a large and growing family, is brought the body of a man hanged for counterfeiting. Excited by this rare chance to advance his knowledge of anatomy, Prestwitch prepares to dissect the body, then discovers that it is still alive. He resuscitates the counterfeiter, a rough, huge man named Jonathan Blinker. Instead of gratitude for having returned Blinker to life, however, Prestwitch receives demands for food, clothing, and money. Unlike Victor Frankenstein, his literary predecessor in revivifying monsters, Prestwitch does what he is asked, funding Blinker from his limited resources. This unequal relationship continues for some time, until Blinker mysteriously discontinues his visits to the doctor. Just as Prestwitch begins to think that he has seen the last of his burden, Blinker reappears. He has become rich in America, and when he dies three years later he leaves an immense fortune to Prestwitch and his family.

This story raises the question of Braddon's literary influences. Certainly her work owes much to Shelley and other authors of Gothic fiction. More significant in this regard are two French authors, Balzac and Zola. A fine novel from this period, Braddon's *Joshua Haggard's Daughter* (1876), employs plot material from classical mythology and descriptive techniques from the realism of Balzac to explore the psychological effects of murder on the murderer. "In Great Waters," a long story from her 1877 collection, *Weavers and Weft, and Other Tales,* is similar in setting and theme to this novel. The action takes place in a fishing village in Normandy, where two sisters compete for the love of the same boatman. Jeanne, the older sister, keeps silent about her feelings, suffering so that her younger sister, Marie, might be happy. Though the boatman, Henri Latouche, asks Marie to marry him, she becomes infatuated with a foppish Parisian gentleman named Hector de Lutrin. Hector dies in a boating accident; Marie, hearing of this, faints and gives way to brain fever. She breaks off her engagement with Henri and becomes a nun; five years later Jeanne and Henri marry. What lends interest to this otherwise conventional plot is Braddon's careful rendering not only of the details of life by the sea but of the complex and conflicting emotions experienced by the characters.

If "In Great Waters" bears a certain resemblance to Balzac's fiction, the rest of the stories in this collection demonstrate another type of influence, looking back to the late 1850s when Braddon was an actress in the provincial theater. "Prince Ramji Rowdedow," a lightweight yet entertaining piece, relates the results of an actor's attempt to impersonate "His Royal Highness Prince Ramji Rowdedow, from the Kingdom of Goojeebadanistan" in order to attract crowds in a dismally slow theater season. In "Her Last Appearance," set in the eighteenth century and containing many heavy-handed references to Horace Walpole, the first Gothic novelist, a London actress draws on the misery of an unhappy marriage to become a great tragedienne. "Too Bright to Last," narrated by an onlooker, tells of the beautiful Lucy Derwent, who takes up acting because her dissipated father is unable to support her. The manager of the provincial company to which she belongs, Mr. Ponsonby, falls in love with her. She, however, only has eyes for Roderick McDonald, a star from the London stage who has come to the provinces for an engagement of two weeks, at the end of which she discovers that he is married. She is crushed by this news but in time comes to forget McDonald and live contentedly as Ponsonby's wife. As such stories indicate, Braddon was just as capable of writing conservative and conciliatory fiction as she was of writing fiction that threatened or subverted.

Braddon's novels from the early 1880s, including *The Golden Calf* (1883) and *Ishmael* (1884), reflect the increasing influence of Zola on her work. Her short fiction from this period, however, returns to sensation. All but one of the stories in *Flower and Weed, and Other Tales* (1883) deal with crime and detection – sometimes involving the theater as in *Weavers and Weft,* at other times exploiting the idea of the respectable criminal. "Thou Art the Man" combines these traits in the person of Michael Elyard, the star of a Drury Lane production about an Italian's murder of his wife and his careful concealment of her body by the banks of a canal. Captain Bywater, disturbed by the uncanny realism Elyard lends to this stage crime, becomes one of Braddon's amateur detectives by establishing, through uncovering a variety of improbable coincidences, that Elyard had actually murdered Bywater's childhood sweetheart, Helen Leeworthy.

In "George Caulfield's Journey" the retiring and shy Reverend George Caulfield agrees to a mysterious man's request that he accompany the man's silent and shrouded sister from one rail station to another. On arrival the woman is discovered to be dead, and Caulfield is arrested for murder. This event introduces one of the most memorable characters in Braddon's short fiction, the worldly vicar Edward Leworthy, who unravels the mystery and frees Caulfield. "The Clown's Quest" features a professional detective, constable James Wormald, and his efforts to locate the missing brother of Signor Grumani, a famous stage clown. "His Secret," an unusual story for Braddon in that a conflict involving love, not money, prompts murder, hinges on a woman's unwitting marriage to the man who killed her husband.

The only nonsensational piece in *Flower and Weed,* "'If She Be Not Fair to Me,'" deals with love more conventionally. The story effectively reverses the relationship between the older and younger sisters of "In Great Waters." The beautiful and ambitious Blanche Ferrier rejects the overtures of Claude Tremayne, a plain but devoted suitor. Tremayne then leaves for military service in India. He is away four years, during which Blanche comes to regret that she did not marry him. On his return Blanche discovers, bitterly but with resignation, that he has fallen out of love with her and deeply in love with her younger sister, Antoinette. Antoinette and Tremayne become engaged, and the end of the story shows them married and leaving England, "off by the next P. and O. steamer – over the hills and far away."

Despite the distance between the concerns of Braddon's novels and those of her short fiction evident in *Flower and Weed, and Other Tales* "Under the Red Flag," the novella that serves as the title story for Braddon's next collection (1886), is, as editor and biographer Robert Lee Wolff points out, the Braddon story most indebted to Zola. Thus, "Under the Red Flag," which appeared first at Christmas 1883 as an entire issue of *The Mistletoe Bough,* violates all expectations for a Victorian Christmas story. The setting is Paris at the time of the Commune; the principal characters are two Irish sisters and their French husbands, a cabinetmaker and a young socialist activist; and the plot is a detailed recounting of the characters' involvements in the Prussian invasion of France and the rise and fall of the Commune. It is characteristic of Braddon that, even in this, her most serious attempt at writing in the style of the French naturalists, she does not follow through: out of dismally unpromising circumstances she manages to produce a happy ending.

The remaining stories in the collection are more closely related to Braddon's earlier themes and plots. "Sir Philip's Wooing" duplicates almost exactly the situation described in "His Secret": a man kills the husband of a woman he has fallen in love with; the man and the widow marry; and years later the woman discovers to her horror that she has married her first husband's murderer. "At Daggers Drawn" and "Across the Footlights" use theatrical settings for their sentimental plots. The only novelty in the collection comes in stories that refer to events of contemporary interest. The polar expedition of Sir John Franklin in the early nineteenth century, for example, provides the premise for "My Wife's Promise," in which the ghost of the wife of a polar explorer leads him to the graves of those lost in an earlier attempt to conquer the Arctic.

Braddon's last collection of stories is included in the three volumes of *All Along the River* (1893).

Like all but one of the stories in *Under the Red Flag,* these deliver little that is new or unusual. "Stapylton's Plot" tells of a young man who lives out the plot of a novel he cannot force himself to write by rescuing a mysterious girl from a suicide attempt. "My Dream" and "His Oldest Friends" are ghost stories of a familiar sort. "One Fatal Moment," though reminiscent of earlier tales involving crimes of passion, is interesting – as is "My Wife's Promise" – for its reliance on contemporary events. Here the Irish Question provides the basic premise: a drunken soldier so infuriates an Irishwoman with his deprecatory remarks on her homeland that she kills him. The crime comes back to haunt her when she falls in love with her victim's brother and is forced to confess to him what she has done.

Braddon continued to write stories after the appearance of *All Along the River,* though those that appeared after 1892 remain uncollected. She continued to produce novels as well, easily adapting to the shift in market demand from the three-volume to the one-volume format that occurred in the mid 1890s. The death on 5 March 1895 of Maxwell, who had for some thirty-four years served as her husband, business manager, and sometime publisher, deeply saddened her. Characteristically, however, she quickly rallied and resumed her former level of activity. With the exception of a brief period in the winter of 1907–1908 spent recovering from the effects of a stroke, the final two decades of her life were nearly as busy and productive as the first six had been. She died on 4 February 1915 at home in Lichfield House.

The overall importance of Braddon's work lies in the effect of her sensation novels of the 1860s on the development of Victorian fiction. These novels, as well as certain sensational stories, introduced themes and techniques into fiction that helped foster new genres such as mystery and detective fiction. Also important, though now little recognized, are her attempts to bring the stylistic and thematic concerns of contemporary French fiction across the Channel. If many of her stories remain untouched by this effort, depending for the most part upon the sensational, the sentimental, or the current, this fact testifies more to the demands of the Victorian readership than to the interests and abilities of Braddon herself.

Letters:

Robert Lee Wolff, ed., "Devoted Disciple: The Letters of Mary Elizabeth Braddon to Sir Edward Bulwer-Lytton, 1862–1873," *Harvard Library*

Bulletin, 22 (January 1974): 1–35; (April 1974): 129–161.

Interviews:

Joseph Hatton, "Miss Braddon at Home," *London Society,* 53 (January 1888): 22–29;

Clive Holland, "Fifty Years of Novel Writing. Miss Braddon at Home. A Chat with the *Doyenne* of English Novelists," *Pall Mall Magazine,* 48 (November 1911): 697–709.

Biography:

Robert Lee Wolff, *Sensational Victorian: The Life and Fiction of Mary Elizabeth Braddon* (New York & London: Garland, 1979).

References:

Thomas Boyle, *Black Swine in the Sewers of Hampstead: Beneath the Surface of Victorian Sensationalism* (Harmondsworth, U.K.: Penguin, 1989);

Patrick Brantlinger, "What Is 'Sensational' about the 'Sensation Novel'?," *Nineteenth-Century Fiction,* 37 (June 1982): 1–28;

Michael Cox and R. A. Gilbert, Introduction to *Victorian Ghost Stories: An Oxford Anthology,* edited by Cox and Gilbert (Oxford & New York: Oxford University Press, 1991), pp. ix–xx;

Winifred Hughes, *The Maniac in the Cellar: Sensation Novels of the 1860s* (Princeton: Princeton University Press, 1977);

Henry James, "Miss Braddon," *Nation,* 1 (9 November 1865): 593–595;

Elaine Showalter, *A Literature of Their Own* (Princeton: Princeton University Press, 1977).

Papers:

Robert Lee Wolff's large collection of Braddon material, including notebooks, essays, letters, the manuscript of her unpublished memoir "Before the Knowledge of Evil," and first editions of many of her novels, is housed at the University of Texas, Austin. Other Braddon notebooks are held at the Houghton Library of Harvard University. Letters may be found in the Lilly Library at Indiana University, the Library of the University of Illinois, the Parrish Collection at Princeton University, and the Beinecke Library at Yale University.

John Buchan

(26 August 1875 – 11 February 1940)

J. Randolph Cox
Saint Olaf College

See also the Buchan entries in *DLB 34: British Novelists, 1890–1929: Traditionalists* and *DLB 70: British Mystery Writers, 1860–1919.*

BOOKS: *Sir Quixote of the Moors* (London: Unwin, 1895; New York: Holt, 1895);

Scholar Gipsies (London: John Lane / New York: Macmillan, 1896);

Sir Walter Ralegh: The Stanhope Essay (Oxford: Blackwell / London: Simpkin, Marshall, Hamilton, Kent, 1897);

John Burnet of Barns (London: John Lane, 1898; New York: Dodd, Mead, 1898);

The Pilgrim Fathers: The Newdigate Prize Poem, 1898 (Oxford: Blackwell / London: Simpkin, Marshall, Hamilton, Kent, 1898);

Brasenose College (London: Robinson, 1898);

Grey Weather: Moorland Tales of My Own People (London: John Lane, 1899);

A Lost Lady of Old Years (London: John Lane, 1899);

The Half-Hearted (London: Isbister, 1900; Boston & New York: Houghton Mifflin, 1900);

The Watcher by the Threshold and Other Tales (Edinburgh & London: Blackwood, 1902; enlarged edition, New York: Doran, 1918);

The African Colony (Edinburgh: Blackwood, 1903);

The Law Relating to the Taxation of Foreign Income (London: Stevens, 1905);

A Lodge in the Wilderness, anonymous (Edinburgh & London: Blackwood, 1906);

Some Eighteenth Century Byways and Other Essays (Edinburgh & London: Blackwood, 1908);

Prester John (London: Nelson, 1910); republished as *The Great Diamond Pipe* (New York: Dodd, Mead, 1910);

Sir Walter Raleigh (London: Nelson, 1911; New York: Holt, 1911);

The Moon Endureth: Tales and Fancies (Edinburgh & London: Blackwood, 1912; New York: Sturgis & Walton, 1912);

The Marquis of Montrose (London: Nelson, 1913; New York: Scribners, 1913);

John Buchan

Andrew Jameson, Lord Ardwall (Edinburgh & London: Blackwood, 1913);

Britain's War by Land (London & New York: Oxford University Press/H. Milford, 1915);

Nelson's History of the War, 24 volumes (London: Nelson, 1915–1919); revised as *A History of the Great War* (4 volumes, London: Nelson, 1921–1922; 8 volumes, Boston & New York: Houghton Mifflin, 1922);

The Achievement of France (London: Methuen, 1915);

Salute to Adventurers (London: Nelson, 1915; Boston & New York: Houghton Mifflin, 1915);

The Thirty-Nine Steps (Edinburgh & London: Blackwood, 1915; New York: Doran, 1916);

The Power-House (Edinburgh & London: Blackwood, 1916; New York: Doran, 1916);

Greenmantle (London: Hodder & Stoughton, 1916; New York: Doran, 1916);

The Battle of the Somme, First Phase (London & New York: Nelson, 1916);

Poems, Scots and English (London & Edinburgh: T. C. & E. C. Jack, 1917; revised and enlarged edition, London: Nelson, 1936);

The Battle of the Somme, Second Phase (Edinburgh, New York & London: Nelson, 1917);

Mr. Standfast (London: Hodder & Stoughton, 1918; New York: Doran, 1919);

These for Remembrance (London: Privately printed, 1919);

The Island of Sheep, by Buchan and Susan Buchan as Cadmus and Harmonia (London: Hodder & Stoughton, 1919; Boston & New York: Houghton Mifflin, 1920);

The History of the South African Forces in France (London: Nelson, 1920);

Francis and Riversdale Grenfell: A Memoir (London: Nelson, 1920);

The Path of the King (London: Hodder & Stoughton, 1921; New York: Doran, 1921);

Huntingtower (London: Hodder & Stoughton, 1922; New York: Doran, 1922);

A Book of Escapes and Hurried Journeys (London: Nelson, 1922; Boston & New York: Houghton Mifflin, 1923);

The Last Secrets (London: Nelson, 1923; Boston & New York: Houghton Mifflin, 1924);

Midwinter (London: Hodder & Stoughton, 1923; New York: Doran, 1923);

Days to Remember: The British Empire in the Great War, by Buchan and Henry Newbolt (London: Nelson, 1923);

The Three Hostages (London: Hodder & Stoughton, 1924; Boston & New York: Houghton Mifflin, 1924);

Lord Minto: A Memoir (London & New York: Nelson, 1924);

The History of the Royal Scots Fusiliers (1678–1918) (London & New York: Nelson, 1925);

John Macnab (London: Hodder & Stoughton, 1925; Boston & New York: Houghton Mifflin, 1925);

The Man and the Book: Sir Walter Scott (London & Edinburgh: Nelson, 1925);

The Dancing Floor (London: Hodder & Stoughton, 1926; Boston & New York: Houghton Mifflin, 1926);

The Fifteenth-Scottish-Division 1914–1919, by Buchan and John Stewart (Edinburgh: Blackwood, 1926);

Homilies and Recreations (London: Nelson, 1926; London & New York: Nelson / Boston: Houghton Mifflin, 1926);

Witch Wood (London: Hodder & Stoughton, 1927; Boston & New York: Houghton Mifflin, 1927);

The Runagates Club (London: Hodder & Stoughton, 1928; Boston & New York: Houghton Mifflin, 1928);

Montrose (London: Nelson, 1928; Boston & New York: Houghton Mifflin, 1928);

The Courts of the Morning (London: Hodder & Stoughton, 1929; Boston & New York: Houghton Mifflin, 1929);

The Causal and the Casual in History (Cambridge: Cambridge University Press, 1929; New York: Macmillan, 1929);

The Four Adventures of Richard Hannay (London: Hodder & Stoughton, 1930);

The Kirk in Scotland, 1560–1929, by Buchan and George Adam Smith (London: Hodder & Stoughton, 1930);

Castle Gay (London: Hodder & Stoughton, 1930; Boston & New York: Houghton Mifflin, 1930);

The Blanket of the Dark (London: Hodder & Stoughton, 1931; Boston & New York: Houghton Mifflin, 1931);

Sir Walter Scott (London & Toronto: Cassell, 1932; New York: Coward-McCann, 1932);

The Gap in the Curtain (London: Hodder & Stoughton, 1932; Boston & New York: Houghton Mifflin, 1932);

Julius Caesar (London: Davies, 1932; New York: Appleton, 1932);

The Magic Walking Stick (London: Hodder & Stoughton, 1932; Boston & New York: Houghton Mifflin, 1932);

The Massacre of Glencoe (London: Davies, 1933; New York: Putnam, 1933);

A Prince of the Captivity (London: Hodder & Stoughton, 1933; Boston & New York: Houghton Mifflin, 1933);

The Free Fishers (London: Hodder & Stoughton, 1934; Boston & New York: Houghton Mifflin, 1934);

Gordon at Khartoum (London: Davies, 1934);

Oliver Cromwell (London: Hodder & Stoughton, 1934; Boston: Houghton Mifflin, 1934);

The Adventures of Sir Edward Leithen (London: Hodder & Stoughton, 1935);

The King's Grace (London: Hodder & Stoughton, 1935); republished as *The People's King, George V* (Boston: Houghton Mifflin, 1935);

The House of the Four Winds (London: Hodder & Stoughton, 1935; Boston & New York: Houghton Mifflin, 1935);

Men and Deeds (London: Davies, 1935);

Four Tales (Edinburgh & London: Blackwood, 1936);

The Island of Sheep (London: Hodder & Stoughton, 1936); republished as *The Man from the Norlands* (Boston & New York: Houghton Mifflin, 1936);

The Adventures of Dickson Mc'Cunn (London: Hodder & Stoughton, 1937);

Augustus (London: Hodder & Stoughton, 1937; Boston: Houghton Mifflin, 1937);

Adventures of Richard Hannay (Boston: Houghton Mifflin, 1939);

Five Fold Salute to Adventure: An Omnibus Volume of Historical Novels (London: Hodder & Stoughton, 1939);

Memory Hold-the-Door (London: Hodder & Stoughton, 1940); republished as *Pilgrim's Way* (Boston: Houghton Mifflin, 1940);

Comments and Characters, edited by W. Forbes Gray (London & New York: Nelson, 1940);

Canadian Occasions (London: Hodder & Stoughton, 1940);

Sick Heart River (London: Hodder & Stoughton, 1941); republished as *Mountain Meadow* (Boston: Houghton Mifflin, 1941);

The Long Traverse (London: Hodder & Stoughton, 1941); republished as *The Lake of Gold* (Boston: Houghton Mifflin, 1941);

Adventurers All (Boston: Houghton Mifflin, 1942);

The Clearing House, edited by Lady Tweedsmuir (London: Hodder & Stoughton, 1946).

Collection: *The Best Short Stories of John Buchan,* 2 volumes, edited by David Daniell (London: M. Joseph, 1980, 1982).

OTHER: *Essays and Apothegms of Francis Lord Bacon,* edited, with an introduction, by Buchan (London: Scott, 1894);

Musa Piscatrix, edited by Buchan (London: John Lane, 1896; Chicago: McClurg, 1896);

Izaak Walton, *The Compleat Angler, or the Contemplative Man's Recreation,* edited, with an introduction and notes, by Buchan (London: Methuen, 1901);

Ralph Waldo Emerson, *Selected Essays,* introduction by Buchan (London: Nelson, 1909);

Edgar Allan Poe, *Tales of Mystery and Imagination,* introduction by Buchan (London: Nelson, 1911);

The Long Road to Victory, edited by Buchan (London: Nelson, 1920);

Archibald Philip Primrose, *Miscellanies, Literary and Historical,* edited, with a prefatory note, by Buchan (London: Hodder & Stoughton, 1921);

Great Hours in Sport, edited by Buchan (London: Nelson, 1921);

A History of English Literature, edited by Buchan (London: Nelson, 1923; New York: Ronald, 1938);

William Morris, *William Morris,* edited by Henry Newbolt, introduction by Buchan (London: Nelson, 1923);

The Nations of Today, 12 volumes, edited by Buchan (London: Hodder & Stoughton, 1923–1924; Boston & New York: Houghton Mifflin, 1923–1924);

The Northern Muse: An Anthology of Scots Vernacular Poetry, edited by Buchan (London: Nelson, 1924);

Modern Short Stories, edited by Buchan (London: Nelson, 1926);

"The Magic Walking Stick," in *Sails of Gold,* edited by Lady Cynthia Asquith (London: Jarrolds, 1927), pp. 12–27;

Mary Webb, *Gone to Earth,* introduction by Buchan (London: Cape, 1930);

"The Strange Adventure of Mr. Andrew Hawthorn," in *The Silver Ship,* collected by Asquith (London: Putnam, 1932), pp. 173–182.

SELECTED PERIODICAL PUBLICATION – UNCOLLECTED: "A Captain of Salvation," *Yellow Book,* 8 (January 1896): 143–158.

Historian, biographer, historical novelist, and statesman, John Buchan found an enduring reputation in popular fiction. The "Buchan touch" is a term applied to fiction that shares his appeal: romantic yet not preposterous characters and a superb sense of setting and climate with swiftly moving plots. Written with unassuming ease, his works of high adventure and political intrigue have had a wide readership. He introduced to spy fiction its basic theme: that evil and worldwide conspiracies can lie just beneath the surface of civilization. According to character Andrew Lumley in his novel *The Power-House* (1916), it is civilization that holds anarchy at bay.

In more than eighty short stories published over a period of forty years in nine collections,

Buchan replicated the themes and subjects of his longer works, including historical adventure, escapes and hurried journeys, essays into the supernatural, taut spy thrillers, portraits of individuals under stress, and playful excursions into satire. All of his stories demonstrate a confidence in technique and are distinctive in style. In his introduction to *Modern Short Stories* (1926), which he edited, he recognized that a short story was not simply a short novel, that there was a difference of quality as well as of length:

> It must deal with a single episode, the *motif* must be narrowed so as to admit of a sharp definition, the impression upon the reader should be not of a piece of life portrayed in all its catholicity and variousness, but of life seen in a dramatic moment. Its parallel in poetry is lyrical concentration as contrasted with epic expansion.

David Daniell has defined the categories appropriate to the Buchan touch: the *locus amoenus* story (about a special and powerful place); the wise, classical scholar story; the "flight North" story; the Scottish moorland romance; and the experience of the power of the irrational. More than half of Buchan's short fiction originally appeared in *Blackwood's Magazine,* but it also appeared in the *Atlantic Monthly,* the *Living Age, The Yellow Book,* and the *Glasgow University Magazine.* Some were written especially for collections, and a few have never been collected.

In four of his collections of short stories – *Sir Walter Raleigh* (1911), *The Path of the King* (1921), *The Gap in the Curtain* (1932), and *The Long Traverse* (1941) – Buchan used a framing device to link the stories into a cohesive narrative so that they resemble novels. In another, *The Runagates Club* (1928), he employed the framework of stories told at a dining club. In each of his collections he gathered stories on common themes or with common settings.

Born in Perth, Scotland, on 26 August 1875, Buchan was a son of John Buchan, a minister in the Free Church of Scotland, and Helen Masterson Buchan. The family moved the following year to Fife, where he grew up along the coast. The woods in which he played with his sister, Anna, and his brothers, Walter and William, became the setting for imaginary adventures based partly on family stories and history and partly on the Bible and John Bunyan's *Pilgrim's Progress* (1678, 1684). In the border country near Peebles and Broughton, where his mother's family lived and where he spent his summers, he found new vistas for his imagination in re-enacting stories from Scottish history. As he grew older and explored the countryside, first on foot

and then by bicycle, he added to a store of places where his fictional characters would live, fight, and die.

Climbing the Tweedside hills led to greater efforts, particularly the Swiss Alps and the Dolomites. At Oxford, where he took his First in Greats in 1899, he did not go out for team sports, but he participated in many strenuous activities. In his autobiography, *Memory Hold-the-Door* (1940), he writes of canoeing, walking to the limit of his strength, or riding a course marked out on a map. His fictional characters followed his example in this, as in other things.

His first fictional characters appeared in *Scholar Gipsies* (1896), a collection of sixteen pieces, primarily essays, previously published in periodicals while Buchan was an undergraduate. Three of these – "Afternoon," "On Cademuir Hill," and "An Individualist" – are short stories based in part on some of the boyhood games played in Peeblesshire and partly on his reading of other authors, such as Kenneth Grahame. In such images of nature and experiences of men and boys are rough drafts for Richard Hannay's pursuit through the Highlands in *The Thirty-Nine Steps* (1915).

In London, Buchan began studying law at the Middle Temple in 1899 and continued the writing he had begun while at Oxford. He intended to support himself with his writing while working for his bar examinations. An introduction to John St Loe Strachey, editor of the *Spectator,* gave him a ready source of income, as he was soon contributing notes and reviews on a regular basis.

Buchan also continued to write short fiction, in 1899 publishing *Grey Weather: Moorland Tales of My Own People,* which collected fourteen stories and a poem, some with such diverse periodical sources as *Chamber's Journal, The Yellow Book,* and *Macmillan's Magazine.* Verses from the poem, "Ballad for Grey Weather," appear as epigraphs for individual stories. The title of the book suggests the way the weather in the stories is so vividly presented as well as the harshness of its effect on the characters.

The stories are all set in the Tweeddale country, which serves as a backdrop to a variety of experiments in storytelling. As Daniell has pointed out, Buchan often focuses on a single moment to give a telling perspective to larger issues. The shepherd in "The Herd of Standlan" risks his own life in detailed agony to save Arthur Mordaunt from drowning, later regretting his altruism when the politician causes a national disaster. In "The Black Fishers" the poaching brothers follow expediency rather than delaying their original plans and notifying the authorities of their father's sudden death. The heroism in "At the Rising of the Waters" is understated through expressions of weariness and discomfort. The religion of the protagonist in "At the Article of Death" is shed during his last hours, leaving him with a feeling of having arrived at even more basic truths.

"Comedy in the Full Moon" and "Politics and the Mayfly" show Buchan in a playful mood and reveal a sound sense of the comic. In the first story six people of varying backgrounds converge on a magic knoll to view the future and find the experience has different meanings for each. In the second story two opposing country politicians share an interest in fly-fishing. The less radical of the two lends a lure to his opponent, who becomes so fascinated with the sport that he fails to show up at the polls on election day. What lies closest to a man's heart thus displaces the fleeting importance of the political arena. "The Moor Song," subtitled "The tale of the respectable whaup and the great godly man," is a playful fable. The story tells of how the "great godly man" on a particular occasion has a conversation with a bird, who takes him to a place where he can hear the entire "Moor Song." The experience makes him leave his home and set out through the world filled with a great yearning.

The rest of the stories in *Grey Weather* use a similar theme. Some of them, as tentative as they might have been for a beginning writer, still stand as remarkably clear and interesting adventures. Some are surprisingly mature, such as "A Reputation," in which the man who seems to have everything life could offer discovers he does not possess the most important and sets out to find what everyone strives for, "the real thing." This story stands in contrast to the later criticism of Buchan as a worshiper of success. This collection is also of interest for his early use of specific personal names, such as Clanroyden and Raden, that appear in some of his later works.

"A Journey of Little Profit" is a folktale about a meeting with the devil; "Summer Weather" shows how a fool can display heroism under the right circumstances; and "The Oasis in the Snow" demonstrates Buchan's grasp of the essentials for a tale of panic in a snowstorm. In "The Oasis in the Snow" the dog avoids the seeming sanctuary of a great green space; in the daylight the space is revealed as a great green bog.

As a successful writer with a steady source of income, Buchan could enjoy London society, and at a dinner party in 1901 he met someone who suggested his name to Lord Milner, high commissioner

Buchan and his daughter, Alice

for South Africa. The Boer War was over (although peace was not formally declared until 1902), and Milner, concerned with reconstruction, had traveled to England to recruit men for his staff. Buchan was offered a two-year appointment, which he accepted. At the time, South Africa seemed to him a land of opportunity and excitement. He had not supported the war, but he was in favor of reconstruction. He set to work in his new administrative duties and learned the value of quick decisions and prompt action. He also took advantage of opportunities to travel to inspect farms and to explore the bush. The two years (1901–1903) he spent there would serve as valuable background for his fiction, in particular for his novel *Prester John* (1910), and he made his most famous character, Richard Hannay, a South African mining engineer.

While Buchan was in South Africa, *The Watcher by the Threshold and Other Tales* (1902) was published. The five stories, two novelettes and three long short stories, are tales of the supernatural, and some have been kept alive by frequent appearances in anthologies. A 1918 American edition included four additional stories. One of these, "The Rime of True Thomas," was the retitled "The Moor Song" from *Grey Weather,* while another, " 'Divus' Johnston," was later included in *The Runagates Club.*

All the stories in the original version of *The Watcher by the Threshold and Other Tales* were written while Buchan was at Oxford and appear in the order in which they were first published. "No-Man's Land" (1898) is narrated by a Mr. Graves, fellow of St. Chad's, Oxford, who while on holiday in Scotland comes upon a remnant of a race, referred to as the Folk, who may have been either the inspiration for the legends of the brownies or else a Pictish survival. The story ends with a suggestion that proof of its truth may still lie in the hills of Allermuir. Biographer Janet Adam Smith has suggested that this story is an example of Buchan's sense of the ever-present reality of evil and how it might break through into the most respectable of lives at any moment – a theme he carried over to his later thrillers.

In "The Far Islands" (1899) Colin Raden's vision of an unattainable goal, an island he can see but not reach, becomes stronger and stronger until it finally becomes a reality at the point of his death in battle. Buchan later used the hereditary hallucination, as well as the contrasts between Oxford and Scotland, in the recurring dream of Vernon Milburne in *The Dancing Floor* (1926). The title story of *The Watcher by the Threshold and Other Tales* is a tale of demonic possession; the skepticism of the protagonist is soon dispelled by experience. Obviously written under the influence of Robert Louis Stevenson, "The Watcher by the Threshold" uses a frame narrative for its structure and is told through a series of unpublished papers, journals, diaries, and letters.

"The Outgoing of the Tide" (1901) is a historical tale told in Scots, another example of the tale of diabolism filled with witchcraft and pagan rites culminating on Beltane's Eve, which precedes the Celtic festival of 1 May. In the final story, "Fountainblue" (1901), a man revisits scenes of his childhood in which he is faced by a self-revelation that points to his true destiny – a foreshadowing of events in Buchan's final novel, *Sick Heart River* (1941), since each protagonist gives up his life for a cause.

Two stories included in the American edition of the book, "Basilissa" and "The King of Ypres," have never been reprinted or collected in any of Buchan's other books. "Basilissa" has elements that were later used in his novel *The Dancing Floor,* in particular Vernon Milburne's recurring dream of moving from room to room, knowing at the end there will be some stranger terror to face. As in the novel, the final adventure occurs on a Greek island, where he becomes the savior of a damsel in distress. In "The King of Ypres" Private Galbraith finds him-

self in charge of a town in France during World War I and succeeds in restoring order, even though it means exceeding his authority.

Another story from this early period, "A Captain of Salvation," has not been collected, although it has appeared in an anthology of stories from its 1898 source, *The Yellow Book.* It relates how a captain in the Salvation Army, having turned from his old life of vice, is reminded of the past when he encounters someone from that old life. Like "The King of Ypres," it is atypical for Buchan except for the struggle of the man against evil.

After his return to London and a period as a barrister while continuing his writing for the *Spectator,* Buchan kept in touch with the political and social scene. At one country-house weekend he met Susan Grosvenor, whose father had been a son of Lord Ebury and whose great-great-uncle had been the Duke of Wellington. Their friendship flourished, and in November 1906 Buchan proposed and was accepted. Her family approved of the liaison, but his family was more skeptical. On 15 July 1907 they were married at St. George's, Hanover Square, and spent part of their honeymoon rock climbing in the Dolomites. Before the proposal Buchan had accepted a position as literary adviser for the publisher Thomas Nelson and Sons in their Edinburgh headquarters, but soon after the wedding the couple returned to London, and Buchan worked in Nelson's office there. The marriage was happy, and the couple had four children.

Much of Buchan's writing before 1910 was nonfiction, including articles and books on Africa and on the tax law. The fiction he published was written in emulation of Sir Walter Scott and Stevenson and drew on the rich romantic traditions of Scotland. In the first decade of the twentieth century he learned how to blend the exaggerated world of romance and adventure with his own style. Later he would write books for some of the new editions he inaugurated for Nelson, including the Sixpenny Classics, the Sevenpenny Library of copyright novels, and others. He was never far from publishing or from a knowledge of what the market required. He even edited a weekly paper, the *Scottish Review.*

In 1910 Buchan published *Prester John,* a boys' adventure novel, which opened new fictional fields for him. That spring he and his wife traveled by the Orient Express to Constantinople, then cruised in the Aegean. While his actual experiences may not have rivaled those of some of his well-known characters, he certainly was observant enough to pick up ideas and background that he could put to good use in later novels and short stories. Some, such as the setting for *The Dancing Floor,* might not be used for a decade or more, but they were never completely forgotten.

The next year Buchan became a Unionist political candidate for Peeblesshire and Selkirk but found time to publish a fictionalized biography, *Sir Walter Raleigh,* composed of eleven distinct stories: "The Luterano," "The Road of the Sunset," "Belphoebe's Smile," "Manoa the Golden," "Cadiz Bar," "New Times, New Men," "Stone Walls," "Fairy Gold," "The King's Path," "The Last Venture," and " 'A Better Indies Than the King of Spain's.' " While intended for young readers, it does not convey the sense of the author having written down to his audience. Each story is told from the point of view of someone who knew Ralegh, either as a close friend or as an observer; the last two stories are told by the same narrator. Some are real people, others fictional; some admired him, others did not. Young Ralegh listens to stories of exploration and is inspired to gain for England "a better Indies than the King of Spain's." The stories, covering the period from 1564 to 1619, tell of his explorations and adventures, his political intrigues, his days in prison, and how bravely he faced his own death. While they are separate incidents, they can best be enjoyed as part of the larger story.

Buchan's visits to his home territory in Peeblesshire or Edinburgh became more frequent when his father retired from the church and his mother's health was failing. In 1911 and 1912 his father and his brother William both died almost a year apart, which, coupled with his mother's depressions and pressures in his public life, adversely affected his health. The duodenal ulcer diagnosed in 1912 was to be with him the rest of his life.

Buchan followed the themes of his first two collections of short stories with more moorland romances and more stories of the supernatural and high adventure in *The Moon Endureth: Tales and Fancies* (1912). The ten stories alternate with verses, in English and Scots, that fit the mood of the collection. Two stories, "Streams of Water in the South" and "The Rime of True Thomas," are reprinted from *Grey Weather,* but the remaining eight, all originally published in *Blackwood's Magazine,* are new. One of the historical stories, "The Company of the Marjolaine," explains how the search for a king for the new American colonies settled on Charles Edward Stewart forty years too late. "A Lucid Interval" conveys social satire, as a group of politicians reacts to an East Indian drug in their food at a country-house dinner by taking up positions opposite to those for which they are best known. "The Lem-

nian," a story with which Buchan was greatly satisfied, concerns a seafaring islander named Atta who is blown to the mainland of Greece in a storm. He meets his death at Thermopylae because of his pride and dignity as a man, although he was not responsible for the quarrel that started the battle.

"Space" is narrated by Edward Leithen, who reappears in the first of Buchan's thrillers, *The Power-House.* The story involves the idea of space as a series of crowded corridors instead of a vacuum. The contemplation of the reality of such a theory drives the erratic genius Holland to his own destruction in the mountains.

In "The Grove of Ashtaroth," classic Buchan in the supernatural mode, the influence of a place on the soul and well-being of its owner becomes all too real. "The Riding of Ninemileburn" recalls the stories from *Grey Weather,* as Sim o' the Cleuch lets his friends talk him into joining them on a raid ("Riding"), for which he pays dearly for his arrogance when he returns home to find his wife dying and his child without food or milk.

In "The Kings of Orion" Tommy Lacelles is searching for something in central Asia with which to build an empire when he fulfills an old legend that the alter ego, good or bad, is always greater than the original person. His daydream becomes a source of practical strength. "The Green Glen" is another story, both touching and sad, of a special place that exerts power or influence over the right person. The narrator tries to learn the secrets of the glen and succeeds in part through historical and genealogical study, but it is the ancestry of two characters that truly unlocks the past when they set foot in the area together and reenact a story from the history of two famous Scottish families.

During World War I Buchan created some of his most enduring characters in fiction – Richard Hannay, Sandy Arbuthnot, John S. Blenkiron, and Peter Pienaar. He continued writing stories about these characters throughout most of the remainder of his literary career.

At the time he was working on *The Thirty-Nine Steps* Buchan proposed a history of the war in monthly parts to Nelson. Originally he suggested Hilaire Belloc as the author, but when Belloc was not available he added the task to his other duties and continued through the rest of the war years. The twenty-four volumes appeared as *Nelson's History of the War* between February 1915 and July 1919 and were revised and published in four volumes as *A History of the Great War* (1921–1922). Having become something of an authority on the progress of the war, he was employed on a regular basis by the

Foreign Office in intelligence and was directly responsible to Sir Edward Grey, the foreign secretary, which resulted in his appointment as first director of the newly established Department of Information. These experiences also influenced his fiction and account for the sense of authenticity in his trilogy set during the war. He wrote few short stories about the war.

The Buchans desired a peaceful postwar existence in a manor house in the Cotswolds. In 1919 he was appointed a director of Reuters, and in 1920 they moved into the manor at Elsfield, a four-mile walk from Oxford, and he achieved the kind of contentment of which he writes in "Fullcircle," a story originally published in *Blackwood's Magazine* in January 1920 that appeared later in *The Runagates Club.* Here he was able to enjoy his family and entertain his friends and the many Oxford students who would walk or bicycle the four miles for tea and conversation.

The first thriller he wrote at Elsfield was *Huntingtower* (1922), but the first collection of short fiction was *The Path of the King,* a series of linked stories that begins with a story of a Viking and ends with the assassination of Abraham Lincoln. There is no record that any of these stories had been published in periodicals, although the whole book appeared as a serial, but one, "The Wife of Flanders," was turned into a play for Samuel French by Buchan's wife.

The theme of *The Path of the King* is that the royal strain is carried through the generations not by the elder sons but by the younger ones. Nature might waste material things, but spiritual qualities are preserved, and the blood drawn from kings will surface again at the proper time. In the first story, "Hightown Under Sunfell," Biorn, the son of Ironbeard the king, receives an armband of gold as his heritage from his father, who is killed in battle. Biorn is taken in by people who do not understand his speech, and the natural progression of the line from king to king is broken. In the early Middle Ages in "The Englishman," Jehan the Hunter passes the armband, now in the form of a large gold ring, to his son and dies in battle. The line goes on in "The Wife of Flanders," when it is apparent that a younger son survives after the death of the older one. In "Eyes of Youth" Sir Aimery of Beaumanoir arrives in the east as an envoy of Louis of France and loses his life. The ring is returned to the Lady Alix, who wears it until her death.

Readers may be pardoned for assuming that somehow the line continues through Joan of Arc, who appears in the next story, "The Maid," but it is actually through Catherine of Beaumanoir, who befriends the maid and is convinced of her sincerity. Her husband, Guy de Laval, has needed no convincing. From here on the connections between generations appear to be clearer, as is the name that changes through the years, each younger son somehow having taken possession of the gold ring. Sometimes the ring is used as a signet to seal a letter, with the remark that it is said to have once belonged to a king. Each character in the line of succession is given an opportunity to perform a heroic act. In "The Wood of Life" it is Catherine's duty to raise the two sons of her son, the younger of whom becomes a scholar and explorer who accompanies Christopher Columbus on his second voyage.

In "Eaucourt by the Waters" the hero's name is Gaspard de Laval; in "The Hidden City" Jasper Lauval is a sailor with Ralegh. In "The Regicide" Nicholas Lovel, lawyer and confidant of Oliver Cromwell, is caught up in the conspiracy to remove the king and replace him with a parliament. His daughter and son-in-law side with the royalists, and they kidnap him. In "The Marplot" the grandson of Nicholas Lovel, also called Nicholas, is murdered when he will not help conceal the true events surrounding a murder. In "The Lit Chamber" Gabriel Lovel, a soldier of fortune in the pay of the Duke of Marlborough, encounters the opposition while drunk in a tavern. He loses his papers but not his honor.

Jim Lovelle is a scout with Daniel Boone who dies at Indian hands in the story "In the Dark Land." Boone takes the ring from Lovelle's dead hand and gives it to Lovelle's daughter, who has just married Abe Hanks. In "The Last Stage" their daughter, Nancy Hanks, married to Tom Linkhorn, gives the ring to her son Abraham, who spells his last name Lincoln. Nancy has had dreams for her son, dreams founded on reading *The Pilgrim's Progress* and *The Arabian Nights.* When Abe comes to tell her that he has lost the ring by using it as a sinker while fishing in the creek, she replies, "Don't you worry about the ring. . . . It ain't needed no more."

The final chapter, "The End of the Road," is divided into four sections: Lincoln at Springfield, Illinois, talking with Edward Stanton, his future war minister; Lincoln at the beginning of his presidency; Lincoln toward the end of the Civil War; and at the time of Lincoln's death and its aftermath. In a brief epilogue the point is made that Lincoln may not have been the first American, but he was the last of the kings. If Buchan never wrote a biography of Robert E. Lee, as he had intended, he certainly made a positive contribution to the dramatic lore of

Lincoln with the last story in *The Path of the King.* Unlike his other collections of linked stories, most of the distinct episodes in *The Path of the King* can be read without knowledge of the framing device.

In 1927 Buchan contributed a short story, "The Magic Walking Stick," to one of Lady Cynthia Asquith's annuals, *Sails of Gold.* This provided the germ of the boys' adventure fantasy of the same name published in 1932. A comparison of the two versions of the same story supports his belief that the short story is not the same as a short novel. While the basic stories are the same, much was added to the book version to give it depth and complexity.

Many Buchan readers turn to *The Runagates Club* for the shorter adventures of Richard Hannay and the good comrades of the World War I trilogy and later novels such as *John Macnab* (1925). Each story is narrated by a member of the dining club of the title. The first, "The Green Wildebeeste," is an unusual story to be narrated by a matter-of-fact character such as Hannay. It is another "special place" story in which an unthinking outsider, here an ignorant young Boer, shoots a creature in a wood held sacred by the natives, releases an evil upon the world, and suffers and dies for his sins.

"The Frying Pan and the Fire" is a miniature thriller in which a ride across the country puts the hero into a situation that becomes a comedy of errors when he stumbles into an asylum and is mistaken for an inmate. The mistaken-identity theme has a noble tradition in the thriller, and Buchan uses it here for both its adventurous and comedic possibilities.

Buchan often excelled in his ability to make the most implausible situations seem plausible. In "Dr. Lartius" a young soldier (it is suggested he may be Sandy Arbuthnot) infiltrates German society during the World War for the British government as a psychic named Dr. S. Lartius. When asked, the soldier says he always told people the *S.* stood for "Sigismund," but in reality it was meant to stand for "Spurius," one of the two men who held the bridge against the Etruscans with Horatius in ancient Roman legend.

"The Wind in the Portico" is another "special place" story, in which an amateur scholar dabbles in unholy matters he does not understand and unleashes the cause of his own destruction. Buchan made good use of his knowledge of classical literature in this story of the remnants of a Roman deity in the British countryside.

" 'Divus' Johnston," reprinted from the American edition of *The Watcher by the Threshold,* tells how

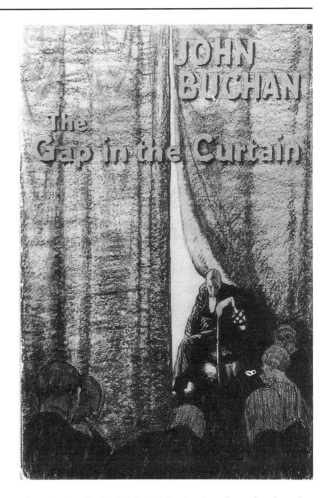

Dust jacket for Buchan's 1932 collection, five related stories about people given a glimpse of a moment one year in the future (Courtesy of the Lilly Library, Indiana University)

a white man became a god to the natives and what the experience did to his outlook on life. It was slightly revised from its original publication for its appearance in *The Runagates Club* in order to fit it into the framed narrative style of the later book.

The next two stories in the collection conform more closely to what might be expected from Buchan, especially by those readers who think of him only as a writer of spy fiction. "The Loathly Opposite" tells of the work by a team in breaking codes and ciphers during the World War. They find they are pitted against a near genius on the German side and try to imagine what he or she might be like. After the war the narrator actually encounters the person and finds the reality is different from what they had fancied. "Sing a Song of Sixpence" is a much-anthologized story of espionage narrated by Edward Leithen. When Leithen encounters the president of a South American nation on the streets of London, he offers him lodging instead of the money he requests (Leithen has only sixpence on his person) and helps to delay the assassination of the man by a group known as the Six.

In "Ship to Tarshish" Jim Hallward flees from the disgrace of losing other people's money in the stock-market crash to a life in Canada, where he just manages to survive but not to succeed at anything he attempts. Returned to London, he feels he has not earned his place there, and he returns to Canada, which he hates, in order to make a proper reentry. The title is taken from the Old Testament story in which Jonah, having been ordered by God to Nineveh, flees to Tarshish instead.

"Skule Skerry" is a typical Buchan story and can be compared favorably with some of his earliest stories about panic experienced in the grip of nature. Anthony Hurrell, steeped in Norse lore and in search of a place from which to observe bird migration, asks to be put on an island that must have been named for Earl Skuli from the *Jarlsaga*. In the storm that follows he senses he is on the very edge of the world and comes face to face with a palpable and living vision of terror.

"Tendebant Manus" takes its name from a misquoted phrase in Virgil's *Aeneid,* "Tendebant que manus ripae ulterioris amore" (they reached out their hands longing for the further shore). Reggie Souldern is killed in battle in the World War, but his older brother George still pictures him as being alive since no body was ever found. George's life is influenced profoundly by his brother from then on, as though he were being guided by him. When George is killed in an automobile accident, it is suggested that he had joined hands with his brother, who had "pulled him over the stream" to him. Readers of Buchan's memoir of the Grenfell brothers, Francis and Riversdale, may find some possible source material for this story.

In "The Last Crusade," another comedy, a journalist's fancy takes the germ of a story and lets it grow into a forest of the imagination. "Fullcircle" tells of a couple who find a house that is not only perfectly suited for them but shapes them to suit its own design.

Buchan alternated his thrillers with historical novels, historical works, biographies, and books on various subjects that engaged him. It is instructive to consider what else he had written during any given year while reading one of his novels or short-story collections, since ideas and enthusiasms spilled over from book to book. For instance, the research for his 1928 biography of the Scottish supporter of Charles I, James Graham, First Marquis of Montrose, was used in the historical novel *Witch Wood* (1927).

Readers of *The Dancing Floor,* a novel about Edward Leithen, would have expected something out of the ordinary for the next account of his doings. They found it in *The Gap in the Curtain,* in which several people, including Leithen, are presented with the opportunity to glimpse a moment of time one year into the future. This work was influenced by Buchan's reading, especially of John William Dunne's *An Experiment with Time* (1927). The fantastic part of the tale is told with such scientific plausibility – the setting is a Whitsuntide party at Lady Flambard's, at which Professor August Moe explains his theory of time as a thing of coils and kinks and not a straight line – that the results of the experiment in time appear equally plausible. The book relates the effect this knowledge has on five lives in five separate accounts. Leithen is distracted and does not see into his own future, but two of the others see their own obituaries. Businessman Arnold Tavenger's glimpse of an international merger actually costs him money, for he does not possess the broad view; David Mayot sees the name of the new prime minister but loses his seat in Parliament; Reginald Daker sees himself as a member of an expedition to Yucatán but not the reason for his trip; and Sir Robert Goodeve and Captain Charles Ottery face the knowledge of their own deaths with different degrees of bravery. The worlds of finance and politics are particularly well depicted in this fine satire. While the book might seem an episodic novel rather than a collection of short stories, each chapter can almost stand on its own merits without depending on the others for comprehension. Leithen seems particularly suited to this sort of story, which requires more introspection than one would expect from Hannay.

Buchan also contributed another short story, "The Strange Adventure of Mr. Andrew Hawthorn," to one of Asquith's annuals, *The Silver Ship* (1932). One day in the eighteenth century Hawthorn steps outside his door for a walk in the garden as he waits for his porridge to cool and disappears for more than five years. In the interim, he has been set upon by thieves and sold into slavery in the Carolinas. His return to his home is achieved, and he steps through his door, where he finds his sister has maintained a vigil for him by setting out two bowls of porridge each morning. He loudly reminds her that she should have set it out a bit earlier, for it is still too hot, but he takes care not to take a walk in the garden while he waits for it to cool.

In 1927 Buchan was elected to Parliament representing the Scottish universities. His speeches were always well received, but he was not successful in getting significant pieces of legislation passed. His new position required that he spend three or four nights a week in London, where he was joined by his wife and his daughter, Alice, in the summer months. He particularly enjoyed the confidence of those in power, who found in him a willing ear and a dispassionate supporter. He served in Parliament until 1935, when he was raised to the peerage as the first Baron Tweedsmuir and appointed governor-general of Canada, a post he held until his death in 1940.

In 1933 Buchan was appointed high commissioner to the General Assembly of the Church of Scotland. The position carried no political significance, but he enjoyed serving. His mother was delighted, more impressed by this accomplishment than by nearly anything else he achieved. He was invited to repeat the appointment the following year.

In spite of the many reasons he could think of not to accept the appointment in Canada – the ease of the job, the distance from his mother, and his health – he accepted. By all accounts he was one of the most successful and best-loved individuals to hold the post. He brought with him a long-standing interest in the country: he had visited Canada in 1924 and was interested in its environment as well as in its political history. He made many tours of the country, but the most significant as well as the most publicized was the one in 1937 down the Mackenzie River to the Arctic. The territory he visited was newly named Tweedsmuir Park in his honor.

His new duties as governor-general did not prevent him from writing books, but they slowed him down. During the 1920s he had continued as regular a routine as possible, traveling daily to London on business for Nelson and Reuters. During the last five years of his life he published only four books, two novels and two biographies, but he gave many speeches and wrote several articles. Following his death at age sixty-four, five books appeared: his autobiography, *Memory Hold-the-Door;* one novel, *Sick Heart River;* two collections of articles and essays, *Comments and Characters* (1940) and *Canadian Occasions* (1940); and one final collection of short stories, about Canada's history told for young people called *The Long Traverse.*

The Long Traverse is a series of eight episodes around a common theme that, like *Sir Walter Raleigh,* can be considered either as a unit or a collection of short stories. Buchan told his sister, Anna, that he wanted to write a proper history of Canada

for young people, a "Canadian *Puck of Pook's Hill,*" to replace the deadly but obligatory reading that Canadian youngsters faced in the schools. Through the power of the Indian, Negog, young Donald sees and feels the significant events in early Canadian history. The first chapter, "The Long Traverse," sets up the premise for the story, somewhat reminiscent of the experiment of August Moe in *The Gap in the Curtain.* In the second, "The Gold of Sagne," Donald is handed his "lucky stone" by Negog, who then burns herbs to produce an odor that awakens all of the boy's senses, and he looks into the water of the river to see the story of Canada's major gold mine, the Hope-Shirras, unfold before him like a motion picture. In "The Wonderful Beaches" Donald watches the arrival of the Norsemen and acquires a remarkable insight into the early history of Canada that surprises his father. In "Cadieux" Buchan tells the story of the coming of the French and their conflict with the Indians. "The Man Who Dreamed of Islands" tells of Alan Macdonnell's quest for the Pacific. "Big Dog" is the story of the role played by the Indians and their horsemanship in the history of Canada. "White Water" is the story of the voyageurs, and "The Faraway People" is about the Eskimos and their ancestors. In each section Donald is allowed to have his vision, but when it is over all that remains is his memory of what he has learned and not how he learned it.

As with *Sir Walter Raleigh* and *The Gap in the Curtain,* the stories cannot be read by themselves without a knowledge of the framing device. The unsigned epilogue suggests that, had Buchan lived, there would have been more to the story and that he would have taken it to 1914 and the discovery of pitchblende and radium. In the Buchan Collection at Queen's University in Kingston, Ontario, there is some manuscript material for a film scenario about the discovery of radium.

Buchan was offered a second five-year appointment as governor-general, but his health would not permit him to accept it. He was planning for the trip back to England when he died on 11 February 1940.

Buchan is remembered for his thrillers today, although some of his other books continue to be read. Even during his lifetime his thrillers outsold his historical novels, which outsold his short-story collections. Criticism on Buchan continues to focus on the thrillers, although since the publication in 1980 and 1982 of Daniell's collections of *The Best Short Stories of John Buchan* this part of his work has not been entirely forgotten, and Daniell's comments on the stories are useful. There has been some at-

Dust jacket for Buchan's 1941 collection of children's stories about Canadian history (Courtesy of the Lilly Library, Indiana University)

tention paid to Buchan's work in the supernatural vein but little outside of reference works and specialized publications.

Critics continue to disagree about what makes Buchan notable and what keeps him in print. Some see the adventures as prosaic but the characters as memorable, while others claim that Buchan's plots are exciting while his characters, heroes and villains both, are dull. However, there is tacit agreement that, unlike many writers of thrillers who depend largely on action for their effects, there is more beneath the surface in Buchan's work, as a careful reading of the short stories confirms. Many of the characters are seen in concentrated moments in their lives, when their most enduring traits, for good or ill, are on display.

The Buchan hero is generally modest – almost too modest to be truly heroic – and part of his success is due to luck or coincidence. Success is also due to patience in waiting for the right moment to

act. He is essentially an amateur and a more plausible figure than many heroes equipped by their creators with special abilities or talents. The talent of a Buchan hero is his common sense. This, plus the matter-of-fact, no-nonsense tone of Buchan's style, explains the high degree of plausibility surrounding even the most improbable events. The reader is drawn into the situation along with the hero, neither knowing what will happen next.

Bibliographies:

Archibald Hanna Jr., *John Buchan, 1875–1940: A Bibliography* (Hamden, Conn.: Shoe String Press, 1953);

B. C. Wilmot, *A Checklist of Works By and About John Buchan in the John Buchan Collection, Douglas Library, Queen's University* (Boston: G. K. Hall, 1961);

J. Randolph Cox, "John Buchan, Lord Tweedsmuir: An Annotated Bibliography of Writings about Him," *English Literature in Transition,* 9, nos. 5–6 (1966): 241–325; 10, no. 4 (1967): 209–211; 15, no. 4 (1972): 67–69;

Robert G. Blanchard, *The First Editions of John Buchan* (Hamden, Conn.: Archon Books, 1981).

Biographies:

Anna Buchan as O. Douglas, *Unforgettable Unforgotten* (London: Hodder & Stoughton, 1945);

Susan Tweedsmuir, *John Buchan, by His Wife and Friends* (London: Hodder & Stoughton, 1947);

Arthur Campbell Turner, *Mr. Buchan, Writer* (London: SCM Press, 1949);

Janet Adam Smith, *John Buchan: A Biography* (London: Hart-Davis, 1965; Boston: Little, Brown, 1965);

William Buchan, *John Buchan: A Memoir* (London: Buchan & Enright, 1982);

Martin Green, *Biography of John Buchan and His Sister Anna: The Personal Background of Their Literary Work* (Lewiston, N.Y.: Mellen, 1990).

References:

Barbara B. Brown, "John Buchan and Twentieth-Century Biography," *Biography,* 2 (Fall 1979): 328–341;

John Cawelti, "The Joys of Buchaneering," in *Essays in Honor of Russel B. Nye,* edited by Joseph Waldmeir (East Lansing: Michigan State University Press, 1978), pp. 7–30; reprinted in *The Spy Story,* by Cawelti and Bruce A. Rosenberg (Chicago & London: University of Chicago Press, 1987), pp. 79–100;

J. Randolph Cox, "John Buchan: A Philosophy of High Adventure," *Armchair Detective,* 2 (July 1969): 207–214;

David Daniell, *The Interpreter's House, A Critical Assessment of John Buchan* (London: Nelson, 1975);

Daniell, Introduction to *The Best Short Stories of John Buchan,* 2 volumes, edited by Daniell (London: M. Joseph, 1980, 1982);

Francis R. Hart, *The Scottish Novel from Smollett to Spark* (Cambridge, Mass.: Harvard University Press, 1979), pp. 169–181;

Gertrude Himmelfarb, "John Buchan, an Untimely Appreciation," *Encounter,* 15 (September 1960): 46–53;

Gavin Lambert, *The Dangerous Edge* (London: Barrie & Jenkins, 1975), pp. 79–104;

Anthony Masters, "John Buchan: The Romantic Spy," in his *Literary Agents: The Novelist as Spy* (New York: Blackwell, 1988), pp. 15–34;

Geoffrey Powell, "John Buchan's Richard Hannay," *History Today,* 37 (August 1987): 32–39;

M. R. Ridley, "A Misrated Author?," in his *Second Thoughts* (London: Dent, 1965), pp. 1–44;

Alan Sandison, *The Wheel of Empire: A Study of the Imperial Idea in Some Late Nineteenth and Early Twentieth-Century Fiction* (London: Macmillan, 1967; New York: St. Martin's Press, 1967), pp. 149–194;

Leland Schubert, "Almost Real Reality: John Buchan's Visible World," *Serif,* 2 (September 1965): 5–14;

Richard Usborne, *Clubland Heroes* (London: Constable, 1953), pp. 83–139; revised edition (London: Barrie & Jenkins, 1974), pp. 81–130;

Robin W. Winks, "John Buchan: Stalking the Wilder Game," in *The Four Adventures of Richard Hannay,* by John Buchan (Boston: Godine, 1988), pp. v–xxii;

Michael Young, "The Rules of the Game: Buchan's *John Macnab,*" *Studies in Scottish Literature,* 24 (1989): 194–211.

Papers:

Buchan's manuscripts, correspondence, notebooks, and much of his private library (with the exception of popular fiction) are in the John Buchan Collection, Douglas Library, Queen's University, Kingston, Ontario. Additional material is in the National Library of Scotland, Edinburgh, and in the Edinburgh University Library.

Bernard Capes
(30 August 1854 – 2 November 1918)

Carolyn Mathews
University of North Carolina at Greensboro

BOOKS: *The Mill of Silence* (Chicago: Rand, Mc-Nally, 1896; London: Simpkin, Marshall, Hamilton, Kent, 1899);

Adventures of the Comte de la Muette during the Reign of Terror (Edinburgh: Blackwood, 1898; New York: Dodd, Mead, 1898);

The Lake of Wine (London: Heinemann, 1898; New York: Appleton, 1898);

The Mysterious Singer (Bristol: Arrowsmith, 1898);

At a Winter's Fire (London: Pearson, 1899; New York: Doubleday & McClure, 1899);

Our Lady of Darkness (Edinburgh: Blackwood, 1899; New York: Dodd, Mead, 1899);

From Door to Door: A Book of Romances, Fantasies, Whimsies, and Levities (Edinburgh: Blackwood, 1900; New York: Stokes, 1900);

Joan Brotherhood (London: Pearson, 1900);

Love Like a Gipsy: A Romance (Edinburgh: Constable, 1901);

Plots (London: Methuen, 1902);

A Castle in Spain: Certain Memoirs of Robin Lois, Ex-Major of His Majesty's 109th Regiment of Foot (London: Smith, Elder, 1903);

The Secret in the Hill (London: Smith, Elder, 1903);

The Extraordinary Confession of Diana Please (London: Methuen, 1904);

A Jay of Italy (London: Methuen, 1905);

The Romance of Lohengrin, Founded on Wagner's Opera (London: Dean, 1905; Boston: Page, 1905);

Loaves and Fishes (London: Methuen, 1906);

A Rogue's Tragedy (London: Methuen, 1906);

Bembo: A Tale of Italy (New York: Dutton, 1906);

The Great Skene Mystery (London: Methuen, 1907);

The Green Parrot (London: Smith, Elder, 1908);

Amaranthus: A Book of Little Songs (London: Unwin, 1908);

The Love Story of St. Bel (London: Methuen, 1909);

Historical Vignettes (London: Unwin, 1910; New York: Stokes, 1910);

Jemmy Abercraw (London: Methuen, 1910; New York: Brentano's, 1910);

Why Did He Do It? (London: Methuen, 1910; New York: Brentano's, 1910);

The Will and the Way (London: John Murray, 1910);

Gilead Balm, Knight Errant: His Adventures in Search of the Truth (London: Unwin, 1911; New York: Baker & Taylor, 1911);

The House of Many Voices (London: Unwin, 1911);

Jessie Bazley (Edinburgh: Nelson, 1913);

Bag and Baggage (London: Constable, 1913);

The Pot of Basil (London: Constable, 1913);

The Story of Fifine (London: Constable, 1914);

The Fabulists (London: Mills & Boon, 1915);

If Age Could (London: Duckworth, 1916);

Moll Davis: A Comedy (Deucalian, U.K.: Allen & Unwin, 1916);

Where England Sets Her Feet: A Romance (London: Collins, 1918);

The Skeleton Key (New York: Doran, 1918; London: Collins, 1919).

SELECTED PERIODICAL PUBLICATIONS – UNCOLLECTED: "Wild Dogs: A Chapter from the Reminiscences of the Comte de Muette," *Blackwood's Magazine,* 162 (August 1897): 220–226;

"Lot 104," *Cornhill Magazine,* 78 (December 1898): 774–782;

"Runner," *Blackwood's Magazine,* 166 (September 1899): 369–380;

"For Literary Use," *Cornhill Magazine,* 82 (July 1900): 101–112;

"Last of the Proctors of Doctors' Commons," *Cornhill Magazine,* 91 (January 1905): 88–95;

"Long Arm," *Cornhill Magazine,* 97 (April 1908): 530–543;

"Bad Relations: Characters in Literature," *Cornhill Magazine,* 98 (August 1908): 223–229;

"Christmas Feast: A Poem," *Current Literature,* 46 (January 1909): 102;

"Clipping the Currency," *Cornhill Magazine,* 100 (September 1909): 404–411;

"Pleasures of Eating," *Living Age,* 282 (19 September 1914): 727–734;

"La Morgue Litteraire," *Cornhill Magazine,* 116 (November 1917): 458–469;

"Middleman," *Cornhill Magazine,* 120 (November 1919): 500–511.

Bernard Capes, a prolific writer in fin de siècle Britain, is virtually unknown today. Remembered, if at all, as a writer of ghost tales and stories of the fantastic and supernatural, his name for the most part lies hidden in late–nineteenth century periodicals or on title pages of books out of print by the mid 1920s. Yet in the course of a writing career that spanned little more than twenty years, Capes published twenty-nine novels, six collections of short fiction, a book of children's poetry, and more than fifty stories and essays in magazines such as *Cornhill Magazine, Blackwood's Magazine,* and *Pall Mall Magazine.* In addition to stories of the supernatural, he wrote historical fiction, romances, tales of adventure, and mystery stories. Compared early in his career to Wilkie Collins, George Meredith, H. G. Wells, and Robert Louis Stevenson, Capes later drew praise or criticism in his own right and was at least a marginal figure in the literary world.

The details of Capes's life are only minimally recorded. Born Bernard Edward Joseph Capes in London on 30 August 1854, he was the son of Fredrick Capes, a proctor of Doctor's Commons. Capes's grandfather had previously held this position, and such familiarity with legal institutions probably inspired Capes's story "Last of the Proctors of Doctors' Commons" (1905). During the Oxford Movement his father had converted to Roman Catholicism, most likely through the influence of his older brother John Moore Capes, also a convert and a major figure in the reform movement aimed at reconnecting the Anglican Church with the early church. Capes was thus raised a Catholic. While he evidently won several literary prizes during his studies at Beaumont College, his interest in literature and the arts likely began at home. His father had contributed articles to Victorian periodicals on topics ranging from John Ruskin's philosophy of art to observations on Chinese life and manners, and his uncle had published two three-volume novels, *The Mosaic Worker's Daughter* (1868) and *The Buckhurst Volunteers* (1869), and had written an opera, *The Druid,* which was performed in 1879. Not surprising, Capes makes frequent allusions to music, painting, and architecture in his fiction, which usually is set in exotic or foreign places.

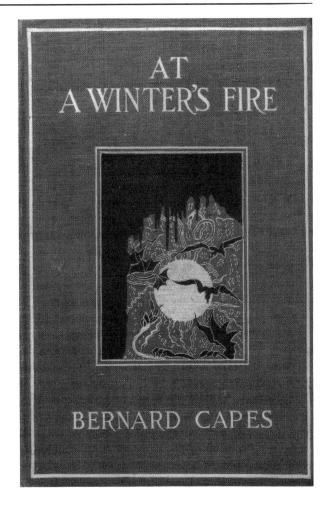

Cover for Bernard Capes's 1899 collection of ghost stories, which many critics faulted for their elaborate style (Courtesy of the Lilly Library, Indiana University)

After leaving school, Capes wanted to enter the army, but, uninformed about age restrictions for entrance examinations, he inadvertently failed to present himself for examination soon enough and was thus prevented from taking a commission. His thwarted interest in the military surfaces in such tales as "The Sword of Corporal Lacoste," collected in *From Door to Door: A Book of Romances, Fantasies, Whimsies, and Levities* (1900), a story about a wounded corporal's bizarre encounter with a perverse priest who leads him through a wolf-infested gorge toward mutilation by a werewolf, and "Chapter's Doom," also collected in *From Door to Door,* an intricately plotted tale of betrayal set during the Napoleonic Wars. Disappointed in his plans for a military career, Capes began work in a tea broker's office, struggling for several years in a job that was at odds with his artistic interests. Finally, he deserted this work to study art at the Slade School in London.

The Slade School was founded in 1871, and its program emphasized students' free use of imagination. Drawing from living models and copying the old masters only as a means of perceiving form and technique, the students were challenged to infuse their drawings and paintings with an original style. While Capes evidently produced no works of distinction while at Slade, the lessons he learned as visual artist surface later in his fiction, since the role of imagination and the development of individual style were to be his main concerns as a writer. While much of his short fiction implicitly explores imagination as a component of the ghastly or fantastic in experience, stories such as "A Danse – Macabre," collected in *From Door to Door,* explicitly draw on philosophical discussions of imagination. As the characters discuss the fourth dimension, they see spirit girls, within motes gyrating in a moonbeam, "beckoning, alluring, with white arms raised." Though the characters come to realize that trees have caused a marvelous optical illusion, they agree that "Imagination is the parent of being, and the true begetter of all visualized Manifestation" – a statement consistent with the Slade School's purpose. While imagination was perhaps the single most important concept for Capes as a writer, style was perhaps his greatest frustration. Though his style drew more comment from critics than any other feature of his fiction, the critics ridiculed his efforts to produce a singular but readable style as often as they praised them.

Capes's studies at the Slade School led in 1888 to a position with the publishing firm of Eglington and Company in London, and by 1890 he was coeditor, with Charles Eglington, of the *Theatre,* a monthly magazine devoted to reviews and articles on drama, music, and the arts. In 1891 he became the magazine's editor, but when Eglington's business closed in 1892 he was again without employment and turned to writing, assuming the career that would sustain him for the rest of his life.

Capes's first break as a writer came in 1896, when he won second place in a fiction contest sponsored by the *Chicago Record.* His winning mystery novel, *The Mill of Silence* (1896), was serialized, running in the *Chicago Record* in thirty-one installments during April and May 1896. As an advertising tactic for the newspaper, each segment appeared with an accompanying invitation to women and girls to submit solutions to the mystery before the publication of the last installment on 8 June 1896: "All may read," the notice read, "but only Women and Girls may guess – and win the $3000." The *Chicago Record* offered a total of 241 prizes, with a thousand

dollars awarded for the best solution. The conventions of nineteenth-century mystery novels dictated that in *The Mill of Silence* Capes choose a narrator who accounts for his access to information and who gradually doles out clues. From this first novel to his later works, he worked both with and against the formulas for popular fiction, trying to create a space where the popular might also be literary. However, his desire for a literary style sometimes led him to overload sentences, to become so engrossed in description that readers could lose the narrative thread, and to choose a voice fraught with affectation. While these qualities ultimately marred rather than distinguished his work, the critics' response and his efforts to counter their opinions are interesting in terms of the late-Victorian debate over the purpose and nature of literature.

Capes produced one or two books each year between the 1896 serialization of *The Mill of Silence* and the posthumous publication of a detective novel called *The Skeleton Key* (1918). Each of his works generated discussion as to whether it could be called literature. Reviewers generally praised Capes's works for their plots and characters, but reviews were usually mixed, with critics either applauding his elaborate descriptions or attacking him for his preciousness.

Capes's reaction to the critics' ridicule appears thinly disguised in his 1908 novel, *The Green Parrot.* The protagonist, John Wisdom, a gifted writer of unsuccessful fiction, has burned his manuscripts and taken up the life of a hermit with a runaway boy. His grievance with critics and the reading public was in all likelihood Capes's own:

> The public ... wanted neither art nor stories. They were both out of date. ... The critics, for the most part, did not want them either. ... One thing there was which they seldom regarded, and that was style; or if they did mention it, it was with some impatient disparagement, as a thing bothering and unnecessary.

Perhaps writing *The Green Parrot* served a therapeutic purpose, allowing Capes thereafter to try less strenuously to write literature. Whatever the case, his later writing is less self-conscious, less loaded with taxing detail, and more direct. During the last half of his writing career his works were met with favorable reviews, and critics at last said his style unobtrusively aided in making general impressions.

The growth Capes made as a novelist parallels his growth as a writer of short fiction. While his early stories become bogged down in superfluous description, his later stories have an intentionally conversational tone. Although critics admired his first collection for its "cleverness and originality," his style drew harsh complaints; *At a Winter's Fire* (1899) was judged difficult reading, and the stories remain much less haunting than they might have been. Discussing his third collection, *Plots* (1902), a reviewer for the *Times Literary Supplement* noted that Capes is too deliberately aesthetic to be a good storyteller. Yet upon the publication of his final collection, *The Fabulists* (1915), a *Times* reviewer could justly write, "Mr. Capes knows the value of words . . . and can paint a landscape or suggest a graveyard or deserted house with . . . dexterous touch."

A comparison of first lines from early Capes stories and from those later in his career demonstrates this change. The most noteworthy story from Capes's first collection, *At a Winter's Fire*, is "An Eddy on the Floor," a tale of mysterious and vengeful forces haunting a vaulted prison cell. The story's characters form the essence of the tale and include a jailed spiritualist driven mad by the unknown presence; a former military man and governor of the jail, who has ordered the cell permanently sealed; a strangely loyal warden, who ultimately unveils a tale of revenge; and Polyhistor, a pseudonym for the narrator, who suffers hysteria upon venturing beyond the closed doors. Capes manages to keep a modern reader's interest despite lengthy introductory material and an excess of sentences such as the story's first: "The eyes of Polyhistor – as he sat before the fire at night – took in the tawdry surroundings of his lodging-house room with nothing of that apathy of resignation to his personal *avaykn* which of all moods is to Fortune, the goddess of spontaneity, the most antipathetic." The story's vaulted cell, fundamental to this seventy-page tale, appears only after twenty-five pages of narration. In order to make the story more palatable for modern readers, the reprint of "An Eddy on the Floor" in *Victorian Ghost Stories* (1991) has been appropriately edited, the pseudonym Polyhistor has been omitted, and the tortured prose of the story's beginning has been reworked. In contrast, "The Dark Compartment" from *The Fabulists,* a concisely presented tale of a haunted railcar compartment, begins, "I remember once, when hunting for a seat in a crowded train, finding unexpectedly an empty compartment, the door of which, when I came to try it, was locked." While "An Eddy on the Floor" relies on letters written by dying characters to reveal seemingly endless details about murder within the vaulted cell, "The Dark Compartment" relies on understatement to convey the narrator's unease.

Capes's short fiction improved markedly over the course of his career, and his development as a

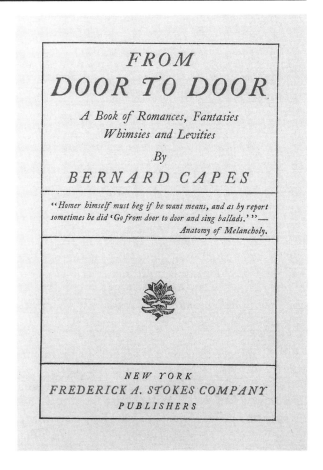

Title page for the first American edition of Capes's 1900 collection of stories, which combine aestheticism and the supernatural (Courtesy of the Lilly Library, Indiana University)

short-story writer makes him an absorbing figure. In terms of the history of short fiction, one can see in his progression the evolution of the short story as a genre in England. As Wendell V. Harris has noted, few British writers before the 1880s regarded the short story as anything other than an exercise in the novelist's craft, but gradually, with the story's move toward economy in dealing with temporal and spatial elements, they developed it into its own form. Compression and the necessary unity of effect came to govern the conventions of the short story, and tedious, mechanical story openers gave way to direct and intriguing first lines. Capes's early stories for the most part follow the conventions of most nineteenth-century short fiction. To modern readers the introductions of these early stories, explaining in vast detail how the narrator came to hear the particular story or possess the manuscript in hand, seem irrelevant, and Capes's continual digressions filling in background information create tedium. Yet not all of his early stories follow formulaic openings. For example, "William Tyrwhitt's 'Copy,' " also collected in *At a Winter's Fire,* begins with uncharacteristic directness, and the story, in which William Tyrwhitt and the ghost of a long-dead buccaneer are pursued by the ghosts of those whom the buccaneer had cruelly murdered, depends almost entirely on dialogue.

Most of the stories in Capes's second collection, *From Door to Door,* also depart from formulaic openings. "The Sword of Corporal Lacoste," for example, begins in medias res, with the wounded corporal dreaming of "a roaring thunder of surf bursting upon jagged rocks." The majority of the stories show influences of aestheticism, a mode that Harris identifies as an important form of late-Victorian short fiction combining fantasy, a mannered style, and the use of a historical setting. Linking William Morris's stories of the late 1880s, Walter Pater's *Imaginary Portraits* (1887), and Arthur Symons's *Spiritual Adventures* (1905), Harris notes that the core similarity of these writers is their use of "a special kind of impressionism: an attempt to render the writer's intense impression not of the actual world he has experienced, but of a past age, a type of mind or a point of view with which he cannot have had direct contact." This sort of impressionism marks the stories in *From Door to Door,* and like those identified by Harris, Capes's stories move style to the forefront as a "glittering ornament" but depend on a control of tone rarely seen in English short fiction before the late 1880s. "The Sword of Corporal Lacoste" displays such control, the sublime terror of the story's beginning changing to fear.

Other stories in the collection can be traced to a corollary stream of aesthetic fiction surfacing in the late 1890s — stories of the mystic or occult. "The Marble Hands" chronicles a vain young woman's commissioning of an artist to sculpt her hands. The hands stand as the only epitaph at her grave, and when the story's narrator touches them he feels "a period of horror and blankness – of crawling, worm-threaded immurements and heaving bones – and then at last the blessed daylight." A similar fascination with mystic occurrences surfaces in "The Footsteps," a story about a woman's dream of a forbidden, closed room that later materializes as her stepchildren's playroom; in "The White Hare," a witch tale wherein the mother of the protagonist's dying fiancée is transformed into a white hare; and in "The Cursing Bell," a story about a woman tormented and sickened by tolling from a bell tower.

Overt comment on aesthetics and the role of the artist forms the core of seven stories. These include "A Danse – Macabre" and "The Queer Pic-

ture," a tale of murder etched into the artist's work, as well as "The Operation," the story of a blind genius whose art deteriorates when she is given sight. In "The Foot of Time" a group of friends debates the meaning of a great artist's final masterpiece. "The Writer and the Prince" is a fairy tale in which the power of words brings a dead girl back to life. "Deux Ex Machina" comments on artists' arrogance, and "The Chapter's Doom" is an odd tale of an artist who fights in the Napoleonic Wars.

"The Chapter's Doom" is perhaps the most interesting in terms of aesthetic fiction because of its implicit critique of aestheticism. In this story the artist-soldier prides himself on his unthinking devotion to observation and impulse. Taking advantage of a nun's love for him and causing the death of his friend, the artist says at the story's end, "I shall paint a picture of him some day – noble, self-sacrificing, burrowing like a red badger after roots, while others no better pull the golden apples in the sunshine above." In this story Capes departs from the philosophy of aesthetes such as Walter Pater, who declared the supreme value of beauty and the love of art for its own sake and who rejected the practical in the pursuit of life's exquisite sensations. Capes, in contrast, pulls in passages of realism to depict the horror of war. This atypical realism, as well as Capes's creation of a most unsympathetic character in the artist, undercuts the philosophy of art for art's sake central to aestheticism.

Perhaps Capes abandoned the affected manner fostered by late-nineteenth-century aestheticism because he saw the limitations of its philosophy. By the same token, critics' opinions may or may not have influenced his evolution as a writer. Most likely the changes were a function of the times, emerging in response to new techniques and approaches marking the British short story during his lifetime. Capes wrote during a transitional period when the genre was moving away from the tedium typical of the nineteenth-century tale and toward the compression and symbolism of the twentieth-century short story. Whatever the reason, his later stories, such as those in *The Fabulists,* are more readable, and it is to his credit that he changed with the new direction in fiction. In terms of subject matter, the stories in *The Fabulists* show the same fascination with the supernatural as the earlier stories. In "The Accident," for example, a traveler with extrasensory powers experiences the recurrence of a fatal accident; in "The Shadow-Dance" the audience sees a dancer "seemingly independent of . . . gravitation" flit above the stage, even as she lies dead in her dressing room. Capes's handling of these subjects depends on psychological insight, suggestion, and compactness more typical of modern than of nineteenth-century short stories. Psychology is central to the concise "Old Harry," a tale exploring motives behind an act of arson, while understatement marks "The Van on the Road," a story in which an abusive husband loses his wife's inheritance. While the early stories tended to let the reader know the characters' every move and to account for passage of time carefully, several of the later stories use chapterlike divisions that allow for succinct shifts between scenes. "The Lady Hope," a story of treasure discovered through examining a work of art, handles time lapses using three such divisions. Published in March 1915, *The Fabulists* falls squarely at the point that Michael Cox and R. A. Gilbert designate as the "symbolic termination-point for the Victorian ghost story." Although Capes's early stories were, as Cox and Gilbert say, "fruit from the Victorian tree," it is to Capes's credit that he could transplant the ghost story into modern soil.

Capes died at his home in Winchester on 2 November 1918 following a bout of influenza. He was sixty-four. His London *Times* obituary notes that he left a widow and three children. Inferences about his family can be gleaned from incomplete bits of information: the dedication of *The Lake of Wine* (1898) to "R. C. Best Counsellor and Helpmate"; a passing reference in an essay, "Clipping the Currency" (1909), to cutting paper dolls by the sea for his little girl; and the note of gratitude from Mrs. Capes to those who helped prepare the manuscript of the posthumously published *The Skeleton Key*. In a short article the *Times* ran the day after his obituary, Capes is described as a "man of many interests and accomplishments, of varied interests, of a broad and independent outlook upon life" who possessed "personal charm, . . . unaffected modesty,

and . . . absolute sincerity." His friends included the critic, poet, and dramatist W. E. Henley and James Ransome, a London architect.

In his introduction to Capes's last book, *The Skeleton Key*, G. K. Chesterton writes, "It may seem a paradox to say that [Capes] was insufficiently appreciated because he did popular things well. But it is true to say that he always gave a touch of distinction to a detective story or a tale of adventure; and so gave it where it was not valued, because it was not expected." While Chesterton notes that Capes's short stories and historical studies are "poetic in a more direct and serious fashion" than his penny dreadfuls, neither the short fiction nor the novels thus far has earned him a secure place in literary history. The evolution of his style, though, makes him an engaging writer. His works evince the changing literary tastes that mark the end of the century and the early years of the twentieth century, and they touch upon issues of social history, including attitudes about class, the "woman question," and morality. Scholars interested in the growth of the short story or in the historical period spanning Capes's career could find much worthy of study in his work.

References:

G. K. Chesterton, Introduction to Capes's *The Skeleton Key* (New York: Doran, 1918; London: Collins, 1919);

"Conditions of the Award of $3000," *Chicago Record*, 24 April 1896, p. 8;

Michael Cox and R. A. Gilbert, eds., *Victorian Ghost Stories: An Oxford Anthology* (New York: Oxford University Press, 1991);

Wendell V. Harris, *British Short Fiction in the Nineteenth Century* (Detroit: Wayne State University Press, 1979).

Joseph Conrad

(3 December 1857 – 3 August 1924)

Monika Brown
Pembroke State University

See also the Conrad entries in *DLB 10: Modern British Dramatists, 1900–1945; DLB 34: British Novelists, 1890–1929: Traditionalists;* and *DLB 98: Modern British Essayists, First Series.*

BOOKS: *Almayer's Folly: A Story of an Eastern River* (London: Unwin, 1895; New York: Macmillan, 1895);

An Outcast of the Islands (London: Unwin, 1896; New York: Appleton, 1896);

The Children of the Sea: A Tale of the Forecastle (New York: Dodd, Mead, 1897); republished as *The Nigger of the "Narcissus": A Tale of the Sea* (London: Heinemann, 1898 [i.e., 1897]);

Tales of Unrest (New York: Scribners, 1898; London: Unwin, 1898);

Lord Jim: A Tale (Edinburgh & London: Blackwood, 1900; New York: Doubleday, McClure, 1900);

The Inheritors: An Extravagant Story, by Conrad and Ford Madox Hueffer [Ford] (New York: McClure, Phillips, 1901; London: Heinemann, 1901);

Youth: A Narrative, and Two Other Stories (Edinburgh & London: Blackwood, 1902; New York: McClure, Phillips, 1903);

Typhoon (New York & London: Putnam, 1902);

The Art of Fiction (Hythe & Cheriton, U.K.: Privately printed by J. Lovick, 1902; Garden City, N.Y.: Doubleday, Page, 1914);

Typhoon and Other Stories (London: Heinemann, 1903); published without "Typhoon" as *Falk, Amy Foster, To-morrow: Three Stories* (New York: McClure, Phillips, 1903);

Romance: A Novel, by Conrad and Hueffer (London: Smith, Elder, 1903; New York: McClure, Phillips, 1904);

Nostromo: A Tale of the Seaboard (London: Harper, 1904; New York: Harper, 1904);

The Mirror of the Sea: Memories and Impressions (London: Methuen, 1906; New York: Harper, 1906);

Joseph Conrad, circa 1922 (Hulton Deutsch Collection)

The Secret Agent: A Simple Tale (London: Methuen, 1907; New York: Harper, 1907);

The Point of Honor: A Military Tale (New York: McClure, 1908); republished as *The Duel: A Military Tale* (Garden City, N.Y.: Garden City Publishing Company, 1923);

A Set of Six (London: Methuen, 1908; Garden City, N.Y.: Doubleday, Page, 1915);

Under Western Eyes (London: Methuen, 1911; New York: Harper, 1911);

A Personal Record (New York: Harper, 1912); also republished as *Some Reminiscences* (London: Eveleigh Nash, 1912); republished as *A Personal Record* (London: Nelson, 1916);

'Twixt Land and Sea: Tales (London: Dent, 1912;
New York: Hodder & Stoughton/Doran,
1912);

Chance: A Tale in Two Parts (London: Methuen,
1913; Garden City, N.Y.: Doubleday, Page,
1913);

Within the Tides: Tales (London & Toronto: Dent,
1915; Garden City, N.Y.: Doubleday, Page,
1916);

Victory: An Island Tale (Garden City, N.Y.: Doubleday, Page, 1915; London: Methuen, 1915);

One Day More: A Play in One Act (London: Privately
printed by Clement Shorter, 1917; Garden
City, N.Y.: Doubleday, Page, 1920);

The Shadow-Line: A Confession (London, Toronto &
Paris: Dent, 1917; Garden City, N.Y.: Doubleday, Page, 1917);

The Arrow of Gold: A Story Between Two Notes (Garden
City, N.Y.: Doubleday, Page, 1919; London:
Unwin, 1919);

The Rescue: A Romance of the Shallows (Garden City,
N.Y.: Doubleday, Page, 1920; London, Toronto & Paris: Dent, 1920);

Notes on My Books (Garden City, N.Y.: Doubleday,
Page, 1921; London: Heinemann, 1921); re-
published as *Conrad's Prefaces to His Works*
(London: Dent, 1937);

Notes on Life and Letters (London & Toronto: Dent,
1921; Garden City, N.Y.: Doubleday, Page,
1921);

The Secret Agent: Drama in Four Acts (Canterbury: Privately printed by H. J. Goulden, 1921);

The Rover (Garden City, N.Y.: Doubleday, Page,
1923; London: Unwin, 1923);

Laughing Anne: A Play (London: Morland Press,
1923);

The Nature of a Crime, by Conrad and Ford Madox
Ford (London: Duckworth, 1924; Garden
City, N.Y.: Doubleday, Page, 1924);

Suspense: A Napoleonic Novel (Garden City, N.Y.:
Doubleday, Page, 1925; London & Toronto:
Dent, 1925);

Tales of Hearsay (London: Unwin, 1925; Garden
City, N.Y.: Doubleday, Page, 1925);

Last Essays (London & Toronto: Dent, 1926; Garden
City, N.Y.: Doubleday, Page, 1926);

The Sisters (New York: Crosby, Gaige, 1928);

Joseph Conrad on Fiction, edited by Walter F. Wright
(Lincoln: University of Nebraska Press,
1964);

*Congo Diary and Other Uncollected Pieces by Joseph Con-
rad,* edited by Zdzislaw Najder (Garden City,
N.Y.: Doubleday, 1978).

Collections: *The Works of Joseph Conrad,* The Uniform Edition, 22 volumes (London: Dent,
1923-1928); reprinted and enlarged, 26 volumes (London: Dent, 1946-1955);

Collected Works of Joseph Conrad, The Kent Edition,
26 volumes (Garden City, N.Y.: Doubleday,
Page, 1926);

The Complete Short Stories of Joseph Conrad (London:
Hutchinson, 1933);

The Complete Short Fiction of Joseph Conrad, 4 volumes,
edited by Samuel Hynes (Bloomington, Ind.:
Ecco Press, 1991-1992).

PLAY PRODUCTIONS: *One Day More,* London,
Royalty Theatre, 25 June 1905;

The Secret Agent, London, Ambassadors' Theatre, 2
November 1922.

OTHER: Alec John Dawson, *Britain's Life-boats: The
Story of a Century of Heroic Service,* foreword by
Conrad (London: Hodder & Stoughton,
1923);

Warrington Dawson, *Adventure in the Night,* foreword by Conrad (London: Unwin, 1924);

Bruno Winawer, *The Book of Job: A Satirical Comedy,*
translated by Conrad (London: Dent, 1931).

The short fiction of Joseph Conrad is central
to his literary achievement. Conrad wrote forty-
three works of fiction, of which thirty-one are short,
ranging from stories of a few pages to novellas of
twenty-five thousand to fifty thousand words. His
short fiction was usually published, after appearing
in periodicals, in collections of three to six stories
on related themes. Friend and fellow novelist Ford
Madox Ford rightly observed that "Conrad never
wrote a true short story." Avoiding the compact,
well-made story popularized by Guy de Maupassant, Conrad preferred tales of "30,000 words or
so," since the effects he aimed for, he explained to
Blackwood's editor David Meldrum in 1902, "depend
upon the reader *looking back* on my story as a
whole." His best short works narrate extended and
complex, yet unified, experiences.

Conrad's novels and stories transmute the adventures of his early life and evoke a godless universe rich in ambiguity. In his fiction, aimed at both
an immediate and a lasting public, modernist experiments coexist with plot devices of popular romance, and unforgettable phrases emerge from
vague description. A writer of high artistic ambition
who compared himself to Gustave Flaubert and
Ivan Turgenev, Conrad wrote fiction that challenged readers and critics alike. His great achieve-

Conrad in 1873

ment, and the impetus behind his experimentation with language and form, is his probing analysis of human character under psychological and moral strain. Concerned, as he explains in *A Personal Record* (1912), that "the ethical view of the universe involves us at last in so many cruel and absurd contradictions . . . that I have come to suspect that the aim of creation cannot be ethical at all," Conrad nonetheless, as Carl D. Bennett notes, wrestles as few modern writers have done with "the ethical dimension of human existence." He explores the obsessive pursuit of goals (material and idealistic), the illusions and limitations that obscure reality and thwart action, and confrontations with natural and human obstacles. He is fascinated by mental states associated with isolation, ambition, moral failure, and the fear of death. His memorable characters, from Kurtz and Marlow in "Heart of Darkness" (1899) to Heyst and Lena in *Victory: An Island Tale* (1915), display weaknesses ranging from egoism and self-deception to hypocrisy and betrayal, yet demonstrate a spectrum of virtues, from love and loyalty to altruism and solidarity. Conrad's fictions are often structured by a decision and its consequences or by a voyage, literal or figurative. His

central characters approach or resist a crucial decision, increased self-knowledge, or deeper insight into an enigmatic person or situation. Paired characters, symbols, allusions to myth and literature, manipulations of time sequence, and single or multiple narrators help him probe individual experiences and link them to public events and the human condition.

The life of Joseph Conrad – a native of the Polish Ukraine who grew up under Russian rule, spoke fluent French, and became a major modern author in English – is as rich and complex as his writing. His fiction and his two autobiographical sketches, *The Mirror of the Sea: Memories and Impressions* (1906) and *A Personal Record,* offer valuable, if not fully reliable, information, and he remains enigmatic in the best biographies, those by Jocelyn Baines, Frederick R. Karl, Zdzislaw Najder, and Jeffrey Meyers. Karl identifies the "three lives" of his subject: an unsettled Polish-Russian childhood, an adventurous young adulthood as a French and British merchant seaman, and a troubled maturity as the British novelist Joseph Conrad, whose subjects derive from his young-adult experience but whose themes are rooted also in his childhood.

Józef Teodor Konrad Korzeniowski (called Konrad in homage to two heroic characters in patriotic poems by Adam Mickiewicz) was born 3 December 1857 in or near Berdichev, now in Ukraine but then in an area that had been Russian since the late-eighteenth-century partitioning of Poland. The families of both parents, Apollo Korzeniowski and Ewa Bobrowska, were landed gentry devoted to the cause of freeing from its occupiers a Poland that no longer existed as a state. While many Polish nationalists lived in western European exile, Conrad's father, a failed farmer, moved to Warsaw to participate in the plans for the ill-fated Polish insurrection of January 1863. Korzeniowski was imprisoned in 1861 and later deported, along with his wife and their four-year-old son, to Vologda, northeast of Moscow. After the family moved south, to Chernikov, near Kiev, his mother died of tuberculosis in 1865. Four years later his father died of tuberculosis in Kraków and was buried a patriotic hero. Orphaned at eleven, Conrad was taken in by a family friend, then by his grandmother, and in 1873 by his devoted uncle, Tadeusz Bobrowski, whose correspondence with his nephew provides a rich source of biographical information about Conrad.

Though he left Poland at sixteen, Conrad retained an obvious accent, Slavic gestures and dress, and a lifestyle appropriate to a Polish country gentleman. In only one late story, "Prince Roman"

(1911), did he write overtly about Poland, calling it "that country which demands to be loved as no country has ever been loved ... with the unextinguishable fire of a hopeless passion." Political issues shape several of Conrad's novels and one story collection, *A Set of Six* (1908), and the values that pervade his fiction – heroic resistance, grace in defeat, and individualism refined by loyalty to larger causes – reflect a time when, writes Gérard Jean-Aubry, he "unconsciously was trained in a secret and inflexible fidelity to ideals divorced from hope." Conrad's boyhood nurtured modernist attitudes as well, including alienation, rejection of bourgeois values, and pessimism about political reform and the human condition.

Conrad received an erratic education from schools and tutors, but literature attracted him. "I don't know what would have become of me," he wrote in *Notes on Life and Letters* (1921), "if I had not been a reading boy." His favorite writers included William Shakespeare, Charles Dickens, Victor Hugo, Miguel de Cervantes, James Fenimore Cooper, and Frederick Marryat. To his readings he traced his impulsive determination, formed at fourteen, to become a seaman, and in October 1874 he left for Marseilles. After training as a sailor and traveling to the West Indies, in 1878 he was ill and in debt. He shot himself in an apparent suicide attempt, which he passed off as a dueling incident.

Unqualified for regular nautical employment without French citizenship, twenty-year-old Konrad Korzeniowski tried his luck in England, which had the world's largest merchant fleet. After early training, including a voyage to Constantinople, in 1879 he began a three-year apprenticeship that took him to Australia and Asia on two clipper ships. During his fifteen years as a British sailor he weathered natural calamities, poor health, a short temper, and poor treatment by superiors. Nonetheless, working hard at his English and at his examinations, he earned the rank of second mate in 1880, first mate in 1884, a master's certificate and British citizenship in 1886, and the command of a small ship in 1888. Lodging in London between voyages, he began a lasting friendship with Adolf Krieger, a partner in a firm of shipping agents who provided loans and other assistance. In 1886 Conrad unsuccessfully submitted his first English story, "The Black Mate," to a magazine contest on "My Experiences as a Sailor."

Among the young officer's voyages of the early 1880s to and from southeast Asia, those best known to readers of Conrad's short fiction involve the disintegration and demise by fire of the anti-quated ship *Palestine,* which provided the basis for "Youth" (1898), and a severe storm and the difficult death of an American seaman suffered on the *Narcissus.* When an 1887 back injury postponed his return to England, he remained in the East. As chief mate on the steamer *Vidar* and as captain of the sailing bark *Otaga,* he transported goods within the East Indies and made excursions to Bangkok, Mauritius, and Australia. As a novelist he would find the Eastern seas his richest resource for fiction. The trying experiences of his first command inspired "The Secret Sharer" (1910) and *The Shadow-Line: A Confession* (1917), while stops on Sumatra, Borneo, and other islands brought contact with the character types who would populate his Eastern novels and stories.

Returning to England in 1889, Conrad expected to receive command of a larger ship, but British sailing ships were reduced by half between 1875 and 1894 as steamships, which were faster and more efficient and required smaller crews, took over international trade. A fascination with central Africa, traced to a childhood curiosity about a blank space on a map, led him to seek work in the Congo (now Zaire), then controlled by King Leopold II of Belgium. A three-year appointment as captain of a steamboat was arranged for him by his friend Krieger and his novelist aunt, Marguerite Poradowska, a resident of Brussels. His experiences in the Congo in 1890, recorded in his first English diary and in letters to his aunt, would inspire his greatest novella, "Heart of Darkness." After a month-long voyage along the West African coast, he took a small ship to Matadi, the farthest navigable port on the lower Congo River. For the next stage of his journey, a 230-mile overland trek to Léopoldville, his diary recorded hot days, cold nights, mosquitoes, menacing drums, and encounters with corpses and graves. In Léopoldville he encountered a supercilious manager and the news that his ship, the *Florida,* needed extensive repairs. A voyage upriver to Stanley Falls on the decrepit *Roi des Belges* included a crew of African cannibals and the death of a white merchant. Upon his return to Léopoldville, ill with malaria and dysentery, he resigned, his health and nerves permanently impaired.

"It may be said that Africa killed Conrad the sailor and strengthened Conrad the novelist," wrote Jean-Aubry. Between 1890 and 1896 he made the transition to a life of authorship and English domesticity. He worked at sea one more time, now as chief mate J. Conrad of the *Torrens,* a sailing ship carrying passengers to Australia. Its second voyage, in 1893, introduced him to two educated Britons who en-

The Roi des Belges, *the Congo steamboat on which Conrad traveled to Stanley Falls in 1890, an experience that inspired "Heart of Darkness" (1902)*

river settings leave a more powerful impression than characters. Reviewers found the novels depressing but compared their exotic settings favorably to those of Rudyard Kipling and Robert Louis Stevenson. H. G. Wells commented, "Only greatness could make books of which the detailed workmanship was so copiously bad, so well worth reading, so convincing, and stimulating."

Conrad earned a meager seventy pounds from the sale of his first books. Short fiction, suitable for magazines and for republication in book form, offered better opportunities for remuneration. Between 1896 and 1897 he wrote six short works, experimenting with subjects and techniques. Five were included in *Tales of Unrest* (1898), while the longest, *The Nigger of the "Narcissus": A Tale of the Sea* (1897), was republished separately. The unifying themes of the tales, moral blindness and the destructive pursuit of dreams, recall those of the early novels. *Tales of Unrest,* published in an edition of three thousand, was well reviewed and helped earn Conrad a fifty-pound award from the *Academy* magazine.

The first of the *Tales of Unrest,* "The Idiots" (published in the "decadent" *Savoy* magazine in 1896), borrows from Maupassant its subject, structure, and compression. After encountering four idiot children in a Breton village, the narrator learns enough to relate their story omnisciently. Farmer Jean-Pierre Bacadou's marriage to Susan produces these four children incapable of human response, and the angry farmer abuses his wife. One night she confesses to her mother that she has murdered her husband, then flees. Imagining herself pursued by her husband's ghost, she plunges into the ocean. This slight story sympathetically portrays the descent into madness of two peasants.

Conrad's next three contributions to *Tales of Unrest* are of enduring quality. In an author's note for the collection he described "An Outpost of Progress," set in an unidentified remote trading post in Africa, as "the lightest part of the loot I carried off from Central Africa." Serialized in *Cosmopolis,* it narrates first the arrival and settling in of the "perfectly insignificant and incapable" white traders Kayerts and Carlier, then their physical, psychological, and moral degeneration as they become implicated in a trade of black servants for ivory and suffer illness and near starvation. In the powerful climax a dispute over a store of sugar leads to a fight that ends when Kayerts shoots Carlier in what he believes is self-defense. A few hours later, wrapped in a symbolic fog as the company ship approaches, Kayerts commits suicide by hanging himself from a cross over a predecessor's grave. Entering the minds of

couraged his writing: Edward Sanderson, who would succeed his father as headmaster of Elstree preparatory school, and novelist John Galsworthy. In October 1894 Conrad's manuscript of *Almayer's Folly: A Story of an Eastern River* (1895), begun in 1888, was accepted by Unwin upon the recommendation of the renowned editor Edward Garnett, henceforth Conrad's friend and supporter. On 24 March 1896, after the publication of his second novel, *An Outcast of the Islands,* Conrad married Jessie George, a young, pleasant typist with little education. They set off for a six-month stay on the Brittany coast, where he began a novel, "The Rescuer," and wrote stories for magazines.

Conrad's first two novels, which imitate Flaubert's realism, introduce several of his thematic concerns. Set on Borneo, each relates the obsessions, moral corruption, and declining fortunes of an isolated Dutch trader. In both novels jungle and

both white and native characters, passing judgments on people incapable of functioning without supervision and on those who make pious remarks about "suffering and sacrifice," and imitating Flaubert's ironic satire of bourgeois stupidity as well as Kipling's ironic descriptions of interactions between colonials and natives, "An Outpost of Progress" blends disparate elements into a disturbing portrait of degeneration.

The other two successful stories have southeast Asian settings. "The Lagoon," published in *Cornhill Magazine,* opens in a jungle, where an unnamed white man visits a Malay living by a stagnant lagoon. From a reminiscence by the Malay, Arsat, the visitor learns a guilty secret: while abducting his intended wife from a rajah's house, Arsat permitted the brutal murder of his own brother. After Arsat tells his story, his wife dies, and though he hopes now to avenge his brother, Conrad's omniscient narrator reflects that Arsat lives in "the darkness of a world of illusions." "The Lagoon" successfully uses its white listener to draw western readers into its eastern world.

More complex is the second Malay story, "Karain: A Memory." With Garnett's assistance it appeared in the prestigious *Blackwood's Edinburgh Magazine.* In its six sections the participant-narrator, a former captain who anticipates Conrad's Charlie Marlow, builds up a portrait of a native chief who, like Arsat, reveals a guilty secret. Karain appears first in theatrical glory as the respected ruler of a bay community on Mindanao but later reveals his private side. When the narrator returns after an absence, his boat is visited by a terrified Karain. The chief recounts a youthful quest for revenge undertaken with his friend Matara. When the two men found Matara's missing sister and the white man with whom she had fled, Karain shot his friend to save the woman's life. Now haunted by Matara's spirit, the chief begs his white friends for a charm. A young British ship's officer ceremonially presents him with a sixpence coined for Queen Victoria's 1887 jubilee, and Karain, relieved, returns to his people. If the charm scene flatters the queen and treats the native condescendingly, it also depicts a gesture of friendship. The impact of "Karain: A Memory" is enhanced by the narrator's reflections about his own storytelling and by an epilogue that takes place in London, where a companion wonders if this bustling life is as "real" as Karain's.

Completing *Tales of Unrest,* though rejected by magazines, "The Return" may be Conrad's worst story. An effective opening describes the arrival at a suburban train station of middle-class Alvan

Hervey; then the story reviews with ironic detachment the five-year marital history of the Herveys, who think well of themselves but merely "skimmed over the surface of life." Hervey enters his sumptuous home and arrives in the drawing room, where a letter informs him that his wife has left with another man. "The Return" follows the self-centered Hervey's reactions: anger, humiliation, sadness, and rationalization. To his surprise his wife returns, and after a long and unconvincing dialogue the self-righteous Hervey concludes that his happiness cannot be restored and leaves. Conrad explained in his author's note that he experimented with a type of "virtuosity" and used "physical impressions" of ordinary objects in order "somehow [to] produce a sinister effect."

In 1897 Conrad also published a major novella, *The Nigger of the "Narcissus,"* in the *New Review.* (In the United States it was published separately as *The Children of the Sea.*) Founded on memories of his 1884 voyage from Bombay to Britain, this first of Conrad's sea tales uses the ship, in the tradition of Samuel Taylor Coleridge and Herman Melville, as a microcosm of human life. The "nigger" of the title, as Conrad explained in a 1914 foreword, is less an individual than "the centre of the ship's collective psychology and the pivot of the action," like the Ancient Mariner's albatross. The opening scenes of arrival on board and roll call introduce a multinational crew. Suddenly the mysterious American James Wait, with his black skin and "deep, ringing voice," makes an operatic entrance on the dark deck. He appears at first "calm, cool, towering, superb," and physically powerful. After relating the orderly departure of the ship, chapter 2 shows how Wait uses his illness and impending death to manipulate and disturb his fellow seamen. He becomes verbally abusive, insists on (but resents) special attention, and "lord[s] over us with a . . . pitiless assertion of his sublime privilege" as a dying man. In chapter 3, near the Cape of Good Hope, a terrible storm washes clear the decks, turns the ship on its side, and draws the crew together as a heroic community that keeps the ship afloat and rescues Wait. Becalmed near the equator and short of food, the crew in chapter 4 again takes interest in Wait. In a rapid sequence of brief scenes he receives two threatening visits, is ordered to remain in bed by the captain, and serves as the pretext for a brief revolt. The crew's visits to Wait continue in chapter 5 as the black man, his frame hollow and his voice a mere croak, fiercely denies his death even as it occurs. After his burial at sea the winds rise and allow the sailors to reach London.

The page from the manuscript for "Heart of Darkness" that includes Kurtz's exclamation "Oh! the horror!" (Beinecke Rare Book and Manuscript Library, Yale University)

A dense narrative of action, *The Nigger of the "Narcissus"* is complex in characterization, description, symbolism, and point of view. The crew, uncertain whether the black man is faking illness or actually dying, project onto him their attitudes toward death. Each major character is both individualized and universalized by his shipboard role and by his relationship to Wait. Old Singleton, the forty-five-year veteran and the helmsman who clings to the wheel through the thirty hours of the storm, represents a passing, dedicated generation, "inarticulate and indispensable." His age keeps him aloof from Wait's fate: "You can't help him; die he must." By contrast, Donkin represents the worst of the younger generation as the articulate but lazy man "that knows all about his rights, but that knows nothing of courage, of endurance, . . . of the unspoken loyalty that knits together a ship's company." Complaining and cursing, inciting rebellion and throwing a heavy object at the captain, Donkin is a villain. For him Wait's fate is something to manipulate for personal gain. Secondary figures reveal other human possibilities: the conscientious cook, who degenerates into fanaticism when he tries to bully Wait into repentance; the blustering Irishman Belfast, who treats Wait with devoted kindness; and the godlike Captain Allistoun, who has the courage during the storm to keep the ship's masts in place and who, though considerate of the dying Wait, refuses to endanger the ship and its crew for his sake.

Like the main characters, the settings and events are both particularized and symbolic. Contrasts of light and dark, sunlight and shadow, and black and white have ambiguous connotations, prefiguring "Heart of Darkness," from the white flower from which the ship takes its name, to the white eyes and teeth that stand out against the obscurity of the black man's skin, to the black storm clouds that spew white hail. Tense moments in the storm are vividly described and personified: the sea is "as mischievous and discomposing as a madman with an axe," and the ship rises "as though she had torn herself out from a deadly grasp."

Of *The Nigger of the "Narcissus"* Conrad stated in 1914, "It is the book by which, not as a novelist perhaps, but as an artist striving for the utmost sincerity of expression, I am willing to stand or fall." His high opinion has been sustained by many readers. Criticism has focused on the shifting point of view, the question of whether Conrad equates Wait's black skin with evil, and the story's psychological and mythic significance. The point of view, alternating between omniscience and the "we" of a participant sailor, reflects the shifting mentality of the crew; at the end a lone "I" reflects, "Haven't we, together and upon the immortal sea, wrung out a meaning from our sinful lives?"

As he finished *The Nigger of the "Narcissus,"* Conrad explained in 1914, "I understood that I had done with the sea, and that henceforth I had to be a writer." He immediately wrote a preface to the novella "to express the spirit in which I was entering on the tasks of my new life." This preface, an epilogue in the *New Review* excluded from the book but published separately as *The Art of Fiction* (1902), is a classic manifesto of critical theory that incorporates ideals of Romanticism, Victorian realism, and modernism. The artist's aim is truth: to reveal, looking within himself, the "enduring and essential" reality behind the surface of experience. The artist appeals to human beings through their feelings – of wonder, of mystery, of pity, of "fellowship with all creation" – but indirectly, by way of their senses. "My task which I am trying to achieve is, by the power of the written word to make you hear, to make you feel – it is, before all, to make you see." The artist must see clearly and depict honestly the "passing phase of life" that he selects, both its surface and its "inspiring secret." When art succeeds, it makes people more alert to life around them and to the human condition. The preface, though dismissed by some critics as vague, has helped others appreciate the purposes of his experimentation.

The task Conrad set for himself required considerable effort, as he found the act of writing slow, tedious, and frustrating. Conrad based his fictions on facts, his memories supplemented by reading and research. Getting started was difficult, and on an average day, struggling with the English language and his emotional involvement, he produced only around three hundred words. "I had to work like a coal miner in his pit, quarrying all my English sentences out of a dark night," he once told Garnett. When inspiration failed he suffered deep depression. His artistic aims made style important, and he reminded novelist Hugh Clifford in a 9 October 1899 letter that carelessness with language distorts truth, since "things 'as they are' exist in words." Influenced by the Polish language, Conrad's style was heavy with adjectives, parallel constructions, and abstract nouns used for rhetorical effect. The English language challenged but rewarded him: "If I had not known English," he told Hugh Walpole in 1918, "I wouldn't have written a line for print in my life."

By 1899 the forty-one-year-old author of four books and reluctant father of a son, Borys (born January 1898), was settled into his new life. He benefited from literary friendships of mutual respect. The American novelist Henry James responded to a gift of *An Outcast of the Islands* with an invitation, and James recognized the merits of Conrad's best fictions despite finding his pessimism uncongenial. The young American novelist and journalist Stephen Crane asked to meet with Conrad, and the two encouraged each other until Crane's untimely death in 1900. Conrad's friendship was also sought by R. B. Cunninghame Graham, an idealistic Scottish aristocrat, South American traveler, and writer of history books and short stories, who received some of Conrad's philosophical letters. Especially important for Conrad was the support of Ford Madox Hueffer, later known as Ford Madox Ford. From 1898 to 1904 Conrad helped Hueffer become a marketable writer by collaborating on two novels and a novella of slight merit, while Hueffer offered Conrad story ideas, suggestions for his English style, and practical help. In October 1898 Hueffer sublet to the Conrads Pent Farm, near his home at Aldington in Kent, southeast of London, an area where Conrad would live for most of his life.

Between 1899 and 1902 publisher William Blackwood, tolerating delays and demands for cash, serialized in *Blackwood's* and published as books the stories for *Youth: A Narrative, and Two Other Stories* (1902), including "Heart of Darkness" and "The End of the Tether" and the novel *Lord Jim: A Tale* (1900), once intended for the 1902 collection. Among the tales, which narrate adventures of seamen in youth, maturity, and old age, respectively, the first two (like much of *Lord Jim*) are told as reminiscences of Charlie Marlow, Conrad's famous alter ego narrator. *Youth: A Narrative, and Two Other Stories,* dedicated to Jessie Conrad and published in an edition of 3,150 copies, was well received by reviewers and is Conrad's most important collection of short fiction.

"Youth: A Narrative" modifies the memory/commentary structure of "Karain: A Memory" by presenting the reminiscences of an Englishman capable of reflecting upon his experiences. After an opening in which the frame narrator presents a group of former seamen – "a director of companies, an accountant, a lawyer, Marlow, and myself " – Charlie Marlow, a forty-two-year-old recalling nostalgically but with ironic distance his first voyage to the East at age twenty, begins speaking. For him it was one of "those voyages that . . . might stand for a symbol of existence," a case in which, despite one's best efforts, "You simply can do nothing." Marlow's account of the disaster-plagued final passage of the

aging *Judea,* carrying a cargo of coal intended for Bangkok, is based on Conrad's experiences on the doomed *Palestine* from 1881 to 1883. As Marlow reminisces about ship and men encountering storms and a collision, fighting a smoldering fire, and suffering burns in a terrifying explosion, he reveals his personality by repeating the "do or die" slogan painted on the *Judea* and by commenting about the courage and enthusiasm, pride and pleasure, of being young: "O youth! The strength of it, the faith of it, the imagination of it!" Even after watching the burning vessel sink, the young second mate Marlow finds fresh delights – his first command, of a small lifeboat, and his first glimpse of an Asian port, "the East of the ancient navigators, so old, so mysterious, resplendent and sombre."

Using the same storyteller and structure, Conrad achieved a far darker impact with his masterwork of short fiction. "Heart of Darkness" was written rapidly in February 1899, appeared in three parts in *Blackwood's,* and was immediately recognized as "the high water mark of the author's talent" by Garnett. The frame narrator of "Youth" introduces the same auditors, now on board a Thames cruiser awaiting the tide at dusk, but here he describes both Marlow, who "resembled an idol," and the setting, which reminds him of the great English explorers. Marlow's association is different: "this also has been one of the dark places of the earth." Anticipating the roles that he and Kurtz play in Africa, Marlow imagines two ancient Romans in Britain: the "commander of a trireme" who avoids contact with the wilderness and a young settler experiencing in a savage setting "the fascination of the abomination." Marlow reflects ambiguously on modern imperialism: "The conquest of the earth, which mostly means the taking it away from those who have a different complexion or slightly flatter noses than ourselves, is not a pretty thing. . . . What redeems it is the idea only . . . and an unselfish belief in the idea."

Marlow's account of his Congo journey, adapted from Conrad's experiences in 1890, presents a corrupt system destructive to Europeans and Africans and redeemed by no ideals. Whereas in "Youth" Marlow keeps separate his youthful reactions and mature perceptions, in "Heart of Darkness" he relives his experiences as he speaks, struggling to comprehend them: "to him," explains the frame narrator, "the meaning of an episode was not inside like a kernel but outside, enveloping the tale." The narrative is replete with surrealistic encounters, beginning with the company's shadowy headquarters in Brussels, where two women knit black wool and a doctor studies human skulls and predicts madness.

Marlow's first stop in the Congo, at the company station, establishes a pattern for his African experiences. After he, to his dismay and horror, encounters a chain gang of emaciated black workers and a grove of trees where natives lie dying, he meets an obsessively neat white chief accountant who tells him about Kurtz, the manager of the inner station who "sends in as much ivory as all the others put together." At each subsequent stage of his journey – a two-hundred-mile overland trek; a frustrating stay at the central station, where Marlow must repair his wrecked steamboat; the boat trip upriver ("Going up that river was like travelling back to the earliest beginnings of the world"); and the arrival at the inner station – the pattern is repeated. The Africans, including a man beaten for causing a fire, a crew of cannibals who show restraint by not consuming their masters, and a helmsman killed by an arrow, behave and suffer in ways that Marlow cannot understand yet seem to him to be fellow human beings. The European colonists – the self-important manager of the central station, the ivory-seeking "faithless pilgrims," the Russian devotee in motley – are self-centered eccentrics who, though alien to Marlow, build up his image of the infamous Kurtz, with whom Marlow becomes increasingly fascinated.

The figure of Kurtz is central to the third section of the novella. He is a paradox: highly educated, destined for high position, and the envy of other managers, Kurtz now acquires his ivory by terrorizing a community of Africans who worship him. Noticing that Kurtz's station is surrounded by posts topped with human heads, Marlow concludes, "Mr. Kurtz lacked restraint in the gratification of his various lusts." When Kurtz does appear he is near death. His tall, emaciated frame is carried on a stretcher to Marlow's boat by threatening men with spears, and he is mourned by a native woman, described as "savage and superb." A few days later, having raved about his "immense plans" for his ivory and his "Intended" wife, he cries out, "The horror! The horror!" These words comprehend the savage jungle, his own moral degeneration, and Western colonial rapacity. A native boy then announces, "Mistah Kurtz – he dead," later T. S. Eliot's epigraph for a poem about spiritual emptiness, "The Hollow Men" (1925).

Idealistic yet consumed by greed and ambition, charismatic yet insane, the enigmatic Kurtz, a mythic figure reminiscent of Prometheus and Faust, intrigues Conrad's critics. For Marlow, Kurtz sinks

'TWIXT LAND & SEA
TALES

BY

JOSEPH CONRAD

A SMILE OF FORTUNE
THE SECRET SHARER
FREYA OF THE SEVEN
ISLES

Life is a tragic folly
Let us laugh and be jolly
Away with melancholy
Bring me a branch of holly
Life is a tragic folly
　　　　　A. SYMONS.

LONDON: J. M. DENT & SONS LTD.
ALDINE HOUSE, COVENT GARDEN · 1912

*Title page for Conrad's collection of three of his
best-known stories*

into an "impenetrable darkness," yet he is superior to other colonists, because he lived by convictions and died speaking "an affirmation, a moral victory paid for by innumerable defeats." For critic Ian Watt, Kurtz's fate symbolizes European imperialism – its subversion, through abuse of power, of those qualities of which Western civilization is most proud.

Marlow, as a character and a narrator, is also a puzzle. The novella is Marlow's journey: he learns more about himself than about Kurtz. Entranced by the wilderness and by Kurtz, Marlow feels that only his self-restraint and devotion to work protect him from going over the edge. He embodies Western morality and humanity, qualities that Kurtz lost in the jungle. For critic Albert J. Guerard, Marlow's jungle voyage reflects the archetypal hero's journey to self-discovery in a dreamlike world where he confronts his suppressed double, or "shadow." Karl, who identifies Kurtz with the id and the desire in individuals and civilizations for unrestrained power, sees in Marlow the rational side of human nature that confronts and restrains these impulses. Critics have puzzled over Marlow's decision, in a portentous final scene in Brussels, to lie to Kurtz's pale and elegant "Intended" by telling her, because the truth is "too dark altogether," that Kurtz's last words were "your name." For feminists Marlow's lie shows condescension, while Karl believes that the lie helps Marlow preserve his own illusions about Kurtz. Others see Marlow's lie as a humane act that distances him from Kurtz's merciless absolutes of good and evil.

Critical understanding of Marlow is bound up also with responses to Conrad's style, imagery, and atmosphere in "Heart of Darkness." The *Manchester Guardian* reviewer was impressed by Conrad's style, but poet and novelist John Masefield noted that the "stately and brilliant prose . . . gives one a curious impression of remoteness and aloofness from its subject." F. R. Leavis admires Conrad's precise descriptions and "sinister and fantastic 'atmosphere' " but criticizes as morally irresponsible his vague philosophizing about the unspeakable. Other critics consider his verbal ambiguities appropriate to a dream journey.

Conrad's stands on social, racial, and gender issues were debated from the start. The *Manchester Guardian* noted that while the novella does not directly attack imperialism, "cheap ideals, platitudes of civilization are shrivelled up in the heat of such experiences." More recently, Nigerian novelist Chinua Achebe – author of an alternative fictional portrayal of colonization, *Things Fall Apart* (1958) – has concluded that Conrad "was a thoroughgoing racist" who uses "Africa as setting and backdrop which eliminates the African as human factor." West Indian novelist V. S. Naipaul explicitly adapted motifs from "Heart of Darkness" for *A Bend in the River* (1979), set in postcolonial Zaire, and filmmaker Francis Ford Coppola, in *Apocalypse Now* (1979), drew from Conrad's novella symbols that indict a modern evil, America's involvement in Vietnam and Cambodia.

"The End of the Tether," the final novella in *Youth,* was published in *Blackwood's* in 1902. Eschewing the grand themes and participant-narrator of its companion pieces, the tale omnisciently relates the final voyage of sixty-seven-year-old Captain Whalley, a once-virtuous and heroic seaman whose poverty and financial commitment to his daughter lead him into moral decline through a series of deceptions. Concealing his poverty, first from a friend and then from Massy, the owner of the steamboat *Sofala,* Whalley gains command of the boat. But he demands so much help of his Asian assistant that

the jealous first mate, Stern, calls Massy's attention to another deception, that the captain is going blind. Taking advantage of Whalley's disability, the owner arranges a shipwreck for the insurance money. As the ship founders, Whalley recognizes what he has lost: " . . . even his own past of honour, of truth, of just pride, was gone. All his spotless life was fallen into the abyss." Whalley wants to bring Massy to justice, but his desire to help his daughter with a share of the insurance money overcomes his scruples, and he decides to "cling to his deception with a fierce determination to carry it out to the end" by going down with the ship. Conrad portrays the captain's moral deterioration, but he creates enough sympathy for Whalley that eventually Conrad himself saw the captain as heroic. Though the story became overly long to meet a publishing commitment, Conrad's characterization of Whalley, which was admired by James, ranks with Thomas Hardy's study of moral decline in *The Mayor of Casterbridge* (1886).

Conrad extended techniques from his short fiction for his first major novel, *Lord Jim,* which uses the participant-narrator Marlow and embedded reminiscences and time shifts to build its mosaic portrait of a young man tormented by shame at his failure to live up to his ideals. Characters are tested also in *Typhoon and Other Stories* (1903). The novella *Typhoon,* first published in *Pall Mall Magazine* in 1901 and published separately in 1902, centers on Captain McWhirr. Unlike Marlow and Jim, the captain is "faithful to facts, which alone his consciousness reflected," having "just enough imagination to carry him through each successive day." As he guides the steamship *Nan-Shan* to the Chinese coast, carrying home two hundred indentured Chinese workers, McWhirr confronts two challenges beyond his experience: a ferocious typhoon and a fight belowdecks among the Chinese. Finding his shipboard manual unhelpful, the literal-minded captain refuses to divert the ship's course and gives orders to head directly into the storm. Amid the "immoderate wrath" of the "passionate sea," the ship is severely damaged, the officers are nearly swept from the deck, the Chinese workers fight as their money and belongings scatter, and the captain's orderly cabin is devastated. Aided by the competent chief engineer Rout, the skeptical first mate Jukes (the second mate goes mad), and a courageous boatswain, the captain stays stubbornly in control, and his ship narrowly survives two assaults by the typhoon. McWhirr, whose motto is "you don't find everything in books," deals with the melee by having the scattered money collected. Later, the captain has the money distributed fairly among the Chinese.

Typhoon creates the immediacy of experience that Conrad advocated in his 1897 preface. Memorable are not only its portrait of McWhirr but also its vivid, fast-paced narration of the storm, the fight, and the heroic struggles of the officers to fulfill their tasks amid darkness and chaos. The novella's framing chapters quote letters home to introduce the main characters and later allow them to interpret their experiences. McWhirr's final letter to his wife resembles a ship's log entry and barely mentions the storm, while Chief Mate Jukes's letter demonstrates a grudging respect for his captain: "I think that he got out of it very well for such a stupid man."

In the long story called "Falk: A Reminiscence," Conrad returns to east Asia. At a gathering of former seamen, a mature storyteller recalls an episode from his youth, when he befriended Hermann, the German captain of the *Diana*. When the Dane or Norwegian Falk, the taciturn and disagreeable owner of a tugboat, suddenly decided to tow the *Diana* out of the harbor but refused to tow the narrator's ship, his motive proved to be his love for Hermann's niece, a blond "built on a magnificent scale." Reassured that the narrator is no rival, Falk revealed his secret to Hermann's family: that once on a stranded ship he survived by murder and cannibalism. Falk, like the legendary Flying Dutchman, met with sympathy, and the girl agreed to be his salvation. The story was first published in *Typhoon*.

An English coastal village setting, compact plots, and well-drawn female characters unite the other two stories in the *Typhoon* collection. "Amy Foster," serialized in the *Illustrated London News* (1901), resembles "The Idiots." A narrator visits Colebrook, meets a "dull creature," and learns her history as told by the local doctor, an outsider who notes that "she had enough imagination to fall in love." The object of her affections was a stranger washed up on shore, the lone survivor among a shipload of central European immigrants. Unable to communicate and odd in his habits, Yanko Goorall was beaten and imprisoned, but after he saved a child from drowning he found work, was given a cottage, and married the kindly servant Amy Foster. But Amy feared his strangeness, and when an illness made him delirious, she fled with their child and left him to die. Conrad, himself an immigrant of unusual habits married to a wife of limited intellect, uses the doctor to present both protagonists sympathetically. In "To-Morrow," first published in *Pall Mall Magazine* (1902), retired Captain Hagberd has waited for his son Harry to return to Colebrook

from the sea and marry his blind neighbor's daughter, Bessie Carvill. But when the son, a self-centered adventurer, visits briefly, the captain fails to recognize him and drives him away. Bessie retreats in despair to "her stuffy little inferno of a cottage," and Hagberd expects Harry to return "tomorrow." This story was adapted as Conrad's first play, *One Day More* (produced 1905, published 1917).

Reviewers were enthusiastic about the *Typhoon* collection. "Not even Kipling," declared the *Times Literary Supplement*, "has quite the same power of intense vividness." Yet Conrad remained troubled: he endured attacks of depression and of malarial gout, and Jessie suffered a serious knee injury in 1904 from which she never fully recovered. A second son, named John Alexander after Galsworthy, was born in 1906. Two moves, to Bedfordshire in 1907 and a farmhouse in Aldington, Kent, in 1909, proved unsatisfactory. Professionally Conrad was more fortunate. He received two awards: £300 from the Royal Literary Fund in 1902 and £500 from the Royal Bounty Fund in 1905. Having alienated Blackwood with demands for money, in 1900 he acquired a literary agent and devoted supporter, James Brand Pinker. Meanwhile, Conrad helped Hueffer write and revise two weak novels – *The Inheritors: An Extravagant Story* (1901), a political satire using science fiction, and *Romance: A Novel* (1903), a West Indies adventure tale imitative of Stevenson – and a novella about a repentant undetected criminal, *The Nature of a Crime* (serialized 1909). Ford gave Conrad story ideas about anarchists and, as editor of the *English Review*, encouraged him to dictate his reminiscences, collected as *The Mirror of the Sea* and *A Personal Record*.

Between 1904 and 1914, the middle phase of his writing career, Conrad extended his reputation and range with five ambitious novels and three story collections. The Eastern nautical settings and isolated individuals of his early works gave way to Western settings and human relationships connected with wider issues, especially political and social problems. Largest in scope of his works is the novel *Nostromo: A Tale of the Seaboard* (1904), whose complex plot using multiple narrators and time shifts centers on a South American revolution and a silver mine, which, like the ivory in "Heart of Darkness," corrupts the major characters. Conrad next wrote two novels about spies. Espionage fiction, popular before World War I, suited his moral concerns and ironic view of humanity. *The Secret Agent: A Simple Tale* (1907), based on a failed terrorist attack in 1894, portrays the destruction of a family within the sordid London underworld of anarchists.

In *Under Western Eyes* (1911), also founded on fact, Conrad tried to capture violence, betrayals, and the expiation of guilt in Russian and Swiss settings. Conrad's ironic political-psychological novels were generally considered sordid by contemporaries and reactionary by Marxists, but they inspired George Orwell, Graham Greene, John le Carré, and Alfred Hitchcock.

Political and social problems receive similarly sympathetic and ironic treatments, though with less experimentation, in *A Set of Six*. To his publisher Conrad described these stories, originally published with illustrations, as "simply entertaining," but his epigraph quotes a French nursery rhyme about helpless marionettes. Reviewers generally recognized the merits of the volume, but many modern critics find its plot contrivances and the conversational tone of most of the stories less attractive.

"Gaspar Ruiz: A Romantic Tale," a twelve-chapter story first published in *Pall Mall Magazine* (1906), shares its South American setting with *Nostromo*. After noting, "A revolutionary war raises many strange characters out of . . . obscurity," the British narrator learns about such a hero from an 1830s conflict in Chile. The aging General Santierra tells his British guests that as a revolutionary lieutenant he encountered some imprisoned deserters condemned to execution. Among them was the powerful but simple Ruiz, a victim of abductions by rival armies. In a series of dramatic episodes Ruiz survived the execution, was sheltered by royalists, rescued Santierra and others during an earthquake, and married a young royalist, Emilia. He became a successful revolutionary fighter, then a renegade leader of Indian tribes. During an attempted rescue of his kidnapped wife and daughter he deployed his strong body as a launcher for artillery shells, causing his own death and Emilia's suicide. Santierra finishes his reminiscence and introduces his heiress, Ruiz's grown daughter. The frame narrator muses about a man "who perished through his own strength: the strength of his body, of his simplicity – of his love." Though Conrad considered this a sentimental "magazine fake," "Gaspar Ruiz" evokes sympathy for common people suffering from war.

"The Brute: An Indignant Tale" is a weak story written for a newspaper, the *Daily Chronicle,* in 1906. It relates a discussion over drinks about *The Apse Family,* an unpredictable ship that kills one person on each voyage and is finally wrecked through an officer's carelessness. Humorous in tone, "The Brute" fits *A Set of Six* because the insensitive ship owners are of higher social standing than the ship's victims.

Each of two short political stories in *A Set of Six,* both published in *Harper's* in 1906, features a narrator whose hobby relates to its theme. "An Anarchist: A Desperate Tale" is recounted by a butterfly collector whose specimen search takes him to a South American island estate, "a penal settlement for condemned cattle," owned by a meat-extracting company. Resembling the doomed butterflies and cattle is the boat mechanic Paul, the story's "anarchist," whose experiences show that "a little thing may bring about the undoing of a man." For an anarchistic comment at a drunken party in Paris, Paul was imprisoned; unemployable when released and implicated in a bank robbery, he was deported to a penal colony and escaped during a mutiny by committing murder. With this past Paul rejects the narrator's offer of a passage home. He is now truly an anarchist, no longer fit for civilized society.

A committed anarchist appears in the companion story, "The Informer: An Ironic Tale." Referred by a friend who "collects acquaintances," the well-dressed revolutionary Mr. X visits the narrator, a "quiet and peaceable product of civilization," to discuss a shared hobby, collecting Chinese bronzes and porcelain. The visitor announces that "there's no amendment to be got out of mankind except by terror and violence" and disdains bourgeois "amateur" terrorists. "Even in England, where you have some common sense, a demagogue has only to shout loud enough and long enough to find some backing in the very class he is shouting at," comments Mr. X. As an example he tells an anecdote about the children of an official who opened their London house to a revolutionary group and wrote pamphlets for them, oblivious to the manufacture of explosives in the upper story. When a faked police raid exposed as an informer the boyfriend of the hostess, she reverted to the values of her class by retreating to an Italian convent.

"Il Conde: A Pathetic Tale," first published in *Cassell's Magazine* in 1908, deals with class conflict. A northern European count meets the narrator in the Naples museum among the bronzes from Pompeii, "whose delicate perfection has been preserved for us by the catastrophic fury of a volcano." Driven south by poor health, the count is a dignified gentleman whose "whole existence had been correct, well ordered, and conventional, undisturbed by startling events." Returning from a ten-day trip, the narrator hears from the dejected count about a devastating experience that occurred during his brief absence. When the count attended an evening concert a moody young Italian confronted him in an alley with a knife at his belly. The count gave up his purse and watch but refused to surrender his rings and expected to be stabbed. Taking flight instead, the attacker, the leader of a criminal student organization, later warned the count, "you are not done with me yet." His composure shattered, the count returns north, though his poor health dooms him. "Il Conde" is a well-crafted story. The count is so movingly characterized that the reader shares his terror during the attack, which is ironically juxtaposed with nearby music and activity.

Conrad's least appreciated major novella, "The Duel: A Military Tale," which concludes *A Set of Six,* was serialized in *Pall Mall Magazine* (1908) and appeared separately as *The Point of Honor: A Military Tale* in 1908. Elaborating on a newspaper anecdote, Conrad tracks the sixteen-year interaction between two officers who "to the surprise and admiration of their fellows, . . . pursued a private contest through the years of universal carnage." Introduced as lieutenants in part 1, the young cavalrymen are both war heroes obsessed with personal honor but otherwise opposites. Feraud, a southerner from the working class, is short and dark, temperamental, aggressive, and fiercely devoted to Napoleon. D'Hubert, an aristocratic northerner from Picardy, is tall, blue-eyed and light-haired, courteous but haughty, and image conscious. Offended by D'Hubert in a trivial incident that neither ever makes public, Feraud insists upon a duel, a spontaneous sword fight that leaves him injured. In part 2, as the imperial armies conquer Europe and the two officers are promoted to captain and colonel, three more duels take place, escalating from swords to cavalry sabers to sabers on horseback. Each time Feraud is the instigator and D'Hubert the reluctant but honor-bound fellow combatant. In part 3 the retreat of the Grand Army from Russia cools the quarrel: each duelist saves the other's life and gains the rank of general. After the battle of Waterloo and the restoration of the monarchy, a convalescent D'Hubert, engaged to marry a neighbor, saves Feraud from execution.

When in part 4 Feraud insists upon another duel, France is at peace and Napoleon in his final exile. The forcibly retired Feraud is not remotely equivalent in rank to the commanding general D'Hubert, and his motive is simply hatred, while D'Hubert, with everything to lose, accepts the challenge as fate. The confrontation is absurd: two aging, battle-scarred soldiers with pistols play a deadly game of hide-and-seek in a forest. After strategy and luck allow D'Hubert to evade Feraud's shots, the victor leaves the loser to live on in disgrace and returns home to his family, a distraught fiancée, and a stable life.

Fast-paced and suspenseful, sympathetic to both protagonists yet steeped in irony, the omnisciently narrated tale is thematically rich. Conrad captured, as he intended, "the spirit of an Epoch": the passionate devotion to glory of the armies of Napoleon, "whose career had the quality of a duel against the whole of Europe." The fanatical upstart Feraud resembles the emperor, with D'Hubert more like Napoleon's royalist enemies in France and elsewhere in Europe, warriors who created lasting peace by their victory at Waterloo. The story also warns against the consequences of European alliances and arms buildups of the early twentieth century. More broadly, *The Duel* depicts two approaches to war and to life: the single-minded Feraud, incapable of growth, is an ideal fighter, while D'Hubert begins as an arrogant young warrior and matures into a leader and lover. The final duel is his great test: " . . . if true courage consists in going out to meet an odious danger from which our body, soul, and heart recoil together, General D'Hubert had the opportunity to practise it for the first time in his life." Garnett considered *The Duel* "a perfect whole" and "worthy of Turgenev," but many critics find it slight or banal. Ridley Scott's motion picture *The Duellists* (1977) movingly evokes the settings and the protagonists.

Between 1910 and 1913 Conrad's fortunes slowly improved, and his works finally reached a wide public. In 1909 conflicts with Hueffer brought an end to their collaboration, and in 1910 his debts to Pinker produced a quarrel between the two men. In January 1910, after completing *Under Western Eyes,* Conrad suffered a nervous breakdown that disabled him for three months. A move to a comfortable home, Capel House in Ashford, Kent, improved his spirits, as did the award of a civil list pension of £100 per year in 1911 and new friendships. Novelist André Gide prepared French translations of Conrad's fiction; philosopher Bertrand Russell admired in Conrad "the boring down into things to get to the very bottom below the apparent facts"; and fellow Polish immigrant Joseph Retinger rekindled Conrad's interest in his native land. In 1909 Conrad met Capt. Carlos Marris, veteran of twenty-one years in Malaya, who told the novelist that British sailors enjoyed his work, prompting him, as he explained to Pinker, to write some "more of the stories they like."

Conrad's three new stories of Eastern seas, collected for *'Twixt Land and Sea: Tales* (1912) after appearing with illustrations in magazines, are unified not only geographically but also in theme: in each a young captain faces challenges for which his

Jessie Conrad, Borys Conrad, American writer Ellen Glasgow, and Conrad in 1914

background has not prepared him. Response to the serials was so positive that Dent published thirty-five hundred copies of the book in its first printing. Reviews of the volume were enthusiastic.

"The Secret Sharer: An Episode from the Coast," serialized in *Harper's* in 1910, draws upon Conrad's first captaincy. Its first-person protagonist is a young captain on his first command. Alone on deck on the first night of the voyage, his ship anchored in the Gulf of Siam near Bangkok, the captain feels himself a stranger, unfamiliar with the ship and alienated from its crew, and wonders "how far I should turn out faithful to that ideal conception of one's own personality every man sets up for himself secretly." Noticing a ladder not pulled up, the captain discovers clinging to its end a naked stranger. Leggatt, the strong, bold intruder who uncannily resembles the captain in appearance and background, explains that he is an escaped prisoner from a nearby ship, the *Sephora*. During a courageous repair effort, which saved the ship in a dangerous storm, he killed an obnoxious sailor who attacked him. The captain for several tense days shelters his double in his cabin and risks discovery. Paradoxically, the narrator's devotion to Leggatt alienates the captain from his crew, yet allows him to demonstrate courage and build confidence. To help

his companion escape, the captain brings his ship dangerously close to the Cambodian island of Koh-Ring. Guided in his rescue maneuvers by a floating hat abandoned by Leggatt, the captain takes his ship to sea and imagines his "second self" as a "free man, a proud swimmer striking out for a new destiny."

Simple on the surface, "The Secret Sharer" has elicited nearly as many interpretations as "Heart of Darkness." Some readers wonder if the captain merely imagines his guest. As a symbol Leggatt may be either an evil counterpart or a better self to the captain. Guerard and others view the escaped murderer as an embodiment of irrational impulses that must be exorcised before the captain is ready to command. Leavis admires the story's affirmation, through both protagonists, of "moral conviction that is strong and courageous enough to . . . defy law and codified morality and justice." When "The Secret Sharer" is read as an initiation story, however, Leggatt may represent something the captain must either overcome or assimilate into himself. "The Secret Sharer," however interpreted, is Conrad's best short story. The author, attributing his achievement to "pure luck," told Garnett in November 1912, "Every word fits and there's not a single uncertain note."

In the two long stories published with "The Secret Sharer," young captains are tested by love. A sexual betrayal, linked with unsavory business dealings, defines the captain who narrates "A Smile of Fortune: A Harbour Story," first published in *London Magazine* in 1910. On a tropical island he obtains a cargo of sugar and supplies through negotiations with the shady Jacobus brothers. He meets Alice, the sensual daughter of one brother. Passive, moody, and rude, Alice lives in a walled garden with a dark pool, where the narrator develops for her a strong attraction that repels him. Escaping, he hauls a cargo of potatoes to a port where a famine brings high prices, his "smile of fortune," but he fails to mature in this weak story.

Enriched by mythic symbolism, "Freya of the Seven Isles: A Story of Shallow Waters" is a successful love story based on an actual incident. Published in 1912 in the American *Metropolitan Magazine* and in *London Magazine,* the story is narrated by an observant friend of the protagonists. The heroine, daughter of a Danish colonist named Nelson, has long golden hair and "health, strength, and what I might call unconscious self-confidence." She loves Englishman Jasper Allen, the proud young captain of his own trading brig, the *Bonito,* from which he watches his beloved through binoculars. To spare her father Freya postpones her elopement with Jasper until her twenty-first birthday and fends off, using Richard Wagner's music and physical force, Captain Heemskirk, a brutal Dutchman who commands the gunboat *Neptun.* The jealous Heemskirk abuses his colonial powers to accuse Jasper of gunrunning and to seize his brig and tow it onto a reef. This drives the young captain to madness and Freya to illness and death.

The last two novels of Conrad's middle period, despite their complexity, enjoyed great popularity. Both *Chance: A Tale in Two Parts* (1913), serialized in the *New York Herald* in 1912, and *Victory: An Island Tale* feature settings at least partially of the sea, romantic plots that the reader must piece together from accounts by witnesses, and well-drawn female characters who suffer cruel exploitation and offer loving devotion to male rescuers. The narrator of *Chance* is Marlow, now detached and moralistic like the narrators of "Freya of the Seven Isles." *Victory* centers on the intellectual recluse Axel Heyst, who overcomes his fear of human feelings to rescue a young woman whom he later proves unable to protect.

The sea, exotic settings, love, and violence also shape Conrad's next story collection, *Within the Tides: Tales* (1915). He gave each story its own "spe-

cial mood" and "special tone," as he tried "several ways of telling a tale" — some used also in *Victory.* Two stories treat innocent characters confronted by satanic forces. In "The Partner," first published in *Harper's* in 1911, a narrator, using four sources of information, pieces together for a hotel audience the truth behind the wreck of the *Sagamore,* whose captain allegedly committed suicide. The reality is unsavory: a greedy businessman hoping with a partner to raise money for a patent-medicine scheme conspired to sink the *Sagamore,* but as the ship was going down the first mate robbed and murdered the well-meaning captain. The conspirators were thwarted, however: their share of the insurance money was insufficient to launch their patent-medicine firm. "The Inn of Two Witches: A Find," first published in 1913 in *Pall Mall Magazine* and *Metropolitan Magazine,* is allegedly reconstructed from an 1850s manuscript describing an incident during the Napoleonic Wars. Creating an eerie, Poesque atmosphere, the modern narrator relates how the manuscript's author — Byrne, a British naval officer suspicious about the fate of his courier, Tom — arrives at an inn near the Spanish coast run by two old women. Byrne feels uneasy in his bedroom, where he seems to hear warnings from young Tom. He discovers Tom's body in a closet, escapes the sudden descent of his bed's canopy, and is rescued by British troops as he flees. Though the story resembles Wilkie Collins's "A Terribly Strange Bed" (1852), Conrad claimed a historical source.

Closer to Conrad's novels are two other tales in *Within the Tides,* both published in *Metropolitan Magazine* in 1914. "Because of the Dollars" ("Laughing Anne" in the magazine) is set in the Malay Archipelago. Captain Davidson, who reappears in *Victory,* is a "*really* good man" entrusted with a cargo of old dollars to be turned in for new ones. After a woman known as Laughing Anne warns the captain that her lover and his unsavory associates plan to steal the dollars and murder him, the captain saves himself, but she is murdered in revenge. The remorseful Davidson takes Anne's young son home and is abandoned by his suspicious wife. Years later, as his child becomes a missionary, Davidson faces a lonely old age "because of those old dollars." Conrad later turned the story into a play, *Laughing Anne* (1923), which was never produced.

In the long final story of the volume, "The Planter of Malata," scientific adventurer Geoffrey Renouard is, like Heyst in *Victory,* a recluse on an island, located near a city (probably Sydney) in the antipodes. When Felicia Moorsom arrives, seeking the fiancé she had abandoned, Renouard falls deeply in love. To forestall her departure he withholds from her the information that her fiancé, his former assistant, is dead. When she learns the truth Felicia rebuffs Renouard and departs, and he later swims out into the ocean, "beyond the confines of life . . . his eyes fixed on a star." Both characters are complex and well drawn. Tall and red-haired, Felicia is a strong, sexually appealing woman, but she is self-absorbed and wants to exercise power over others. To Renouard she is a misbegotten Venus: "only, O Divinity, it isn't your body, it is your soul that is made of foam." Renouard, in contrast, is a consummate romantic. Captivated by Felicia into a fatal obsession that compromises "the last shred of his rectitude," he sustains by sheer force of will his fantasy of keeping her with him.

Within the Tides was published by Dent and in the United States by Doubleday, Page, with an author's note in which Conrad describes his aesthetic values: a "romantic feeling of reality . . . disciplined by a sense of personal responsibility and a recognition of the hard facts of experience." Treating subjects "outside the general run of everyday experience," he said, increased his sense of obligation to truthfulness. *Within the Tides,* the last story collection of Conrad's lifetime, is often linked by critics to his weaker late novels, but its characters and themes are similar to *Chance* and *Victory.*

In July 1914, undisturbed by the fateful assassination in Sarajevo of Archduke Franz Ferdinand of Austria, the Conrads and the Retingers set out for Poland. While they were visiting Kraków, Britain declared war on Austria, which controlled the city. The Conrads spent two months in hiding before receiving permission to leave for Vienna and proceed to still-neutral Italy and back to England. World War I interfered with his writing: "I have been affected mentally and physically more profoundly than I thought it possible," he wrote on 27 February 1916 to a friend, John Quinn. His son Borys joined an artillery unit in France, Hueffer volunteered and was injured by gas, and in 1916 Conrad worked as an inspector of ships in the Royal Navy. He also became infatuated with an American journalist named Jane Anderson, a woman with a history of seducing important men. Whether or not Conrad and Anderson were lovers, as his biographer Meyers argues, Conrad was energized by this romantic episode. Also, in 1918, in the wake of the Russian Revolution, Poland finally received its independence.

During the war Conrad wrote a few stories and a novella, and after 1917 he dictated four more novels. Of these late works, only the novella *The Shadow-Line: A Confession* was on a par with his masterpieces. First published in 1916–1917 in the *English Review* and the *Metropolitan Magazine,* it appeared as a book in 1917. For a Britain appalled by suffering and death in the trenches, Conrad offered this dedication: "To Borys, and all others who like himself have crossed in early youth the shadow line of their generation." Like "The Secret Sharer," *The Shadow-Line* is a first-person retrospective account of a young captain's coming of age through his first command. But the later work, following more closely events associated with Conrad's first captaincy, avoids obvious symbolism. The first three chapters in *The Shadow-Line* reveal the narrator's character before he is tested at sea. The dissatisfied young man impulsively resigns as first mate of a ship and checks in at a sailor's home, where he meets two contrasting seamen who recall for readers Singleton and Donkin of *The Nigger of the "Narcissus."* The wise Captain Giles helps him obtain the command of a ship, and the arrogant Hamilton is denied the position he covets. The narrator's lethargy gives way to enthusiasm when he travels to Bangkok and sees his ship. On board he is filled with wonder: "In that community I stood, like a king in his country, in a class by myself." Yet he soon faces two serious problems: an envious chief mate obsessed with the previous captain's irresponsible behavior and death and a fever among crew members that delays their departure. When the ship departs the captain feels not elation but "weariness after an inglorious fight." He can depend only on one man: Ransome, an experienced mate whose heart condition has reduced him to the position of cook.

In the last three chapters the young captain is tested and suffers. Within a day after the ship sets sail, as it nears the island of Koh-Ring and the latitude where the old captain's body was buried at sea, two parallel natural forces, which the superstitious chief mate, Burns, attributes to the old captain's spirit, bring stagnation: a total calm in the ocean and a fever that spreads rapidly because the old captain secretly sold the ship's quinine. Only the young captain and Ransome escape infection. When the weather changes, a threatening darkness envelops the becalmed ship, whose pathetic crew somehow manages to haul up the mainsail. The chief mate urges the captain to challenge the spirit of his predecessor. When a breeze finally arises, only the captain and the fragile Ransome remain on deck to unfurl the sails. Their efforts allow the ship to return to port and obtain desperately needed medical assistance.

The title of *The Shadow-Line* refers both to a latitude that the becalmed ship cannot cross and to the transition each person makes from youth into youthful maturity. After his initial pride at his unforeseen appointment and his rediscovery of his devotion to the sea and ships – "the test of manliness, of temperament, of courage and fidelity – and of love" – the captain blames himself for not checking the quinine and falls into despair and a sort of madness. Yet he fulfills his responsibilities and responds calmly to challenges from the crew, the ship, and natural forces. His companions, the insecure and distraught chief mate and the confident though weakened Ransome, symbolize aspects of the captain's personality, as do the stagnant sea and crew. The captain's sense of guilt, the forces that overwhelm the ship and leave him almost alone, and the mature narrative voice invoke "The Ancient Mariner" and the legend of the Flying Dutchman. The stillness and darkness that overtake the ship also suggest to the captain primordial chaos and the creation of the world, "the formidable Work of the Seven Days into which mankind seems to have blundered unbidden." At the end of *The Shadow-Line* the captain has learned how dependent he is on his crew, yet he must release his faithful Ransome, as his own captain once freed him.

Well received by reviewers, *The Shadow-Line* is among Conrad's best works. Though some critics find the opening chapters slow and awkwardly structured, others consider them suitable to the captain's uncertainties. When comparisons, invited by Conrad, are made with "The Secret Sharer," most critics prefer the former for its modernist symbolism, while a few find the latter story richer, its commitment to communal values recalling *The Nigger of the "Narcissus."*

Also completed during the Great War were Conrad's last two stories, which with two earlier tales were published posthumously, following Conrad's intentions, as *Tales of Hearsay* (1925). First came "The Black Mate," written for *London Magazine* in 1908, using the title of his 1886 magazine contest story, which was probably lost. Chief Mate Bunter, whose hair color changes from black to white during a voyage, tells his spiritualist captain that he was terrified by a ghost. To the tale's narrator the mate later recounts what actually happened: after facing age discrimination, he dyed his hair black to earn a berth, lost the dye in a storm, and invented the ghost story. "The Black Mate" is typical Conrad in using a reminiscence to reveal the truth behind an incomplete report of events.

Historical subjects and themes inform the three later stories in *Tales of Hearsay*. "Prince Roman" was published in the *Oxford and Cambridge Review* in 1911 and in the *Metropolitan Magazine* as "The Aristocrat" in 1912. Conrad's only story set in Poland relates the life of a war hero from the nobility, a friend of the author's grandfather. The narrator reviews the career of a hero, Prince Roman, whom he met as a child. In 1831, in despair after the death of his beloved young wife, Roman anonymously joins a rebellion as a noncommissioned officer. Captured by the Russians, the prince turns down an opportunity to excuse his participation. "I joined the national rising from conviction," he insists; the price is twenty-five years in the Siberian mines and broken health. Related in its heroic subject is "The Warrior's Soul," first published in *Land and Water* in 1917. An aging Russian officer, Tomassov, relates his experiences from the Napoleonic wars. While serving as a Russian diplomat in Paris he was warned by a Frenchman, De Castel, of an impending arrest of diplomats; in gratitude the Russian offered that "if ever I have an opportunity . . . you may command my life." Tomassov must fulfill his promise during the retreat of the French from Moscow when De Castel, a weary, disfigured prisoner of war, persuades a reluctant Tomassov to show "the soul of a warrior" and shoot him.

Though Conrad's last short story, "The Tale," first published in *The Strand* in 1917, also involves a morally repugnant decision, its fictional art sets it above the others in *Tales of Hearsay*. In a dialogue between two characters, a man enters a dark room and speaks to a reclining woman, revealing that he is home on leave for a few days. "Tell me a tale," she asks, and he relates a nocturnal episode from the early months of World War I, based on Conrad's brief stint as an inspector of ships. The commander of a British ship looking out for enemy submarines sees an object that could have contained fuel for a submarine. Retreating in the fog to a small bay, he encounters a concealed ship. After its Scandinavian captain fails to persuade him that he is not transporting contraband, the British captain orders the ship to leave the bay and deliberately suggests a course that causes it to wreck on the rocky coast. The narrator, admitting that the captain's experience is his own, muses that he shall never know whether this action was justified retribution or murder. Modern critics acknowledge the power of "The Tale," Conrad's only story with a woman as the audience, but disagree about its morality. Does Conrad condone murder when patriotic duty requires it, or is the captain's choice a typical Conradian di-

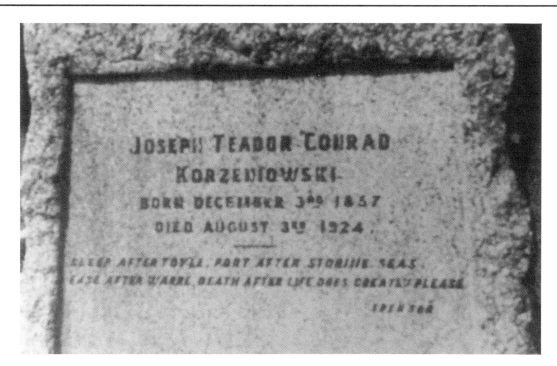

Conrad's tombstone in Canterbury

lemma in which a character must make an impossible decision and bear its consequences?

Conrad's last four novels revive his favorite themes. *The Arrow of Gold: A Story Between Two Notes* (1919), set in the 1870s amid French weapons smugglers, draws on the author's youth in Marseilles and his involvement with Jane Anderson. *The Rescue: A Romance of the Shallows* (1920), begun twenty years earlier and completed at the instigation of an American publisher, centers on the betrayal of a friend by Tom Lingard, the employer of the protagonists of *Almayer's Folly* and *An Outcast of the Islands*. Conrad's last completed novel, *The Rover* (1923), as well as the novel he left unfinished at his death, *Suspense: A Napoleonic Novel* (1925), return to familiar settings. Some features of *The Rover*, especially the spare descriptions of Mediterranean landscapes, influenced Ernest Hemingway. *Suspense* is a weak novel, though projected as an ambitious rival to Leo Tolstoy's *War and Peace* (1863–1869). It is concerned with "the state of suspense in which all classes live here from the highest to the lowest, as to what may happen next."

The last decade of Conrad's life was his most successful professionally, and he recognized the irony of his celebrity status, which allowed his later works to appear in large editions and earn far more money than his best writings. He issued a collected American edition of his works in 1921 and a deluxe British edition in 1922; sold manuscripts and film rights; wrote a silent-film scenario, "The Strong Man," based on "Gaspar Ruiz," and a play based on *The Secret Agent* (1921); and settled in 1919 in a stately old residence, Oswalds, in Bishopsbourne, near Canterbury. In 1920 he made a new friend, the adventurer T. E. Lawrence, and in 1922 suffered the death of his close friend and agent Pinker.

The American publisher Frank Doubleday persuaded Conrad to travel across the Atlantic in 1923. Highlights of this stressful trip included travel through New England and a lecture in New York City to a select audience, whom he moved to tears by reading from *Victory*. He declined a knighthood in 1924 along with offers of honorary degrees from several British universities; he never received the one award he coveted, the Nobel Prize. On 3 August 1924, at age sixty-six, Conrad died of a heart attack. A Catholic funeral was arranged on 7 August at St. Thomas's Catholic Church, Canterbury, by his wife, who was too crippled to attend. On the granite tombstone was carved a quotation from Edmund Spenser's *The Faerie Queene* (1590, 1596): "Sleep after toyle, port after stormie seas, / Ease after warre, death after life does greatly please."

Assessing Conrad's career, critics and biographers of the 1950s and 1960s identified three stages: apprenticeship, achievement, and decline. More-recent studies hold that his fiction matured as he elaborated and explored means of artistic expression for a few central concerns, among them patterns shaping his personal experiences, his widening ethical awareness, a political philosophy of organicism, the effects of his fiction on readers, and moral awareness and responsible action. Neither his seriousness of purpose nor his commitment to his art ever declined.

Conrad contributed to English literature a dozen undisputed classics of long and short fiction among outwardly similar works with few claims to permanence. His insights into human experience and his literary craft are as evident in his stories as in his novels. Unique in his writings are not only an unusual style, traceable to his native Polish, but also a range of features that resist classification. Conrad is romantic in his idealism and pessimism, his exceptional characters (men of action or reflection), and such symbolic motifs as personified nature and doubles. Like nineteenth-century realists, Conrad is committed to truth, interested in the effects of literature on readers, and concerned with characters and situations that are both individual and of wider significance. Impressionism shapes his descriptive style, while modernism manifests itself, though less in the stories than in the novels, in his complex and ambiguous themes and symbols and in his manipulations of time, point of view, and genre. A major British modernist, Conrad had few direct imitators but passed along a rich artistic legacy.

Letters:

Joseph Conrad, Life and Letters, 2 volumes, edited by G. Jean-Aubry (Garden City, N.Y.: Doubleday, Page, 1927; London: Heinemann, 1927);

Conrad to a Friend: 150 Selected Letters from Joseph Conrad to Richard Curle, edited by Richard Curle (Garden City, N.Y.: Doubleday, Doran, 1928; London: Sampson Low, Marston, 1928);

Letters from Joseph Conrad, 1895–1924, edited by Edward Garnett (Indianapolis: Bobbs-Merrill, 1928; London: Nonesuch, 1928);

Lettres françaises de Joseph Conrad, edited by Jean-Aubry (Paris: Gallimard, 1929);

Letters of Joseph Conrad to Marguerite Poradowska, 1890–1920, translated and edited by John A. Gee and Paul J. Sturm (New Haven: Yale University Press, 1940; London: Oxford University Press, 1941);

Letters to William Blackwood and David S. Meldrum, edited by William Blackburn (Durham, N.C.: Duke University Press, 1958);

Conrad's Polish Background: Letters to and from Polish Friends, edited by Zdzislaw Najder, translated by Halina Carroll (London: Oxford University Press, 1964);

Joseph Conrad and Warrington Dawson: The Record of a Friendship, edited by Dale B. J. Randall (Durham, N.C.: Duke University Press, 1968);

Joseph Conrad's Letters to Cunninghame Graham, edited by C. T. Watts (Cambridge: Cambridge University Press, 1969);

The Collected Letters of Joseph Conrad, 4 volumes, 8 volumes projected, edited by Frederick R. Karl and Laurence Davies (Cambridge: Cambridge University Press, 1983–   ).

Interviews:

Joseph Conrad: Interviews and Recollections, edited by Martin Ray (Houndmills, Basingstoke: Macmillan, 1990).

Bibliographies:

Thomas J. Wise, *A Bibliography of the Writings of Joseph Conrad (1895–1921),* revised and enlarged edition (London: Dawson's, 1921);

Kenneth A. Lohf and Eugene P. Sheehy, *Joseph Conrad at Mid-Century: Editions and Studies, 1895–1955* (Minneapolis: University of Minnesota Press, 1957);

Theodore G. Ehrsam, *A Bibliography of Joseph Conrad* (Metuchen, N.J.: Scarecrow, 1969);

Bruce E. Teets and Helmut E. Gerber, *Joseph Conrad: An Annotated Bibliography of Writings about Him* (De Kalb: Northern Illinois University Press, 1971).

Biographies:

Ford Madox Ford, *Joseph Conrad: A Personal Remembrance* (London: Duckworth, 1924; Boston: Little, Brown, 1924);

Jessie Conrad, *Joseph Conrad As I Knew Him* (London: Heinemann, 1926; Garden City, N.Y.: Doubleday, 1926);

Conrad, *Joseph Conrad and His Circle* (London: Jarrolds, 1935; New York: Dutton, 1935);

Jocelyn Baines, *Joseph Conrad: A Critical Biography* (London: Weidenfeld & Nicolson, 1959; New York: McGraw-Hill, 1960);

Bernard Meyer, *Joseph Conrad: A Psychoanalytic Biography* (Princeton: Princeton University Press, 1967);

Gustave Morf, *The Polish Shades and Ghosts of Joseph Conrad* (New York: Astra, 1976);

Frederick R. Karl, *Joseph Conrad: The Three Lives* (New York: Farrar, Straus & Giroux, 1979);

Zdzislaw Najder, *Joseph Conrad,* translated by Halina Carroll-Najder (New Brunswick, N.J.: Rutgers University Press, 1983);

Jeffrey Meyers, *Joseph Conrad: A Biography* (New York: Scribners, 1991);

Owen Knowles, *A Conrad Chronology* (Boston: G. K. Hall, 1991).

References:

Richard Ambrosini, *Conrad's Fiction as Critical Discourse* (Cambridge: Cambridge University Press, 1991);

Carl D. Bennett, *Joseph Conrad* (New York: Continuum, 1991);

Keith Carabine, ed., *Joseph Conrad: Critical Assessments,* 4 volumes (Robertsbridge, East Sussex: Helm, 1992);

Avrom Fleishman, *Conrad's Politics: Community and Anarchy in the Fiction of Joseph Conrad* (Baltimore: Johns Hopkins University Press, 1967);

John Dozier Gordan, *Joseph Conrad: The Making of a Novelist* (Cambridge, Mass.: Harvard University Press, 1940);

Lawrence Graver, *Conrad's Short Fiction* (Berkeley: University of California Press, 1969);

Albert J. Guerard, *Conrad the Novelist* (Cambridge, Mass.: Harvard University Press, 1958);

Eloise Knapp Hay, *The Political Novels of Joseph Conrad* (Chicago: University of Chicago Press, 1963);

Irving Howe, *Politics and the Novel* (New York: Horizon, 1957), pp. 76–113;

Frederick R. Karl, *A Reader's Guide to Joseph Conrad,* revised edition (New York: Farrar, Straus & Giroux, 1969);

Robert Kimbrough, ed., *Heart of Darkness: Norton Critical Edition,* third edition (New York & London: Norton, 1988);

Kimbrough, ed., *The Nigger of the "Narcissus": Norton Critical Edition* (New York & London: Norton, 1979);

F. R. Leavis, *The Great Tradition* (London: Chatto & Windus, 1948; New York: Stewart, 1949), pp. 173–226;

J. Hillis Miller, *Poets of Reality: Six Twentieth-Century Writers* (Cambridge, Mass.: Harvard University Press, 1966), pp. 13–67;

Thomas Moser, *Joseph Conrad: Achievement and Decline* (Cambridge, Mass.: Harvard University Press, 1957);

Ross C. Murphin, ed., *Heart of Darkness: A Case Study in Contemporary Criticism* (New York: St. Martin's Press, 1988);

Norman Page, *A Conrad Companion* (New York: St. Martin's Press, 1986);

John A. Palmer, *Joseph Conrad's Fiction: A Study in Literary Growth* (Ithaca, N.Y.: Cornell University Press, 1968);

Edward Said, *Joseph Conrad and the Fiction of Autobiography* (Cambridge, Mass.: Harvard University Press, 1966);

Norman Sherry, *Conrad's Eastern World* (Cambridge: Cambridge University Press, 1966);

Sherry, *Conrad's Western World* (Cambridge: Cambridge University Press, 1971);

Sherry, ed., *Conrad: The Critical Heritage* (London & Boston: Routledge & Kegan Paul, 1973);

Ian Watt, *Conrad in the Nineteenth Century* (Berkeley: University of California Press, 1979).

Papers:
The following libraries have collections of Conrad's papers: the Beinecke Library at Yale University; the New York Public Library; the British Library; the Brotherton Collection at Leeds University; Colgate University Library; Dartmouth College Library; the Houghton Library at Harvard University; the Harry Ransom Humanities Research Center, University of Texas at Austin; the Lilly Library at Indiana University; the J. Pierpont Morgan Library; the William T. Perkins Library at Duke University; the Princeton University Library; the Philip H. and A. S. Rosenbach Foundation; the University of Birmingham Library; and the University of Virginia Library.

Marie Corelli

(April–May 1855? – 21 April 1924)

Janet Galligani Casey
College of the Holy Cross

See also the Corelli entry in *DLB 34: British Novelists, 1890–1929: Traditionalists.*

BOOKS: *A Romance of Two Worlds* (London: Bentley, 1886; New York: McNally, 1887);

Vendetta! or, The Story of One Forgotten (3 volumes, London: Bentley, 1886; 1 volume, New York: Burt, 1886?);

Thelma: A Society Novel, 3 volumes (London: Bentley, 1887); republished as *Thelma: A Norwegian Princess,* 1 volume (Chicago: Weeks, 1893);

Ardath: The Story of a Dead Self (3 volumes, London: Bentley, 1889; 1 volume, New York: Lovell, Coryell, 188?);

My Wonderful Wife: A Study in Smoke (London: White, 1889; New York: Ivers, 1890);

Wormwood, A Drama of Paris (3 volumes, London: Bentley, 1890; 1 volume, Chicago: Donohue, Henneberry, 1890);

The Soul of Lilith (3 volumes, London: Bentley, 1892; 1 volume, New York: Lovell, 1892);

The Silver Domino; or, Side Whispers, Social and Literary, as Domino (London: Lamley, 1892);

Barabbas: A Dream of the World's Tragedy (3 volumes, London: Methuen, 1893; 1 volume, New York: Grosset & Dunlap, 1893);

The Sorrows of Satan; or, The Strange Experience of One Geoffrey Tempest, Millionaire (London: Methuen, 1895; Philadelphia: Lippincott, 1896);

The Silence of the Maharajah (New York: Merriam, 1895);

The Mighty Atom (London: Hutchinson, 1896; Philadelphia: Lippincott, 1896);

Cameos (London: Hutchinson, 1896; Philadelphia: Lippincott, 1896);

The Murder of Delicia (London: Skeffington, 1896; Philadelphia: Lippincott, 1896);

"Three Wise Men of Gotham." A "New" Reading of an Old Rhyme (Philadelphia: Lippincott, 1896);

The Distant Voice: A Fact or a Fancy? (Philadelphia: Lippincott, 1896);

Ziska: The Problem of a Wicked Soul (London: Methuen, 1897; New York: Stone & Kimball, 1897);

Jane: A Social Incident (London: Hutchinson, 1897; Philadelphia: Lippincott, 1897);

The Song of Miriam, and Other Stories (New York: Munro, 1898);

Angel's Wickedness: A True Story (New York: Beers, 1900);

Patriotism or Self-Advertisement? A Social Note on the War (London: Simpkin, Marshall, Hamilton, Kent, 1900; Philadelphia: Lippincott, 1900);

The Greatest Queen in the World: A Tribute to the Majesty of England (London: Skeffington, 1900);

Boy: A Sketch (London: Hutchinson, 1900; Philadelphia: Lippincott, 1900);

The Master-Christian: A Question of the Time (London: Methuen, 1900; New York: Dodd, Mead, 1900);

A Christmas Greeting (New York: Dodd, Mead, 1901);

Christmas Greeting of Various Thoughts, Verses, and Fancies (London: Methuen, 1901);

The Passing of the Great Queen: A Tribute to the Noble Life of Victoria Regina (London: Methuen, 1901; New York: Dodd, Mead, 1901);

"Temporal Power": A Study in Supremacy (London: Methuen, 1902; New York: Dodd, Mead, 1902);

The Vanishing Gift: An Address on the Decay of the Imagination (Edinburgh: Philosophical Institution, 1902);

The Plain Truth of the Stratford-upon-Avon Controversy (London: Methuen, 1903);

Angel's Wickedness: A True Story (New York: Beers, 1903);

The Strange Visitation of Josiah McNason (London: Newnes, 1904; New York: International News, 1904);

God's Good Man: A Simple Love-Story (London: Methuen, 1904; New York: Dodd, Mead, 1904);

An authorized photograph of Corelli, circa 1906 (left), and the original photograph (right) before it was retouched to make her look younger

Free Opinions Freely Expressed on Certain Phases of Modern Social Life and Conduct (London: Constable, 1905; New York: Dodd, Mead, 1905);

The Spirit of Work (Edinburgh: Privately printed, 1906);

Faith versus Flunkeyism: A Word on the Spanish Royal Marriage (London: Rapid Review, 1906);

The Treasure of Heaven: A Romance of Riches (London: Constable, 1906; New York: Dodd, Mead, 1906);

Delicia, and Other Stories (London: Constable, 1907);

Woman, or Suffragette? A Question of Rational Choice (London: Pearson, 1907);

Holy Orders: The Tragedy of a Quiet Life (London: Methuen, 1908; New York: Stokes, 1908);

America's Possession in Shakespeare's Town: The Harvard House (Edinburgh: Morrison & Gibb, 1909);

The Devil's Motor: A Fantasy (London: Hodder & Stoughton, 1910);

The Life Everlasting: A Reality of Romance (London: Methuen, 1911; New York: Hodder & Stoughton/Doran, 1911);

Innocent: Her Fancy and His Fact (London & New York: Hodder & Stoughton, 1914; New York: Doran, 1914);

Eyes of the Sea: A Tribute to the Grand Fleet and the Grand Fleet's Commander (London: Marshall, 1917);

Is All Well with England? A Question (London: Jarrolds, 1917);

The Young Diana: An Experiment of the Future (London: Hutchinson, 1918; New York: Doran, 1918);

My "Little Bit" (London: Collins, 1919; New York: Doran, 1919);

The Love of Long Ago, and Other Stories (London: Methuen, 1920; Garden City, N.Y. & Toronto: Doubleday, Page, 1921);

The Secret Power (London: Methuen, 1921; Garden City, N.Y. & Toronto: Doubleday, Page, 1921);

Love – and the Philosopher: A Study in Sentiment (London: Methuen, 1923; New York: Doran, 1923);

Praise and Prayer, A Simple Home Service (London: Methuen, 1923);

Open Confession to a Man from a Woman (London: Hutchinson, 1924; New York: Doran, 1925);

Poems, edited by Bertha Vyver (London: Hutchinson, 1925; New York: Doran, 1926).

OTHER: "The Modern Marriage Market," in *The Modern Marriage Market,* by Corelli, Lady Jeune, Flora Annie Steel, and Susan, Countess of Malmsbury (London: Hutchinson, 1898; Philadelphia: Lippincott, 1900).

SELECTED PERIODICAL PUBLICATIONS – UNCOLLECTED: "Man's War Against Women," *Harper's Bazaar,* 41 (May–June 1907): 425–428, 550–553;

"The World's Great Need," *Good Housekeeping,* 66 (January 1918): 30–32, 112.

On the day following Marie Corelli's death in 1924 a journalist in the London *Times* attempted to articulate the reasons for her enormous, though curious, popularity:

> Even the most lenient critic cannot regard Miss Corelli's works as of much literary importance. They were chiefly tracts, written in an emotional and melodramatic style of invective against some of her pet aversions, of which, being a good hater, she had many. . . . She was deficient in humour, a sense of proportion, and an understanding sympathy with human nature. But she possessed in large measure the magic gift of telling a story, however wild and improbable it might be, and to that more than to anything else her great popular success is attributable.

Corelli did have a fervid imagination that infused her fiction with a passion that held her readers spellbound, regardless of the bizarre machinations or cloying sentimentality of her often-fantastic plots. Yet her loyal public was fascinated not only by her stories but by their creator, a woman of small stature (less than five feet) who managed to maintain a gargantuan public image largely through her own devices. While literary critics mocked Corelli's works, preventing her from achieving the serious acclaim she felt was her due, the press focused on the writer herself, whose outrageous behavior was as colorful as her sensational fiction. Her immense success is a complex phenomenon, comprised equally of the woman and of her works, and merits attention from both a social and a literary perspective.

Corelli was quite prolific. In addition to the twenty-five romantic novels for which she is remembered, she also wrote thirty-four short stories published in four collections that spanned her career: *Cameos* (1896); *The Song of Miriam, and Other Stories* (1898); *Delicia, and Other Stories* (1907); and *The Love of Long Ago, and Other Stories* (1920). These short pieces reveal in microcosm virtually all of the same problems and preoccupations as Corelli's major works. Her short fiction was not, like that of other writers of the period, published initially in periodicals; however, many of her stories appeared in more than one collection or were initially published separately as novellas. The resulting overlap frustrates efforts to position individual short stories either chronologically or from the perspective of Corelli's artistic development. Moreover, some of the pieces in these collections can scarcely be called fiction. A few are closer to vignettes, and one or two are thinly disguised essays. A thematic approach to these works, exploring the ways in which they extend the interests of both Corelli's life and her novels, is perhaps the most fruitful way to consider their relative importance.

Corelli's recycling of previously published stories in new venues was one way in which she kept herself and her works in the public eye in order to maintain her extraordinary popularity. Nearly half of her books were international best-sellers, and it was not unusual for a new Corelli novel to sell out on its first day of publication. *The Sorrows of Satan; or, The Strange Experience of One Geoffrey Tempest, Millionaire* (1895), for example, had an initial sale larger than that of any previous novel in the English language (at the time of her death it was in its sixtieth printing), while *"Temporal Power": A Study in Supremacy* (1902) required an initial printing of 120,000, a record for a six-shilling volume, with another 30,000 ordered within a week. Such successes were not isolated; throughout her life publishers sold approximately 100,000 Corelli books per year, more than the annual averages of Hall Caine, Mrs. Humphry Ward, and H. G. Wells combined. Owing to the speed with which she produced new works – a result largely of her working method,

Eric Mackay, Corelli's half brother, who later served as inspiration for villainous men in her fiction

lescent (even as the seams were about to burst) and frequently would "admit" to being as much as fifteen years younger than she actually was. While Minnie might be privately insecure about her talents and pained by the jibes of critics, Corelli could hotly and publicly declare that the literary world had yet to recognize her true genius. In short, plain Minnie Mackay of Box Hill re-created herself in what she believed was the dauntless and enchanting form of Marie Corelli, even going so far as to assert later in her life that Minnie Mackay was dead.

Immersed in the creation of a persona she came to cherish as real, Corelli never perceived that many who knew her, especially the influential people she tried hard to befriend, laughed at her vanities and pretensions. She did have several famous admirers, all of whom she shamelessly advertised. Queen Victoria requested copies of her books, and Corelli was the only writer invited to the coronation of Edward VII; she was complimented by Oscar Wilde; William Gladstone honored her with a visit; and George Meredith, who had known her as a child, remained a lifelong supporter. Usually, however, the prestigious company she sought found her amusing at best, silly and tiresome at worst. Mark Twain, aware that she was courting him as part of "a self-advertising scheme," wrote in his autobiography that she was "a conscienceless fool" and a "most offensive sham" and that his visit with her in 1907 was "the most hateful day my seventy-two years have ever known."

Perhaps fortunately for Corelli, few if any of her adoring fans enjoyed a personal audience with her, being forced instead to rely on the carefully contrived public image that she consciously and vigorously fought to preserve. She understood that she was selling herself as well as her books; consequently, she jealously guarded the persona she chose to project, that of a demure maiden whose ladylike demeanor only served to emphasize the vitality of her intellect and talent. Her tactics for preserving this image were varied. She lied freely about her accomplishments, blatantly claiming a scholarly background that could not have been further removed from her haphazard and informal education. She was relentless in her attempts to manipulate the press, submitting "anonymous" reports of her philanthropic gestures and illustrious houseguests. When a journalist dared to make a negative comment about her or when her name was omitted from the list of distinguished guests at a public function, she responded with a barrage of angry letters. Perhaps most important was her determination to limit the circulation of photographs of herself that might

which eschewed even the most cursory attempt at revision – she remained a formidable commercial force in the publishing world until her death. More surprising is her continuing endurance: her books have never been entirely out of print.

During Corelli's life there were conflicting rumors about her origins – rumors that she deliberately compounded in order to shroud herself in a cloak of mystique and romance. The details of her early life, including the precise circumstances of her parentage and birth, remain uncertain, although it is known that she was born in London in April or May 1855 and was raised from age ten as the "adopted daughter" of Dr. Charles Mackay, a minor journalist. (Biographer Brian Masters suggests that she was Mackay's illegitimate daughter.) Mary "Minnie" Mackay created the persona of Marie Corelli, perhaps the most elaborate artistic creation of her entire career, out of her own fantasies and insecurities. As Marie, Minnie was not tainted with the illegitimacy that dogged her throughout her life. Indeed, she insistently claimed a highly respectable birth, at different times asserting American, Scotch, and Venetian ancestry. Similarly, she refused to be subjected to the natural aging process: until her death she wore the frilly dresses of an ado-

challenge the persona she had taken pains to create. A published snapshot of her could incite her to fury, and she assiduously avoided stray cameras throughout her career. When she became convinced in 1906 of the need for an "official" representation of herself, she had an authorized photograph printed as the frontispiece to *The Treasure of Heaven: A Romance of Riches* (1906), but only after it had been heavily doctored. In the photo she wears her trademark lace dress, and her face appears smoothly youthful. Although she looks about thirty years old, she was actually fifty-one.

The general dearth of photographs of Corelli heightened the air of mystery surrounding her. Combined with the insatiable hunger for personal details that characterizes the adoration of the masses, this made her a kind of cult figure for some and the persistent object of speculation for many others. In 1900 she took up residence in Stratford-upon-Avon, inviting what she assumed were obvious parallels between herself and William Shakespeare; her house, Mason Croft, soon became the second biggest attraction in town. (To the dismay of city officials, her presence was further publicized through her celebrated feud with the Shakespeare Birthplace Trust, whose plan to establish a public library endowed by Andrew Carnegie she vehemently opposed.) Together with her lifelong companion, Bertha Vyver, Corelli could be seen riding daily in her pony chaise, laden with bells and whimsical decorations, or gliding down the Avon in her specially imported gondola, complete with an Italian gondolier.

Corelli's outlandish behavior is reflected in the excesses of her books. While she enjoyed vast popular acclaim, serious literary success eluded her, and literary history has reaffirmed the negative evaluations of contemporary critics. To her dismay and anger, they repeatedly ridiculed her style, which was by turns mawkish and sensational and always preposterously overwritten. Her prose was melodramatic, verbose, rife with clichés, and often sprinkled with archaisms such as *thee, loveth,* and *methinks.* The number of exclamation points in an average Corelli paragraph far exceeds the bounds of appropriate usage, and her penchant for setting her stories in ancient times and exotic places, regardless of her lack of knowledge of such things, resulted in historical inaccuracies that were gleefully noted by malicious commentators. Her symbolism was ridiculously heavy-handed, including the use of such names as "Rose" and "Angel" for spotless heroines; "Theos Alwyn" (God All-wise) for an agnostic who comes to believe in the power of the Creator; and

"Claudia Strange" for an American broker who challenges an English lord's staid expectations of women. Perhaps most offensive to contemporary reviewers, and certainly most disruptive to her narratives, are her liberally inserted diatribes against social evils ranging from women who smoke and read fashion magazines to mean-spirited critics who deny true artists their due. Reviewers often perceived her works as little more than vehicles for her vituperation, which sometimes approached hysterical proportions.

However, the middle class, no better educated than Corelli and holding many of the same uninformed opinions and inflated fears, swallowed her pronouncements, ignoring the critics (to whom she refused advance review copies in the later years of her career) and eagerly purchasing her books by the thousands. Unaware of her stylistic excesses and intellectual blunders, they were mesmerized by her fantastic narratives and her subject matter, which often consisted of pseudoreligious or false scientific ideas made intelligible for the larger public. Much of her success is certainly due to her range: she naively tackled such disparate topics as Christian orthodoxy, electromagnetic currents, and the supernatural, and she relished setting her stories in such unlikely and exotic locales as morgues and absinthe dens. Her lurid tales of occult proceedings and mysterious visions were rivaled only by her equally popular melodramatic romances.

Like her novels, Corelli's short pieces vacillate between mysticism or occultism and, more commonly, maudlin sentimentality. But while the stylistic faults of the novels are at least partially redeemed by their colorful and elaborate plots, the brevity of the short fiction often serves to emphasize its defects. Trite or exaggerated descriptions that might occasionally be overlooked in a larger work seem glaring in a story of several pages. For instance, in *The Silence of the Maharajah,* published as a novella in 1895 and collected in *The Song of Miriam,* the narrator describes a telescope as "man's peephole of inquiry at world's [*sic*] inscrutable"; in "Tiny Tramps," collected in *Cameos,* homeless children reveal "pinched faces begrimed with dirt and tears, and their tiny voices [are] attuned to the beggar's whine, while too often, alas! their young hearts are already withered by the corroding influences of deceit and cunning." An excerpt from the opening paragraph of "The Boy," a story first published as *Boy: A Sketch* (1900) and collected in *The Love of Long Ago,* about a youth who falls in with a prostitute, betrays all of Corelli's worst traits:

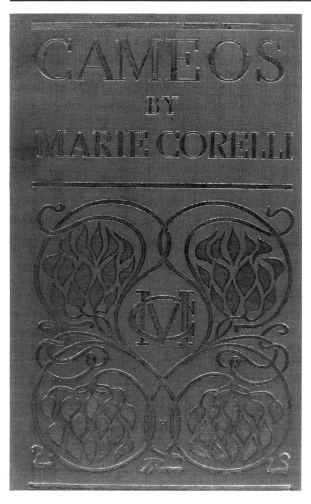

Cover for a 1907 American edition of the first collection of Corelli's short stories, compiled in 1896 to capitalize on her popularity as a novelist

She was older than the Boy, but by reason of her artistic make-up, delicately-tinted cheeks and over-rubied lips, passed muster for being as young, or younger.... [She] engaged him in conversation with many provocative flashes of the roving eyes aforesaid, with the result that the Boy was somewhat dazzled and attracted by her prettiness, and asked her to lunch with him next day. Very rash and silly of him! – but "Boys will be boys"! She told him she was "in the War-Office" – (by the way, it *is* remarkable what a number of "painted-lady" butterflies found work in that important section of Government activity!) – a statement which he confidingly accepted.

Corelli's most typical short stories are grossly oversentimental, their characteristic heroes and heroines destitute but honorable wanderers, unjustly spurned lovers who remain inhumanly faithful, and children and maidens whose snow-white innocence is threatened by all manner of evildoers and ne'erdo-wells. Her short fiction also includes ghost stories, such as "The Lady with the Carnations" from *Cameos;* tales of mystical religious experiences, such as "The Distant Voice" from *Cameos* and "The Trench Comrade" from *The Love of Long Ago;* and idealized representations of artists, as in "Rejected! The Story of a Picture," or scientists, as in "Lead, Kindly Light," both from *The Love of Long Ago.* Perhaps the topic most important to her, however, and the one that recurs most frequently in her short fiction as well as her novels concerns the situation of women.

Particularly interesting are the physical characteristics of Corelli's feminine ideal: her heroines are virtually always small, delicate, and childlike, literary manifestations of the image she wished to project. Similarly, her fictional conceptions of gender roles generally reflect her complex personal experiences. For instance, several Corelli narratives, such as *The Master-Christian: A Question of the Time* (1900) and "Nehemiah P. Hoskins, Artist" from *Cameos,* betray her obsession with tales of female artists whose works are deliberately undervalued or even stolen by less gifted men. Her constant sparring with reviewers could account for her interest in this theme, yet the treachery of her half brother, Eric Mackay, provided the real impetus for these particular works. Mackay, a self-indulgent man entirely supported by Corelli's earnings for the fifteen years prior to his death in 1898, allowed rumors to circulate that he was the author of her best books. Pained by these lies, Corelli later used him as a model for several deceitful and untalented male characters who prey on female artists of genius. In these stories her bitterness toward not only Mackay but also men in general comes through clearly.

More often, though, the correlation between Corelli's life and fiction is less specific, and her renderings of gender roles are less predictable. Her depictions of women are complex and contradictory, revealing her as an epitome of turn-of-the-century attempts both to repudiate and to support Victorian versions of femininity. On the one hand, she was an unconventional woman for her time and had a personal stake in the positive representation of women like her. Self-supporting and unmarried, she was sensitive to criticism aimed at her professional skills or her spinsterhood. The abuse she endured at the hands of the male literary establishment only led her to reaffirm her own talents and to claim for herself, and a minority of women with similar qualities, an intellectual position equal to or even superior to that of men. She also adamantly insisted that she was content as a single woman: when, in 1906, Emil Reich implied in a public lecture that Corelli was an old maid, she responded vehemently in a 25 February letter to her agent, saying that "if Reich is a specimen of manhood, my single estate is truly blessed." Her need to validate her lifestyle expressed itself in frequent characterizations of single women who lead happy, productive lives and in narrative asides concerning the joys of the single life and intellectual attainment. For example, the unmarried female scientist in "The Stepping Star," collected in *The Love of Long Ago*, explains to a horrified male companion that she remains single because her married friends are miserable, reinforcing her sense that her solitary life of study is preferable: "Some of [my married women friends] are physical wrecks – some have children who are the misery and despair of their lives – and all have lost the illusion of 'love' which first captivated their fancy. *My* [scientific inquiry] keeps me in good health at any rate, and gives me happiness and freedom – so there is something to be said for it."

On the other hand, Corelli's narratives also betray her loyalty to the Victorian ideal of passive femininity. The superficial self-possession of her heroines – usually marked by some combination of professional achievement, financial independence, and unmarried status – is persistently undermined by their determination not to compromise their positions as proper ladies. Even those female characters who are blatantly abused by men are too well bred to indulge in spiteful retaliation or even a healthy display of anger. The female artist whose works have been unjustly claimed by a man in "Nehemiah P. Hoskins, Artist," for instance, sanctions the continuation of her exploitation and argues that the money she receives from her oppressor enables her to maintain her quiet life at home, making her "happier than she thinks she is likely to be as an art 'celebrity.'" She is a typical Corelli heroine because she embodies the problematic combination of superior attainments and a completely submissive nature. Corelli's works reveal her constant efforts to reconcile the Victorian ideal – with which she was raised of woman as domestic goddess – with a newer, twentieth-century version of independent womanhood more in keeping with her personal experience. Yet her intrusive discourses on the happiness of unmarried life cannot wholly conceal her sentimental nostalgia for old-fashioned femininity. As a result, her fiction seems to offer a feminist surface without really challenging the Victorian status quo for women. Such inconsistency may frustrate modern readers but probably appealed to many of her female fans, who saw reflected in her books the same conflicts and contradictions with which they struggled in their more mundane lives.

At least half of Corelli's short stories address issues of gender in some way. Typical patterns can be seen in her last collection, *The Love of Long Ago;* most often a woman is unjustly rebuffed or even abused by a man, yet her superior moral nature allows her to rise above such treatment. A particularly dramatic instance of this basic pattern is seen in "The Sculptor's Angel," in which a monk initiates a sexual relationship with a young peasant girl, who drowns herself when he ultimately repents of his lust and rejects her. Later, as the monk sculpts an angel for the abbey chapel, he realizes that his statue has mystically taken the form of the abused girl, who speaks to him and forgives him just prior to his dramatic death upon completion of the work. Until his final moment of repentance the monk had unjustly blamed the girl for his own sin, "as Adam urged before him." The narrator adds, "So will men, in their pitiless egotism, argue in their own defense till time shall be no more."

Other stories in this collection similarly stress the degradation and chauvinism of men and the superior nature of women. In "Claudia's Business," for instance, Corelli presents for ridicule a male character who perceives the ideal woman as "half-drudge, half-toy – devoted to the interests of her sovereign ruler, Man!" In "Why She Was Glad" readers are told that a good woman need not be ashamed when she fails to lament the death of a tyrannical and abusive husband, while the heroine of "The Stepping Star" proclaims that "the meaning of Christianity and the ultimate goal of all science" is the "uplifting of Man through the purity of Woman." Yet overall Corelli's views of relations between the sexes were neither so simplistic nor so radical as these stories might suggest, and her indignation was not reserved solely for men who fail to appreciate and nurture women. She was equally infuriated by women who in her view refused to accept their natural roles as moral beacons and obliging companions. Her fictional heroines, often bright and engaging, are also uniformly virtuous and sweet, and she railed throughout her works against women who participated in "inappropriate activities," such as riding bicycles. She was also a lifelong opponent of women's suffrage, partly because she associated it with what she saw as the "unladylike" behavior of suffragettes.

Apparently Corelli cherished the idea of a more traditional female role for herself as well. From 1906 to 1917 she was engaged in a tempestuous relationship with painter Arthur Severn, her neighbor and the object of her unrequited love. Her initial relations with Severn and his wife, Joan Rus-

Bertha Vyver, Corelli's lifetime companion, dressed for a costume ball

The relationship, known at the time to few, reveals her emotional neediness and the deep schism that existed between her public and private selves. Outwardly she was haughtily certain of virtually everything; inside, however, she was desperately insecure, as many of her letters to Severn indicate. In addition, her overtures to a happily married man at a late point in both their lives (when they met, Severn was sixty-four and Corelli fifty-one) suggest that she was virtually starved for romantic, if not sexual, love. Biographers and critics have observed that, despite her exaggerated affectation of modesty, her fiction is filled with sensational love scenes that are unself-consciously titillating. Similarly, while Corelli insisted to both Severn and his wife that her affection for him was purely platonic, her private journal records poetry of great sexual intensity.

Although Corelli remained single her life was not entirely without intimacy, as she shared her life and home for almost fifty years with Bertha Vyver. During Corelli's lifetime and beyond there were occasional rumors of a lesbian relationship between the women, but there is little evidence to support this. Instead, it seems that the amiable Vyver was simply a sincere friend and warm supporter, providing Corelli with a loving stability that is remarkable given the notorious difficulty of her personality. Corelli's will was intended to provide handsomely for Vyver, but because of the author's dwindled fortune and certain miscalculations on her part regarding the potential sale value of her manuscripts, Vyver died in poverty in 1942.

Corelli can best be understood as a phenomenon of popular culture. By literary standards she was not a good writer, and she did not even possess the skill of commercial writers who respond to the demands of the market. In fact, Corelli worked in precisely the opposite way: she wrote what she felt, trusting that her audience would share her particular combination of passions, prejudices, and dreams. While she never achieved literary acclaim, she has repeatedly attracted the notice of serious readers who have attempted to characterize the nature of her peculiar talent. Leonard Woolf, for instance, wrote of the "passionate conviction with which [Corelli's books] are written," and Rebecca West acknowledged her "demoniac vitality." Indeed, Corelli's unflagging enthusiasm for embracing any and all topical issues, reflected in the voracious appetites of a newly emerging mass culture, largely ensured her immense success. Her works, while they reveal a great deal about the idiosyncratic concerns and opinions of their creator, per-

kin Severn, were amicable, but Corelli's eagerness for friends and her obvious infatuation with Severn led to intrusive efforts for his attention. She pestered Joan constantly about her husband's health and even renovated part of Mason Croft as a studio for Severn so he could work in peace – which proved to be virtually impossible with Corelli constantly in attendance. When he was not at Mason Croft she wrote him daily, frequently using embarrassing baby talk. Initially he was amused by her affectations, but he soon found her jealous outbursts and attempts to monopolize his time tedious, and their relations took on a sour tone. Throughout the decade or so of their "affair" Corelli kept a journal that records in poetry her intense pain during those years. She also wrote a thinly disguised account of the relationship, *Open Confession to a Man from a Woman* (1924), prepared and published posthumously by Vyver, which dramatizes both the distress and the festering bitterness wrought in Corelli by her association with Severn.

haps tell even more about the culture that eagerly devoured them.

Interview:

Arthur H. Lawrence, "Illustrated Interview with Miss Marie Corelli," *Strand,* 16 (July 1898): 17–26.

Biographies:

Kent Carr, *Marie Corelli* (London: Drane, 1901);

Thomas F. G. Coates and R. S. Warren-Bell, *Marie Corelli: The Writer and the Woman* (London: Hutchinson, 1903);

Bertha Vyver, *Memoirs of Marie Corelli* (London: Alston Rivers, 1930);

George Bullock, *Marie Corelli: The Life and Death of a Best-Seller* (London: Constable, 1940);

Eileen Bigland, *Marie Corelli: The Woman and the Legend* (London: Jarrolds, 1953);

William Stuart Scott, *Marie Corelli: The Story of a Friendship* (London: Hutchinson, 1955);

Brian Masters, *Now Barabbas Was a Rotter: The Extraordinary Life of Marie Corelli* (London: Hamilton, 1978).

References:

Q. D. Leavis, *Fiction and the Reading Public* (London: Chatto & Windus, 1932);

Rebecca West, *The Strange Necessity: Essays and Reviews* (London: Cape, 1928; Garden City, N.Y.: Doubleday, Doran, 1928);

Leonard Woolf, "The World of Books," *Nation and Atheneum,* 36 (7 March 1925): 777.

Papers:

Most of Corelli's manuscripts are in private hands, although thousands of her letters are scattered in collections throughout the United States and the United Kingdom. The most significant of these are the letters to Arthur and Joan Severn housed at the University of Detroit library and those to George Bentley housed in the Beinecke Library at Yale University.

Sir Arthur Conan Doyle

(22 May 1859 – 7 July 1930)

Michael S. Helfand
University of Pittsburgh

See also the Doyle entries in *DLB 18: Victorian Novelists After 1885* and *DLB 70: British Mystery Writers, 1860–1919.*

BOOKS: *A Study in Scarlet* (London: Ward, Lock, 1888; Philadelphia: Lippincott, 1890);

The Mystery of Cloomber (London: Ward & Downey, 1889; New York: Fenno, 1896);

Micah Clarke (London: Longmans, Green, 1889; New York: Harper, 1889);

Mysteries and Adventures (London: Scott, 1890); republished as *The Gully of Bluemansdyke* (London: Scott, 1892); republished as *My Friend the Murderer and Other Mysteries and Adventures* (New York: Lovell, Coryell, 1893);

The Captain of the Polestar and Other Tales (London & New York: Longmans, Green, 1890);

The Firm of Girdlestone: A Romance of the Unromantic (London: Chatto & Windus, 1890; New York: Lovell, 1890);

The Sign of Four (London: Blackett, 1890; New York: Collier, 1891); republished as *The Sign of the Four; or, The Problem of the Sholtos* (Philadelphia: Lippincott, 1890);

The White Company (3 volumes, London: Smith, Elder, 1891; 1 volume, New York: Lovell, 1891);

The Doings of Raffles Haw (London, Paris & Melbourne: Cassell, 1892; New York: Lovell, Coryell, 1892);

The Adventures of Sherlock Holmes (London: Newnes, 1892; New York: Harper, 1892);

The Great Shadow (Bristol: Arrowsmith / London: Simpkin, Marshall, Hamilton, Kent, 1892; New York: Harper, 1893);

The Great Shadow and Beyond the City (Bristol: Arrowsmith / London: Simpkin, Marshall, Hamilton, Kent, 1893);

The Refugees: A Tale of Two Continents (3 volumes, London: Longmans, Green, 1893; 1 volume, New York: Harper, 1893);

Arthur Conan Doyle

Jane Annie; or, The Good Conduct Prize: A New and Original English Comic Opera, by Doyle and J. M. Barrie (London: Chappell, 1893);

The Memoirs of Sherlock Holmes (London: Newnes, 1894; New York: Harper, 1894);

An Actor's Duel and The Winning Shot (London: Dicks, 1894);

Round the Red Lamp: Being Facts and Fancies of Medical Life (London: Methuen, 1894; New York: Appleton, 1894);

The Parasite (London: Constable, 1894; New York: Harper, 1895);

The Stark Munro Letters (London: Longmans, Green, 1895; New York: Appleton, 1895);

The Exploits of Brigadier Gerard (London: Newnes, 1896; New York: Appleton, 1896);

Rodney Stone (London: Smith, Elder, 1896; New York: Appleton, 1896);

Uncle Bernac: A Memory of the Empire (London: Smith, Elder, 1897; New York: Appleton, 1897);

Sons of Action (London: Smith, Elder, 1898; New York: Doubleday & McClure, 1898);

The Tragedy of the Korosko (London: Smith, Elder, 1898); republished as *A Desert Drama: Being the Tragedy of the Korosko* (Philadelphia: Lippincott, 1898);

A Duet with an Occasional Chorus (London: Richards, 1899; New York: Appleton, 1899);

Hilda Wade: A Woman with Tenacity of Purpose, by Doyle and Grant Allen (London: Richards, 1900; New York & London: Putnam, 1900);

The Green Flag and Other Stories of War and Sport (London: Smith, Elder, 1900; New York: McClure, Phillips, 1900);

The Great Boer War (London: Smith, Elder, 1900; New York: McClure, Phillips, 1900);

The Immortal Memory (Edinburgh: Mitchell, 1901);

The Hound of the Baskervilles (London: Newnes, 1902; New York: McClure, Phillips, 1902);

The War in South Africa: Its Cause and Conduct (London: Smith, Elder, 1902; New York: McClure, Phillips, 1902);

Adventures of Gerard (London: Newnes, 1903; New York: McClure, Phillips, 1903);

A Duet (A Duologue) (London & New York: French, 1903);

The Return of Sherlock Holmes (London: Newnes, 1905; New York: McClure, Phillips, 1905);

The Fiscal Question: Treated in a Series of Three Speeches (Hawick: Henderson, 1905);

An Incursion into Diplomacy (London: Smith, Elder, 1906);

Sir Nigel (London: Smith, Elder, 1906; New York: McClure, Phillips, 1906);

The Story of Mr. George Edalji (London: Roberts, 1907); republished as *The Case of Mr. George Edalji* (Putney: Blake, 1907);

Through the Magic Door (London: Smith, Elder, 1907; New York: McClure, 1908);

The Croxley Master: A Great Tale of the Prize Ring (New York: McClure, Phillips, 1907);

Waterloo (London & New York: French, 1907);

Round the Fire Stories (London: Smith, Elder, 1908; New York: McClure, 1908);

The Crime of the Congo (London: Hutchinson, 1909; New York: Doubleday, Page, 1909);

Divorce Law Reform: An Essay (London: Divorce Law Reform Union, 1909);

Songs of the Road (London: Smith, Elder, 1911; Garden City, N.Y.: Doubleday, Page, 1911);

Why He Is Now in Favour of Home Rule (London: Liberal Publication, 1911);

The Last Galley: Impressions and Tales (London: Smith, Elder, 1911; Garden City, N.Y.: Doubleday, Page, 1911);

The Speckled Band: An Adventure of Sherlock Holmes (New York & London: French, 1912);

The Case of Oscar Slater (London, New York & Toronto: Hodder & Stoughton, 1912; New York: Hodder & Stoughton/Doran, 1913);

The Lost World (London, New York & Toronto: Hodder & Stoughton, 1912; New York: Hodder & Stoughton/Doran, 1912);

The Poison Belt (London, New York & Toronto: Hodder & Stoughton, 1913; New York: Hodder & Stoughton/Doran, 1913);

Great Britain and the Next War (Boston: Small, Maynard, 1914);

To Arms! (London: Hodder & Stoughton, 1914);

The German War (London, New York & Toronto: Hodder & Stoughton, 1914);

The Valley of Fear (London: Smith, Elder, 1915; New York: Doran, 1915);

A Visit to Three Fronts (London, New York & Toronto: Hodder & Stoughton, 1916; New York: Doran, 1916);

The British Campaign in France and Flanders, 6 volumes (London, New York & Toronto: Hodder & Stoughton, 1916–1920; New York: Doran, 1916–1920);

His Last Bow: Some Reminiscences of Sherlock Holmes (London: John Murray, 1917); republished as *His Last Bow: A Reminiscence of Sherlock Holmes* (New York: Doran, 1917);

The New Revelation (London, New York & Toronto: Hodder & Stoughton, 1918; New York: Doran, 1918);

Danger! and Other Stories (London: John Murray, 1918; New York: Doran, 1919);

The Vital Message (London, New York & Toronto: Hodder & Stoughton, 1919; New York: Doran, 1919);

The Guards Came Through and Other Poems (London: John Murray, 1919; New York: Doran, 1920);

Spiritualism and Rationalism (London: Hodder & Stoughton, 1920);

The Wanderings of a Spiritualist (London: Hodder & Stoughton, 1921; New York: Doran, 1921);

The Evidence for Fairies (New York: Doran, 1921);

The Coming of the Fairies (London, New York & Toronto: Hodder & Stoughton, 1922; New York: Doran, 1922);

The Poems of Sir Arthur Conan Doyle: Collected Edition (London: John Murray, 1922);

Tales of the Ring and Camp (London: John Murray, 1922); republished as *The Croxley Master and Other Tales of the Ring and Camp* (New York: Doran, 1925);

Tales of Pirates and Blue Water (London: John Murray, 1922); republished as *The Dealings of Captain Sharkey and Other Tales of Pirates* (New York: Doran, 1925);

Tales of Terror and Mystery (London: John Murray, 1922); republished as *The Black Doctor and Other Tales of Terror and Mystery* (New York: Doran, 1925);

Tales of Twilight and the Unseen (London: John Murray, 1922); republished as *The Great Keinplatz Experiment and Other Tales of Twilight and the Unseen* (New York: Doran, 1925);

Tales of Adventure and Medical Life (London: John Murray, 1922); republished as *The Man from Archangel and Other Tales of Adventure* (New York: Doran, 1925);

Tales of Long Ago (London: John Murray, 1922); republished as *The Last of the Legions and Other Tales of Long Ago* (New York: Doran, 1925);

The Case for Spirit Photography (London: Hutchinson, 1922; New York: Doran, 1923);

Our American Adventure (London, New York & Toronto: Hodder & Stoughton, 1923; New York: Doran, 1923);

Three of Them: A Reminiscence (London: John Murray, 1923);

Our Second American Adventure (London: Hodder & Stoughton, 1924; Boston: Little, Brown, 1924);

Memories and Adventures (London: Hodder & Stoughton, 1924; Boston: Little, Brown, 1924; revised, London: John Murray, 1930);

Psychic Experiences (London & New York: Putnam, 1925);

The Land of Mist (London: Hutchinson, 1926; New York: Doran, 1926);

The History of Spiritualism, 2 volumes (London, New York, Toronto & Melbourne: Cassell, 1926; New York: Doran, 1926);

Pheneas Speaks (London: Psychic Press and Bookshop, 1927; New York: Doran, 1927);

The Case-Book of Sherlock Holmes (London: John Murray, 1927; New York: Doran, 1927);

The Maracot Deep and Other Stories (London: John Murray, 1929; Garden City, N.Y.: Doubleday, Doran, 1929);

Our African Winter (London: John Murray, 1929);

The Edge of the Unknown (London: John Murray, 1930; New York: Putnam, 1930);

The Field Bazaar (London: Atheneum, 1934; Summit, N.J.: Pamphlet House, 1947);

The Professor Challenger Stories (London: John Murray, 1952);

The Crown Diamond: An Evening with Sherlock Holmes — A Play in One Act (New York: Privately printed, 1958);

Strange Studies from Life: Containing Three Hitherto Uncollected Tales (New York & Copenhagen: Candlelight Press, 1963);

The Best Science Fiction of Arthur Conan Doyle, edited by Charles G. Waugh and Martin H. Greenberg (Carbondale & Edwardsville: Southern Illinois University Press, 1981);

The Unknown Conan Doyle: Uncollected Stories, edited by John Michael Gibson and Richard Lancelyn Green (London: Secker & Warburg, 1982; Garden City, N.Y.: Doubleday, 1934);

Masterworks of Crime and Mystery, edited by Jack Tracy (New York: Dial, 1982);

The Unknown Conan Doyle: Essays on Photography, edited by Gibson and Green (London: Secker & Warburg, 1982; North Pomfret, Vt.: David & Charles, 1983);

The Illustrated Sherlock Holmes (New York: Potter, 1985).

PLAY PRODUCTIONS: *Jane Annie; or, The Good Conduct Prize,* by Doyle and J. M. Barrie, London, Savoy Theatre, 13 May 1893;

Foreign Policy, London, Terry's Theatre, 3 June 1893;

A Story of Waterloo, Bristol, Prince's Theatre, 21 September 1894;

Halves, Aberdeen, Scotland, Her Majesty's Theatre, 10 April 1899; London, Garrick Theatre, 10 June 1899;

Sherlock Holmes, by Doyle and William Gillette, London, Duke of York's Theatre, 12 June 1899;

Brigadier Gerard, London, Imperial Theatre, 3 March 1906;

The Fires of Fate, Liverpool, Shakespeare Theatre, 11 June 1909;

The House of Temperley, London, Adelphi Theatre, 11 February 1910;

A Pot of Caviare, London, Adelphi Theatre, 19 April 1910;

The Speckled Band, London, Adelphi Theatre, 4 June 1910;

The Crown Diamond, Bristol, Hippodrome, 2 May 1921.

Arthur Conan Doyle is best known for his short stories and novels about Sherlock Holmes, whom Jon L. Lellenberg describes in *The Quest for Sir Arthur Conan Doyle: Thirteen Biographies in Search of a Life* (1987) as "the most universally recognized fictional character of English literature." Even though Doyle wrote a large amount of historical fiction, science fiction, and stories of romance, war, sports, horror, and the supernatural, it is the phenomenal popularity of Holmes that has shaped the questions, problems, and projects of the people who have written about Doyle. His life may provide answers to these questions.

One can learn about Doyle's life from his autobiography, *Memories and Adventures* (1924; revised, 1930), which he wrote late in life and revised in the year of his death. He was born 22 May 1859 in Edinburgh, Scotland, the eldest son of Mary Foley Doyle and Charles Altamont Doyle. His paternal grandfather came from an impoverished Irish Catholic landowning family and as a young man had gone to England and achieved fame and prosperity as a political caricaturist. Doyle's father failed to achieve either fame or fortune, working most of his life as a poorly paid minor civil servant while suffering from epilepsy, alcoholism, and worsening bouts of depression. While Doyle was generous to his father in his autobiography, he was often bitter elsewhere about his father's emotional withdrawal and financial failures. His mother was the strength and center of the family, successfully sustaining and nurturing the family despite a life of poverty.

Doyle was her eldest and favorite son, and her early influence on him was profound. She wanted him to be a gentleman and passed on to him an obsessive concern with genealogy and a romantic conception of the feudal past. The tales of adventure, chivalry, and romance he heard from her as a child (such as Sir Walter Scott's novels) considerably shaped his ideals of behavior, his concept of the heroic, and the content and style of his historical fiction.

Beginning in 1869 Doyle was sent to Jesuit schools, Hodder and Stonyhurst, where he received an education consisting of authoritarian methods, corporal punishment, spartan living conditions, and the tedious study of Latin and Greek that left him hating the classics. His love of the feudal past did not extend to its educational methods or goals, but

he also played and enjoyed sports, an interest he sustained throughout his life.

In 1875 Doyle moved to another Jesuit institution, the Feldkirch School in Austria, where he spent a pleasant year studying German. He also lost his faith in orthodox Catholicism and Christianity in general. He particularly rejected, he wrote in his autobiography, "the uncompromising bigotry of Jesuit theology" because of his belief in the usefulness of reason and the methods of scientific inquiry.

Doyle's interest in science was probably sparked by a man he never mentions in his autobiography, Bryan Charles Waller. Only six years older than Doyle, Waller shared a house with the Doyles in 1875, admitted Charles Doyle to a nursing home, and provided a home for Mary Doyle for more than thirty years. Recent biographers have speculated that he was an important intellectual influence on Doyle, since he advised him on his education and tutored him for his medical examinations. Doyle probably resented Waller's assumption of a paternal role in his family, but the rest of the family maintained warm and close relations with him for the rest of his life.

For Doyle, the rejection of a specific faith and its theology led him to agnosticism rather than atheism. Recalling his crisis of faith in his autobiography, he reminds his readers that T. H. Huxley and Herbert Spencer as well as Charles Darwin, John Tyndall, and John Stuart Mill were the "chief philosophers" of the day, and his study of their work led him to doubt Christianity. He resolved to believe nothing without "positive proofs" or "definite demonstrations."

Like many at the time, Doyle believed in the inheritance of acquired characteristics first proposed by Jean-Baptiste Lamarck. In human beings, according to this theory, racial characteristics represented the sum of the physical and mental experiences passed on biologically to the living members of the race. Doyle's understanding of human psychology was also shaped by this theory. He believed that at birth the individual psyche possessed a collective unconscious made up of the mental habits and traits of one's ancestors. In his autobiography he remarks that a writer cannot "spin a character out of his own inner consciousness and make it really life-like unless he has some possibilities of that character within him," then quotes a poem of his describing "our multiplex personalities." Both his recognition of consciousness as many selves and his interpretation of them as racial memory are important for understanding his literary development. He wrote many stories in which contemporary English

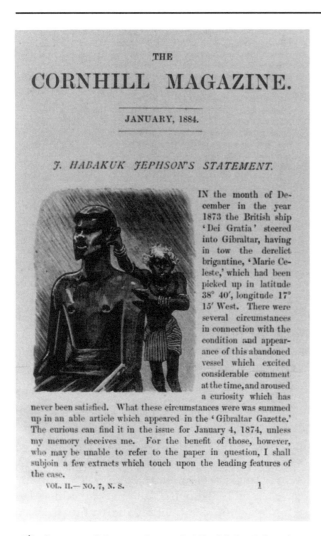

THE

CORNHILL MAGAZINE.

JANUARY, 1884.

J. HABAKUK JEPHSON'S STATEMENT.

IN the month of December in the year 1873 the British ship 'Dei Gratia' steered into Gibraltar, having in tow the derelict brigantine, 'Marie Celeste,' which had been picked up in latitude 38° 40', longitude 17° 15' West. There were several circumstances in connection with the condition and appearance of this abandoned vessel which excited considerable comment at the time, and aroused a curiosity which has never been satisfied. What these circumstances were was summed up in an able article which appeared in the 'Gibraltar Gazette.' The curious can find it in the issue for January 4, 1874, unless my memory deceives me. For the benefit of those, however, who may be unable to refer to the paper in question, I shall subjoin a few extracts which touch upon the leading features of the case.

VOL. II.— NO. 7, N. S.   1

The first page of the story that marked Doyle's breakthrough as a professional writer

characters recollect or reexperience a fragment of their consciousness from the past, and the general belief that the past remains alive in the present appears regularly as a theme in his fiction. For instance, in his favorite collection of stories, *The Last Galley: Impressions and Tales* (1911), he included a story, "Through the Veil" (1911), in which a contemporary Scottish couple briefly reexperience through dream and reawakened memory an incident involving their previous selves hundreds of years before.

In the mid 1890s August Weissmann disproved the theory of the inheritance of acquired characteristics, but many writers, including Doyle, continued to believe it. At the beginning of *The Lost World* (1912), for instance, Professor Challenger, Doyle's hero, has given a paper on "The Underlying Fallacy of Weissmannism," which is hotly contested at a conference of scientists in Vienna. Doyle

elsewhere shows his loyalty to this theory, which allowed him to believe in a spiritual reality and reject philosophical materialism. The possibility of supernatural reality, of the existence of the inexplicable, forms an important theme for his short fiction.

After his year at Feldkirch, Doyle returned to Edinburgh and lived in straitened circumstances with his family and Waller while he studied medicine, receiving his degree in 1881. At Edinburgh University he observed his teacher Joseph Bell, the man he claims provided the model for Holmes's methods. "After the study of such a character," he wrote in his autobiography, "I used and amplified his methods when in later life I tried to build up a scientific detective."

Doyle published his first short story, "The Mystery of Sasassa Valley," in *Chamber's Journal* in 1879. An action-adventure story with a first-person narrator — by far Doyle's favorite point of view — it involves a conflict between science and superstition in Africa. The Kaffirs up-country believe that a god with an evil eye casts a spell on the Sasassa Valley. The enlightened English lads Tom and Jack, the narrator, decide to ignore this superstition and explore the area. They discover, after a difficult trip, that the evil eye is really a diamond. The story ends happily since "we had certainly got possession of a jewel of great value; and with light hearts we turned from the valley bearing away with us the 'fiend' which had so long reigned there." The scientific perspective not only makes the boys rich, it frees the Kaffirs to use the valley. Western imperialism, benevolent and paternal, exercises its enlightenment for the benefit of the unenlightened Africans. The story is slight, interesting only because it shows that even in his earliest work Doyle dealt with the conflict of science and the supernatural. It is also typical of several of his earliest stories — including "Bones: The April Fool of Harvey's Sluice" (1882), "The Gully of Bluemansdyke" (1881), and "The American's Tale" (1880) — in being poorly crafted and derivative. Doyle later dismissed them in his autobiography as "feeble echoes of Bret Harte," and it is understandable why he left most of them uncollected. Readers may now find all these stories and many others in *The Unknown Conan Doyle: Uncollected Stories* (1982), edited by John Michael Gibson and Richard Lancelyn Green.

These stories share problems with Doyle's more accomplished efforts. Many modern critical readers would dismiss them because, as Don Richard Cox explains in *Arthur Conan Doyle* (1985), "there is no sub-text . . . to study. . . . There is essentially no covert theme to be teased out of the character and the action." The changing standards of readers account for the lack of interest in most of Doyle's fiction, which perhaps for this reason mainly appeals to those who read for the simple pleasures of action, thrills, and humor.

While still a student, in 1880 Doyle decided to sign on as a surgeon for the whaler *Hope,* which was hunting in Arctic waters. He drew on this experience to write some of his first tales of the supernatural, later collected in *The Captain of the Polestar and Other Tales* (1890). Shortly after returning from the voyage in 1881, he graduated from medical school and, short of funds, took a position as a doctor on a passenger ship bound for West Africa. When he returned he accepted an invitation to go into medical practice with a strange, flamboyant physician, George Budd, whom he had met while they were medical students in Edinburgh. Doyle describes Budd as "half genius and half quack" in the semi-autobiographical novel *The Stark Munro Letters* (1895). Budd's work was apparently unorthodox and verged on the criminal. He drew large crowds to his offices with offers of free consultations and used drugs excessively to achieve dramatic but dangerous results. He and Doyle practiced together in Plymouth for only four months because Budd secretly read a letter Doyle's mother wrote voicing disapproval of Budd's methods. He broke off the partnership, promising to support Doyle in a new practice. When he moved to Southsea, a suburb of Plymouth, in 1882, Budd refused to send the promised funds, and Doyle was left financially distressed but with experience he could use in fiction. *The Stark Munro Letters* uses this experience as the basis for a spiritual autobiography.

During these financially hard times Doyle maintained his honorable standards of behavior and his sense of humor. He steadfastly refused offers of help, financial or otherwise, from his Catholic relatives to establish his medical practice because he had left the church. After a lean first year in Southsea, when he earned and declared on his income-tax form only £154, the form was returned with the comment, "Most unsatisfactory." Doyle returned the form with the comment, "I entirely agree."

During the next seven years Doyle's medical practice failed to flourish. He continued to write and publish stories sporadically in various magazines, including *London Society, All the Year Round, Temple Bar,* and *The Boy's Own Paper.* His literary breakthrough came when James Payn, editor of the prestigious *Cornhill Magazine,* accepted "J. Habakuk Jephson's Statement" in 1884. "I was ceasing to be a hack writer and getting into good company," he wrote in his autobiography. The story, like some of Edgar Allan Poe's, masquerades as a nonfictional, first-person narrative, explaining the mysterious happenings on the ship *Mary Celeste.* It appeared anonymously and was taken by the advocate-general of Gibraltar as factual; he sent telegrams to major newspapers denouncing the story as "a fabrication" and followed it up with a written report to the government, which was also released to the press. Doyle considered this response a triumph of his art and began to devote more time to writing fiction than to his medical practice.

Doyle received his Master of Surgery degree in July 1885 and married Louise "Touie" Hawkins on 7 August 1885. They met when Doyle unsuccessfully tried to save her brother's life; he became close to the family during their mourning, and eventually he and she married. She contributed a small income, which allowed him to devote more time to his writing. Together they had two children, Mary Louise in 1889 and Kingsley in 1892, before she contracted tuberculosis. Doyle wrote little about his wife, but he said in his autobiography that "no man could have had a more gentle and amiable life's companion" and that throughout their life together their mutual affection remained intact.

Doyle's marriage marked a turning point in all areas of his life. In his bachelor days he lived, like Holmes, a bohemian existence and mainly attended to his medical work; after his marriage he enjoyed a more comfortable and stable home life. Philosophically he began a slow movement from agnosticism to a belief in the existence of a spiritual realm that had nothing to do with orthodox religions.

The first result of his intensified literary work was a novel, *The Firm of Girdlestone: A Romance of the Unromantic,* published in 1890. He had begun working on this "sensational book of adventure" in 1884 and finally finished it in 1886. Its setting is the University of Edinburgh, and the hero, Tom Dimsdale, bears some resemblance to the young Doyle. As Doyle admitted, the book is badly written and derivative. It is important, however, because it shows his growing interest in crime fiction.

During this period Doyle also wrote and published several Gothic tales of terror and mystery in which his heroes do not triumph over the supernatural, as they do in his earlier tales, but succumb to evil or ambiguous forces despite heroic efforts. Such stories as "The Captain of the 'Pole-star'" (*Temple Bar,* 1883), "John Barrington Cowles" (*Cassell's Saturday Journal,* 1884), "The Man from Archangel" (*London Society,* 1885), and "The Ring of Thoth"

(*Cornhill Magazine,* 1890) end with the madness or death of a hero who has become emotionally and intellectually obsessed with his love for a dead woman. In these stories women are sometimes untrustworthy, luring men to death and destruction, and sometimes simply part of a tragic tale of passion. The seeds of Holmes's misogyny may be seen in these stories, but other Doyle stories demonstrate no such attitudes. Indeed, in his later political activities he showed contradictory attitudes toward women's issues, favoring reforms in the divorce code but opposing women's suffrage.

Set on a whaling ship in the Arctic Ocean, "The Captain of the 'Pole-star' " tells of a captain, Nicholas Craigie, who is haunted by the specter of a woman he loved. She is in fact a siren who lures him farther and farther into the ice floes. Eventually the captain's obsession isolates him from his men, who occasionally hear the woman but cannot see her, as Craigie can. He abandons the ship to pursue her image, and the crew finds him frozen to death. But with the body they see the shape of a woman made from ice crystals and snow bending over to kiss the corpse. In this story, at least, the supernatural is not a delusion. There are clear echoes of Mary Shelley's *Frankenstein* (1818) in the story, including a self-destructive hero, a central character obsessed by love, and a trip to the Arctic.

A more interesting story is "The Man from Archangel." Doyle described it in *Memories and Adventures* as "perhaps as good honest work as I have ever done," and it constitutes a kind of reflection on and criticism of romantic obsession. It features two obsessed heroes: McVittie, a scientist, and Ourganeff, the captain of a ship and the doomed lover of a woman named Sophie. Both men disdain domesticity and the unheroic bourgeois life. McVittie, the misanthropic narrator, lives away from society and devotes himself to science. His solitude is disrupted when Ourganeff's ship is wrecked at sea and Sophie is washed up on the beach next to his cottage. The two men are clearly doubles, similar in appearance and in their fiery, obsessional temperaments, and they are aware of this when they meet. Ourganeff abducts Sophie, and they go off to their deaths in a storm. McVittie's misanthropic attitude ceases because of his experience with the doomed couple. He becomes more sympathetic to human problems and feelings and recognizes that his scientific work should serve human needs. The story echoes Thomas Carlyle's injunction "Close thy Byron, open thy Goethe" by rejecting self-destructive passion in favor of practical work for humanity. McVittie the scientist becomes the model for the de-

tective, turning his passion for knowledge to the solution of practical problems. However, the scientist, and later the detective, does not deny the reality of metaphysics and passion. McVittie accepts the reality of the spirit and learns from it but limits his research to the practical, empirical realm.

Around 1884 Doyle began writing detective fiction. He did not invent the form, though admiring critics argue that he reinvented it. He was influenced by the earlier detective fiction of Poe, Emile Gaboriau, Charles Dickens, and Wilkie Collins. He was also fascinated by the dramatic flair and deductive method of Bell, his teacher at Edinburgh University.

In one of his early detective stories – "The Recollections of Captain Wilkie" (1895), first published in *Chamber's Journal* – Doyle features a medical narrator. His style and methods are clearly those of Sherlock Holmes: "I did not feel quite satisfied even then with my deduction. However, as a leading question would – to pursue my chemical analogy – act as my litmus paper, I determined to try one." What is missing from the story is a Watson, the medical narrator whose common sense hides the thoughts of the great deducer and keeps him a man of mystery. In this story the man of mystery is the criminal the doctor meets on a train. Rather unrealistically, Captain Wilkie tells the doctor of his life of crime as a fake and a cracksman who enjoys the stories about him. What is most interesting about the story is Wilkie's comparison of the lives of the criminal and the artist. Crime, he insists, is the "triumph of intellect over brute force," and a good cracksman, he claims, is as much concerned with the originality of his plans and the perfection of their execution as he is with getting the jewels: "It is not the mere jewels or plate, you know. . . . The neatness of the job and his reputation for smartness are almost as important in his eyes." The story ends with Wilkie successfully stealing the doctor's purse but after a pang of conscience returning it.

Doyle first introduced Holmes in *A Study in Scarlet* in *Beeton's Christmas Annual* for 1887, but not before it was, much to his regret, rejected by James Payn and two other publishers. Surprisingly, it was neither a critical nor a popular success. Two years later an American editor, J. M. Stoddart, who liked the novel commissioned Doyle to write another Holmes novel, *The Sign of Four* (published in the United States as *The Sign of the Four*). The novel appeared in *Lippincott's* in February 1890, in the same issue as Oscar Wilde's *The Picture of Dorian Gray,* and from that point Holmes became his most successful creation.

Tennyson Road.
Nov 11 /91.

Dearest mam -

　　　I have done five of the
Sherlock Holmes stories of the new Series.
They are 1. The adventure of the Blue
Carbuncle 2. The Adventure of the Speckled
Band 3. The Adventure of the Noble
Bachelor 4 The Adventure of the Engineer's
Thumb 5. The Adventure of the Beryl
Coronet. I think that they are up to the
standard of the first series, & the
twelve ought to make a rather good
book of the sort. I think of slaying
Holmes in the sixth & winding him
up for good & all. He takes my mind
from better things. I think your golden
haired idea has the making of a tale
in it, but I think it would be better
not as a detective tale, but as a
separate one.

The first page of the letter in which Doyle tells his mother of his desire to kill his popular character Sherlock Holmes (from John Dickson Carr, The Life of Sir Arthur Conan Doyle, *1949)*

Doyle's primary passion, however, was not the crime story, which he considered mere entertainment. He wanted to write historical fiction because, he said in his autobiography, it combined "literary dignity" with "scenes of action and adventure." His growing success and financial stability allowed him to try a novel about Monmouth's Rebellion, *Micah Clarke* (1889). Written in three months, the novel achieved enough critical and popular success to encourage Doyle to begin researching and writing a second historical romance immediately.

Doyle put an enormous amount of effort into his historical novels in order to re-create times and events. Like other writers of historical fiction of the period he was influenced by Scott's novels, in Doyle's case the romances of chivalry, such as *Ivanhoe* (1819), rather than the more-realistic novels, such as *The Heart of Midlothian* (1818). But Doyle was also influenced by two popular historians, Thomas Babington Macaulay and Carlyle. Both held progressive views of history, and both glorified aspects of the Puritan revolution. Like Macaulay, Doyle accepted the Whig belief in political liberty and was fascinated by social history – the customs, clothing, manners, speech, and military technology of the periods he studied. *Micah Clarke* is based on incidents described in Macaulay's *History of England* (1849–1855). Like Carlyle, Doyle was interested in creating and celebrating heroes of British history.

Just before *The Sign of Four* appeared Doyle published two other novels, *The Mystery of Cloomber* (1889) and his early project *The Firm of Girdlestone*. By 1891 he had finished his second historical romance, *The White Company,* his favorite novel and the one he hoped would be remembered. The book was a popular success, eventually going through more than fifty printings, and he became momentarily depressed because with this book he felt he had said all he had to say.

For a while Doyle planned to return to medicine, and in 1890 he went to Vienna and Paris to train as an eye specialist. He returned to London with his family in March 1891, became critically ill with pneumonia, saw no eye patients, and determined to make his living by writing. Then he wrote and sold six Sherlock Holmes short stories to the *Strand* for thirty-five pounds each. All six were enormously popular, and the editors begged for more. Because he did not want to write more, Doyle asked for fifty pounds per story, assuming the editors would demur – but they did not. He wrote six more stories, which with the first six were published in book form as *The Adventures of Sherlock Holmes* (1892).

By this time Doyle was immersed in literary London and writing another historical novel, this time about the Napoleonic Wars, called *The Refugees: A Tale of Two Continents* (1893). His nascent friendship with J. M. Barrie also encouraged him to try his hand at writing drama. Once he collaborated with Barrie on an opera, *Jane Annie; or, The Good Conduct Prize* (1893), which failed miserably. He also began to write a successful series of comic tales about the exploits of a French colonel, Etienne Gerard, during and after the Napoleonic Wars. Doyle wanted nothing more to do with Holmes and had even mentioned to his mother that he would kill him off in the last story sold to the *Strand*. She urged against the execution, and he reluctantly complied. Again the editor of the *Strand* bothered him for more Holmes stories; again, imagining that he would be refused, he offered to write a dozen for one thousand pounds, and again he was accepted. After finishing *The Great Shadow* (1892) – yet another novel on the Napoleonic Wars, a subject that obsessed both Doyle and his mother – he began to write the stories, which appeared in the *Strand* between December 1892 and November 1893 and were collected as *The Memoirs of Sherlock Holmes* (1894). Despite his mother's earlier objections, Doyle resolved to end his hero's life in the last of these commissioned stories, "The Final Problem," primarily because he feared, as he noted in his autobiography, that he would be "entirely identified with what I regarded as a lower stratum of literary achievement." When the story was published the public response amazed him, and he finally learned how real Holmes had become to the reading public. The attachment of the reading public to this character was so great that twenty thousand subscriptions to the *Strand* were canceled when readers learned that Professor Moriarty and Holmes had supposedly tumbled into the Reichenbach Falls. People went into mourning. Letters were sent to Holmes (and sometimes Watson) via Doyle, requesting that he solve mysteries or offering to keep house for him when he retired. Doyle also received hate mail to "protest against my summary execution of Holmes." In fact, an organization called the Baker Street Irregulars is dedicated to carrying on the pretense of Holmes's actual existence.

The popularity of the stories is due in part to Watson, Holmes's perfect Boswell and a flattering surrogate for the reader: he is brave, loyal, and always part of the action. Watson's solidity makes Holmes believable, while his lack of intuition keeps Holmes's mental activities mysterious. As Doyle pointed out in his autobiography, what fascinated him and others about his teacher Bell was the drama of his diagnostic method: "To his audience of Watsons it all seemed very miraculous until it was explained, and then it became simple enough." The effect, of course, was created not by the empirical method of explanation but by asserting the conclusions before the explanation. But there was more to Bell's method than this dramatic trick; Bell, said Doyle, had an "eerie trick of spotting details" that transcended his analytic skill. Doyle said it was this process that he later "used and amplified" in writing his stories. Holmes's genius lies in his intuitive ability to choose the relevant facts as well as in his analysis of them. It is precisely his intuitive ability that shines forth in the often-cited moment when he identifies the crucial clue as the absence of a dog's bark in "The Adventure of Silver Blaze" (1892).

Holmes reaffirms his audience's faith in the practical value of the scientific method and, symbolically at least, confirms its sense of security and justice in the modern world. At the same time, Doyle always insisted upon the ultimately mysterious power of Holmes's intuition in the solution of his cases. Nothing demonstrates this better than Holmes's left-handed compliment to Watson in "A Case of Identity" (1891): " 'Pon my word, Watson, you are coming along wonderfully. You have really done very well indeed. It is true that you have missed everything of importance, but you have hit upon the method."

Holmes is a hero who embodies the qualities of the romantic genius and the scientist, an elitist and nonconformist who defends the common and respectable members of society. Holmes may not have Superman's powers, but he is for London what Superman is for Metropolis, a benign presence who reassures all levels of society that the good are protected and the wicked will not prevail. A man of contemplation and action, his ethical purity allows him to break the law and dispense justice without benefit of the courts. He is a mythical hero who resolves in his character and actions many of the contradictions of late-Victorian society, and his stories combine the entertainment of adventure and magic with a gentle introduction to the wonders of the scientific method.

Holmes also combines qualities of the heroes from Doyle's Gothic and chivalric tales. He is often as eccentric, secretive, and obsessive as the heroes of Gothic fiction, but he is also a man of action who lives by the chivalric code. Doyle's public could more easily identify with the unsystematic intellectual omnivore, urban bohemian, practical scientist,

and moody bachelor recluse than with his heroes from preindustrial times.

Despite his dislike for Holmes, Doyle resurrected him – in a purely rational way, of course – in 1902, explaining that he was never really dead but working underground. In the intervening years Doyle was able to exercise his imagination in new directions as he became one of the richest and most famous writers of his age. But as his professional life blossomed, he had to deal with loss and illness in his family. His father, institutionalized since 1875, finally died in 1893. Shortly afterward his wife contracted the tuberculosis that made her an invalid and eventually caused her death in 1906.

In 1893 Doyle moved the family to Switzerland, where his wife's health improved. There he wrote *The Stark Munro Letters;* introduced skiing, which he had learned in Norway, to the Swiss; and continued to write stories about Brigadier Gerard. He also made an enormously successful reading tour in the United States, where he met Rudyard Kipling, then living in Vermont.

While the clamor for more Holmes stories continued, Doyle finished and published *The Exploits of Brigadier Gerard* (1896), which continued his interest in stories of military action and romance during the Napoleonic Wars. As in his serious historical fiction, his settings are accurate, based on historical research. Gerard is based on a real French soldier, General Baron de Marbot. He is brave in battle, getting into scrapes because he takes on seemingly impossible military assignments and carries them off by the skin of his teeth. He is honorable and chivalrous to his opponents and to women in distress who, in the quiet after the storm, often succumb to his charm and strength. But Gerard is also a comic buffoon. He tells his own stories and frequently boasts of his bravery as well as his military and amorous successes. He engages at times in absurdly brave pranks, and he clearly plays on British patriotic sentiments and their stereotypes of French men and common soldiers. The stories were so popular that Doyle produced a second volume, *Adventures of Gerard* (1903).

Though the stories are based on reality, they are nevertheless extraordinary in their plots. They begin with Gerard's earliest exploits and end with his last military duty. In *The Exploits of Brigadier Gerard* Gerard is introduced at age twenty-five in "How the Brigadier Came to the Castle of Doom." He is already known as the best horseman and swordsman in ten regiments of hussars. He joins a young soldier named Duroc in search of Jean Carabin, a radical of the French Revolution who killed

Duroc's father, destroyed his mother, and became the Baron Straubenthal. Arriving at the Castle of Doom, the Baron's home, Duroc and Gerard call out the villain and ask for satisfaction. He tricks them into dungeon confinement, from which they escape. In a sword fight between Duroc and the Baron the Baron succeeds until Gerard steps in to save the day. The Baron has a shamefully mistreated stepdaughter, and upon his demise she falls in love with Duroc, who eventually marries her.

In another story, "How the Brigadier Held the King," Gerard is recuperating from a wound and is anxious to return to battle. He takes a coach to Spain that is waylaid by Spanish bandits. Gerard is captured, taken to their mountain hideaway, and threatened with torture and death. Just before he is to be roasted over an open fire, Gerard is rescued by an English officer and carried back to the British army camp. There Gerard, knowing the officer's love of gambling, wagers for his freedom in a card game. He holds a king in the crucial game and wins his freedom, only to have the Duke of Wellington interpose at the last moment and send him off to prison in England. In the following story, "How the King Held the Brigadier," Gerard manages to escape from prison and steal a cloak containing a letter addressed to the head of the prison. Gerard outfoxes the search party by staying close to the prison, but eventually he needs food and water, and he wanders into the home of the local boxing champion who manages to hold him until the prison authorities retrieve him. Gerard chivalrously offers the warden the letter he found, and it turns out to be an order to release Gerard, who has been traded to the French for a captured English officer.

In *Adventures of Gerard* Gerard is older but no wiser. For instance, in "How the Brigadier Lost His Ear" Gerard has foolishly seduced Lucia, who was engaged to the son of the doge of Venice. Gerard is thrown into a cell next to Lucia, who is sentenced to have her ear cut off. Gerard manages to slip into her cell; he impersonates her and has his ear removed instead. Just as he is discovered the French forces storm the cells, and Gerard is released. In "How the Brigadier Slew the Fox" Gerard watches the British prepare for a foxhunt during a lull in a battle with the French. Gerard decides that he will put on a British uniform and take part in the hunt. He does so and manages to outdo the British at their own game. Naturally, when the British discover he is a French officer and an enemy, they cheer his great act of sportsmanship and daring.

Other stories are more military in character, such as "How the Brigadier Bore Himself at Water-

loo," but they are no more realistic. The mixture of chivalrous heroics and comic high jinks was no doubt appealing to British readers with ambiguous feelings about a French hero. Certainly they would admire his bravery, but his overly amorous nature, an English stereotype of the French, often makes him look and act foolish.

This double attitude, however, is not a major problem in a comic tale. Gerard was one of Doyle's most popular characters, and Cox calls the Gerard stories "Doyle's best Napoleonic fiction." In another historical novel of the Napoleonic period, *Uncle Bernac: A Memory of the Empire* (1897), Doyle's ambiguous feelings for the French and especially for Napoleon, a brilliant and brave man and yet a threat to the British, create major aesthetic flaws. Gerard appears as a minor character in this novel, which was Doyle's least favorite work.

During this period Doyle wrote and published a collection of stories about doctors, *Round the Red Lamp: Being Facts and Fancies of Medical Life* (1894). Like *The Stark Munro Letters,* these stories are loosely based on his own medical practice and experience. The stories vary considerably in tone from comic to starkly realistic, but the book includes some of his best short fiction. Some, such as "Behind the Times" (1894) and "A Straggler of '15" (1891), first published in *Black and White,* are portraits of people who are old and old-fashioned. In "Behind the Times" he contrasts brusque, scientific young doctors with the old-fashioned, gentle Doctor Winter, who has a talent for healing. "A Straggler of '15" features a common soldier from the Napoleonic Wars who had one great moment of military heroism but is now poor and physically decrepit. He is visited by a young doctor who cares for him and by a young member of his regiment, the only people who have not forgotten him. The story is sentimental but is saved from mawkishness by the comic-grotesque behavior of the old soldier.

Another kind of story might be called clinical realism. In "The Third Generation" (1894) a young aristocrat visits a physician because he is about to marry and knows that his family suffers from a "constitutional and hereditary taint" caused by the sinful behavior of his grandfather. The sins, he says, have been passed on to his father and to him, an example of the inheritance of acquired characteristics. He wonders if he should take the chance and marry the woman he deeply loves. The doctor advises against it and reads later that the man has committed suicide. In "The Curse of Eve" (1894) a husband suffers intolerably when his wife gives birth. To the doctors attending, the problems are routine, while to the husband they are extraordinary, and he is angry and upset by the doctors' apparent nonchalance. A particularly chilling example of this kind of story is "A Medical Document" (1894), in which a doctor tells of seeing a sickly and deformed child in a crib. He is expecting to treat a baby and looks into the crib:

> The head on the pillow turned, and I saw a face looking up at me which seemed to me to have more malignancy and wickedness than ever I had dreamed of in a nightmare. It was the flush of red over the cheek-bones, and the brooding eyes full of loathing of me, and of everything else, that impressed me. I'll never forget my start as, instead of the chubby face of an infant, my eyes fell upon this creature. I took the mother into the next room. 'What is it?' I asked. 'A girl of sixteen,' said she, and then throwing up her arms, 'Oh, pray God she may be taken!'

Such stories recall contemporary realistic portraits of the London poor. Toward the end of the story the doctors who have been relating odd, scary, and weird experiences turn to the third doctor, who has been taking notes. They wonder why: " 'We've done nothing but talk shop,' says the general practitioner. 'What possible interest can the public take in that?' "

In *Round the Red Lamp* there are also tales of comic misunderstanding, a tale of the courtship of two doctors that ends unhappily, and tales dwelling on the unlimited possibilities for strangeness in a post-Darwinian world. In "Lot 249" (*Harper's Monthly Magazine*, 1892), a story of murder and madness at Oxford University, the narrator announces a theme that dominates much of Doyle's later fiction: "Yet when we think how devious this path of Nature is, how dimly we can trace it, for all our lamps of science, and how from the darkness which girds it round great and terrible possibilities loom ever shadowly upwards, it is a bold and confident man who will put a limit to the strange by-paths into which the human spirit may wander." The same theme is realized in comic form in "The Los Amigos Fiasco" (1896), a fantasy about the attempt to execute a man by electrocution. Rather than killing him, the electricity makes him so strong that he is able to live through attempts to hang and shoot him.

Doyle returned to England in 1895 when he learned that his wife's tuberculosis could be kept under control in Surrey. Since both wanted to return, he had a house built at Hindhead. Then he returned to Switzerland, where he wrote *Rodney Stone* (1896), a fine novel about boxing set in the time of

An illustration by Sidney Paget for Doyle's "The Final Problem," published in The Strand Magazine *(July–December 1893)*

the Regency. By this time he was so famous that he earned £5,500 in advances for the serial rights and book publication.

Doyle also wrote a few stories about sports, which he, like many Victorians, associated with war. "The Croxley Master" (1899), published in *The Strand Magazine,* is an often-reprinted tale typical of his attitude toward sports since it celebrates prizefighting and its culture. The plot is simple: Montgomery, a young medical student working for a stingy and puritanical doctor, is short of the cash he needs to finish his professional training. He floors the local boxing champion in a brawl and is prevailed upon by miners to represent them in a match against the cagey, old, and powerful Croxley Master, who represents the neighboring town. The rest of the story describes, with all the skill of a seasoned ring reporter, the bout and Montgomery's victory. Doyle handles the working-class dialect well and sprinkles the story with amusing minor characters, including the aggressive, red-haired mistress of the Croxley Master, who knocks Montgomery unconscious after he wins the bout. Montgomery is, like all Doyle's heroes, chivalrous, physically powerful, intelligent, brave, and decent, a man who respects and is respected by people of all classes. His opposite is his employer, a selfish, weak, religious hypocrite more concerned with respectability than social responsibility or Christian charity. But the interest of the story is in the action, especially in the description of the boxing match itself.

After he finished *Rodney Stone,* the Doyles visited Egypt, and shortly thereafter Doyle returned as a correspondent from the *Westminster Gazette* to cover the early phases of Horatio Herbert Kitchener's campaign to capture the Sudan. In the spring of 1896 the Doyles returned to England, and Doyle wrote *Uncle Bernac* in Surrey while waiting for Undershaw, the home he ordered, to be completed.

In 1897 Doyle met Jean Leckie, the twenty-four-year-old woman who would become his second wife. According to Doyle they fell in love immediately, saw each other often, and wrote to each other almost daily but kept the relationship a secret from everyone, except Doyle's mother, as long as Doyle's wife was alive. It was perhaps Doyle's chance to live out the courtly ideal of love: passion and devotion without consummation. Yet the relationship made his busy and complicated life even more complex, and he admitted to his mother that maintaining the platonic relationship was a strain.

In the same year the Doyles moved into Undershaw he tried his hand at a play featuring Sherlock Holmes. Eventually it was performed in the United States, with William Gillette acting the part of Holmes, with such success and popularity that he was identified with the role for the rest of his life. Doyle also wrote a domestic novel, *A Duet with an Occasional Chorus* (1899), which was not a popular success, and a series of twelve stories for the *Strand,* later collected as *Round the Fire Stories* (1908). These stories, among the finest Doyle wrote, and favorites among Doyle aficionados, have little in common save an interest in the grotesque and the terrible. One of the best known is a brilliantly told tale of sheer terror, "The Brazilian Cat" (1898), in which the narrator visits his rich cousin, who owns a black puma. The cousin lures the narrator into a room with the cat, which tries unsuccessfully to kill him. The narrator escapes with an injury when the cousin opens the door and the maddened cat attacks and kills him.

Another story of the same type is "The Beetle Hunter" (1898), in which a doctor is invited for a weekend visit to talk with an aristocrat who is an expert on beetles. The expert, it turns out, is also a homicidal maniac, and the doctor was invited to serve as a witness to his madness and criminality. Other stories, such as "The Lost Special" (1898) and "The Man with the Watches" (1898), are closer to detective stories. Seemingly impossible crimes are committed, and only at the very end are explanations offered for the mysterious events. Doyle is at the top of his form here as an entertainer.

With the exception of the later Holmes stories and some science-fiction stories, including the Professor Challenger series, these stories were among Doyle's last major fictional projects. Having become the most popular writer of fiction since Charles Dickens, he turned his attention primarily to nonfiction and drama. Some of his nonfiction developed from his experiences in the Boer War, which began in 1899. Doyle volunteered to serve, although he was forty years old. He was rejected but managed to see action as a physician. After the war he wrote a history, *The Great Boer War* (1900), and a defense of the actions of British soldiers, *The War in South Africa: Its Cause and Conduct* (1902). For this work he was knighted at the coronation of Edward VII in August 1902.

In 1900 Doyle ran for a seat in Parliament as a Liberal Unionist (opposing Irish independence) and lost by an unexpectedly small margin. In the same year the *Strand* began the serialization of *The Hound of the Baskervilles,* featuring Holmes in a novel with supernatural aspects later explained rationally. Possibly, having achieved the literary fame he desired, Doyle no longer feared the popularity of his most famous creation. Furthermore, despite his success, his mood had grown dark, no doubt because of his wife's lingering illness, his failure in politics, and his prolonged and frustrating relationship with Leckie. Perhaps he hoped to bring back happier days by returning to his famous detective.

Again Doyle was besieged by demands for more Holmes stories. Finally, offered $5,000 per story by the American magazine *Collier's Weekly* and half as much by the *Strand* for the English rights, Doyle wrote a series of thirteen stories, which began serial publication in 1903 and appeared in book form as *The Return of Sherlock Holmes* (1905). When the first story of the series, "The Adventure of the Empty House," appeared, people lined up for blocks to buy the magazine, and the series was commercially a wild success. Many readers believe these stories are not as good as those in the first two collections, but Doyle did not agree. Having brought Holmes back, he allowed him to flourish in

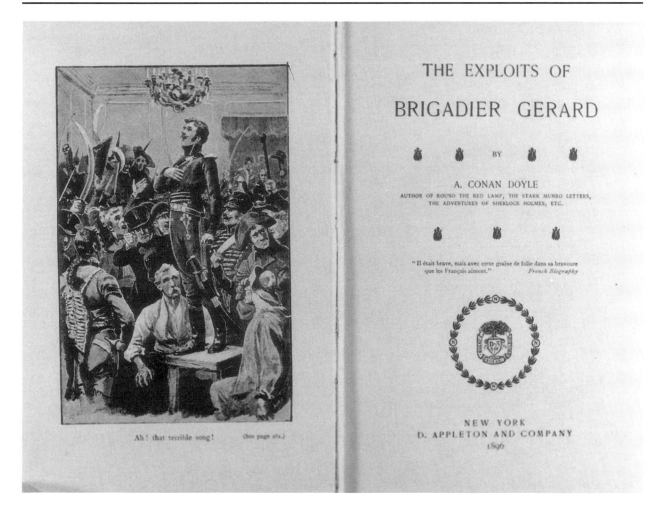

THE EXPLOITS OF

BRIGADIER GERARD

BY

A. CONAN DOYLE

AUTHOR OF ROUND THE RED LAMP, THE STARK MUNRO LETTERS,
THE ADVENTURES OF SHERLOCK HOLMES, ETC.

"Il était brave, mais avec certe graine de folie dans sa bravoure
que les Français aiment."   *French Biography*

NEW YORK
D. APPLETON AND COMPANY
1896

Ah! that terrible song!   (See page 262.)

*Frontispiece and title page for the American edition of the first collection of Doyle's stories featuring a French soldier in the
Napoleonic Wars*

two further collections, *His Last Bow: Some Reminis-cences of Sherlock Holmes* (1917) and *The Case-Book of Sherlock Holmes* (1927), gathering stories originally published in the *Strand* between 1908 and 1927, and a novel, *The Valley of Fear* (1915).

The differences between the later works and the earlier stories are primarily in the character of Holmes. In them he is more even-tempered, more interested in culture and the fine arts, and surer of himself. Holmes remains the practical problem solver and the protector of all good people, but he also remains, like Carlyle's heroes of action, ready to break or ignore the law if he feels it is justified. This characteristic is most obvious in "The Adventure of Charles Augustus Milverton" (1904), in which Holmes and Watson illegally enter a house, then secretly watch a woman kill the man who wronged her. They offer the police no help in solving this particular case.

This pattern of justice privately achieved occurs frequently in the later stories and hints at Doyle's growing elitism and distrust of the normal institutions of justice. He had involved himself deeply in the cases of two men, George Edalji and Oscar Slater, whom he considered victims of legal injustice. In both cases his strenuous and time-consuming efforts resulted in vindicating his beliefs and liberating the wronged men. He was equally pessimistic about the fate of honor, fair play, and decency, the feudal and paternalistic values he felt should supercede institutional religion. In "His Last Bow" (1917) a German diplomat, Baron Von Herling, remarks that Britain might ignore its responsibility to Belgium if Germany invaded it: "we live in a utilitarian age. Honor is a medieval conception." But in fiction Holmes had not abandoned these values, and in his life Doyle held to them as well. He remained true to his wife until her death in 1906. A year later he married Leckie, and together they had five children.

The last part of Doyle's life was dominated by his commitment to various causes. His successful defense of Edalji took more than a year. Thereafter, he exposed the brutal mistreatment of Africans by the Belgians in *The Crime of the Congo* (1909). He spoke and wrote in favor of Irish home rule, a reversal of his previous position, and of reform of the divorce laws; he also spoke against women's suffrage. *The Case of Oscar Slater* (1912) demolishes the logic and evidence offered to convict Slater of murder, and Doyle continued to support Slater until his conviction was reversed in 1928 and Slater was paid £6,000. The dominant crusade of his last years was the spiritualist movement, to which he gave unselfishly of his time, his money, his writing, and his voice, traveling extensively to promote the cause.

Doyle managed to enjoy himself in these years as well. He built a home for his second wife in Sussex, and they both took part in a European auto race and traveled twice to the Mediterranean, exploring Greece and Egypt. In Constantinople he received a letter from the sultan of Turkey, who said he had read and enjoyed Doyle's books. In an odd incident, which may have inspired *The Lost World,* Doyle claimed, writing in his autobiography, that he and his wife saw in the waters near Aegina "a creature which has never, so far as I know, been described by Science. It was exactly like a young ichthyosaurus, about 4 feet long, with thin neck and tail." Noting that in later years an admiral saw a similar creature near Ireland, he concluded that "this old world has got some surprises for us yet." In 1914 the couple also traveled to western Canada, touring the Canadian Rockies as guests of the government but managed to return to England before World War I began.

Doyle also undertook some adventures in sports and finance. He organized various groups supporting the British team that was to compete in the 1916 Olympic Games, which were canceled when the war began. His many adventures in finance were often unsuccessful. Doyle admitted in his autobiography to a "certain speculative element in my own nature," which led him to invest in a bicycle factory, a sculpting machine, a brass factory, guano islands, coal mines, and the search for gold in mines and sunken ships.

Doyle also continued his lifelong interest in sports. He played primarily for enjoyment, admitting he was "a second-rater in all things," including boxing, rugby, shooting, fishing, billiards, cricket, fencing, golf, skiing, flying, and auto racing. Doyle fought some prizefights, played soccer at age forty-four, and participated in some international cricket matches. He also taught Kipling golf in a Vermont field.

With all this extraliterary activity, Doyle still managed to complete a few plays, including one on his favorite character, Brigadier Gerard, and another historical novel, *Sir Nigel* (1906), which involves characters from *The White Company* but antedates its action. The book was praised, but Doyle believed it was his masterpiece and was dissatisfied because the critics liked the story as an adventure and ignored his painstaking re-creation of the era.

Doyle also created *The Lost World,* a novel in which prehistory and contemporary life are synthesized. The first of four Professor Challenger stories, *The Lost World* dramatizes Doyle's belief in the theory of the inheritance of acquired characteristics through the description of his hero, the professor, and through the action itself, which suggests the existence of prehistoric nature in the present.

The plot involves Challenger and other scientists exploring a South American jungle and discovering the existence of prehistoric animals and human beings. The past remains alive in the present. This is also true in the character of Professor Challenger, who after Holmes and Watson is Doyle's most memorable creation. In particular, Doyle compares Challenger's appearance to that of the apes. In part, Doyle uses Challenger to criticize concerns about safety and utility that he sees as dominating modern society. Modern heroes need the physical aggressiveness and courage of their prehistoric ancestors, and Challenger has these. He is a brilliant scientist, and he is strong, courageous, and adventurous. In him the best qualities of the past survive and unite with the superior knowledge of the present.

Doyle identified closely with his brave and intellectually arrogant but chivalrous hero. He even suggested to his publisher that the book be illustrated with photographs of himself disguised as Challenger. He also fooled some relatives when he arrived at their home disguised as the professor. Like Holmes, Doyle loved wearing disguises and playing roles, which might explain why he created so many and such diverse first-person narrators for his stories.

Doyle wrote a few science-fiction tales apart from the Professor Challenger series, mostly during the last third of his life. Although their subjects are diverse — some dealing with air travel, some with creatures from prehistory, some with the effects of imaginary technology on contemporary life — they share a common vision with the themes of *The Lost World*. As George E. Slusser writes in his introduction to *The Best Science Fiction of Arthur Conan Doyle* (1981):

> As vision, it not only radically qualifies the turn-of-the-century myth of empire built on technological mastery of the natural environment, on the taming of elemental and racial savagery into institutionalized civility, but also contradicts the world view that sustains Doyle's own creation, Sherlock Holmes, the age's most popular incarnation of rationalistic positivism.

Doyle's science fiction rests mostly in the tradition of cautionary tales about human experiment. Some of these tales are comic. "The Great Keinplatz Experiment" describes the farcical confusion that results when the personalities of a professor and his student are exchanged by an experimental machine. "The Adventure of the Creeping Man" (1923), first published in *The Strand Magazine,* is a rare Sherlock Holmes story on the same theme. In it, a Professor Presbury attempts to rejuvenate himself with experimental drugs because he is in love with a young woman. As a result he reverts to animal-like behavior, and Holmes offers the moral, "When one tries to rise above nature one is liable to fall below it. The highest type of man may revert to the animal if he leaves the straight road of destiny." "The Horror of Heights" (1913), also published in *The Strand Magazine,* points the moral in another direction. The story involves a man who tries to fly a plane higher than anyone else. He disappears, and only a log from his plane is ever found. In it the pilot describes monstrous creatures that float in the sky and destroy anyone who ventures too high.

Such stories exalt the bravery of the spirit of exploration even as they warn against its excesses. "Through the Veil" (1911), written about the same time as *The Lost World,* is, like the novel, a parable exploring the idea of the inheritance of acquired experience and the related concept of racial memory. A contemporary married couple literally relive a moment from their racial past at the site of an archeological dig. The husband tells his wife that he had been present at a fight between savages and a Roman soldier. She says she has a similar memory, and he remarks, "Yes, it was just you. Not merely like you, you understand. It was you – you yourself. I saw the same soul in your eyes." The narrator concludes, "For an instant the curtain of the past had swung aside, and some strange glimpse of a forgotten life had come to them."

A more interesting story, based on concepts of racial characteristics and technological danger, is "The Great Brown-Pericord Motor" (1911). Pericord, a Celtic creative genius, has planned a motor for a flying machine, and Brown, a practical man of Anglo-Saxon background, has put it together. Pericord is emotionally sensitive and a bit unstable, while Brown is somewhat crude and brutal. Obviously Doyle has dramatized the mind/body split as a division of labor along racial lines in a story published a month after the Wright brothers' flight at Kitty Hawk. Pericord and Brown fight over who created the machine and should get the patent. Pericord accidentally kills Brown, straps his body to their invention, and sends it off to sea and oblivion, then goes mad. At one level the story is a parable about the destructiveness of English-Irish relations and the value of a reconciliation of the two racial characteristics. In another way the story suggests that technological progress is wonderful but at the same time impossible because of primitive qualities in the organic human world.

Yet another example is one of the last Challenger stories, "The Disintegration Machine" (1929). Here a Mr. Nemor, whose physical description suggests he is primitive, has invented a doomsday device and has come to Challenger with a threat to blow up England, if not the world. Challenger saves the world by disintegrating the man in his own machine. He concludes, "We make the matter worse if we experiment with the unknown." Of course, Challenger continues to experiment with the unknown. Again the physically primitive and the technologically advanced cancel each other or, rather, remain in uneasy conflict.

Both "Through the Veil" and "The Great Brown-Pericord Motor" are from *The Last Galley: Impressions and Tales,* which Doyle thought contained some of his best historical tales. He later republished only the historical stories in *Tales of Long Ago* (1922), which includes others as well. The stories often focus on what the Victorians considered moments of historical transformation. For instance, "The Last Galley" tells about the triumph of a young and vigorous Roman empire over the naval forces of Carthage. Told from the losers' perspective, it focuses on a theme Doyle increasingly emphasized in his later fiction: the failure of empire growing from love of wealth and luxury. In "The Centurion" (1922), which first appeared in *Storyteller,* he offers a fragment of a letter from a Roman legate to his uncle written thirty years after the crucifixion of Christ. The legate, present at the siege of Jerusalem, writes in passing of a centurion who sees the burning of Jerusalem as a possible punishment for those, presumably the Jews, who insisted that

William Gillette, Doyle's collaborator on the 1899 play Sherlock Holmes *and the first actor to play Doyle's detective*

Pilate kill Jesus. Neither the writer nor the centurion is Christian, but the latter is deeply impressed by Jesus and recollects, in naturalistic detail, some of the incidents on Calvary. The story resembles some of Robert Browning's dramatic monologues, creating irony by telling a familiar story from an unfamiliar perspective – a narrative device Doyle used well in the Brigadier Gerard stories also. The story suggests the spiritual longing of good Romans and foreshadows the eventual triumph of Christianity over both Jewish and pagan cultures. Like most of the later fiction Doyle wrote, the focus is less on character than on culture.

During World War I Doyle volunteered his services to his country. In 1913 he had written a prescient article in the *Fortnightly Review* about the possibility of war with Germany, "Great Britain and the Next War." In this essay he argued that the major dangers to England would be from submarines and airships. Submarines, he said, could seriously weaken England by destroying a significant part of its merchant fleet, diminishing food supplies, and causing privation and inflation. They could also directly affect military operations by controlling the English Channel, and he argued strongly for the construction of a Channel tunnel. Doyle was so concerned about this matter that he dramatized this possibility in the short story "Danger!" (1914), a powerful projection of English weakness first pub-

lished in the *Strand* and later collected in *Danger! and Other Stories* (1918). In the story Capt. John Sirius, a submarine commander from an unnamed country, brings England to its knees with six submarines because its merchant fleet is totally unprotected. The theme is obvious: progress in technology must be dealt with as logically and remorselessly as possible. Otherwise the new will be used by the unscrupulous to destroy civilization since war is a struggle for victory by any means, not a feudal game.

The military establishment ignored Doyle's warning because it did not believe Germany would sink nonmilitary ships, and Doyle had the grim satisfaction of seeing his prediction come true. However, the navy did take up Doyle's suggestion to create inflatable life preservers and formally thanked him for an innovation that saved many lives.

Doyle's family, like many others in Europe, lost several men to the war. His patriotism and public persona remained steadfast in the face of these losses, which included his son, Kingsley; his wife's brother; and his sister's husband. He devotes almost a third of his memoirs to his experiences of the war. He wrote five books on the subject, including the six-volume *The British Campaign in France and Flanders* (1916–1920).

During the war Doyle became totally converted to and committed to a belief in spiritualism. He admitted in his autobiography that without his "absolute conviction that the change of vibration which we call death did not destroy our personality and that communication was still possible," he would have found it hard to bear his family's losses. Doyle claimed to have received such communications and to be granted moments of foreknowledge, and he believed others who claimed similar psychic experiences. He devoted most of the rest of his life to this cause, seeing himself as a knight fighting a great war against "materialism and annihilation." Doyle's evolution of belief – from orthodox religious conviction to an agnosticism influenced by science and philosophy to a rejection of materialism in favor of a nonsectarian belief in the reality of spirit – is typical of many Victorian intellectuals.

Doyle's later writings were primarily devoted to spiritualism. Holmes remained untouched by Doyle's conversion, even in his last adventures, but the agnostic Professor Challenger was converted to the cause in *The Land of Mist* (1926). The final wisdom of the book is delivered by Challenger's daughter: "The most dangerous condition for a man or a nation is when his intellectual side is more developed than his spiritual." This statement corresponds with Doyle's criticism of H. G. Wells's *The*

Outline of History (1920) in his memoirs: "He has never shown any perception of the true meaning of the psychic, and for want of it his history of the world, elaborate and remarkable as it was, seemed to me to be a body without a soul."

Doyle produced one other book of short fiction, *The Maracot Deep and Other Stories* (1929), and among the other stories were two short Challenger tales, "The Disintegration Machine" (1929) and "When the World Screamed" (1928), which first appeared in *The Strand Magazine*. Both show Challenger to be his usual humorous, brash, and bullish self, but he still, like Holmes, defies and outrages the respectable, living his life to pursue knowledge and in accord with chivalric values.

"When the World Screamed" is a strange tale on the familiar theme of the scientist as violator; it is strange because in this case the scientist is Challenger. Still seemingly sane, Challenger decides to shoot "an iron dart into the nerve ganglion of old Mother Earth." The result is "a howl in which pain, anger, menace and the outraged majesty of Nature all blended into one hideous shriek." While the narrator suggests that nature has developed means "to defend Mother Earth from intrusive Challengers," it also shows Challenger lauded for his mighty achievement: "To set the whole world screaming was the privilege of Challenger alone." Is the story a joke, an attempt to show the absurdity of Challenger's ego? Perhaps, yet it also seems to affirm the grandeur of his enterprise. In any case, it certainly confirms that throughout his career Doyle's fiction continued to display a tension between his desire to explore the unknown and his fear and doubts about doing so.

"The Maracot Deep" (1927), which appeared in *The Strand Magazine,* is a more substantial work, using the story of a failed scientific experiment to criticize modern society. Three scientists exploring the ocean in a diving bell are accidentally cut loose from their mother ship, which subsequently sinks with all aboard. The diving bell drops to the lowest point in the ocean, where the men prepare to die but are unexpectedly rescued by people from Atlantis. The story is filled with descriptions of new technology such as a thought visualizer, "a combination of such telepathy and television as we dimly comprehend upon earth," which turns thought into pictures by transforming "etheric impressions back into terms of matter," thus allowing the two groups to communicate. The didactic thrust of the story comes from the thoughts of a prophet who visualizes racial memories, the history of a civilization that was once more advanced than modern England but declined because of "dissipation and

moral degeneracy, of the accretion of matter and decline of spirit." The narrator, Cyrus Headley, feels an identity with and knowledge of the old civilization because, he says, "I, the latest product of modern civilization, had myself once been part of this mighty civilization of old." This knowledge "came from the depth of my own subconscious self where memories of twelve thousand years still lingered." The scientist who returns from Atlantis a wise and chastened man echoes almost word for word Challenger's daughter in *The Land of Mist:* "the greatest danger which can come to a state is when its intellect outruns its soul." Thus, the author who created the most famous intellect in literary history believed at last that it was soul that mattered. His message to the world in his lectures and writings on spiritualism was that the West was sick from the dominance of commerce, materialism, reason, and skepticism.

In his last years Doyle wrote *Memories and Adventures,* a book rich in description of his public acts and thoughts but reticent about much of his private life and family relationships. He also continued to lecture on spiritualism, befriending for a brief period Harry Houdini, who specialized in exposing fraudulent spiritual mediums. Doyle favored this activity because he felt the movement was constantly compromised by charlatans. The friendship ended abruptly, however, when Jean Doyle told Houdini, who was Jewish, that she had communicated with his dead mother and seen her wearing a crucifix. Doyle's advocacy of spiritualism tainted his reputation and cost him a peerage, but this in no way persuaded him to abandon his beliefs.

In 1929 Doyle's health deteriorated, and he found he was suffering from angina pectoris. Nine months later he died of a heart attack and was buried on his estate at Windlesham. His epitaph, "Steel True, Blade Straight," deftly captures his knightly character and reveals his distance from a generation of writers whose experience of wars involved barbed wire, poison gas, tanks, and machine guns.

Doyle hoped his writing would reshape the social and political beliefs of his country, and he was deeply disappointed when his work was praised and appreciated primarily as entertainment. Certainly he wanted to amuse, but he also wanted to instruct. His fate, however, was to live in an age of great achievements in science, technology, history, and literature and to write in the first age of mass publication and consumption. At this time writers could earn great wealth by reaching a large and newly literate audience, created by the national education acts, through the new magazines that emerged to serve them.

When a reaction set in against all things Victorian, Doyle's reputation sank, causing critics to wonder how it was possible for him to create a character as eccentric and aesthetic as Sherlock Holmes. Recent biographies have revealed that Doyle's self-portrait was selective, that he omitted significant information about his life, especially his early life, that did not fit his public image. This information makes him seem a more complex person, one capable of creating Holmes and other interesting characters. When Doyle died, his most famous creations continued to flourish in fiction, in motion pictures, and on television. His literary reputation rests securely where he least wanted it, in Baker Street and its fictional environs.

Furthermore, it is in the Holmes short stories, rather than the novels, that Doyle was most successful. His creation of a series of stories related by common central characters made them a commercial bonanza for the new mass-circulation magazines and influenced many later writers, including Dorothy Sayers and Agatha Christie. The classic form of short fiction – exposition, action, and resolution – is perfectly suited to these tales of ratiocination involving a few characters and a single problem. His work in detective fiction decisively shaped its great first wave. As Sayers says in her introduction to *The Omnibus of Crime* (1929), "Conan Doyle took up the Poe formula and galvanized it into life and popularity." If Doyle did not always play fair with readers, not always giving them the same clues that the detective has, he did introduce his stories as one standard by which later detective stories might be judged. Many writers still play the game as Doyle defined the rules.

Doyle's other writings, including his short fiction, are widely considered less significant in his career, but they constitute a substantial body of creative work in various forms of popular fiction. Critics and scholars use them for what they reveal about Doyle's life, beliefs, and feelings. Certainly they can supply evidence of the development of his craft and in the process shed light on the achievement and special qualities of the Holmes stories. Some critics have also recognized literary merit in some of these pieces. Like most writers of adventure stories, Doyle was successful because of his imaginative plots, vivid settings, and careful pacing of narrative developments. In his later stories he created a variety of vivid characters who add another dimension to his art. Finally, in a few of his stories of contemporary life, such as his medical fiction, he was capable of an uncompromising naturalism that approaches the grotesque and sensational. What is common to all is a quality of wonder. Doyle's aesthetic notions were simple: he felt a writer's primary job was, working within the bounds of the morally acceptable, to capture a reader's interest with whatever subject matter and techniques he or she chose.

After years of neglect some of these other writings have returned to print. Scholars have identified and reissued previously uncollected stories, some published anonymously, and collections of his best crime, mystery, and science-fiction stories have recently appeared. Professor Challenger – after Holmes, Doyle's most lively character – is also gaining in interest. As Jacqueline A. Jaffe remarks in *Arthur Conan Doyle* (1987), "Even without Holmes, Professor Challenger should be enough to ensure Doyle's place among the best writers of scientific romances."

With the growing interest in popular fiction and increasing respect for Victorian achievements, Doyle's literary career will command more professional attention, even as the cult of Holmes and Watson continues unabated. His short fiction displays the variety of his interests and his ability to write successfully in most genres. His production was enormous, but by no means will all of these stories appeal to contemporary readers. However, beyond the Holmes fiction there are mysteries; stories of horror, adventure, and humor; and realistic tales that are entertaining and illuminating. Exploring the lost world of Doyle's fiction will yield discoveries that will enrich the understanding of late Victorian culture and of a man of letters who, as much as anyone, entertained and instructed it.

Letters:

Letters to the Press, edited by John Michael Gibson and Richard Lancelyn Green (London: Secker & Warburg, 1986; Iowa City: University of Iowa Press, 1986).

Interviews:

R. Blathwayt, "Talk with Dr. Conan Doyle," *Bookman* (London), 2 (May 1892): 50–51;

Harry How, "A Day with Dr. Conan Doyle," *Strand Magazine,* 4 (August 1892): 182–188;

Robert Barr, "A Chat with Conan Doyle," *Idler,* 6 (October 1894): 340–349; published in *McClure's Magazine,* 3 (November 1894): 503–513.

Bibliographies:

Harold Locke, *A Bibliographical Catalogue of the Writings of Sir Arthur Conan Doyle, M.D., LL.D.,*

1879–1928 (Tunbridge Wells: Webster, 1928);

Edgar W. Smith, *Baker Street Inventory: A Sherlockian Bibliography* (Summit, N.J.: Pamphlet House, 1945);

Jay Finley Christ, *The Fiction of Sir Arthur Conan Doyle* (N.p.: Privately printed, 1959);

Ronald Burt De Waal, *The World Bibliography of Sherlock Holmes and Dr. Watson* (Boston: New York Graphic Society, 1974);

De Waal, *The International Sherlock Holmes: A Companion Volume to the World Bibliography of Sherlock Holmes and Dr. Watson* (Hamden, Conn.: Archon, 1980; London: Mansell, 1980);

Richard Lancelyn Green and John Michael Gibson, *A Bibliography of A. Conan Doyle* (Oxford: Clarendon Press, 1983).

Biographies:

John Lamond, *Arthur Conan Doyle: A Memoir* (London: John Murray, 1931; Port Washington, N.Y.: Kennikat Press, 1972);

Hesketh Pearson, *Conan Doyle: His Life and Art* (London: Methuen, 1943; New York: Coward-McCann, 1946);

Adrian Conan Doyle, *The True Conan Doyle* (London: John Murray, 1945; New York: Harper, 1946);

John Dickson Carr, *The Life of Sir Arthur Conan Doyle* (London: John Murray, 1949; New York: Harper, 1949);

Carr, *Sir Arthur Conan Doyle Centenary, 1859–1959* (London: John Murray, 1959; Garden City, N.Y.: Doubleday, 1959);

Michael and Mollie Hardwick, *The Man Who Was Sherlock Holmes* (London: John Murray, 1964; Garden City, N.Y.: Doubleday, 1964);

Pierre Nordon, *Sir Arthur Conan Doyle: L'Homme et l'oeuvre* (Paris & Brussels: Didier, 1964); translated by Frances Partridge as *Conan Doyle: A Biography* (London: John Murray, 1966; New York: Holt, Rinehart & Winston, 1967);

Ivor Brown, *Conan Doyle, a Biography of the Creator of Sherlock Holmes* (London: Hamish Hamilton, 1972);

Charles Higham, *The Adventures of Conan Doyle: The Life of the Creator of Sherlock Holmes* (New York: Norton, 1976; London: Hamish Hamilton, 1976);

Ronald Pearsall, *Conan Doyle: A Biographical Solution* (London: Weidenfeld & Nicolson, 1977; New York: St. Martin's Press, 1977);

Julian Symons, *Portrait of an Artist – Conan Doyle* (London: Whizzard Press/Deutsch, 1979; New York: Mysterious Press, 1987);

Owen Dudley Edwards, *The Quest for Sherlock Holmes: A Biographical Study of Arthur Conan Doyle* (Edinburgh: Mainstream, 1983);

Jon L. Lellenberg, ed., *The Quest for Sir Arthur Conan Doyle: Thirteen Biographies in Search of a Life* (Carbondale: Southern Illinois University Press, 1987).

References:

Jack Adrian, Introduction, *Detective Stories from the Strand Magazine* (Oxford & New York: Oxford University Press, 1991);

Adrian, Introduction, *Strange Tales from the Strand Magazine* (Oxford & New York: Oxford University Press, 1991);

Don Richard Cox, *Arthur Conan Doyle* (New York: Ungar, 1985);

John Michael Gibson and Richard Lancelyn Green, Introduction, *The Unknown Conan Doyle: Uncollected Stories* (London: Secker & Warburg, 1981; Garden City, N.Y.: Doubleday, 1984);

Jacqueline A. Jaffe, *Arthur Conan Doyle* (Boston: Twayne, 1987);

Dorothy L. Sayers, Introduction, *The Omnibus of Crime* (New York: Harcourt, Brace, 1929);

George E. Slusser, Introduction, *The Best Science Fiction of Arthur Conan Doyle,* edited by Charles G. Waugh and Martin H. Greenburg (Carbondale & Edwardsville: Southern Illinois University Press, 1981);

Jack W. Tracy, Introduction, *Masterworks of Crime and Mystery by Sir Arthur Conan Doyle* (New York: Dial, 1982).

Papers:

Manuscript materials of Arthur Conan Doyle are housed in the Berg Collection, New York Public Library; the Lilly Library, Indiana University, Bloomington; and the Humanities Research Center, University of Texas at Austin. The largest collection of Doyle materials, including correspondence, is in the Arthur Conan Doyle Collection, Metropolitan Toronto Library, Toronto, Ontario; the largest collection of Sherlockiana in a public institution is the Philip S. and Mary Kahler Hench Collection, O. Meredith Wilson Library, University of Minnesota, Minneapolis; the largest private collection of Sherlockiana belongs to John Bennett Shaw, Santa Fe, New Mexico, and is designated for deposit at the University of Minnesota.

Lord Dunsany
(Edward John Moreton Drax Plunkett, Baron Dunsany)
(25 August 1878 – 25 October 1957)

Siobhan Craft Brownson
University of South Carolina

See also the Dunsany entries in *DLB 10: Modern British Dramatists, 1900–1945; DLB 77: British Mystery Writers, 1920–1939;* and *DLB 153: Late Victorian and Edwardian Novelists, First Series.*

BOOKS: *The Gods of Pegana* (London: Elkin Mathews, 1905; Boston: Luce, 1916);

Time and the Gods (London: Heinemann, 1906; Boston: Luce, 1913);

The Sword of Welleran and Other Stories (London: George Allen, 1908; Boston: Luce, 1916);

A Dreamer's Tales (London: George Allen, 1910; Boston: Luce, 1916);

Selections from the Writings of Lord Dunsany (Churchtown, Ireland: Cuala Press, 1912);

The Book of Wonder (London: Heinemann, 1912; Boston: Luce, 1913);

Five Plays (London: Richards, 1914; New York: Kennerley, 1914);

Fifty-One Tales (London: Elkin Mathews, 1915; New York: Kennerley, 1915);

Tales of Wonder (London: Elkin Mathews, 1916); republished as *The Last Book of Wonder* (Boston: Luce, 1916);

A Night at the Inn (New York: Sunwise Turn, 1916; London: Putnam, 1922);

Plays of Gods and Men (Dublin: Talbot, 1917; London: Unwin, 1917; Boston: Luce, 1917);

A Dreamer's Tales and Other Stories (New York: Boni & Liveright, 1917);

Tales of War (Boston: Little, Brown, 1918; Dublin: Talbot / London: Unwin, 1918);

Unhappy Far-Off Things (Boston: Little, Brown, 1919; London: Elkin Mathews, 1919);

Tales of Three Hemispheres (Boston: Luce, 1919; London: Unwin, 1920);

If (London & New York: Putnam, 1921);

The Chronicles of Rodriguez (London & New York: Putnam, 1922); published as *Don Rodriguez:*

Lord Dunsany

Chronicles of Shadow Valley (New York & London: Putnam, 1922);

The Laughter of the Gods (London: Putnam, 1922);

Plays of Near and Far (London & New York: Putnam, 1922); expanded as *Plays of Near and Far (Including If)* (London & New York: Putnam, 1923);

King Argimenes and the Unknown Warrior (London & New York: Putnam, 1923);

The Glittering Gate (London & New York: Putnam, 1923);

The Lost Silk Hat (London & New York: Putnam, 1923);

The King of Elfland's Daughter (London & New York: Putnam, 1924);

Alexander and Three Small Plays (London & New York: Putnam, 1925);

Alexander (London & New York: Putnam, 1925);

The Charwoman's Shadow (London & New York: Putnam, 1926);

The Blessing of Pan (London & New York: Putnam, 1927);

Seven Modern Comedies (London & New York: Putnam, 1928);

Fifty Poems (London & New York: Putnam, 1929);

The Old Folk of the Centuries (London: Elkin Mathews & Marrot, 1930);

The Travel Tales of Mr. Joseph Jorkens (London & New York: Putnam, 1931);

The Curse of the Wise Woman (London: Heinemann, 1933; New York & Toronto: Longmans, Green, 1933);

If I Were Dictator (London: Methuen, 1934);

Jorkens Remembers Africa (New York & Toronto: Longmans, Green, 1934); republished as *Mr. Jorkens Remembers Africa* (London & Toronto: Heinemann, 1934);

Mr. Faithful (New York, Los Angeles & London: French, 1935);

Up in the Hills (London & Toronto: Heinemann, 1935; New York: Putnam, 1936);

Rory and Bran (London & Toronto: Heinemann, 1936; New York: Putnam, 1937);

My Talks with Dean Spanley (London & Toronto: Heinemann, 1936; New York: Putnam, 1936);

My Ireland (London: Jarrolds, 1937; New York & London: Funk & Wagnalls, 1937);

Plays for Earth and Air (London & Toronto: Heinemann, 1937);

Patches of Sunlight (London & Toronto: Heinemann, 1938; New York: Reynal & Hitchcock, 1938);

Mirage Water (London: Putnam, 1938; Philadelphia: Dorrance, 1939);

The Story of Mona Sheehy (London & Toronto: Heinemann, 1939; New York & London: Harper, 1940);

Jorkens Has a Large Whiskey (London: Putnam, 1940);

War Poems (London: Hutchinson, 1941);

Wandering Songs (London: Hutchinson, 1943);

A Journey (London: Macdonald, 1944);

Guerrilla (London & Toronto: Heinemann, 1944; Indianapolis: Bobbs-Merrill, 1944);

While the Sirens Slept (London: Jarrolds, 1944);

The Donnellan Lectures (London & Toronto: Heinemann, 1945);

The Sirens Wake (London: Jarrolds, 1945);

The Year (London: Jarrolds, 1946);

Glimpse from a Watch Tower (London: Jarrolds, 1946);

The Fourth Book of Jorkens (London: Jarrolds, 1947; Sauk City, Wis.: Arkham House, 1948);

To Awaken Pegasus (Oxford: Ronald, 1949);

The Man Who Ate the Phoenix (London: Jarrolds, 1949);

The Strange Journeys of Colonel Polders (London: Jarrolds, 1950);

Carcassonne (Boston: Luce, 1950);

The Last Revolution (London: Jarrolds, 1951);

His Fellow Men (London: Jarrolds, 1952);

The Little Tales of Smethers and Other Stories (London: Jarrolds, 1952);

Jorkens Borrows Another Whiskey (London: M. Joseph, 1954);

The Sword of Welleran and Other Tales of Enchantment (New York: Devin-Adair, 1954);

At the Edge of the World, edited by Lin Carter (New York: Ballantine, 1970);

Beyond the Fields We Know, edited by Carter (New York: Ballantine, 1972);

Gods, Men and Ghosts: The Best Supernatural Fiction of Lord Dunsany, edited by E. F. Bleiler (New York: Dover, 1972);

Over the Hills and Far Away, edited by Carter (New York: Ballantine, 1974);

The Ghosts of the Heaviside Layer and Other Phantasms, edited by Darrell Schweitzer (Philadelphia: Owlswick, 1980);

An Enemy of Scotland Yard and Other Whodunits / Ein Feind vom Scotland Yard und andere Kurzkrimis, translations by Elisabeth Schnack (Munich: Deutscher Taschenbuch, 1985);

Verses Dedicatory: Eighteen Previously Unpublished Poems, edited by Carter (Montclair, N.J.: Charnel House, 1985).

PLAY PRODUCTIONS: *The Glittering Gate,* Dublin, Abbey Theatre, 29 April 1909; London, Court Theatre, 6 June 1910;

King Argimenes and the Unknown Warrior, Dublin, Abbey Theatre, 26 January 1911;

The Gods of the Mountain, London, Haymarket Theatre, 1 June 1911;

The Golden Doom, London, Haymarket Theatre, 19 November 1912;

A Night at an Inn, New York, Neighborhood Playhouse, 23 April 1916; London, Palace Theatre, 6 November 1917;

Frontispiece and title page for Dunsany's first book, a collection of sketches about an invented mythology (Special Collections, Thomas Cooper Library, University of South Carolina)

The Queen's Enemies, New York, Neighborhood Playhouse, 14 November 1916;

The Laughter of the Gods, New York, Punch and Judy Theatre, 15 January 1919;

If, London, Ambassadors' Theatre, 30 May 1921;

Cheezo, London, Everyman Theatre, 15 November 1921;

Lord Adrian, Birmingham, Prince of Wales's Theatre, 12 November 1923;

Fame and the Poet, Leeds, Albert Hall, 8 February 1924;

His Sainted Grandmother, London, Fortune Theatre, 8 December 1926;

The Jest of Hahalaba, London, Playroom 6, 22 March 1927;

Mr. Faithful, London, Q Theatre, 22 August 1927.

OTHER: Francis Ledwidge, *The Complete Poems of Francis Ledwidge,* introduction by Dunsany (London: Jenkins, 1919);

Mary Lavin, *Tales from Bective Bridge,* introduction by Dunsany (London: M. Joseph, 1945);

George Meredith, *The Egoist,* introduction by Dunsany (London: Oxford University Press, 1947);

The Odes of Horace, translated by Dunsany (London & Toronto: Heinemann, 1947);

Arthur Machen, *The Hill of Dreams,* introduction by Dunsany (London: Richards, 1954);

The Collected Works of Horace, translated by Dunsany and Michael Oakley (London: Dent, 1961; New York: Dutton, 1961).

SELECTED PERIODICAL PUBLICATIONS – UNCOLLECTED: "A Walk in the Waste of Time," *Smart Set,* 53 (October 1917): 1;

"Cheng Hi and the Window Framer," *Smart Set,* 60 (November 1919): 2;

"England Language Conditions!," *Essays and Studies,* 13 (1928): 138–144;

"The Story of Tse Gah," *Tomorrow,* 7 (December 1947): 19–20;

"An Ancient Mariner," *Punch,* 217 (6 July 1949): 4–5;

"Two Christmas Dinners," *Punch,* 217 (7 November 1949): 3–4;

"A Crime Story," *Punch,* 218 (4 January 1950): 22–23;

"A Talk in the Dark," *Tomorrow,* 10 (July 1951): 19;

"The Awakening," *Poetry Review,* 44 (July–September 1953): 375–377.

Extraordinarily prolific in the fields of fiction, poetry, essay, translation, autobiography, and memoir, including fifteen short-fiction collections and at least one hundred uncollected short stories, Edward John Moreton Drax Plunkett, the eighteenth Baron Dunsany, fought the charge of literary dilettantism during his fifty-year career. His title sat uneasily on him: he was known more for his love of games; his humor; his idiosyncratic declaiming on such subjects as furniture polish, food additives, and the removal of dogs' tails; and his sartorial ineptitude than for his peerage. He spent much of his time shooting game, going on safari in Africa, and playing chess, a game he loved – he was once chess champion of Ireland and played the world champion to a draw in 1929. He wrote his stories quickly, without revision, with a goose-quill pen in a flowing, indecipherable hand. Readers in England and the United States especially appreciated his early fantasy stories for their ingenious settings, strange gods and heroes, and imaginative description. Perhaps because of their greater accessibility, his later stories – largely tall tales, ghost stories, and detective mysteries – received even wider popular acceptance. His stories cover an immense range of categories, and he tried almost every form of short fiction, including mythological fantasies, heroic fantasies, sword-and-sorcery tales, fables, short-shorts, frame-within-a-frame stories, horror fiction, humorous fiction, mood pieces, and the Jorkens "you can't top this" chronicles. He was productive until shortly before his death in 1957.

Perhaps because of his active life and productivity, critics during his lifetime tended to discount Dunsany's literary efforts, and subsequent critical attention has focused on his early fantasy stories. Despite some critical reservations about the depth of his fantasy and its lack of important female figures, Dunsany reveals in his short fiction a thoroughly engaged and romantic vision of nature, and he was capable of crafting haunting and enchanting images of ethereal and real worlds alike. In addition, he invested his stories with the spontaneity and vigor with which he confronted his own experiences. Enthusiasm for his successful work in fantasy is justified by his expert creation of mythical leg-

ends and has ensured that his short stories of all types are remembered.

Dunsany's family moved shortly after his birth in London on 25 August 1878 to a house in Kent, Dunstall Priory, which he loved for the beauty of its setting. After his father became the seventeenth Baron Dunsany in 1889, he and his younger brother, Reggie, alternated between Dunstall; Dunsany Castle, twenty miles northwest of Dublin; and school. In 1891 he entered Eton, where he spent an undistinguished few years before his father sent him to various academic crammers in preparation for attendance at the Royal Military Academy at Sandhurst. He served with the Coldstream Guards at Gibraltar and in the Boer War in 1899–1900, and he cheerfully left the army in 1901. He married Lady Beatrice Villiers in 1904; their only son, Randal Arthur Henry, was born in 1906. Dunsany was the Conservative candidate for Wiltshire that same year, lost the election, and gladly turned away from a career in politics. Rejecting soldiering, farming, and politics left him time for chess, cricket, hunting, travel, and, most important to him, writing. The common view of his work as the mere dabblings of a bored landowning peer dogged him for the remaining half-century of his life.

Dunsany's first book, *The Gods of Pegana* (1905), is composed of brief sketches, rather than stories, of the cosmos Pegana, created by Mana-Yood-Sushai, and gods designated by names such as Skarl the Drummer, Slid, and Mung; Dunsany continued this pattern of choosing strange names throughout his writing career. Though L. Sprague de Camp believes that some readers are "exasperated by such unfamiliar word shapes," Vernon Hyles claims that Dunsany's "supreme gift was the coining of magical and evocative names." A certain malice and caprice characterize these gods, whose stories are recorded in sometimes less than two hundred words. Later critics particularly admire his rhythmic, biblical style in *The Gods of Pegana.* Because fantastic elements of place mark these vignettes – which also lack traditional fictional elements of plot, theme, and character – critics are sometimes tempted to view them, and indeed all of his fantasy stories, as human allegories; yet Dunsany warns in *Patches of Sunlight* (1938) that "once you start looking for allegories you are lost in a maze that has no centre." In fact, he claimed that he wrote "the history of lands that [he] had known in forgotten wanderings" and preferred to attribute his inventions to creative power rather than any kind of erudition.

A contemporary review of *The Gods of Pegana* in the *Observer* – "the sheer originality of it encourages high hopes for Lord Dunsany" – typifies the calm yet appreciative audience that greeted the book. A few years later, critics expressed much more enthusiasm for Dunsany's mythology. For example, Ernest A. Boyd in "Lord Dunsany – Fantaisiste" (1917) says that "it is difficult in summary to give an adequate idea of the wealth of [its] fantasy and imagination." While George Brandon Saul, writing in 1963, calls Dunsany's first collection "a series of notations on an invented pantheon [rather] than a set of stories," most posthumous critical reactions to *The Gods of Pegana* celebrate its novelty. A balanced reaction is that of Jules Zanger, who concludes that "although it is too slight a work to stand by itself, as the first element in the whole body of Dunsany's fantasy, it has a claim to attention."

Fantasy writers and critics praise Dunsany's early short stories; giving him the title "father of modern fantasy," many of them, as does Darrell Schweitzer in "Lovecraft and Lord Dunsany" (1987), consider him "probably the most brilliant fantasy writer who ever lived." The works of twentieth-century writers in the field, including J. R. R. Tolkien, Ray Bradbury, Arthur C. Clarke, Ursula K. Le Guin, and particularly H. P. Lovecraft, markedly reveal Dunsany's influence, and a particular type of story has even been classified "Dunsanian." In a 3 June 1923 letter to Frank Belknap Long, Lovecraft, whom critics consider a master of supernatural fiction, writes, "His distant, emotionless vistas of the beauty of the moonlight on quaint and ancient roofs are the vistas I know and cherish." Further, in his frequently reprinted essay "Supernatural Horror in Literature" (1927) Lovecraft calls Dunsany the "inventor of a new mythology and weaver of surprising folklore." Fantasy-literature advocates tend to emphasize his first five collections, becoming apologists for his middle work; because his later work, particularly the Jorkens series, does not fit the fantasy genre, they deplore what John D. Rateliff regards as a decline in imagination. Later critical response to Dunsany's short stories from experts in fantasy is valuable; however, modern readers of his work should remember that he wrote many successful stories of other types.

Time and the Gods (1906) introduces the concept of time not merely as the tool of the gods but as the source of their destruction. By the standards of short fiction the volume fulfills more regular expectations. Here the gods are more substantial; the archaic language, in re-creating time long past, makes sense; and the plots, though fantasic, are more reasonable. It is virtually impossible to select illustrative fragments from *The Gods of Pegana,* but the

pieces in *Time and the Gods* are more distinct from one another and stand more easily on their own as short stories. As critics have pointed out, a new element appears – that of humankind. Most contemporary reviews were mixed on Dunsany's second collection of tales. A few years after its publication, however, critics maintained their early appreciation of *The Gods of Pegana,* and reactions to *Time and the Gods* ranged from the complimentary to the adulatory. Recent criticism, while perhaps more moderate, exhibits the same range.

Dunsany explored, to great critical acclaim, heroic fantasy in his next collection, *The Sword of Welleran and Other Stories* (1908). In "The Fortress Unvanquishable Save for Sacnoth," for example, the hero, Leothric, must thwart the dragon, Tharagavverug, in order to gain the sword, Sacnoth, and save his village from the nightmares sent to it by the sorcerer, Gaznak. John Wilson Foster calls the story a "splendidly titled quest romance, . . . one of Dunsany's best stories, full of felicitous and imaginative strokes." Contemporary reviews of the collection were positive, with the *Times Literary Supplement* calling the title story "the best Lord Dunsany has yet written." Commentators in the next decades also lauded his continuing imagination and deft evocation of archaic events. W. B. Yeats found in Dunsany's description of a desert that "he can show us the movement of sand, as we have seen it where the sea shore meets the grass, but so changed that it becomes the deserts of the world." Later critics of *The Sword of Welleran* are equally enthusiastic, mentioning in particular "The Kith of the Elf-folk." The story's appearance in recent fantasy anthologies attests to a continuing appreciation of its charms.

In 1908–1909 Dunsany and Lady Beatrice made an expedition up the Nile to Aswan, which certainly influenced the later Jorkens stories of the last thirty years of Dunsany's career. At about this time Dunsany began a somewhat troubled relationship with Yeats, who encouraged him to write a one-act play. The well-known story is that Dunsany wrote the play, *The Glittering Gate,* one afternoon between luncheon and tea; it premiered at the Abbey Theatre on 29 April 1909 and thus began Dunsany's career in drama. Yeats wrote to his father in April 1909 that "Dunsany is man of genius I think . . . I want to get him into 'the movement,' " the movement being the Irish Renaissance. Dunsany gladly contributed money to keep the Abbey afloat during hard times, and though the theater produced his second play, *King Argimenes and the Unknown Warrior,* in January 1911, he was displeased when Lady

Gregory staged one of her plays, strikingly similar in plot, a week earlier, and his already tenuous relationship with Yeats began to deteriorate. Indeed, though almost every recent fantasy critic reminds readers of Yeats's comment from his introduction to *Selections from the Writings of Lord Dunsany* (1912) – "Had I read 'The Fall of Babbulkund' or 'Idle Days on the Yann' when a boy I had perhaps been changed for better or worse, and looked to that first reading as the creation of my world" – few reprint his remarks from the same piece – "Not all Lord Dunsany's moods delight me, for he writes out of a careless abundance."

The movement to which Yeats referred in his letter represented a tremendous explosion of Irish artistic creativity at the end of the nineteenth century and the beginning of the twentieth. Its importance in Dunsany's career is that, despite his living in Ireland and being somewhat involved with contributors such as Yeats and Irish poet James Stephens, he decidedly does not play a part in the Irish Renaissance. Although his early plays were produced at the Abbey, they are not in the same class as those of Yeats, John Millington Synge, or Sean O'Casey, for they often explore the same subjects of his early short stories rather than the native Irish culture and Celtic imagination that typifies the plays, poetry, and fiction of the Irish Renaissance. S. T. Joshi and Schweitzer suggest in their *Lord Dunsany: A Bibliography* (1993) that, among other reasons, because "Dunsany made a conscious decision not to restrict his imagination to purely 'Irish' subjects" and because of his "unwavering Unionist position," his willingness to be "co-opt[ed] . . . into the Irish literary movement" was fleeting at best.

Dunsany's next collection of short fiction, *A Dreamer's Tales* (1910), continues in the supernatural vein of his previous work yet moves again in a different direction. He abandons his personal mythology for tales of great cities, such as Bethmoora and Carcassonne, and fairy tales such as "Poltarnees, Beholder of the Ocean," in which the young men of Mondath cannot resist climbing the mountain Poltarnees in order to gaze upon the sea, which is so mesmerizing and exquisite that they never return. Other stories, such as "Blagdaross," "The Hashish Man," and "Poor Old Bill," depart from Dunsany's earlier myths and heroic fantasies because of their realistic settings and characters. Most reviewers liked the tales, while Stephens was particularly complimentary, in a 17 November 1910 letter to Dunsany calling the volume "one of the finest books of recent years." Both contemporary and posthumous critics tend to analyze those stories that differ from

Dunsany in 1914, during his service with the Fifth Inniskilling Fusiliers

Dunsany's earlier fantasies because of their new elements of humor and horror. Boyd and Schweitzer both note this new tone of horror in "Where the Tides Ebb and Flow," in which a London dreamer finds himself tossed in the mud because his crime against a secret society forbids a proper burial; Schweitzer alleges that the story was written "on a dare to see if [Dunsany] really could write a story about the mud at the bottom of the Thames." Many critics consider *A Dreamer's Tales* the pinnacle of Dunsany's achievement; for those readers who do not care for fantasy, it offers a richer array of fantasy, horror, humor, and irony.

Many fantasy critics, however, believe that Dunsany's next short-story collection, *The Book of Wonder* (1912), was the apex of his writing career, and contemporary reviewers found it Dunsany's best collection yet. As with much of his fiction, both professional and amateur critics find what they want in the collection. In his preface Dunsany invites those "who are in any wise weary of London: come with me: and those that tire of the world we know: for we have new worlds here." Critics frequently remark on the ease with which the stories move from London to wonderlands such as Ag, Bombasharna, Zeroora, and Ool as if the city actually lay at the end of the world. Though the stories characteristically lack traditional symbolic or thematic development, Dunsany's simple expectation that readers will follow his imagination works surprisingly well in stories such as "Miss Cubbidge and the Dragon of Romance," in which a dragon takes the heroine from her house at Number 12A Prince of Wales's Square across the "mystical sea" to a marble palace. The greater accessibility of these stories may be the result of their more familiar details.

Tales of Wonder (1916; published in the United States as *The Last Book of Wonder*) contains stories written before World War I, despite its publication date. Mark Amory believes its appearance during the war "suspended any chance of great success." The stories include characters who, though undeveloped, are more recognizable than those in earlier works, as well as fewer fanciful settings and less fantastic subject matter. Though Boyd in "Lord Dunsany – Fantaisiste" thinks "there is enough" in the volume "to justify the faith of those who were lured by the author's original narratives of fabulous beauty and wonder," later fantasy critics find its lack of personal mythology, ancient lands of mystery, and extraordinary heroic feats disappointing. Marshall B. Tymn, Kenneth J. Zahorski, and Robert H. Boyer, for example, dismiss it as "a collection of low fantasy, alcohol tales, and semi-allegorical visions of London." Certainly some of the stories fail because they seem pointless, invested with none of the startling descriptive moments or irony of his earlier efforts. Other critics find much to admire in its new kinds of stories, such as "Thirteen at Table," a ghost story that succeeds largely because of its unpredictability and Dunsany's skilled description of an eerie dinner party.

Because Dunsany never again wrote of what Lovecraft calls that "gorgeous and languorous world of iridescent exotic vision," some scholars, such as Mike Ashley, believe "the First World War soured Dunsany's outlook and no longer could he produce his light-hearted brand of imaginative fantasy." Though he was productive during the 1920s, writing fantasy novels such as *The Chronicles of Rodriguez* (1922; published in the United States as *Don Rodriguez: Chronicles of Shadow Valley*) and *The King of Elfland's Daughter* (1924), he labored in these longer works to expand his narratives, incorporate symbols, and develop themes, often simple ones such as good versus evil or humanity versus nature. However, these highly stylistic novels are enjoyed by many fantasy advocates, and most consider *The King of Elfland's Daughter* a classic of the genre. Dunsany also continued to write plays during this decade, such as *If* (1921), his most popular, and *Cheezo* (1921). In 1929 he published the first of his collections of poetry, *Fifty Poems;* he was as prolific in poetry as he was in all the forms of literature he explored but much less successful. He was adamant in his rejection of both eighteenth- and twentieth-century poetry, and labored rhymes, purple imagery, and overbearing themes typify his poems.

Dunsany wrote the five Jorkens books – *The Travel Tales of Mr. Joseph Jorkens* (1931); *Jorkens Remembers Africa* (1934; republished as *Mr. Jorkens Remembers Africa*); *Jorkens Has a Large Whiskey* (1940); *The Fourth Book of Jorkens* (1947); and *Jorkens Borrows Another Whiskey* (1954) – during the next two decades. The collections feature the shameless canvasser of drinks and incomparable teller of tall tales, Joseph Jorkens, whose stories fall into categories such as mystery, ghost story, science fiction, and horror. All are tinged with humor, but none include the mythology or heroic fantasy of Dunsany's earlier works. A narrator prefaces each collection with a statement testifying to the tales' veracity and potential for the advancement of science. Dunsany thereby establishes the frame-within-a-frame narrative technique, which he handles with skill. Another feature of the stories is the character of the harassing Terbut, who frequently disputes the truth of Jorkens's claims, usually becoming the butt of humorous put-downs – Jorkens withstands any assault on his integrity. A further element in the series is Dunsany's development of the "club tale": Jorkens tells his stories in the Billiards Club of London (though the club has no billiards table), usually after lunch, while the members congregate in a desultory fashion. Later in the twentieth century science-fiction writers such as Clarke, Isaac Asimov, and Spider Robinson took a cue from the Jorkens stories in developing their otherworldly bar-yarns books. Though the club setting is a mere device for telling the stories, Dunsany skillfully creates a sense of atmosphere that juxtaposes the chilly darkness outside and the boredom of the members with the stimulation they feel at hearing a Jorkens story. Finally, while readers repeatedly meet such standard fare as the island or river that cannot be located on a map ("A Drink at a Running Stream," "Mgamu"), the treasure that slips from the grasp of Jorkens and his compatriots ("Jorkens Retires from Business," "The Pearly Beach," "The Jorkens Family Emeralds"), the bewitching woman ("A Grecian Singer," "The Lost Romance"), and the scientific invention too clever to be useful ("The Invention of the Age," "Making Fine Weather," "The Lost Invention"), Dunsany treats each story with freshness and vigor, eliciting from the reader not boredom but a delighted sense of recognition.

Readers might speculate on what Dunsany's reputation would have been had he composed only the Jorkens stories. J. F. La Croix, for example, calls Jorkens "one of the most memorable persons in twentieth century fiction" and judges the books "Dunsany's supreme achievement." Most fantasy critics tend to dismiss these collections, though Brian Stableford concludes that while "Dunsany is not quite as impressive in this irreverent Wodehousian vein as when he is at his most self-indulgently romantic, . . . all the tales are amusing and some are very funny."

Dunsany explains in his second autobiography, *While the Sirens Slept* (1944), that Jorkens was "my reply to some earlier suggestion that I should write of my journeys after big game, and, being still reluctant to do this, I . . . invented a drunken old man who, whenever he could cadge a drink at a club, told tales of his travels." Perhaps to excuse the underpinnings of reality in the Jorkens stories, Dunsany, who thought his best stories were those that "seemed to come from pure inspiration," says in *Patches of Sunlight* that "the lie is the tale itself, worked up with this [true] material as a goldsmith will make a winged goddess from honest gold." Criticism of the Jorkens series ranges widely, from the enthusiastic to the polite to the vexed, as does the criticism of the fantasy stories.

At the start of World War II Dunsany returned to Dunstall, where he joined the Home Guard in preparation for the Battle of Britain. He saw little action, especially when the Germans failed to invade England. At least partly because of his government's request, he accepted an offer to hold the Byron Chair of English Literature at the University of Athens. He and his wife escaped from Greece in anticipation of the German invasion. He continued to write short stories and submit them to magazines through 1956. In the autumn of 1957, while living in Ireland as he had for the previous six years, he was stricken with appendicitis. He never recovered consciousness after an

appendectomy and died, at age seventy-nine, on 25 October 1957.

Dunsany's view that true literature resulted from inspiration rather than craft is well documented in his hundreds of short stories. His writing, governed by plot rather than an exploration of human complexity and motivations, broadened rather than evolved, shifting in subject matter from gods, ancient heroes, and the supernatural to tall tales, ghosts, and murder. His work is often classified and summarized rather than analyzed, and his tales engage the imagination but rarely the intellect. Yet his tales appeal to many readers, and his best work would fill several volumes. Despite the fact that he will probably never achieve a wide or general readership, the recent explosion in fantasy fiction and the respect critics of the genre hold for his early work assure continuing attention to his place in the field of short fiction.

Interviews:

Clayton Hamilton, "Lord Dunsany: Personal Impressions," *Bookman* (New York), 50 (February 1920): 537–542;

Bertrand de La Salle, "Une Visite à Lord Dunsany," *Revue de Paris,* 8 (August 1956): 39–43.

Bibliography:

S. T. Joshi and Darrell Schweitzer, *Lord Dunsany: A Bibliography* (Metuchen, N.J. & London: Scarecrow Press, 1993).

Biographies:

Hazel Littlefield, *Lord Dunsany: King of Dreams – A Personal Portrait* (New York: Exposition Press, 1959);

Mark Amory, *Biography of Lord Dunsany* (London: Collins, 1972).

References:

Mike Ashley, "Lord Dunsany," in his *Who's Who in Horror and Fantasy Fiction* (London: Elm Tree Books, 1977), pp. 70–72;

Edward Hale Bierstadt, *Dunsany the Dramatist* (Boston: Little, Brown, 1917; revised, 1919);

E. F. Bleiler, Introduction to *Gods, Men, and Ghosts: The Best Supernatural Fiction of Lord Dunsany,* edited by Bleiler (New York: Dover, 1972), pp. v–x;

Bleiler, "Lord Dunsany," in his *The Guide to Supernatural Fiction* (Kent, Ohio: Kent State University Press, 1983), pp. 165–172;

Zack Bowen, "Lord Dunsany," in *The Dictionary of Irish Literature,* edited by Robert Hogan (West-

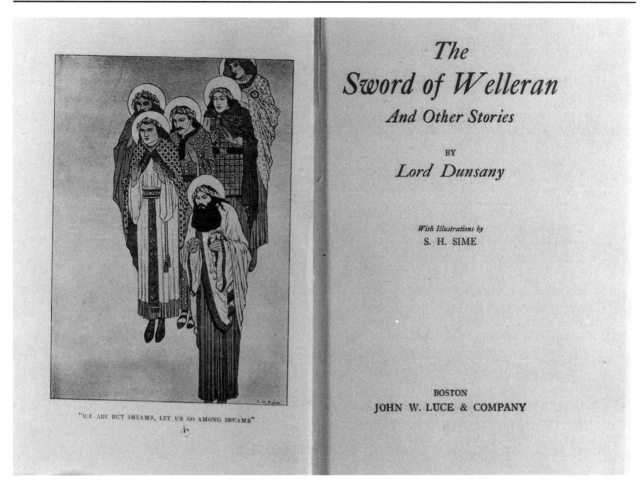

"WE ARE BUT DREAMS, LET US GO AMONG DREAMS"

Frontispiece and title page for the 1916 American edition of Dunsany's 1908 collection of heroic fantasy stories

port, Conn.: Greenwood Press, 1979), pp. 217–220;

Ernest A. Boyd, "Lord Dunsany and James Stephens," in his *Ireland's Literary Renaissance,* revised edition (New York: Barnes & Noble, 1968), pp. 412–414;

Boyd, "Lord Dunsany – Fantaisiste," in his *Appreciations and Depreciations: Irish Literary Studies* (London: Talbot, 1917), pp. 71–100;

Donald R. Burleson, "Major Literary Influences: Dunsany and Machen," in his *H. P. Lovecraft: A Critical Study* (Westport, Conn.: Greenwood Press, 1983), pp. 221–227;

Lin Carter, "The Dreams of Mana-Yood-Sushai," in Dunsany's *At the Edge of the World,* edited by Carter (New York: Ballantine, 1970), pp. vii–xi;

Carter, "Happy Far-Off Things," in Dunsany's *Over the Hills and Far Away,* edited by Carter (New York: Ballantine, 1974), pp. ix–xii;

Carter, "Return to the World's Edge," in Dunsany's *Beyond the Fields We Know,* edited by

Carter (New York: Ballantine, 1972), pp. vi–x;

William Chislett, "New Gods for Old," in his *Moderns and Near-Moderns* (New York: Grafton, 1928), pp. 171–188;

Padraic Colum, Introduction to Dunsany's *A Dreamer's Tales and Other Stories* (New York: Boni & Liveright, 1917), pp. xiii–xviii;

L. Sprague de Camp, "Two Men in One: Lord Dunsany," in his *Literary Swordsmen and Sorcerers: The Makers of Heroic Fantasy* (Sauk City, Wis.: Arkham House, 1976), pp. 48–63;

Shaw Desmond, "Dunsany, Yeats and Shaw: Trinity of Magic," *Bookman* (New York), 58 (November 1923): 260–266;

Grace Eckley, "The Short Fiction of Lord Dunsany," in *Survey of Modern Fantasy Literature,* 5 volumes, edited by Frank N. Magill (Englewood Cliffs, N.J.: Salem, 1983), pp. 1507–1510;

John Wilson Foster, "A Dreamer's Tales: The Stories of Lord Dunsany," in his *Fictions of the Irish*

Literary Revival: A Changeling Art (Syracuse: Syracuse University Press, 1987), pp. 291–298;

Martin Gardner, "Lord Dunsany" in *Supernatural Fiction Writers,* 2 volumes, edited by Bleiler (New York: Scribners, 1985), I: 471–478;

Oliver St. John Gogarty, "Lord Dunsany," *Atlantic Monthly,* 195 (March 1955): 67–72;

Frank Harris, "Lord Dunsany and Sidney Sime," in his *Contemporary Portraits: Second Series* (New York: Harris, 1919), pp. 141–157;

Vernon Hyles, "Lord Dunsany: The Geography of the Gods," in *More Real Than Reality: The Fantastic in Irish Literature and the Arts,* edited by Donald E. Morse and Csilla Bertha (Westport, Conn.: Greenwood Press, 1991), pp. 211–218;

S. T. Joshi, *Lord Dunsany: Master of the Anglo-Irish Imagination* (Westport, Conn.: Greenwood Press, 1995);

Joshi, "Lord Dunsany: The Career of a *Fantaisiste,*" in his *The Weird Tale: Arthur Machen, Lord Dunsany, Algernon Blackwood, M. R. James, Ambrose Bierce, H. P. Lovecraft* (Austin: University of Texas Press, 1990), pp. 42–86;

T. E. D. Klein, "A Dreamer's Tales," in *Dagon and Other Macabre Tales,* by H. P. Lovecraft, edited by August Derleth and S. T. Joshi (Sauk City, Wis.: Arkham House, 1987), pp. xiii–xxiii, xliii–xlv;

J. F. La Croix, "Lord Dunsany," dissertation, Trinity College, Dublin, 1956;

Ursula K. Le Guin, "From Elfland to Poughkeepsie," in her *The Language of the Night: Essays on Fantasy and Science Fiction,* edited by Susan Wood (New York: Putnam, 1979), pp. 83–96;

H. P. Lovecraft, "Supernatural Horror in Literature," *Recluse,* no. 1 (1927): 55–56; reprinted in revised and corrected form in his *Dagon and Other Macabre Tales,* edited by August Derleth and Joshi (Sauk City, Wis.: Arkham House, 1987), pp. 429–431;

Chris Morgan, "*The Book of Wonder,*" in *Survey of Modern Fantasy Literature,* 5 volumes, edited by Frank N. Magill (Englewood Cliffs, N.J.: Salem, 1983), pp. 161–163;

John D. Rateliff, " 'Beyond the Fields We Know': The Short Stories of Lord Dunsany," dissertation, Marquette University, 1990;

George Brandon Saul, "Strange Gods and Far Places: The Short Stories of Lord Dunsany," *Arizona Quarterly,* 19 (Autumn 1963): 197–210;

Darrell Schweitzer, Foreword to Dunsany's *The Ghosts of the Heaviside Layer and Other Phantasms,* edited by Schweitzer (Philadelphia: Owlswick, 1980), pp. 1–10;

Schweitzer, "Lovecraft and Lord Dunsany," in *Discovering H. P. Lovecraft,* edited by Schweitzer (Mercer Island, Wash.: Starmont House, 1987), pp. 91–112;

Schweitzer, *Pathways to Elfland: The Writings of Lord Dunsany* (Philadelphia: Owlswick, 1989);

Odell Shepard, "A Modern Myth-Maker," in his *The Joys of Forgetting: A Book of Bagatelles* (Boston: Houghton Mifflin, 1929), pp. 30–47;

Brian Stableford, "Lord Dunsany," in *Fantasy Literature: A Reader's Guide,* edited by Neil Barron (New York: Garland, 1990), pp. 158–160;

James Stephens, *The Letters of James Stephens,* edited by Richard J. Finneran (London: Macmillan, 1974);

Peter Tremayne, "Lord Dunsany (1878–1957)," in his *Irish Masters of Fantasy* (Postmarnock, Ireland: Wolfhound Press, 1979), pp. 205–210;

Marshall B. Tymn, Kenneth J. Zahorski, and Robert H. Boyer, *Fantasy Literature: A Core Collection and Reference Guide* (New York: Bowker, 1979);

Warren S. Walker, " 'Tales That One Never Wants to Hear' – A Sample from Dunsany," *Studies in Short Fiction,* 22 (Fall 1985): 449–454;

W. B. Yeats, Introduction to *Selections from the Writings of Lord Dunsany* (Churchtown, Ireland: Cuala Press, 1912), pp. xix–xxvii;

Jules Zanger, "*The Gods of Pegana,*" in *Survey of Modern Fantasy Literature,* 5 volumes, edited by Frank N. Magill (Englewood Cliffs, N.J.: Salem, 1983), pp. 625–627.

Papers:

Many of Dunsany's short stories, plays, poetry, and novels, particularly in the fantasy genre, are held in the L. W. Currey Science Fiction and Fantasy Collection at the Harry Ransom Humanities Research Center, University of Texas at Austin. In addition, a selection of letters from Dunsany to Mary Lavin can be found in the manuscript collection of the library at the State University of New York at Binghamton.

H. Rider Haggard

(22 June 1856 – 14 May 1925)

P. T. Whelan
Francis Marion University

See also the Haggard entry in *DLB 70: British Mystery Writers, 1860–1919.*

BOOKS: *Cetywayo and His White Neighbours; or, Remarks on Recent Events in Zululand, Natal and the Transvaal* (London: Trübner, 1882; enlarged, 1888; revised, 1889);

Dawn (3 volumes, London: Hurst & Blackett, 1884; 1 volume, New York: Lovell, 1887);

The Witch's Head (3 volumes, London: Hurst & Blackett, 1885; 1 volume, New York: Appleton, 1885);

King Solomon's Mines (London, Paris, New York & Melbourne: Cassell, 1885);

She: A History of Adventure (New York: Harper, 1886; London: Longmans, Green, 1887);

Jess (London: Smith, Elder, 1887; New York: Harper, 1887);

Allan Quatermain, Being an Account of his Further Adventures and Discoveries in Company with Sir Henry Curtis, Bart., Commander John Good, R. N. and One Umslopogaas (London: Longmans, Green, 1887: New York: Munro, 1887);

A Tale of Three Lions (New York: Lovell, 1887);

Maiwa's Revenge; or, The War of the Little Hand (London & New York: Longmans, Green, 1888; New York: Harper, 1888);

Mr. Meeson's Will (London: Blackett, 1888; New York: Harper, 1888);

My Fellow Laborer (New York: Munro, 1888);

Colonel Quaritch, V. C.: A Tale of Country Life (3 volumes, London: Longmans, Green, 1888; 1 volume, New York: Lovell, 1888);

Cleopatra, Being an Account of the Fall and Vengeance of Harmachis, the Royal Egyptian, as Set Forth by His Own Hand (New York: Munro, 1889; London: Longmans, Green, 1889);

Allan's Wife and Other Tales (London: Blackett, 1889; New York: Lovell, 1889);

Beatrice: A Novel (London: Longmans, Green, 1890; New York: Munro, 1890);

H. Rider Haggard

The World's Desire, by Haggard and Andrew Lang (London: Longmans, Green, 1890; New York: Harper, 1890);

Eric Brighteyes (London: Longmans, Green, 1891; New York: Lovell, 1891);

Nada the Lily (London & New York: Longmans, Green, 1892);

An Heroic Effort (London: Butler & Tanner, 1893);

Montezuma's Daughter (London: Longmans, Green, 1893; New York: Longmans, Green, 1894);

The People of the Mist (London & New York: Longmans, Green, 1894);

Church and State (New Style), An Appeal to the Laity (London: McCorquodale, 1895);

Speeches of the Earl of Iddesleigh and Mr. Rider Haggard (London: Published for the National Society for the Prevention of Cruelty to Children by Kegan Paul, Trench, Trübner, 1895);

Joan Haste (London & New York: Longmans, Green, 1895);

Heart of the World (New York: Longmans, Green, 1895; London, New York & Bombay: Longmans, Green, 1896);

The Wizard (Bristol: Arrowsmith / London: Simpkin, Marshall, Hamilton, Kent, 1896; New York, London & Bombay: Longmans, Green, 1896);

Dr. Therne (London, New York & Bombay: Longmans, Green, 1898);

Swallow: A Tale of the Great Trek (London, New York & Bombay: Longmans, Green, 1899);

A Farmer's Year, Being His Commonplace Book for 1898 (London, New York & Bombay: Longmans, Green, 1899);

The Last Boer War (London: Kegan Paul, Trench, Trübner, 1899); republished as *A History of the Transvaal* (New York & London: New Amsterdam/Kegan Paul, Trench, & Trübner, 1899);

Black Heart and White Heart and Other Stories (London, New York & Bombay: Longmans, Green, 1900); republished in part as *Elissa* (New York: Longmans, Green, 1900);

Lysbeth: A Tale of the Dutch (London, New York & Bombay: Longmans, Green, 1901);

A Winter Pilgrimage, Being an Account of Travels through Palestine, Italy, and the Island of Cyprus, Accomplished in the Year 1900 (London, New York & Bombay: Longmans, Green, 1901);

Rural England, Being an Account of Agricultural and Social Researches Carried Out in the Years 1901 and 1902, 2 volumes (London, New York & Bombay: Longmans, Green, 1902);

Pearl-Maiden: A Tale of the Fall of Jerusalem (London, New York & Bombay: Longmans, Green, 1903);

Stella Fregelius: A Tale of Three Destinies (New York: Longmans, Green, 1903; London, New York & Bombay: Longmans, Green, 1904);

The Brethren (London, Paris, New York & Melbourne: Cassell, 1904; New York: McClure, Phillips, 1904);

A Gardener's Year (London, New York & Bombay: Longmans, Green, 1905);

Report on the Salvation Army Colonies in the United States and at Hadleigh, England (London: Printed for His Majesty's Stationery Office, 1905); enlarged as *The Poor and the Land, Being a Report on the Salvation Army Colonies in the United States and at Hadleigh, England with Scheme of National Land Settlement and an Introduction* (London, New York & Bombay: Longmans, Green, 1905);

Ayesha: The Return of She (London: Ward, Lock, 1905; New York: Doubleday, Page, 1905);

The Way of the Spirit (London: Hutchinson, 1906);

Benita: An African Romance (London, Paris, New York & Melbourne: Cassell, 1906); republished as *The Spirit of Bambatse* (New York: Longmans, Green, 1906);

Fair Margaret (London: Hutchinson, 1907); republished as *Margaret* (New York: Longmans, Green, 1907);

Reports of the Royal Commission on Coast Erosion, 3 volumes, by Haggard and others (N.p., 1907–1911);

The Real Wealth of England (London: Ward, Lock, 1908);

The Ghost Kings (London, Paris, New York, Toronto & Melbourne: Cassell, 1908); republished as *The Lady of the Heavens* (New York: Lovell, 1909);

The Yellow God: An Idol of Africa (New York: Cupples & Leon, 1908; London, New York, Toronto & Melbourne: Cassell, 1909);

The Lady of Blossholme (London: Hodder & Stoughton, 1909);

Morning Star (London, New York, Toronto & Melbourne: Cassell, 1910; New York: Longmans, Green, 1910);

Queen Sheba's Ring (London: Eveleigh Nash, 1910; Garden City, N.Y.: Doubleday, Page, 1910);

Regeneration, Being an Account of the Social Work of the Salvation Army in Great Britain (London & New York: Longmans, Green, 1910);

Rural Denmark and Its Lessons (London, New York, Bombay & Calcutta: Longmans, Green, 1911);

Red Eve (London, New York & Toronto: Hodder & Stoughton, 1911; Garden City, N.Y.: Doubleday, Page, 1911);

The Mahatma and the Hare: A Dream Story (London, New York, Bombay & Calcutta: Longmans, Green, 1911; New York: Holt, 1911);

Reports of the Dominions Royal Commission, 24 volumes, by Haggard and others (N.p., 1912–1917);

Marie (London, New York, Toronto & Melbourne: Cassell, 1912; New York: Longmans, Green, 1912);

Child of Storm (London, New York, Toronto & Melbourne: Cassell, 1913; New York: Longmans, Green, 1913);

Umslopogaas, a Swazi prince Haggard met during his service in Africa and the model for several of Haggard's heroic Zulu characters

The Wanderer's Necklace (London, New York, Toronto & Melbourne: Cassell, 1914; New York: Longmans, Green, 1914);

A Call to Arms to the Men of East Anglia (London: Privately printed, 1914);

The Holy Flower (London, Melbourne & Toronto: Ward, Lock, 1915); republished as *Allan and the Holy Flower* (New York: Longmans, Green, 1915);

The Ivory Child (London, New York, Toronto & Melbourne: Cassell, 1916; New York: Longmans, Green, 1916);

The After-War Settlement and Employment of Ex-Service Men in the Overseas Dominions: Report to Royal Colonial Institute (London: Published for the Royal Colonial Institute by the Saint Catherine Press, 1916);

Finished (London, Melbourne & Toronto: Ward, Lock, 1917; New York: Longmans, Green, 1917);

Love Eternal (London, New York, Toronto & Melbourne: Cassell, 1918; New York: Longmans, Green, 1918);

Moon of Israel: A Tale of the Exodus (London: Murray, 1918; New York: Longmans, Green, 1919);

When the World Shook, Being an Account of the Great Adventure of Bastin, Bickley and Arbuthnot (London, New York, Toronto & Melbourne: Cassell, 1919; New York: Longmans, Green, 1919);

The Ancient Allan (London, New York, Toronto & Melbourne: Cassell, 1920; New York: Longmans, Green, 1920);

Smith and the Pharaohs and Other Tales (Bristol & London: Arrowsmith/Simpkin, Marshall, Hamilton, Kent, 1920; New York: Longmans, Green, 1921);

She and Allan (London: Hutchinson, 1921; New York: Longmans, Green, 1921);

The Virgin of the Sun (London, New York, Toronto & Melbourne: Cassell, 1922; Garden City, N.Y.: Doubleday, Page, 1922);

Wisdom's Daughter: The Life and Love Story of She-Who-Must-Be-Obeyed (London: Hutchinson, 1923; Garden City, N.Y.: Doubleday, Page, 1923);

Heu-Heu; or, The Monster (London: Hutchinson, 1924; Garden City, N.Y.: Doubleday, Page, 1924);

Queen of the Dawn: A Love Tale of Old Egypt (London: Hutchinson, 1925; Garden City, N.Y.: Doubleday, Page, 1925);

The Treasure of the Lake (London: Hutchinson, 1926); republished as *Treasure of the Lake* (Garden City, N.Y.: Doubleday, Page, 1926);

The Days of My Life: An Autobiography, 2 volumes, edited by C. J. Longman (London, New York, Toronto, Bombay, Calcutta & Madras: Longmans, Green, 1926); republished in part as *A Note on Religion* (London, New York, Toronto, Bombay, Calcutta & Madras: Longmans, Green, 1927);

Allan and the Ice Gods: A Tale of Beginnings (London: Hutchinson, 1927; Garden City, N.Y.: Doubleday, Page, 1927);

Mary of Marion Isle (London: Hutchinson, 1929); republished as *Marion Isle* (Garden City, N.Y.: Doubleday, Doran, 1929);

Belshazzar (London: Paul, 1930; Garden City, N.Y.: Doubleday, Doran, 1930);

The Private Diaries of Sir H. Rider Haggard, edited by D. S. Higgins (New York: Stein & Day, 1980).

OTHER: "In Memoriam," preface to *Life and Its Author, An Essay in Verse* by Ella Haggard (London: Longmans, Green, 1890);

"The Tale of Isandhlwana and Rorke's Drift," in *The True Story Book,* edited by Andrew Lang (London: Longmans, Green, 1893), pp. 132–152;

"Wilson's Last Fight," in *The Red True Story Book,* edited by Lang (London: Longmans, Green, 1895), pp. 1–18.

SELECTED PERIODICAL PUBLICATIONS –
UNCOLLECTED: "The Transvaal," *Macmillan's Magazine,* 36 (May 1877): 71–79;

"About Fiction," *Contemporary Review,* 51 (February 1887): 172–180;

"Suggested Prologue to a Dramatised Version of *She,*" *Longman's Magazine,* 11 (March 1888): 492–497;

"The Real *King Solomon's Mines,*" *Cassell's Magazine* (July 1907): 144–151.

Sir Henry Rider Haggard was not a great artist in anyone's estimation, least of all his own. Still less was he a great writer of short fiction; one seeks in vain for his name in critical surveys of the short story of the nineteenth or early twentieth century. By far the greater part of his fictional output was novels – more than fifty novels, as opposed to three volumes of shorter fiction – and of those novels he is remembered for three of his earliest works: *King Solomon's Mines* (1885), *She: A History of Adventure* (1886), and *Allan Quatermain* (1887). The rest of his work, which he continued to write until his death in 1925, is now forgotten – for the most part deservedly so. Yet in his day Haggard was the most popular writer in England and among the highest earning, commanding large sums from publishers' advances, magazine serializations, and the sheer volume of sales of his romances. Thus Haggard is a literary phenomenon essential to any history of nineteenth- and twentieth-century British culture.

Born on 22 June 1856 at Bradenham, Norfolk, Rider Haggard was the son of William Haggard, a Norfolk squire, and his wife, Ella. Their eighth child, he was a sickly baby saved only by his mother's devotion. His early life conforms to a pattern familiar to readers of literary biography: nursed through infancy by a sensitive, artistic, and loving mother, he grew up under the contempt of his father, whose lack of imagination rendered his son incomprehensible to him. The father's obtuseness turned the boy more exclusively toward his mother, to whom he attributed his literary talent.

She first aroused his interest in ancient Egypt, the spiritual center of his fiction.

Haggard's childhood memories seem to have been especially vivid, and certain images return in his fiction, some of them frequently. One of his childhood nurses somehow discovered the power of his imagination and used it to keep him quiet at night. After she had put him to bed, according to his daughter Lilias Rider Haggard, Rider's nurse opened a cupboard in the room, disclosing "a disreputable doll of particularly hideous aspect, with boot-button eyes, hair of black wool and a sinister leer on its painted face." She then committed the young Rider to the charge of "She-who-must-be-obeyed" and left him alone in the dark. In his memoirs John Kotzé, who knew Haggard in Africa, confirms that Haggard's imagination could occasionally run away with the facts: "Those who knew Haggard recognized in him a man of honour and truth. But his . . . imagination impelled him into a world of fancy which for the time had complete hold of his sense, and hence he described as fact what was mere fiction." Thus one should not take the doll anecdote as fact, as his biographers have tended to do, but as a vital image, the original version of the femme fatale archetype often manifested in his fiction. Here is the common root of the sinister sorceresses with which his work abounds: both the repulsive, such as the ancient Gagool in *King Solomon's Mines,* and the fascinating, such as Ayesha in *She.*

In his diary for 15 November 1920, Haggard recalled hearing as a boy a tale concerning a Peruvian tomb whose inner chamber contained "a dead and mummified man at the head of about a dozen other persons ranged round the table." The ring on the dead chieftain's hand was owned – so at least the boy believed – by the man who told the tale. Haggard comments, "The tale made a deep impression on my youthful mind and, in fact, turned it towards Romance." To this image, as well as to his mother's interest in ancient Egypt, can be traced Haggard's fascination with mummified corpses, which recur often enough in his fiction to bear out his assertion.

After secondary education at Ipswich Grammar, Haggard failed an entrance examination for the army, and his father sent him to a London "crammer," a private institution that undertook to prepare the boy for the Foreign Office. Haggard never took the exam but made use of his new freedom to become acquainted with spiritualism and to fall in love. In *The Days of My Life: An Autobiography* (1926) Haggard records that he had something of a gift for seeing visions at séances. One of the more spectacular was of two young, beautiful women wrapped, like his character Ayesha, in white, gauzy drapery. More important than any vision he may have experienced was the conviction, which he shared with the spiritualists and may have derived from them, that this world and the next are in intimate contact and that life in the world after death is not very different from this life. Biographer D. S. Higgins notes the affinity between the spiritualists' notions and the esoteric doctrines of ancient Egypt. There is also an affinity between Haggard's metaphysical assumptions in his novels and the teachings of the theosophists, including Madame Blavatsky and her followers, who were also in vogue in London around the turn of the century. A metaphysics combining the spiritualist belief in communication between the worlds and the theosophical doctrine of multiple reincarnation is evident throughout Haggard's fiction.

Love most obviously gave Haggard the personal need for such convictions. Haggard's daughter Lilias refers in her memoir of her father to "Lilith," with whom he fell violently and permanently in love during this period; Higgins names her as Mary Elizabeth Jackson, who was known to her friends as Lilly. Haggard's father effectively destroyed the relationship by sending Haggard out to Natal. He left in July 1895 as an unpaid member of Sir Henry Bulwer's staff.

Haggard flourished in Africa, becoming a personal friend of the first governor of the Transvaal, Sir Theophilus Shepstone. This relationship led to Haggard's first salaried appointment, which was quickly followed by promotion to master and registrar of the high court of the Transvaal, a considerable accomplishment for one so young. His duties involved traveling all over the province with the court and the judge in a small caravan of ox wagons that he conducted. He was also responsible for security and for supplying fresh meat. The position carried a salary that would have enabled him to marry, but by this time Lilly had accepted an older, richer suitor.

Haggard, however, apparently clung to the belief that Lilly was not lost to him. Lilias Rider Haggard testifies that "it was to be his fate that the deep emotional experiences, his loves and tragedies . . . remained active, insistent, his daily companions until the hour of his death." Throughout his life he needed to believe that in some future existence Lilly and he would be together, an echo of the story of *She*. The parting and reunion of lovers over a span of many lives is Haggard's monomyth, for which Africa, particularly Egypt, provides the most suc-

cessful of his fictional settings. In Haggard's beautiful yet savage fictional Africa, projections and displacements of his own imagined spiritual biography are dramatized repeatedly.

In Africa, Haggard acquired some of the most impressive types in his limited dramatis personae. Almost always Zulu, Haggard's noble savage is typically strong, fleet, fierce, unforgiving, courageous, honorable, proud, and unshakably loyal to those he loves; always a warrior of legendary endurance and prowess, he is also philosophical and able to be tender and nurturing when occasion demands. Based on a Swazi prince whom Haggard met on his travels, Umslopogaas in *Allan Quatermain* and *Nada the Lily* (1892) is perhaps the purest example of this archetype, but his type also appears in Umbopa in *King Solomon's Mines,* Magepa in "Magepa the Buck" (1912), and Nahoon in "Black Heart and White Heart" (1896). Often he is a magician with uncanny abilities as a seer and witch doctor, like Indabazimbi in "Allan's Wife" (1889), Hokosa in "The Wizard" (1896), or Menzi in "Little Flower" (1920). His attitude to the Europeans whom he serves is that of the noble follower; he is never subservient and often looks upon his white companions as willful children in his charge, whom he must protect from the consequences of their own folly. He is, especially in his magician form, immensely wise, fully aware of theosophical mysteries at which the white people in their simpleminded Christian orthodoxy have not even begun to guess. In this aspect the noble savage is the mouthpiece of Haggard himself.

This figure is often found in tandem with Allan Quatermain, the other great "discovery" of Haggard's African years. Based perhaps on the hunter F. C. Selous, though Haggard denied it, Quatermain is a presence felt throughout Haggard's work. Like Joseph Conrad's Marlow, whom he predates, Quatermain is a second narrator, the tales being offered to the reader by an anonymous "editor" who claims to have taken them posthumously from Quatermain's papers or from Quatermain as he talked after dinner at Sir Henry Curtis's home in Yorkshire. Many of Haggard's novels and several of his shorter fictions are Quatermain stories, which begin in 1887 with *Allan Quatermain* and end in 1927 with *Allan and the Ice Gods: A Tale of Beginnings*.

Haggard's sojourn in Africa from 1875 to 1881, brief though it was, occurred at a politically active time. Among the events to which Haggard recurred in his fiction were the Zulu War with Cetywayo and the massacre of British troops by Zulus at Isandhlwana in 1879. During these years Haggard matured greatly, acquired the confidence his difficult relationship with his father had hitherto denied him, and through both personal and vicarious experience amassed a fund of anecdotes that in many forms and repetitions was to last him throughout his career as a writer.

On his return to England Haggard met and became engaged to Louisa Margitson, whom he married in August 1880. The couple returned to South Africa just before the outbreak of the first Boer War, a brief campaign in which the British were decisively defeated. Their adventures provided material for the novel *Jess* (1887). Their son, Jock, was born in Africa in 1881, but before a year had passed they returned to England to begin farming in their native Norfolk. It soon became clear, however, that farming in England, now in an intense agricultural depression, would not provide the new family with a living, so Haggard began reading for the law. He also began his first book, *Cetywayo and His White Neighbours; or, Remarks on Recent Events in Zululand, Natal and the Transvaal* (1882).

Haggard quickly became a compulsive writer. His first novel, *Dawn* (written in 1883), was an apprentice piece followed shortly by three masterpieces in the first phase of his career as a fiction writer – *King Solomon's Mines, Allan Quatermain,* and *Jess,* all written in 1885. The publication of these early works placed him among the practitioners of romantic adventure fiction, a genre to which Robert Louis Stevenson's *Treasure Island* (1883) and *The Black Arrow* (serialized in 1883) had just given a considerable boost. This period was also the eve of the creation of Sherlock Holmes by Sir Arthur Conan Doyle and of the emergence of Rudyard Kipling as a major writer of short fiction.

Allan's Wife and Other Tales (1889), the first of Haggard's three volumes of shorter fiction, is also of this period but compares unfavorably with his best work. The title story, the longest and most substantial work in the volume, is a considerable contribution to the Quatermain saga, as it deals with the character's early childhood, his marriage to Stella, and the birth of his son, Harry.

Structurally "Allan's Wife" has the characteristic fault of the quest-romance in that the thematic portion of the novella is preceded by a picaresque journey whose incidents have nothing to do with the theme. After the first chapter, which deals with Allan's and Stella's infancies and their separate departures for Africa, the plot becomes a series of events that for five chapters are connected only chronologically, until eventually Quatermain and his Zulu witch-doctor companion, Indaba-zimbi, are rescued from a waterless desert by Stella and her

Haggard shortly after returning from Africa in 1881

servant, Hendrika the "Baboon-woman." Hendrika has been taken into Stella's household after being stolen as a baby and brought up by baboons; in the process, she has acquired not only a great deal of baboon psychology but several of their physical features, too: a long face, for example, as well as superhuman strength and agility.

Stella takes her guests back to the village where her father, though not a minister, is a kind of unofficial lay preacher to the native Basutos. Stella and Allan naturally fall in love (the love scenes are among Haggard's worst writing), but the Baboon-woman is insanely jealous of her mistress's affection, and when Stella marries Allan, Hendrika musters an immense army of baboons, which descends on the village and carries off the bride. Stella never fully recovers from the experience; though she is rescued, she survives only long enough to bear Quatermain's child.

In this tale, as often in reading Haggard, there is a sense of wasted potential. The reader is constantly jarred out of even the most willing suspension of disbelief by the careless construction of the plot, by the lifelessness of Stella and of Quatermain as lover, and by the love scenes themselves, which are wordy and overloaded with metaphysics. Particularly irritating are the prophecies and philosophizing of Indaba-zimbi. Almost to the end Quatermain remains skeptical of the Zulu's ability as a seer – inexplicably so, as every one of his many predictions comes true, usually almost immediately – but to the reader Indaba-zimbi is obviously Haggard's mouthpiece on the subjects of love, the afterlife, and human nature in general. Perhaps as a result, Indaba-zimbi's idiolect is grossly inconsistent, ranging from the Zulu/biblical to the chummy/colloquial. Cordy Jeaffreson, a supportive reader of Haggard's first attempt at a novel, wrote in the spring of 1883 to Haggard, "You have written it with your *left hand* without strenuous pains; you must rewrite it with your *right hand,* throwing all your force into it." Haggard took the advice then, but he did not make it a guiding principle for his career; for more than forty years he was driven to produce adventure after adventure, never pausing to make them into art.

The shorter Quatermain stories in the same volume – "Hunter Quatermain's Story," "Long Odds," and "A Tale of Three Lions" – are hunter's yarns presented as after-dinner stories at the table of Sir Henry Curtis, Quatermain's companion in *King Solomon's Mines.* Structured episodically, these are slight, sensational pieces, of interest perhaps only to readers who wish to complete their surveys of the Quatermain saga.

"A Tale of Three Lions" features Quatermain's son, Harry, a bloodthirsty youth long dead when Quatermain tells the story. The episodes are lively, with Haggard's occasional trademark touch of vivid horror. At one point Quatermain, searching for a servant who has been dragged away by a lion during the night, finds the man's severed head floating in a beautiful pool. The scene symbolizes much that Africa means to Haggard: an ancient and serene beauty liable at any time to be disrupted by terror. Modern tastes are less endeared to a man introduced as the age's most successful slayer of elephants and lions, and it is difficult to rejoice in Quatermain's slaughtering several lions in deliberate revenge for his servant's death. The desire for revenge also motivates his lion hunting in "Long Odds," though the lions have eaten his ox rather than his servant. On this occasion one of the lions manages to sink its teeth into Quatermain's leg before it dies, leaving him with the limp that, like his bereavement, is part of his persona as a spinner of yarns.

Haggard's career was established by 1887, in which year he earned more than £10,680 sterling. His critical reception was less favorable: critics said his style was faulty and his writing careless. Most negative criticism was directed at the sheer bloodiness of the fiction, though now his battle scenes do not seem exceptional in this respect.

Haggard took more seriously several accusations of plagiarism, more than one of which was undoubtedly justified. In *Allan Quatermain* Umslopogaas's terrifying display of axmanship is much like Sergeant Troy's display of swordsmanship in Thomas Hardy's *Far From the Madding Crowd,* published the previous year, and the scene in which Quatermain's party is threatened by giant land crabs occurs almost word for word in E. F. Knight's *The Cruise of the "Falcon"* (1884). Also, the plot of *She* coincides in many details with that of Edward George Earle Bulwer-Lytton's *A Strange Story* (1862). Given Haggard's character, such plagiarism was probably unconscious.

During this period Haggard made friends as well as enemies. Attacked by Frank Harris and George Moore, he was defended by Andrew Lang, with whom he developed a friendship that led eventually to collaboration on a novel, *The World's Desire* (1890). A lifelong friendship with Kipling began in 1889, and in 1890 there was even a word of praise from Matthew Arnold, who, according to John Murray, rated Haggard among "the greatest living masters of English prose."

In December 1890 Haggard's mother died. The following year he finished *Nada the Lily,* the last work of his most fertile period, seven years in which he had written fifteen novels. His mother's death had a disastrous effect on Haggard. It was fifteen years before he took up the sequel to *She,* which he had already planned, and longer still before his next Quatermain tale. Higgins believes that he had been writing obsessively for his mother; with her death the drive to create departed. In addition, the death of Haggard's son, Jock, little more than a year later had an equal or greater effect. None of the thirty-nine novels that followed had the impact or originality of the earlier ones, and the activity that began as a deep-seated drive became for Haggard a chore undertaken out of the need to maintain his family's lifestyle.

After the completion of *Nada the Lily,* Haggard was no longer so exclusively devoted to writing. He farmed; he moved to London to edit the *African Review*; and he campaigned for Parliament. He still wrote fiction, but without the conviction or drive of the early years of his career. From this period come the tales in *Black Heart and White Heart and Other Stories* (1900). This volume includes only one short story, the sixty-page tale titled "Black Heart and

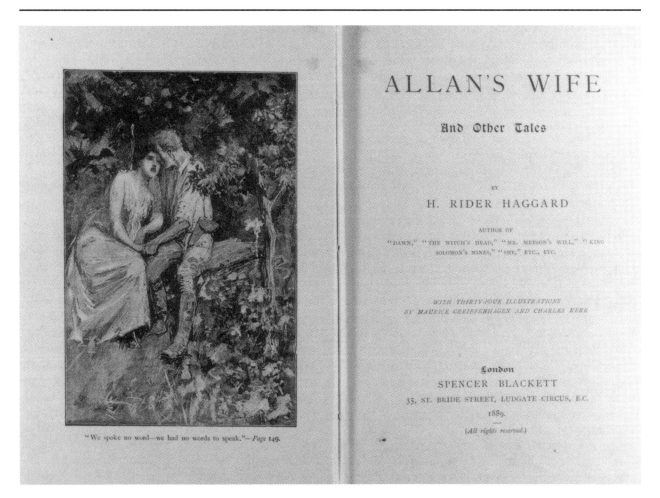

ALLAN'S WIFE

And Other Tales

BY

H. RIDER HAGGARD

AUTHOR OF

"DAWN," "THE WITCH'S HEAD," "MR. MEESON'S WILL," "KING
SOLOMON'S MINES," "SHE," ETC., ETC.

WITH THIRTY-FOUR ILLUSTRATIONS
BY MAURICE GREIFFENHAGEN AND CHARLES KERR

London
SPENCER BLACKETT
35, ST. BRIDE STREET, LUDGATE CIRCUS, E.C.
1889.
(All rights reserved.)

"We spoke no word—we had no words to speak."—Page 149.

Frontispiece and title page for Haggard's first collection of short fiction

White Heart: A Zulu Idyll." The other two works are novellas: "The Wizard" and "Elissa; or, The Doom of Zimbabwe," published serially in *The Long Bow* in 1898. "The Wizard" was not included in the first American edition of the collection, which was published as *Elissa.*

"Black Heart and White Heart," as its subtitle implies, is set in Zulu territory in 1878, at the time when King Cetywayo was preparing for war with the British. As is typical in Haggard's writing, the historical and geographical setting of the tale is precise, and it refers to the battle of Isandhlwana, at which a British force was wiped out by Zulu warriors. The tale is unusual among Haggard's short fiction in that the only European in the tale, its center of consciousness, is also its villain, and the evil of this corrupt scion of British aristocracy is contrasted with the nobility of the Zulu hero and heroine. Philip Hadden is an effective character. His experience as hunter and trader and his expertise in Zulu language and customs make him a negative Quatermain. He deliberately stifles any vestiges of

conscience left in him in order to arrange the death of Nahoon, the Zulu hero who has saved his life, and the abduction of Nanea, Nahoon's bride-to-be.

The story also contains elements of racism, which makes a portion of Haggard's prolific output unattractive. Nahoon is the archetypal noble savage, "a savage gentleman of birth, dignity and courage," black outside but "white-hearted" in contrast to Hadden, who has, in the words of a witch who is the author's mouthpiece, a "[b]eautiful white body with a black heart." Nanea, as well as being "white-hearted," is presented so as to be attractive to Haggard's white readers: "As is occasionally the case among Zulu women, she was beautiful – so beautiful that the sight of her went straight to the white man's heart . . . her face had little in common with that of the ordinary native girl, showing as it did strong traces of the ancestral Arabian or Semitic blood. It was oval in shape, with delicate aquiline features . . . the wavy coal-black hair hung down to the shoulders." In short, she is beautiful because she is unlike most Africans. When Bushmen appear in the stories, Haggard's racism turns from the offensive to the ludicrous. Stella remarks in *Allan's Wife* that she believes baboons to be "almost as human as the Bushmen." In "Black Heart and White Heart" there is a small group of Bushmen who nourish their grotesque bodies with corpses that float downriver from a Zulu place of execution, or, executions being scarce, with their own children. The tale also offers staples of adventure fiction: hairbreadth escapes from death, a stirring battle between the Zulu warrior and a leopard, and justice done in the end.

"Black Heart and White Heart" is a fairly ordinary adventure story, but the other two tales in the volume are not: "The Wizard" offers breathtaking battle scenes in an unconvincing metaphysical framework, while "Elissa" is one of Haggard's best tales. "The Wizard" begins with a prosperous English rector, Thomas Owen, receiving a spiritual call to convert the Amasuka, who resemble the Zulus. Pausing only long enough to learn the language, he marches into the stronghold of these witch doctor–ridden murderers of missionaries. Owen's path is made straight with a series of unlikely marvels and visions, which he exploits with shameless equivocation and mummery, convincing part of the tribe that he is a greater wizard than those empowered by their ancestors. He becomes embroiled in a dispute over succession involving "good" and "evil" "savages," a femme fatale, and, most striking, a wizard named Hokosa, Owen's most powerful antagonist and later his most significant convert. After poisoning Owen, Hokosa leads the side of good in the final battle and, though the good of course triumphs, dies at the end of the battle in one of the most astonishing deaths in literature. Treacherously captured, he is crucified at the top of the Tree of Doom, a tree on which so many men have been hanged that the very exhalations of its leaves have become poisonous. From this position, however, he inspires his troops with his words and his stoic suffering until, at the moment of victory, he is slain by the femme fatale, who climbs the tree to thrust a knife into his side. Thus Hokosa becomes a Christ figure to whom Owen seems finally a mere precursor. Perhaps this tale, more than any other by Haggard, illustrates the phenomenon he represents: he is a second-rate artist generally unable to create a satisfying form, but the flow of archetypal material through his extraordinary imagination generates brief tours de force.

"Elissa; or, The Doom of Zimbabwe" is the best of Haggard's shorter fiction in the adventure genre. Zimbabwe is an ancient ruined city in south-ern Africa whose origin in Haggard's day was the subject of much wild speculation; most assumed that a civilization such as Zimbabwe apparently represented could not have been the work of native Africans. Haggard concurs in "The Marble Kraals" chapter of "Allan's Wife," where it is asserted that buildings in stone could not be the work of black Africans, even if the buildings were designed like Basuto huts. For Haggard in "Elissa," Zimbabwe was "an inland Phoenician city . . . weakened by luxury and the mixture of races" and destroyed when "hordes of invading savages stamped it out of existence."

"Elissa" is set in Zimbabwe's latter days during the tenth century B.C. King Solomon still reigns in Israel, but Zimbabwe is decadent, a place of fleshpots and of "unholy orgies" in honor of Baaltis, a mother goddess who delights in the sacrifice of infants. Two travelers, reminiscent of other pairs in Haggard's fiction, have come to this place. Tall, handsome, aristocratic, and openheartedly naive, Aziel is the grandson of Solomon and an Egyptian woman; Metem is a Phoenician merchant with Quatermain's combination of hard-bitten experience and a soft heart. Hiram, king of Tyre, has assigned Metem to guard Aziel. Yet Metem at least is not a mere repetition of a formula. He has a love of fast bargains that gets him into scrapes, but his quick wits and courage keep him and Aziel from disaster. There is also an element of the comic in his character.

On the outskirts of the city Metem and Aziel have the good fortune to save Elissa, daughter of the king of Zimbabwe and neophyte priestess of Baaltis, from being abducted by an immense savage. Abductions are not uncommon in these troubled times, Elissa tells them, as "savages such as he haunt the outskirts of the city seeking to steal white women to be their wives." The naive Elissa allegorizes the whole scene: "is [the black giant] not a symbol of the evil and the ignorance which are on the earth and that seek to drag down the beauty and wisdom of the earth to their own level?" Aziel and Elissa are beginning to fall in love when the Levite Issachar, another figure of some originality, comes upon the party. Issachar is a fanatical monotheist and the guardian of Aziel's soul; as such he is the enemy of Elissa, priestess of Baaltis.

The party enters the city, where the last of the central characters is introduced – Ithobal, son of a Phoenician and an African queen, and king of the land around the city. Elissa's attacker was his emissary. The tale plays out the drama of Ithobal's struggle to gain possession of Elissa. The plot is complex but handled well. Particularly enjoyable are the machinations of Metem, whose avowed aim is wealth but whose heart is with the lovers. The story is full of action and romance, with erotic interludes in the worship of Baaltis and an exciting culminating battle. Apart from the usual racist elements in the setting and characterization, its only real flaw is the overworking of prophecy. Most of the main characters utter doom-laden prophecies, every one of which is bound to come true. The tale is in Haggard's grandest style, and though many of the characters and situations are recognizable from other works, there is much originality.

The decade 1900–1910 was a difficult one for Haggard, resulting in indifferent romances, including *Ayesha: The Return of She* (1905), the long-awaited sequel to *She*. Much of his energy was spent researching and writing on English agrarian reform and on the activities of the Salvation Army, which in 1905 led to his appointment as a royal commissioner. He served on various government committees and did a great deal of traveling almost until the end of his life without receiving an honorarium for his work. He was rewarded in 1912 with a knighthood, but meanwhile his publishers advanced smaller sums, and his work was no longer serialized before publication in book form. As a result, Haggard had to work even harder at his fiction to keep his income from declining.

In 1903 Haggard also made a visit to Egypt, where, guided by the renowned Egyptologist Howard Carter, he viewed the newly unearthed tomb of Queen Nefertiti. Several of Haggard's romances from this decade are set in Egypt around the theme of reincarnation, as is the title story of Haggard's third and final volume of stories, *Smith and the Pharaohs and Other Tales* (1920). The volume includes six tales, all but one of which were published years earlier: "Smith and the Pharaohs" (1912–1913), "Magepa the Buck," "The Blue Curtains" (1886), "Little Flower" (no earlier publication recorded), "Only a Dream" (1905), and "Barbara Who Came Back" (1913).

"Only a Dream" is a tale in the manner of Edgar Allan Poe: a widower on the eve of his second marriage dreams that his first wife's ghost visits him and makes him a wedding present of her own polished skull. "Magepa the Buck" is another Allan Quatermain story, effectively presented in the context of the Zulu War between Cetywayo and the British. Haggard casts Cetywayo in the role of villain; the hero is Magepa, a Zulu who has fallen from favor with his bloodthirsty chief. Quatermain narrates the story of Magepa's heroic death for the sake of his beloved daughter and grandson.

"The Blue Curtains" has its foundation in the author's biography. The hero, whose nickname is Bottles, is a penniless army officer in Natal. His English sweetheart, Madeline Spenser, deserts him for a rich man, pleading pressure from her family. Twelve years later Bottles inherits a small legacy and returns to England, where Madeline is now a widow. He seems to be greeted favorably by her, but his brother, who is a good deal richer than he, proves her false by proposing to her while Bottles eavesdrops. Bottles is found dead the next morning with his sleep-inducing medicine by his bedside. "The Blue Curtains" is a well-told story, tightly organized and economical. The mystical meditations are kept brief and placed appropriately in the mind of an eccentric hero, and the hard superficiality of Madeline and the amused cynicism of the elder brother are convincing.

"Little Flower," like "The Wizard" and "Allan's Wife," concerns the activity of missionaries in an African village. As in "The Wizard," the missionary's chief antagonist is a Zulu witch doctor, but here the author sides with the witch doctor against the bullying, arrogant missionary Thomas Bull, known as "Tombool." The narrator despises the villagers of Basuto stock, who have donned tattered European clothing with their new religion. Their Zulu neighbors remain staunchly pagan and lightly clad. Whereas Owen in "The Wizard" produced all kinds of wonders to convert his flock, here only the pagan Menzi has any ability of this kind, producing rain that falls only on the pagans' fields and uttering frequent prophecies of predictable accuracy. Tombool's daughter Tabitha is the center of Menzi's interest, and he names her "Little Flower." A beautiful and charming child, she arouses a Victorian kind of avuncular-romantic sentiment in the witch doctor. He protects her with his charms, so that while her parents are harrowed with evil dreams, having built their house on an ancient Zulu execution site, she flourishes, becoming more and more sympathetic to the Zulu way of life.

The feud between Tombool and Menzi continues amusingly, with Menzi the victor at every turn until the mission church bell tower is brought down by a storm. Menzi is fatally injured by the clapper, which flies through the air and catches him squarely in the chest. Menzi is thus brought to acknowledge the superiority of Christianity. He requests baptism from Tabitha's hand at the same time as he makes her his heir and dies convinced that he will be with his Little Flower in the life to come. The remainder of the tribe converts at Tabitha's order, and

Haggard during a 1924 visit to Egypt

Tombool goes off to a more civilized post, leaving Tabitha as ruler of the tribe.

"Smith and the Pharaohs" is the story of a bank clerk. At the British Museum, Smith falls in love with the stone head of the Egyptian queen Ma-Mee, and over the next several years he becomes an expert amateur Egyptologist, finally discovering her tomb. The tomb has been robbed, but not everything is taken, and Smith finds some interesting items to hand over to the French director-general of antiquities at the Cairo Museum. For himself he reserves a statuette and the hand of the mummy with one of its rings. The director discerns that Smith is in love with the queen he has exhumed; he points out, in his tolerant French manner, that her name would be more conventionally spelled Ma-Mé, and that Smith's pronunciation sounds like the French "*Ma mie* – my darling." The reader acquainted with Haggard's early life may discern a connection here with his interest in Egypt, his association of corpses with feminine beauty, and his love for his mother.

After his interview with the director Smith is inadvertently locked in the museum with the ghosts of the pharaohs whose mummies are housed there. They charge Smith with tomb robbing, but Ma-Mee, recognizing him as the reincarnation of the artist she once loved, intercedes for him. This portion of the tale is unsuccessful. The dialogue of the pharaohs begins in an idiom indistinguishable from that of Sir Henry Curtis's dinner guests, then drifts into the ponderous diction of romance, but the episode replays one of Haggard's key motifs, that of the lover's rediscovery of the beloved in a subsequent life. Smith's unconscious quest, like that of Leo Vincy in *She,* is for a bride lost millennia before.

This motif of love across generations is also present in "Barbara Who Came Back," the other tale of reincarnation in the volume. The lively Barbara is a poor clergyman's daughter who marries the son of the local squire. The two are "twin souls": "Had they been one ancient entity divided long ago by the working of Fate . . . their union could not have been more complete." They have a child who is passionate, uncontrollable, and a terrible burden to his mother. Both parents then die, the husband first, and Haggard offers an account of their life in the other world, where they live with their entire family and even the husband's dog, which is posthumously endowed with speech. Meanwhile, Barbara is still worried about her son, now married to his former nurse, a gypsy, and gone thoroughly to the bad. Through Barbara's spiritualized vision the reader watches him degenerate until Barbara sets out to rescue him; she begins by being reincarnated as his daughter. The plot is a farrago, yet it displays more clearly than elsewhere in Haggard's work the imaginative possibilities of a reincarnation whose mechanism is flexible enough to allow a woman voluntarily to become her own granddaughter. One may hope, implies Haggard in these two stories, to marry in a future life a beloved whom circumstances have denied in this life.

One of Haggard's later works, *The Mahatma and the Hare: A Dream Story* (1911) is undoubtedly one of his finest pieces of fiction, and its characterization and setting leave it free of racism. A satire against blood sports in the form of a conversation between a man and a hare, it could not be further in spirit from his gory lion-hunting yarns of the 1880s. Rather than harking back to African days or to times when men were heroes or slaves and women were queens or hags, the story grows out of Haggard's experience as a squire, an enthusiastic student of agriculture, and a lover of the English countryside. It is linked to his other short fiction by its frame-story method of narration and by the author's theosophical metaphysics, wry humor, and ability to paint vivid scenes of action. It contrasts with it in its artistic success.

By the time *Smith and the Pharaohs* was published, Haggard's fortunes had risen from their low point in 1910 and 1911. Neither the quality nor the sales of his fiction had improved, but by 1914 the developing motion-picture industry was expressing interest in his work, which in 1915 and 1916 brought him more than nine thousand pounds in sales of film rights. He was also encouraged by his old friend Kipling, who genuinely admired his work and had helped sustain Haggard's morale through all the difficulties of his bereavement and declining creative power. Haggard was invigorated by the onset of World War I. War work called forth another surge of energy as, in addition to his writing, he traveled the world negotiating the future migration of demobilized military personnel to the colonies. By the end of the war his health was poor, but he wrote another eight novels in his remaining six-and-a-half years.

During Haggard's lifetime he was part of the brief revival of romance and as such was compared by the critics, almost always unfavorably, with Kipling and Stevenson. Both these authors admired him, however; Kipling frankly admitted Haggard's inspiration for his own work, and his letters to Haggard are consistent in their praise of his writing.

More recently, critics as diverse as C. S. Lewis, V. S. Pritchett, and Nina Auerbach have written on Haggard, and a complete annotated bibliography of Haggard criticism was published in 1991. Contemporary criticism of Haggard tends to center around the extent to which he was or was not sexist, racist, and a propagandist of imperialism. Attempts to absolve him of racial prejudice are not entirely successful, and critics have argued persuasively that he has been to some extent responsible for certain aspects of a past imperialistic ethos and current racial stereotypes. The racism and sexism that were such a powerful part of the ethos of his time are undeniably present in his works, more egregiously in some than in others. Yet the theosophical wisdom and love that are Haggard's highest values transcend boundaries of race and gender. Wisdom and love are the basis of a non-stereotypical heroic strength manifest in Africans such as Menzi and Hokosa, in women such as Barbara and Tabitha, and in the hare. White males in Haggard's work can be stupid, arrogant, cowardly, or treacherous; even white heroes may be naive, irresolute, and in need of rescue by Africans or women who are wiser, braver, and unhesitating in their commitment to the consequences of love.

It is Haggard's popular novels that have been most influential, for good or for ill; it cannot be maintained that Haggard's legacy derives from his short fiction. Of the few pieces in this genre collected in Peter Haining's 1981 anthology *The Best Short Stories of Rider Haggard,* only *The Mahatma and the Hare* fully deserves to be remembered. Haggard's comparative insignificance in short fiction is illustrated by Haining, who fills out his collection with autobiographical anecdotes and chapters from a serialized novel.

Through two of his romances, however, Haggard's influence on certain kinds of fiction has been enormous, out of all proportion to the literary value most critics would ever have assigned to him. Kipling acknowledged his inspiration for *The Jungle Book* (1894), and Conrad's work also has obvious affinities with Haggard's. Haggard's closest literary affinities, however, are with writers of popular fiction. Doyle, whose career also included a South African sojourn, an interest in spiritualism, the defense of British colonial policy, and a knighthood, was a contemporary, and Haggard's immediate successors include adventure writers Edgar Wallace and John Buchan, who began to publish in the 1890s but did not fully develop as writers until later. Wallace's trademark character – Sanders, colonial commissioner of some indefinite location in West Africa – seems to owe much to Quatermain, as do some of Buchan's heroes.

Haggard's influence is still discernible in popular fiction, particularly science fiction and fantasy. In film, not only have Haggard's own works appealed to directors, but every children's animated film or television serial about lost cities or Egyptian curses owes something to him directly or indirectly. Finally, his reputation rests and will continue to rest on *King Solomon's Mines* and *She,* romances never out of print since they were first published more than a century ago.

Interviews:
Frederick Dolman, "How I Write My Books," *Young Man,* 8 (June 1894): 21–23;
"An Interview with H. Rider Haggard," *Christian Commonwealth,* 25 (1 November 1906): 75–76.

Bibliographies:
J. E. Scott, *A Bibliography of the Works of Sir Henry Rider Haggard, 1856–1925* (London: Mathews, 1947);
D. E. Whatmore, *H. Rider Haggard: A Bibliography* (Westport, Conn.: Meckler / London: Mansell, 1987);

Lloyd Siemens, *The Critical Reception of Sir Henry Rider Haggard: An Annotated Bibliography, 1882–1991, English Literature in Transition, 1880–1920,* Special Series Number 5 (1991).

Biographies:

Lilias Rider Haggard, *The Cloak That I Left: A Biography of Rider Haggard* (London: Hodder & Stoughton, 1951);

Morton Cohen, *Rider Haggard: His Life and Works* (London: Hutchinson, 1960);

Peter Berresford Ellis, *H. Rider Haggard: A Voice from the Infinite* (London & Henley: Routledge & Kegan Paul, 1978);

D. S. Higgins, *Rider Haggard: The Great Storyteller* (London: Cassell, 1981).

References:

Norman Etherington, *Rider Haggard* (Boston: Twayne, 1984);

Margery Fisher, *The Bright Face of Danger: An Exploration of the Adventure Story* (London: Hodder & Stoughton, 1986; Boston: Horn Book, 1986);

Wendy R. Katz, *Rider Haggard and the Fiction of Empire: A Critical Study of British Imperial Fiction* (Cambridge: Cambridge University Press, 1987);

John Kotzé, *Biographical Memoirs and Reminiscences* (Cape Town: Maskew Miller, n.d.);

Murray Pittock, "Rider Haggard and *Heart of Darkness,*" *Conradiana,* 19 (Autumn 1987): 206–208;

Alan Sandison, *The Wheel of Empire* (London: Macmillan, 1967; New York: St. Martin's Press, 1967).

Papers:

Haggard collections in England are housed at the Norfolk Record Office, Norwich; Cassell in London; and A. P. Watt & Son, London. Collections in the United States are housed at the Columbia University library; the Huntington Library, San Marino, California; and the Lockwood Memorial Library, State University of New York, Buffalo.

Frank Harris

(14 February 1856 – 26 August 1931)

Patricia Roberts
University of Missouri at Columbia

BOOKS: *Elder Conklin and Other Stories* (London: Heinemann, 1895 [i.e., 1894]; New York & London: Macmillan, 1894);

How to Beat the Boer: A Conversation in Hades (London: Heinemann, 1900);

Montes, the Matador and Other Stories (London: Richards, 1900; New York: Kennerley, 1910);

The Bomb (London: Long, 1908; New York: Kennerley, 1909);

The Man Shakespeare and His Tragic Life Story (London: Palmer, 1909; New York: Kennerley, 1909; revised edition, London: Palmer, 1911);

Shakespeare and His Love (London: Palmer, 1910);

The Women of Shakespeare (London: Methuen, 1911; New York: Kennerley, 1912);

Unpath'd Waters (London: John Lane, 1913; New York: Kennerley, 1913);

Great Days (London: John Lane, 1914 [i.e., 1913]; New York: Kennerley, 1914);

The Yellow Ticket, and Other Stories (London: Richards, 1914; New York: Published by the author, 1920);

Contemporary Portraits (London: Methuen, 1915; New York: Kennerley, 1915);

England or Germany? (New York: Wilmarth, 1915);

The Veils of Isis, and Other Stories (New York: Doran, 1915);

Love in Youth (New York: Doran, 1916);

Oscar Wilde: His Life and Confessions, 2 volumes (New York: Published by the author, 1916; augmented edition, New York: Published by the author, 1918; augmented edition, Garden City, N.Y.: Garden City, 1932; London: Constable, 1938);

Contemporary Portraits. Second Series (New York: Published by the author, 1919);

A Mad Love: The Strange Story of a Musician (New York: Published by the author, 1920);

Contemporary Portraits. Third Series (New York: Published by the author, 1920);

My Life and Loves, 4 volumes (Paris: Privately printed, 1922–1927; London: W. H. Allen,

Frank Harris in 1927

1964); revised & abridged as *My Life: Frank Harris* (London: Richards, 1947); republished as *Frank Harris: My Life and Adventures* (London: Elek, 1958);

Contemporary Portraits. Fourth Series (New York: Brentano's, 1923; London: Richards, 1924);

Undream'd of Shores (London: Richards, 1924; New York: Brentano's, 1924);

New Preface to "The Life and Confessions of Oscar Wilde," by Harris and Lord Alfred Douglas (London: Fortune, 1925);

Joan La Romée (London: Fortune, 1926; New York: Harris, 1926);

Latest Contemporary Portraits (New York: Macaulay, 1927);

Confessional: A Volume of Intimate Portraits, Sketches and Studies (New York: Panurge, 1930);

On the Trail: Being My Reminiscences as a Cowboy (London: John Lane, 1930); republished as *My Reminiscences as a Cowboy* (New York: Boni, 1930);

Pantopia (New York: Panurge, 1930);

Bernard Shaw: An Unauthorized Biography Based on Firsthand Information, with a Postscript by Mr. Shaw (London: Gollancz, 1931; New York: Simon & Schuster, 1931);

Mr. and Mrs. Daventry, by Harris and Oscar Wilde (London: Richards, 1956).

Collection: Elmer Gertz, ed., *The Short Stories of Frank Harris: A Selection* (Carbondale: Southern Illinois University Press, 1975).

According to his four-volume autobiography, Frank Harris was so gifted with intelligence, virility, and natural talent that his ability to triumph at any endeavor, from boxing to writing, threatened the small minds by which he was surrounded and resulted in his lifelong persecution. But in his autobiography Harris admits that he may have misremembered much of his life, saying, "I am no longer a trustworthy witness." He remains best known for his sexually explicit autobiography, *My Life and Loves* (1922–1927), his biographies of Oscar Wilde and George Bernard Shaw, and his fictional memoirs *On the Trail: Being My Reminiscences as a Cowboy* (1930). During his lifetime his short fiction was overshadowed by the controversies raised by his other writings and by his personal and professional dealings. Since his death scholars have paid most attention to questions of biography, especially his relations with Wilde and Shaw, while his volumes of short fiction have not received the attention they deserve.

Harris lived his life in the realm of extravagant promises, fabulous plans, spectacular gestures, and dramatic poses. His friends and acquaintances generally reacted to him in equally extreme manners; it was apparently difficult for him to have anything other than admirers or enemies, with quite a few people shifting from one category to the other.

He was a gifted listener and storyteller, with a tendency to relate incidents in others' lives with himself as the protagonist. In the second volume of his autobiography he describes the actions of his memory: "It began to color incidents dramatically. For example, I had been told a story by someone, it lay dormant in me for years; suddenly some striking fact called back the tale and I told it as if I had been present and it was fulfilled with dramatic effects, far beyond the first narration." He was not, for example, a ranch hand, as he claimed, but he probably picked up the stories that make up *On the Trail* from the cowhands he met when he was a young man working in his family's butcher business and while traveling across the United States by train. He probably never met many of the people who make up his five volumes of *Contemporary Portraits* (1915–1927), and he certainly was not close enough to them to have been the recipient of the sort of intimate confidences he relates.

Born James Thomas Harris in Galway, Ireland, on 14 February 1856, he was the son of a cantankerous, heavy-drinking coastguardsman, Thomas Vernon Harris, and a weak mother, Anne Thomas Harris, who died when he was three. He was raised primarily by his oldest brother, Vernon, with intermittent periods under the supervision of their strict and demanding father. Probably because of his friendship with an Irish Catholic boy and his resulting absorption of Fenian sentiments, which enraged his Protestant father, Harris was sent in 1869 to Ruabon Grammar School in Denbighshire, Wales. Harris claims he performed spectacularly there in mathematics and Latin but that he was ostracized for his Anglo-Irish origins, his small stature, and his willingness to stand up to the school bullies.

In April 1871 Harris ran away from the school and went to the United States, where he spent some time in New York and Colorado before ending up in Lawrence, Kansas, sometime in 1872. The next three years were spent studying law, attending lectures at the University of Kansas, and working in his brothers' butcher business. After his autobiography was published what exactly happened in Lawrence came to be the source of considerable controversy. In his autobiography Harris claims that he was the confidant of a promising young classics scholar, Byron Smith, whose frail health was quickly deteriorating because of nearly incessant wet dreams. Despite Harris's ingenious application of a whipcord, Smith's health continued to decline and, after leaving Lawrence for Colorado, he died. The incident as Harris tells it is typical of his autobiography and of the kind of controversies in which he continually found himself. It is easy to recognize the story as part of a recurrent pattern in the autobiography: Harris attributes some humiliating sexual habit or weakness (most frequently impotence but sometimes incest, sodomy, or compulsive masturbation) to anyone who made him angry or envious. Biographer Philippa Pullar suggests that Harris was motivated by his own impotence while writing the autobiography, and biographer Hugh Kingsmill suggests that he was motivated by having read a mildly insulting letter that Smith had written about him. Whatever caused Harris to invent the story in the autobiography, the consequences were that Smith's now-aged fiancée, Kate Stephens, who had never married, was enraged enough to edit a book called *The Lies and Libels of Frank Harris* (1929) in response, portraying Harris in the worst possible light. The pettiness and prurience of the controversy were typical for Harris, whose impressive abilities were dissipated in the many unnecessary battles he carried out in his magazines, memoirs, autobiographies, and libel suits. These battles frequently alienated friends and collaborators, became libel suits against him, and at least once resulted in his going to jail. As John Dos Passos wrote in an introduction to a later edition of Harris's *The Bomb* (1908), "He might have developed into a first-rate novelist if he hadn't been such a damn liar."

These battles were particularly likely to develop, and were probably most destructive, with or regarding someone whom Harris once admired. For example, it is clear from his early short stories that Harris once idolized Smith, who is obviously the model for the hero of one of Harris's best stories, "The Boss of Gullmore," collected in *Elder Conklin and Other Stories* (1895). In this story Roberts, a professor of Greek at the state university who has espoused a Pateresque cultural deism, gets involved in trying to break the power of the town's corrupt political boss. The boss retaliates by playing on the religious bigotry of the town and faculty who, in a righteous terror at the prospect of having a professor who is not a conventional Christian, fire Roberts. The story, like several of Harris's best, is a highly effective portrait of the narrow-mindedness and hypocrisy of western towns. As in the work of Sinclair Lewis, the villain of the story is not so much the corrupt political boss as the passion for conformity on the part of the townspeople.

The controversy over Smith has also tended to overshadow the real importance that Harris's time in Lawrence had for him as a writer. In addition to providing him with an identity – he forever after claimed to have been a cowboy, although he

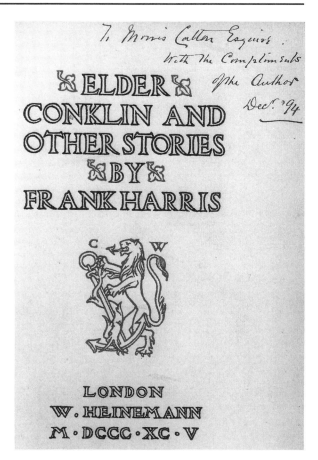

Inscribed title page for Harris's first book, a collection of stories praised for their characterization and straightforward prose (Courtesy of the Lilly Library, Indiana University)

probably never got closer to the cowboy life than working as a butcher – it provided him with the material for many of his best stories, such as "A Modern Idyll," "Elder Conklin," and "The Boss of Gullmore."

In 1875 Harris returned to Europe, first living in England and then traveling to Germany to study. In 1878, while in Germany, he married Florence Adams, a sickly woman who lived only ten months after their wedding. After her death he spent some time in Russia, Vienna, and Ireland before returning to England. He corresponded with Thomas Carlyle and apparently impressed him as a man of considerable promise. The letter of introduction Carlyle wrote for him was useful for meeting some of the editors of the more prominent British journals. In 1883, after writing some reviews and essays for some of those journals, Harris met one of the owners of the politically conservative *Evening News* and convinced him that he should be made editor. There has been considerable speculation as to how someone with so little experience and such politically liberal sentiments managed to attain such a position in a conservative paper. It has even been suggested that he did so through having affairs with the owners' wives, but Pullar has persuasively argued that it was probably because the owners were desperate to improve the disastrously bad financial situation of the paper. Although Harris's sensationalistic techniques did precisely that, he was released from the paper and moved on to the *Fortnightly Review*, a journal with a more liberal tradition, in 1886.

In 1887 Harris married a rich widow named Emily Clayton, who was well connected in conservative political circles. As editor of a prestigious journal he demonstrated excellent judgment in the authors he selected; his wife's money enabled him to entertain in the extravagant manner he had long admired; and her connections made it possible for him to indulge seriously his dreams of entering politics – in fact, in 1889 he became the Conservative candidate for South Hackney. There is something unintentionally pathetic in his descriptions of this period, however. Having attained what he had always wanted – wealth, class, and power – he did not seem to know what to do with them other than annoy people. As he says in his autobiography, "And so now, having won a secure position in the best English life, I found I was out of place." One of his problems was that he remained deeply self-conscious and defensive of his height and of his class origins. Another was that his dramatic gestures, ranging from spending hours regaling friends and acquaintances with enthralling stories to spontaneously inviting large numbers of people to nearly endless lunches at expensive restaurants, did not fit well with the mundane cares of running a paper.

Perhaps most important, Harris simply did not have the discretion and tact necessary for a political career in Victorian Britain. When the Charles Stewart Parnell scandal broke during the 1889 election campaign, for example, Harris condemned the British public for hypocrisy and skewed priorities in pillorying a man for adultery when other politicians regularly did the same or worse. He may have been right in his attack, but he was not shrewd; the majority of his campaign committee immediately resigned. Perhaps his stance on the Parnell issue was largely motivated by his own unhappy marriage and adulterous relationship with a young woman, but throughout his life – in his fiction, his editorial tirades, the Wilde controversy, the calculated offensiveness of his autobiography – Harris returned to the theme of sordid motives hypocritically cloaked in Christian virtue. In his fiction, for example, this is the theme of "A Modern Idyll," "Profit and Loss," "The Boss of Gullmore," "An English Saint," and "The Magic Glasses."

Harris's political career limped along after the Parnell outburst, and the marriage languished as well. He gave up both the political aspirations and the marriage that would help him achieve them around the same time that he was dismissed as editor from the *Fortnightly Review* in 1894. He went through a period of depression before buying the *Saturday Review* and then hiring an impressive group of writers, among them Shaw, H. G. Wells, Max Beerbohm, and Arthur Symons.

In 1895 Harris's first book, *Elder Conklin and Other Stories,* was published and was generally received favorably. The story of a vain young schoolmaster who leaves his bourgeois family to travel west to study law, "Elder Conklin" was immediately identified as the strongest in the collection and praised for its depth of characterization and spare prose. The schoolmaster is alternately aroused and repulsed by the forthright, willful, and sensual daughter of Elder Conklin. The characterization of the daughter is especially powerful, showing Harris's capacity to give depth and compassion to characters who might easily be unattractive. The story is particularly sensitive to the conflicts of the middle-class morality of the eastern schoolmaster and the straightforwardness of the daughter; she recognizes that he is both aroused and repulsed but cannot imagine the cause, and her aggressive attempts to capture the schoolteacher simply repel him the more.

"A Modern Idyll," the story of a young and somewhat self-absorbed minister who chooses to refuse a prosperous and prestigious call from a Chicago church in order to remain close to his deacon's wife, whom he hopes to seduce, has strengths similar to "Elder Conklin." It is not surprising that it was condemned by some reviewers for immorality – a reviewer in the *Nation* condemned all of the stories for the sensuality of the women, especially "A Modern Idyll" – but other critics recognized the story's depth of characterization, including the minister's becoming persuaded by his fascination with his own eloquence, his mistaking an effective peroration for a call from God, and his spiritual struggles that degenerate into self-absorption. The other stories in the collection – "The Sheriff and His Partner," "Eatin' Crow," and "The Best Man in Garotte" – are true Westerns, stories of life in gold-mining towns. They were initially praised in England as superior to those of Bret Harte for their simpler narrative style; now they seem inferior because of their complete lack of humor.

Wilde's trial also took place in 1895. Harris responded with foresight, courage, and generosity during his friend's trial and imprisonment, although his actions were not always as generous as his promises. Unfortunately for his reputation, those letters in which Wilde berates Harris for failing to fulfill promises have become better known than those in which he thanks Harris for gifts and loans. After Wilde's release they collaborated on a moderately successful play, eventually published in 1956 as *Mr. and Mrs. Daventry,* but neither profited much from it because of various disagreements over whether Wilde had simultaneously sold the plot to several other people, the amount of work Wilde put into Harris's version, and whether (or how much) Wilde owed Harris and vice versa. It is probable that the disagreements could have been resolved or prevented had Harris been either more magnanimous or better organized. It was typical of Harris that the friendship, and any further possibility of literary collaboration, soured because of his extravagant promises and financial disarray.

In 1900 Harris published his second collection, *Montes, the Matador and Other Stories.* Prior to its publication George Meredith is said to have praised the title story. Critics have frequently remarked on the clear influences of Stendhal, Guy de Maupassant, and Leo Tolstoy, particularly in the two best-known stories, "Montes the Matador" and "Sonia." Harris's interest in the common person's life, his affection for stories with simple plots and depth of characterization, and his sympathy for the unsavory are particularly evident in these two stories. "Montes the Matador" tells of a matador's success, his love for a young woman, and his reaction to discovering she has become the lover of an inferior bullfighter. As several critics have remarked, it is the kind of story that Ernest Hemingway has done better, but it was very striking in its day. A serious problem with the story is indicated in Vincent Brome's comment regarding the narration, "told in the first person by Montes alias Harris," referring to Harris's inability to write a story from any perspective other than his own. In this collection, for instance, "Profit and Loss" is the only story that does not rely on a Harris-like first-person narrator. This story, about a man who becomes a hero for saving a child from a fire he himself has set in order to solve his financial difficulties, combines two themes recurrent in Harris's fiction: the heartlessness of contemporary business practices and the confusion of sinners for saints. "Sonia," like Harris's novel *The Bomb,* is a highly sympathetic account of an anarchist. The narrator, a young man who sounds much

Caricature of Harris by Max Beerbohm (by permission of Mrs. Eva Reichmann)

like Harris, falls in love with a passionate and headstrong Russian aristocrat. She breaks off the relationship, but he finds her again in Saint Petersburg, where he discovers that she is at the center of an anarchist conspiracy. "First Love" and "The Interpreter" are both very short stories. The second is about an interpreter who is tricked into betraying a hiding criminal, while the first is about the attempted seduction of a girl.

After a trip to South Africa, Harris began to use the *Saturday Review* as a vehicle to promote his personal investments by running articles that were little more than advertisements. Some have suggested that the journal was also used as a means to raise money through blackmail, with Harris threatening to publish private letters or embarrassing articles unless paid, but his biographers generally agree that he had no part in such activity. In any case, his interest in the world of high finance turned him away from his own literary career; he wrote little fiction between *Mr. and Mrs. Daventry* (completed in 1901) and his novel *The Bomb.*

When Harris sold the *Saturday Review* in 1898 he founded or edited a series of journals intended to protect or enhance his own investments in the stock market in one way or another: *The Candid Friend,* a gossipy society paper that lasted two years; the "Automobile Review," which apparently never actually produced a single issue; and Dunlop Tyres's magazine *Motorist and Traveller,* which ran for approximately one year. His most successful publishing venture from 1898 to 1910 was *Vanity Fair,* an enterprise he ran from 1907 to 1909 that Pullar sees as a milestone because it caused him to begin writing the kind of material for which he would become famous, such as his memoirs and his portraits of contemporaries. Despite attempts to use the various journals as advertisements for his financial ventures and as representations of himself as a financial genius, throughout the rest of his life his finances were precarious. He had occasional prosperous periods during which he would order expensive pieces of art, buy property, and begin projects, but there were also periods when his prospects were bleak.

In February 1909 Harris finished *The Man Shakespeare and His Tragic Life Story,* in which he argues that Hamlet, who he claims is the type for most of William Shakespeare's heroes, is a self-portrait. The book was favorably reviewed but not popular. He proceeded to write *The Women of Shakespeare* (1911), which was published serially in the *English Review* and was less well received but more profitable.

In 1913 Harris published his third collection of short stories, *Unpath'd Waters,* which was favorably reviewed. In the best-known of the stories, "The Miracle of the Stigmata," Jesus has survived the Crucifixion, moved to Caesarea, married, and settled down to life as a carpenter. When Paul preaches in the area Jesus is the only one not converted to Christianity, and the story becomes a vehicle for Harris's belief that Jesus' gospel of love was corrupted by Paul's hatred of the flesh. In "King of the Jews," in the form of a short play, Simon of Cyrene tells his wife about helping Jesus carry the cross. In "The Holy Man" Harris has taken a plot from Tolstoy. An orthodox bishop visits an isolated village where there is a holy man. The bishop is concerned about the lack of proper religious instruction, and he teaches the Lord's Prayer to the saint. He comes to think that the saint's unconscious revision of the prayer is an improvement, and the story ends with the holy man walking across the water to ask the departing bishop one more question about the prayer. "The Irony of Chance" and "The Magic Glasses" are short pieces of science fiction in the style of Harris's own protégé Wells. The first is about a scientist who

ruins his reputation by adding a mechanism to assist a genuine scientific discovery; the second tells of a scientist who is prosecuted for fraud because he invents and sells glasses that enable the wearer to see the truth. "The Spider and the Fly," another story in the form of a play, and "The Ring" are both about how contemporary monetary practices victimize people. The victims are not lower class but rather aristocrats who are impoverished or threatened with impoverishment.

The best of the stories is "An English Saint," a powerful tale of a vacuous young man whose passivity is mistaken for wisdom. Kingsmill begins his biography of Harris with an incident regarding this story, which he sees as typical of Harris's life. John Middleton Murry had been a disciple of Harris and had written a piece praising "An English Saint" in extravagant terms. According to Kingsmill, just before the essay was to be published Harris alienated Murry by publicly ridiculing him and a piece he had just written; Murry never published the essay on Harris and ceased to be a friend and ally.

Harris next purchased *Hearth and Home,* a journal run primarily by himself and Enid Bagnold that lasted until 1913. He proceeded to buy *Modern Society,* and for various reasons his finances reached a new low. Bagnold said in his autobiography that the final blow was when Harris was jailed for contempt of court during a libel trial at a time when the magazine and his finances were already extremely precarious. He lost the magazine and left England for Nice. He spent the next year writing the first series of his *Contemporary Portraits* (1915). This concept, Harris's impressions of his famous contemporaries, was popular, and it turned into a profitable series. It also seriously annoyed many of those whose portraits Harris sketched, both because Harris claimed intimate knowledge of people whom he barely knew and because he took credit for saving or discovering innumerable people. In a 1917 letter to Harris, Shaw aptly parodied the latter quality in a short essay called "How I Discovered Frank Harris":

One cold winter day I was walking along the embankment: the benches of which are the only furniture of the homeless, frozen, penniless outcasts of London. At one of the outcasts I looked a second time, struck by his fine eyes and something familiar in his expression. Suddenly I recognized him as Frank Harris, who had edited an obscure rag called The Fortnightly Review for a miserable pittance. In a flash it came to me that Frank was the man I needed. I spoke to him; told him to wait on his bench for my return; pressed a shilling into his frozen fingers; and left the poor wretch, who was unable to speak and could only sob with gratitude. At that moment the once famous Saturday Review was on the brink of the abyss. I jumped into a hansom and drove to the office. I wasted no time in preliminaries. I said bluntly "Nothing can save you but a feuilleton by G.B.S., and you know it. Well, I will fill two pages of any paper that is edited by Frank Harris." Ten minutes later I returned to the embankment, and said "Frank: you are the editor of the Saturday Review." He tried to say "Thank God!"; but his mouth was full of the sausage roll he had purchased with my shilling. His heart was full too. The rest is history.

While in Nice, Harris became involved in negotiations closely related to blackmail: Lady Frances Warwick's threats to publish her love letters from the king of England unless someone from the palace paid her substantial debts. At the same time that she contacted Harris, she let friends of the king know of her plans and her willingness to suppress the letters in exchange for a large sum. The negotiations with Harris were promptly confused when Buckingham Palace acquired an injunction against publication and used the Defence of the Realm Act to threaten Lady Warwick with imprisonment. She turned the letters over to the palace in exchange for her substantial debts being paid. There is little doubt that she was engaged in blackmail; it is less clear whether Harris was. Even after her debts were paid and the letters were returned to the palace, Harris and Lady Warwick continued to negotiate regarding her memoirs.

While Harris was in Nice he published another collection of short stories, *The Yellow Ticket, and Other Stories* (1914). This collection has probably received the least attention of any, presumably because, apart from "A Daughter of Eve," it contains his weakest work. At his best he was capable of giving depth and complexity to unsavory characters; at his worst, as in this collection, many of his stories seem overworked. In addition, the qualities that make his fiction stand out strikingly from that of his contemporaries – especially the depth, sensuality, and contradictions of his women – tend in this collection to deteriorate into redundant portraits of the type of woman that aroused Harris. "A Daughter of Eve" is the exception, and it is justifiably considered one of his masterpieces by many scholars. While discussing the death of a much-admired prominent lady, a judge proceeds to tell an apparently unrelated story about how unpredictable women are. In his youth, he says, while he was on a sailing voyage, he saw a sensual, attractive young woman seduce the husband of her pregnant sister. The pregnant wife promptly commits suicide, and a few days later the distraught husband does as well. The seductress

Harris near the end of his life

who appears to have caused all the misery becomes a respectable and kindly society matron whose kindness and charity are a great benefit to her family and community. After her death, and after the judge has realized her identity, he receives a letter she left for him that explains that she was actually the victim of her sister and her sister's husband. Thus what appears to be a conventional narrative of a pure and loving wife betrayed by her sensual sister's seduction of her husband is turned so that the sensual sister becomes the true victim and virtuous heroine.

With the outbreak of World War I Harris wrote a series of articles urging the United States to take the German side of the conflict; they were collected as *England or Germany?* (1915) and caused him permanent harm. He next finished his biography of

Wilde, *Oscar Wilde: His Life and Confessions,* which he published himself in February 1916. Although the book has become central in discussions of Wilde and impressions of Lord Alfred Douglas, it was largely ignored initially. It is probable that a defense of a homosexual written by a pro-German author who had previously defended anarchists was simply too much for the American or British press to review favorably.

Still, Harris was able to acquire an American magazine, *Pearson's,* which he edited from October 1916 to 1922. Kingsmill claims that, although Harris was constantly sending letters claiming that the journal was about to fold and was in desperate need of money, he lived a magnificent life. Pullar, however, suggests that it was precisely because of his extravagant living and financial schemes that he was constantly trying to raise money; thus, in a sense, the pleas for help were sincere. One of these schemes was his autobiography, which he began writing in Nice and continued writing in the Catskills. During this time he was also working on a second series of *Contemporary Portraits* (1919), various short stories and lectures, and a new edition of the Wilde biography, and he was still negotiating regarding Lady Warwick's memoirs.

One of these short stories, *A Mad Love: The Strange Story of a Musician,* was published by the author in New York in 1920. It has received little attention, although Elmer Gertz included it in his 1975 selection of Harris's short fiction. Like much of Harris's writing, it concerns obsessive love and disillusionment, but it lacks the depth of characterization or conflict that marks his best work. The narrator, a man much like Harris, meets a brilliant musician contemplating suicide because of his wife's betrayal. The narrator both convinces the musician to postpone the suicide and manages to find the misunderstood wife. Although the musician acknowledges that he misinterpreted the situation to see it as betrayal, he still feels that love is gone and commits suicide. The story, already weak, is further flawed by a long digression into Harris's music criticism. It is also flawed by his limitations in narrative style; with the exception of those done as plays, his stories are almost always narrated by a person extremely similar to the narrator of the autobiography, and some stories might have been improved by experimenting with point of view, tone, or voice.

Harris published a final collection of short stories, *Undream'd of Shores,* in 1924. In this collection he included some extremely short stories, "The Extra Eight Days" and "St. Peter's Difficulty," that work particularly well. "St. Peter's Difficulty" reads

like a folktale from Fyodor Dostoyevsky; "The Extra Eight Days" could have been written by Maupassant or W. Somerset Maugham. "Love Is My Sin," a retelling of the Andrea del Sarto story, is similar to *A Mad Love.* The narrator, again a man much like Harris, manages to postpone but not prevent the suicide of a brilliant artist, this time a painter, who is ruined by his obsession with an unworthy woman. "Akbar: The Greatest," "A Chinese Story," and "In Central Africa" are hampered by Harris's inability to convey foreign settings in a convincing manner. Some critics highly praise one of the longer stories, "The Temple of the Forgotten Dead." Robert Brainard Pearsall predicts, "When Harris is finally awarded a serious literary biography, many of its chief psychological and esthetic concepts will be illustrated by 'The Temple of the Forgotten Dead.'" Brome praises the collection as a whole: "A not unexpected blend of cynicism and sentimentality, brutality and tenderness marked these stories."

The first volume of Harris's autobiography, the explicit and appropriately titled *My Life and Loves,* came out in 1922. Some biographers have suggested that the book was relentlessly explicit in order to ensure good sales; Pullar argues that Harris, by this time impotent, was attempting to titillate the secretaries to whom he dictated the memoirs. Whatever his intentions, it is clear that he did not predict the consequences. He must have known there would be a furor, and he always liked to see himself as a martyr for art and truth, but it is unlikely that he thought his autobiographies would be banned in so many countries. Because of the autobiography, Harris was threatened with prosecution by the French government, the American distributor was imprisoned, copies were confiscated in England, and he was told he could not travel to the United States without risking imprisonment. Although the volumes were apparently fairly well read, the fact that they were banned meant that they were read in pirated forms that provided no income for Harris. Perhaps more important, they immediately cast a long shadow over any of his other work. He claims, probably correctly, that he was ostracized after their publication, and his other writings could not get the attention they deserved.

Despite the problems created by the first two volumes of the autobiography, he continued to write more. The last few years of his life were spent dictating additional volumes, meeting people whom the book impressed, fighting off various illnesses and infirmities, and making plans for other literary and financial ventures. When he died in Nice on 26

August 1931, he was in the middle of a biography of Shaw and the final volume of the autobiography, both of which were published posthumously.

Modern unexpurgated versions of the autobiography have created little if any controversy. The book continued to exert an unwelcome effect on the reception of Harris's short fiction, however, since Gertz's 1975 selection of Harris's short fiction was discussed in the context of the autobiography. The anonymous reviewer for the *Virginia Quarterly Review,* for example, said, "While these stories ... have much of the easy narrative style of *My Life and Loves* they have neither its psychological force nor its dramatic proportion. Harris has a tin ear for characterization and dialogue and an unfortunate penchant for mediocre aphorisms that reduce his stories to the level of transparent fable of sociopolitical morality." Gertz's analysis of Harris epitomizes a more favorable response: "Harris's stories, like everything he has written, bear witness to the combination of diverse qualities that has always distinguished his work at its best and at its worst — an irresistible attraction for all sorts and conditions of men and women, striking and diversified scenes and situations, variety almost for its own sake, always dramatic and sometimes shocking changes and chances, conversation from the most naturalistic to the poetic and unreal, a preoccupation with the most primitive passion no less than the most sub[t]le nuances of action and contemplation so intertwined as to be indistinguishable."

Perhaps because Harris dissipated his energies in so many different areas and controversies, he never fully developed the fully distinctive style or approach for his short fiction that is suggested in "Elder Conklin," "The Boss of Gullmore," "Profit and Loss," or the other stories in which he demonstrated a shrewd judgment of American Victorianism. Thus, at its worst his work verges on the derivative, particularly showing the influence of Harte, Tolstoy, Maupassant, and Stendhal. Even if not fully distinctive, much of his other short fiction is valuable as well, especially "Sonia," "St. Peter's Difficulty," "The Extra Eight Days," "An English Saint," and "A Daughter of Eve."

Letters:

Autobiographical Letters of John Galsworthy: A Correspondence with Frank Harris, Hitherto Unpublished (New York: English Book Shop, 1933);

Frank Harris to Arnold Bennett: Fifty-Eight Letters, 1908–1910 (Merion Station, Pa.: Privately printed for the American Autograph Shop, 1936);

Dan H. Laurence, ed., *Bernard Shaw: Collected Letters* (London: Reinhardt, 1965);

Stanley Weintraub, ed., *The Playwright and the Pirate: Bernard Shaw and Frank Harris – A Correspondence* (University Park: Pennsylvania State University Press, 1982).

Biographies:

Kate Stephens, ed., *The Lies and Libels of Frank Harris* (New York: Antigone, 1929);

Elmer Gertz and A. I. Tobin, *Frank Harris* (Chicago: Mendelsohn, 1931);

Samuel Roth, *The Private Life of Frank Harris* (New York: Faro, 1931);

Hugh Kingsmill, *Frank Harris* (London: Cape, 1932; New York: Farrar & Rinehart, 1932);

E. M. Root, *Frank Harris* (New York: Odyssey, 1947);

Vincent Brome, *Frank Harris* (London: Cassell, 1959);

Philippa Pullar, *Frank Harris* (London: Hamish Hamilton, 1975; New York: Simon & Schuster, 1976).

References:

Elmer Gertz, Introduction to *The Short Stories of Frank Harris: A Selection* (Carbondale: Southern Illinois University Press, 1975);

Robert Brainard Pearsall, *Frank Harris* (New York: Twayne, 1970).

Papers:

Harris's papers are located at the New York Public Library.

Maurice Hewlett

(22 January 1861 – 15 June 1923)

George M. Johnson
University College of the Cariboo

See also the Hewlett entry in *DLB 34: British Novelists, 1890–1929: Traditionalists.*

BOOKS: *Earthwork Out of Tuscany* (London: Dent, 1895; revised, London: Dent, 1899; New York: Putnam, 1899; revised again, London & New York: Macmillan, 1901);

A Masque of Dead Florentines (London: Dent, 1895; Portland, Maine: Mosher, 1911);

Songs and Meditations (Westminster: Constable, 1896);

The Forest Lovers (London & New York: Macmillan, 1898);

Pan and the Young Shepherd (London & New York: Lane, 1898; abridged edition, London: Heinemann, 1906);

Little Novels of Italy (London: Chapman & Hall, 1899; New York & London: Macmillan, 1899);

The Life and Death of Richard Yea-and-Nay (London & New York: Macmillan, 1900);

The New Canterbury Tales (Westminster: Constable, 1901);

The Road in Tuscany, 2 volumes (London & New York: Macmillan, 1904);

The Queen's Quair (London & New York: Macmillan, 1904);

Fond Adventures: Tales of the Youth of the World (London: Macmillan, 1905; New York & London: Harper, 1905);

The Fool Errant (London: Heinemann, 1905; New York & London: Macmillan, 1905);

The Stooping Lady (London: Macmillan, 1907; New York: Dodd, Mead, 1907);

The Spanish Jade (London: Cassell, 1908; New York: Doubleday, Page, 1908);

Halfway House: A Comedy of Degrees (London: Chapman & Hall, 1908; New York: Scribners, 1908);

Letters to Sanchia (London: Privately printed, 1908); revised as *Letters to Sanchia upon Things as They*

Courtesy of the Lilly Library, Indiana University

Are (London: Macmillan, 1910; New York: Scribners, 1910);

Open Country: A Comedy with a Sting (London: Macmillan, 1909; New York: Scribners, 1909);

Artemision: Idylls and Songs (London: Elkin Mathews, 1909; New York: Scribners, 1909);

Rest Harrow: A Comedy of Resolution (London: Macmillan, 1910; New York: Scribners, 1910);

146

Brazenhead the Great (London: Smith, Elder, 1911; New York: Scribners, 1911);

The Song of Renny (London: Macmillan, 1911; New York: Scribners, 1911);

The Agonists: A Trilogy of God and Man (London: Macmillan, 1911; New York: Scribners, 1911);

Mrs. Lancelot: A Comedy of Assumptions (London: Macmillan, 1912; New York: Century, 1912);

Bendish (London: Macmillan, 1913; New York: Scribners, 1913);

Lore of Proserpine (London: Macmillan, 1913; New York: Scribners, 1913);

Helen Redeemed and Other Poems (London: Macmillan, 1913; New York: Scribners, 1913);

A Lover's Tale (London, Melbourne & Toronto: Ward, Lock, 1915; New York: Scribners, 1915);

The Little Iliad (London: Heinemann, 1915; Philadelphia & London: Lippincott, 1915);

Frey and His Wife (London, Melbourne & Toronto: Ward, Lock, 1916; New York: McBride, 1916);

Love and Lucy (London: Macmillan, 1916; New York: Dodd, Mead, 1916);

Gai Saber: Tales and Songs (London: Elkin Mathews, 1916; New York: Putnam, 1916);

The Song of the Plow (London: Heinemann, 1916; New York: Macmillan, 1916);

The Loving History of Peridore and Paravail (London: Collins, 1917);

Thorgils of Treadholt (London, Melbourne & Toronto: Ward, Lock, 1917; New York: Dodd, Mead, 1917);

Gudrid the Fair (London: Constable, 1918; New York: Dodd, Mead, 1918);

The Village Wife's Lament (London: Secker, 1918; New York & London: Putnam, 1918);

The Outlaw (London: Constable, 1919; New York: Dodd, Mead, 1920);

The Light Heart (London: Chapman & Hall, 1920; New York: Holt, 1920);

Mainwaring (London: Collins, 1920; New York: Dodd, Mead, 1920);

Flowers in the Grass (London: Constable, 1920);

In a Green Shade: A Country Commentary (London: Bell, 1920);

Wiltshire Essays (London & New York: Oxford University Press, 1921);

Extemporary Essays (London & New York: Oxford University Press, 1922);

Last Essays of Maurice Hewlett (London: Heinemann, 1924; New York: Scribners, 1924).

PLAY PRODUCTIONS: *Pan and the Young Shepherd,* London, Court Theatre, 27 February 1906;

The King's Son, Chelsea, Margaret Morris Theatre, 25 February 1917;

The Ladies' Comedy, Chelsea, Margaret Morris Theatre, 4 March 1917.

On 31 December 1900, the same day that Thomas Hardy penned "The Darkling Thrush," Maurice Hewlett wrote to his wife:

> I hope I have a good deal of work before me, – indeed I hope that my name will be known, if known at all, as of a man who led the 20th Century, rather than one who came at the end of the 19th. I like to look on what I have done so far as a beginning; but if I die next year, it is a beginning which I hope will count for something. Whether I live or die, I hope it will be as a baddish man, trying to be better, and as a writer taking his art seriously.

Though he did not begin writing until age thirty-six and almost immediately was labeled a writer of romances, Hewlett certainly took his art seriously. He achieved both popular and critical success in a diverse variety of genres, including historical romance in both novel and short-story form, literary and travel essays, poetry, and drama – a feat that irritated or baffled both his public and those critics who tried to categorize him. He considered himself a poet above all, claiming that he had never written a novel but instead had expanded poetic intuition about a subject using prose. He was frequently praised for his poetic style, particularly in his short stories. In 1912, for instance, Frederic T. Cooper wrote that "in the earlier Maurice Hewlett we have the chief living champion of purely romantic fiction, and a stylist of the first order, whose cadenced prose is a delight to the ear, whose verbal colour has the gleam of many jewels, and who has given us at least two novels and many short stories which the epicures of literature will not willingly allow to die."

Nevertheless, unlike Hardy's reputation, Hewlett's was already in decline in 1912, and Hewlett has retained neither his readership nor much critical interest. As Samuel Hynes has more recently pointed out, in ironic deflation of Hewlett's hopes of leading the twentieth century, he "was a man who came at the end of a tradition in everything he did. At the height of his popularity he was already old-fashioned, and it is perhaps only in the Edwardian era, with its odd mixtures of the old and new, that he could have enjoyed such status as he did." During his career Hewlett published four volumes of short stories and tales in the vein of historical romance. These stories are worth revisiting now for their psychological insights and their imaginative and entertaining glimpses into distant times.

Hewlett's family background and interests seem to have played a large role in shaping his literary interests. His mother, Mary Emmeline Knowles, came from a cultured family: her father was a prominent London architect, and her brother, James Knowles, founded and edited the *Nineteenth Century Review*. His father, Henry Gay Hewlett, had produced two volumes of poetry along with several books on English history. The Hewletts had practiced law for three generations, and his father became the crown expert in antiquarian law, a position that Maurice eventually obtained in 1897. His long study of this field gave him the historical depth that informs his medieval romances.

Hewlett's parents married in 1860 and moved to Oatlands Park, Weybridge, Surrey, where Maurice, the first of eight children, was born on 22 January 1861. Though doted on by his mother, he was a difficult child. He once said that he "lived alone in a household of a dozen friendly persons," consoling himself by developing in his imagination a "thronged and busy life, a secret life, full of terror, triumph, wonder, [and] frantic enterprise." As early as he could remember he read and wrote, probably as further consolation for his isolation. Beginning with a child's version of Thomas Malory's *Le Morte D'Arthur* (1470), he quickly peopled his world with characters as diverse as Lancelot, Don Juan, Socrates, and Tom Jones.

Precocious and reserved, Hewlett found his schooling an intrusion on his imaginative world and a torment. He attended a succession of schools as his father moved the family farther from London into the countryside that he loved. After a move to West Molesey, Hewlett began his education at Hampton grammar school and then entered a school at Sevenoaks following the family's removal to Farningham, Kent, in 1872. Though he had attained a good grounding in Latin, French, and Greek by the time he left his next school, Enfield, he became increasingly unhappy after being sent as a boarder in 1875 to the International College at Spring Grove, where he spent several "barren, profitless" years. In an essay, "Gods in the Schoolhouse," he claimed, "The cruel, dull, false gods of English convention held me fast; master and pupils alike were gaolers to me." Nevertheless, he was later able to retrieve three happy memories: he discovered the gods of Greece through Homer; poetry

through John Milton; and romance in a "brief idyllic attachment" ambiguously described in the same essay. In his leisure he wrote about fictitious members of the peerage in a couple of Conservative weekly papers that he created, and he took up fly-fishing with his brother, Edward.

On leaving college in 1878 without a degree, Hewlett entered into his cousin's law practice at Gray's Inn. His choice to pursue antiquarian law, his father's specialty, is ironic, since he had never been able to speak to his father, who was typically bothered by his son's complete apathy to his enthusiasms, notably for long tramps over the countryside. This source of irritation for his father and depression for himself became an issue again in 1882 after his ever-restless father moved the family to Addington, which meant that father and son had a long daily walk and rail commute to London. Their relationship improved somewhat when Hewlett moved to London around 1883 and even more so when in 1888 he married Hilda Beatrice Herbert, for whom his father had a great affection.

The early years of their marriage seem to have been happy and productive, judging from Hewlett's affectionate letters to his wife. They had a son, Cecco, in 1890 and a daughter, Pia, in 1895. During the first year of his marriage he was called to the bar and became a partner in his cousin's firm. On a trip to Tangiers in 1889 he began writing in earnest. Back in London he developed an energetic routine of reading and writing from six until ten in the morning. At ten, he began work, and he resumed reading and writing until late in the evening. In 1892 he began to make visits to Italy on his holidays. His attraction to Italian history and culture inspired some of the poems first published in the *Academy* and *Nineteenth Century* and later collected in his first poetry volumes, *A Masque of Dead Florentines* (1895) and *Songs and Meditations* (1896). He corresponded with John Addington Symonds and visited Robert Bridges, who thought him good enough to be called a poet.

In 1895 Hewlett's first prose book, *Earthwork Out of Tuscany*, was published. It includes impressionistic essays and stories woven together by his obvious love of Italy and his fascination with the painter Sandro Botticelli. Though, as he acknowledged, the collection shows traces of Walter Pater and Paul Bourget, Hewlett's imaginative re-creations or "parables" are his own. He is certainly no aesthete, claiming, "Art is Nature made articulate, Nature's soul inflamed with love and voicing her secrets through one man to many."

Of the four pieces in *Earthwork Out of Tuscany* that might be considered short stories, or at least contes, the first, "A Sacrifice at Prato," imaginatively explores how a pagan with a wide knowledge of Greek myths might interpret Catholicism. In "Of Boils and the Ideal" Hewlett, who appears as a character, holds a conversation with the Renaissance painter Pietro Vannucci, known as Il Perugino. Hewlett portrays him in human terms as "an urbane little painter" well past middle age with a young wife whose heart lies elsewhere. Hewlett mischievously shows the contradictions between Il Perugino's life and art, centering on his wish to avoid including a boil on Saint Roch's face in a commissioned painting. In "Quattrocentisteria," called "the pearl of the book" by early critic Milton Bronner, Hewlett weaves a tale of romantic encounter and loss based on Botticelli's portrait of Simonetta Vespucci, the beloved of Giuliano Medici. Again Hewlett shows an artist's conflicting impulses, this time as Botticelli first observes Simonetta and then accepts her offer to paint her as Venus. Botticelli's passions are aroused as the tale builds to her disrobing, but at the crucial moment the artist in him asserts control, and he becomes immersed in his task. Though Simonetta wants to love him, his neglect angers her, and she repudiates him at the end of the session. Following her unexpected death three days later, the tormented Botticelli sees her as a victim of the strivings of the Florentines rather than as a goddess, and he "painted her a rapt Presence floating evenly to our earth." "The Soul of a City" presents a contrast to "Quattrocentisteria" in its earthy treatment of Mariola (Maso) Cecci's petty jealousy and hatred of Marco Zoppa, a fellow fig farmer. Most of the other pieces comprise what Hewlett in the preface to the revised edition called "criticism by trope and figure," filling out his image of Italy. However, the volume was misunderstood and criticized for lack of unity, which exasperated him. On 20 February 1899 he wrote to an American admirer, Royal Cortissoz, "I don't believe a single reviewer in England knew what I was driving at; the book (and my first too) fell dead flat; I was very much discouraged."

The same complaint could not be made of his first novel, *The Forest Lovers* (1898), hailed by the *Academy* as the best fiction of 1898 along with Joseph Conrad's *Tales of Unrest*. In this medieval romance Hewlett traces the adventures of a knight who marries a poor beauty, Isoult La Desirous, to save her from death, titillatingly deferring the consummation of their relationship until the denouement. Through the popular success of the novel he was able to realize the goal he had pursued since 1892, to support himself entirely by writing (though not within seven years, as he had hoped), and in 1901 he retired from his appointment at the Land Records Office, a position he had held since 1897. However, this novel, which according to Cooper spawned a whole school of cardboard medieval romance, fixed his readers' expectations and created a reputation by which he felt constrained and grew to hate.

During the late 1890s, as Hewlett became successful as a professional writer, shadows began to appear in his personal life. His 1889 trip to Tangiers had been prompted by nervous fatigue, and he subsequently suffered several nervous breakdowns. He became increasingly estranged from his wife as their interests diverged. Beginning in 1897, his expressions of loneliness in his diaries became more frequent. According to Marie Belloc-Lowndes, Hilda Hewlett's "only interest in life appeared to be centred in what can only be called machinery." After participating in European road races as one of the first women drivers, she took up flying and in 1911 became the first Englishwoman to obtain a pilot's license.

Hynes links Hewlett's unfulfilling marriage with his frequent treatment "not of romantic love, but of frustration, denial, temptation, and sexual torment" and of marriages without love, a claim that can be easily substantiated in his subsequent works. However, in what several critics consider to be his best collection of short stories, *Little Novels of Italy* (1899), he seems wistfully attracted to young, beautiful heroines whose attitudes toward love are as simple as they, though their lives are complicated by their lack of freedom in choosing husbands. Each of the five tales features "a madonna of the region" or city forming the backdrop. These tales grew out of his travels to Italy, including a particular journey in April 1898, and from his extensive knowledge of Italian art and literature, though he later claimed there were no particular historical sources for the tales. In "Madonna of the Peach Tree," fifty-four-year-old Baldassare pays a dowry to wed twenty-one-year-old Giovanna (Vanna) Scarpa, a lowly washerwoman. After two years without a child, Vanna is advised to seek a lover but rejects the idea until she falls under the spell of the famous Carmelite preacher Fra Battista. She has a child, and the rival preachers "nose for a scandal." The Carmelite prior, who interviews her when her husband leaves town for a week, is ironically offended by her innocence; she is ejected from his presence, only to be stoned by the waiting mob. Cast out from the city in the dark, she wanders through a peach orchard until encountered by three shepherds who, not recognizing her, suppose her to be the Madonna with child. A legend is thus born and grows as she appears at various places. The final "miracle" occurs after Verona has returned to routine as Baldassare returns to the city to find his winsome wife, Vanna, exactly as before with "bambinaccio." Throughout the story Hewlett treats the emotional life of Verona colorfully and light-heartedly. The highest praise for the tale came from the seasoned critic Frederic Harrison, who said, "I hold 'The Madonna of the Peach Tree' to be as perfect a short story as we have had in our time. It has humour, poetry, pathos, mystery, imaginative history, and pure humanity."

Both "Ippolita in the Hills" and "The Duchess of Nona" similarly portray simple and beautiful women who are raised onto pedestals with unfortunate results. In the former the poets of Padua are responsible. Alessandro, a young poet, sees in a humble stonecutter's daughter, Ippolita, the Greek Madonna Elena and proceeds to worship her from a distance. Other artists join in, and she finds that her image inspires every art form, from canzone to faience, in roles as diverse as Daphne and Leda. The artists purchase the terrified girl from her father, who expects that Alessandro will make her his wife, but instead they crown her queen of their Collegio d'Amore, imprisoning her in order to extol her incomparable virtues. Baffled and then bored, she escapes disguised as a boy with some goatherds under the pretense of having killed a Jew. Eventually she rides off into the scented night with one of these goatherds, Pilade, but not before he has been falsely accused of the crime that Ippolita supposedly committed.

This tale of the projection of an image onto an innocent girl gently mocks the courtly love tradition, as does "Messer Cino and the Live Coal." In this story, the aging Cino da Pistoja rejects his fourteen-year-old goddess of inspiration when she demonstrates kindness toward him, since there is no literary precedent for such an act. She dies soon after, thwarting his plan to feature her in an epic, but he thrives nonetheless in a state of melodious sadness.

The final tale, "The Judgement of Borso," turns to comedy, tracing the fortune-hunting of the unfashionably thin but beautiful Bellaroba and her bosom and buxom friend, Olimpia Castaneve. En route to Ferrara, Bellaroba becomes attached to a young fop called Angioletto, while her more forward friend enters into negotiations with a Captain Mosca. At Ferrara, Angioletto performs a do-it-yourself marriage ceremony with Bellaroba and then sets out to win his way at court. With his "throstle-pipe" he succeeds better than he intended,

and his employer, Madama Lionella d'Este, falls in love with him. To complicate matters, her husband, Count Guarino Guarini, pursues Bellaroba. Captain Mosca does not fare well, being rejected by both Olimpia and Guarini. His desperate attempt to use information about Bellaroba and Angioletto to secure Guarini's favor backfires and he is killed. In a contrasting scene straight out of French bedroom farce, the Duke Borso, Lionella's father, wanders into a bedroom with an empty bed, which happens to be Bellaroba's, and in the morning discovers that he has been joined by Angioletto. Borso enjoys the lad's wit and shows leniency, preparing the reader for his Solomon-like decision about whether Bellaroba or Olimpia is the true murderer of Mosca.

Whereas Hewlett's technique in most of these tales is to draw fleeting associations between a famous figure, often of the period being described, such as Desiderius Erasmus or Dante, and the protagonist of the tale, in his next novel, *The Life and Death of Richard Yea-and-Nay* (1900), he focuses directly on the great historical figure of Richard Coeur de Lion. Though more historically accurate than Sir Walter Scott's account in *The Talisman* (1825), the novel is also a psychological study of a man obsessed and deeply divided between his quest for love and religion.

These themes preoccupy Hewlett in his next and equally ambitious project, *The New Canterbury Tales* (1901), composed of six stories by various pilgrims en route to Canterbury in 1450, sixty-two years after those of Geoffrey Chaucer. In a clever and concise prologue Hewlett justifies his adoption of Chaucer's structure, claiming "that is a poor-hearted chronicler who withholds from a tale because some other has told one well," and he points out that the tales were told in common speech. Initially the scrivener proposes telling tales as a means of averting a conflict between two of the pilgrims. His compelling and historically based tale of King Edward III's unlawful pursuit of Countess Alys, the wife of a loyal subject, presumably has a cathartic function, since it involves treachery and climaxes in a violent jousting match.

Dan Costard, a "mild old priest," narrates the next tale, "The Loving History of Peridore and Paravail," a bizarre story of a religious hermit with a twisted mind who nearly ruins the lives of two lovers. The Blessed Vigilas rescues a baby, whom he names Paravail, from a witch's sacrificial slab and takes her to a wet nurse with an infant son, Peridore. However, Paravail has aroused the love of the hermit, and he retrieves her after only a month. Another of Hewlett's wild beauties, she

Hewlett in 1922, portrait by Victor Tittle (from Arthur Bruce
Sutherland, Maurice Hewlett, *1938)*

seems soulless. Here Hewlett draws on a medieval superstition that children weaned before five months lack souls. Predictably, she falls in love with Peridore, whose marriage proposal arouses the hermit's jealousy. Tormented by his delusion that Paravail is a she-devil, Vigilas digs a grave for himself, but a witch's prophecy comes true and Paravail dies instead. An enraged Peridore knocks out Vigilas and absconds with Paravail, bringing her back to life by applying dove's blood to her lips and cheeks. She continues to lack a soul, however, and he must take her to a woman in a chapel to be suckled for five months. This powerful tale of an ascetic whose desperate need for love overpowers his sanity was Hewlett's favorite of the collection.

Captain Salomon Brazenhead, a wily mercenary, then takes up the narrative gauntlet, providing a tale of Italian intrigue reminiscent of *Little Novels of Italy*. Based on the age-old theme of one brother's betrayal of another over a woman, the tale ends conventionally and tragically with the deaths of all three.

With the Prioress of Ambresbury's Tale of Saint Gervase of Plesy the book moves back into the realm of the bizarre and psychologically fascinating. The counterpart to "Peridore and Paravail," this tale depicts the overbearing love of a childless Jewess, Sornia, for Gervase, a boy she abducts originally with the intention of having him sacrificed in the quest of some of her fellow Jews for a messiah. However, her neediness prompts her to rescue him and raise him secretly. Only after a young girl, Persilla, captures Gervase's heart does the possessive Sornia return to the Jewish quarter and present him as the King of the Jews. This action prompts the Jews to convert en masse and the leaders of the Roman Catholic Church to consider Gervase for canonization. Gervase convinces Persilla to live a saintly life with him, and the love-hungry Sornia is left alone.

The final two tales bring to a head the theme of confused identity that has been developing among the pilgrims themselves. "The Cast of the Apple," narrated by the shipman, deals with a bloody feud between a Welsh family, headed by Sir Caradoc, and an English one, headed by Sir Belem, the eldest of three brothers. Belem captures or kills five of Caradoc's sons and is about to finish off in battle the remaining two children, a twin brother and sister, when Belem's more humane younger brother Sir Sagramor steps in. He falls in love with the female twin, Audiart, but the vengeful Belem hatches a plot to wed Audiart by force. Unknown to Sagramor, the twins use their identical appearance to enable the brother to murder Belem in his bedroom. The bewildered but grateful Sagramor finally determines the identity of his love by observing whether each is able to catch an apple between his or her knees, and the tale ends predictably. The shipman has presumably chosen this story because he incorrectly believes the next and final narrator, Percival Perceforest, to be Jenny Perceforest, an old flame. Ironically, Percival has taken on a false identity, since he is illicitly in love with the higher-born niece of the Prioress, also on the pilgrimage. His amusing story of the impetuous Galeotto, his love Isotta, his cousin Donna Camillo, and her lover, Eugenio, represents a more complex treatment of the confusion-of-identity theme involving marriages of same-sex partners. Its denouement is also less predictable than the shipman's tale and causes the pilgrims at the end of their quest to identify with various characters in it.

Hewlett uncharacteristically published nothing in the following year, 1902, though he had begun writing *The Queen's Quair* (1904), a historical novel attempting to capture the essence of Mary Stuart's life. The writing was interrupted by a spring visit to Tuscany, where he gathered material for his novel *The Road in Tuscany* (1904). In May 1903 the Hewletts leased the Old Rectory, Broad Chalke, and spent an enormous amount of energy transforming the neglected garden into what he considered a paradise. In a 1903 letter to his wife he wrote, "I have the sort of love for it one has for one's mother."

In 1905 his final volume of stories was published. The four stories in *Fond Adventures: Tales of the Youth of the World* are all novellas, and all deal with the vicissitudes of the young in love. This collection was generally received well, the critic for the *Nation* (1 June 1905) making the representative comment that the "splendid" stories are "full of action and passion, with an undercurrent of laughter, all carried off with great spirit and style."

"Brazenhead the Great" not only knows characters but provides a thematic connection with *The New Canterbury Tales,* since it delightfully exposes the real motivations of the pilgrims in those tales, focusing particularly on Percival Perceforest and Captain Brazenhead. The swashbuckling, bombastic captain, who owes something to Falstaff and Cy-

rano de Bergerac among others, comes alive in this tale and is one of Hewlett's most endearing, as well as most enduring, characters. Hewlett self-consciously draws on mock-epic elements, as in his paean on Brazenhead's nose. While gathering men in aid of his friend Jack Cade, Brazenhead comes across the lovelorn Perceforest and promises to help him gain his lady, Mawdleyn, perceiving that Perceforest will be perfect to act as the brains of his own operation. When Jack Cade identifies Perceforest as the heir of his enemy, Lord Say, Perceforest refuses to participate in the murder of his newfound relation, and he parts ways with the captain. However, the captain reappears in the guise of a cardinal and dramatically rescues Perceforest, a victim of mistaken identity. At the denouement Perceforest attains his title, fortune, and lady while Brazenhead, who "does furiously thirst," gets his desired drink and an appointment as "Steward of the manors of Westerham, Knockholt, and Froghole."

"The Heart's Key," set in France, and "Buondelmonte's Saga," another Italian tale, both deal with young people who aspire to have different lovers from those with whom they are involved and who are brought low as a consequence. In the former, a romance, the proud and remote Lady Saill's rejection of three lovers causes them to attack her castle and lock her out, demanding her heart's key, a jeweled girdle. With the aid of a fourth lover, the servant Guillam, she escapes from the situation, only to descend into beggary before she finally realizes Guillam's true quality. In the second story, a tragedy, Buondelmonte breaks his lackluster betrothal to Cunizza, a member of the powerful Uberti family, when he is introduced to the ravishing Piccarda, who has been brought up in seclusion and kept for Buondelmonte by her ambitious mother. Once the Uberti family learns of Buondelmonte's maneuver, which is offensive to their pride, they lose little time in barbarously murdering him.

In the final tale, "The Love Chase," Hewlett deftly pulls back from tragedy. The story follows the fortunes of a triangle of Emilia Fiordispiana's lovers, all by now familiar types in Hewlett's stories: the demon warrior, Simone, the Black Dog; the powerful political warrior, Cardinal Gonzaga; and the clever humanist, Nello Nelli. Envoy for the cardinal, Nello wins the heart of Emilia despite a much earlier pledge she had made to Simone and also despite the cardinal's romantic pursuit of her. Once the cardinal discovers Nello's treachery he stabs him, and Emilia rides off with Simone; however, all is not lost, since Nello recovers, returns to his studies, and weds another woman he had earlier saved from the gallows.

After 1905 Hewlett's writing career developed mainly in forms other than the short story. He continued to churn out novels, which he considered a dismal duty born of financial necessity. In a trilogy beginning with *Halfway House: A Comedy of Degrees* in 1908, he turned to contemporary themes, reflecting his mildly progressive stance in support of divorce and women's issues. His typically Edwardian fascination with the spirit world, as well as his autobiographical reminiscences, are captured in *Lore of Proserpine* (1913), a collection of essays that attempt to convey an essence of truth rather than be factual. They reveal his dividedness and a strong need for solitude, increased by his "conviction that behind the world of appearance lies another and vaster with a thronging population of its own" and specifically by his belief in fairies, whose appearance in his own life he details throughout. Reviewers are divided about the book's merits, calling it both odd and fascinating.

During the late Edwardian period Hewlett referred more and more in his letters to his desire of developing as a poet, and in 1913 he embarked in earnest on an epic poem in praise of the English peasant class. Originally titled "The Hodgiad," after the colloquial name of Hodge for farmworker, the volume was published to some critical acclaim as *The Song of the Plow* (1916). More recently Hynes has hailed it as "one of the best *terza rima* poems in English." In this poem is the fullest expression of a change in attitude that had been evolving from at least 1910, when Hewlett wrote to Walter Woodford on 19 January, "We have Privilege to clear out of the way, and War to abolish."

By 1917 Hewlett had joined the Fabians and was asserting that his favorite idea was "that happiness lies in having as little as possible, not as much." This belief prompted him to enter local politics, first as a district councillor and then as a member of the Wiltshire County Council, and to work for the board of agriculture and his district housing committee in the postwar years. Hewlett continued his stance as a moralist in four volumes of impressionistic essays published in his final years. These essays are enormously varied and appropriately sum up an extraordinarily versatile career.

This versatility impeded his success, as several critics, including S. K. Ratcliffe and J. B. Priestley, have observed. Several commentators would also agree with Priestley's claim:

Hewlett did some magnificent work, and always showed himself an artist, bent on grappling with and overcoming new difficulties, and not a manufacturer, turning out the required article; but nevertheless I do not think he ever completely found himself; his work had echoes of other voices in it, and often suggested that its author had derived his inspiration at second-hand, from other books, rather than from his own interpretation of what was stirring about him; and it always looked as if the man was greater than his theme and task.

If Hewlett's plots could be derivative and predictable and his style unfashionably affected, his settings and backgrounds betray vast knowledge of and insight into the historical periods about which he wrote. His characterization is often delightful and broadly humane, supporting the assertion of his friend E. V. Lucas that "I can't remember anyone with a more vivid personality than Hewlett's" and J. C. Squire's tribute following his death on 15 June 1923: "He was an extraordinarily full man. . . . He never said a thing twice in different words, and never pretended to knowledge that he did not possess. The knowledge that he did possess sufficed him. It was almost impossible to mention to him in conversation a thing which he did not know about; and everything was alive to him. His knowledge and imagination working together made the whole past, and the whole of literature, live for him."

Letters:

The Letters of Maurice Hewlett, edited by Laurence Binyon (London: Methuen, 1926; Boston: Small, Maynard, 1926).

Bibliographies:

P. H. Muir, "A Bibliography of the First Editions of Books by Maurice H. Hewlett (1861–1923)" Supplement to the *Bookman's Journal,* 15 (London, 1927);

B. D. Cutler and V. Stiles, *Modern British Authors: Their First Editions* (New York: Greenberg, 1930).

References:

Milton Bronner, *Maurice Hewlett: Being a Critical Review of His Prose and Poetry* (Boston: Luce, 1910);

Richard Church, "Maurice Hewlett Reconsidered," *Fortnightly,* 141 (January 1934): 96–102;

Frederic T. Cooper, "Maurice Hewlett," in his *Some English Story Tellers: A Book of the Younger Novelists* (New York: Holt, 1912), pp. 54–93;

John Freeman, "Maurice Hewlett," in his *English Portraits and Essays* (London: Hodder & Stoughton, 1924), pp. 115–147;

H. W. Graham, "Maurice Hewlett," *Fortnightly,* 124 (July 1925): 47–63;

Stephen Gwynn, "Maurice Hewlett," *Edinburgh Review,* 239 (January 1924): 61–72;

Frederic Harrison, *Memories and Thoughts* (New York: Macmillan, 1906);

Samuel Hynes, "Maurice Hewlett: An Edwardian Career," in his *Edwardian Occasions: Essays on English Writing in the Early Twentieth Century* (New York: Oxford University Press, 1972), pp. 173–190;

E. V. Lucas, "The Academy," in his *Reading, Writing, and Remembering* (London: Methuen, 1932), pp. 178–180;

Barrington O'Reardon, "Maurice Hewlett," *Sewanee Review,* 21 (January 1913): 99–107;

J. B. Priestley, "Maurice Hewlett's Later Verse and Prose," in his *Figures in Modern Literature* (London: Lane, 1924), pp. 63–89;

S. K. Ratcliffe, "Maurice Hewlett," *New Statesman,* 21 (23 June 1923): 328;

J. C. Squire, "Maurice Hewlett, Man of Many Talents," *Language Arts* (25 August 1923): 363–364;

Arthur Bruce Sutherland, *Maurice Hewlett: Historical Romancer* (Philadelphia: University of Pennsylvania, 1938);

Edith Wharton, "Maurice Hewlett's 'The Fool Errant,'" *Bookman* (New York), 22 (September 1905): 64–67.

Papers:
Typescripts of selected entries of Hewlett's diaries are deposited in the British Library. There is a collection of letters sent by Hewlett from 1902 to 1913 in the Bancroft Library, University of California, Berkeley.

William Hope Hodgson

(15 November 1877 – 17 April 1918)

Adrian Eckersley
Birkbeck College, London University

See also the Hodgson entries in *DLB 70: British Mystery Writers, 1860–1919* and *DLB 153: Late-Victorian and Edwardian Novelists, First Series.*

BOOKS: *The Boats of the "Glen Carrig"* (London: Chapman & Hall, 1907);

The House on the Borderland (London: Chapman & Hall, 1908);

The Ghost Pirates (London: Paul, 1909);

The Night Land (London: Eveleigh Nash, 1912);

"Poems" and "The Dream of X" (London: Watts, 1912; New York: Paget, 1912);

Carnacki the Ghost-Finder (London: Eveleigh Nash, 1913; enlarged edition, Sauk City, Wis.: Mycroft & Moran, 1947);

Men of the Deep Waters (London: Eveleigh Nash, 1914);

Cargunka, and Poems and Anecdotes (New York: Paget / London: Watt, 1914);

The Luck of the Strong (London: Eveleigh Nash, 1916);

Captain Gault: Being the Exceedingly Private Log of a Sea Captain (London: Eveleigh Nash, 1917; New York: MacBride, 1918);

The Calling of the Sea (London: Selwyn & Blount, 1920);

The Voice of the Ocean (London: Selwyn & Blount, 1921);

The House on the Borderland and Other Novels (Sauk City, Wis.: Arkham House, 1946) – includes *The Boats of the "Glen Carrig," The Ghost Pirates,* and *The Night Land;*

Deep Waters (Sauk City, Wis.: Arkham House, 1967);

Out of the Storm: Uncollected Fantasies, edited, with a critical biography, by Sam Moskowitz (West Kingston, R.I.: Grant, 1975);

Spectral Manifestations: William Hope Hodgson, edited by Ian Bell (Oxford: Bellknapp, 1984);

William Hope Hodgson (Hulton Deutsch Collection)

The Haunted Pampero: Uncollected Fantasies and Mysteries, edited by Moskowitz (Hampton Falls, N.H.: Grant, 1995).

Never a member of the literary establishment, William Hope Hodgson achieved no great fame as a writer, but he is one of the few minor Edwardian writers of horror fiction whose work is regularly republished. The unfettered quality of his best work has ensured him continued representation to this day on shelves beside more-lurid writers such as Stephen King. Hodgson saw himself primarily as a writer of sea tales, and many of his best short stories, as well as some of his longer works, combine a nautical setting with the sense of horror, isolation, and decay paralleled in works such as Oscar Wilde's *The Picture of Dorian Gray* (1891), H. G. Wells's *The Time Machine* (1895), and Arthur Machen's *The Hill of Dreams* (1907). As well as creating monsters from the deep, he was also interested in the more conventional ghostly and occult tale, as is evident in the series of tales whose hero is Carnacki, the Ghost-Finder; and he also went on to write more-conventional sea stories outside the horror mold. His ability to think outside narrow moral codes led to success with the creation of heroes who lived by their wits, wily seamen who, while at heart good men and true, have little respect for the law and order of nations. Nonetheless, it is for his work in horror, which in his case cannot always be divorced from science fiction, that he is remembered and republished today. He wrote about forty published short stories and four longer fictional works. Some of the stories were published in the United States before they appeared in Britain, though none of his longer works appeared in the United States until 1946.

Hodgson was born on 15 November 1877 in Wethersfield, a small North Essex village. Like several of his literary contemporaries, he was the son of an Anglican clergyman; brought up in semi-genteel poverty, he was one of nine surviving children. His family moved a good deal in his early years as his father sought a living. He was unhappy at home and quarreled with his overbearing father. When he was only eight years old he was sent to boarding school in Margate, Kent, and he ran away twice, once in 1890 and again in 1891. His schooling ended at age thirteen through the second of these escapades, which resulted in his joining the merchant marine as an apprentice. He was physically small but had the resilience and courage to combat the bullying and humiliation that were an inevitable part of apprentice life. He stuck to his training, and in 1895 he became a qualified seaman. For the next four years he followed the sea, achieving distinction briefly by rescuing a fellow sailor in shark-infested waters off New Zealand, for which he received a medal from the British Humane Society.

Hodgson finally quit the sea in 1899. He returned to his family (his father had died in 1892), now living in Blackburn, Lancashire, and there in 1900 he opened his School of Physical Culture. Like a modern health farm, the business promoted exercise as a key to improvement in health and the creation of an attractive body. His aims in establishing his school can be best understood through his first published work, a series of articles for *Sandow's Magazine of Physical Culture and British Sport* between 1901 and 1904 in which he discussed in quasi-medical terms the benefits of particular exercise regimes. He backed up the business venture with a knack for self-publicizing, engaging in stunts such as riding down a dangerous flight of steps on a bicycle and taking up Harry Houdini's challenge to allow Hodgson to bind Houdini in a way from which he could not free himself. Hodgson succeeded, but Houdini alleged that he had cheated, an accusation Hodgson firmly rebutted in more than one newspaper. These and other stunts were reported in the local press, which made Hodgson something of a celebrity and enabled him to keep his unlikely business venture afloat until 1904, the year he joined the Society of Authors. In 1905 he moved with his family from Blackburn to Borth in north Wales.

Hodgson's early tales and his first longer work show a remarkable homogeneity. Together they make up what Peter Tremayne in *William Hope Hodgson: Voyages and Visions* (1987) calls "Hodgson's Sargasso Sea Mythos." The Sargasso Sea in Hodgson's work is a realm of absolute, windless calm, a kind of kingdom of decay peopled through his imagination with continents of drifting weed banks from which no ship is likely to return, with the hulks of ships lost over the centuries, and with monsters unimaginable elsewhere. His first real success came in 1906, with the publication in the *Monthly Story Magazine* of Chicago of his short piece "From the Tideless Sea." A tarred barrel fished up from the sea contains a manuscript titled "The Losing of the Homebird," which the finder recognizes as the name of a ship recently lost. The manuscript tells how the ship was taken by a tidal wave to the desolate Sargasso, "the Cemetery of the Ocean." In the account captain and crew fall prey to disease and giant octopuses, until the sole survivors are the writer and the captain's daughter, who after a hasty marriage ceremony find they have become the Adam and Eve of the Sargasso, destined to live out their lives on the forever-trapped hulk of their ship with no hope of return to civilization.

The excitement of the story lies in the menace of the giant octopuses, whose presence necessitates the building of a great superstructure on the ship, but it is the setting and situation of the story that ensure its power. The sense of desolation and loneliness communicated by the description of weed banks and hulks is a subject to which Hodgson returned many times; it underlies the surface excitement of much of his best work. Little more than a year later he published a sequel, "More News of the 'Homebird,'" in which narrator and wife face an invasion of giant crabs. In this tale they have a baby, and the implied invitation to the reader to superimpose the details of domestic life on so hopeless a situation and to imagine the possibilities for the future of the family is the author's most powerful device.

Hodgson's first novel, *The Boats of the "Glen Carrig"* (1907), concerns a group of men imprisoned in the same "weed-choked sea" who must fight creatures of slime unknown in reality, but with a less hopeless outcome. At last they make contact with survivors of another ship in a similar condition and together regain the open sea. This first longer work is an extension of rather than a contrast to his short stories: like the stories, it is governed by the atmosphere of seascapes and an episodic excitement more typical of the romance than the novel. Another early short tale that places similar emphasis on a sense of isolation and decay in a sea setting is "The Voice in the Night," published in the *Blue Book Magazine*, the successor to the *Monthly Story Magazine*. Here the narrator, at sea but near an unnamed land, is hailed by what he assumes to be a man in a rowboat who will not show himself. After he has received kindness from the narrator and his shipmates the invisible oarsman whispers his tale of how he and his woman have taken refuge on this island of fungus, of how they have succumbed to the temptation to eat it (another curious parallel to the story of Adam and Eve), and of how they are now creatures of fungus themselves. In the dawn light the narrator catches a glimpse of what appears to be a "great grey nodding sponge" as it (or he) rows away to an isolation and presumable death similar to those of the family imprisoned in the *Homebird*.

Thus far in his career as a writer Hodgson had not called upon the mystical, occult, or spiritual. Though not exactly science fiction, the fantasies within the tales are loosely reconcilable with the biological and geographical possibilities of the post-Darwinian era, when the fear of biological degeneration was treated as a reality by the science of the day. In 1908 and 1909 he concentrated more on longer fiction. His most famous and often republished novel, *The House on the Borderland* (1908), explodes beyond these boundaries; it includes occult, mystical, spiritual, biological, and scientific elements and might be defined as science fiction, mystical bildungsroman, or biological fantasy. This is the result, according to Brian Stableford and others, of the novel's evolution as a combination of two or more shorter pieces. The most important of these

are two visionary "interludes," in both of which the beleaguered narrator visits a place the reader comes to know as "the Plain of Silence," a space bounded by mountains, in the center of which stands a replica of his house – the setting of most of the story, though now huge and made of a green jadelike substance. Around the rim of the plain and above the mountains loom huge shapes, which the narrator recognizes as the gods who have been worshiped by humanity through the ages, and there is a suggestion that the narrator has journeyed through a space-time warp to a place that is the concrete manifestation of inner space. The work as a whole, smoothly integrating disparate elements, defies both attempts to consign it to a genre and to interpret it smoothly and logically. What cannot be denied is that this is one of the works in which post-Victorian horror most nearly approaches surrealism.

Hodgson's other longer work of this period, *The Ghost Pirates* (1909), though in the familiar setting of the sea, also breaks new ground in dealing with occult phenomena, ghosts, and inexplicable events with which the crew of the *Mortzestus* seem unable to grapple. The book may be read as an allegory of humanity besieged in the castle of rational science.

After these expansions of his imaginative horizons, though Hodgson returned to the imagery of the Sargasso Sea, his work expanded in its range to take in a more conventional kind of tale. Most notable is the series of tales, mostly published in the *Idler* from 1910 to 1912, collected in book form in 1913 as *Carnacki the Ghost-Finder*. The idea of an occult detective was not new: Machen's Dyson, who features in *The Great God Pan and the Inmost Light* (1894) and *The Three Impostors* (1895), is one of the first of the breed, and another, Algernon Blackwood's eponymous John Silence, appeared in book form in 1908. Dyson, Silence, and Carnacki all share a common debt to Arthur Conan Doyle's Sherlock Holmes, and in the Carnacki stories the narrator has a relationship with Carnacki parallel to that of Mr. Watson to Holmes. Carnacki, though, is not like Holmes. The latter, with his indulgence in cocaine and his violin playing, is at heart an aesthete of the earlier 1890s. In contrast, Carnacki is interested in photography (as was Hodgson) and uses in his work an "electric pentacle," perhaps the most bizarre blending of the technological and the occult on record; he is a down-to-earth, straightforward figure who treats the narrator and his circle of fellow admirers as a public-school rugby captain might treat a group of admiring youngsters.

The Carnacki stories, as the book title indicates, involve the macabre. However, several are

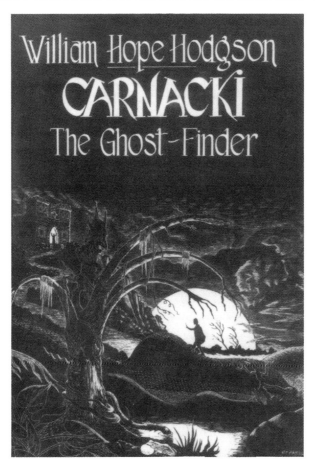

Dust jacket for the 1947 enlarged edition of Hodgson's stories
about a detective who investigates the supernatural

not occult tales at all but deal with phenomena that appear to be occult but have discoverable, rational explanations. "The Thing Invisible" is one such story: the reader is given a minute account of Carnacki's vigil in a lonely family chapel where a servant has been unaccountably struck down by a dagger that cannot have been wielded by a human presence. The scene takes place in utter darkness, and the sounds Carnacki hears suggest the movements of a monstrous armed man. However, all turns out to be imagination when the reader finds that the flying dagger is no more than a booby trap that a neurotic elderly relative has forgotten to turn off. Though the excitement in the reading of such tales matches the others, they are less satisfying. The most satisfying are those in which the occult promise is not betrayed: in "The Whistling Room," for example, the reader is led to suspect that the room whistles furiously when the young man enters with his intended because of the machinations of a romantic rival, but it turns out that the room is haunted by a jester who was wronged by the remote ancestors of the girl and that "the room had become the material expression of the ancient Jester — that his soul, rotted with hatred had bred into a monster."

This story conforms to the pattern of the classic ghost story, in which events buried in the past reach out to disturb the present, but what is new here is the imagined manner of that disturbance, where the material of something as factual as a building can be molded by the malevolent ghost. Most complex of the Carnacki stories is "The Hog," in which Carnacki acts as "minder" to Bains, a terrified neurotic who cannot sleep, as he is haunted by hog noises. Carnacki passes a night with Bains asleep in his electric pentacle, but this proves disastrous, as Bains is a traitor both to himself and Carnacki, and through him the Hog — an "ab-human" monstrosity with ties to similar creatures in *The House on the Borderland* — materializes within the pentacle. Carnacki imperceptibly takes on the role of analyst in a materialized Jungian nightmare, but even his resourcefulness seems to fail. Rescue comes, magically, from some force triggered in the beyond to which Carnacki and Bains are as children, after which the Hog can be treated by "suggestion." In this story, as in *The House on the Borderland,* Hodgson has a capacity to take the reader to a place where conventional signposts, whether of science or mysticism, fail to be of use.

Carnacki is an Edwardian detective-hero, not a Victorian. There is a strong emphasis in the tales on excitement for its own sake, and there are many occasions when the overall cohesion of a story is sacrificed to create more excitement and tension in a first reading. It is a reasonable assumption that many of the tales were written to be read only once, for without the element of surprise and suspense their impact is weakened.

In 1911 Hodgson moved to London. By this time he was involved in his most ambitious project, the romance *The Night Land* (1912). Basically the tale is a love quest, written in a seventeenth-century pastiche English justified by the central story being framed as the reported dream of a young man of that era. What he reports is set far in the future, when the sun has gone out, the upper world has grown absolutely cold, and all life exists in a vast rift valley warmed by volcanic fire. Within this setting humanity occupies a vast, technologically sophisticated pyramidal structure known as the Great Redoubt, surrounded by darkness and horrific enemies. The hero receives telepathic knowledge of another Redoubt far off in the night, where lives the reincarnation of his seventeenth-century lover, whom he must journey through terrible danger to rescue. Taken as a love tale, the work is unremarkable and has moments of bathos, but it is redeemed by the somber splendor of its visual imagery and by the palpable sense of isolation and horror that marks most of Hodgson's best work. Many readers have judged the intentionally archaic style of the book a failure.

Around the same time as he was writing *The Night Land* Hodgson returned to his Sargasso idiom, several tales of which were published in the *Red Magazine* in 1912 and 1913 and a collection of which was published as *Men of the Deep Waters* (1914), undoubtedly his finest and most representative collection of short fiction. One of these stories, "The Derelict," is an extremely gruesome biological fantasy. The story is told by a ship's old doctor: after a terrible storm the *Bheotpte* finds herself in an unknown region near an ancient hulk with "a pretty old-fashioned look about her" that, it is speculated, may have been drifting for centuries. A volunteer party rows to the hulk; near it the sea has become as thick

as treacle, full of decaying flotsam. When they board they find the whole ship is like sponge. When a kick breaks part of the surface of the deck a purplish fluid pours out in jets, and the mariners hear sounds that indicate a living organism, from which they must now escape. Over the centuries the ship in its process of decay has become a living organism, and the old doctor speculates, "If we could know exactly what that old vessel had originally been loaded with, and the juxtaposition of the various articles of her cargo, plus the heat and time she had endured, plus one or two other only guessable quantities, we should have solved the chemistry of the Life Force."

Like this one, most of the stories in the collection can be taken as science fiction. Others, however, are more traditional. "The Sea Horses" weaves the fantasies of a child and the guilt of an old man into a sentimental denial of death, while two pieces, "On the Bridge" and "Through the Vortex of a Cyclone," are straightforward descriptions of intense moments at sea.

In 1913 Hodgson married Bessie Farnworth and went to live with her in France. He returned to England on the outbreak of war in 1914, and in 1915 he joined the officer training corps of the University of London. He continued to write, though for the second time in his career he turned away from the Sargasso and looked for ways of making a more conventional contribution to the literature of the sea. In the collection *The Luck of the Strong* (1916) the tendencies of the Carnacki stories are at work: the poetry of the tales set in the Sargasso Sea and the horror of degenerate life forms are sacrificed for more-momentary excitement. Many of these tales are also linked with Carnacki in that Hodgson attempts to create a hero transferable across more than one tale. His attempts are interesting but not always successful. The first of these heroes is Captain Jat, who features in two tales, "The Island of the Ud" and "The Adventure of the Headland." In both he is accompanied by Pibby Tawles, the cabin boy, who admires him but fears his brutality. The captain is a suspicious and violent man. When Pibby spills the captain's grog in the first tale he must fetch a rope's end with which to be beaten, yet Pibby admires him, and in the second he both saves the captain's life and is saved by him in turn. In both tales the adventure is a result of the captain's indomitable greed, and both bring captain and cabin boy in contact with primitive civilizations. In "The Island of the Ud" they go in quest of sacred pearls and are menaced by the Ud, a giant crab, whereas in "The Adventure of the Headland" they are hunted by man-eating dogs the size of donkeys and bestial cannibal-priests who run with them. Both tales raise issues of male bonding and loyalty but sacrifice any serious exploration of them to the creation of excitement.

Hodgson's second attempt at a hero yielded the marginally more attractive figure of D. C. O. Cargunka. The initials are not for forenames but stand for "dot and carry one," as the diminutive but plucky Cargunka is lame and compares himself frequently and rather pathetically with Lord Byron. Both the tales in which he appears are marred by unlikely coincidence. "The Bells of the Laughing Sally" concerns a castaway girl who made a recording of a song with this title and who is wrecked on a ship coincidentally of the same name, whose mad captain treats her would-be rescuers to supernatural suggestion through chicanery with bells. In both Cargunka tales the hero makes a friend through mutual respect arising out of a fight and is drawn into a quest on his behalf. Relationships between males are most important in this least impressive of Hodgson's collections. Revenge against bullies is a common mainspring to the action, and the sentimental British love for the underdog is exploited to the full. The most interesting aspect of the collection is Hodgson's delight in the morally ambiguous hero, with whom readers may side because they sense him as wronged or as a victim but who is not in the conventional sense a good man.

In Hodgson's last collection of short pieces he succeeded in doing what he had attempted in *The Luck of the Strong:* he created a sea hero whom he could use in a variety of tales. Captain Gault, hero of the collection *Captain Gault: Being the Exceedingly Private Log of a Sea Captain* (1917), is the heir to Captains Jat and Cargunka, but the format has changed, since there is no cabin boy or admirer, and Gault is narrator of his own tales. Gault's great interest in life, from which he derives both income and intellectual satisfaction, is the evasion of excise duty and customs. As an inhabitant of the sea and a follower of its morality, he owes nothing to the powers of the land, who are his enemies, though except in one or two cases they machinate against him according to the rules of gentlemanly sport. Gault is not quite a parallel to Robin Hood, but in moral terms he shares the same paradoxical honorable outlawry. The pleasure of the tales consists not in the knowledge that Gault will win – he always does – but how he will do so when his enemies have full knowledge of his cargo and his intention to deceive them.

The type of fiction Hodgson created through his outlaw captain allowed him to touch upon ideas and bring talents to bear that had not previously figured in his work. Though Gault's intellectual powers are as legendary as Holmes's powers of deduction, the kinds of situation in which he finds himself are part of a real world of subterfuge, not the boyish never-never land of Captain Jat's adventures. The people for whom he smuggles and the agents and agents provocateurs who are ranged against him provide opportunities for a kind of characterization not present before in Hodgson's work.

In the most memorable of the tales, "The Adventure of the Garter," Miss Malbrey, an attractive young woman, shows Gault her jewel-runner's garter. She tells him she has been spotted by a treasury spy and needs his help, flattering him by showing that his ingenuity is known to her. Through a romantic entanglement to which Gault likely is by no means immune, she makes him reveal what the reader believes to be his ultimate hiding place. It is gradually revealed that she is herself a treasury spy, and the tension of the story begins to hinge on whether or not Gault has revealed too much to her in the earlier stages of their relationship. When in port she attempts to unmask him the reader finds that he has not trusted her and has used the revealed hiding place. In her chagrin she dishonorably accuses him of thieving the diamonds she had asked him to smuggle for her, though she cannot press the accusation without declaring a real guilt in her own intention to smuggle. Gault reveals to her after this scene, "I kept hoping against hope, that you would find it impossible to 'sell' me, when it came to the point. I felt that your womanhood would make that impossible to you." This makes her blush deeply, as she has calculatingly used her intimacy with him as a weapon. Finally, Gault returns her diamonds to her: he has successfully smuggled them, and some of his own, in the collar of her own lapdog. Gault's misogyny – in an early tale he declares that a woman is "apt to be a bit mixed in her ideas of fair play" – is confirmed, and his distrust proves to have been right. What makes this group of tales thoroughly modern for their time is their urbanity; just as the setting of the modern ocean liner has replaced the primitive island peopled by devil worshipers, so Gault's smooth individualism transcends the fisticuffs of Victorian adventure fiction.

Hodgson joined the Royal Field Artillery as lieutenant in 1915 but did not see action in France until 1917. On 17 April 1918 he was killed by a German shell while acting as forward observing officer, a duty for which, with characteristic courage, he had volunteered.

Hodgson was not a novelist in the conventional sense. His longer works are romances, their rhythms governed by the interest in suspense and excitement that marks his shorter pieces. His greatest gift as a writer was his capacity to convey feeling through the powerful description of imaginary landscapes, and through this gift he gave poetic shape to some of the inchoate fears of his age. In *William Hope Hodgson: Voyages and Visions* Stableford suggests that Hodgson was willing and able to use the imagery of his own dreams, and this claim is borne out in his best work, where there is a vividness that is often rich in suggestion but that defies any easy attempt at logical interpretation. If his personal imagery links him with the generation that preceded him, the tempo of his work, with its necessity for action and excitement, links him with the fiction of the later twentieth century. When he could balance these two needs against one another he was capable of excellent work, yet it is noticeable that when he fell back too far upon the mere creation of excitement, as in the tales of Captains Jat and Cargunka, his imagination failed him. The closing stages of his career show that he recognized the need to conquer new fields, and with the publication of *Captain Gault* he found a new and stylish idiom, which he did not live to explore further.

Hodgson's longer work has survived well in the late twentieth century, though his short stories are not widely known. His works do not reach a wide readership but are capable of inspiring devotion in minorities such as the collectors and connoisseurs of horror fiction. His influence upon those who followed him in this genre, such as H. P. Lovecraft and Dennis Wheatley, was great. His importance to the cultural history of his period lies most of all in his work's complex relationship with the prevailing scientific ethos. At a simple level Hodgson was one of many in revolt against the banishment of wonder by science, yet at a deeper level his best work was a vehicle for the doubts and fears created by the science whose vision he eschewed.

Bibliographies:

L. W. Currey, *Science Fiction and Fantasy Authors: A Bibliography of First Printings of Their Fiction* (Boston: G. K. Hall, 1979);

Roger C. Schlobin, *The Literature of Fantasy: A Comprehensive Annotated Bibliography of Modern Fantasy Fiction* (New York & London: Garland, 1979);

Ian Bell, *Spectral Manifestations: William Hope Hodgson* (Oxford: Bellknapp Books, 1984).

References:

Ian Bell, ed., *William Hope Hodgson: Voyages and Visions* (N.p.: Bell, 1987);

H. P. Lovecraft, *Supernatural Horror in Literature* (New York: Abramson, 1945);

Roger C. Schlobin, ed., *The Aesthetics of Fantasy Literature and Art* (Notre Dame, Ind.: University of Notre Dame Press / Brighton, U.K.: Harvester, 1982);

Brian Stableford, *Scientific Romance in Britain, 1890–1950* (London: Fourth Estate, 1985).

Anthony Hope
(Sir Anthony Hope Hawkins)
(9 February 1863 – 8 July 1933)

John R. Holmes
Franciscan University of Steubenville

See also the Hope entry in *DLB 153: Late Victorian and Edwardian Novelists, First Series.*

BOOKS: *A Man of Mark* (London: Remington, 1890; New York: Holt, 1895);

Father Stafford (London & New York: Cassell, 1891); republished as *Father Stafford: A Lover's Fate and Friend's Counsel* (Chicago: Tennyson, 1896);

Mr. Witt's Widow: A Frivolous Tale (London: Innes, 1892; New York & Chicago: United States Book Company, 1892);

Sport Royal and Other Stories (London: Innes, 1893; New York: Holt, 1895);

A Change of Air (London: Methuen, 1893; New York: Holt, 1894);

Half a Hero (2 volumes, London: Innes, 1893; 1 volume, New York: Harper, 1893);

The Prisoner of Zenda: Being the History of Three Months in the Life of an English Gentleman (Bristol: Arrowsmith / London: Simpkin, Marshall, Hamilton, Kent, 1894; New York: Holt, 1894);

The Dolly Dialogues (London: Westminster Gazette, 1894; New York: Holt, 1894);

The Indiscretion of the Duchess, Being a Story Concerning Two Ladies, a Nobleman, and a Necklace (Bristol: Arrowsmith / London: Simpkin, Marshall, Hamilton, Kent, 1894; New York: Holt, 1894);

The God in the Car (2 volumes, London: Methuen, 1894; 1 volume, New York: Appleton, 1894);

The Lady of the Pool (New York: Appleton, 1894);

The Chronicles of Count Antonio (London: Methuen, 1895; New York: Appleton, 1895);

Frivolous Cupid (New York: Platt, Bruce, 1895); republished in altered, unauthorized form as *Comedies of Courtship* (London: Innes, 1896; New York: Scribners, 1896) and *A Cut and a Kiss* (Boston: Brown, 1899);

Anthony Hope (Sir Anthony Hope Hawkins); photograph by Lenare (Courtesy of the Lilly Library, Indiana University)

The Heart of Princess Osra (London: Longmans, Green, 1896; New York & London: Stokes, 1896); republished in abridged form as *The Happiness of Stephen the Smith* (New York: Stokes, 1896);

Phroso (London: Methuen, 1897; New York: Stokes, 1897);

La Mort à la Mode (New York: Stokes, 1897);

Simon Dale (New York: Stokes, 1897; London: Methuen, 1898);

Rupert of Hentzau (Bristol: Arrowsmith, 1898; New York: Holt, 1898);

The Adventure of Lady Ursula: A Comedy in Four Acts (New York: Russell, 1898);

The King's Mirror (New York: Appleton, 1898; London: Methuen, 1899);

Quisanté (London: Methuen, 1900; New York: Stokes, 1900);

Captain Dieppe (New York: Doubleday & McClure, 1900; London: Skeffington, 1918);

Tristram of Blent: An Episode in the Story of an Ancient House (London: John Murray, 1901; New York: McClure, Phillips, 1901);

The Intrusions of Peggy (New York: Harper, 1901; London: Smith, Elder, 1902);

Double Harness (London: Hutchinson, 1904; New York: McClure, Phillips, 1904);

A Servant of the Public (London: Methuen, 1905; New York: Stokes, 1905);

Sophy of Kravonia (Bristol: Arrowsmith, 1905; New York & London: Harper, 1905);

Tales of Two People (London: Methuen, 1907); published in abridged form as *Love's Logic* (New York: McClure, 1908);

Helena's Path (New York: McClure, 1907);

The Great Miss Driver (London: Methuen, 1908; New York: McClure, 1908);

Pilkerton's Peerage: A Comedy in Four Acts (New York: French, 1908);

Dialogue, as Anthony Hope Hawkins (Oxford: Printed by Horace Hart at the University Press, 1909);

Second String (London & New York: Nelson, 1910; Garden City, N.Y.: Doubleday, Page, 1910);

Mrs. Maxon Protests (New York & London: Harper, 1910; London: Methuen, 1911);

The New (German) Testament: Some Texts and a Commentary (London: Methuen, 1914; New York: Appleton, 1915);

Militarism: German and British (London: Darling, 1915);

A Young Man's Year (London: Methuen, 1915; New York: Appleton, 1915);

Why Italy Is with the Allies (London: Clay, 1917);

Beaumaroy Home from the Wars (London: Methuen, 1919); published as *The Secret of the Tower* (New York: Appleton, 1919);

Lucinda (London: Hutchinson, 1920; New York: Appleton, 1920);

Little Tiger (London: Hutchinson, 1925; New York: Doran, 1925);

The Philosopher in the Apple Orchard: A Pastoral in One Act (New York, Los Angeles & London: French, 1926);

Memories and Notes (London: Hutchinson, 1927; Garden City, N.Y.: Doubleday, Doran, 1928).

PLAY PRODUCTIONS: *Rupert of Hentzau,* New York, Lyceum Theatre, 10 April 1898; Glasgow, Theatre Royal, 5 October 1899; London, St. James Theatre, 2 January 1900;

The Adventure of Lady Ursula, New York, Lyceum Theatre, 1 September 1898; London, Duke of York's Theatre, 11 October 1898;

When a Man's in Love, London, Court Theatre, 19 October 1898;

Phroso, New York, Empire Theatre, 26 December 1898;

English Nell, London, Prince of Wales's Theatre, 21 August 1900;

Pilkerton's Peerage, London, Garrick Theatre, 28 January 1901;

La Princess Osra, London, Covent Garden, 14 July 1902;

Helena's Path, London, Duke of York's Theatre, 3 May 1910;

Mrs. Thistleton's Princess, London, Royalty Theatre, 13 November 1921.

Sir Anthony Hope Hawkins is best known as Anthony Hope, author of *The Prisoner of Zenda: Being the History of Three Months in the Life of an English Gentleman* (1894), the adventure tale that in his lifetime became a best-selling novel, a successful play in New York and London, and three popular motion pictures. The story proved so enduring that three additional screen versions were made after his death. The novel's influence on turn-of-the-century fiction in England and the United States was immense: its fictional setting, Ruritania, gave a name to a whole subgenre of adventure fiction, the "Ruritanian romance." In the short-story genre his most enduring works are *The Dolly Dialogues* (1894), which in the 1890s rivaled his adventure novels in popularity. In fact, when he was invited to do public readings, he was invariably asked to read from the comic and domestic *Dolly Dialogues* rather than his exotic adventure tales. His fellow writers considered him a master of dialogue, and the *Dolly* pieces remain models of rapid story development through dialogue.

Anthony Hope Hawkins was born on 9 February 1863 in the London suburb of Clapton. His father, the Reverend Edwards Comerford Hawkins, established Saint John's Foundation School for the

Sons of Poor Clergy and for more than twenty years served as its headmaster. His mother, Jane Isabella (Grahame) Hawkins, claimed descent from the Scots hero Robert the Bruce; her brother's son, Kenneth Grahame, also achieved literary fame as author of *The Wind in the Willows* (1908). The youngest of three children, Hawkins remained close to his older brother, Geoffrey, and his sister, Joan, throughout their lives; he survived them both.

His early education was at his father's school. His earliest literary influence was the *Spectator,* the politically independent newsweekly that helped set the standard for prose style through much of the nineteenth century. The *Spectator* gave young Hawkins a precocious knowledge of British and world politics, which not only prepared him for his later dabbling in national politics but also won him a public-school scholarship at Marlborough in 1876. The entrance exam that year required candidates to name as many cabinet ministers as they could; Hawkins named the entire cabinet and the office held by each.

In his four years at Marlborough, Hawkins excelled at athletics, especially rugby. He also served as editor of the *Marlburian* and president of the speaking society, and he finished fourth in his class. Despite his work on the *Marlburian,* Hawkins did not distinguish himself as a writer in public school. Once in a competition for a school prize in poetry, headmaster G. C. Bell returned his entry, informing him that only one other poem had been submitted. Of the two entries, Hawkins recalled in *Memories and Notes* (1927), Bell added, "One was very feeble and the other very grotesque. Do you care to know which yours was?"

Matriculating from Marlborough, Hawkins entered Balliol College of Oxford University in the fall of 1881. As in public school, he distinguished himself more as a speaker than a writer, though he contributed sports articles to the new *Oxford Magazine.* Oxford at that time enjoyed three debating societies; Hawkins joined all three and became president of the most prestigious, the Oxford Union.

Upon graduation in 1885 Hawkins remained at Oxford, reading law in preparation for the bar and supporting himself by tutoring. In the summer of 1886 he moved to London to live with his father, who three years earlier had resigned his headmaster position to accept a pastoral office at Saint Bride's parish in Fleet Street. Living on Fleet Street, the center of journalism and publishing in London, proved tempting to the aspiring man of law. Though he was called to the bar at the Middle Temple in 1887 and apprenticed with attorney Ashworth James, Hawkins found his pen more active in "scribbling" for the newspapers than in any legal work.

What led to the demise of any legal career for Hawkins was the revelation that newspapers would actually pay cash for his favorite leisure activity, writing. His first success was a small satiric piece on libel in the London *Globe* in 1888, for which he received a guinea — a good rate, because the story was a "turnover," an entertaining piece on the bottom right corner of the front page continuing on the next, enticing the casual reader to "turn over" to the editorials.

Encouraged by what seemed to be easy money, Hawkins tried his hand at short fiction, which he soon published in the *Illustrated London News, Sketch,* and the *St. James Gazette.* In 1890 he finished his first novel and published it at his own expense under the pseudonym Anthony Hope. *A Man of Mark* anticipates the technique of the mythical setting that proved so successful in his later fiction.

The reviews of *A Man of Mark* were positive enough for Hawkins to chance sending another novel, which he had finished even before his first was printed, to commercial publishers. *Father Stafford,* a tale of an Anglican priest swearing a personal vow of celibacy and then falling in love, appeared in October 1891. While *Father Stafford* was seeking a publisher, the Liberal Party drafted Hawkins to oppose the incumbent member of Parliament in South Buckinghamshire. He campaigned hard but lost the election, though he valued the experience of running.

As with his first novel, his second was not even through the press before Hawkins had completed another, *Mr. Witt's Widow: A Frivolous Tale,* published in March 1892. While writing a fourth novel he collected his short stories published in various magazines into a volume named after the longest, *Sport Royal and Other Stories* (1893). The early title story is one of his finest, including most of the elements that led to the success of *The Prisoner of Zenda* and that his first four novels lacked. While the setting is not mythical, the royal characters are, though they sound vaguely authentic. "Sport Royal" marks Hawkins's first use of the doppelgänger motif, which, as its first reviewers noted, was reminiscent of the work of Robert Louis Stevenson. The narrator, Mr. Jason, is the first of many Hope heroes who is mistaken for another, with the mistaken identity precipitating the adventure. The tale typifies his most successful short stories in its pacing, its jumping immediately into the action, and its deft use of dialogue to advance the plot, sometimes with nothing but speeches for several pages.

In the dialogue of "Sport Royal" Hawkins first showed the versatility of one of his characteristic techniques, hesitation. Jason is mistaken for a man who is to fight a duel for the honor of a countess; instead of revealing his identity, he duels anyway, though he knows nothing of the cause. The scene in which he meets the countess is virtually all dialogue and is riddled with effective hesitations – the countess's revealing her need for secrecy, and Jason's his ignorance of the facts:

> "But how did you know anything about it? Did he tell you about the pr – about the affair?"
> "No. I only heard – "
> "From him?"
> "Yes – that you wanted a champion."
> "Oh, that's absurd! Why, you never heard of me!"
> "Ah, indeed I have!"
> "And – did you recognize me under my new name?"
> "Your – "
> "My – my title. You know."
> "The – he told me that. Must I confess? I jumped at the chance of serving you."
> "You had never seen me!"
> "Perhaps I had seen your photograph."

Later in his career, in his 1909 lecture on dialogue before the London English Association, Hawkins explained the versatility of hesitation in dialogue: "The hesitation, the aposiopesis, the interruption, are all ready and flexible devices, apt to convey limits, innuendoes, doubts, objections."

In addition to *Sport Royal,* two other books by Hawkins appeared in 1893: *A Change of Air* and *Half a Hero,* both political adventures like his first novel. More significant to his development as a short-story writer was the inauguration that February of the *Westminster Gazette,* to which he submitted the first of his "Dolly Dialogues." These witty stories, told almost exclusively through dialogue, captured the parlor talk of the 1890s. Though comfortably married – except in the first three dialogues, in which she is betrothed – Lady Dorothy "Dolly" Mickleham harmlessly flirts through every story with a former flame, the narrator, Mr. Samuel Carter.

In *The Dolly Dialogues* Hawkins perfected his dialogue technique of hesitation and interruption. The Dolly stories are often called sketches or dialogues, but each has conflict, a plot, and characterization, even though all are told mostly through dialogue. In the very first, "A Liberal Education," Mr. Carter reveals, without ever saying so, that he is still attracted to Dolly as she cruelly praises another man's features. In most of the dialogues the readers

must piece together the plot from snatches of information given in the dialogue. Sometimes the gaps are between stories: "Cordial Relations," which takes place before Dolly marries Lord Mickleham, ends with the butler announcing the lord's arrival just as Carter was showing her a locket depicting a broken heart. "Retribution" opens with Dolly's aunt upbraiding Carter for the breach of taste in showing such a thing to an engaged woman.

As popular as *The Dolly Dialogues* became, they were not as lucrative as the next Anthony Hope novel, written concurrently with the first dialogues. The genesis of *The Prisoner of Zenda* can be dated almost to the hour: in the late afternoon of 28 November 1893 Hawkins conceived the idea for the novel while walking from the courts to his rooms in the Middle Temple. He wrote the first chapter the next morning and exactly a month later, on 29 December, completed the novel. Four months later it was in the bookstores and became his all-time bestseller.

With the twin successes of *The Dolly Dialogues,* which appeared in book form early in 1894, and *The Prisoner of Zenda,* Hawkins was convinced that a writing career would support him as well as a legal one, if not better. He left the bar in July 1894 and moved from the court district to fashionable Buckingham Street. The next few months saw the publication of two very different novels: *The Indiscretion of the Duchess, Being a Story Concerning Two Ladies, a Nobleman, and a Necklace,* in which he shows more of the domestic sensibility that made Dolly seem real; and *The God in the Car,* a serious novel unlike anything he had written before. *The God in the Car* is a portrait of an empire builder named Willie Ruston, seemingly modeled after British financier Cecil Rhodes. According to biographer Sir Charles Mallet, Rhodes is reputed to have said, "I'm not such a brute as that" after reading the novel, and Hawkins, when he later met Rhodes, wrote in his diary that he agreed. H. G. Wells sent Hawkins a postcard praising *The God in the Car* as soon as he finished reading it.

Hawkins's adventure tales in his first year as a full-time writer focused on one character, the *Zenda*-style swashbuckler Count Antonio of Monte Velluto; these stories were published in the spring of 1895 as *The Chronicles of Count Antonio.* Each chapter of the book is structurally a separate story about the Robin Hood–like count, exiled from the court of Duke Valentine, who robs the duke's tax collectors and gives the booty to the poor. Hawkins uses the same technique in *The Heart of Princess Osra* (1896), which like the *Chronicles* is a short-story collection

Hope in the early 1880s

masquerading as a novel. Each "chapter" of *The Heart of Princes Osra* tells the story of a different unsuccessful suitor for Osra's hand until the last, in which she marries the grand duke of Mittenheim. The characters in the Princess Osra stories are the early-eighteenth-century ancestors of the royal family in *The Prisoner of Zenda,* whose popularity helped to sell *The Heart of Princess Osra,* leading Hawkins to consider a sequel. In 1902 the Osra stories were made into a musical drama, which ran for only two performances in London's historic Covent Garden.

Not all of Hawkins's love stories are set in exotic mythical kingdoms. Six of his domestic love stories of this period, along with two fairy-tale romances, were collected in *Frivolous Cupid* (1895). The same love stories were renamed and repackaged in two unauthorized editions, *Comedies of Courtship* (1896) and *A Cut and A Kiss* (1899). In these stories Hawkins attempted to create characters who, like Dolly, would become recurring figures of a variety of tales. Two such characters are Jack Dexter and Mark (or George) Wynne, each of whom appears in two stories in the collections.

The Jack Dexter stories are narrated by an unnamed table companion of Colonel Holborow's. Whatever the after-dinner conversation happens to be, it is always topped by a self-aggrandizing tale by Jack Dexter punctuated at the end by his leaving and closing the door, cutting off any doubts or objections to his exaggerations. Mark Wynne is the narrator of his two stories (and of two more in 1907), in which he is an onlooker at the upper-class society of his wealthier relatives. He records with barely perceptible irony the way of lovers in high society.

Though Hawkins confided to his diary that his knowledge of love was mostly theoretical, his female friends commended his insight into the hearts of women of the 1890s. One in particular, Millicent, Duchess of Sutherland, knew him first through his stories and then commenced a close platonic relationship with him in November 1896. The duchess became a cherished friend and a sounding board for both his personal and literary ideas.

The popularity of *The Prisoner of Zenda* in the United States brought Hawkins many requests to cross the Atlantic for a series of readings and talks, which he declined until the offers grew too lucrative to refuse. In February 1897, as his new novel *Phroso* appeared, he agreed to an American tour, which he began in October. His readings from *The Dolly Dialogues* proved tremendously popular, and he dined with President William McKinley, former president Benjamin Harrison, and future president Theodore Roosevelt. Visiting Harvard, Yale, Princeton, and Cornell Universities, the former Marlborough athlete found himself puzzled by American football.

Though 1898 began with the British publication of another Anthony Hope novel, *Simon Dale,* and July saw *Rupert of Hentzau,* the much-anticipated sequel to *The Prisoner of Zenda,* most of that year's literary activity for Hawkins was dramatic. For most of the 1898 season an Anthony Hope play was onstage in London, *The Adventure of Lady Ursula* running for 262 performances and *When a Man's in Love* running 35 performances through 11 November.

Hawkins's dramatic activity at the turn of the century brought him into contact with London theatrical society, which began to bring him out of the personal isolation his busy writing schedule had created. He began falling in love with the actresses he met, including the American Ethel Barrymore, whom, he told his diary, "I should like to marry . . . if I could make the time." Theatrical society also brought him into contact with other playwrights, and a lifelong friendship with dramatist J. M. Barrie began in 1899, sparked to some extent by the British publication that year of *The King's Mirror,* which Barrie considered Hawkins's best novel. The personal reminiscences of King Augustin about an unnamed but vaguely Germanic principality, *The King's Mirror* offers endless variations on the theme that royalty is more a burden than a privilege. Here, as in all his fiction, Hawkins humanizes royalty more than did most of his contemporaries.

From the day he abandoned law for literature Hawkins made it his duty to support British writing as a profession and writers as a group. He joined the British Author's Society in 1894 and in January 1900 was named its chair. He established and contributed heavily to a pension fund for writers whose royalties were not commensurate with their merits and took delegations to visit the nation's great authors on their birthdays.

In January 1900 *Rupert of Hentzau* failed as a stage play in London, though *English Nell,* the stage version of *Simon Dale,* did quite well, starting in August and running for 176 performances. Shortly after its opening, he was asked again to run for Parliament, though his doctor halted his campaigning when Hawkins developed heart trouble from the stress.

Around this time the loneliness of the writing profession, the fear of death, and the fear of losing his creative powers began to worry Hawkins: he began the century with a letter to the Duchess of Sutherland dated "Hades. 1 January 1900," and his diary for the rest of his life would note with shock each time a celebrated author died. He was conscious of the onus of reaching middle age still living with his father in the vicarage and of being unmarried at forty. A second trip to the United States on his fortieth birthday proved a solution to both problems. Seeking the society of Ethel Barrymore, he ended up paying more attention to a younger member of the actress's set. Hawkins had met Betty Sheldon on his first trip to America, but she was then only thirteen; now, in 1903, she was eighteen and, in the novelist's words in his diary, "dangerously prettier." By 21 May they were engaged, and on 1 July they were married in his father's parish by an old Balliol chum, C. G. Lang, now an Anglican bishop. Barrymore was the maid of honor.

Hawkins was sure that family life would decrease his output of fiction, but a collected edition of his novels by Appleton in America brought him more income than any new novel could. In 1903 there was no new Anthony Hope novel for the first time in his thirteen years of writing, but by the spring of 1904 he had three completed novels in manuscript, which he published over the next two years: *Double Harness* (1904), *A Servant of the Public* (1905), and *Sophy of Kravonia* (1905).

August 1904 brought both sorrow and joy to Hawkins. First, his father was bedridden with a lingering illness that claimed his life eighteen months later. Then, on 21 August, his first child was born, whom Betty insisted on naming Millicent after his friend the duchess. With his family growing quickly – his first son, Richard, was born in November 1905 – Hawkins felt the need for a larger home. Early in 1905 he bought a house at 41 Bedford Square; a year later he owned one of the newest status symbols, a motorcar.

One of Hawkins's only two books in 1907 was *Tales of Two People,* another collection of love stories, which was published in the United States with one story omitted as *Love's Logic* (1908). At a time when he was attempting to get more serious in his novels (with the exception of *Sophy of Kravonia,* which he called "a yarn" in his diary), these simple and direct stories recalled the "old" Anthony Hope, and reviewers hailed the book as such. Most of the *Tales of Two People* are intrigues of matchmaking among the titled, but two of them, "Mrs. Thistleton's Princess" and "The Necessary Resources," merge the two strains of Anthony Hope short stories: the domestic love story and the adventure tale in a mythical foreign country. In these two stories he domesticates the *Prisoner of Zenda* formula: both have a monarch deposed by trickery, yet in both the monarch is exiled in England. In "Mrs. Thistleton's Princess" the narrator, a lawyer, helps Princess Vera of Boravia regain her throne, and in "The Necessary Resources" an English widow helps Prince Julian, whose kingdom is never named, in the same cause. The prince's coup fails, but it leaves him free to marry the Englishwoman. *Tales of Two People* also includes the creation of the last of Anthony Hope's recurring characters, the Duke of Belleville. The fun-loving duke likes to masquerade as a commoner: in "The Lady and the Flagon" he impersonates a policeman to rescue a young lady from a thief intent on stealing both her heart and his priceless antique. In "The Duke's Allotment" he poses as a day laborer, is mistaken for a criminal, and runs from the police with the chief constable's fiancée. Both stories end with the duke's reluctant return to the life of a British peer.

In the years leading up to World War I, Hawkins's writing schedule slowed, though the filming of the first motion-picture version of *The Prisoner of Zenda* in 1913 made up for the absence of book royalties. When the war came in 1914 the British government recruited him and two dozen other

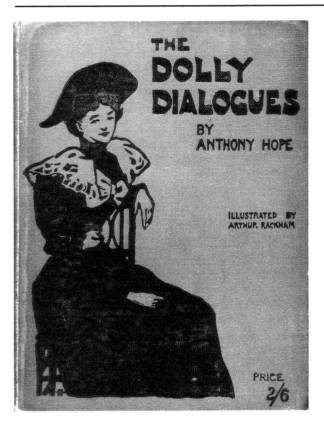
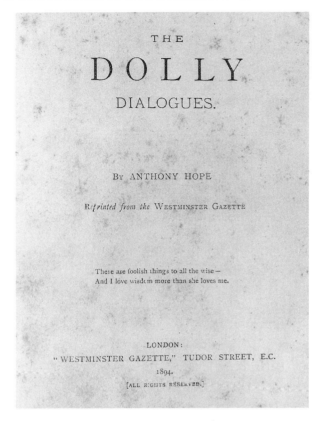

Cover and title page for Hope's most successful collection of stories, which reflect parlor conversations of the 1890s (Courtesy of the Lilly Library, Indiana University)

popular writers to counter German propaganda. This work resulted in his three wartime books, *The New (German) Testament: Some Texts and a Commentary* (1914), *Militarism: German and British* (1915), and *Why Italy Is with the Allies* (1917). The work often kept him away from his growing family – a second son, David, was born in January 1916 – but they accepted this sacrifice as a patriotic duty. For this wartime service Hawkins was offered a knighthood; on 6 January 1918 he became Sir Anthony Hope Hawkins.

The psychological devastation of the war in Europe gave Hawkins his material for his next novel. Many authors wrote novels of the changes in personal ethics among young men coming home from the war, but Hawkins's *Beaumeroy Home from the Wars* (1919) preceded them all. Many of his friends and fellow writers lost sons in the war, but the deaths of two young men after the war hit Hawkins more severely. His nephew Geoffrey survived a serious wound in the battlefield but recovered only to die at home in a cycling accident in March 1920, and two months later Hawkins was a pallbearer at the Oxford funeral of his cousin Alistair Grahame,

the boy whose father had written the children's classic *The Wind in the Willows* for him.

In the 1920s Hawkins's fear of losing his creative powers became increasingly justified. He was still able to produce two more novels, *Lucinda* (1920) and *Little Tiger* (1925), but he relied on reprints and film rights to maintain his income, which had already slipped from its prewar zenith. A well-timed renegotiation of the film rights for *The Prisoner of Zenda* in 1920 paid off when it was refilmed in 1922, the last film version in its author's lifetime. By the late 1920s, with his children grown and gone, Hawkins was able to accept the declining income his dwindling literary output entailed.

With the 1930s Hawkins stopped looking backward and apparently finally accepted the inevitability of what lay ahead. On 8 June 1931, the day of his son Richard's wedding, Hawkins wrote his last diary entry. He stopped writing altogether and also stopped giving the after-dinner speeches for which he had been known over the past forty years. He died at his farm outside London on 8 July 1933 and was buried in his father's old parish of Saint Brides in London. In a letter of consolation to

Betty, Barrie wrote, "He made more people happy than any other author of our time." If true, this alone should entitle Anthony Hope Hawkins to a place in the hall of letters.

Hawkins is likely to remain always, in critic S. Gorley Putt's phrase, "The Prisoner of *The Prisoner of Zenda*." The phenomenal popular success of that adventure novel has obscured, perhaps permanently, his artistic success in other forms of fiction. His fame as a short-story writer is assured by *The Dolly Dialogues,* but Hawkins wrote artful, well-told, tightly constructed short stories of virtually every type, which are still occasionally anthologized.

It is not altogether unjust, however, that the name "Anthony Hope" is inextricably linked with "Ruritanian" swashbuckling romance, for in that genre or subgenre Hawkins shone brightly, and, perhaps more important, such tales emblemize the last hurrah for European monarchism that the Great War obliterated, even from Hawkins's fiction.

For if Hawkins was truly a romantic, as those critics who pay him any notice have styled him, he was a romantic of monarchism, which is ironic because his personal politics were decidedly liberal. Yet unlike Continental liberalism, British liberalism did not generally entail an aversion to royalty and peerage. His unabashed admiration for the aristocracy in both his private life and his writing is the common factor in his two most typical kinds of story: his *Zenda*-like romances of royalty and his *Dolly*-like domestic conversations. The light tales of modern courtship may at first seem far removed from tales of commoners giving all for their prince or princess, but at least one of the lovers in such stories is usually a peer, and the plot often hinges, sometimes satirically, sometimes seriously, on the special problems of courtship among lords and ladies.

Hawkins is a rarity: a transitional figure obviously aware of being a transitional figure. Launching his career in the last decade of the Victorian age, he imbibed in his short fiction the nostalgic romanticism of earlier writers such as Stevenson, to whom he is often compared and who honored him by writing a letter of appreciation for *The Prisoner of Zenda*

that proved to be the last thing he ever wrote. Yet Hawkins wrote through the first three decades of the twentieth century and became conscious, especially after the war, of being a literary fossil. In a 1905 address to the Philosophical Institution in Edinburgh he observed that the English novel, once devoted to the study of manners, had now given itself over to philosophy. "The centre of gravity of the book, so to say, is changed," he said. "The analysis and exhibition of human character tend to become a means toward the statement and illustration of a problem." For Hawkins, however, the delineation of character and manners was an end in itself, which he knew made him old-fashioned. He also knew that it made his fiction sell. "If we are amusing," he concluded, "you can afford to forgive us our philosophising, and if we're not amusing, all the philosophising in the world won't make you read ten pages of us."

Hawkins's *Memories and Notes* concludes with a similarly frank assessment of his place in the world of letters as a Victorian who lived to see a generation of younger writers snicker at Victorianism and as a popular writer who seemed content with the role of a craftsman rather than an artist. This assessment seems fair: there may be little in his stories to interest a literary critic today, but there is much to commend them to a lover of adventure fiction in any era.

Biography:
Sir Charles Mallet, *Anthony Hope and His Books* (London: Hutchinson, 1935).

References:
Arthur St. John Adcock, *Gods of Modern Grub Street* (New York: Stokes, 1923);

Edward J. Fluck, Afterword to Hope's *Sport Royal and Other Stories* (Emmaus, Pa.: Story Classics, 1952);

Hugh Greene, Introduction to Hope's *Sophy of Kravonia* (London: Bodley Head, 1975), pp. 5–7;

S. Gorley Putt, "The Prisoner of *The Prisoner of Zenda,*" in his *Scholars of the Heart* (London: Faber & Faber, 1962), pp. 110–131.

M. R. James
(1 August 1862 – 12 June 1936)

William Atkinson
Appalachian State University

BOOKS: *Ghost-Stories of an Antiquary* (London: Arnold, 1904; New York: Longmans, Green, 1905);

More Ghost Stories of an Antiquary (London: Arnold, 1911; New York: Longmans, Green, 1911);

A Thin Ghost, and Others (London: Arnold, 1919; New York: Longmans, Green, 1919);

The Five Jars (London: Arnold, 1922; New York: Longmans, Green, 1922);

A Warning to the Curious, and Other Ghost Stories (London: Arnold, 1925; New York: Longmans, Green, 1925);

Abbeys (London: Great Western Railway, 1925; Garden City, N.Y.: Doubleday, Page, 1926);

Eton and King's: Recollections, Mostly Trivial, 1875–1925 (London: William & Norgate, 1926);

Suffolk and Norfolk (London: Dent, 1930);

The Collected Ghost Stories of M. R. James (London: Arnold, 1931; New York: Longmans, Green, 1931); republished as *The Ghost Stories of M. R. James* (London: Arnold, 1974); republished as *The Penguin Complete Ghost Stories of M. R. James* (London: Penguin, 1984).

OTHER: Walter Map, *De Nugis Curialium (Courtiers' Trifles)*, translated by James (Cymmrodorion Record Series 9, 1923);

Joseph Sheridan Le Fanu, *"Madam Crowl's Ghost" and Other Tales of Mystery by Joseph Sheridan Le Fanu*, edited by James (London: Bell, 1923);

V. H. Collins, ed., *Ghosts and Marvels: A Selection of Uncanny Tales from Daniel Defoe to Algernon Blackwood*, introduction by James (London: Oxford University Press, 1924);

The Apocryphal New Testament, Being the Apocryphal Gospels, Acts, Epistles, and Apocalypses, with Other Narratives and Fragments, translated by James (Oxford: Clarendon, 1924);

Le Fanu, *Uncle Silas: A Tale of Bartram-Haugh*, introduction by James (London: Oxford University Press, 1926);

Hans Andersen: Forty Stories, translated by James (London: Faber, 1930); republished as *Forty-Two Stories* (London: Faber, 1953).

SELECTED PERIODICAL PUBLICATIONS –

UNCOLLECTED: "The Experiment: A New Year's Eve Ghost Story," *Morning Post*, 31 December 1931, p. 8;

"The Malice of Inanimate Objects," *Masquerade*, 1 (June 1933): 29–32;

"A Vignette," *London Mercury*, 35 (November 1936): 18–22.

While M. R. James is best remembered as the author of thirty-four ghost stories, most of which have seldom been out of print, during his lifetime he was acknowledged as a leading authority on medieval manuscripts and biblical apocrypha. He published descriptions of the Western manuscripts of all the principal Cambridge libraries and several other significant collections and made an influential translation of the apocryphal New Testament in 1924. This antiquarian expertise is evident in all his stories and is explicit in the title of his first collection of supernatural tales, *Ghost-Stories of an Antiquary* (1904). His deeply informed fascination with the past and its artifacts, particularly those written or drawn, not only generates a surface verisimilitude but is at the heart of his conception of the ghost story. In an uncharacteristically revealing moment of his memoir, *Eton and King's: Recollections, Mostly Trivial, 1875–1925* (1926), James wrote of his dissertation, "I had cherished for years, I still cherish, a quite peculiar interest in any document that has claimed to be a Book of the Bible, and is not. Nowadays I suppose it would be proper to say that I had a complex about it." A recurring theme in his ghost stories is the attempt by some power from the past, usually immanent in a manuscript of some sort, to manifest itself in the present, to find a denied place in the "book." These same preoccupa-

M. R. James

tions can be seen both in his scholarship and in his occasional ghost stories.

Montague Rhodes James was born on 1 August 1862 in Goodnestone next Wingham in Kent, the youngest of the four children of the Reverend Herbert James and Mary Emily James (née Horton). In 1865 his father left the curacy of Goodnestone for the living of Livermere, near Bury St. Edmunds in Suffolk. The older James favored the evangelical wing of the Church of England.

After being tutored by his father, James was sent to Temple Grove School near London in 1873. After three years he had profited well enough to win a scholarship to Eton College. At Eton, James was at the center of English privilege, and although never a wealthy man – his education was largely financed by scholarships – he was very much an establishment figure, as his extremely successful academic career demonstrates. To the extent that his ghost stories present a moral world, it is one infused by the ethics of the Edwardian establishment.

James had been fascinated with churches from an early age, and at Eton he began to collect rare books and, as he writes in *Eton and King's,* "browse untrammelled" among the manuscripts of the school's eighteenth-century library. His ghost stories dem-

onstrate a facility for imitating the language of old documents, sometimes even in Latin, and while still at school he fabricated a manuscript that purported to reveal the site of a buried treasure; one of his teachers was convinced of its authenticity. During this period he started telling ghost stories, possibly his own: in a December 1878 letter he wrote, "I must depart for a while, as I am engaged for a 'dark seance' i.e. a telling of ghost stories, in which capacity I am rather popular just now." One of his papers for the school's Literary Society was titled "The Occult Sciences," and he contributed an essay on ghost stories to the *Eton Rambler* for the 21 June 1880 issue. This essay included an anecdote about a wanderer's experience at night in a churchyard. The story's ghostly apparition already has the hallmarks of a Jamesian horror: "Nothing less than two glassy eyes belonging to a form that crouched there in the long grass. It was covered with what looked like a stained and tattered shroud, and he could dimly discern its long skinny clawed hands, eager, as it seemed, to grasp something." Rather than a sheeted ghost or the manifestation of someone as she was in life, the figure is plainly a reanimated corpse.

In October 1882 James won a scholarship to King's College at Cambridge University. He gained his baccalaureate in 1885 with Firsts in both parts of the Classical Tripos. In order to stay at King's as a don he needed to write a dissertation. While still at Eton he had bought the four volumes of John Albert Fabricius on the apocrypha of both Testaments; in his memoir he recalls the day as one when "life seemed to have little more to offer," and so his decision to write on the apocryphal Apocalypse of Saint Peter came easily.

The word *apocrypha* comes from the Greek and means "hidden away." James's ghost stories are reiterations of the theme of apocrypha revealed: an illustration from a manuscript scrapbook generates a demon; a narrative reveals itself in a mezzotint; a will is hidden in a book; an allegory's explanation lies in a bronze sphere at the center of a maze; a secret reveals itself through a pattern copied for some drapes; the uncovering of the ancient crown of the kings of East Anglia leads to a man's death. *Apocalypse* means a revelation or uncovering, and as a child James had dreamed of opening a Bible and finding, on a single page, an unknown book. His dissertation can be seen as an attempt to fulfill that dream and reveal a lost book of the Bible through logical inference. He admitted in his memoir to having no more than half a dozen lines, quoted in various manuscripts, to go on. "Those six lines, however, contained enough clues to suggest what the subject of the book had been: and I wove about them a web of considerable size. A few years later a large piece of the text, found in Egypt in 1884, was printed, and served to confirm my main guesses or conclusions, while of course it put others out of court." In the ghost stories the method reveals itself as very similar to that which Arthur Conan Doyle had been perfecting for Sherlock Holmes. A few fragments of a puzzle are sufficient for the detective or scholar to re-create a narrative that will bring a sequence of apparently random events within a single explanation. In this both James and Doyle are products of the late nineteenth century: although they have abandoned the omniscient narrator of high Victorian fiction, they still offer narratives depicting a comprehensible world.

A more evident influence on James's fiction was the work of the Irish writer Joseph Sheridan Le Fanu, whose short stories and novels he frequently mentioned with approval. In 1923 James collected and edited twelve of Le Fanu's stories as *"Madam Crowl's Ghost" and Other Tales of Mystery by Joseph Sheridan Le Fanu*. Most interesting for the study of James's own stories is his praise for Le Fanu's deft use of detail in scene-setting and "the leisureliness of his style." He writes in his introduction to the volume that "the ghost-story is in itself a slightly old-fashioned form; it needs some deliberateness in the telling." These characteristics are widely considered by critics to be among James's own strengths. Three years later he wrote an introduction for Le Fanu's novel *Uncle Silas* (1864) for the Oxford University Press.

James had been working on the illustrated manuscripts of the Fitzwilliam Museum at Cambridge since his sophomore year, and in 1886, while he was writing his dissertation, he was appointed assistant director of the museum. By 1889 he was junior dean of King's College, and in 1893 he became director of the Fitzwilliam Museum.

Bicycling trips to France with friends had been James's preferred vacation since his undergraduate years and remained so for most of his life. They generally consisted of visits to the great churches of France. In 1892 the itinerary included the church of St. Bertrand at Comminges. On 28 October in the following year James read to the Cambridge Chitchat Society a ghost story set in Comminges. Early in 1894 he sent "A Curious Book" to the *National Review*. Retitled "The Scrap-Book of Canon Alberic," it was published in the March 1895 issue; James was paid ten shillings a page. An extremely accomplished performance, this was apparently James's first written ghost story. He seems to have mastered his limited genre early and thereafter worked the same vein. His first story is entirely characteristic of his later work and demonstrates some of his favorite themes and motifs.

The narrative begins with a description of place: Comminges and its church. The narrator says that the small town is decayed and that the cathedral does not attract many tourists. This hint of the sinister is elaborated in the person of the sacristan who shows Denistoun, the English visitor, around the cathedral; the sacristan's back and shoulders suggest someone in constant fear of finding himself "in the clutch of an enemy." Even Denistoun, the narrator says, thinks he hears voices in the church, but he remains unperturbed. After they have finished, his guide takes Denistoun to his home and shows him a scrapbook of pages from a variety of medieval illuminated manuscripts gathered by Alberic de Mauléon, a seventeenth-century canon of Comminges. The last illustration depicts King Solomon, a corpse, some soldiers, and a figure familiar from James's Eton anecdote: exceptionally thin, covered with coarse dark hair, eyes glowing and hands taloned.

The sacristan is only too happy to sell Denistoun the scrapbook, and the antiquary eagerly carries it away to his own room. When he puts aside the cross that the sacristan's daughter hung round his neck, the taloned creature is freed from its textual existence and shows itself, but Denistoun frightens it away with the crucifix. All those who saw the picture affirmed that the subject must have been drawn from life. The art is so fully mimetic that its contemplation can summon up the signified object, which crosses from its original medium to Denistoun's room. The reader may be chilled to think that it could just as easily cross from the page of the story to the reader's own room.

The demon's manifestation is not in itself the most important part of the story. James establishes various puzzles: Why is the sacristan so nervous? What is the significance of the dark picture of Saint Bertrand delivering a man from a devil? Whom was Canon Alberic questioning about treasure on the page before the illustration of Solomon and the demon? The answer to all these questions is effectively the chthonic phenomenon that Denistoun experiences in his hotel room. Just as his examination of the scrapbook releases the devil, so the reading of the story releases the answer to the puzzles. Whereas the ghost stories that he translated in Walter Map's *De Nugis Curialium (Courtiers' Trifles)* (1923) simply record the appearance of a ghost, James's narrative implies an explanation for the resurgence of the past into the present. Not to do so would be like having a detective story with no culprit. It would seem that Canon Alberic, in a quest for treasure, conjured up a dangerous entity he was unable to control, and the demon has haunted his house ever since; the unfortunate modern sacristan lives in the same building. Denistoun exorcises the spirit by taking the book away and later destroying the picture.

James published a second story that same year: "Lost Hearts" appeared in the *Pall Mall Gazette* in December 1895. However, he probably would have regarded these stories as minor achievements when set against his other publications of the year, which included his first five descriptive catalogs covering the Western manuscript collections of the Eton College Library, the Fitzwilliam Museum, and three Cambridge colleges.

James liked to use a narrator in his stories. This technique probably was an attempt to reproduce the original oral narrative experience. Evidently a James ghost story, read by the author, was a central element in the Christmas festivities among his circle at King's. In a letter of 24 December 1902 to A. T. Loyd, H. E. Luxmoore, James's tutor at Eton and a lifelong friend, wrote, "Last night

James in 1895

Monty James read us a new Christmas story of most blood curdling character . . . ." S. G. Lubbock recalls James's manner of reading as being "entirely untheatrical and immensely effective."

By 1904 James felt he had enough stories to publish a collection. Part of the impetus seems to have come from James McBryde, a companion of many cycling expeditions who offered to illustrate some of the ghost stories. James thought that he had six publishable stories: "The Scrap-Book of Canon Alberic," "The Mezzotint," "The Spiders" (finally called "The Ash-tree"), "Number 13," "Count Magnus," and "Oh, Whistle, and I'll Come to You, My Lad." He excluded "Lost Hearts," telling McBryde in a 13 March letter, "I don't much care about it." When McBryde died in June 1904, he had completed four drawings: two each for "Canon Alberic" and "Oh, Whistle, and I'll Come to You, My Lad." The publisher, Edward Arnold, wanted two more tales to make up a volume of six-shilling length, so James wrote a new story, "The Treasure of Abbot Thomas," and included "Lost Hearts." The title, *Ghost-Stories of an Antiquary,* was decided on by July 1904, and the book came out at the end of the year in time for the Christmas trade.

A handful of journals noticed it. The *Athenaeum* believed the stories "cannot fail to produce a series of thrills" and remarked how James's erudition produced "a background of vraisemblance." The reviewer for the *Spectator* acknowledges "the literary merit" and ingenuity in construction of the stories but confesses to having no fondness for "constructed ghost stories" as opposed to "the real thing," a conclusion echoed by *The New York Times*. Nonetheless, readers and critics have admired the stories' painstaking details and undefined horrors. The collection had gone through fifteen printings by 1937.

The book opens with "Canon Alberic's Scrapbook," followed by "Lost Hearts," a story about an antiquarian who hopes to gain magical powers by ingesting the hearts of children. Mr. Abney has already killed two and has now invited his orphaned eleven-year-old nephew to live with him. The boy experiences a variety of supernatural phenomena, whose explanation is both the answer to various other puzzles and his deliverance. Justice is served by the two earlier victims, who are able to cross from one realm to another and avenge themselves upon Mr. Abney. Revenge is also the explanation of the mysteries in "The Ash-Tree" and "The Mezzotint."

"The Ash-Tree" concerns an executed witch whose corpse takes up residence in an ash tree. Sir Matthew Fell's testimony that he had seen her gathering sprigs from the tree, which grew close to his bedroom window, played an important part in her conviction. She vowed revenge, and Sir Matthew is found "dead and black" in his bed several weeks after her death. Sixty-four years later Sir Richard Fell dies suddenly upon moving into his grandfather's bedroom. When the ash tree is accidentally set ablaze, huge spiders emerge from the conflagration. Beneath the tree is the body of a woman dead some fifty years. When opened a few years earlier, the witch's coffin was found to be empty; evidently she had moved to the tree, whence she had sent out her poisonous spiders to fulfill her vengeance on the descendants and cattle of the man she held responsible for her death.

"The Mezzotint" is a companion piece to "Canon Alberic's Scrap-book." Mr. Williams is responsible for the drawings and engravings in his university's museum, and one day his usual London dealer sends him an unimpressive mezzotint of a country manor house. The name on the back is partially torn, so its location is a puzzle. The first colleague to whom he shows it is impressed by the moonlight and the figure in the foreground, but

when Williams first looked there had been no figure. Over the course of the narrative a sequence of changes in the picture occurs: a skeletal figure approaches the building, opens a window, and enters, then reemerges with a child in his arms and disappears. While the mezzotint itself establishes an unexplained narrative, the story explains the mystery. The college bursar knew the house and its legend. When a poacher had killed a gamekeeper, the hall's last owner had seen to it that the man was hanged. The bursar speculates that the mezzotint represents the poacher's revenge, for the only son of the hall's last owner had indeed disappeared. With the puzzle solved and the poacher's story told, the picture was not known to change again.

The story takes place among academic men, and they show many of the characteristics of their trade. Williams writes careful descriptions of the picture at its various stages and has witnesses sign them; another of them photographs the print after each of its transformations. As in "Canon Alberic's Scrap-book," careful, dispassionate observation brings a mystery into the light of learning and thereby defuses it. Canon Alberic's sin of greed had caused him to release a demon into the world. Denistoun is able to exorcise it by burning the picture, and the fact that he donates the enormously valuable "scrap-book" to a public collection will ensure his safety, for disinterested scholarship is surely virtuous. Similarly, in "The Treasure of Abbot Thomas" an antiquary locates the abbot's gold by solving the riddle he left in the abbey's stained glass. The treasure is hidden in a well, but the antiquary does not know that the abbot left a toadlike creature to protect it. The gold is tainted, so he has someone else return it to the hiding place and seal up the niche.

The danger of raising devils is shown in "Number 13," set in a hotel in the Danish town of Viborg. Although there is no room 13, the occupants of both numbers 12 and 14 are disturbed by noisy cavortings in the room that would be between them. It transpires that number 13 is haunted by the ghost of Nicolas Francken, who sold his soul to the devil. As in the story of Canon Alberic, the source of the ghostly activity is a document, hidden in the floor between rooms 12 and 14. It is presumably neutralized by being removed from its hiding place and placed in the museum.

This story shows an interesting development of the detective element, since there are two puzzles that appear to be unconnected. First, who is in room 13, and why is he dancing? The second mystery arises from the protagonist's research. Mr. Anderson had gone to Viborg to look into the early years

Illustration by James McBryde for "Canon Alberic's Scrap-book," James's first story, in his Ghost-Stories of an Antiquary *(1904)*

of Danish Protestantism, and he came upon some correspondence that denounced Nicolas Francken as a satanist. There was a gap before the next letter, which defends Francken but states that he "hath been suddenly removed from among us." Room 13 fills the gap, since Francken's Faustian pact with the devil accounts for both his disappearance in the sixteenth century and the contemporary noises from the room.

"Count Magnus," set in Sweden, is another story of raising the devil and also reflects James's three Scandinavian cycling tours. The narrator represents himself as having pieced together the story from various fragments, and Mr. Wraxall, the protagonist, is similarly engaged in filling in the lacunae in the life of the mysterious Count Magnus. This desire leads him unwittingly to say the spell that will release the undead count, who, with a hooded companion, pursues Wraxall to his death in England. The protagonist of "The Treasure of

Abbot Thomas" is an amateur antiquary who almost comes to grief; "Count Magnus" tells of another amateur. The narrator comments, "His besetting fault was pretty clearly that of over-inquisitiveness." The reader might infer that professionals such as Denistoun, Williams, and Anderson are the only ones who can deal with the dangers of the past.

"Oh, Whistle, and I'll Come to You, My Lad," one of James's most admired stories, picks up the same idea, with an additional warning against skepticism. Professor Parkins, a scientist, is planning a golfing holiday on the East Anglian coast, and when one of his colleagues hears of it he asks him to take a quick look at the site of a Templars' preceptory in the neighborhood. Although Parkins has little respect for such antiquarian pursuits, he agrees to do so. The reader next learns that his room will contain a spare bed, and another colleague, Mr. Rogers, jokes that his presence would "keep the ghosts off." Parkins deprecates such remarks, refusing to concede even the possibility of the existence of the supernatural. Like many scholars of his time, James resented the threat posed by science to the traditional preeminence of the humanities; Parkins's positivist hubris will soon be punished.

He goes to East Anglia without Rogers, and between golf matches he finds the remains of the preceptory. "Few people," the narrator observes, "can resist the temptation to try a little amateur research in a department quite outside their own," and Parkins is no exception. He discovers a small cavity and removes a cylindrical object, about four inches long. He pockets it and on his way back to his hotel notices that there is always behind him "a rather indistinct personage, who seemed to be making great efforts to catch up with him, but made little, if any, progress." The object from the preceptory is, after a little cleaning, revealed as a whistle. It has Latin inscriptions on both sides, but the professor can only translate one of them: *Quis est iste qui venit,* "Who is this who is coming?" In other stories the potency of the past is released in the reading of a manuscript. Here an artifact carries the supernatural charge, and when Parkins blows the whistle, an image immediately comes to his mind of a figure in a wide expanse of windy night. Then a sudden wind rises, and he has to close the shutter. The image haunts him throughout the night; he dreams of a man being chased by "a figure in pale, fluttering draperies."

The next morning he finds that the second bed is disordered; the following night something sits up in the bed. Although apparently blind, it almost forces Parkins out the window before his golfing partner comes to his aid. The manifestation appears to have been little other than an animated sheet, but Parkins is nearly driven out of his wits by the "intensely horrible, face *of crumpled linen.*" The narrator dryly concludes that the professor's "views on certain points are less clear cut than they used to be."

Early in 1905 the provost of King's College died, and in May James was elected to lead his college. The years that followed do not show any significant diminution in his output, scholarly or fictional, and in 1911 he published *More Ghost Stories of an Antiquary.* Only one of the seven had been published before: "The Stalls of Barchester Cathedral" in the *Contemporary Review* in 1910.

The stories are similar to those in the first collection, reiterating many of the same themes and techniques. Texts and artifacts are frequently invested with ghostly power, and in the first three cases revenge is the motivating force. "A School Story" tells of a teacher who is harassed by a spirit, which communicates its threats through Latin grammar drills. In "The Stalls of Barchester Cathedral" it is the statuettes on the dean's prayer desk that are charged. Carved from an oak said to have been a hanging tree, they take on the tactile characteristics of those they represent when the dean touches them, for he had murdered his aged predecessor. There is no written text or artifact in "Martin's Close" that functions in the same way as the stalls or the Latin drills; instead a song, "Madam, Will You Walk?," is the conduit between murderer George Martin and his victim, Ann Clark.

Two stories concern the malicious investment of texts. "The Tractate Middoth" is a talmudic volume in which the older Mr. Eldred perversely had hidden a will, leaving all his property to his niece. In the meantime the nephew inherits everything according to an earlier will. Some years later the niece meets a young man who works in the university library and is able to track down the volume. Although the nephew has already secured it, his selfish greed seems to undo him, and a black, spidery form smothers him just as he is about to destroy the later will. Mr. Karswell in "Casting the Runes" is even more malicious than Mr. Eldred. He will not tolerate criticism of his books or articles on magic and takes revenge by writing a death sentence on a slip of paper, which he then ensures his victim will unwittingly accept. The story's protagonist manages to circumvent his fate by passing the death sentence back to Karswell.

"Mr. Humphreys and His Inheritance" represents the most elaborate of texts, a maze. At its center is a copper globe, which is finally revealed as holding the ashes of Mr. Humphreys's ancestor, who appears to have been an alchemist of sorts. Humphreys finds a book in the library, *A Parable of this Unhappy Condition,* that compares the world to a labyrinth with a jewel at its center, which represents "the Satisfaction which a Man may bring back with him from the Course of this World's Pleasures." However, writes the author of the parable, "I have brought back that with it that will leave me neither Rest at Night nor Pleasure by Day." The mystery is presumably related to the inscription Humphreys' ancestor placed above the entrance to his maze, *Secretum meum mihi et filiis domus meae* (My secret is for me and the sons of my house). The reader later learns that there had been stones leading to the center that spelled out the words *Penetrans ad interiora mortis* (penetrating to the interior of death). The secret is in some way connected with death, but the reader cannot be sure of much more than that, although the key might lie in James's familiarity with alchemical lore. A similarly perplexing story in this volume is "The Rose Garden," which tells how the attempted removal of a wooden post in a garden leads to fearful visions connected with a late-seventeenth-century trial and execution. The reader is never sure exactly what happened or to whom.

These stories are characteristic of a tendency in James's later work for the background narratives, which generate the supernatural energy, to remain vague and inchoate. Their very narratability seems to be in question. James was thus, to a small extent, a figure of his time, for the modernist movement in all the arts questioned the possibility of unequivocal representation.

From 1913 to 1915 James was vice chancellor of Cambridge University, but his later years at King's were increasingly unsatisfying, so when he was offered the provostship of Eton College he was glad to accept it. In the early fall of 1918, at age fifty-six, he returned to the school he had first joined when he was fourteen.

In 1919 James produced a third volume of stories, titled *A Thin Ghost, and Others*. It is a small collection, containing only five tales, and they are not much favored by his admirers. "The Diary of Mr. Poynter" is perhaps most closely related to his classic stories. James Denton and his aunt find a piece of printed fabric in the diary of a local eighteenth-century squire. They have the pattern copied and curtains made from it. The design suggests long, wavy hair, and the second night after the drapes are hung Mr. Denton, dozing in his chair, senses a head of hair against his hand. He feels "a soft ineffectual tearing at his back" as he flees. A closer examination of the diary reveals that the original piece of fabric had come from the rooms of the dissolute Sir Everard Charlett, who was so proud of his hair that he had hangings made in imitation of it. His debaucheries led to an ignominious death. Copying the fabric has drawn the dead man's spirit into Mr. Denton's world.

"The Residence at Whitminster" tells of the Irish Lord Saul, who brings about the death of the senior prebendary's orphaned nephew and is then hounded to death by furies. The later inhabitants of the cathedral residence are troubled by flies and ghostly manifestations associated with the Irish boy's room. Although he finds some documents that would recount what Lord Saul "brought with him from Ireland" and thus fully explain the circumstances of the boys' deaths, the new prebendary elects to ignore the papers and locks them in the

Cover for James's 1911 collection, More Ghost Stories of an Antiquary *(Courtesy of the Lilly Library, Indiana University)*

room. They are, as one character comments, "a jack-in-the-box, awaiting some future occupant of the residence of the senior prebendary."

The lamia in "An Episode of Cathedral History" behaves in much the same way when its dwelling is disturbed. It is released from a tomb as a result of the kind of restoration project that James plainly deplored. But though the lamia looks like a standard Jamesian horror, "a thing like a man, all over hair, and two great eyes to it," the creature seems almost afraid of the modernizing dean and darts out of the cathedral, never to be seen again. Perhaps the story implies that such phenomena are losing their powers in a world of skeptics.

The *Cambridge Review* first published this story and "The Story of a Disappearance and an Appearance," an epistolary story showing James's fondness for pastiches. For example, Sir Everard's death in "The Diary of Mr. Poynter" was written in the style of the early eighteenth century; "Mr. Humphreys and His Inheritance" includes the impressive "Parable of this Unhappy Condition"; and "Martin's Close" is a masterly imitation of a late-seventeenth-century trial. "Two Doctors," however, takes the pastiche technique to such an extreme as to be barely comprehensible, and it is not much admired.

The provostship of Eton did not involve James in the day-to-day running of the school, and he found more time for the things he enjoyed. In 1922 he published a short children's book called *The Five Jars*. Written for Jane, the daughter of his late friend McBryde, it tells of five jars whose contents so elevate the five senses as to allow the narrator to meet with a normally invisible fairy people. His editions of Le Fanu's works came out in 1923 and 1926, and in 1924 he produced his best-known scholarly work, a translation of *The Apocryphal New Testament*.

In the same year James wrote an introduction to V. H. Collins's *Ghosts and Marvels: A Selection of Uncanny Tales from Daniel Defoe to Algernon Blackwood*. This essay contains his best-known remarks on the craft of the ghost story. He values "atmosphere and the nicely managed crescendo" above all. His account of these two qualities epitomizes his own most successful stories:

> Let us, then, be introduced to the actors in a placid way; let us see them going about their ordinary business, undisturbed by forebodings, pleased with their surroundings; and into this calm environment let the ominous thing put out its head, unobtrusively at first, and then more insistently, until it holds the stage. It is not amiss sometimes to leave a loophole for a natural explanation; but, I would say, let the loophole be so narrow as not to be quite practicable.

He favors "a slight haze of distance" for the setting – "thirty years ago," for example; too antique a setting will make a "spectator" of the reader, rather than one who identifies with "the patient."

In 1925 James brought out his last collection of ghost stories. *A Warning to the Curious, and Other Ghost Stories* includes six tales, five of which had already been published. "A Haunted Dolls' House" was written for the library of Queen Mary's Dolls' House at Windsor and appeared in the February 1923 issue of the *Empire Review*. The story is a reworking of "The Mezzotint." The dolls' house becomes like a theater where a murdered father takes revenge by killing his grandchildren. In "The Mezzotint" all the events are explained, with the loose ends tied up, but in "A Haunted Dolls' House" the characters are more shadowy, the crime more diffi-

cult to comprehend. History can be seen but not fully comprehended.

"A Neighbour's Landmark," first published in a school ephemeral publication called the *Eton Chronic*, begins in a library, where the narrator comes across a reference in an eighteenth-century pamphlet to the haunting of some local woods. The land is still haunted, and the narrative is able to offer a full explanation as to why. It seems that an earlier owner had removed a landmark in order to defraud others out of the land. Their curse lay upon "them that removes the landmark." Here James returns to his earlier manner of fully accounting for a supernatural experience.

Two stories touch on the dangers of looking into the past. Mr. Baxter in "A View from a Hill" is killed by the dead men whose bones he had rendered down to make a pair of fieldglasses that enables the viewer to see the past. In "An Evening's Entertainment" Mr. Davis's fascination with history leads him and his "young man" to human sacrifice.

"A Warning to the Curious," like "A View from a Hill," was first published in the *London Mercury* in 1925. It is the story of a young man who finds the lost crown of the kings of East Anglia. Even though he returns the crown to its hiding place, the treasure's skeletal guardian pursues him to his death. "The Uncommon Prayer-book," first published in the *Atlantic Monthly* (June 1921), also tells of the revenge taken by a treasure's guardian spirit on one who would steal it. In this case the treasure is a set of prayer books privately published at a time in English history when such an act would have been considered treason. The warnings to the curious have grown fiercer since "The Treasure of Abbot Thomas," when the antiquary received no more than a bad fright.

By 1925 James's reputation as a writer of ghost stories was well established, and *A Warning to the Curious* was widely reviewed. While Edwin Muir in *The Nation and the Athenaeum* found that the stories are well-told anecdotes but nothing more, the anonymous reviewer for the *New Statesman* offers an unusual judgment: that "Dr. James has written the best modern ghost stories of the playful kind. By playful we mean ghost stories written to amuse and gently thrill, not to horrify or suggest the reality of the uncanny." A review in the *Times Literary Supplement* finds the stories more sinister and is appreciative of James's artistry with details or "facts." *The New York Times* was still more favorably impressed: "No other ghost stories remotely approach the authentic James touch of actuality."

In 1931 Edward Arnold published *The Collected Ghost Stories of M. R. James,* and the *Times Literary Supplement* devoted its front page to a review of stories of the supernatural. *The Collected Ghost Stories* includes five new pieces, three of which had already appeared in Eton magazines. "There Was a Man Dwelt by a Churchyard" takes its inspiration from the story begun by Mamilius, in William Shakespeare's *A Winter's Tale* (1610–1611), who got no further than the words of James's title. "Rats" is a locked-room story in which the protagonist sees more than he would have wished. It is another warning to the curious, but this time the offender escapes with his life. The invisible population of "After Dark in the Playing Fields," although more sinister, is reminiscent of the little people of *The Five Jars.*

"Wailing Well," written for the Eton Boy Scouts, tells of the terrible death of Stanley Judkins, who disobeyed the adults and took water from a forbidden well. His vulgar skepticism relates him to Professor Parkins. "Some Stories I Have Tried to Write" outlines ideas that James never worked out fully. The discussion indicates that his modus operandi was to begin with a place and a situation and work up a narrative explanation for the supernatural events afterward.

Three stories remain uncollected: "The Experiment," which appeared in the *Morning Post* of 31 December 1931; "The Malice of Inanimate Objects," published in *The Masquerade,* an Eton ephemeral of June 1933; and "A Vignette," James's last story, published posthumously in the *London Mercury* in 1936. It contains what is in some ways his purest and most medieval ghost story. The setting is probably his childhood home at Livermere. He begins with the garden of a country rectory. A belt of trees separates the world of the garden from an adjacent park, suggestive of an older and more privileged world than that of a rector's son. The writer insists that there is nothing sinister about the trees. The point of intersection between one world and the other is a gate that leads from the trees to a path surrounding the garden. One afternoon he sees a face peering malevolently at him through a hole in the gate: "a border of white linen drapery hung down from the brows." There is no text wherein the horror subsists; instead, James describes the hole in the fence as "a frame," as if he were looking at a picture that looks back at him. Having retreated well within "my own precincts," he sees "a draped form shambling away among the trees," back to its own world.

In the final decade of his life James received honorary doctorates from both Oxford and Cam-

Dust jacket for James's last collection, published in 1925 (Courtesy of the Lilly Library, Indiana University)

bridge, and in 1930 he joined the select group of those awarded the Order of Merit. His health began to fail in 1934, and he died in Eton on 12 June 1936.

Arnold's 1931 edition of *The Collected Ghost Stories of M. R. James* was reprinted ten times; a second edition, *The Ghost Stories of M. R. James,* came out in 1974 and was reprinted the next year. The same publisher produced a pocket volume in 1942. The first paperback collection, *Thirteen Ghost Stories,* was published by the Albatross Continental Library in 1935. Penguin offered *Ghost Stories of an Antiquary* in 1937 and brought out *More Ghost Stories of an Antiquary* in 1959. They combined the two volumes in 1974 and published *The Complete Ghost Stories of M. R. James* in 1984. By this time his reputation was secure, and *Booklist* in July 1985 called him "an acknowledged master of the ghost story."

Ghost stories are usually considered peripheral to the canon of modern literature, so there has not been much scholarship on James's fiction.

Three analyses are part of larger discussions of supernatural literature as a whole, in which James is always regarded as preeminent. Peter Penzoldt in *The Supernatural in Fiction* (1952) finds no deep meaning in James's stories, simply a desire to frighten; Penzoldt is therefore mainly interested in the analysis of form. The most successful ghost stories, he argues, have a single climax, but he acknowledges a variant that he calls the "double climax," which is characteristic of James's fiction. Here the supernatural apparition is followed by the necessary explanation. He cites as examples "The Treasure of Abbot Thomas" and "Mr. Humphreys' Inheritance."

Julia Briggs in *Night Visitors: The Rise and Fall of the English Ghost Story* (1977) places the golden age of the English ghost story between 1850 and 1930. During this period faith and doubt were still of central importance in intellectual debate, and the ghost story reasserted the existence of an earlier world where the spiritual held sway. However, a credulous tone will not convince, and James's understated narrative tone suggests a contemporary critical detachment. "His stories," Briggs writes, "assert a total acceptance of the supernatural that his scepticism apparently denies." This skepticism combined with nostalgia for the supernatural are central to her understanding of the ghost story. Jack Sullivan in *Elegant Nightmares: The English Ghost Story from Le Fanu to Blackwood* (1978) argues that nostalgia turns into horror in James's stories. Indeed, he claims that the antiquarians cannot connect with anything in the present and that the supernatural materializes out of such voids in their lives.

M. R. James created the antiquarian ghost story and wrote some of the most artful and perfectly finished ghost stories in the English language. While his body of work shows relatively little development and its range is acknowledged to be narrow, few readers and critics have questioned his mastery of his chosen form.

Bibliographies:

A. F. Scholfield, "Montague Rhodes James: A List of His Writings," in *A Memoir of Montague Rhodes James* by S. G. Lubbock (Cambridge: Cambridge University Press, 1939), pp. 47–86;

Richard William Pfaff, "A Bibliography of the Scholarly Writings of M. R. James," in his *Montague Rhodes James* (London: Scolar, 1980), pp. 427–438.

Biographies:

S. G. Lubbock, *A Memoir of Montague Rhodes James* (Cambridge: Cambridge University Press, 1939);

Richard William Pfaff, *Montague Rhodes James* (London: Scolar, 1980);

Michael Cox, *M. R. James: An Informal Portrait* (Oxford & New York: Oxford University Press, 1983).

References:

Lance Arney, "An Elucidation (?) of the Plot of M. R. James's 'Two Doctors,' " *Studies in Weird Fiction,* 8 (Fall 1990): 26–35;

Julia Briggs, "No Mere Antiquary: M. R. James," in her *Night Visitors: The Rise and Fall of the English Ghost Story* (London: Faber & Faber, 1977), pp. 124–141;

Mary Butts, "The Art of Montagu[e] James," *London Mercury,* 29 (February 1934): 306–317;

Richard Holmes, "Of Ghosts and King's," *Times* (London), 23 November 1974, pp. 7+;

Michael A. Mason, "On Not Letting Them Lie: Moral Significance in the Ghost Stories of M. R. James," *Studies in Short Fiction,* 19 (1982): 253–260;

Peter Penzoldt, "Dr. M. R. James," in his *The Supernatural in Fiction* (London: Nevill, 1952; New York: Humanities Press, 1965), pp. 191–202;

Jack Sullivan, "The Antiquarian Ghost Story: Montague Rhodes James," in his *Elegant Nightmares: The English Ghost Story from Le Fanu to Blackwood* (Athens: Ohio University Press, 1978), pp. 69–90;

Austin Warren, "The Marvels of M. R. James, Antiquary," in his *Connections* (Ann Arbor: University of Michigan Press, 1970), pp. 86–107.

Rudyard Kipling

(30 December 1865 – 18 January 1936)

Donald Gray
Indiana University

See also the Kipling entries in *DLB 19: British Poets, 1880–1914; DLB 34: British Novelists, 1890–1929;* and *DLB 141: British Children's Writers, 1880–1914.*

BOOKS: *Schoolboy Lyrics* (Lahore: Privately printed, 1881);

Echoes, by Kipling and Alice Kipling (Lahore: Privately printed, 1884);

Departmental Ditties and Other Verses (Lahore: Privately printed, 1886; enlarged edition, Calcutta: Thacker, Spink, 1886; enlarged edition, Calcutta: Thacker, Spink / London: Thacker, 1888; enlarged edition, Calcutta: Thacker, Spink / London & Bombay: Thacker, 1890); enlarged as *Departmental Ditties, Barrack-Room Ballads and Other Verses* (New York: United States Book Company, 1890); republished as *Departmental Ditties and Ballads and Barrack-Room Ballads* (New York: Doubleday & McClure, 1899);

Plain Tales from the Hills (Calcutta: Thacker, Spink / London: Thacker, 1888; New York: Lovell, 1890; London & New York: Macmillan, 1890);

Soldiers Three: A Collection of Stories Setting Forth Certain Passages in the Lives and Adventures of Privates Terence Mulvaney, Stanley Ortheris, and John Learoyd (Allahabad: Pioneer, 1888; London: Sampson Low, Marston, Searle & Rivington, 1890);

The Story of the Gadsbys: A Tale Without a Plot (Allahabad: Wheeler, 1888; Allahabad: Wheeler / London: Sampson Low, Marston, Searle & Rivington, 1890; New York: Lovell, 1890);

In Black and White (Allahabad: Wheeler, 1888; Allahabad: Wheeler / London: Sampson Low, Marston, Searle & Rivington, 1890);

Under the Deodars (Allahabad: Wheeler, 1888; Allahabad: Wheeler / London: Sampson Low, Marston, Searle & Rivington, 1890; New York: Lovell, 1890);

Rudyard Kipling in 1915, exhorting young Englishmen to enlist for military service in World War I

The Phantom 'Rickshaw and Other Tales (Allahabad: Wheeler, 1888; Allahabad: Wheeler / London: Sampson Low, Marston, Searle & Rivington, 1890);

Wee Willie Winkie and Other Child Stories (Allahabad: Wheeler, 1888); republished as *Wee Willie Winkie and Other Stories* (Allahabad: Wheeler / London: Sampson Low, Marston, Searle & Rivington, 1890);

"Turnovers," by Kipling and others, 9 volumes (Lahore: Privately printed, 1888-1890);

Soldiers Three [and In Black and White] (New York: Lovell, 1890);

Indian Tales (New York: Lovell, 1890);

The Courting of Dinah Shadd and Other Stories (New York: Harper, 1890);

The Light That Failed (London & Melbourne: Ward, Lock, Bowden, 1891; Philadelphia: Lippincott, 1891; revised edition, London & New York: Macmillan, 1891);

The City of Dreadful Night and Other Places (Allahabad: Wheeler, 1891; Allahabad: Wheeler / London: Sampson Low, Marston, 1891);

Letters of Marque (Allahabad: Wheeler, 1891; republished in part, London: Sampson Low, Marston, 1891);

American Notes (New York: Ivers, 1891);

Mine Own People (New York: United States Book Company, 1891);

Life's Handicap: Being Stories of Mine Own People (London & New York: Macmillan, 1891);

The Story of the Gadsbys and Under the Deodars (New York: United States Book Company, 1891);

The Naulahka: A Story of West and East, by Kipling and Wolcott Balestier (London: Heinemann, 1892; New York & London: Macmillan, 1892);

Barrack-Room Ballads and Other Verses (London: Methuen, 1892; republished as Ballads and Barrack-Room Ballads (New York & London: Macmillan, 1892; enlarged edition, New York & London: Macmillan, 1893);

Soldiers Three, The Story of the Gadsbys, In Black and White (London: Sampson Low, Marston, 1892; London & New York: Macmillan, 1895; enlarged edition, New York & London: Macmillan, 1895);

Wee Willie Winkie, Under the Deodars, The Phantom 'Rickshaw and Other Stories (London: Sampson Low, Marston, 1892; London & New York: Macmillan, 1895); republished as Under the Deodars, The Phantom 'Rickshaw, Wee Willie Winkie (New York & London: Macmillan, 1895);

Many Inventions (London & New York: Macmillan, 1893; New York: Appleton, 1893);

The Jungle Book (London & New York: Macmillan, 1894; New York: Century, 1894);

The Second Jungle Book (London & New York: Macmillan, 1895; enlarged edition, 1895; New York: Century, 1895);

Out of India: Things I Saw, and Failed to See, in Certain Days and Nights at Jeypore and Elsewhere (New York: Dillingham, 1895) – includes The City of Dreadful Night and Other Places and Letters of Marque;

The Seven Seas (New York: Appleton, 1896; London: Methuen, 1896);

Soldier Tales (London & New York: Macmillan, 1896); republished as Soldier Stories (New York & London: Macmillan, 1896);

The Kipling Birthday Book, compiled by Joseph Finn (London & New York: Macmillan, 1896; New York: Doubleday & McClure, 1899);

"Captains Courageous": A Story of the Grand Banks (London & New York: Macmillan, 1897; New York: Century, 1897);

An Almanac of Twelve Sports, text by Kipling and illustrations by William Nicholson (London: Heinemann, 1898; New York: Russell, 1898);

The Day's Work (New York: Doubleday & McClure, 1898; London: Macmillan, 1898);

A Fleet in Being: Notes of Two Trips with the Channel Squadron (London & New York: Macmillan, 1898);

Kipling's Poems, edited by Wallace Rice (Chicago: Star Books, 1899);

Stalky & Co. (London: Macmillan, 1899; New York: Doubleday & McClure, 1899);

From Sea to Sea, 2 volumes (New York: Doubleday & McClure, 1899); republished as From Sea to Sea and Other Sketches, 2 volumes (London: Macmillan, 1900);

A Ken of Kipling (New York: New Amsterdam Book Company, 1899);

The Kipling Reader: Selections from the Books of Rudyard Kipling (London & New York: Macmillan, 1900; revised, 1901);

Kim (New York: Doubleday, Page, 1901; London: Macmillan, 1901);

Just So Stories: For Little Children (London: Macmillan, 1902; New York: Doubleday, Page, 1902);

The Five Nations (London: Methuen, 1903; New York: Doubleday, Page, 1903);

Traffics and Discoveries (London: Macmillan, 1904; New York: Doubleday, Page, 1904);

Puck of Pook's Hill (London: Macmillan, 1906; New York: Doubleday, Page, 1906);

Collected Verse (New York: Doubleday, Page, 1907; London: Hodder & Stoughton, 1912);

Letters to the Family: Notes on a Recent Trip to Canada (Toronto: Macmillan, 1908);

Actions and Reactions (London: Macmillan, 1909; New York: Doubleday, Page, 1909);

Abaft the Funnel (New York: Dodge, 1909; authorized edition, New York: Doubleday, Page, 1909);

Kipling Stories and Poems Every Child Should Know, edited by Mary E. Burt and W. T. Chapin (New York: Doubleday, Page, 1909; abridged edition, New York: Garden City, 1938);

Rewards and Fairies (London: Macmillan, 1910; Garden City, N.Y.: Doubleday, Page, 1910);

A History of England, by Kipling and C. R. L. Fletcher (Oxford: Clarendon Press / London: Frowde/Hodder & Stoughton, 1911; Garden City, N.Y.: Doubleday, Page, 1911);

The Kipling Reader for Elementary Grades (New York & Chicago: Appleton, 1912);

The Kipling Reader for Upper Grades (New York & Chicago: Appleton, 1912);

Songs from Books (Garden City, N.Y.: Doubleday, Page, 1912; London: Macmillan, 1913);

The New Army, 6 pamphlets (Garden City, N.Y.: Doubleday, Page, 1914); republished as *The New Army in Training,* 1 volume (London: Macmillan, 1915);

France at War (London: Macmillan, 1915); republished as *France at War on the Frontier of Civilization* (Garden City, N.Y.: Doubleday, Page, 1915);

The Fringes of the Fleet (London: Macmillan, 1915; Garden City, N.Y.: Doubleday, Page, 1915);

Sea Warfare (London: Macmillan, 1916; Garden City, N.Y.: Doubleday, Page, 1917);

A Diversity of Creatures (London: Macmillan, 1917; Garden City, N.Y.: Doubleday, Page, 1917);

The Eyes of Asia (Garden City, N.Y.: Doubleday, Page, 1918);

Twenty Poems (London: Methuen, 1918);

The Graves of the Fallen (London: Imperial War Graves Commission, 1919);

The Years Between (London: Methuen, 1919; Garden City, N.Y.: Doubleday, Page, 1919);

Rudyard Kipling's Verse, Inclusive Edition, 1885–1918 (3 volumes, London: Hodder & Stoughton, 1919; 1 volume, Garden City, N.Y.: Doubleday, Page, 1919);

Letters of Travel (1892–1913) (London: Macmillan, 1920; Garden City, N.Y.: Doubleday, Page, 1920);

Q. Horati Flacci Carminum Librum Quintum a Rudyardo Kipling et Carolo Graves Angelice Redditum et Variorum Notis Adornatum ad Fidem Codicum Mss. Edidit Aluredus D. Godley, by Kipling and others (Oxonii [Oxford]: Blackwell, 1920; Novo Portu [New Haven]: Yalensi [Yale Alumni Association], 1921);

Selected Stories from Kipling, edited by William Lyon Phelps (Garden City, N.Y. & Toronto: Doubleday, Page, 1921);

A Kipling Anthology: Verse (London: Methuen, 1922; Garden City, N.Y.: Doubleday, Page, 1922);

A Kipling Anthology: Prose (London: Macmillan, 1922; Garden City, N.Y.: Doubleday, Page, 1922);

Kipling Calendar (London: Hodder & Stoughton, 1923; Garden City, N.Y.: Doubleday, Page, 1923);

Land and Sea Tales for Scouts and Guides (London: Macmillan, 1923); republished as *Land and Sea Tales for Boys and Girls* (Garden City, N.Y.: Doubleday, Page, 1923); republished as *Land and Sea Tales for Scouts and Scout Masters* (Garden City, N.Y.: Doubleday, Page, 1924);

The Two Jungle Books (London: Macmillan, 1924; Garden City, N.Y.: Doubleday, Page, 1925);

Songs for Youth (London: Hodder & Stoughton, 1924; Garden City, N.Y.: Doubleday, Page, 1925);

A Choice of Songs (London: Methuen, 1925);

Debits and Credits (London: Macmillan, 1926; Garden City, N.Y.: Doubleday, Page, 1926);

Sea and Sussex (London: Macmillan, 1926; Garden City, N.Y.: Doubleday, Page, 1926);

Songs of the Sea (London: Macmillan, 1927; Garden City, N.Y.: Doubleday, Page, 1927);

Rudyard Kipling's Verse, Inclusive Edition, 1885–1926 (London: Hodder & Stoughton, 1927; Garden City, N.Y.: Doubleday, Page, 1927);

A Book of Words: Selections from Speeches and Addresses Delivered Between 1906 and 1927 (London: Macmillan, 1928; Garden City, N.Y.: Doubleday, Page, 1928);

The One Volume Kipling (Garden City, N.Y.: Doubleday, Doran, 1928);

The Complete Stalky & Co. (London: Macmillan, 1929; Garden City, N.Y.: Doubleday, Doran, 1930);

Poems 1886–1929, 3 volumes (London: Macmillan, 1929; Garden City, N.Y.: Doubleday, Doran, 1930);

Selected Stories (London: Macmillan, 1929);

Thy Servant a Dog, Told by Boots (London: Macmillan, 1930; Garden City, N.Y.: Doubleday, Doran, 1930);

Selected Poems (London: Methuen, 1931);

East of Suez (London: Macmillan, 1931);

Humorous Tales (London: Macmillan, 1931); republished as *The Humorous Tales of Rudyard Kipling* (Garden City, N.Y.: Doubleday, Doran, 1931);

Animal Stories (London: Macmillan, 1932; New York: Doubleday, Doran, 1938);

Limits and Renewals (London: Macmillan, 1932; Garden City, N.Y.: Doubleday, Doran, 1932);

Souvenirs of France (London: Macmillan, 1933);

All the Mowgli Stories (London: Macmillan, 1933; Garden City, N.Y.: Doubleday, Doran, 1936);

Rudyard Kipling's Verse, Inclusive Edition, 1885–1932 (London: Hodder & Stoughton, 1933; Garden City, N.Y.: Doubleday, Doran, 1934);

Collected Dog Stories (London: Macmillan, 1934; Garden City, N.Y.: Doubleday, Doran, 1934);

All the Puck Stories (London: Macmillan, 1935);

A Kipling Pageant (Garden City, N.Y.: Doubleday, Doran, 1935);

Something of Myself for My Friends Known and Unknown (London: Macmillan, 1937; Garden City, N.Y.: Doubleday, Doran, 1937);

Rudyard Kipling's Verse, Definitive Edition (London: Hodder & Stoughton, 1940; New York: Doubleday, Doran, 1940).

Collections: *The Sussex Edition of the Complete Works of Rudyard Kipling,* 35 volumes (London: Macmillan, 1937–1939); republished as *The Collected Works of Rudyard Kipling, The Burwash Edition,* 28 volumes (Garden City, N.Y.: Doubleday, Doran, 1940);

Kipling's India: Uncollected Sketches, 1884–1888, edited by Thomas Pinney (London: Macmillan, 1985);

Early Verse by Rudyard Kipling 1879–1889: Unpublished, Uncollected, and Rarely Collected Poems, edited by Andrew Rutherford (Oxford & New York: Oxford University Press, 1986);

Something of Myself and Other Autobiographical Writings, edited by Pinney (Cambridge: Cambridge University Press, 1990).

OTHER: André Chevrillon, *Britain and the War,* preface by Kipling (London, New York & Toronto: Hodder & Stoughton, 1917); republished as *England and the War* (Garden City, N.Y.: Doubleday, Page, 1917);

The Irish Guards in the Great War, 2 volumes, edited by Kipling (London: Macmillan, 1923; Garden City, N.Y.: Doubleday, Page, 1923).

It is easy to underestimate the variety, complexity, and subtlety of Rudyard Kipling's writing. He became an extraordinarily popular writer in the 1890s with short stories and poems enlivened by strange and interesting settings, a brisk narrative economy, and the fresh energy of the voices that told his tales, sometimes in working-class dialects and usually in the smart, confident tone of someone who affected to know how the world really worked. Readers and critics who esteemed the refined melancholy and stylistic elaborations of the fin de siècle often thought his effects coarse and common. The

loose colloquial forms and development of his tales and fables came to seem obvious and old-fashioned to early-twentieth-century readers learning to enjoy the compression and elliptical styles of James Joyce, Katherine Mansfield, and Virginia Woolf and the rhetorical intensity of D. H. Lawrence. Kipling's popularity itself sometimes made him suspect to readers who had learned from literary modernism that popularity was necessarily purchased by undignified concessions to vulgar tastes and conventional expectations.

The themes of Kipling's short stories have also been criticized by contemporaries and increasingly by later critics and readers as simple-minded and even pernicious. He often seems to honor white men and Western technology as agents of a desirable dominion over less-progressive peoples and parts of the world. He has been read as the eulogist of an oligarchy of effective administrators, soldiers, engineers, doctors, and an occasional journalist who belong, formally or informally, to a club almost always closed to women. Such men are also almost always British, bred in the schools and ethical code of a professional middle class in which they learned how to obey the law that work be honorable and honest while making up their own rules for getting the job done.

These assessments are just but incomplete. From the beginning, especially in his short stories, Kipling wrote as powerfully, and more often, of the waste and cost of the work of empire as he did of its efficiencies. He was always aware of the impermanence of dominion, the inevitable decline and succession of empires. He knew that Western perspectives – sometimes he even seemed to recognize that masculine perspectives – were inescapably limited. There is much in the world that a European male simply cannot comprehend, and much that he comprehends quite differently from the equally valid understanding of someone who organizes experience by the interests and values of another culture or a different gender. The mystery of the world and the burden of human fallibility and mortality can sometimes baffle attempts to do orderly work in the world and tell coherent and conclusive stories about it.

In his best short stories, early and late, Kipling found ways to play these uncertainties and contingencies against his desire for order and his trust in the kinds of men and work he thought could create and sustain it. He wrote fiction that moved not only by the conventions of realism but also by those of fable, ghost stories, and science fiction, and sometimes he incorporated one of these fantastic modes

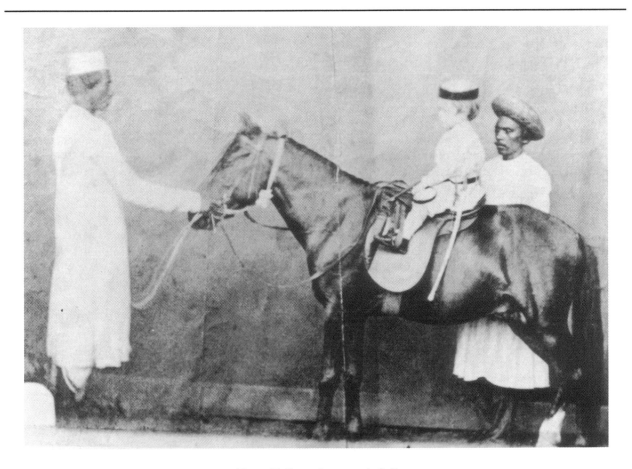

Young Kipling and servants in India

into a realistic story in order to show the instability or surprise in what is taken to be real life. The many voices of his fiction — of Americans, Indians, women, an Irish soldier and a cockney sailor, animals, and machines — sometimes testify to what is common and fundamental in experience and sometimes remind readers that they are always hearing only one version of the story. Especially in his later stories Kipling liked to suggest what the story left out or to take in matter that the story left unexplained. He could be as confident, sure-minded, and repetitive in his narrative practices as some readers since the 1890s have judged him to be. He could also use his considerable craft as a short-story writer, a talent that he learned to take seriously and to enlarge as he matured, to complicate and call into question the structure of belief and practice by which he wanted to order the world.

In his fragmentary autobiography, *Something of Myself for My Friends Known and Unknown* (1937), Kipling wrote, "Everything in my working life has been dealt to me in such a manner that I had just to play it as it came." Certainly one of the most powerful cards dealt to Kipling was his birth and experience

in India, and as a young man he played it masterfully. His father, John Lockwood Kipling, had worked as a sculptor during the construction of the Victoria and Albert Museum in London in the 1860s. He traveled to India in 1865 as professor of sculptural history at the University of Bombay. His mother, Alice Macdonald Kipling, had also moved in the company of artists in London. His family was affectionate and talented, giving support and encouragement that Kipling was later to depend on as "the family square."

When Kipling was not yet six years old he was sent away with his younger sister, Alice, to begin his education in England. They were lodged at Southsea with a religiously evangelical family who held strict views about the upbringing of children. Kipling perhaps exaggerated the meanness of this period when he recalled it in his autobiography and the short story "Baa, Baa Black Sheep" (1888). He remembered himself as the black sheep. His energy and curiosity about books and almost everything else consistently brought punishments at home, and undiagnosed problems with his eyesight created difficulties at school. When he was eleven his mother returned to England, probably summoned by a friend who had discovered his predicament. She placed him in the United Services College, a school organized to prepare the sons of military officers and colonial administrators for similar careers.

Kipling flourished in his new school. Here the code of the boys and the rules of the masters created a discipline that was masculine and institutional, with clear premises and hierarchies and consistent administration. He read widely, learned Latin well enough to amuse himself as an adult by translating and imitating Horace, and wrote for the school paper. He formed the close friendships memorialized in his school novel *Stalky & Co.* (1899) and became what he admired the rest of his life, a capable, knowledgeable, eminent member of a group of like-minded males. At Southsea he learned, as he wrote in "Baa, Baa Black Sheep," that "when young lips have drunk deep of the bitter waters of Hate, Suspicion, and Despair, all the Love in the world will not wholly take away that knowledge; though it may turn darkened eyes for a while to the light, and teach Faith where no Faith was." At the United Services College he learned to balance his dark knowledge that one day the apparently secure world will collapse into confusion with the satisfaction of freely accepting a set of rules that give hard work its reasons and rewards.

At the end of 1882 Kipling returned to India to work as subeditor (the editor was the only other staff member) of the *Civil and Military Gazette,* a daily newspaper in Lahore. He wrote, edited, and translated scraps of news: "Wrote in course of year 230 columns matter," he noted in his diary in 1884. As a reporter he traveled to public events and the courts of native rulers, and he spent his evenings at home in the "family square" or at clubs where, he wrote in his autobiography, he met "none except picked men at their definite tasks." In 1885 he wrote the first two stories he thought worthy of inclusion in later editions of his works for a family magazine subsequently issued as a Christmas number by the newspaper. Then he began to write stories for the newspaper that had to fit into columns of two thousand words. When in 1887 he moved to a bigger paper as a reporter and editor of its supplement, the *Week's News,* he immediately contracted to supply fiction to the supplement.

The matter of his stories was India, usually the events of the offices, garrisons, and bungalows of the British in India, occasionally the character and customs of India itself as it could be known by an Englishman. The teller of the stories was often someone like Kipling – a detached observer, a re-

tailer of the tales he heard in railway carriages and at the club. When he collected some of the stories he wrote for the *Civil and Military Gazette* as *Plain Tales from the Hills* in 1888 for an Indian publisher, they were widely read and discussed by the British in India, although the one thousand copies the publisher sent to England were little noticed. Kipling followed this mixed success in the same year by collecting some of the stories he had written for the *Week's News* in six volumes of the Indian Railway Library, published by the proprietors of his newspaper. He retained the titles of these volumes when he later combined them in two volumes of his collected works: *Soldiers Three, The Story of the Gadsbys,* and *In Black and White* in one volume (1892) and *Wee Willie Winkie, Under the Deodars,* and *The Phantom 'Rickshaw and Other Stories* in the other (1892). After serving what he called a seven-year apprenticeship in India, he left in 1889, sailing east to visit China, Japan, and California, then traveling across the United States to sail for England.

Kipling arrived in London in the fall of 1889, three months short of his twenty-fourth birthday. By the end of the next year he was famous. All through 1890 he wrote about India in new stories and poems – among them some of his best known, including "Gunga Din," "Danny Deever," and "Mandalay" – that appeared monthly, sometimes weekly in British and American periodicals. He collaborated on one novel, *The Naulahka: A Story of West and East* (1892), with Wolcott Balestier, and completed another, *The Light That Failed* (1891), that was also published in England and the United States in an American magazine. British and American publishers reprinted the stories of *Plain Tales from the Hills,* which went through three printings in six months in England, and the volumes of the Indian Railway Library. At the end of 1890 Kipling put his new stories together with some unpublished fiction and a dozen stories from Indian newspapers to make his first substantial volume of short stories first published outside India, *Life's Handicap: Being Stories of Mine Own People* (1891).

At the end of this first phase in his career, Kipling had seen into print more than one hundred short stories, more than half the number written for adults that he finally admitted into authorized editions of his work. Often composed to meet the deadlines and space requirements of newspapers, many of these stories nonetheless hold together to compose a body of writing marked by complicated themes and ambitious practices. In these stories he found his hero, the competent man (and, only occasionally, woman) of deeds rather than talk who did the real work of the world. He made India into a place that expressed his abiding sense of reality as a finally incomprehensible mystery within which humans constructed different codes of belief and conduct, some more honorable and availing than others but none essentially more true than others. He became known for a kind of literary realism within which he could register the costs as well as the material and moral benefits of the work people do. But his laconic style of anecdote occasionally turned his stories into something like parables, and he began to experiment with stories that left the conventions of realism entirely to move into fable.

Private Terence Mulvaney, described in "The Three Musketeers" (1887) – collected in *Plain Tales from the Hills* – as one of "the worst men in the regiment as far as genial blackguardism goes," fairly represents the hero of Kipling's early stories. Mulvaney gets drunk, gets into fights, flirts with other peoples' wives, and finally loses his corporal's stripes. But when it comes down to it, Mulvaney is capable, a brave and effective soldier. He leads a group of naked men in "The Taking of Lungtungphem" (1887), collected in *Plain Tales from the Hills,* and helps to turn an ambush into a vividly described victory in "With the Main Guard" (1888), collected in *Soldiers Three.* In "The God from the Machine" (1888), another story in *Soldiers Three,* he prevents the inappropriate elopement of the colonel's daughter. In "The Incarnation of Krishna Mulvaney" (1888), collected in *The Courting of Dinah Shadd and Other Stories* (1890), he destroys a scheme in which a contractor is cheating his coolie workers and then, after a farcical sequence created by his drunkenness, impersonates the Hindu deity Krishna and extorts 434 rupees and a gold necklace from a priest. After he marries and leaves the army, there is no place for Mulvaney in England. He returns to India in "The Big Drunk Draf'" (1888), gathered in *Soldiers Three,* as a civilian, "a great and terrible fall." Even out of uniform, he helps to discipline an unruly regiment of men waiting to go home by advising its young officer to tie one of the men spread-eagle to tent pegs and leave him out one frosty night. "You look to that little orf'cer bhoy. He has bowils. 'Tis not ivry child that wud chuck the Rig'lations to Flanders an' stretch Peg Barney on a wink from a brokin' an' dilapidated ould carkiss like mesilf."

Competence and effectiveness in these stories often require a bending of regulations or a neglect of protocol. When in "Thrown Away" (1888), a story in *Plain Tales from the Hills,* a sheltered boy breaks under the strain of his work and shoots himself in the head, a major and the teller of the story organize the lie that he died of cholera to protect his honor and the sensibilities of his mother. "The tale had credence as long as was necessary; for everyone forgot about The Boy before a fortnight was over. Many people, however, found time to say that the Major had behaved scandalously in not bringing in the body for a Regimental funeral." Strickland, a police officer who appears in several stories and later in Kipling's novel *Kim* (1901), uses his intimate knowledge of native ways to disguise himself in order to defeat an accusation of adultery against an innocent woman in "The Bronckhorst Divorce Case" (1888) and to be near and finally to win the woman who becomes his wife in "Miss Youghal's Sais" (1887), both collected in *Plain Tales from the Hills.* The narrator of the latter story refers to Strickland's "crowning achievement" of "spending eleven days as *faquir* or priest in the gardens of Baba Atal at Amristar, and there picking up the threads of the great Nasiban Murder Case. But people said, justly enough, 'Why on earth can't Strickland sit in his office and write up his diary, and recruit, and keep quiet, instead of showing up the incapacity of his seniors?'"

Even competent men can be defeated by the reality of British India and of India itself. Bureaucratic rigidity in "In the Pride of His Youth" (1887), a story in *Plain Tales from the Hills,* frustrates Dicky Hatt, who works "like a horse" to save money to bring his wife and child out from England. But "pay in India is a matter of age, not merit, you see, and if their particular boy wished to work like two boys, Business forbid they should stop him." By the time Dicky is given a salary that will enable him to pay the cost of passage, his child is dead and his wife has divorced him. He quits at age twenty-three: "I'm tired of work. I'm an old man now."

Other careers are destroyed, and sometimes made, because of tedium. Her gender deprives Mrs. Hauksbee, a clever, manipulative woman who appears in half a dozen stories, of a field in which she can openly exercise her intelligence and ambition. Out of boredom she incites callow young men to waste their time by riding miles to flirt with her and tries to become influential by intriguing to make the careers of cheats and fools. In "At the Pit's Mouth" (1888), collected in *Under the Deodars,* another woman, named only the Man's Wife, relieves her boredom by manufacturing "some semblance of intrigue to cloak even her most commonplace actions." She conducts an affair in a cemetery until her lover, the Tertium Quid, becomes depressed by the presence of shallow graves filling with water. When he is killed in an accident, she goes to bed for three days, "which were rainy; so she missed attending the funeral of the Tertium Quid, who was lowered into eighteen inches of water, instead of the twelve to which he had first objected." The condition of people at Simla, the hill town to which British administrators and their families retreat in the hot weather, and in the married quarters of garrisons is presented at its extreme in "A Wayside Comedy" (1888), collected in *Under the Deodars.* Each of the five men and women isolated in the "rat-pit" of a remote station is in some way unfaithful to friend and spouse. By the end of the story everyone knows about and has been hurt by these betrayals, but all stay in their marriages and their jobs, visiting one another as before, singing to the banjo and laughing "the mirthless mirth of these men on the long white line of the Narkarr Road."

Beneath what the British do to one another in India lies what India does to them. Kipling's India is violent and dangerous, only lightly marked by British rule. One of his first published stories – "The Strange Ride of Morrowbie Jukes" (1885), collected in *The Phantom 'Rickshaw* – describes a grotesque community of Hindus who have "had the misfortune to recover from trance or catalepsy" before their bodies were burned. They are dumped into a crater whose walls are unscalable cliffs, like the trap "the ant-lion sets for its prey," and left to scramble against one another in a brutal contest of survival. In "Dray Wara You Dee" (1888), included in *In Black and White,* one of several stories Kipling tells in the voice of a native, the speaker recounts how he has beheaded his wife because she was unfaithful and then cut off her breasts to advertise her crime. "Your Law!" he says. "What is your Law to me!"

When Englishmen cross into this India, even the most compassionate and competent are baffled. John Holden in "Without Benefit of Clergy" (1890), a story in *The Courting of Dinah Shadd,* buys a fourteen-year-old "Mussleman's daughter" from her mother, falls in love with her, fathers a son, and lives happily in a house in the native precincts of the city. "The delight of that life was too perfect to endure. Therefore it was taken away as many things are taken away in India – suddenly and without warning." His lover and son die of fever; the house is torn down; and Holden is called away to relieve a British colleague dying in the epidemic. Trejago, the hero of "Beyond the Pale" (1888), gathered in *Plain Tales from the Hills,* is undone because of his intimate knowledge of India. A young woman, Biesa, who has spoken to him from behind a grated window in an alley sends him a letter made of objects whose meaning he must interpret. "Trejago knew far too much about these things, as I have said. No Englishman should be able to translate object-letters." His translation begins an affair that lasts until one night, after an interval of three weeks, he knocks at the grating and the girl "held out her arms into the moonlight. Both hands had been cut off at the wrists, and the stumps were nearly healed." Trejago never discovers what has happened. "He cannot get Biesa – poor little Biesa – back again. He has lost her in the City where each man's house is as guarded and as unknowable as the grave; and the grating that opens into Amir Nath's Gully has been walled up."

India baffles the British even when they do not venture into its mysteries. "False Dawn" (1888), collected in *Plain Tales from the Hills,* tells of a midnight picnic in the ruined gardens of an old tomb during which Saumerez, a civil servant, intends to propose to Edith Copleigh. A dust storm blows up, and in the "roaring, whirling darkness" he proposes by mistake to Maud, her older sister. The narrator rides after the distressed Edith and, "ringed with the lightning and the storm," brings her back to correct the mistake, but the mistake cannot really be corrected. He ends his story "tired and limp, and a good deal ashamed of myself." He knows that this trivial tale carries a deep, sad lesson about the cost of trying to stage picnics and decorous courtships in the ruins and violent weather of this alien place. He also knows that from another perspective the story is even sadder. "There is a woman's version of this story, but it will never be written . . . unless Maud Copleigh cares to try."

Kipling's manner in these stories is that of a realist. He suggests that he tells the real story beneath the official narrative and superficial glamour of empire. Kipling fills the stories with the place-names of India, words from its languages, and the dialects, jargon, and shoptalk of British soldiers and administrators. Most often the narrator has heard his stories from someone else, but rather than diluting his authority, this enhances it: he knows all the stories, more about the British in India than anyone else. His tone, with a few lapses, is matter-of-fact. He wants to shock his readers, but he is not shocked, and some of his most devastating stories concern events that at home would be quite ordinary. For example, in "Bitters Neat" (1887), a story from the *Civil and Military Gazette* that Kipling did not put into *Plain Tales from the Hills* until an 1897 collected edition of his writing, a young woman falls in love with Surrey, an efficient yet dull man unaware of her infatuation. She refuses a proposal from another man, goes somewhat crazy, and is sent home. When Surrey learns why the young woman has gone, he is unstrung: "I didn't see, I didn't see. If I had *only* known." The narrator, who has known the whole story all along, spends no other words of pity or irony on Surrey. He drops directly to what he has also always known, what this story is really about – "the hopelessness and tangle of it – the waste and the muddle."

In some of these stories Kipling leaves realism to make his skepticism about certainty and permanence into parables about empire itself. The heroes of "The Man Who Would be King" (1888), competent men in the style of Terence Mulvaney, use their knowledge of India to disguise themselves to make a dangerous journey beyond the northern frontier. Then they use their training as soldiers to drill an army and organize the region into their kingdom. The region once had been conquered by Alexander, who introduced Masonic rituals, and the two Englishmen use their knowledge of Masonry to pass themselves off as gods. The ambitious Daniel Dravot has himself crowned king. "I won't make a Nation," he says, "I'll make an Empire. . . . Two hundred and fifty thousand men, ready to cut in on Russia's right flank when she tries for India! . . . Oh, it's big! It's big, I tell you. But there's so much to be done in every place." After Dravot is tricked and killed by suspicious priests, his partner, Peachy Carnahan, survives a crucifixion and is set free, maimed and mad, to make his way back to India, carrying Dravot's head and crown in a sack. When Carnahan dies in an asylum, the narrator, who has seen the contents of the sack, asks " 'if he had anything upon him by chance when he died?' 'Not to my knowledge,' said the Superintendent. And there the matter rests." Like Alexander yesterday, like England tomorrow, another empire has come to nothing, this time leaving no trace at all.

The tactics of the stories of Kipling's first collections eventually extend his ironic sense of the contingency of systems to the premise of his own kind of realism, which is founded on the secular, materialistic creed that people can know the world, even if they cannot always command it. He plays with this creed in ghost stories in which he allows the inexplicable to stand unexplained. Is the apparition of "The Phantom 'Rickshaw" (1887) a hallucination, or is it retribution for the lover's heartless rejection of the woman whose ghost haunts his rides with his fiancée? The narrators of many of these stories occasionally admit that their compressed forms leave complicated questions unanswered and

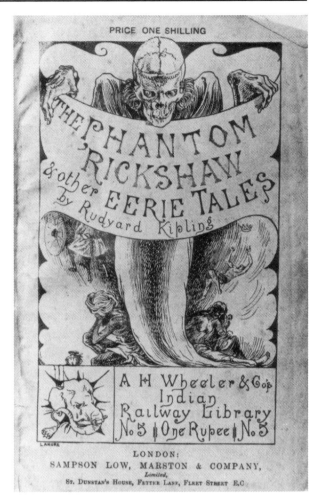

Cover for one of the 1888 story collections that launched Kipling to fame

intricate characters unrealized. The narrator poses a conundrum to himself at the end of "The Bronckhorst Divorce Case": "What I want to know is, 'how do women like Mrs. Bronckhorst come to marry men like Bronckhorst?'" In "The Last of the Stories," a fantasy that Kipling wrote in 1888 but left unpublished until 1909, when it was collected in *Abaft the Funnel,* the narrator visits a hell populated by grotesque dolls who tell him that they suffer from his botched attempts to make them seem real. Even so, " 'I've touched 'em raw. . . . I show you what they ought to be. You must find out for yourself how to make 'em so.'"

The one hundred stories of these first collections are told by a chorus of voices. Each voice contributes a piece to a mosaic that collectively represents a stable, comprehensible reality. But as the narrator acknowledges at the end of "False Dawn," another voice would tell a different story. Thus, each perspective offers not a piece of the whole but a singular, subjective version of it. In "To be Filed for Reference," the last story in *Plain Tales from the Hills,* police officer Strickland and the narrator study a manuscript left by McIntosh Jellaludin, a drunken Scot who changed his religion, went to live with a native woman, and descended into India. Neither Strickland nor the narrator can make any sense of the manuscript, but Kipling gives it the title of his own never-finished novel of native life, "The Book of Mother Maturin." There are stories that Kipling as a Western realist can neither understand nor write. Writing of the tales of Gobind, a Hindu holy man he invents for the preface of *Life's Handicap,* he says his "tales were true, but not one in twenty could be printed in an English book, because the English do not think as natives do." Kipling then introduces his own stories, "collected from all places, and all sorts of people." He adds, "The most remarkable stories are, of course those which do not appear – for obvious reasons."

In the two decades after the publication of his first collections of short stories Kipling consolidated and enlarged his fame. After traveling to South Africa, Australia, and (for the last time) India, he married Carrie Balestier, an American, in 1892 and moved to Brattleboro, Vermont. There he began to write the children's stories of *The Jungle Book* (1894) and *The Second Jungle Book* (1895), in which the boy Mowgli learns the law of the jungle and becomes leader of its creatures before marrying and settling on the boundary of the forest, a master of the two cultures, the wild and the civilized. Kipling's novel *"Captains Courageous": A Story of the Grand Banks,* was published in 1897, and he followed the great success of *Barrack-Room Ballads and Other Verses* (1892) with collections of poems in 1896 and 1903 and in the United States the first collected edition of his verse in 1907. He visited President Grover Cleveland in the White House and met Theodore Roosevelt, whose energy he admired. He picked up the notion, which he still seemed to hold when he wrote his autobiography at the end of his life, that the United States was in decline, its hardy stock devastated in the Civil War and replaced by less vigorous immigrants. A rancorous dispute with his brother-in-law, which ended in court, precipitated Kipling's return to England in 1896.

Back in England, Kipling rose from fame and affluence to eminence. When he visited Scotland Andrew Carnegie offered him his house; he spent his winters in South Africa in a house provided by Cecil Rhodes. The editorial page of the *Times* was open to him whenever he wanted to address his contemporaries in verse on public issues, as he did

when he warned them of the obligations and costs of empire in "Recessional" (1897) and "The White Man's Burden" (1899). He witnessed some of the Boer War (1899–1902), during which he contributed to and helped to edit a newspaper for the troops. He received honorary degrees from Cambridge and Oxford but refused a knighthood in 1899 and declined to stand as a Conservative for Parliament. In 1907 he became the first British writer to be awarded the Nobel Prize for Literature.

Kipling continued to write for children and young adults; his efforts include his school novel *Stalky & Co.; Just So Stories: For Little Children* (1902), a collection of fables about animal origins; and *Puck of Pook's Hill* (1906) and *Rewards and Fairies* (1910), fanciful retellings of stories from British history. He wrote about India again in *Kim,* probably his most successful novel.

Now at home in England, Kipling bought Bateman's, a seventeenth-century house in Sussex, and knit himself into the life of a member of a high professional caste. He explored the countryside in the automobiles he enthusiastically acquired; prosecuted a steady commerce with magazine editors, publishers, and literary agents in Britain, the United States, and Canada; and enjoyed his fraternity with other leading men in their professions at London clubs and public dinners. Two more collections of short stories published before 1900, *Many Inventions* (1893) and *The Day's Work* (1898), include stories about India, but increasingly in the stories collected in the two volumes published in the first decade of the twentieth century, *Traffics and Discoveries* (1904) and *Actions and Reactions* (1909), Kipling reflected the experience and opinions of a man making himself comfortable not in the outposts but at the center of empire.

In the short stories of these collections Kipling sometimes attacked the complacency and enervation of the comfortable English at home. In a few stories published in the 1890s – for example, "Love-o-Woman," told by Mulvaney and first published in *Many Inventions* – he continues to try to shock people at home by retailing the self-destructive appetites for drink and women that can be set loose out on the margins. He urged the support of a large volunteer army in the tractlike fantasy "The Army of a Dream" (1904), collected in *Traffics and Discoveries.* In "One View of the Question" (1890), a story in *Many Inventions,* he reversed his usual perspective so that an Indian visitor to London could conclude that "the fountain-head of power is putrid with long standing still" and predict, with a smugness that Kipling surely intended as cautionary, that "the Sa-

hibs die out at the third generation in our land."
That prediction seems already to be coming true in
"A Deal in Cotton" (1902), collected in *Actions and
Reactions,* in which the narrator revisits Strickland,
now retired to a seaside resort in the west of England, and hears of how Strickland's son, helpless
with fever, was made to look good in his African
post by the contrivance of his Indian servant.

When Kipling looks from England at the work
of the empire at this stage of his career, however, he
usually tends to remember not war and waste but
the benefits whites bring to natives. "William the
Conqueror" (1895), gathered in *The Day's Work,*
opens with the observation, "famine was sore in the
land, and white men were needed." Scott, a civil servant, and William, the oddly but revealingly named
sister of a British officer in the police, alleviate the
disaster in a heroic bout of work that also turns out
to be their courtship. A third-generation Anglo-
Indian in "A Tomb of His Ancestors" (1897), another story in *The Day's Work,* uses the natives' belief that he is the reincarnation of his grandfather,
an administrator of fabled effectiveness, to complete
a successful vaccination campaign. In "Little Foxes"
(1909) in *Actions and Reactions,* British administrators
in Africa settle land disputes during ingeniously organized fox hunts: "One gets at the truth in a hunt-
ing-field a heap quicker than in your law courts."
Generally in these stories, white people do good for
natives, and the British do more good than anyone.
Certainly they do more than the engaging American
who thinks of war as a game and tries to sell the gun
he has invented to the Boers in "A Captive" (1902),
collected in *Traffics and Discoveries;* more than the
Boers with their dishonorable guerrilla tactics in "A
Sahib's War" (1901), also in *Traffics and Discoveries;*
and more than the Jewish shipowners cleverly out-
witted in "Bread Upon the Waters" (1896), collected in *The Day's Work.*

A set of fables in these four collections epitomizes some of these themes and the convictions
they express. Kipling loved modern machinery –
the railways and steamships of the old century, the
motorcars, wireless, and airplanes of the new.
When he installed a turbine in an old mill on his
Sussex property, he wrote a fable – "Below the Mill
Dam" (1902), collected in *Traffics and Discoveries* – in
which the Waters and the Spirit of the Mill discuss
the innovation. All approve except an old English
rat, who is discovered by the electric lights turned
on by the turbine and killed. Yet Kipling was deeply
hostile to political innovation. When in "A Walking
Delegate" (1894), a story in *The Day's Work,* a Kansas horse brings socialist views to a Vermont stable –

" 'As usual,' he said, with an underhung sneer –
'bowin' your heads before the Oppressor, that
comes to spend his leisure gloatin' over you'" – he
is argued down and beaten by the other horses.
" 'There's jest two kind o' horse in the United States –
them ez can an' will do their work after bein' properly broke an' handled, an' them as won't.' " A wax
moth that insinuates itself into "The Mother Hive"
(1908), included in *Actions and Reactions,* so subverts
the work of the hive that it produces a batch of
Oddities who destroy it with theories that honey-
combs should be built of democratic circles and that
bees can live on the honey of the hive without producing more. As the plates and rivets of "The Ship
That Found Itself" (1895), gathered in *The Day's
Work,* tell one another during its first Atlantic run,
each must learn its place in the hierarchy of the Design, "how to lock down and lock up on one another." Then "the talking of the separate pieces
ceases and melts into one voice, which is the soul of
the ship." Waste in these fables is not a natural condition within which humans build more or less adequate shelters of work and rule. Instead, Kipling
here imagines existences governed by design and
law that creatures, to their ruin or profit, choose to
resist or accept.

As his convictions settled in the two decades
before World War I, Kipling's narrative practices
became expansive and adventurous. No longer constrained by the limitations of space imposed on his
early stories, he constructed elaborate plots, sometimes around nothing more than a practical joke. He
began his practice of prefacing and concluding his
stories with verses that sometimes enforced, sometimes complicated, their themes. He told some stories in several voices, giving them the feel, oblique-
ness, and surprise of conversation. If the stories of
the *Jungle Books* and *Just So Stories* are included, he
wrote as many fables as realistic short stories in
these years. He even toyed with science fiction. At
the end of "With the Night Mail: A Story of 2000
A.D." (1905), a fantasy about airplanes and a world
benevolently regulated by the Aerial Board of Control that was collected in *Actions and Reactions,* his invention spills over into appendices of mock news
stories, a book review, and advertisements for used
dirigibles and aerial chauffeurs ("Must be member
of the Church of England, and make himself useful
in the garden"). The best measure of the development of Kipling's talent as a short-story writer in
these years is that the four collections published between 1893 and 1909 contain five or six of his most
accomplished and interesting stories, and none is
like any of the others.

For example, "The Bridge-Builders" (1893), collected in *The Day's Work,* begins as a typical Kipling story celebrating capable men doing good work in India despite the heat, disease, and interference of remote and ignorant superiors. Trying to protect their uncompleted bridge from a flood, the British engineer Findlayson and his lascar overseer Peroo are swept in their boat into the river, out of realism and into fable. In a trance of weariness smoothed with opium, they witness the gods debate the plea of the river to destroy the bridge that obstructs her. "Be certain that is only for a little," Krishna says, and then tells the gods that except for Brahma, the principle of life, they themselves are only for a time: "The fire-carriages shout the names of new Gods that are *not* the old under new names." When morning comes the bridge still stands. Findlayson and Peroo are rescued by a westernized Indian in his steam launch on his way to the temple "to sanctify some new idol." The realistic part of the story honors Findlayson's work in careful descriptions of it; the fable both subverts and sanctifies it. Although it too will ultimately be washed away, Findlayson's work, like the "fire-carriages" of the railway, speaks the name of gods. The bridge is an idol rightly to be worshipped, an authentic contemporary expression of reverence for Brahma.

" 'They' " (1904), a story in *Traffics and Discoveries,* is to an early Kipling ghost story such as "The Phantom 'Rickshaw" what "The Bridge-Builders" is to some of Kipling's early realistic anecdotes about good work in India. The narrator clatters in his motorcar through a magically beautiful southern English landscape to find by accident a lovely Elizabethan house behind a lawn full of topiary yew cut as knights and ladies. Gradually it comes to him that the children he entertains with his motorcar are ghosts summoned by the need of the gracious blind woman who lives alone in the house. Kipling's young daughter Josephine, born in 1892, had died during his visit to the United States in 1899, and his loss underwrites the poignancy of the narrator's decision not to return to the house. Kipling prefaced " 'They'" with a poem in which the Virgin Mary releases children from heaven so that their spirits will comfort people on earth. The ghostliness in this story is not a realist's playful reminder that he cannot know everything. It is rather a possibility of belief, an earthly paradise, from which the narrator is shut out because of his commitment to the valuable, practical work that makes and purchases motorcars.

Each of these four collections of short stories includes one or two stories governed by the physical action of farce. The deft timing of "My Sunday at Home" (1895), a story in *The Day's Work,* tops its principal plot, in which an American doctor mistakenly administers a purgative to a perfectly healthy workingman, with a final scene in which the enraged victim is approached by yet another doctor intent on doing him good. Kipling then caps the story with a lightly ironic comment on "man who is immortal and master of his fate." Included in *Actions and Reactions,* "The Puzzler" (1906), named for a densely branched tree, is more ambitiously metaphorical. A group of important men – politicians and government ministers – set a monkey loose in the tree to test its impenetrability. One of the puzzles of the story is how to catch the monkey after it has escaped into a house. Another puzzle is how to get an idea about the governing of colonies through the dense thicket of British government at home. The solution to the first puzzle also solves the second: bonded by the fun of their adventure in catching the monkey and facing down the indignant residents of the house, the important men work together to get the idea through, "a little chipped at the edges."

"Mrs. Bathurst" (1904), collected in *Traffics and Discoveries* and perhaps Kipling's finest short story, begins with its tellers reminiscing about a farcical episode of their youths, turns into something like a ghost story, and ends as a commentary about the difficulty of catching reality in the frame of narrative. Vickers, a naval warrant officer, is haunted by a sequence he sees in a "cinematograph" shown in a carnival at Cape Town. Night after night he takes Pyecroft, the principal teller of the story, to watch a woman step out of a train in Paddington Station and walk toward the camera, looking "out straight at us . . . till she melted out of the picture – like – like a shadow jumpin' over a candle, an' as she went I 'eard Dawson in the tickey seats be'ind sing out, 'Christ! there's Mrs. B!'" Two other people help Pyecroft tell the story. One, like Pyecroft, has known Ada Bathhurst as the generous proprietor of a small hotel near Auckland. The other knows what happened to Vickers. None of them know what Mrs. Bathhurst was doing in London – "She's lookin' for me," Vickers says – or what Vickers has done to be haunted by her, or what he tells the captain of his ship before he is sent upcountry alone on a detail, or why he deserts, or who is with him when he is found with another person on a railway track in a teak forest, both "burned to charcoal" by lightning. The artful ramble of the story, as its several tellers exchange information and opinions that end without resolving its plot, testifies both to the ambition of realistic narrative to

Cartoon from the July 1906 issue of the Westminster Gazette *satirizing Kipling as an imperialist*

take in everything and to the futility of that ambition. By this time Kipling has learned to accommodate his own skepticism about ascertaining fact within the structure of a story that defeats its drive for closure. Ten years earlier, in the preface to *Life's Handicap,* he marked the limit of his craft by referring to stories he could not tell. In "Mrs. Bathhurst" he makes the same point not by withholding the story but by trying, and failing, to tell it.

Three collections of Kipling's short stories were published in the last twenty years of his life: *A Diversity of Creatures* (1917), *Debits and Credits* (1926), and *Limits and Renewals* (1932). He was now a wealthy man: except for *Thy Servant a Dog, Told by Boots* (1930), three sketches about the faithfulness of dogs told by one of them, his new books sold only modestly, but editions of his children's stories, anthologies of his stories and poems, editions of his collected works, and the *Inclusive Editions* of his poems (first published in 1919) brought him a large annual income. One of his biographers, C. E. Carrington, estimates that in his lifetime Kipling

earned more than $4 million, mostly from his writing and the rest from investments its income purchased.

During his cousin Stanley Baldwin's terms as prime minister in the 1920s, Kipling's advice to the Conservative party acquired a quasi-official status, and when he visited Scotland he stayed at Balmoral with the king. He suffered a stomach disease that he incorrectly feared was cancer, and his wife carefully guarded his privacy at Bateman's. But when he believed the world was going wrong, he used his public presence to try to set it right. With his friend H. Rider Haggard he founded a short-lived Liberty League to oppose socialism. He bitterly regretted the 1921 treaty that set Ireland on its way toward independence of England, and he resigned from the Rhodes Trust in 1925 because he thought its policies encouraged the growth of a commonwealth of autonomous nations to replace an empire ruled by white men from home.

In the short stories of his last three collections, Kipling's conviction that at least some of the time right-minded people know exactly what to do coexists with his persistent sense of the uncertainties of knowing and doing. A set of stories about the consequences of World War I shows this mix of skepticism and sometimes belligerent certainty. Like many of his contemporaries, Kipling at first welcomed the war as an occasion to renew and test courage and honor. He enlisted his talent and name in a series of pamphlets and newspaper articles about the army in France and the work of the navy. When his only son, John, was reported missing in action in France in 1915 – his body was never found – Kipling responded in part in the manly code in which he had been schooled: "it's something to have bred a man." (Interestingly, he used a woman's voice to express his grief in the 1916 ballad "My Boy Jack.") He soon undertook to edit a history of his son's regiment, *The Irish Guards in the Great War* (1923), and to serve on the Imperial War Graves Commission, which established and supervised military cemeteries outside England.

Before his son's death Kipling wrote three short stories that express a simple morality about the war. In "Swept and Garnished" (1915), collected in *A Diversity of Creatures*, the house of a tidy German woman is haunted by the ghosts of children killed by German shells and bombs. In "Sea Constables" (1915), included in *Debits and Credits*, one of Kipling's competent, affluent gentlemen serving as a volunteer forces a neutral vessel trying to run the blockade into a remote port, where he lets its captain die of pneumonia unattended. After a child in an English village is killed by a bomb dropped from a German airplane in "Mary Postgate" (1915), a story in *A Diversity of Creatures*, a middle-aged spinster finds the injured German pilot in her garden. Already grieving over a young friend killed while training to be a pilot, she lets the German die, takes a hot bath, and comes down looking "quite handsome."

However, in some of the stories he wrote after the war, Kipling considers that it is not so easy to watch men die. All these stories are about the psychic damage of war and how friends or small communities protect or cure its victims. When the narrator discovers Masonic Lodge Faith and Works 5837 E.C. in " 'In the Interest of the Brethren' " (1918), collected in *Debits and Credits*, this creation of merchants and professional men provides food, lodging, and the comforts of ritual to young men on leave from the war. In two later stories, "The Janeites" (1924) and "A Madonna of the Trenches" (1924), both collected in *Debits and Credits*, the members of the lodge do what they can to hold together

men who might never be able to leave the war behind. During the war Brother Strangwick in "A Madonna of the Trenches" saw an apparition of his recently deceased aunt in a trench. Shocked out of his certainties about life and death, he now refuses to get married and get on with life. Brother Humberstall, who tells most of "The Janeites," returns to the front after the explosion of an ammunition dump "knocked all 'is Gunnery instruction clean out of 'im." He is kept going by officers who induct him into a select society of initiates in the details of Jane Austen's fiction. None of the officers survives the collapse of the front at Sommes, and back home after the war Humberstall fills his days by shuffling through his memories of the war and by trying to play his Janeite game with his sister. Strangwick and Humberstall tell their stories at the lodge, presumably not for the first time, to sympathetic men who listen to them and send them home, only temporarily relieved of their burdens.

In other stories about the trauma of the war, friends conspire not just to sustain but to cure the victims. For example, the several tellers of a story in *Limits and Renewals,* "Fairy-Kist" (1927) – some of them members of Lodge 5837 who also meet occasionally with other successful men as an Eclectic *but* Comprehensive Fraternity – not only solve the mystery of a dead body much more neatly than the tellers of "Mrs. Bathurst" manage to do, they also diagnose and make harmless the obsession of a man who, "wounded and gassed and gangrened in the War," goes around England planting flowers. In "The Woman in His Life" (1928), collected in *Limits and Renewals,* a servant, once his orderly, helps a man who was a sapper in the war recover from the lethargy and hallucinations of his delayed reaction to the horrors of his experience beneath no-man's-land in France. In another story from the volume, "The Tender Achilles" (1929), a group of colleagues, one of them a member of Lodge 5837, combine to return to his important research a scientist unstrung by memories of his inevitable failures as a surgeon in field hospitals during the war: "Everything that a man's brain automatically shoves into the background was out before the footlights, and dancing Hell's fox-trot, with drums and horns." Unlike Strangwick and Humberstall, the men saved in these stories belong to the same mercantile and professional classes as the men who do most of the saving. Kipling here does not put at permanent risk the caste on which he often depended in his later stories to do the real work of making order.

In other stories in these three final collections, such men manage triumphs as complete as those in

"Fairy-Kist" and "The Tender Achilles." Returning to the scientific fantasy of a world run by the technicians of the Aerial Board of Control in "As Easy as A.B.C." (1912), included in *A Diversity of Creatures,* Kipling describes how these powerful masters of machines and electricity effortlessly and bloodlessly suppress a revolt in Chicago of malcontents who want to bring back the days of crowds, sensational journalism, and democracy. In "The Honours of War" (1914), collected in *A Diversity of Creatures,* Kipling returned to Stalky, the hero of his school novel, to tell how grown-up, hearty army men discipline the unrest of subalterns, just as back in India in their own young manhoods they once gave Elliot-Hacker a bath on his veranda, and "his lady-love saw it and broke off the engagement, which was what the Mess intended, she being an Eurasian." In "Unprofessional" (1930), included in *Limits and Renewals,* a group of doctors and scientists, "tried and proved beneath glaring and hostile moons in No Man's Land," marry biology and astrology to cure a cancer and hold off death long enough for one of them to marry the woman they have cured.

On the other hand, at the end of "Unprofessional" two of the successful team, from opposite ends of the middle classes, recall the unrelieved sorrows of their marriages to drunken wives. In this story and others Kipling allows pain to be felt beneath or beyond the resolutions of his plots. A woman in a story in *Debits and Credits,* "The Wish House" (1924), whose fantasy is solidly rendered in the dialect and details of working-class life, cures the cancer of her faithless lover by wishing it to herself. She is troubled only by the worry that he will marry before she dies. "But the pain do count, don't ye think, Liz?" she says on her deathbed. "The pain *do* count to keep 'Arry — where I want 'im. Say it can't be wasted, like." In "The Gardener" (1925), gathered in *Debits and Credits,* an unmarried woman visiting the grave of a man she has always called her nephew in a military cemetery in France is guided to it by a gardener who might be Christ and who in any event pleases her by speaking her secret and referring to her son. But the story leaves unexplained and unresolved a curious episode in which she fails to comfort, and even inadvertently insults, another woman who lives without relief in the troubles of her secret: she must invent subterfuges to give herself reasons to visit the grave of a man who never acknowledged her as his lover when he was living. A story collected in *Debits and Credits,* "The Eye of Allah" (1920), one of several historical fantasies Kipling wrote in the last phase of his career, ele-

vates the difficulties that create such incomplete resolutions into a social and cultural dilemma. A thirteenth-century abbot knows that the prototype of a microscope one of his monks has brought back from the Moors in Spain will lead to the cure of disease. He also knows that its revelation of a hellish world of bacteria in a drop of water will lead to persecution for magic and blasphemy. After a collegial conversation in which some of his monks freely exchange opinions about the significance of this technological advance, the abbot puts on the ring of his authority and smashes the instrument. His act, decisive but unsatisfying, preserves his community, but it also helps to preserve a backward and rigidly dogmatic church that requires such sacrifices.

Two similar, well-managed stories demonstrate how in these stories at the end of his career Kipling sometimes drove toward clear resolutions and sometimes drifted to what he had always known as "the hopelessness and tangle of it." Both stories work out elaborate hoaxes, of which Kipling was always fond. Caught in a speed trap in a small village, a couple of journalists, a member of Parliament, and the proprietor of a music hall combine their talents to revenge themselves in "The Village That Voted the Earth Was Flat" (1913), collected in *A Diversity of Creatures.* Kipling calls on his exuberant invention and his close knowledge of politics and popular media to describe how the conspirators concoct newspaper stories, commission a music-hall song, and arrange a question in Parliament to convince the public of the lie that the villagers of Huckley are fools who have voted their belief in a flat earth. In this story Kipling exercises his scorn at the ease with which popular opinion can be created by the instruments of politics and popular culture, while at the same time he maneuvers an absolute triumph of sound men who know their jobs over officious incompetents who have risen to an authority and status beyond their talents.

The hoax of "Dayspring Mishandled" (1924), included in *Limits and Renewals,* is also sponsored by revenge. Castorley, who has risen from writing for a fiction syndicate in the 1890s to become an expert on Geoffrey Chaucer, says something insensitive (it remains unrevealed) about a paralyzed woman Manallace cares for and loves. Manallace, who writes historical novels "in a style that exactly met, but never exceeded, every expectation," spends years fabricating and arranging for the discovery of the manuscript of a supposedly lost tale by Chaucer. Castorley falls into the trap, but before he publishes the book that Manallace lies in wait to ambush, he dies, perhaps of kidney disease, perhaps at

Honorary-degree recipients at Oxford University, 27 June 1907: 1) Gen. William Booth, 2) Samuel Langhorne Clemens, and 3) Kipling. Other recipients were Auguste Rodin and Camille Saint-Saëns.

the hands of the physician to whom Lady Castorley turns her eyes as her husband's coffin crawls into the crematorium. Here the joke does not clap shut, as it does in the Huckley hoax. Like Manallace's clever machine of vengeance, the plot pulls up short before a deep trouble that cannot be comprehended by farce, then tumbles into other troubles that were there all along – not just the mystery of Lady Castorley and the possible malignity of her lover but also the unspecified cruelty of her husband and the unexamined affection of Manallace for the sad woman who may never have loved him.

The writer of Kipling's obituary in the 25 January 1936 *Times Literary Supplement,* trying to figure out "Rudyard Kipling's Place in English Literature," acknowledged that by the time of his death "many had lost interest in him and many others had been repelled." What repels mid- and late-twentieth-century readers is most often the politics of Kipling's endorsement of empire. George Orwell, writing a few years after Kipling's death, judged his colonial politics not only repellent but ignorant in his neglect of the economic basis of empire. But Orwell also thought that because of what he left out as well

as what he included, Kipling accurately described the life and attitudes of British colonial administrators and soldiers, providing "not only the best but about the only literary picture we have" of late-nineteenth-century Anglo-India. Lionel Trilling, who found Kipling unreadable after his own adoption of liberal politics, nonetheless remarked the "anthropological view" that Kipling learned in India: "the perception that another man's idea of virtue and honor may be different from one's own but quite to be respected." Noel Annan has argued that this awareness of the relativity and individual integrity of cultural institutions and authority assures Kipling's place in the history of ideas. This view has made Kipling interesting to an increasing number of literary and cultural critics and historians who go to his writing not just for a picture of the lives of colonialists but also for a sensitive register of the tensions and contradictions in their exercise of dominion over ways of knowing that Kipling at least sometimes thought of as valid and valuable.

Other commentators who have sustained or revived interest in Kipling's writing since his death have not troubled so much with his politics but instead honored his craft. Despite his disappointment in Kipling's fiction after *Traffics and Discoveries,* Edmund Wilson presented to formalist literary critics a Kipling who was attractive because of his themes of loneliness and isolation and his accounts of a perilous fortitude. J. M. S. Tompkins has written of the sophisticated use of irony by which Kipling maintains his equilibrium on the edge; Bonamy Dobrée of Kipling's modulation in and out of the fabulist forms in which he tended to express his certainties; and Elliot K. L. Gilbert of the tactics that mediate between Kipling's notion of "the irrationality of the universe and man's need to find some order in it." These fundamentally existentialist ideas about how Kipling's craft fashioned order in and against the void are consistent with the interests and language of late-twentieth-century literary criticism. Sandra Kemp, for example, writes of how Kipling's recognition that identity, like everything else, is constructed and contingent informs self-consciously fictional narratives in which he tries out a repertory of identities, no longer resisting the void but rather inhabiting it as a condition that enables him to explore the exhilarating possibilities of otherness.

One reason to attend to Kipling's craft is that such attention makes clear the continuity and development of his talent during the nearly half century in which he wrote short stories. He now is probably best known outside academic literary criticism as the author of the *Jungle Books* and *Just So Stories,* and perhaps after that as a writer of short stories, poems, and a novel, *Kim,* about the British in India. Recent attention to his colonial politics, although it makes him freshly interesting, also helps to fix him in the moment of his first fame at the turn of the century, as if he wrote little that matters after 1901 or what he wrote has little to do with the books that made him famous. But Kipling's practice was always various, and it grew more supple as he graduated to long forms. He continually experimented with voices and points of view. The connected narratives of *The Story of the Gadsbys* are told entirely in the dialogue of quick, fluid scenes that read like scripts for short films. The comic effects of Mulvaney's dialect point up the ravages of the losses he describes in the same way that the working-class dialect in "The Wish House" plays against and makes poignant the fantastic event that is the hinge of the plot. Kipling learned to move in the same story from one set of conventions and expectations to another and so to reproduce his sense of a reality in which the meaning of things would not settle and stay fixed. He also learned in stories such as "Mrs. Bathhurst" to let the voices mix with one another to tell their tales in pieces and layers and so to express his skepticism that the whole story could ever be told.

As a young man Kipling sometimes deprecated his calling. Throughout his life he spoke of his "Daemon," who brought the words from somewhere beneath his will. "When your Daemon is in charge, do not try to think consciously," he wrote in his autobiography. "Drift, wait, and obey." At the end of his life, however, Kipling proudly owned the craft that deliberately selected and refined the welter of experience. In the chapter on "Working Tools" in his autobiography he mentions first as instruments of the "Higher Editing" a pot of India ink and a brush. He advises that writers "consider faithfully every paragraph, sentence and word, blacking out where requisite," repeating the process after letting the manuscript "lie by to drain as long as possible," and then repeating it again after reading the words aloud. He habitually read his writing aloud, testing the "weights, colours, perfumes, and attributes of words in relation to other words. . . . There is no line of my verse or prose which has not been mouthed till the tongue has made all smooth."

In "Proofs of Holy Writ" (1934), the last short story by Kipling published in his lifetime (it was collected in volume thirty-four of *The Sussex Edition of the Complete Works of Rudyard Kipling*), he compared his method of composition to that of William Shakespeare. Shakespeare, with occasional help from an outclassed Ben Jonson, has agreed to help the translators of the King James Bible with the rhythms of their sentences:

> "Quiet man!" said he. I wait on my Demon! . . . How shall this open? 'Arise.' No! 'Rise.' Yes. And we'll have no weak coupling. 'Tis a call to a City! 'Rise – shine'. . . . Nor yet any schoolmaster's 'because'. . . . 'And the glory of God!' No! 'God's' over-short. We need the long roll here. *'And the glory of the Lord is risen on thee.'* "

Kipling started out by presenting himself as a clever young man who wrote "penny farthing tales" in which he pretended to transmit the words of men he met at the club and in railway carriages. He ended by imagining how a craft such as his can find words and a sound that will wake the lessons of a great prophet.

Letters:

Rudyard Kipling to Rider Haggard: The Record of a Friendship, edited by Morton Cohen (London: Hutchinson, 1965; Rutherford, N. J.: Fairleigh Dickinson United Press, 1965);

'O Beloved Kids': Rudyard Kipling's Letters to His Children, edited by Elliot L. Gilbert (London: Weidenfeld & Nicolson, 1983; New York: Harcourt Brace Jovanovich, 1984);

The Letters of Rudyard Kipling, edited by Thomas Pinney, volume 1, 1872–1889; volume 2, 1890–1899 (London: Macmillan, 1990; Iowa City: University of Iowa Press, 1991).

Interview:

Kipling: Interviews and Recollections, 2 volumes, edited by Harold Orel (Totowa, N. J.: Barnes & Noble, 1983).

Bibliographies:

Flora V. Livingston, *Bibliography of the Works of Rudyard Kipling* (New York: Wells, 1927); *Supplement* (Cambridge, Mass.: Harvard University Press, 1938; London: Oxford University Press, 1938);

Lloyd H. Chandler, *A Summary of the Work of Rudyard Kipling* (New York: Grolier Club, 1930);

James McG. Stewart, *Kipling: A Bibliographical Catalogue,* edited by A. W. Yeats (Toronto: Dalhousie University Press and University of Toronto Press, 1959);

Helmut E. Gerber and Edward Lauterbach, "Rudyard Kipling: An Annotated Bibliography of Writings About Him," *English Literature in Transition,* 3, nos. 3–5 (1960): 1–235; 8, nos. 3–4 (1965): 136–241.

Biographies:

C. E. Carrington, *The Life of Rudyard Kipling* (London: Macmillan, 1955; Garden City, N.Y.: Doubleday, 1955; revised edition, 1978);

John Gross, *Rudyard Kipling: The Man, His Work, and His World* (London: Weidenfeld & Nicolson, 1972; New York: Simon & Schuster, 1972);

Martin Fido, *Rudyard Kipling* (London & New York: Hamlyn, 1974);

Philip Mason, *Kipling: The Glass, the Shadow and the Fire* (London: Cape, 1975; New York: Harper, Row, 1975);

Kingsley Amis, *Rudyard Kipling and His World* (London: Thames & Hudson, 1975; New York: Scribners, 1975);

Angus Wilson, *The Strange Ride of Rudyard Kipling: His Life and Works* (London: Secker & Warburg, 1977; New York: Viking, 1978);

Lord Birkenhead, *Rudyard Kipling* (London: Weidenfeld & Nicolson, 1978; New York: Random House, 1978);

Martin Seymour-Smith, *Rudyard Kipling* (London: Macdonald, 1989);

Harold Orel, *A Kipling Chronology* (Boston: G. K. Hall, 1990; London: Macmillan, 1990).

References:

Noel Annan, "Kipling's Place in the History of Ideas," *Victorian Studies,* 3 (June 1960): 323–348;

Stephen D. Arata, "A Universal Foreignness: Kipling in the Fin-de-Siècle," *English Literature in Transition,* 36 (1993): 7–38;

Tim Bascom, "Secret Imperialism: The Reader's Response to the Narrator in 'The Man Who Would Be King,' " *English Literature in Transition,* 31 (1988): 162–173;

John Bayley, "The False Structure," *English Literature in Transition,* 29 (1986): 19–27;

Bayley, " 'Mrs. Bathhurst' Again," *Essays in Criticism,* 38 (July 1988): 233–236;

Harold Bloom, ed., *Rudyard Kipling* (New York: Chelsea House, 1987);

C. A. Bodelson, *Aspects of Kipling's Art* (Manchester: Manchester University Press, 1964; New York: Barnes & Noble, 1964);

David Bromwich, "Kipling's Jest," *Grand Street,* 4 (Winter 1985): 150–179;

Terry Caesar, "Suppression, Textuality, Entanglement, and Revenge in Kipling's 'Dayspring Mishandled,' " *English Literature in Transition,* 29 (1986): 54–63;

John Coates, " 'Proofs of Holy Writ': Kipling's Valedictory Statement on Art," *Kipling Journal,* 61 (September 1987): 12–20;

Louis L. Cornell, *Kipling in India* (London: Macmillan, 1966; New York: St. Martin's Press, 1966);

Nora Crook, *Kipling's Myths of Love and Death* (London: Macmillan, 1989; New York: St. Martin's Press, 1989);

Bonamy Dobrée, *Rudyard Kipling: Realist and Fabulist* (London & New York: Oxford University Press, 1967);

John deLancey Ferguson, "Kipling's Revision of His Published Works," *Journal of English and Germanic Philology,* 22 (1923): 114–124;

Peter E. Firchow, "Kipling's 'Mary Postgate': The Barbarians and the Critics," *Etudes Anglaises,* 29 (January–March 1976): 27–39;

Elliot L. Gilbert, *The Good Kipling: Studies in the Short Story* (Athens: Ohio University Press, 1971; Manchester: Manchester University Press, 1971);

Gilbert, "Silence and Survival in Rudyard Kipling's Art and Life," *English Literature in Transition,* 29 (1986): 115–126;

Gilbert, ed., *Kipling and the Critics* (New York: New York University Press, 1965; London: Owen, 1966);

Robert Gish, "The Exotic Short Story: Kipling and Others," in *Twayne's Critical History of the Short Story,* edited by Joseph M. Flora (Boston: Twayne, 1985), pp. 1–37;

Roger Lancelyn Green, ed., *Kipling: The Critical Heritage* (New York: Barnes & Noble, 1971; London: Routledge & Kegan Paul, 1971);

James Harrison, *Rudyard Kipling* (Boston: Twayne, 1982);

T. R. Henn, *Kipling* (Edinburgh & London: Oliver & Boyd, 1967);

Sukeshi Kamra, *Kipling's Vision: A Study in His Short Stories* (New Delhi: Prestige, 1989; New York: Advent, 1989);

Sandra Kemp, *Kipling's Hidden Narratives* (Oxford & New York: Blackwell, 1988);

Lisa A. Lewis, "Some Links between the Stories in Kipling's *Debits and Credits," English Literature in Transition,* 25 (1982): 74–85;

W. J. Lohman, *The Culture Shocks of Rudyard Kipling* (New York: Lang, 1990);

Robert H. MacDonald, "Discourse and Ideology in Kipling's 'Beyond the Pale,' " *Studies in Short Fiction,* 23 (Fall 1986): 413–418;

Phillip Mallett, ed., *Kipling Considered* (New York: St. Martin's Press, 1989);

Philip Mason, "The Birth of a Story," *Kipling Journal,* 62 (June 1988): 20–26;

John McBratney, "Lovers Beyond the Pale: Images of Indian Women in Kipling's Tales of Miscegenation," *Works and Days,* 8 (Spring 1990): 17–36;

John A. McClure, *Kipling and Conrad: The Colonial Fiction* (Cambridge, Mass.: Harvard University Press, 1981);

B. J. Moore-Gilbert, *Kipling and "Orientalism"* (New York: St. Martin's Press, 1986);

Harold Orel, ed., *Critical Essays on Rudyard Kipling* (Boston: G. K. Hall, 1989);

Orel, "Rudyard Kipling and the Establishment: A Humanistic Dilemma," *Cahiers Victoriens et Edouardiens* (November 1983): 21–37;

George Orwell, "Rudyard Kipling," in his *Dickens, Dali and Others* (London: Secker & Warburg, 1946; New York: Harcourt Brace Jovanovich, 1946), pp. 140–160;

Mark Paffard, *Kipling's Indian Fiction* (New York: St. Martin's Press, 1989);

Norman Page, *A Kipling Companion* (London: Macmillan, 1984);

Ann Parry, "Imperialism in 'The Bridge-Builders': Metaphor or Reality?," *Kipling Journal,* 60 (March 1986): 12–22; (June 1986): 9–16;

Parry, "Reading Formations in the Victorian Press: The Reception of Kipling 1888–1891," *Literature and History,* 11 (Autumn 1985): 254–263;

Kanatur Bhaskara Rao, *Rudyard Kipling's India* (Norman: University of Oklahoma Press, 1967);

Harry Ricketts, "Kipling and the War: A Reading of *Debits and Credits,*" *English Literature in Transition,* 29 (1986): 29–39;

Angus Ross, ed., *Kipling 86* (Brighton: University of Sussex Library, 1987);

Andrew Rutherford, ed., *Kipling's Mind and Art: Selected Critical Essays* (Stanford: Stanford University Press, 1964; Edinburgh & London: Oliver & Boyd, 1964);

Vasant Anant Shahane, *Rudyard Kipling: Activist and Artist* (Carbondale: Southern Illinois University Press, 1973; London & Amsterdam: Feffer & Simmons, 1973);

Shamsul Islam, *Kipling's "Law": A Study of the Philosophy of His Life* (London: Macmillan, 1975; New York: St. Martin's Press, 1975);

Edward Shanks, *Rudyard Kipling: A Study in Literature and Political Ideas* (London: Macmillan, 1940; New York: Doubleday, Doran, 1940);

S. T. Sharma, "Kipling's India: A Study of Some Short Stories," *Literary Criterion,* 22, no. 4 (1987): 54–61;

David Stewart, "Kipling's Portraits of the Artists," *English Literature in Transition,* 31 (1988): 265–283;

J. I. M. Stewart, *Rudyard Kipling* (London: Gollancz, 1966; New York: Dodd, Mead, 1966);

T. C. W. Stinton, "What Really Happened in 'Mrs. Bathhurst'?," *Essays in Criticism,* 38 (January 1988): 55–74;

Zohreh T. Sullivan, *Narratives of Empire: The Fictions of Rudyard Kipling* (London & New York: Cambridge University Press, 1993);

J. M. S. Tompkins, *The Art of Rudyard Kipling* (London: Methuen, 1959);

Lionel Trilling, "Kipling," in his *The Liberal Imagination* (New York: Viking, 1950), pp. 118–128;

Ruth Waterhouse, " 'That Blindish Look': Signification of Meaning in 'Mrs. Bathhurst,' " *Studia Neophilologica,* 60 (1988): 193–206;

Edmund Wilson, "The Kipling That Nobody Read," in his *The Wound and the Bow* (Boston: Houghton Mifflin, 1941; London: Secker & Warburg, 1942), pp. 105–181;

Lewis D. Wurgaft, *The Imperial Imagination: Magic and Myth in Kipling's India* (Middletown, Conn.: Wesleyan University Press, 1983);

W. Arthur Young and John H. McGivering, *A Kipling Dictionary* (London: Macmillan, 1967; New York: St. Martin's Press, 1967).

Papers:

The most extensive archive of Kipling's letters, manuscripts, and family papers is housed at the University of Sussex Library in Brighton. Other significant collections of letters and manuscripts are in the British Library, the Berg Collection of the New York Public Library, the Library of Congress, the Doubleday Collection of the Princeton University Library, the Bodleian Library, and the university libraries of Syracuse, Harvard, Cornell, and Dalhousie.

Vernon Lee
(Violet Paget)
(14 October 1856 – 13 February 1935)

Jane Bowman Smith
Winthrop University

See also the Lee entries in *DLB 57: Victorian Prose Writers After 1867* and *DLB 153: Late-Victorian and Edwardian Novelists, First Series.*

BOOKS: *Studies of the Eighteenth Century in Italy* (London: Satchell, 1880; Chicago: McClurg, 1908);

Belcaro: Being Essays on Sundry Aesthetical Questions (London: Satchell, 1881);

Ottilie: An Eighteenth-Century Idyl (London: Unwin, 1883); republished with *The Prince of the Hundred Soups* (New York: Harper, 1886);

The Countess of Albany (London: Allen, 1884; Boston: Roberts, 1884);

Euphorion: Being Studies of the Antique and Mediaeval in the Renaissance (2 volumes, London: Unwin, 1884; Boston: Roberts, 1884; revised edition, 1 volume, London: Unwin, 1885);

Miss Brown: A Novel (3 volumes, Edinburgh & London: Blackwood, 1884; 1 volume, New York: Harper, 1885);

A Phantom Lover: A Fantastic Story (Edinburgh & London: Blackwood, 1886; Boston: Roberts, 1886);

Baldwin: Being Dialogues on Views and Aspirations (London: Unwin, 1886; Boston: Roberts, 1886);

Juvenilia: Being a Second Series of Essays on Sundry Aesthetical Questions (2 volumes, London: Unwin, 1887; 1 volume, Boston: Roberts, 1887);

Hauntings: Fantastic Stories (London: Heinemann, 1890; New York: Lovell, 1890);

Vanitas: Polite Stories (London: Heinemann, 1892; New York: Lovell, Coryell, 1892; enlarged edition, London: John Lane / New York: John Lane, 1911);

Althea: A Second Book of Dialogues on Aspirations and Duties (London: Osgood, McIlvaine, 1894);

Renaissance Fancies and Studies: Being a Sequel to "Euphorion" (London: Smith, Elder, 1895; New York: Putnam / London: Smith, Elder, 1896);

Portrait of Vernon Lee (Violet Paget) by Berthe Nouffland (Courtesy of Irene Cooper Willis and the Librarian, Library of Colby College)

Limbo, and Other Essays (London: Richards, 1897; enlarged, London: John Lane / New York: John Lane, 1908);

Genius Loci: Notes on Places (London: Richards, 1899; London: John Lane / New York: John Lane, 1908);

The Child in the Vatican (Portland, Maine: Mosher, 1900);

Chapelmaster Kreisler: A Study of Musical Romanticists (Portland, Maine: Mosher, 1901);

In Umbria: A Study of the Artistic Personality (Portland, Maine: Mosher, 1901);

Ariadne in Mantua: A Romance in Five Acts (Oxford: Blackwell, 1903; Portland, Maine: Mosher, 1906);

Penelope Brandling: A Tale of the Welsh Coast in the Eighteenth Century (London: Unwin, 1903);

Hortus Vitae: Essays on the Gardening of Life (London: John Lane / New York: John Lane, 1904);

Pope Jacynth and Other Fantastic Tales (London: Richards, 1904; London: John Lane / New York: John Lane, 1907);

The Enchanted Woods, and Other Essays on the Genius of Places (London: John Lane / New York: John Lane, 1905);

Sister Benvenuta and the Christ Child: An Eighteenth-Century Legend (New York: Kennerley, 1905; London: Richards, 1906);

The Spirit of Rome: Leaves from a Diary (London: John Lane / New York: John Lane, 1906);

The Sentimental Traveller: Notes on Places (London: John Lane / New York: John Lane, 1908);

Gospels of Anarchy and Other Contemporary Studies (London & Leipzig: Unwin, 1908; New York: Brentano's / London: Unwin, 1909);

Laurus Nobilis: Chapters on Art and Life (London: John Lane / New York: John Lane, 1909);

Beauty and Ugliness and Other Studies in Psychological Aesthetics, by Lee and Clementina Anstruther-Thomson (London: John Lane / New York: John Lane, 1912);

Vital Lies: Studies of Some Varieties of Recent Obscurantism, 2 volumes (London: John Lane / New York: John Lane / Toronto: Bell & Cockburn, 1912);

The Beautiful: An Introduction to Psychological Aesthetics (Cambridge: Cambridge University Press, 1913; New York: Putnam, 1913);

The Tower of the Mirrors, and Other Essays on the Spirit of Places (London: John Lane / New York: John Lane / Toronto: Bell & Cockburn, 1914);

Louis Norbert: A Two-Fold Romance (London: John Lane / New York: John Lane, 1914);

The Ballet of the Nations: A Present-day Morality (London: Chatto & Windus, 1915; New York: Putnam, 1915);

Peace with Honour: Controversial Notes on the Settlement (London: Union of Democratic Control, 1915);

Satan, the Waster: A Philosophic War Trilogy (London: John Lane / New York: John Lane, 1920);

The Handling of Words and Other Studies in Literary Psychology (London: John Lane, 1923; New York: Dodd, Mead, 1923);

The Golden Keys and Other Essays on the Genius Loci (London: John Lane, 1925; New York: Dodd, Mead, 1925);

Proteus; or, The Future of Intelligence (London: Kegan Paul, Trench, Trübner / New York: Dutton, 1925);

The Poet's Eye: Notes on Some Differences between Verse and Prose (London: Leonard & Virginia Woolf at the Hogarth Press, 1926);

For Maurice: Five Unlikely Stories (London: John Lane, 1927);

A Vernon Lee Anthology: Selections from the Earlier Works, edited by Irene Cooper Willis (London: Lane, Bodley Head, 1929);

Music and Its Lovers: An Empirical Study of Emotional and Imaginative Responses to Music (London: Allen & Unwin, 1932; New York: Dutton, 1933).

Collections: *The Snake Lady, and Other Stories,* edited, with an introduction, by Horace Gregory (New York: Grove, 1954);

Supernatural Tales, edited by Cooper Willis (London: Owen, 1955); published as *The Virgin of the Seven Daggers* (London: Corgi, 1962);

Pope Jacynth and More Supernatural Tales: Excursions into Fantasy (London: Owen, 1956).

OTHER: *Tuscan Fairy Tales, Taken Down from the Mouths of the People,* transcribed and edited anonymously by Lee (London: Satchell, 1880);

The Prince of the Hundred Soups: A Puppet-Show in Narrative, edited, with an introduction, by Lee (London: Unwin, 1883; New York: Lovell, 1886);

Clementina Anstruther-Thomson, *Art and Man: Essays and Fragments,* edited, with an introduction, by Lee (London: John Lane, Bodley Head, 1924; New York: Dutton, 1924);

"J. S. S. In Memoriam," in *John Sargent,* by Evan Charteris (London: Heinemann, 1927), pp. 233–255.

SELECTED PERIODICAL PUBLICATIONS –
UNCOLLECTED: "Les Aventures d'une pièce de monnaie," *La Famille* (Lausanne), no. 10 (May 1870): 233–237; no. 12 (June 1870): 268–271; no. 14 (July 1870): 327–334;

"Vivisection: An Evolutionist to Evolutionists," *Contemporary Review,* 41 (May 1882): 788–811;

Review of *Florentine Painters of the Renaissance,* by Bernard Berenson, *Mind,* new series 2 (1896): 270–272;

"Psychologie d'un écrivain sur l'art (observation personnelle)," *Revue Philosophique,* 56 (September 1903): 225-254;

"Essais d'esthétique empirique: l'individu devant l'oeuvre d'art," *Revue Philosophique,* 59 (January-February 1905): 43-60, 133-146.

Although Vernon Lee (born Violet Paget) was widely respected for her intellect during her lifetime – Henry James, for example, wrote to his brother William on 20 January 1893 that Lee's "vigour and sweep of intellect are most rare and her talk superior altogether" – her literary reputation peaked early in her life and gradually diminished. Like many of her contemporaries, she wrote in several genres; besides her five volumes of short stories, she published novels, collections of travel essays, romances, philosophy, and psychological and aesthetic explorations of the arts. Like other female Victorian writers, she believed that few people would take a woman author seriously, especially in the field of aesthetics, and thus created the pseudonym "Vernon Lee," which she used both professionally and personally.

While her short fiction has been reprinted in several editions since her death in 1935, her stories have never been widely popular. Her biographer, Peter Gunn, praises the stories, "all of which have a quality deeper than the charm and sensitivity in the re-creation of time and place which are so immediately apparent – a power to haunt us in our profounder levels of consciousness." In his introduction to *The Snake Lady, and Other Stories* (1954) Horace Gregory writes that "if genius can find a definition within writing of less than monumental scope, genius was hers."

Violet Paget's powerful intellect probably served as her escape from an unhealthy family. Born at Chateau Saint-Leonard near Boulogne on 14 October 1856, she was raised as an expatriate. Her mother, Matilda, was highly intellectual and passionate in her convictions but hated society. The Paget family continually moved around Europe, living primarily in Germany; in 1866 they began wintering in Italy. They settled in Florence in 1873, and she lived there for the rest of her life. Her mother's letters to Eugene, her older stepbrother, as well as his replies (now in the Colby College Collection), suggest that her mother and Eugene were obsessively devoted to one another. Her father, Henry Ferguson Paget, seems to have been treated as an outsider by her mother and stepbrother, and Violet was trained to be an intellectual prodigy. Although her earliest education came at the hands of German governesses, her mother and stepbrother intended for her to be another Mme. de Staël and educated her accordingly; apparently her mother substituted books for maternal love.

When Violet was ten she met John Singer Sargent, also born in 1856, and his family. His mother introduced her to the churches and historic monuments of Rome, and she had what can only be described as an epiphany that shaped her entire life's work: in *Juvenilia: Being a Second Series of Essays on Sundry Aesthetical Questions* (1887) Lee describes herself as being "wild to be taken into those dark, damp little churches, resplendent with magic garlands and pyramids of lights, and full of the long, sweet, tearful, almost infantine notes of voices." This need to visit and understand places and capture their essences in language became a lifelong quest. She wrote several books of essays in which she described the genius loci, the "spirit of the place," and her short fiction reveals this same fascination with the past and an uncanny ability to re-create its ambience. During this same period she read and reread Nathaniel Hawthorne's *The Marble Faun* (1860) and William Wetmore Story's *Roba di Roma* (1862); in each of these books she recognized a deep response to Italy similar to her own. The Paget family wintered in Rome from 1868 to 1870, maintaining contact with the Sargents, but then her brief period of companionship was over as the Sargents moved to Florence. Her friendship with Sargent continued throughout their lives, however, and he painted her portrait in 1881.

This rigorous training paid off in that Violet published her first essay in 1870 at age thirteen. Written in French, "Biographie d'une monnaie" – published as "Les Aventures d'une pièce de monnaie" in *La Famille,* the Lausanne newspaper – traces the adventures of a coin, made from an old Macedonian helmet, throughout Rome's history. Apparently already feeling strongly possessive about her work, she was outraged when the editor made minor changes in the story, such as the title. She also wrote fiction; one unpublished story, written when she was about thirteen, displays one of her major themes. In "Capo Serpente" an artist, apparently ignoring warnings from the more knowledgeable peasants, seeks out a "haunted" spot in which to paint. As he works, a huge snake with the head of a beautiful prince suddenly appears before him: "The artist wishes to fly, he is rooted to the ground; he cannot take his eyes off the beautiful but terrible face." The half-human, half-snake reappears in a later work, as does the helpless fascination of an artist or scholar for a beautiful yet clearly deadly creature.

By 1870 Lee was seriously researching eighteenth-century Italian music with an intensity that frightened some of her family's friends. Henrietta C. Jenkin, who had helped Lee find publishers, wrote in 1871, "I have so much belief in your powers . . . – at the same time, my dear little friend, don't forget that you are a complex machine – body, soul, mind and heart – and that all your component parts must have a due share of attention." However, she was unable to take this advice; absolutely focused on her work in adulthood, she lived with "passionate intellectuality," as her biographer says. Known for her brilliant conversation, she was extremely self-assured, with a reputation for caustic comments and a desire to hold center stage. Many people who admired her intellect actively disliked her because, as Percy Lubbock stated in his *Portrait of Edith Wharton* (1947), "It was impossible to control or to civilize Vernon Lee." In middle age, after suffering several breakdowns, she wrote on 9 August 1894 to a close friend, Carlo Placci, that she realized that her family was "on one side acutely neuropathic and hysterical; and that my earlier years were admirably calculated, by an alternation of indiscipline and terrorism, by excessive overwork and absolute solitude, to develop these characteristics."

In 1875 her stepbrother, Eugene, left a successful political career and returned home an invalid, completely incapacitated by an apparently psychosomatic case of neurasthenia. Despite demands that she become his almost constant companion, Lee insisted on privacy and her right to have time in which to read and write. To better her understanding of eighteenth-century music she studied voice and assiduously collected old scores. This passion led to the short story "A Culture-Ghost; or, Winthrop's Adventure," written in 1874 when she was eighteen and published in *Fraser's Magazine* in 1881.

Lee was undoubtedly a lesbian, but according to her literary executrix, Irene Cooper Willis, "she never faced up to sexual facts. She was perfectly pure. . . . She had a whole series of passions for women, but they were all perfectly correct. Physical contact she shunned." Lee's friend Dame Ethel Smyth said that Lee never admitted that she loved these women nor indulged "in the most innocent demonstration of affection, preferring instead to create a fiction that to her these friends were merely *intellectual* necessities." The first of these relationships began in 1878, when Lee met Annie Meyer. Their friendship failed in 1880, the same year in which Lee met Mary Robinson, a talented poet. This new relationship continued for seven years.

Violet Paget in 1871, the year after she published her first essay, "Les Aventures d'une pièce de monnaie," at age thirteen

In 1877 *Fraser's Magazine* published four of her essays on eighteenth-century Italy; three of these bear the pseudonym Vernon Lee. Her first major publication, *Studies of the Eighteenth Century in Italy* (1880), changed the way in which the importance of Italian music was viewed. In this same year she also published a book of short stories, *Tuscan Fairy Tales, Taken Down from the Mouths of the People.* Although her name does not appear on this second book, Lee clearly transcribed the stories and edited them; she was sent twelve copies, and it was later advertised on a flier together with her book *Belcaro: Being Essays on Sundry Aesthetical Questions* (1881). The absence of her name on the book has become a minor mystery. In the preface she hints at a "scholarly aim" when she refers to other collections of Italian folklore published by "Miss Busk, Professor Bernoni, and Fraulein Laura Gonzenbach." She hopes that her collection of "ten of the most striking of those [she] heard" will help to preserve the folklore of this region. She claims that she reproduced these tales as closely as possible to the way she heard them, yet she alters her role as silent transcriber on several occasions when she interrupts the story to ask questions or to add explanatory notes. In her later fiction she often writes as the transcriber of a tale told to her by another, and even more common, she takes on the role of the educated guide to the past.

Of the ten tales she chose, five are retellings of tales found in the Brothers Grimm but with intriguing variations. For example, the first story, "The Little Convent of Cats," which is told in two versions in the book, is similar to the Grimms' "The Widow's Two Daughters." "The Beautiful Glutton" is similar to the Grimms' "The Three Spinning Fairies," while "The Three Cauliflowers" is essentially "Bluebeard." She even presents a version of "Snow White and the Seven Dwarfs" called "The Glass Coffin," but the seven dwarfs are replaced with seven robbers. Lee's authorial comment at the end of this story displays both her knowledge of cultural history and her scholarly voice:

> I may remark, by way of note, that although the seven brothers were called robbers by the narrator, she seemed to consider them as highly respectable persons, and was much puzzled when I asked her how robbers could be anything but rascals. I fancy the explanation of this anomaly must be sought for in the fact that these brothers were originally *outlaws,* and that as after some time outlaws ceased to exist, and the fact of their having existed was forgotten by the people, they were turned into *robbers.*

Lee does not mention the Brothers Grimm in the preface to the book. Given her German governesses in childhood, it is hard to imagine that she would not have known their work. Apparently she was not interested in a comparative study but simply in these tales for themselves as a reflection of her beloved Italy.

The next works Lee published, although fictional, resulted at least in part from her research. *Ottilie: An Eighteenth-Century Idyl* (1883) is of interest, according to critic Vineta Colby, because "it is a personal history framed in the cultural history of eighteenth-century German Romanticism." Ottilie's half brother is a poet who depends upon her as a muse; she essentially sacrifices her own life to help him write. The story escapes morbidity because of the romantic scenes of Germany that Lee creates. *The Prince of the Hundred Soups: A Puppet-Show in Narrative* (1883), another volume "edited" by Lee, displays her knowledge of commedia dell'arte in a charming fairy-tale setting.

Beginning in 1881 Lee began to make yearly visits with Robinson to England to meet other writers and, particularly, publishers for her work. She met Robert Browning, Oscar Wilde, William Morris, Leslie Stephen, and the Humphry Wards, among others. Longmans, Green began to pressure her to write a novel, but at first she hesitated: "even had I time, I would shrink from writing what would certainly be vastly inferior to my other work," she replied in a letter. However, she became convinced and proceeded. The book, *Miss Brown: A Novel* (1884), was even more hastily written than usual – Lee's typical composing style was to write quickly and revise little, if at all – and created a scandal because of its attack on the London art scene. Henry James, whom Lee had met sometime in 1884, was embarrassed by her having dedicated the novel to him. The thin plot concerns Anne Brown, who is educated by Walter Hamlin, a poet who hopes to marry her. Although Anne eventually realizes she loathes Hamlin's world, with its posturings, drugs, and neglect of social responsibility, she agrees to marry him because it is her duty to attempt to save him. Most readers recognized Lee's characters as actual people, and several Pre-Raphaelites were offended by her portrayals of them in the book. Cosmo Monkhouse, a friend of Lee's, reviewed the book negatively and then wrote her privately to say he found it "very nasty." Lee's response, written in her diary, suggests that she had no idea readers would see the novel as a roman à clef. She wrote that she feared her idealism hid something "base": "May I be indulging a more depraved appetite for the loathesome, while I *fancy* that I am studying disease and probing wounds for the sake of diminishing both?"

The Countess of Albany (1884), a biography for the Distinguished Women Series, and *Euphorion: Being Studies of the Antique and Mediaeval in the Renaissance* (1884) were both overshadowed by the scandal caused by her novel. Two more collections of aesthetic essays quickly followed.

In 1887 Robinson, who had been Lee's nearly constant companion since 1880, suddenly announced her engagement to James Darmsteter, whom she had only seen three times. Lee was horrified by this news, not only because her relationship with Mary would be irremediably changed but because Darmsteter was severely crippled. After the marriage Lee suffered a complete nervous collapse and was forbidden to work. Clementina Anstruther-Thompson, whom Lee had met earlier, helped her to recover. Their relationship lasted ten years and furthered Lee's interest in social causes. With "Kit" she visited socialists and social reformers and sought firsthand knowledge of conditions among the poor.

Hauntings: Fantastic Stories (1890), a collection of ghost stories, was Lee's first major collection of short fiction. Prepared during this convalescent period, the book included four previously published stories: "Amour Dure," first published in *Murray's Magazine* (1887); "Dionea"; "Oke of Okehurst," first published as a penny dreadful in 1886; and "The Wicked Voice," first published as "A Culture-Ghost: or, Winthrop's Adventure" in *Fraser's Magazine* (January 1881). Most of her short fiction, including these works, owes more to the leisurely storytelling of the Victorian tale than to the modern short story, which demands greater conciseness and unity of effect. The narrators of these tales, as was common in the period, are scholars and artists. Lee's work is reminiscent both of Walter Pater's in her attempt to define the essential spirit of the historical period and of E. T. A. Hoffmann's in her blending of the supernatural with psychological realism. Her descriptions, particularly of settings, create a haunted atmosphere, such as in one passage from "Amour Dure":

> I take refuge in long rambles. . . . This town is a handful of tall black houses huddled on to the top of an Alp, long narrow lanes trickling down its sides, like the slides we made on hillocks in our boyhood, and in the middle the superb red brick structure, turreted and battlemented, of Duke Ottobuono's palace, from whose windows you look down upon a sea, a kind of whirlpool, of melancholy grey mountains.

Contemporary reviews praised both Lee's ability to create suspense and her knowledge of the past. On 27 April 1890 James wrote her a positive letter in response to this book, saying, "I always taste, deeply, in all your work, the redolence of the unspeakable Italy, to whose infinite atmosphere you perform the valuable function of conductor or condenser." Many modern critics agree, concurring with Colby that Lee's supernatural stories are her "best works of fiction, where scholarship and imagination both flourish." Colby observes, however, that Lee's success resulted from the genre's less stringent demands on "plotting, realistic characterization, and dialogue," areas in which Lee's writing was weak.

In the preface to *Hauntings,* which was dedicated to artists Flora Priestley and Arthur Lemon, Lee describes her theory of the supernatural: "That is the thing – the Past, the more or less remote Past, of which the prose is clean obliterated by distance – that is the place to get our ghosts from. . . . My ghosts are what you call spurious ghosts (according to me the only genuine ones), of whom I can affirm

only one thing, that they haunted certain brains." In all four stories Lee presents characters whose obsessions with figures from the past lead to destruction. The accuracy of her psychological description is particularly impressive. Although the plots are similar – the protagonist is at first only intellectually intrigued, then gradually drawn in until nothing matters but the bewitching, beloved object of the obsession – Lee uses different points of view and narrative techniques: sometimes the narrator is the protagonist; sometimes an observer is. In "Amour Dure" the narrator, Spiridion Trepka, a Polish professor, falls passionately in love with the long-dead Medea da Carpi, an Italian duchess of the sixteenth century. In "Dionea" an artist becomes obsessed with a mysterious orphan, Venus in human form, who demands that the artist sacrifice himself to free her from mortal existence. In "The Wicked Voice" a musician becomes obsessed with a long-dead opera singer's beautiful voice.

Although critic Burdett Gardner suggests in *The Lesbian Imagination (Victorian Style): A Psychological and Critical Study of "Vernon Lee"* (1987) that these lamialike figures always meet "the affront of passionate love by the . . . rebuff of murder" and connects this with Lee's psychological "problems," at least "Oke of Okehurst" demands a different and more complex interpretation. In the story's past, set in the 1620s, Alice Oke dressed in men's clothing and acted as her husband's groom when he rode out to kill Lovelock, the poet who hoped to become Alice's lover. As the men fought, Alice shot Lovelock in the back. The present Alice Oke is obsessed by this story. "Such love as that," she tells the narrator, "is very rare, but it can exist. It becomes a person's whole existence, his whole soul. . . . It is unextinguishable, and goes on in the spiritual world until it meets a reincarnation of the beloved . . . takes shape and surrounds the beloved one once more." The present Alice's fixation eventually causes her husband to murder her in jealous madness. Although unstated, it seems clear that Alice's death is an expiation for the earlier Alice's crime and that her soul will be united with Lovelock's. This story gains power from its point of view: an artist, modeled on Sargent, at work painting portraits of the modern couple, watches this drama as it unfolds but is powerless to prevent it.

Two years later Lee published *Vanitas: Polite Stories* (1892). Similar in theme to *Miss Brown,* these stories offer harsh criticism of women's lives in society. Most critical attention to these stories has dealt not with Lee's theme but with the scandal caused by "Lady Tal." Jervase Marion, a central figure in

Portrait of Lee by her friend John Singer Sargent (Tate Gallery, London)

"Lady Tal," was widely recognized as Henry James, who believed himself to be the victim of deliberate satire. William James wrote Lee an angry letter defending his brother; her mortified response did not mollify Henry James, and he avoided her until 1912. Ironically, Lee was already in James's debt when this occurred: he had been kind to her during the earlier scandal, and she had grown as a writer after careful reading of his work. Others have suggested that Lee compounded the damage to her reputation by modeling Lady Tal on Alice Callander, a member of Anglo-American society in Italy who had asked her advice about a novel she had written. Although it is difficult to determine Lee's motivations in writing the story, she apparently felt free to use material at hand in her own life, unaware that this could cause offense.

Lee's presumption also diverted attention from the point she wished to make. In the preface, addressed to the Baroness Elena French-Cini, she states that "round these sketches of frivolous women, there have gathered some of the least frivolous thoughts, heaven knows, that have ever come into my head. . . . Indeed, how can one look from outside on the great waste of precious things, del-

icate discernment, quick feeling and sometimes stoical fortitude, involved in frivolous life, without a sense of sadness and indignation?" What Gunn calls her "peculiarly period cast of integrity and humanity" surfaces in these stories. She intensely scrutinizes the lives of wealthy aristocrats, disdaining the limited lives women lead within a society that views them as artifacts. In all three of the stories in the first edition, the female protagonists have been or will be "sold into marriage." Each woman struggles, as Lee says, against the great goddess Vanitas, but with varying degrees of success. Lee's point of view in each of these stories adds to the effect – none of the women tells her own story; instead, they are viewed by male characters who cannot fully free themselves of society's blinders in evaluating the women, thus misjudging them.

"A Worldly Woman," which was first published in the October 1890 *Contemporary Review,* and "Lady Tal" have similar plots. In each a woman with artistic ability but not genius must depend on a man to gain entry into the artist's world. Lady Tal, according to the preface, "abandoned freely the service of the great Goddess Vanitas," while Valentine Flodden, the central character of "A Worldly Woman," is ultimately martyred. "The Legend of Mme Krasinska," first published in *Fortnightly Review* (March 1890), presents the woman who is "saved." Lee's fascination with those who are haunted reappears here: Mme Krasinska, who has lived exclusively for her own pleasure, gradually begins to assume the identity of a pathetic, impoverished widow who has hanged herself in despair. Lee impressively suggests the gradual breakdown of Mme Krasinska's mind. When her suicide attempt miraculously fails, Mme Krasinska becomes a nun, one of "the Little Sisters of the Poor." In the enlarged edition of *Vanitas* (1911) Lee added a previously unpublished story, "A Frivolous Conversion," with a male protagonist who struggles futilely to free himself from society's limitations.

Lee's relationship with Anstruther-Thomson resulted in collaborative work in what Lee called "the science of the Mind and the Mind's relations with Body," a shift away from what she would later call her juvenile interests. She and Anstruther-Thomson studied human reactions, both physical and mental, to art. During their relationship Lee published *Althea: A Second Book of Dialogues on Aspirations and Duties* (1894), *Renaissance Fancies and Studies: Being a Sequel to "Euphorion"* (1895), *Limbo, and Other Essays* (1897), and *Genius Loci: Notes on Places* (1899).

Then another feud occurred. In 1897 Lee sent Bernard Berenson, whose *Florentine Painters of the Re-*

naissance (1896) she had reviewed, an essay titled "Beauty and Ugliness." Berenson replied with a sarcastic letter accusing her and Anstruther-Thomson of plagiarism. A series of letters failed to resolve the problem, but more than twenty years later Berenson's wife finally succeeded in reconciling Lee and Berenson. This feud, however, apparently worsened Anstruther-Thomson's health, which had been affected by overwork and research. She moved out of Lee's villa in 1899. The two remained friends but never resumed their intimate relationship. Lee's letters reveal how deeply she suffered as a result.

Lee published five books, including *Ariadne in Mantua: A Romance in Five Acts* (1903) and *Penelope Brandling: A Tale of the Welsh Coast in the Eighteenth Century* (1903), before collecting and publishing another book of short stories. *Penelope Brandling,* a short novel, is similar to many of her short stories in that the sinister past impinges on the present.

Favorably reviewed for its richness, color, and imagination, *Pope Jacynth and Other Fantastic Tales* (1904) is less thematically focused than Lee's earlier collections and has no preface. Three of the stories — "St. Eudaemon and His Orange Tree," "Pope Jacynth," and "The Lady and Death" — are unified by mild criticism of the Roman Catholic Church. Lee had similarly attacked religion in *Baldwin: Being Dialogues on Views and Aspirations* (1886), questioning the believer's expectations of justice in heaven, as God, she said, had not provided justice on earth. Instead, she proposed a morality that derived from responsible human relationships.

In both "Prince Alberic and the Snake Lady," first published in *The Yellow Book* (July 1896), and "The Wedding Chest" Lee returns to the theme of obsession. Of the stories in this collection "Prince Alberic and the Snake Lady" has attracted the most attention. Gardner in *The Lesbian Imagination (Victorian Style)* finds it a story "of unwholesome weirdness . . . the evidence of diseased sensibility is not to be found merely in the perverse and brutal plot. The style is everywhere loaded with an unhealthy excess of color and jewelled ornament." Colby disagrees, calling it "a work of love and imagination, but also a subtle allegory of the struggle of pure beauty and art against worldliness and carnality." Gardner possibly overlooks the story's roots in the darker fairy tales. As in "Capo Serpente," the Snake Lady is part human and part snake; she seems to wish only good for Prince Alberic, who longs to save her from her enchantment and allow her to live again in human form. The villain, Alberic's grandfather Duke Balthasar, cares only for money and sophisticated pleasures. When Alberic refuses to marry well to

save the duke from debt, both Alberic and the Lady die. Within the fairy-tale format Lee has opposed romance and idealism, as represented by Alberic, with sophistication, corruption, and artifice.

Both "Prince Alberic and the Snake Lady" and "The Wedding Chest" present the disturbing image of a woman's naked body stabbed to death. This same image occurs in a story-within-an-essay, "Ravenna and Her Ghosts," first published in *Macmillan's* (September 1894) and included in Gregory's collection, *The Snake Lady, and Other Stories.* It also recalls the final description of Alice Oke, whose blood made "a pool of red . . . in her white dress." Gardner sees this image as a reversal of Lee's powerful lamialike figures, saying that the woman "characteristically appears in one of two conditions: either she is brutally sacrificed as in 'Prince Alberic' or she ruthlessly demands the sacrifice of others." However, the image of the brutalized woman could also be seen, in context with *Vanitas,* as Lee's reaction to women's place in society. The disturbing image suggests a woman's fate when men control her: she loses her own identity to become an object, the helpless victim of male aggression.

Between the publication of *Pope Jacynth and Other Fantastic Tales* and Lee's final volume of short stories, *For Maurice: Five Unlikely Stories* (1927), Lee published eighteen books. *Louis Norbert: A Two-Fold Romance* (1914) is a complex work in which two protagonists mirror Lee's own passion for historical research. Five other books were collections of her "genius loci" essays, written weekly for the *Westminster Gazette. The Handling of Words and Other Studies in Literary Psychology* (1923) was one of the first works to demonstrate close stylistic analyses of literary texts. Critic Kenneth Graham praises the book: it "contains not only a full exposition of point of view in its modern sense, but is in many respects one of the most remarkable of all late-Victorian pronouncements on the craft of fiction — and one that appears to have gone largely unremarked."

Perhaps most notable in this period was Lee's pacifism, which contributed both to her failure to secure a lasting reputation as a writer and to her growing isolation and loneliness as she aged. Lee strongly opposed the Boer War, an act that angered many of her English friends. She was alarmed by the growth of nationalism and worked strenuously against World War I, believing that international armaments manufacturers were playing on national fears to increase preparedness for war and thus maximize profits. After the war broke out she worked for a negotiated peace, fearing that the defeat of either side would eventually result in further hostilities. *Satan, the Waster: A Philosophic War Trilogy* (1920) included her

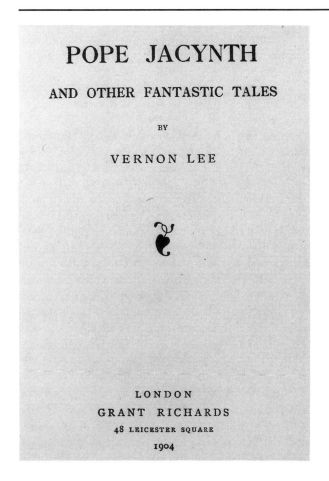

POPE JACYNTH

AND OTHER FANTASTIC TALES

BY

VERNON LEE

LONDON
GRANT RICHARDS
48 LEICESTER SQUARE
1904

Title page for Lee's second collection of stories with supernatural subjects (Courtesy of the Lilly Library, Indiana University)

earlier *The Ballet of the Nations: A Present-day Morality* (1915). Coming after the war, the book's ardent pacifism was somewhat accepted, and Bernard Shaw wrote a lengthy review of it in the *Nation,* congratulating her for her "intellectual force" and for keeping "her head when Europe was a mere lunatic asylum." Yet Shaw's praise did not restore her earlier reputation. Further, she was devastated by the damage done to the countryside she loved as well as by the changes that occurred in society as a result of the war. No longer sure of her power to sway people, to lead by her own moral and ethical principles, she lost self-confidence. Yet she achieved at least academic recognition when in 1924 the University of Durham made her an honorary doctor of letters.

For Maurice: Five Unlikely Stories was compiled for one of her closest friends and most loyal admirers, Maurice Baring, who was nearly twenty years her junior. In the introduction to this work, written in the same intimate style as both earlier prefaces, Lee places the stories in an autobiographical framework. One

part of this background recounts her inadvertent "cheating" of Baring as a child: he purchased *The Prince of the Hundred Soups* and enjoyed it so much he went back to the shop and bought *Belcaro,* believing it to be another fairy tale. When they met he told her this story, and she writes that she had "long determined to make amends to that Little Boy by giving him a book more like what he thought he was buying all those many, many years ago."

Like *Pope Jacynth, For Maurice* lacks thematic unity. The book received mixed reviews. Two of the tales, "The Gods and Ritter Tanhûser" and "Marsyas in Flanders," are retellings of legends; "The Doll," a story told to Lee by her friend Pier Desiderio Pasolini, returns to the obsession theme. "The Virgin of the Seven Daggers," subtitled "A Moorish Ghost Story of the Seventeenth Century," was first published in French as "La Madone aux sept glaives" in *Feuilleton du Journal des Debats du Samedi* (February 1896). The story is an account of Don Juan's loyalty to an image of the Virgin Mary.

"Winthrop's Adventure," the original version of "The Wicked Voice" from *Hauntings,* is the most intriguing of the stories because of its connection with Lee's own history. In 1872 Lee and Sargent found in Bologna a portrait of the Italian singer Carlo Broschi, a castrato who performed as Farinelli. In the introduction to *For Maurice* she writes that after seeing the portrait she felt "mingled love and wonder at the miracle of the human voice. . . . That was one half. The other was the attraction and terror, the mysteriousness, of bygone times." The time Lee devoted to this story suggests a personal significance: "The Culture-Ghost; or, Winthrop's Adventure" was first published in 1881 in *Fraser's Magazine;* then Lee completely reworked the story and republished it as "Voix Maudite" in *Les Lettres et les Arts* (1887) before including it in *Hauntings.* In discussing the two stories, with more emphasis on "A Wicked Voice," Carlo Caballero claims that "the alluring music she chose to perpetrate on Magnus ["The Wicked Voice"] haunted her, too." The story seems to have been significant for her in that it represents, as she says in the introduction, her "longing for the unattainable, with the passion only unattainable objects seem to inspire." Colby suggests that the theme of this story is similar to all of her supernatural tales with the past invading the present: "Because these are ghost stories, the influence is usually sinister, but there is no suggestion that either the past or its pursuit in the form of scholarship is intrinsically evil – simply that these are isolated incidents produced by the obsession of individuals, neurotics and madmen sometimes, but more often dedicated scholars exhausted and overwrought by their labors." Surely Lee had experienced such exhaustion firsthand.

In the last years of her life Lee became increasingly reclusive. Having gradually grown almost completely deaf, she maintained her friendships through letters. An earlier one to Placci, written in 1920, suggests her general attitude late in life: "Having what I want of you safely in the Past, I am reluctant to run risks with the present. We are neither of us the same and these war years have completed the transformation." Her last work, *Music and Its Lovers: An Empirical Study of Emotional and Imaginative Responses to Music* (1932), was the result of more than twenty-five years of study, yet it was both too academic for a popular audience and not rigorous enough for the academy. Lee died on 13 February 1935 after suffering for some years from heart trouble. She was buried near her stepbrother in Allori Cemetery in Florence.

Several collections of Lee's short stories have been published since her death. In the United States Gregory edited *The Snake Lady, and Other Stories*, a collection of several of her best stories; in England Cooper Willis edited *Supernatural Tales* (1955), a similar collection. Two collections were published in England: *Pope Jacynth and More Supernatural Tales: Excursions into Fantasy* (1956) and *The Virgin of the Seven Daggers* (1962), a reprint of the earlier *Supernatural Tales*. Reviewers found these collections dated and of interest primarily because the ghost tales could be viewed as psychological studies.

Royal A. Gettmann, who edited *The Handling of Words*, suggests that "variety and volume" have contributed to Lee's present neglect, adding that "her merits are not fully represented in any one work." Her failure to reach the public during her lifetime may be attributed to her distance – physically because she lived in Italy and had an expatriate's response to the English, intellectually because for all of her study of human responses to art she remained unaware of her own audience's preferences. Gunn sums up her importance as a short-story writer, claiming, "To readers of a certain type of mind – those who find pleasure in the psychological revivisence of the feelings and emotions of people in other places and other times – the short stories of Vernon Lee will always appeal."

Letters:

Vernon Lee's Letters (London: Privately printed, 1937).

Bibliographies:

Phyllis F. Mannocchi, " 'Vernon Lee': A Reintroduction and Primary Bibliography," *English Literature in Transition 1880–1920*, 26, no. 4 (1983): 231–267;

Carl Markgraf, "'Vernon Lee': A Commentary and Annotated Bibliography of Writings about Her," *English Literature in Transition 1880–1920*, 26, no. 4 (1983): 268–312.

Biography:

Peter Gunn, *Vernon Lee: Violet Paget, 1856–1935* (London, New York & Toronto: Oxford University Press, 1964).

References:

Maurice Baring, "Stimulants," in his *Lost Lectures* (London: Davies, 1932), pp. 82–90;

Carlo Caballero, " 'A Wicked Voice': On Vernon Lee, Wagner, and the Effects of Music," *Victorian Studies*, 35 (Summer 1992): 385–408;

Richard Cary, "Vernon Lee's Vignettes of Literary Acquaintances," *Colby Library Quarterly*, 9 (September 1970): 179–199;

Vineta Colby, "The Puritan Aesthete: Vernon Lee," in her *The Singular Anomaly: Women Novelists of the Nineteenth Century* (New York: New York University Press, 1970), pp. 235–304;

Burdett Gardner, "An Apology for Henry James's 'Tiger-Cat,' " *PMLA*, 68 (September 1953): 688–695;

Gardner, *The Lesbian Imagination (Victorian Style): A Psychological and Critical Study of "Vernon Lee"* (New York & London: Garland, 1987);

Kenneth Graham, *English Criticism of the Novel 1865–1900* (London: Oxford University Press, 1965);

Horace Gregory, "The Romantic Inventions of Vernon Lee," introduction to Lee's *The Snake Lady, and Other Stories*, edited by Gregory (New York: Grove, 1954), pp. 1–24;

Richard Ormond, "John Singer Sargent and Vernon Lee," *Colby Library Quarterly*, 9 (September 1970): 154–178;

Carl J. Weber, "Henry James and His Tiger-Cat," *PMLA*, 68 (September 1953): 672–687.

Papers:

The Vernon Lee Collection is at Colby College, Waterville, Maine.

Amy Levy

(10 November 1861 – 10 September 1889)

Audrey F. Horton
University of Miami School of Medicine

BOOKS: *Xantippe, and Other Verse* (Cambridge: Johnson, 1881);

A Minor Poet and Other Verse (London: Unwin, 1884);

The Romance of a Shop (London: Unwin, 1888; Boston: Cupples & Hurd, 1889);

Reuben Sachs: A Sketch (London & New York: Macmillan, 1888);

Miss Meredith (London: Hodder & Stoughton, 1889);

A London Plane-Tree, and Other Verse (London: Unwin, 1889; New York: Stokes, 1890).

Collection: *The Complete Novels and Selected Writings of Amy Levy, 1861–1889,* edited by Melvyn New (Gainesville: University of Florida Press, 1993).

OTHER: Jean Baptiste Pérès, *Historic and Other Doubts; or, The Non-Existence of Napoleon Proved,* translated by Levy (London: E. W. Allen, 1885);

Translations of works by Jehudah Halevl and Heinrich Heine in Katie (Lady) Magnus, *Jewish Portraits* (London: Routledge, 1888).

SELECTED PERIODICAL PUBLICATIONS –
UNCOLLECTED: "Mrs. Pierrepoint: A Sketch in Two Parts," anonymous, *Temple Bar,* 59 (June 1880): 226–236;

"Euphemia: A Sketch," *Victoria Magazine,* 36 (August–September 1880): 129–141, 199–203;

"James Thomson: A Minor Poet," *Cambridge Review,* 4 (February 1883): 240–241, 257–258;

"The Diary of a Plain Girl," anonymous, *London Society,* 44 (September 1883): 295–304;

"Olga's Valentine," anonymous, *London Society,* 45 (February 1884): 152–157;

"The New School of American Fiction," *Temple Bar,* 70 (March 1884): 383–389;

"In Holiday Humour," anonymous, *London Society,* 46 (August 1884): 177–184;

"In Retreat: A Long Vacation Experience," anonymous, *London Society,* 46 (September 1884): 332–335;

Amy Levy

"In the Black Forest," anonymous, *London Society,* 46 (October 1884): 392–394;

"Revenge," *London Society,* 47 (April 1885): 389–399;

"Easter-Tide at Tunbridge Wells," anonymous, *London Society,* 47 (May 1885): 481–483;

"Out of This World," anonymous, *London Society,* 49 (January 1886): 53–56;

"The Jew in Fiction," *Jewish Chronicle,* New Series 897 (June 1886): 13;

"Jewish Humour," *Jewish Chronicle,* New Series 908 (August 1886): 9–10;

"Jewish Children," *Jewish Chronicle,* New Series 919
(November 1886): 8;

"The Poetry of Christina Rossetti," *Woman's World,*
1 (1888): 178–180;

"A Woman's Club," *Woman's World,* 1 (1888): 364–
367;

"At Prato," *Time,* 19 (July 1888): 168–174;

"Eldorado at Islington," *Woman's World,* 2 (1889):
488–489.

In a letter to Helena Sickert dated October
1887, Oscar Wilde called "The Recent Telepathic
Occurrence at the British Museum" a "real literary
gem" and wrote that its author, Amy Levy, "has a
touch of genius in her work." He published this
story and others by Levy in his literary magazine
Woman's World. During her short lifetime she wrote
three novels, three volumes of poetry, a privately
published drama, translations, and several essays in
addition to her frequent short stories for Victorian
periodicals, some of which appeared unsigned. She
is perhaps best known as a minor poet and novelist
who committed suicide at age twenty-seven. While
she remained forgotten during most of the twentieth
century, interest in her work is growing. A 1993 collection of her works, edited by Melvyn New, includes her complete novels and selections from her
poems, short stories, and nonfiction. As he notes in
his introduction to the collection, "Amy Levy's
work deserves a modern audience it does not presently have."

Levy's short stories provide more than a
glimpse of her ability to write both light tales and
serious fiction; they illustrate the development of
her talents up to her death in 1889, when she had
earned a reputation as a promising young writer.
Their increasing attention to plot and detail hint at
her potential for greatness. Her stories focus upon
the disappointments and despair the world often
brings, revealing a characteristic frustration and depression as romantic idealism clashes with the realities of changing nineteenth-century society. Such
emotional responses are not limited to the women
Levy portrays through her light stories, such as
"Olga's Valentine" or "Revenge," but are also evident in the male characters of her more poignant
stories, such as "Sokratics in the Strand" and her
best-known story, "Cohen of Trinity" (1889).

The second daughter of Isabelle Levin Levy
and Lewis Levy, Amy Levy was born on 10 November 1861 in Clapham, England. In 1876 her family
moved to Brighton, where she began school. In
1879 she became the first Jew to study at Newnham
College, Cambridge, remaining there until 1881.

While at Cambridge she published a short story,
"Mrs. Pierrepoint: A Sketch in Two Parts," in the
June 1880 issue of *Temple Bar.* This light story of a
newly widowed and wealthy woman who attempts
to renew the relationship she forsook to marry well
exemplifies the themes of marriage and thwarted aspirations that later characterized Levy's fiction.
Death eventually came to dominate both her fiction
and her poetry.

While at Cambridge, Levy also published a
second story, "Euphemia: A Sketch," in *Victoria
Magazine* (August–September 1880), about a young
girl whose heritage is half-Jew, half-gentile. The
story is the first of only three instances in which
Levy portrays Jews in her fiction, but as Beth Zion
Lask points out, "there is no specific Jewish treatment of the characters." Levy's other two portrayals
of Jews occur in her novel *Reuben Sachs: A Sketch*
(1888) and "Cohen of Trinity."

Recorded biographical facts about Levy are
few and sometimes erroneous. One critic pronounced her to be a Clapham factory girl, but this
claim is not supported by any known evidence; her
publishing history contradicts the possibility of its
truth. Several sources report that she was a teacher;
one claims that she lived in a garret at some point.
However, both a tribute by Wilde in *Woman's World*
(1890) and a letter by Clementina Black to the *Athenaeum* (5 October 1889) attest that she "spent the
greater part of her short and uneventful life in London," except for visits to the sea or to Europe on
holidays. Details from her stories and her essays for
the *Jewish Chronicle* in 1886 provide evidence of her
travels. She had a knowledge of Greek and knew
French well enough to translate Jean Baptiste
Pérès's brochure *Comme quoi Napoléon n'a jamais existé*
in 1885. She was secretary of the Beaumont Trust
in 1886, when her father was president, and letters
confirm that just prior to her death in 1889 she traveled with writer Olive Schreiner to the seashore.
Another source mentions visits with her friend Vernon Lee, and Deborah Epstein Nord has found evidence that Levy was part of a female community in
the 1880s that included Schreiner, Beatrice Webb,
Margaret Harkness, Eleanor Marx, and others.

Levy anonymously published "The Diary of a
Plain Girl" in the September 1883 issue of *London
Society.* In keeping with the magazine's subtitle, "An
Illustrated Magazine of Light and Amusing Literature for the Hours of Relaxation," the story is seemingly a simple tale of rivalry between sisters Milly,
the plain girl, and her beautiful sister, Dalia. However, Levy takes subtle swipes at a society that so
highly values female beauty and fosters female van-

ity. Reminiscent of those of Jane Austen, Levy's characters reveal society's focus upon assuring that young ladies marry well: "Mamma called me downstairs, and lectured me after breakfast. She said I was a disgrace to the family and her training. That I had no more breeding than a housemaid. That a woman who is not beautiful has her own career to make. That a well-bred and charming woman can always hold her own in society, whatever be her physical disadvantages." Levy uses marriage as a traditional sentimental device as the story ends. Just when Milly thinks she "shall always be a lonely woman," dashing Ralston Owens proposes marriage and she accepts. "But, strange to say, in a few short hours I have grown to believe it; it seems the most natural thing in the world as though we had belonged to one another from the beginning to all time."

"Between Two Stools," one of Levy's many epistolary stories, appeared in the November 1883 issue of *Temple Bar,* a popular middle-class literary magazine. The six letters from Nora Wycherly to her friend Agnes Crew at Newnham College, Cambridge, chronicle ten months of activity, during which Nora rejects a marriage proposal from Stephen Broke because she imagines herself in love with Reginald Talbot. The story is well paced and suspenseful up to the point when, faced with both men at a dinner party, Nora realizes her mistaken ideas about Talbot: "An awful sense of humiliation, of terror, rushed across me. What had I done? And then it flashed through my mind that here again was the old, old story of substance and shadow!"

Throughout the otherwise light prose, Levy includes interesting details of women's rebellion. Nora's "new dress," in a style fashionable at Cambridge, causes a stir: "The absence of stays and crinollette almost wrung tears from the various members of my family." On her reception in society Nora writes, "A woman is held to have no absolute value; it is relative, and depends on the extent of the demand for her among members of the other sex . . . Nobody wants a girl for her soul and a rather fine critical perception." Living "in the very heart and centre of Philistia," Nora describes life after Cambridge, expressing what might have been Levy's own feelings: "I am willing enough to smoke the pipe of peace with the philistines, but the philistines will have none of me. They distrust me: the girls think I want to 'come it over' them; and the young men are continually on the look-out for covert snubbing. One is afraid to call a thing by its right name for fear of being thought pedantic; it is not young-ladylike to have one's facts right or one's sentences

logical. A pretty haziness, a charming inconsequence – these are the qualities the Philistine male would fain see in this womankind." As New points out, "One cannot read two paragraphs of Nora's correspondence without appreciating Levy's self-parody of intellectual pretensions, her recognition of and amusement over the incipient snobbery and self-importance that almost surely accompanied a career as successful as hers gave promise of being."

Levy's early short stories fluctuate between leisure reading and serious fiction. Nowhere is this more apparent than in a comparison of her simultaneous magazine publications for February 1884. While her light, amusing story "Olga's Valentine" was being consumed by the readers of *London Society,* readers of the *Cambridge Review* were challenged by the philosophical dialogue of her "Sokratics in the Strand." As the tale of a young woman who, despite being considered an old maid by her family, receives a "valentine," a marriage proposal, "Olga's Valentine" is similar to "The Diary of a Plain Girl." However, Levy's literary development is evident in its conciseness and increased sympathy for Olga: "O, if I were only a man, the veriest fogey in the doorway, it would be better than this."

"Sokratics in the Strand" is a more complex and disturbing venture. Unlike Levy's earlier stories, no dances, dinner parties, or travels are mentioned here, only the harsh realities of the contrasting lives of the two characters, the barrister Vincent and the poet Horace. Levy eschews romantic images for realistic ones, describing both the characters and the setting in great detail. At the poet's meager residence, "not far from Charing Cross Station" in the Strand, a dirty, working-class section of London, the two discuss suicide. Horace passionately expresses his idea that suicide is not a surrender but a logical choice for one "unfit for life"; it is an option he eventually chooses.

A two-part review of the works of James Thomson (B.V.), which Levy published in the February 1883 *Cambridge Review,* is important in understanding her treatment of death in "Sokratics in the Strand." The review, written a few months after Thomson's death, indicates that she felt a kinship with this poet, who is best known for his pessimistic look at London, *The City of Dreadful Night and Other Poems* (1880). In his work she found "a great human soul, horribly vital and sensitive in all its parts, struggling with a great agony." She laments that he never became more than "a minor poet" before his death. However, she denied any personal over-identification with his pessimism: "He dwells on a view of things which is morbid, nay false, which does not exist for the perfectly healthy human being." Nonetheless, Thomson's works influenced Levy, both in her poetry and prose. The final paragraph of "Sokratics in the Strand" expresses her feelings on a poet's suicide almost a year after Thomson's: "Poets, and those afflicted with the so-called 'poetic temperament,' although constantly contemplating it, rarely commit suicide; they have too much imagination. The click of the self-slaughterer's pistol (I speak with due allowance for metaphor) is oftener to be heard in Mincing Lane and Capel Court than in the regions of Grub Street and Parnassus Hill."

"In Holiday Humour," published in *London Society* (August 1884), is another light story in the vein of "The Diary of a Plain Girl." Taking its title from William Shakespeare's *As You Like It* (1599), the story centers on Olivia, who while "in holiday humour" consents to marriage, only to decline the offer later when her mood changes. Levy uses nature throughout the story as an appropriate background to Olivia's emotions; she realizes her mistake during a violent storm, and later, as she rejects Mr. Tresidder, "the moon went suddenly behind a cloud, and the place grew dark."

In September 1884 Levy began a series of four epistolary travel sketches in *London Society* that continued until January 1886. Written by Melissa to her friend Blanche and later to her friend Psyche, the sketches chronicle Melissa's travels through the Continent and the English countryside. In addition to the sketches, "Revenge," another of Levy's tales of young girls hoping to marry well, also appeared in *London Society* in April 1885.

There is evidence that Levy based at least one of the travel sketches on her own experiences. After her death the Shakespeare scholar Harry Quilter wrote in the April 1890 *Universal Review* of having traveled into the West Country years before "to an old stone manor house, which has now for many a year been used as a convent by the nuns of Lanherne." During his stay at a country hostel his hostess told him about Levy, who had visited there previously:

she had been a dweller in Bloomsbury all her life, and knew nothing about the country; and my landlady had, in her capacity of nurse, taken her into the woods and fields, and down amongst the caves on the Porth, and taught her all those strange, hidden trifles of earth, sea, and air, which only the dwellers in, and lovers of, the country know, and the girl – for she was quite a girl then – had taught her instructress – what? Had you asked Miss ——, she would have told you that there was little or nothing of which she had not talked with her

patient, on which her patient had not some store of knowledge and thought.

In the last of Levy's travel sketches, "Out of This World," which was published in *London Society* (January 1886), Melissa writes to Psyche from the "Yale of Lanherne, Cornwall," and in addition to detailing a visit to the Lanherne convent, she mentions, "My kind hostess has instructed me in bread-making and cream-scalding, and is quite capable of giving instructions in a great many other things. We mix Matthew Arnold with our pastry, and wage war on questions of 'the infinite' as we chop meat for pies. . . ."

Levy did not publish another story until "Griselda," which appeared in *Temple Bar* (September 1888). As in her earlier stories of girls longing to marry well, the plot centers around Griselda MacRonan, daughter of an Irish viscount, and her social turmoil as her family is forced to live anonymously in England as "only the MacRonans, obscure Irish strangers, in poor lodgings." The longest of Levy's short stories, it stretches through six chapters and a "postscript." New notes that while "clearly [Levy] is generating material for which readers – and hence publishers – were willing to pay," there is an evident stylistic development in this story: "Levy is beginning to develop some distinction of style to accompany her clarity and exquisite observations."

The stories that follow "Griselda" are characterized by their brevity. Indeed, the length of "The Recent Telepathic Occurrence at the British Museum," as well as the great passion it contains, was what prompted Wilde to publish it in the first volume of *Woman's World* in 1888. He called it "a good example of Miss Levy's extraordinary power of condensation. The story occupied only about a page of this magazine, and it gives the whole history of a wasted and misunderstood love. There is not so much as a name in it, but the relation of the man and woman stands out vivid as if we had known and watched its growth." The story signifies a further development in both her style and theme. In the short narrative space she carries readers from a young woman's deathbed to the British Museum, where an apparition appears before "the Professor," the man who had refused the dying woman's love. Leaving both characters nameless heightens the universal nature of "the wasted days, the wasted loves, the wonderful wasted chances!"

Equally well-crafted is "At Prato," published in the July 1888 issue of *Time*. A young photographer, Ivan Callander, finds himself entranced by a beautiful woman as they both wait for the next train to Florence. Levy combines realistic details with romantic imagery as, during the two-hour wait, the man falls in love with and is utterly defeated by the enchanting Elinor, who reveals herself as "not a good woman" and eventually abandons him. As the plot unfolds in a hotel sitting room, Levy juxtaposes images of life and death outside in the piazza. The story ends in a transformation reminiscent of, but counter to, that experienced by the wedding guest in Samuel Taylor Coleridge's *The Rime of the Ancient Mariner* (1798). The man experiences a profound change: "Sometimes he wonders if it were indeed a living woman, or a beautiful, sad vision, that talked with him that night in Prato." Others around him notice: "Meanwhile, Ivan Callander's friends shake their heads over the change in him; unaccountable, indescribable, yet in some painful and subtle manner, a change affecting his whole personality."

Levy's next contribution to *Woman's World* was "Eldorado at Islington" (1889). Though not as successful as her earlier contribution, the story reveals an interesting contrast between two women, the dreaming Eleanor and her practical mother. A poor family suddenly faces the prospect of wealth, only to learn that the money to be theirs had been taken from other poor people; they cannot accept it. The two women react in opposite ways to the bad news. Although Eleanor maintains that she "knew it could not be true" all along, she is nonetheless angry and saddened. Levy presents the contrast in describing the mother's actions: "Meantime, in the parlour, the mother comforted her children. It was Eleanor who had believed in Eldorado, and yet who had cried, 'I knew it!' The mother, whose heart had throughout refused to accept the glad tidings, made no such proclamation. She quieted the crying child, handed Eddy his tea, and taking up the loaf, began to cut it." The mother returns her household to normal.

In May 1889 *Gentleman's Magazine* featured Levy's "Cohen of Trinity." It would become her best-known short story largely because of its parallels to the author's life, since the character Cohen is a Jew and commits suicide. Critic Edward Wagenknecht calls "Cohen of Trinity" the "most important of the author's other writings about Jews" after *Reuben Sachs,* her most acclaimed novel, which provides an engrossing look at hypocrisy and despair in London Jewish society through the actions of the title character, his family, and his friend Judith.

Told by a character who had known and admits a fair disdain for the "desperately lonely and desperately unapproachable" Cohen, the story begins in the present and then flashes back to events leading up to the suicide. Despite the success of his brilliant book, *Gubernator,* Cohen remains unsatisfied with his life and his achievements. Levy vividly profiles his cravings. At one point the narrator recalls telling Cohen, "I should say the difference from your point of view was a very great one. But you always chose to cry for the moon." Cohen replies that "it's the only thing worth having." Critic Linda Gertner Zatlin compares Levy's experience with *Reuben Sachs* to the fictional character Cohen's disappointment regarding *Gubernator:* "It is not known whether Levy committed suicide for the same reason [as Cohen] – her novel about Jews had met with an unfavorable reaction – but the story does detail a Jew's despair at not finding the exact success of which he dreamed."

Levy's last contribution to *Temple Bar* was "A Slip of the Pen" (July 1889). Despite its loose construction and a somewhat frivolous plot, it is an amusing tale about Ethel, a young girl whose "slip" in writing a luncheon invitation causes embarrassment but reveals an inner desire. Levy mixes humor throughout the story, as in her description of Ethel's reaction to her mistake: "Ethel astonished her family at dinner that evening by enquiries as to the state of the female labour-market in New Zealand." Like all of Levy's stories about girls longing to marry well, it reveals details about the protocols of Victorian society and the issues that young unwed women faced.

Levy took her own life by inhaling charcoal fumes at her parents' house on 10 September 1889. She had corrected the proofs of her volume *A London Plane-Tree, and Other Verse* less than one week earlier. Cremated at Woking on 13 September, Levy became the second Jew and the first Jewish woman to be cremated in England. On 15 September 1889 her ashes were buried at Balls Pond cemetery in London. A will signed on 4 December 1888 left all her books, papers, letters, and "documents of every kind and copyright" to friend and writer Clementina Black. To dispel rumors surrounding Levy's suicide, Black wrote a letter, published in the 5 October 1889 issue of the *Athenaeum,* disputing the rumor that her depression was caused by increasing blindness, "the loss of her sense of humour," or for always being treated "coldly" by family members and the Jewish community for *Reuben Sachs.* Black maintains that while Levy "did suffer for several years from slight deafness," her "fits of extreme depression" and eventual death resulted from "her lack of physical robustness and . . . the exhaustion produced by strenuous brain work."

While the reason for Levy's suicide remains unclear, clues to her feelings on being a woman writer may be discerned from her last short story, "Wise in Her Generation," published after her death in *Woman's World* (1890). Similar in theme to her earlier romances, the plot is much more complex. The narrator, Virginia, has become "wise" in the year that has passed since Philip Shand broke her heart to marry a wealthier girl. Virginia has learned "the game" well enough to win a marriage proposal from Sir Guy Ormond. In reference to a female poet named Medora Grey, who is older, unwed, and vying for Ormond's attention, Virginia protests, "Heaven save me from the laurels of third-rate female celebrity! Unless she happens to be Patti, or Lady Burdett-Coutts, or Queen Elizabeth, there is only one way of success open to a woman: the way of marriage." New believes "Wise in Her Generation" to be "Levy's clearest look at female cynicism, a product of the 'marriage game' that seems to have engaged so many Victorian women, Jew and non-Jew alike."

Although never more than a minor writer during her lifetime, as a Jew and a woman Levy remains an important writer of the Victorian era. Her short fiction reveals her development as a writer who learned to craft language meticulously in order to reveal the complexities of life in condensed, compact, and memorable scenes. As Wilde wrote after her death, "her work was not poured out lightly, but drawn drop by drop from the very depth of her own feeling. We may say of it that it was in truth her life's blood."

References:

Beth Zion Abrahams, "Amy Levy: Poet and Writer," *Anglo-Jewish Association Quarterly*, 6, no. 3 (1960): 11–17;

Clementina Black, letter, *Athenaeum* (5 October 1889): 457;

Brian Cheyette, "From Apology to Revolt: Benjamin Farjeon, Amy Levy, and the Post-Emancipation Anglo-Jewish Novel," *Jewish Historical Society of England Transactions* (January 1985): 254–265;

Linda Hunt, "Amy Levy and the 'Jewish Novel': Representing Jewish Life in the Victorian Period," *Studies in the Novel*, 26 (Fall 1994): 235–253;

Beth Zion Lask, "Amy Levy," *Jewish Historical Society of England Transactions*, 11 (1924–1927): 168–189;

Deborah Epstein Nord, "'Neither Pairs Nor Odd': Female Community in Late Nineteenth-Century London," *Signs: Journal of Women in Culture and Society*, 15 (Summer 1990): 733–754;

Harry Quilter, "Amy Levy," *Universal Review*, 6 (April 1890): 492–507;

Edward Wagenknecht, "Amy Levy," in his *Daughters of the Covenant: Portraits of Six Jewish Women* (Amherst: University of Massachusetts Press, 1983), pp. 55–93;

Oscar Wilde, "Amy Levy," *Woman's World*, 3 (1890): 51–52;

Linda Gertner Zatlin, *The Anglo-Jewish Novel in the Nineteenth Century* (Boston: Twayne, 1981), pp. 90–97.

Arthur Machen

(3 March 1863 – 15 December 1947)

Adrian Eckersley
Birkbeck College, London University

See also the Machen entry in *DLB 36: British Novelists, 1890–1929: Modernists.*

BOOKS: *Eleusinia, by a Former Member of H.C.S.* (Hereford: Privately printed, 1881);

The Anatomy of Tobacco: or Smoking Methodised, Divided, and Considered after a New Fashion, by Leolinus Siluriensis, Professor of Fumifical Philosophy in the University of Brentford (London: Redway, 1884; New York: Boni & Liveright, 1923); as Arthur Machen, with new introduction (New York: Knopf, 1926);

The Chronicle of Clemendy (London: Privately printed, 1888; Carbonnek, N.Y.: Privately printed, 1923);

The Great God Pan and The Inmost Light (London: John Lane, 1894; Boston: Roberts, 1894);

The Three Impostors (London: John Lane, 1895; Boston: Roberts, 1895);

Hieroglyphics (London: Richards, 1902; New York: Kennerley, 1913);

The House of the Hidden Light (London: Privately printed, 1904);

The House of Souls (London: Richards, 1906; Boston: Estes, 1906; with different contents, New York: Knopf, 1922);

Dr. Stiggins: His Views and Principles (London: Griffiths, 1906; New York: Knopf, 1925);

The Hill of Dreams (London: Richards, 1907; Boston: Estes, 1907);

The Angels of Mons: The Bowmen and Other Legends of the War (London: Simpkin, Marshall, Hamilton, Kent, 1915; New York: Putnam, 1915);

The Great Return (London: Faith Press, 1915);

The Terror: A Fantasy (London: Duckworth, 1917); republished as *The Terror: A Mystery* (New York: McBride, 1917);

War and the Christian Faith (London: Skeffington, 1918);

The Secret Glory (London: Secker, 1922; New York: Knopf, 1922);

Arthur Machen in 1909

Far Off Things (London: Secker, 1922; New York: Knopf, 1922);

Things Near and Far (London: Secker, 1923; New York: Knopf, 1923);

The Grand Trouvaille: A Legend of Pentonville (London: Privately printed, 1923);

The Shining Pyramid (Chicago: Covici-McGee, 1923; with different contents, London: Secker, 1925; New York: Knopf, 1925);

The Collector's Craft (London: Privately printed, 1923);

Strange Roads (London: Classic Press, 1923);

Caerleon Edition of the Works, 9 volumes (London: Secker, 1923);

Dog and Duck (New York: Knopf, 1924; London: Cape, 1924);

The London Adventure (London: Secker, 1924; New York: Knopf, 1924);

The Glorious Mystery, edited by Vincent Starrett (Chicago: Covici-McGee, 1924);

Precious Balms (London: Spurr & Swift, 1924);

Ornaments in Jade (New York: Knopf, 1924);

The Canning Wonder (London: Chatto & Windus, 1925; New York: Knopf, 1926);

Dreads and Drolls (London: Secker, 1926; New York: Knopf, 1927);

Notes and Queries (London: Spurr & Swift, 1926);

A Souvenir of Cadby Hall (London: Lyons, 1927);

Tom O'Bedlam and His Song (Westport, Conn.: Apellicon, 1930);

Beneath the Barley: A Note on the Origins of Eleusinia (London: Privately printed, 1931);

In the 'Eighties (Amersham: Privately printed, 1931);

The Glitter of the Brook (Dalton, Ga.: Postprandial, 1932);

The Green Round (London: Benn, 1933; Sauk City, Wis.: Arkham House, 1968);

The Cosy Room and Other Stories (London: Rich & Cowan, 1936);

The Children of the Pool and Other Stories (London: Hutchinson, 1936);

Holy Terrors (London: Penguin, 1946);

Tales of Horror and the Supernatural, edited by Philip Van Doren Stern (New York: Knopf, 1948; London: Richards, 1949);

Bridles and Spurs (Cleveland: Rowfant Club, 1951);

A Critical Essay (Lakewood, Ohio: Privately printed, 1953);

A Note on Poetry (Wichita, Kans.: Four Ducks Press, 1959);

Eleusinia and Beneath the Barley (West Warwick, R.I.: Necronomicon Press, 1988);

Ritual and Other Stories (Lewes, U.K.: Tartarus, 1992);

The Secret of the Sangraal (Lewes, U.K.: Tartarus, 1995).

OTHER: Marguerite, Queen of Navarre, *The Heptameron,* translated by Machen (London: Dryden Press, 1886; New York: Scribner & Welford, 1887);

Beroalde de Verville, *Fantastic Tales or The Way to Attain,* translated by Machen (London: Privately printed, 1890; Carbonnek, N.Y.: Boni & Liveright, 1923);

The Memoirs of Jacques Casanova, 12 volumes, translated by Machen (London: Privately printed, 1894); republished as *The Memoires of Jacques Casanova,* 12 volumes (New York: Society of Bibliophiles, 1920); republished as *The Memoirs of Giacomo Casanova di Seingalt,* 12 volumes (London: Casanova Society, 1922); republished as *The Memoirs of Jacques Casanova de Seingalt,* 12 volumes (New York: Aventuros, 1925); republished as *Giacomo Casanova: His Life and Memoirs,* 2 volumes (New York: Knopf, 1929); republished in abridged form as *My Life and Adventures by Casanova Chevalier de Seingalt* (London: Joiner & Steele, 1932); republished as *The Memoirs of Jacques Casanova de Seingalt: 1725–1798,* 8 volumes (Edinburgh: Limited Editions Club, 1940).

Arthur Machen's long career was diverse in both interest and achievement. Beginning in the 1880s and 1890s as an aesthete, he later became a master of the horror tale, moved on to create almost single-handedly what might be called the tale of spiritual awakening, wrote three volumes of autobiography often judged classics of the genre, and as journalist and essayist fought passionately against the prevalent materialistic values of the age in which he lived. His best-known short story, "The Bowmen" (1915), was set in World War I and became a cause célèbre, as many people believed that the supernatural events he had invented were a record of what had truly taken place. Yet his earnings from literature were meager. He inspired intense enthusiasms in a variety of discerning minorities, many of them younger writers, but achieved real popularity only briefly, in the 1920s in the United States, when the proselytizing of August Derleth, Vincent Starrett, and H. P. Lovecraft gave him a powerful following, creating a genre in his image.

Arthur Llewellyn Jones Machen was born in the Welsh border town of Caerleon on Usk, the ancient Isca of the Romans and the legendary seat of King Arthur. He was the only son of John Edward Jones, an Anglican clergyman, and Janet Machen, a Scot, and was brought up in the rectory at Llandewi, the tiny parish near Caerleon served by his father. His isolated childhood led him to a passionate, Wordsworthian identification with the landscape of the Gwent district around Caerleon, which informs much of his fiction and autobiography. He was sent to Hereford School, where he was known as Jones-Machen and where he acquired some of the tools of scholarship. He was unable, however, to follow in his father's footsteps either to

Oxford or into the priesthood because of his family's lack of means. In June 1880 he took the exam for the Royal College of Surgeons, but his plans for a medical career soon faded and were replaced by the urge to write.

In the early 1880s Machen lived a lonely and poverty-stricken existence in a variety of London lodgings. He fell into an awed love/hate relationship with London's infinite variety and supported himself as best he could with tutoring while he read and explored the city. By 1884 he had met George Redway, an antiquarian bookseller, publisher, and magazine editor, who began to employ Machen as a catalouger and subeditor and who published, at Machen's expense, *The Anatomy of Tobacco: or Smoking Methodised, Divided, and Considered after a New Fashion,* by Leolinus Siluriensis, Professor of Fumifical Philosophy in the University of Brentford (1884), a work neither of fact nor fiction but actually a parody of a standard philosophy textbook written in a pastiche of seventeenth-century English. All of Machen's longer work published in the 1880s is written in this deliberately archaic style, an early indication of how passionately at odds he was with the spirit of his own time.

Much of Machen's work in the 1880s involved translation from the French. In his first work of fiction – *The Chronicle of Clemendy* (1888), a frame tale in the manner of Giovanni Boccaccio's *The Decameron* (1351–1353) and of the *Heptameron* (1559) of Marguerite of Navarre, which he had translated in 1886 – he began to explore the short tale. The overall aim of this work is to paint an ideal picture of a preindustrial Gwent, set in a seventeenth-century past, with a sense of festival and well-being. Within this context narrators come forward and tell their best tales. Several of the themes later important to Machen are already apparent. In "The Story of a Red Jar," for example, a monk drinks a vintage left over from pagan times and has a visionary experience of dancing maenads, the first example of a surfacing of primitive paganism. In "The Rubrican's First Tale" an alchemist-necromancer seduces an otherworldly girl through his unspeakable powers, linking black magic with a dark sexuality. Many of the tales are concerned with the trials of romantic love, and some show a keen sense of the darkly fantastic – for example, "Signor Piero Latini's Tale," in which a Renaissance Italian duke builds a vast doorless and windowless wall around his wife and her lover, whom he has caught flagrante delicto. Machen's aim in the book as a whole, however, which is to communicate a sense of wonder at the beauty of a community dedicated to wholesome fes-

tival, is at odds with the darker notes of some of the best stories in the collection: the writer will not allow the mood to grow dark enough to cloud the sense of merriment. Many of the framed short tales succeed where the work as a whole does not.

Though Machen did not publish much in periodicals, the shorter tale is central to his fiction: only two of his many works really qualify as novels, and *The Chronicle of Clemendy* is not his only longer work that is effectively a collection of short pieces. In the earlier stages of his career he was uninterested in the creation of character or social commentary. He worked toward creating a sense of evil, above all by suggesting the material presence of dark and primitive pagan powers.

With the turn of the decade he abandoned his attempts at archaism. Though his prose from this point consists of the measured music and sonorous vocabulary of the 1890s, he writes in a way that calls no attention to his artistry. The reader is invited implicitly to look not at the surface of the writing but through it to the narrative it conveys. His break with the archaism beloved of an older generation of writers, such as William Morris, constitutes his artistic coming of age, a placing of trust in his imagination rather than his considerable stylistic flair. His decision to leave archaism behind might also have been prompted by minor subeditorial and journalistic successes as well as by emulation of the successes of Arthur Conan Doyle and Robert Louis Stevenson.

About this time Machen began to publish some very short pieces, rather anecdotal in tone, in journals such as *The Globe* and the *St. James's Gazette,* several of which explore the possibility of fantastic events in a contemporary London setting. Most notable of these is "A Double Return" (1890), in which a man returns home to find that an actor has successfully impersonated his return the night before. The result of the presumable impropriety, to which the text makes no reference, is rather savage: the husband leaves for America, and the wife dies within a year. The text leaves the reader in doubt as to how to connect these events but succeeds well in communicating the sense of a hidden sexuality at work.

In 1894, with the publication by John Lane in book form of Machen's long short story "The Great God Pan," together with "The Inmost Light," he achieved notoriety if not fame. In the tale a doctor believes he can perform an operation to restore a vital, primitive vision to modern humanity – a process to which he refers metaphorically as "seeing the god Pan." He experiments on a female dependent, who on awaking from the operation seems indeed to have realized ecstasy but collapses into idiocy. The later result of the treatment is that she has a child, whom the reader understands as having been fathered by Pan himself. The child grows up to become a devil-woman, consorting with Pan and driving the libertine men who associate with her to suicide. She is tracked down slowly but relentlessly by Villiers, a kind of occultist version of Edgar Allan Poe's Auguste Dupin or Doyle's Sherlock Holmes who appears in more than one of Machen's short tales. When Villiers finally corners the daughter of Pan, she degenerates spectacularly into primeval slime.

Through this story Machen shares with his readers a sense of horror at the possibility of an evil that may be seen as rooted in sexuality, a sense no doubt based in the idea of degeneration, the reverse side of Charles Darwin's evolutionary theories. The other story in the volume, "The Inmost Light," also contains a mad scientist, a devil-woman, and a detective, Dyson. While wandering in the remote London suburb of Harlesden, Dyson glimpses something that is and is not a woman's face at a window. He reports, "I knew I had looked into another world – looked through the window of a commonplace, brand-new house, and seen hell open before me." He learns that this woman's husband, Dr. Black, has given in to a lust for knowledge that has made a subhuman monster of his suffering and complaisant wife. Thus both tales document the irruption into the everyday of the hideously primeval through the action of a scientist upon a woman.

The book was widely noticed but criticized on two counts. One was its refusal to go into detail: the scenes in "The Great God Pan" in which the devil-woman drives her lovers to suicide are left to the imagination, and many critics complained of this lack of substance. The other criticism was that through its frame of reference, which was much wider than the conventional supernatural tale, the story was in bad taste. One female reviewer found it "an unmanly tale," no doubt responding to its powerful negative sexuality. Both criticisms, though somewhat mutually contradictory, have some justice. To a modern reader both tales are strong on atmosphere, but the moments in which frisson is intended are not always successful.

In these tales the main characteristics of Machen's early short fiction can be seen clearly. His aim was always to create a sense of wonder or of horror, yet two factors make his work stand out from others of the genre. First, he draws extensively on a world that is known to him and to the reader;

Cover for the first American edition of Machen's 1894 collection of two stories featuring mad scientists and the supernatural

the settings for most of his stories are a London or Gwent that he knows intimately. Second, he is uninterested in the merely fanciful. The horrible and, later, the marvelous are imagined as partaking of the world of physical and social reality, available to the senses of all. Machen often emphasizes this by using a wide range of narrators and viewpoints. Though he was not a writer of science fiction, he shared with writers of that genre the ability and the wish to impart a sense of concrete particularity to what he imagined. Yet his is not a great inventive imagination; he works with a limited palette, and many of his stories can be read as close variations upon one another.

In 1895 John Lane published *The Three Impostors,* another frame tale more celebrated in its parts, the best of which have often been anthologized, than as a whole. The constituent tales are designated as "novels." "The Novel of the White Powder" concerns a brilliant young man who, suffering from neurasthenia, takes a mistaken remedy that causes him to decompose into primeval slime. "The Novel of the Black Seal" is the tale of another scientist, Professor Clegg, who discovers in the "grey hills" a degenerate species of protohumans, on whom superstitions of the fairies are based, whose unstable protoplasm may be commanded by ancient words of power. These stories detail a horror connected to the primeval and primitive in one form or another, and this theme may be linked with the concern of the 1880s and 1890s in general with the figure of the degenerate beast, as evinced in stories such as Stevenson's *The Strange Case of Dr. Jekyll and Mr. Hyde* (1886), Oscar Wilde's *The Picture of Dorian Gray* (1891), and Bram Stoker's *Dracula* (1897). At the root of the sense of horror in all these tales, in none more than Machen's, is humanity's horror at the image of its own animality, as adumbrated by Darwin and Thomas Henry Huxley.

Machen married his first wife, Amy Hogg, in 1887. By the later 1890s he had found a stable if not well-remunerated way of life in London, had found faithful friends, and was a member of the Golden Dawn occult circle. He was a writer of pronounced aesthete sympathies, though not quite part of the inner circle of Aubrey Beardsley, Arthur Symons, or William Butler Yeats. Nonetheless, he suffered their fate. The changing climate of the times increasingly judged the "decadent" aesthetes as degenerate; Wilde, who fell from grace in 1895, was an early victim of this trend. The result for Machen was that, though the years around 1897 were his best in terms of the creation of fiction, nothing he wrote then was published until much later. "The White People" is the testament of a young girl haunted by pagan powers. His most often anthologized piece and judged his finest by Lovecraft, this work is remarkable for its juxtaposition of the narrator's naiveté and the evil that surrounds her. It was first published in *Horlick's Magazine* in 1904.

Machen's longest and best work, the novel *The Hill of Dreams,* finally appeared in 1907 after magazine serial publication in 1904 in *Horlick's Magazine* as "The Garden of Avallaunius," but another major achievement, a linked series of very short pieces, did not appear until 1924, when they were published in the United States as *Ornaments in Jade.* In "The Turanians" a girl who is chided for saying to her mother that a rose she has seen "burnt like a flame" is drawn to a group of Gypsies she observes. At the end of the story she lies suffused with pleasure, clutching "a small green stone . . . awful with age." In "The Ceremony" a girl watches in terror as another makes a painful blood sacrifice to an ancient stone that as an initiate she herself will make later. In these pieces there are secret watchers drawn into mystery, which is both visionary and often ambiguously sexual. They draw their power from a revaluation of the pagan roots from which horror is derived in stories such as "The Great God Pan."

The last of the *Ornaments in Jade,* "The Holy Things," is an account of a mystical vision unconnected with paganism, sacrifice, or the primitive. A disillusioned artist contemplates the town of Holborn, which suddenly throbs with a sense of spiritual wonder and regeneration, and a heavenly choir begins to sound as everything around him is transfigured. If Machen's horror stories of the 1890s derive from the frame tales within *The Chronicle of Clemendy,* then this piece, and others that echo its concerns, derive from the main aim of that work — to describe a world reborn. The first of such pieces to appear was the novella "A Fragment of Life," published in the collection *The House of Souls* (1906), in which "The White People" and *The Three Impostors* were republished. "A Fragment of Life" is the antithesis of the pagan tales. Darnell, the hero, is a quiet clerk who lives in the suburbs. The reader follows his day-to-day decisions about furnishing his small house and coping with minor domestic crises relating to a servant girl and a relative of his wife. In Machen's quiet crafting of a credible existence his rarely exhibited novelistic powers are at work. Gradually Darnell confides to his wife some experiences he had dismissed as almost trivial: an awakening to a sense of splendor in the city and in nature around him. Slowly and hesitantly he comes spiritually alive and begins to make tentative decisions to move to his native Wales, giving up the materially bound life of a city clerk and seeking the distant heritage of his ancestors.

Its quietness of tone and absolute authenticity make "A Fragment of Life" the most impressive of Machen's works concerning rebirth or spiritual awakening. It is less overtly powerful but more convincing than many of his later efforts in this vein. Perhaps he was documenting his own experience in the 1890s, when he looked back to his days in Gwent and began to make sense of the experiences he had had as a child. On this foundation he built his increasingly orthodox Anglo-Catholic faith, which gave him in turn the standpoint from which he became in fiction and in polemics an archenemy of Protestantism and the materialism he saw as its child.

At the end of 1899 Machen's wife died, and he was plunged into personal breakdown and crisis.

The first page of the manuscript for an introduction to a new edition of Machen's 1895 book The Three Impostors *(from Adrian Goldstone and Wesley Sweetser,* A Bibliography of Arthur Machen, *1965)*

Perhaps as a therapeutic measure, he temporarily abandoned the solitary craft of writing and became an actor with Frank Benson's troupe of repertory players. Through the troupe he met his second wife, Purefoy Hudleston, whom he married in 1903; they had two children, Hilary and Janet. During the Edwardian decade his fortunes as a writer improved: *Hieroglyphics,* his book of literary theory, was published in 1902, and his friend A. E. Waite became the editor of the literary periodical *Horlick's Magazine,* which gave a first, though not a wide, exposure to "The White People," "A Fragment of Life," and *The Hill of Dreams.* But his successes of this decade were mainly based upon work conceived and largely executed in the 1890s. His relatively few new ideas did not find publication until a later decade.

Had Machen died young he would be remembered as a member of the aesthete brotherhood who had an unparalleled sense of the demonic, which was linked with paganism, sexuality, and the primeval. Though he continued until old age to write in this vein, in the 1910s the promise implicit in "A Fragment of Life" was fulfilled. He had always hated the world of business, especially the prostitution of talent he found implicit in the very idea of journalism, but he became in this decade a newspaper journalist. Ironically, his power to create fiction was not destroyed by the experience but revitalized. In those days newspapers frequently published fiction, and some of his more important works appeared in the *Evening News* during World War I. One of these was "The Bowmen" (1914). In his introduction to the tale in his 1915 collection, *The Angels of Mons: The Bowmen and Other Legends of the War,* he says that the germ of the story was his reading in the news about the British retreat from the Battle of Mons. His brief tale concerned the appearance at Mons of ghostly bowmen, who might have been seen at Agincourt, who fire upon the Germans and turn defeat into victory. The other stories in *The Angels of Mons* celebrate the power of God and his angels working for the British. In "The Soldier's Rest" a soldier-hero slowly gathers that he is in heaven; in "The Monstrance" the wicked German sergeant Karl-Heinz betrays a German advance because of madness brought on by guilt at his murder of a child.

The memorableness of "The Bowmen" is not, as Machen was first to point out, in its literary quality but in the response it received. Some people refused to accept it as a work of fiction. At first parish magazines wrote asking for "the exact authorities for the story," and when he denied its truth others

stepped forward with accounts of conversations with people who claimed to have experienced in battle what Machen had merely imagined. When Machen demurred, those who believed in the story's literal truth countered with the suggestion that he had been vouchsafed a vision and had misunderstood its nature. Four books were published dealing with the veracity of the story. In his introduction to *The Angels of Mons* Machen shrewdly blamed this insistent credulity on the materialist spirit of the age.

Machen was scrupulously honest in his disavowal of the truth of "The Bowmen." Yet, as S. T. Joshi points out, his claim may seem ironic since some of Machen's later work seems deliberately to foster a confusion similar to "The Bowman." One example is *The Great Return* (1915), which was serialized in the *Evening News.* The story concerns the appearance of the Holy Grail in Llantrisant, a small Welsh seaside town. Confusion between fiction and reality is created when Machen appears in his own tale as a journalist, and the fictitious priest refers to Machen's actual ancestors. The appearance of the Grail causes old enemies to be reconciled, the nearly dead to be revived, and the community to go about its life in regenerate joy. What is perhaps most important about this phase of his work is that it shows vividly the tensions under which the credulous and incredulous confronted one another in this era of materialism, when scientists were often appalled at the sheer inhuman mechanism of the cosmos they envisioned and religion became a counterweight and comfort against the inhumanity of their vision.

When the war ended, Machen was fifty-five years old, and much still lay before him. His three works of autobiography – *Far Off Things* (1922), *Things Near and Far* (1923), and *The London Adventure* (1924) – were a new departure and in a new voice. The intense, diffident youth of the 1890s had become the raconteur, and his work found a conversational tone. Another long work of fiction, *The Secret Glory,* was published in 1922. This work adds to his autobiography an intense spiritual dimension and a character – Ambrose Meyrick, the schoolboy who goes in quest of the Holy Grail – who is to his stories of regeneration what Dyson had been to his pagan works.

During the 1920s Machen briefly became a popular writer, and all of his major work was republished in both the United States and Britain. Fame came first in the United States, where knowledge of his work spread through the appreciative labors of Starrett, who backed the first American publication of some of his best stories in *The Shining Pyramid*

(1923). In 1918 Starrett had published a book on Machen's work, *Arthur Machen: A Novelist of Ecstasy and Sin,* which established Machen as a focus of interest for writers, such as Lovecraft and James Branch Cabell, who would revive interest in the supernatural. Though he did not profit greatly from this attention financially, Machen found himself the recipient of much admiration.

Still, his long career was not over. In 1933 he published *The Green Round,* a novel or romance that, though often judged a failure because of its rambling, episodic quality, nonetheless shows an engagement with the fantastic that points toward the absurd and provides a loose parallel with the work of younger European contemporaries such as Franz Kafka. In 1936 two short-story collections, both containing significant new work, appeared. *The Cosy Room and Other Stories* includes the first popular publication of the *Ornaments in Jade* pieces and others that celebrate neither horror nor ecstasy but rather a sharp sense of irony. In the title piece, for example, the "cosy room" is a condemned cell so described because a murderer's long and terrible flight is over. The best of the collection is "N," which unites in one tale Machen's senses of horror and ecstasy, previously kept separate. The story concerns the narrator's eventually successful quest for evidence of a lost primal reality, glimpsed by only a few, that underlies part of the distant and dusty suburb of Stoke Newington in North London. In his closing words the narrator tells his listeners, who are gathered at the fireside in a cozy flat near the Strand, "It is possible, indeed, that we three are now sitting among desolate rocks, by bitter streams." Such has been the suggestion that has gone before that the moment works powerfully.

The second 1936 collection, *The Children of the Pool and Other Stories,* includes only tales written for the volume. There are stories, like "N," with the power simultaneously to shock and to awaken a sense of transcendence. "The Children of the Pool" is the tale of James Roberts, a middle-aged man staying at a farmhouse in Wales near a peculiar landscape – "a level, half marshland and half black water lying in still pools, with green islands of iris and all manner of rank and strange growths that love to have their roots in slime." There he experiences what turns out to be an intense hallucination of a blackmailing threat from a young girl, which turns out to hinge on relatively minor sexual misconduct some thirty years before, about which Roberts has been unable to speak. Nothing in the story is incompatible with modern psychology: the narrator observes that "Roberts had nothing in him of

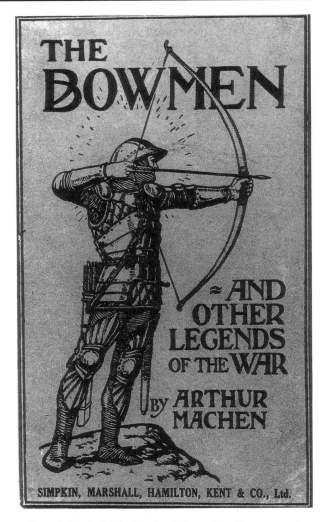

Cover for Machen's The Angels of Mons: The Bowmen and Other Legends of the War *(1915); the title story is about angels who helped the British during World War I*

the poetic faculty, nothing of the shaping power of the imagination," and Machen clearly relates his capacity to be gripped by such dark fantasies to this failure of the imaginative faculty, which he saw as the disease of his age. Some of the stories are less successful. "Change" concerns a marvelous nanny who turns out to be of demonic or fairy stock; she steals a child and leaves a changeling. Here Machen's novelistic imagination fails him; he is uninterested in the plight of the family left with the changeling, and the story goes off in pursuit of an acrostic puzzle.

Machen spent his declining years in Amersham, Buckinghamshire, in reach of the London he loved. In 1943 a national appeal was made through the newspapers to rescue him from indigence, which he had never managed to shake off despite much labor. On his eightieth birthday, at a feast in his honor, he was presented with a check for twelve hundred guineas. He and his wife lived quietly at Amersham through World War II, and he died on 15 December 1947, shortly after his wife, whose loss had disoriented him.

Machen's work has retained its capacity to awaken powerful enthusiasms. Since his death four books on his life and work have been published and two societies created in his honor, with one still thriving at the end of the twentieth century. His work is also of importance to the literary and cultural historian, especially as closer attention is paid to the relationship between popular culture and the literary establishment, which his work bridges. He used his considerable conventional novelistic powers only rarely, though often to good effect; his main contribution to fiction is in the short story. His work stands out in comparison with other writers because it is not easily consigned to one genre. While most writers of the weird tale work within a close set of conventions toward the creation of an unambiguous effect, Machen's best short work is neither greatly bound by conventional plot structure nor by an effort toward unambiguous excitement or horror. The best of his work has an ambiguity that might often be seen as a bringing together of disparate or opposite factors: the juxtaposition of evil and innocence in "The White People," of the familiar and the strange in "N," and of sexuality and mysticism in some of the pieces in *Ornaments in Jade* are examples. It was perhaps through his fortunate link with an aesthete past and an ability to take the world of his imagination on its own terms that he was able to bring such richness to his work.

Letters:

Arthur Machen: Selected Letters, edited by Roger Dobson, Godfrey Brangham, and R. A. Gilbert (Wellingborough, U.K: Aquarian Press, 1988);

Arthur Machen and Montgomery Evans: Letters of a Literary Friendship, 1923–1947, edited by Sue Strong Hassler and Donald M. Hassler (Kent, Ohio & London: Kent State University Press, 1994).

Bibliographies:

Henry Danielson, *Arthur Machen: A Bibliography* (London: Danielson, 1923);

Adrian Goldstone and Wesley Sweetser, *A Bibliography of Arthur Machen* (Austin: University of Texas Press, 1965).

References:

William Francis Gekle, *Arthur Machen: Weaver of Fantasy* (Millbrook, N.Y.: Round Table Press, 1949);

S. T. Joshi, "Arthur Machen: The Mystery of the Universe," in his *The Weird Tale: Arthur Machen, Lord Dunsany, Algernon Blackwood, M. R. James, Ambrose Bierce, H. P. Lovecraft* (Austin: University of Texas Press, 1990), pp. 12–41;

D. P. M. Michael, *Arthur Machen* (Cardiff: University of Wales Press, 1971);

Aidan Reynolds and William Charlton, *Arthur Machen: A Short Account of His Life and Work* (London: Richards, 1963);

Vincent Starrett, *Arthur Machen: A Novelist of Ecstasy and Sin* (Chicago: Hill, 1918);

Wesley D. Sweetser, *Arthur Machen* (New York: Twayne, 1964).

Papers:

There is a collection of Machen's drafts, letters, and some photographs at Newport Reference Library, Wales. His correspondence with John Lane is part of the collection of Lane's correspondence at the University of Texas at Austin. Other letters exist in the National Library of Wales.

Richard Middleton

(28 October 1882 – 1 December 1911)

Anne-Elizabeth Murdy
University of Chicago

BOOKS: *The Ghost Ship and Other Stories* (London: Unwin, 1912; New York: Kennerly, 1913);

The Day Before Yesterday (London: Unwin, 1912; New York: Kennerly, 1913);

Poems and Songs (London: Unwin, 1912; New York: Kennerly, 1913; enlarged as *Poems and Songs: Second Series,* London: Unwin, 1912; New York: Kennerly, 1913);

Monologues (London: Unwin, 1913; New York: Kennerly, 1914);

The District Visitor (Baltimore: Norman, Remington, 1924);

Queen Melanie and the Wood-Boy (San Francisco: Johnck & Seeger, 1931);

The Pantomime Man, edited by John Gawsworth (London: Rich & Cowan, 1933).

PLAY PRODUCTION: *The District Visitor,* London, Vagabond Theatre, 3 January 1921.

Richard Middleton's biography, written by his close friend Henry Savage, opens with a disclaimer: "While we were acquainted I had not only no inclination to gather facts relating to him, but an excessive contempt for facts in general. . . . Middleton himself was no fact-lover. He preferred fancies." Most accounts of Middleton describe him as a man of childlike egotism, "Shaggy Peter Pan with a briar pipe" in the words of poet Louis McQuilland. While Middleton always considered himself a poet, his prose earned him a living and his highest, albeit posthumous, reviews. He is best known for "The Ghost Ship," a lighthearted ghost story. His prose ranges from fanciful, mostly melancholy tales for children to essays celebrating childhood and criticizing the decrepit state of English letters.

Middleton did not achieve much critical attention until after his suicide in 1911 at age twenty-nine, when Savage collected and published his works. *The Ghost Ship and Other Stories* (1912) consists entirely of ghost stories, ten supernatural and ten about children's experiences with death. *The*

Richard Middleton (photograph by E. O. Hoppé)

Day Before Yesterday (1912) is a volume of twenty-two nostalgic stories of childhood fantasies and many essays about children's simple wisdom. *The Pantomime Man* (1933) includes his autobiographical pieces, what seem to be early stories, and several essays. *Poems and Songs* (1912) collects all of his poetry, and *Monologues* (1913) compiles thirty-two essays. *The District Visitor* (1924), a one-act, is Middleton's only play.

Middleton is striking in his acute sociopolitical commentary, found in essays and stories alike, his apparent ill-fittedness to his time, his Wildean spirit

225

of the 1890s, and his brilliant children's stories and ghost stories. Norman Foerster wrote in a 1914 *Dial* review of Middleton's works, "The true attitude toward life, Middleton suggests, is a combination of that of the Bohemian, who sucks joy from the passing moment; of the rebel, who hates passionately what is not beautiful; of the pirate, whose enfranchised spirit breathes diviner air than it is the general lot of mankind to enjoy. . . . [B]ecause the child is at once Bohemian, rebel, and pirate, Middleton yearned, in his weariness of soul, for 'The Day Before Yesterday.' "

Throughout his life Middleton remained fascinated with children and acutely critical of adults' apparent misguidedness. As charming as many of his children's tales are, he wrote of his own childhood in a draft of his unpublished autobiography, "I hope I shall never have to endure that state of aggrieved helplessness again. I had some good games and some good dreams. But on the whole the atmosphere was charged with ugly mysteries like an Ibsen play, and I was too introspective to be a happy child." Born on 28 October 1882 in Middlesex, one of three children, he was sent to various London schools that seem to have been indistinguishable in their attendant miseries. His autobiographical short story "A Drama of Youth," first published in the *English Review* (May 1911) and collected in *The Ghost Ship and Other Stories,* describes his walk to one school each morning "through Farringdon Meat Market, which aesthetic butchers made hideous with mosaics of the intestines of animals, as if the horror of suety pavements and bloody sawdust did not suffice. . . . Worst of all was the society of my cheerful, contented comrades, to avoid which I was compelled to mope in deserted corridors, the prey of a sorrow that could not be enjoyed, a hatred that was in no way stimulating. At the best of times the place disgusted me."

Similarly, his story "The New Boy," published in the *English Review* (October 1911) and collected in *The Ghost Ship and Other Stories,* is a poignant account of being sent off to school and terrorized by boys and masters alike; it ends with the young boy preparing to go home for a holiday, having finally gotten used to school life. "I saw that my whole school life would be punctuated by these violent uprootings, that the alternation of term-time and holidays would make it impossible for me to change life into a comfortable habit, and that even to the end of my school-days it would be necessary for me to preserve my new-found courage." Later Middleton attended the University of London and passed the Oxford and Cambridge Higher Certificate Exami-

nation in elementary and additional mathematics, English, and natural philosophy in July 1900.

In 1901 Middleton was hired as a temporary clerk at the Royal Exchange Assurance Corporation; nine months later he officially joined the staff. For five years he was a diligent but uninspired employee, spending his evenings reading and writing and his weekends entertaining William, Elsie, and Lily, several children he knew through his sister Margaret and friends. Entries in his "Journal of a Clerk," collected in *The Pantomime Man,* alternate between accounts of the number of words written that day and tales of his escapades with the children. "I am frightfully fond of children," he writes on 12 May 1903. "I know nothing nicer than looking into the eyes of a pretty little girl and trying to catch the madcap thoughts that slip to and fro within. Thoughts are frozen words. But my little rascal tries to melt as many as she can, for her tongue is never silent."

Late in 1905 Middleton saw an ad in the *Academy* for a literary tavern club: "The New Bohemians, an unexpected society, mainly devoted to the encouragement of intelligent conversation among journalists, bookmen, critics, artists, and others. . . ." In his successful letter of application Middleton replied that "owing to the folly of editors I am one of the 'others.' " His membership in the "N.B." gave him the literary and social community he had longed for during years of writing alone. In 1906 he was finally able to move out of his parents' home near Hampton Court and take bachelor quarters in Blackfriars in London, and in April 1907 he began publishing in the *Academy* and quit his clerkship to devote himself to writing full time.

Middleton was disdainful of journalistic writing and hated deferring to editors, but he submitted to writing reviews and essays as cheerfully as possible so that he could support himself. Within the next four years he was published in *Vanity Fair,* the *Century,* and the *Pall Mall Gazette;* he regularly contributed essays and reviews to the *Academy* and the *English Review;* and he was compiling a collection of poems in hopes of publication.

Middleton's favorite writer was Robert Browning; he also admired the poetry of A. E. Housman – Savage notes that Middleton marked the most "morbid and dark passages" in his copy of *A Shropshire Lad* (1896) – and the literary careers of Andrew Lang and Frank Harris. In 1913 Ezra Pound reviewed Middleton's *Poems and Songs* in *Poetry,* saying that "[h]e proves that English poetry did not stop with the nineties. . . . There can be no hesitation in granting him a permanent place among the personalities of English verse, among the post-Victorians." While Savage and other members of the New Bohemians applauded the poems Middleton brought to them, his contemporaries agreed that his prose outshone his poetry. The poems are sentimental and romantic – and melancholy, like most of his stories. Many of the poems are dedicated to Christine, a woman whom he dated intermittently. Reviews of *Poems and Songs* in the *Athenaeum* criticized it for "diffuseness, deftness, obviousness, and the wrong sort of vagueness" and dubbed Middleton "seldom more than a charming literary butterfly."

While living in Blackfriars, Middleton threw himself wholeheartedly into the New Bohemians and its motto, "talk for talk's sake." The best meetings, in his opinion, consisted of drinking, reciting verses, drawing caricatures, and arguing well after the taverner had closed up and kicked them out. Through the New Bohemians he befriended writers Frank Harris, Arthur Machen, Hilaire Belloc, G. K. Chesterton, and George Francis Wilson as well as Savage and McQuilland, all of whom became significant influences in his career. Middleton and his literary circle simultaneously maintained a self-conscious intellectual elitism and a romantic notion of the absolute purity and accessibility of poetic expression; the terms "poet," "seer," "prophet," and "child" seem interchangeable for them. Disillusioned by the rise of what they saw as a humdrum middle class, the New Bohemians nursed a post–Industrial Revolution nostalgia for the patronage system of a mercantile economy. Their political dissent permitted them to love England in only the most anachronistic and aristocratic senses; these young men reserved their more boisterous nationalism for the utopian bohemia they sought to discover.

Two essays from *Monologues,* which collects essays from 1906 to 1911 – "The Poet and the People" and "The True Bohemia," both published in the *Academy* (28 December 1907) – illustrate these paradoxical politics and Middleton's particular critique of his own position in literary history. In "The Poet and the People," a key text for Harris's portrait, Middleton scoffs at the commercialization of poetry and details a bleak cultural forecast in which, as far as he is concerned, middle-class British conventions turn literature into a parody of itself. He ends the essay noting that "the cost of one *Dreadnought* would provide an annual sum sufficient to keep twenty poets from emotional starvation"; after all, he says, "the finer luxuries of the rich are the mere necessaries of poets." For all his sentimentality about the life of the poet, he entertained no romantic notions of poverty.

In "The True Bohemia" Middleton focuses on a utopian intellectual aristocracy of young male writers who privilege any sort of "illogical enthusiasm" over rationalized conventions and prize the capability to think over the possession of knowledge. He urges readers to follow the maxim of his favorite bohemian, Robert Louis Stevenson: "Youth, taking fortune by the beard, demands joy like a right." The essay revels in the sentimental nostalgia of "this bittersweet country of Bohemia – sweet because it is the ultimate expression of youth, bitter because, like youth itself, it is evanescent." As he laments in the conclusion, modernity and maturity will inevitably conspire to contaminate the private space and the imaginative powers of the individual: "Yet as I sit in my castle in Bohemia and write these lines I hear the songs of the citizens rising from the street and their laughter echoing among the housetops, and I dread the day when my palaces shall change to factories and my domes to chimneys and I shall be able to see the truth no more." Both "The True Bohemia" and "The Poet and the People" figure prominently in the essays Middleton's contemporaries wrote about him after his death. Harris's remembrance of Middleton depicts the young writer's experience of England's "ineffable and callous contempt" for poets, and almost half the essay decries the "decay and dissolution" of a "body-politic" that kills off its most important citizens, its struggling writers.

Many of Middleton's essays and much of his life seem marked with a graceful acrimony and proud discontent reminiscent of Oscar Wilde. In his biography Savage remarks on the similarities between the two writers, but he makes an emphatic attempt to disassociate Middleton from Wilde. Because Middleton committed suicide, Savage was already in the position of having to defend his friend's sanity, and it was in the interest both of Middleton's posthumous success and Savage's professional investment for him to place Middleton in explicit opposition to Wilde. In a long passage on Middleton's literary influences – Housman, Stevenson, Wilde, Kenneth Grahame, J. M. Barrie, Thomas Ashe, and later Theodore Dreiser and Emile Zola – Savage interrupts with a caveat to deny rumors of Middleton's homosexuality. Savage states that his "own slight impression that [Middleton] had leanings towards this form of perversity was due mainly to his habit, in the earlier days of our acquaintance, of making himself out to be other than he was, acting after the fashion of Barrie's Sentimental Tommy." Savage attempts to separate Middleton from Wilde, convicted for his sexual prac-

Caricature of Middleton by H. R. Millar (from Henry Savage,
Richard Middleton: The Man and His Work, *1922)*

tices and noted for his pioneering role in an incipient gay male literary tradition, by reaffirming his connection with writers now indentified by many critics with that same tradition, such as Stevenson, Barrie, and Grahame. Indeed, he inserts Middleton into that literature himself with the comparison to Sentimental Tommy. For Savage to refute such rumors was requisite for Middleton's posthumous literary success; for Savage and others to indentify Middleton's life and work as part of this circle of English letters was and remains similarly salient.

An avid fan of Barrie's *Peter Pan,* first performed on 27 December 1904, Middleton wrote many children's stories that share the spirit of *Sentimental Tommy* (1896), most of them collected in *The Day Before Yesterday* and *The Pantomime Man.* In these stories he follows Barrie and Grahame by referring to adults as "Olympians" who have inexplicable power and whose capacities for creativity are sadly deficient. Throughout these volumes he rehearses the theme of the precision and accuracy of children's and poets' self-expression. Any effort to reorganize this sort of knowledge is actually an attempt to distort, homogenize, and obstruct truth. For example, "Children and the Sea" in *The Day Before Yesterday* claims:

The sea, like all very large things, can only be intimately understood by children. If we can conceive a sensible grown-up person looking at the sea for the first time, we feel that he should either yawn or wish to drown himself. But a child would take a sample of it in a bucket, and consider that in all its aspects; and then it would know that the sea is a great many bucketfuls of water, and further that by an odd freak of destiny this water is not fit to drink.

Middleton's point is not simply antiscientific or antirational; the child is calculating in its own way while investigating the sea. Rather, Middleton seems to be coloring in the possibilities outlined in Walter Pater's philosophy of experience when he says that: "for [children] the universe is merely an aggregate of details, some agreeable and some stupid, while I must needs depress myself by regarding it as a whole. And this is the proved distinction between juvenile and adult philosophies.... Life is a collection of little bits of experience; the seaside bits are pleasant, and there is nothing more to be said."

"Fate and the Artist," collected in *The Ghost Ship and Other Stories,* is a poignant story on this same theme, a touching allegory concerning the marginalization of both children and artists. The story is set in a London tenement, where a sickly, lonesome boy named George tells wonderful stories to the other children. Their favorite is George's story about a beautiful fish who lives in the rainwater tank on the roof of their building. "But no one ever saw it clearly except George, though most of the children thought they had seen its tail disappearing in the shadows at one time or another." All this is spoiled when a new boy moves in, "one of those masterful stupid boys who excel at games and physical contests, and triumph over intellectual problems by sheer braggart innocence." He calls George a liar, and he is so convincing that George must creep up to the roof that night to be certain that his fish is real. There in the dark he finds that the fish is "even more beautiful than he had said." After this George becomes extremely ill, and in his absence the other children forget the fish. But when the dry summer weather has emptied the tank, it occurs to the bully to look in and confirm his suspicions. At the bottom of the tank, dead, lies a gorgeous rainbow-colored fish. He runs downstairs to tell George, but he is too late; George too has died.

This story, particularly with its heavy-handed title, is striking in its similarity to Middleton's experience. The feminized storyteller-artist cannot survive the brute, hypermasculinized force of those who can regulate the expectations and requirements of the storyteller's audience. The artist is silenced, threatened, and finally killed by the power and ugliness of this bully – someone who, like commercial publishers, measures the creation of something beautiful according to its potential for producing profit. Young George is a seer whose stories are even truer than he needs to account for, but he and his art die prematurely. Only in retrospect, casting a glance on the sacrificed fish, can George's survivors begin to understand what they have lost.

Middleton also wrote excellent ghost stories, and it is for two of these that he is best remembered. "On the Brighton Road," collected in *The Ghost Ship and Other Stories,* shares with other Middleton stories its quiet eeriness, the subjects of solitary children and dying, and the conviction that youth is somehow wiser than adulthood. It was inspired by a bit of artistic recklessness on Middleton's part. According to Savage, in 1908 Middleton was so far behind on rent payments in Blackfriars that "[c]haracteristically, he spent his last few shillings on a seat at a play and then walked out into the night towards Brighton. But no material good came of the adventure. It gave him only an illness and a short story."

The story opens with a cold dawn and a tramp awakening to find himself sprawled haphazardly on the roadside. To his surprise, he feels well-rested. As he walks on toward London he comes upon and joins "an unspeakably fragile" boy, who despite his apparent youth is eighteen years old and far more experienced in the ways of the road than the tramp. As they talk the older man mentions that he slept where he must have fallen the night before. " 'It's a wonder I didn't die,' the tramp said. The boy looked at him sharply. 'How do you know you didn't?' "

The boy then reveals that he has died many times, but every time he returns to the road. As the boy coughs and shivers more and more violently, he rebukes the tramp's clumsy attempts at kindness: "I was telling you about the road. You haven't got down to it yet, but you'll find out presently. We're all dead, all of us who're on it, and we're all tired, yet somehow we can't leave it. There's nice smells in the summer, dust and hay and the wind smack in your face on a hot day; and it's nice waking up in the wet grass on a fine morning." Just as the boy collapses in pain, a doctor drives by in a car, diagnoses pneumonia, and carries the boy off to the infirmary. The story closes with the fulfillment of the boy's prophecy: he and the tramp meet farther down the road. " 'But the pneumonia!' cried the tramp aghast. 'I died at Crawley this morning,' said the boy."

Middleton's best-known story, "The Ghost Ship," first published in the *Century* (April 1912), is a

much cheerier tale. After being rejected by English journals the story was finally accepted by the New York magazine one week after Middleton's death. Machen writes in his preface to *The Ghost Ship and Other Stories,* "I declare I would not exchange this short, crazy, enchanting fantasy for a whole wilderness of seemly novels, proclaiming in decorous accents the undoubted truth that there are milestones on the Portsmouth Road." The narrator's conversational style, almost that of a dramatic monologue, creates a mood at once fantastic and matter-of-fact. The narrator inhabits a world in which family and community relations are reordered and ordinary physics becomes unimaginable, while a sturdy adherence to decent bourgeois manners and a healthy provincialism persevere.

The setting is 1897 in Fairfield, a village just off the Portsmouth Road, which is described as always having been "the ghostiest place in all England." A huge storm has hit and left a three-hundred-year-old pirate ship in a turnip field. The concern is not for the ship so much as for the endangered turnips. Fortunately, the ship's captain is a gentleman and offers his gold brooch to the worried local landlord as rent and as payment for the smashed turnips. Once this is settled, not much is made of the ship, though the villagers are pleased to note that the captain participates in Jubilee Day, celebrating Queen Victoria's sixtieth year on the throne – not anticipating, of course, that shooting off his ghost guns would knock real holes in a nearby barn. The guidelines for distinguishing "real" from "ghost" are blithely arbitrary, but the narrator is clear that social class lines, however temporary, are observed: "Landlord, he saw his tenant once or twice when he was hoeing his turnips and passed the time of day, and landlord's wife wore her new brooch to church every Sunday. But we didn't mix much with the ghosts at any time, all except an idiot lad there was in the village, and he didn't know the difference between a man and a ghost, poor innocent!"

Problems begin when Joshua, one of the town's ancestral ghosts who died young, repeatedly gets drunk and wakes everyone up when he gets home at three in the morning. Joshua's living great-great-nephew, the shoemaker, threatens to throw him out, and the narrator comments, "This kind of talk shocked me, I can tell you, for I don't like to hear a man abusing his own family, and I could hardly believe that a steady youngster like Joshua had taken to drink." The problem is that the captain has a store of magical rum, and no ghost in town can resist it. The matter is resolved when the narra-

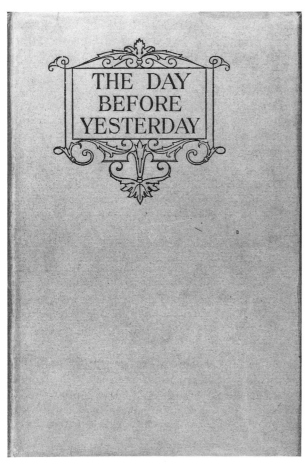

Dust jacket for one of Middleton's posthumous 1912 works, a collection of childhood fantasies and essays on the wisdom of children (Courtesy of the Lilly Library, Indiana University)

tor and the parson have a talk with the captain. They are received with utmost respect, and while the parson addresses the problem the narrator tastes what no mortal has tasted before, the magic rum. He drinks himself silly and watches "the fishes swimming to and fro over landlord's turnips."

The next day, in a huge tempest, the ship sails "very comfortably through the windy stars," taking along all of Fairfield's male ghosts as apprentice sailors. The villagers miss their ancestors for some time after, but eventually the whole affair is virtually forgotten. The tale ends with the return of "the daft lad who had gone away with the ship, without waiting till he was dead to become a ghost. . . . The worst of it was that he had come back as softheaded as he went, and try as we might we couldn't get anything reasonable out of him."

"The Ghost Ship" is typical of Middleton's work in its reversal of the power dynamic between young and old; the shoemaker is a professional adult, while Joshua is both a "lad" and an ancestor

to be respected. This kind of complicated family relationship allows Middleton to play with traditional notions of respect for one's elders and to upset the way age and wisdom are measured. By this means familiar systems of order – gentlemanliness, sobriety, fair prices on rent and turnips – are mixed with images of chaos – ships landing in fields fifty miles inland, for instance. Also, the reference to the Jubilee of 1897 echoes a nostalgia for the patronage of a stronger monarchy that was typical among the New Bohemians.

Middleton wrote "The Ghost Ship" during the several months he lived in Brussels, where he had moved in the spring of 1911 to escape the poverty and restlessness he felt in England. He loved Brussels for its noisy cafés and relative freedom from English conventions, but financial troubles plagued him there as they had in England. He had had to borrow money from Savage many times while still in London; now, penniless and sick with neuralgia and Hale's disease, Middleton was owed money by the *Academy,* and by summer he again had to borrow from Savage.

Middleton's essay writing by this time was successful if not lucrative, but the collection of poems he had sent to Harris in the spring of 1911 in order to find a publisher had found no success, which devastated him. By October he grew depressed more and more frequently. On 5 November 1911 he wrote to Savage, "Do you remember the end of my *New Boy* where he realised that all his life he would be uprooted and flung back and so would find no peace? It's awful true of my life. Up and down, up and down."

Middleton's last letter to Savage was a postcard found in his Brussels room after his suicide. Dated 26 November 1911 and then crossed out and dated 1 December 1911 in a different ink, it reads, "Goodbye! Harry I'm going adventuring again, and thanks to you I shall have some pleasant memories in my knapsack. As for the many bitter ones, perhaps they will not weigh so heavy now as they did before. 'A broken and contrite heart, oh Lord, thou shalt not despise.' " Middleton ended his life with chloroform. Savage went to Brussels immediately and buried his friend outside the city at Calvoet.

After Middleton's death Savage published literary eulogies in both the *Academy* and the *English Review,* and by 1913 he was able to collect, edit, and publish the bulk of Middleton's poetry and prose with T. Fisher Unwin. Harris included Middleton in his first *Contemporary Portraits* volume in 1915, and Savage's biography followed in 1922. As told by Harris and Savage, the romantic melodrama of

Middleton's literary and political disenfranchisement and his suicide secured the marketability that he had been unable to produce himself. All four of the books Savage published appeared in American editions within a year following British publication, and both *The Ghost Ship and Other Stories* and *Poems and Songs* went into their fourth printings at Unwin.

Reviews of these volumes varied widely, from the reverent speculation in the *American Review of Reviews* that Middleton "died because he could not compass in objective life the greatness that lay within him" to the dismissal of the *Saturday Review:* "posthumous notoriety has so pranked and veiled this work as to have earned it already several certificates of immortality, but . . . we seem to find an ordinary performance." The *Spectator* praises the "care and distinction" of Middleton's writing but "doubt[s] the wisdom of republishing work which is for the most part of an obviously ephemeral nature." Notable but measured critical attention was given to Middleton just after the collections were published but diminished by 1914. "The Ghost Ship" and "On the Brighton Road," however, are frequently anthologized in ghost-story collections.

What is most intriguing about Middleton is not simply his role in the tradition of children's and ghost stories, although this is a noteworthy part of the history of short fiction, but rather his affinity for children's prose in conjunction with biting social commentary and a stubbornly anachronistic position. His prose adroitly conveys simultaneous joy and bitterness, easy access to a carefree past and utter despair for the future. As McQuilland wrote of Middleton, "His mind was a remarkably sane, lucid and logical one, but his imagination was whimsically and delightfully freakish, giving continual expositions of realism in fairyland, of flashes of joy shooting through forests of nightmare."

Letters:

Richard Middleton's Letters to Henry Savage, edited by Savage (London: Mandrake Press, 1929).

Biography:

Henry Savage, *Richard Middleton: The Man and His Work* (London: Palmer, 1922).

References:

John Alexander Chapman, *Papers on Shelley, Wordsworth and Others* (London: Oxford University Press, 1929);

Frank Harris, *Contemporary Portraits* (London: Methuen, 1915; New York: Kennerley, 1915);

Stuart Petre Brodie Mais, *From Shakespeare to O. Henry: Studies in Literature* (London: Richards, 1917);

Vincent Starrett, *Buried Caesars: Essays in Literary Appreciation* (Chicago: Covici-McGee, 1923).

William Morris

(24 March 1834 – 3 October 1896)

Charlotte H. Oberg
University of Richmond

See also the Morris entries in *DLB 18: Victorian Novelists After 1885, DLB 35: Victorian Poets After 1850,* and *DLB 57: Victorian Prose Writers After 1867.*

BOOKS: *The Defence of Guenevere and Other Poems* (London: Bell & Daldy, 1858; Boston: Roberts Brothers, 1875);

The Life and Death of Jason: A Poem (London: Bell & Daldy, 1867; Boston: Roberts Brothers, 1867);

The Earthly Paradise: A Poem, 3 volumes (London: Ellis, 1868–1870; Boston: Roberts Brothers, 1868–1870);

The Lovers of Gudrun: A Poem (Boston: Roberts Brothers, 1870);

Love Is Enough; or, The Freeing of Pharamond: A Morality (London: Ellis & White, 1873; Boston: Roberts Brothers, 1873);

The Story of Sigurd the Volsung and the Fall of the Niblungs (London: Ellis & White, 1876; Boston: Roberts Brothers, 1876);

Hopes and Fears for Art: Five Lectures Delivered in Birmingham, London, and Nottingham 1878–81 (London: Ellis & White, 1882; Boston: Roberts Brothers, 1882);

A Summary of the Principles of Socialism Written for the Democratic Federation, by Morris and H. M. Hyndman (London: Modern Press, 1884);

Textile Fabrics: A Lecture (London: Clowes, 1884);

Art and Socialism: A Lecture; and Watchman, What of the Night? The Aims and Ideals of the English Socialists of Today (London: Reeves, 1884);

Chants for Socialists: No. 1. The Day is Coming (London: Reeves, 1884);

The Voice of Toil, All for the Cause: Two Chants for Socialists (London: Justice Office, 1884);

The God of the Poor (London: Justice Office, 1884);

Chants for Socialists (London: Socialist League Office, 1885; New York: New Horizon Press, 1935);

The Manifesto of the Socialist League (London: Socialist League Office, 1885);

William Morris

The Socialist League: Constitution and Rules Adopted at the General Conference (London: Socialist League Office, 1885);

Address to Trades' Unions (The Socialist Platform – No. 1) (London: Socialist League Office, 1885);

Useful Work v. Useless Toil (The Socialist Platform – No. 2) (London: Socialist League Office, 1885);

For Whom Shall We Vote? Addressed to the Working-Men Electors of Great Britain (London: Commonweal Office, 1885);

What Socialists Want (London: Hammersmith Branch of the Socialist League, 1885);

The Labour Question from the Socialist Standpoint (Claims of Labour Lectures – No. 5) (Edinburgh: Co-operative Printing, 1886);

A Short Account of the Commune of Paris (The Socialist Platform – No. 4) (London: Socialist League Office, 1886);

The Pilgrims of Hope: A Poem in Thirteen Books (London: Buxton Forman, 1886; Portland, Maine: Mosher, 1901);

The Aims of Art (London: Commonweal Office, 1887);

The Tables Turned; or, Nupkins Awakened: A Socialist Interlude (London: Commonweal Office, 1887);

True and False Society (London: Socialist League Office, 1888);

Signs of Change: Seven Lectures Delivered on Various Occasions (London: Reeves & Turner, 1888; New York: Longmans, Green, 1896);

A Dream of John Ball and A King's Lesson (London: Reeves & Turner, 1888; East Aurora, N.Y.: Roycroft, 1898);

A Tale of the House of the Wolfings and All the Kindreds of the Mark (London: Reeves & Turner, 1889; Boston: Roberts Brothers, 1890);

The Roots of the Mountains Wherein Is Told Somewhat of the Lives of the Men of Burgdale, Their Friends, Their Neighbours, Their Foemen, and Their Fellows in Arms (London: Reeves & Turner, 1890; New York: Longmans, Green, 1896);

Monopoly; or, How Labour is Robbed (The Socialist Platform – No. 7) (London: Commonweal Office, 1890);

News from Nowhere; or, An Epoch of Rest: Being Some Chapters from a Utopian Romance (Boston: Roberts Brothers, 1890; London: Reeves & Turner, 1891);

Statement of Principles of the Hammersmith Socialist Society, anonymous (Hammersmith: Hammersmith Socialist Society, 1890);

The Story of the Glittering Plain Which Has Been Also Called the Land of Living Men or the Acre of the Undying (Hammersmith: Kelmscott Press, 1891; London: Reeves & Turner, 1891; Boston: Roberts Brothers, 1891);

Poems by the Way (Hammersmith: Kelmscott Press, 1891; London: Reeves & Turner, 1891; Boston: Roberts Brothers, 1892);

Address on the Collection of Paintings of the English Pre-Raphaelite School (Birmingham: Osborne, 1891);

Under an Elm-Tree; or, Thoughts in the Country-side (Aberdeen: Leatham, 1891; Portland, Maine: Mosher, 1912);

Manifesto of English Socialists, anonymous, by Morris, H. M. Hyndman, and G. B. Shaw (London: Twentieth Century Press, 1893);

The Reward of Labour: A Dialogue (London: Hayman, Christy & Lilly, 1893);

Concerning Westminster Abbey, anonymous (London: Women's Printing Society, 1893);

Socialism: Its Growth and Outcome, by Morris and E. B. Bax (London: Sonnenschein, 1893; New York: Scribners, 1893);

Help for the Miners: The Deeper Meaning of the Struggle (London: Baines & Searsrook, 1893);

Gothic Architecture: A Lecture for the Arts and Crafts Exhibition Society (Hammersmith: Kelmscott Press, 1893);

The Wood beyond the World (Hammersmith: Kelmscott Press, 1894; London: Lawrence & Bullen, 1895; Boston: Roberts House, 1895);

The Why I Ams: Why I Am a Communist, with L. S. Bevington's Why I Am an Expropriationist (London: Liberty Press, 1894);

Child Christopher and Goldilind the Fair (2 volumes, Hammersmith: Kelmscott Press, 1895; 1 volume, Portland, Maine: Mosher, 1900);

Gossip about an Old House on the Upper Thames (Birmingham: Birmingham Guild of Handicraft, 1895; Flushing, N.Y.: Hill, 1901);

The Well at the World's End: A Tale (Hammersmith: Kelmscott Press, 1896; 2 volumes, London: Longmans, Green, 1896);

Of the External Coverings of Roofs, anonymous (London: Society for the Protection of Ancient Buildings, 1896);

How I Became a Socialist (London: Twentieth Century Press, 1896);

Some German Woodcuts of the Fifteenth Century, edited by S. C. Cockerell (Hammersmith: Kelmscott Press, 1897);

The Water of the Wondrous Isles (Hammersmith: Kelmscott Press, 1897; London: Longmans, Green, 1897);

The Sundering Flood (Hammersmith: Kelmscott Press, 1897; London: Longmans, Green, 1898);

A Note by William Morris on His Aims in Founding the Kelmscott Press, Together with a Short Description of the Press by S. C. Cockerell and an Annotated List of the Books Printed Thereat (Hammersmith: Kelmscott Press, 1898);

Address Delivered at the Distribution of Prizes to Students of the Birmingham Municipal School of Art on 21 February 1894 (London: Longmans, Green, 1898);

Art and the Beauty of the Earth (London: Longmans, Green, 1899);

Some Hints on Pattern-Designing (London: Longmans, Green, 1899);

Architecture and History, and Westminster Abbey (London: Longmans, Green, 1900);

Art and Its Producers, and the Arts and Crafts of Today (London: Longmans, Green, 1901);

Architecture, Industry, and Wealth: Collected Papers (London: Longmans, Green, 1902);

Communism (Fabian Tract No. 113) (London: Fabian Society, 1903);

The Hollow Land and Other Contributions to the Oxford and Cambridge Magazine (London: Longmans, Green, 1903);

The Unpublished Lectures of William Morris, edited by Eugene D. LeMire (Detroit: Wayne State University Press, 1969);

Icelandic Journals of William Morris (Fontwell, U.K.: Centaur Press, 1969; New York: Praeger, 1970);

A Book of Verse: A Facsimile of the Manuscript Written in 1870 (London: Scolar Press, 1980);

Socialist Diary, edited by Florence Boos (Iowa City: Windhover Press, 1981);

The Novel on Blue Paper, edited by Penelope Fitzgerald (London: Journeyman Press, 1982); *Dickens Studies Annual: Essays on Victorian Fiction,* volume 10, edited by Michael Timko, Fred Kaplan, and Edward Guiliano (New York: AMS Press, 1982), pp. 153–220;

The Ideal Book: Essays and Lectures on the Arts of the Book, edited by William S. Peterson (Berkeley & London: University of California Press, 1982);

The Juvenilia of William Morris, edited by Boos (New York: William Morris Society, 1983);

The Widow's House by the Great Water, edited by Helen A. Timo (New York: William Morris Society, 1990).

Collections: *The Collected Works of William Morris,* edited by May Morris, 24 volumes (London & New York: Longmans, Green, 1910–1915; New York: Russell & Russell, 1966);

William Morris: Artist, Writer, Socialist, edited by Morris, 2 volumes (Oxford: Blackwell, 1936; New York: Russell & Russell, 1966).

OTHER: "Mural Decoration," by Morris and J. H. Middleton, in *Encyclopaedia Britannica,* ninth edition, volume 17 (Edinburgh: Black, 1884; New York: Allen, 1888);

John Ruskin, *The Nature of Gothic: A Chapter of the Stones of Venice,* preface by Morris (London: G. Allen, 1892);

Thomas Moore, *Utopia,* foreword by Morris (Hammersmith: Kelmscott Press, 1893);

Robert Steele, ed., *Medieval Lore,* preface by Morris (London: Stock, 1893; Boston: Luce, 1907);

Arts and Crafts Exhibition Society, *Arts and Crafts Essays,* preface and three articles by Morris (London: Rivington, Percival, 1893; New York: Scribners, 1893).

TRANSLATIONS: *The Story of Grettir the Strong,* translated by Morris and Eiríkr Magnússon (London: Ellis, 1869; New York: Longmans, Green, 1901);

The Story of the Volsungs and the Niblungs, translated by Morris and Magnússon (London: Ellis, 1870; New York: Longmans, Green, 1901);

Three Northern Love Stories, and Other Tales, translated by Morris and Magnússon (London: Ellis & White, 1875; New York: Longmans, Green, 1901);

The Aeneid of Virgil Done Into English Verse (Boston: Roberts Brothers, 1875; London: Ellis & White, 1876);

The Odyssey of Homer Done Into English Verse, 2 volumes (London: Reeves & Turner, 1887);

The Saga Library, translated by Morris and Magnússon, 6 volumes (London: Quaritch, 1891–1905);

The Ordination of Knighthood, from William Caxton's translation of *The Order of Chivalry* (London: Reeves & Turner, 1892);

The Tale of King Florus and the Fair Jehane (Hammersmith: Kelmscott Press, 1893);

Of the Friendship of Amis and Amile (Hammersmith: Kelmscott Press, 1894);

The Tale of the Emperor Coustans and of Over Sea (Hammersmith: Kelmscott Press, 1894);

The Tale of Beowulf, translated by Morris and A. J. Wyatt (Hammersmith: Kelmscott Press, 1895; London & New York: Longmans, Green, 1898);

Old French Romances (London: Allen, 1896; New York: Scribners, 1896);

The Story of Kormak, the Son of Ogmund, translated by Morris and Magnússon, edited by Grace Calder (London: William Morris Society, 1970).

William Morris was a prolific writer who worked in many genres. His literary works that continue to receive considerable attention include his early short Pre-Raphaelite poems, his socialist writings, and his late prose romances. His works of short fiction are relatively few and tend to be overshadowed by his other writings but are important for their originality and for the insights they provide into his writing as a whole. For instance, the medieval setting of most of his short fiction is a significant aspect of Morris's well-known medievalism.

Further, because his writings are intrinsically linked to his many other endeavors, political as well as artistic, these works of short fiction may ultimately be seen as essential elements in the mosaic of a varied career.

It is difficult to say whether Morris is now better known for his writings, for his designs, or for his part in the development of British socialism – and these are only the most visible of his accomplishments. His influence in printing and typography, architecture, historic preservation, and environmentalism has been considerable. His influence on the genre of short fiction is undoubtedly slighter, but, as Wendell Harris has noted, his foundational contributions to Aesthetic fiction had effects on several important later writers. Though diverse, his many achievements and interests were linked as expressions of the same basic impulses, and upon examination his life can be seen as a unified, if varied, whole. Thus, students of his work have found their understanding of Morris enhanced by familiarity with the circumstances of his life and the development of his aesthetic and social philosophy. Biographers have discerned the beginnings of this development in his early childhood, particularly his early fascination with things medieval.

Morris was born on 24 March 1834 in Walthamstow, Essex, the eldest son of William and Emma Shelton Morris. The family, of Welsh background, seems to have been happy and loving, enjoying a middle-class affluence made possible by his father's success as a London bill broker. The family home in Walthamstow, then a rustic eastern suburb of London, was a large estate where an idyllic approximation of traditional manor-house life was maintained. In 1840 the family moved to Woodford Hall, on the edge of Epping Forest, which became a playground for Morris and his brothers and where Morris could ride his pony, wearing the toy suit of armor provided by his indulgent parents. By age seven Morris, having read all of Sir Walter Scott's Waverley novels, was already on his way to becoming an authority on the medieval period.

At Woodford Hall, Morris enjoyed a close relationship with his elder sisters, especially Emma, with whom he read Clara Reeve's *The Old English Baron* (1778). This Gothic romance was especially meaningful to the pair: in it one of the heroes, named William, loses his beloved sister, Emma, to a friend. Morris's biographers have noted that this early favorite reading was strangely prophetic not only of the later circumstances of his life but of patterns that became prevalent in his writings. In 1848, a year after the death of Morris's father, the family moved to Water House, Walthamstow (now the William Morris Gallery), which provided him and his eight siblings with another idealized natural setting, a moated island. The gardens and forests of his childhood had a profound effect upon his developing aesthetic ideals and were the prototypes for the paradisal settings found in many of his writings. Similarly, the close family unit in which he grew up prefigured the ideal communities of his later romances as well as the socialist utopia he would strive to establish in later years. But the private paradise of his childhood came to an end when his favorite sister, Emma, married a clergyman in 1850. The prevalent theme of lost love, noticeable in his writings from the beginning, may stem from his feelings of abandonment upon her marriage.

When his father died in 1847, Morris, the eldest son, inherited a large fortune. He had earlier attended a local preparatory school, but in 1848 he entered a public school, Marlborough College, where his father had purchased a nomination for him. Marlborough had opened only five years before and was still loosely organized. In 1883 Morris wrote in a letter to a socialist friend that he had "learned next to nothing there, for indeed next to nothing was taught," but, as he also admitted, he "perhaps learned a good deal," mostly history, from the school's well-stocked library, as well as from the many prehistoric, Roman, and medieval remains in the surrounding countryside. During this period he educated himself impressively in the areas of archaeology and ecclesiastical architecture, becoming something of an authority on English Gothic by the time he left Marlborough. He would always retain, however, an attitude of contempt toward formal education; his Marlborough experience, together with his disillusioning Oxford years, may have formed the convictions expressed by the Nowhereians in *News from Nowhere; or, An Epoch of Rest: Being Some Chapters from a Utopian Romance* (1890) about how and what children should learn.

Morris remained at Marlborough until 1851, when a highly disruptive student revolt occurred. Although there is no evidence that he was involved, he remembered in later years, when he had become a socialist and was advocating revolution, that "rebellion" was the chief thing he had learned during his school days. Also, at Marlborough, with its High Church emphasis, Morris first came under the influence of the Anglo-Catholic movement; the Morris family had tended toward evangelicalism. The attraction of Anglo-Catholicism for Morris would lead him into some of the most important associations of his life when he went to Exeter Col-

Morris at age twenty-three

lege, Oxford, in 1853, intending to prepare himself for the Anglican priesthood.

Upon his arrival at Oxford, Morris almost immediately became fast friends with another young man who intended to take holy orders, Edward Burne-Jones. Soon the two were planning to form a monastic brotherhood; although these plans were abandoned as they became more devoted to art than to religion, in a sense this brotherhood was realized: the two remained friends for life, and their artistic collaboration was formalized a few years later under the aegis of the Morris firm. In a larger sense, the ideal of fellowship was always compelling to Morris and underlies much of his later writing, whether overtly socialist or not.

Morris gained little from the formal instruction offered at Oxford but gained a great deal from the circle of friends with whom he and Burne-Jones shared reading and discussion. As at Marlborough, Morris read voraciously – poetry, mythology, history – and, inspired by the buildings of Oxford, continued his study of medieval architecture. He pursued this study during his vacations, first in visits to English churches, then to the churches of Belgium and France. But his fascination with ecclesiastical architecture did not ensure his continued devotion to the church; he seems to have experienced a spiritual crisis about this time and never regained his Christian faith. In the summer of 1855, at the end of a tour of the churches and cathedrals of northern France, Morris and Burne-Jones made final their decision to become not clergymen but artists: Burne-Jones would become a painter and Morris an architect. Burne-Jones's ambition was directly and brilliantly realized, while Morris's artistic development was tortuous and took forms these young men could not yet envision.

In the autumn of 1855 Morris completed the requirements for his B.A. and arranged to be articled to the well-known neo-Gothic architect of Oxford, G. E. Street, with whom he remained less than a year. Although Morris never designed a building, his knowledge and love of architecture undergirded his approach to interior design and historic preservation. More important for students of literature, his acute awareness of the manner in which architecture determines how people live is not only an important aspect of setting in much of his writing but also lies at the heart of his socialist vision, in which redeemed humanity creates for itself an ideal community realized in neomedieval architectural settings. During these same busy months Morris and his friends, who called themselves the "Brotherhood," made plans for a new periodical, the *Oxford and Cambridge Magazine*. Of the many short-lived undergraduate magazines of the nineteenth century, this one is chiefly notable for first publishing poems and stories by Morris, who had begun writing poetry some years earlier. It is also notable as the first communal enterprise Morris spearheaded and financed.

The *Oxford and Cambridge Magazine, Conducted by Members of the Two Universities* first appeared in January 1856. It was to a large extent inspired by its predecessor, the *Germ*, which had appeared in four issues, from January through April 1850, as the official journal of the Pre-Raphaelite Brotherhood. Morris and Burne-Jones were familiar with the journal of the brotherhood as well as their paintings, which had startled the art world in 1848. On the strength of several poems he had published in the *Germ*, the two friends had adopted the most notorious of the "Brothers," the charismatic painter-poet Dante Gabriel Rossetti, as one of their chief heroes. Rossetti was pleased by Burne-Jones's complimentary remarks in the first issue of the *Oxford and Cambridge Magazine* about one of his illustrations and eventually contributed three poems to the new publication. Through the *Oxford and Cambridge Magazine* Rossetti's attention first became drawn to the new Brotherhood at Oxford, setting the stage for the most fateful personal events of Morris's life.

The *Oxford and Cambridge Magazine* had no official connection with either of the universities; it was the joint project of the seven "Brothers," including Morris, Burne-Jones, Richard Watson Dixon, William Fulford, and Cormell Price of Oxford and Wilfred Heeley and Vernon Lushington of Trinity College, Cambridge. The enterprise was entirely financed by Morris, who had come of age and was in command of a large private income; he was also initially named as the editor, although he almost immediately turned over editorial duties to Fulford. Whereas the *Germ* was intended to help bring about a reform in art, the founders of the *Oxford and Cambridge Magazine* did not limit themselves to aesthetic concerns. Like Thomas Carlyle and John Ruskin, whose joint influence is evident in the content of the magazine, they aimed at nothing less than saving the world, or at least correcting most of the social ills of Victorian England. This youthful endeavor clearly shows the dedication to reform that later drew Morris into political action.

Reviewers were remarkably tolerant of the occasional presumptuousness of these young idealists who so freely lectured their elders on what they must do to be saved, and the *Oxford and Cambridge Magazine* was generally well received by its influential if small readership, though circulation figures did drop throughout the year. But the Brothers' youthful enthusiasm could not long be sustained in the face not only of the world's reluctance to be reformed but of the inevitable changes in circumstances and interests natural to their stage of life, and the magazine ended with its twelfth issue at the end of 1856. By that time the burden of responsibility for writing and editing had largely fallen upon Morris and Fulford, who together had written more than half of the magazine's contents for the year. Morris had by then been persuaded by Rossetti to become a painter under his supervision along with Burne-Jones, who had left Oxford in 1855 to study with Rossetti in London.

The *Oxford and Cambridge Magazine* did not carry attributions of authorship. Morris's known contributions include, in addition to several poems, essays, and a review, eight short prose tales or romances: "The Story of the Unknown Church" (January 1856), "A Dream" (March 1856), "Frank's Sealed Letter" (April 1856), "Gertha's Lovers, Part I" (July 1856), "Gertha's Lovers, Part II" (August 1856), "Svend and His Brethren" (August 1856), "Lindenborg Pool" (September 1856), "The Hollow Land, Part I" (September 1856), "The Hollow Land, Part II" (October 1856), and "Golden Wings" (December 1856). Strong arguments have been made for the attribution of two additional tales to Morris, "The Two Partings" (February 1856) and "A Night in a Cathedral" (May 1856).

Although few would argue that any of these tales should be counted among Morris's best work – he later felt that they were immature – critics agree that their collective originality of conception and technique makes them a remarkable and significant literary achievement. They generally anticipate the medieval subject matter of much of his later writing: all, except "Frank's Sealed Letter" and the two attributed tales, have medieval settings. Appropriately for their medieval settings, the most intriguing tales are in the tradition of Gothic romance: their subjects include death, frustrated sexuality, guilt, retribution, supernatural happenings, and paranormal psychological states and dreams. He would go on to other genres, but his fascination with these themes was lifelong, and they recur in his most important mature works. In their settings, subjects, and inventiveness, the early prose tales have much in common with his early poems, most of which were published in March 1858 in *The Defence of Guenevere and Other Poems*. These early romances invite psychological interpretation, and commentators attempting to explain his artistic or psychosexual development have found them particularly fruitful subjects for study and explication. Morris wrote these tales as he was coming of age, and it is natural that initiatory motifs and patterns should be prominent. The frequently recurring pattern of crime, guilt, and expiation may reflect the emotional conflicts he had recently undergone during his loss of religious faith and his decision not to go into the priesthood.

The majority of the *Oxford and Cambridge Magazine* tales defy literal interpretation because of Morris's extraordinary departures from accustomed conventions of storytelling, particularly in his creation of several narrators who are either dead, ambiguously located, or both. This group of tales anticipates surrealism, not only because their narrative technique tends to subvert the normal expectations of realistic fiction but also because of their irrational and dreamlike plots and characters. A striking example is the first published tale, "The Story of the Unknown Church," in which the narrator, the master mason of the church, says at the outset that he has been dead for six hundred years. As Wendell Harris has pointed out, this tale – with its medieval setting, strange style, slight plot, and art theme – was undoubtedly inspired by Rossetti's "Hand and Soul," published in 1855 in *The Germ*. Further, Morris's *Oxford and Cambridge Magazine* tales, together with "Hand and Soul," comprised the original corpus of Aesthetic fiction, which would influence in varying degrees many later short-fiction writers, most notably Walter Pater, Arthur Symons, Robert Louis Stevenson, Oscar Wilde, and William Butler Yeats.

At the time Morris was writing "The Story of the Unknown Church" he was also working on an article that appeared in the next issue of the magazine, "Shadows of Amiens," an appreciative recounting of the architectural features of the cathedral, which he had visited in 1854 and 1855. It is clear that the narrator of "The Story of the Unknown Church" is one of the "passed-away [cathedral] builders . . . still surely living" whom Morris envisions in "Shadows of Amiens." This narrator tells of the doomed love of his sister Margaret and her betrothed, Amyot, also the narrator's friend; of the elaborate tomb he created for the dead lovers; and of his own death upon completing their tomb after twenty years' work. The church is now entirely vanished, existing only in the memory of its dead builder; the narrator thus seems to exist only as a disembodied memory of the past. This complex little tale has inspired various interpretations, centering either on the narrator as artist or on the autobiographical resonances of the triangular relationship underlying the slight plot. Related to "The Story of the Unknown Church" and "Shadows of Amiens" in several ways is the apocryphal tale "A Night in a Cathedral," which appeared in the magazine's May issue. Its first-person narrator is a Victorian student of architecture, much like Morris, who spends a terrifying night in Amiens Cathedral after being mistakenly locked in.

The highly unusual narrative structure of "A Dream," which appeared in the March issue of the *Oxford and Cambridge Magazine,* is even more complex than that of "The Story of the Unknown Church." In this initially confusing and unsettling tale a first-person narrator relates his dream of the four reincarnations of two lovers, Lawrence and Ella, who seem to undergo some kind of purgatorial experience. Four internal narrator-witnesses, who themselves transcend the limitations of death and time, are required to complete the telling of the story, which stretches over four centuries.

Another narrator who transcends death in order to tell his story is Lionel, the protagonist of "Golden Wings." In an overtly Oedipal plot, the narrator, controlled by his vengeful mother, becomes a patricide under her influence. Fatherless and powerless, Lionel is unable to gain status at court and, after eloping with Alys, the king's daughter, brings vengeance upon himself. Lionel's narration ends with a graphic description of his own death.

The longest of this group of surrealistic tales is "The Hollow Land"; its complicated plot centers on revenge and atonement. Florian, the narrator-protagonist, has joined in a plot to murder the queen and is overcome in battle by her son, Red Harald. He finds himself in the Hollow Land, where he wanders with Margaret, his beloved, until he is inexplicably ejected from this paradisal otherworld back into the real world. Here years of disjointed and nightmarish encounters with mysterious characters culminate in a prolonged purgatorial rapprochement with his enemy, during which, for a period of many years, they together paint pictures of "God's judgments" on the walls of Florian's castle. Florian is eventually reunited with Margaret and finds once more the entrance to the paradisal Hollow Land. As in "The Story of the Unknown Church," the protagonist's experiences can be seen as relevant to the significance of art and the role of the artist. Commentators have pointed out the complexity of the color symbolism in this tale as well as its relationship to Robert Browning's "Childe Roland to the Dark Tower Came" (1855).

The wasteland imagery of "Lindenborg Pool," the only one of Morris's early prose tales with neither a love interest nor an original plot, may also owe something to Browning's poem, as it certainly does to Edgar Allan Poe's "The Masque of the Red Death" (1842) and "The Fall of the House of Usher" (1839). Nearly all the *Oxford and Cambridge Magazine* tales show evidence of Morris's wide reading in Gothic romance, but "Lindenborg Pool" is the most derivative; it was directly inspired by a specific source, Benjamin Thorpe's *Northern Mythology* (1851). Yet the tale is not without originality. Here again the innovation lies chiefly in narrative technique: the narrator has a dual identity, becoming a thirteenth-century priest without losing consciousness of his "proper nineteenth-century character." The narrator's double awareness prefigures to some degree the time-traveling narrators of Morris's mature socialist romances *A Dream of John Ball* (published with *A King's Lesson,* 1888) and *News from Nowhere.* Summoned to attend a dying baron, the priest finds himself amid a macabre saturnalian revel and realizes that he has been tricked into administering the sacraments to a pig, which strangely resembles the murder victim of his guilt-ridden Victorian aspect.

Thorpe's *Northern Mythology* was one of Morris's favorite books; he had been interested in mythology since his time at Marlborough, and it is clear from these early romances that by 1856 northern myth had begun to fire his imagination. The plots of "Gertha's Lovers" and "Svend and His Brethren" are original, but the action and the straightforward third-person narration of these tales are appropriate to the world of the saga, as opposed to the world of romance. The supernatural occurrences concluding each tale are not intrinsic to the plots but suggest the kind of folkloric embroidery often decorating historical accounts that have become melded into ethnic or national tradition. These two tales thus anticipate the large body of poetry based on the literature and folklore of the north that Morris began to write in the 1860s, beginning with *The Earthly Paradise: A Poem* (1868–1870). Both "Svend and His Brethren" and "Gertha's Lovers" employ his favorite plot situation, a love triangle. In "Svend" the self-sacrificing heroine, Cissela, gives up her artisan lover, the blacksmith Siur, and marries the king in order to secure peace for her people. Following the death of the king and Cissela, the faithful Siur aids the escape of Svend and his six brothers from the mob fury of civil war, providing them with swords on which are inscribed the word "WESTWARD." Some five centuries later their descendants return to find the streets of the city still wet with fresh blood and clogged with the undecayed corpses of the impious crowd. The figure of Siur, artisan and rejected lover, is oddly prophetic of what Morris himself would become before many years had passed.

Leuchnar is the unsuccessful suitor in "Gertha's Lovers." When he renounces his love for Gertha to free her for his friend and king, Olaf, he also loses his preeminent place in Olaf's affections. After Olaf is killed in battle, all that is left for Leuchnar is to give his life for his queen. Gertha and Olaf attain a kind of apotheosis when his ghost welcomes her at the moment of her death, but the church that was intended to commemorate their lives and deeds is never completed.

"Frank's Sealed Letter," yet another triangle story, is narrated by Hugh, the rejected lover. Critics generally agree that, of all Morris's tales published in the *Oxford and Cambridge Magazine,* this is the least successful by any artistic standard. Though mawkish, however, this tale has several points of interest. First, it is the only one of the tales with a modern setting and the only one that does not violate the tenets of literary realism. Morris made few attempts to write about contemporary events and characters; his imagination lived in the past. Second, Mabel, the cruel, beautiful heroine

Jane Burden Morris, circa 1860

who rejects Hugh, her faithful lover, because he is deformed and ugly – and who is described as having "heavy sweeping black hair," "dreamily passionate eyes," "full lips," and "long hands" – seems to foreshadow Morris's wife, Jane, whom he did not meet until 1857. The apocryphal tale "The Two Partings" has much in common with "Frank's Sealed Letter": the setting is modern, the narrator is the rejected lover, and the heroine is shallow and fickle.

High spirits and optimism characterized Morris's personal life during this exciting period, in which he was initiated into the world of art by his mentor and friend Rossetti, whom he met for the first time in 1856 while visiting Burne-Jones in London. When Street moved his architectural offices to London later that year, Morris became a part of Rossetti's circle, which included other Pre-Raphaelite painters and Ruskin. Determined to become a painter, Morris moved with Burne-Jones to Red Lion Square into lodgings formerly occupied by

Rossetti. Morris took his first step toward becoming a designer when, unable to find furniture suited to their medieval tastes, he and Burne-Jones were forced to design their own. This bohemian period of Morris's life, although provoking the disapproval of his mother, was a happy time for him and his friends, characterized by camaraderie, horseplay, and much joking at his expense; his various eccentricities and his ample girth were sources of endless amusement to his circle. Morris was stocky and rather short, with a handsome head of curly hair that won him the nickname "Topsy." During the Red Lion Square period he let his beard grow and formed a lifelong habit of paying little attention to his personal appearance. He was inclined to be shy with women and was in general rather inept socially. Of a nervous, excitable temperament, perhaps inherited from his father, he had a quick, violent temper, which sometimes led him into absurd incidents. These seemingly unprepossessing traits tended to endear him to his close friends, who loved to collect and repeat amusing anecdotes about him.

In the summer of 1857 Morris was one of a group of Rossetti's artist friends assembled to paint murals depicting Arthurian scenes on the walls of the Oxford Union debating hall. Morris's painting characteristically was based upon the triangular love relationship of Iseult, Tristram, and Palomydes. Having executed it, he astonished his friends with an unprecedented display of his designing talent, decorating the roof beams with paintings of animals and birds. Unfortunately, none of these young painters knew the proper techniques for painting frescoes, and their work has deteriorated.

That autumn, while attending the theater in Oxford, Rossetti was struck with the unusual beauty of a young woman in the audience. He managed to introduce himself and prevailed on her to sit for him and his friends as an artist's model. The young woman was Jane (Janey) Burden, daughter of an Oxford groom, and her exotic brunette looks, memorialized in many of Rossetti's paintings, would make her famous as a prototype of the Pre-Raphaelite style of beauty. Soon Morris was in love with her, and by the following year the couple were engaged, despite their inequality of wealth and social position. Jane's humble circumstances probably made her all the more attractive to the romantic and idealistic Morris, if not to his family. It is possible that Rossetti was also in love with Jane during this period, and she with him, but that he encouraged her to marry Morris because he was obliged by con-

science and duty to marry his longtime fiancée and favorite model, Elizabeth (Lizzie) Siddal, then already dying. Meanwhile, Morris, still under Rossetti's spell, strove unsuccessfully to become a painter. At the same time he wrote, with seemingly little effort, some of the finest and most original poems of the nineteenth century.

In March 1858 Morris published at his own expense a volume of poetry titled *The Defence of Guenevere*. Sir Thomas Malory and Jean Froissart were Morris's chief sources for these inventive, complex, surprising, sometimes gruesome, and sometimes bewildering poetic glimpses of the Middle Ages. *The Defence of Guenevere* was not well received at the time of its publication, but many critics now consider it his finest literary accomplishment. Morris's plans for an Arthurian cycle of poems were preempted by the huge success of the first volume of Alfred Tennyson's *Idylls of the King* in 1859.

In the spring of 1859 Morris and Jane were married quietly. The ceremony was attended by a few friends; none of his family was present, nor was Rossetti. The first years of their marriage seem to have been happy. Much of his attention and time were taken up with the building and furnishing of Red House, named for its unassuming but handsome red brick exterior. Located in an orchard in Kent, Red House was designed for Morris in a sophisticated neo-Gothic style by Philip Webb, with whom Morris had become friends during his time in Street's architectural offices. As at Red Lion Square, Morris insisted upon medieval-style furnishings, found nothing that suited his requirements, and remedied the deficiency by designing his own with the help of his friends. The collaboration worked well, and, as his private income was diminishing at this time, he conceived the idea of forming a company to manufacture furnishings and decorative articles of all kinds for private houses as well as for churches and public buildings. The primary aim of the projected company, however, was to bring about a reform, on Ruskinian principles, in the production of household goods and decorative items — handcrafted objects were to replace those made by machine. Thus, in 1861, just a few months after the birth of the Morrises' first daughter, Jane Alice (Jenny), the firm, known as Morris, Marshall, Faulkner and Company, was founded and began operations in Red Lion Square near Morris's old lodgings. Over the years the firm, subsequently named Morris and Company, moved several times to various locations. Morris not only provided most of the capital for the enterprise but from the beginning did most of the firm's work.

In the prospectus of Morris, Marshall, Faulkner and Company the members, who included Burne-Jones, Rossetti, and Philip Webb among others, advertised themselves as "Fine Art Workmen in Painting, Carving, Furniture, and the Metals." Fortunately for Morris, whose private income continued to decline, the firm was soon a success, accepting many prestigious commissions following the favorable reception of their exhibit in the 1862 International Exhibition at South Kensington. In its early years its main work was in ecclesiastical furnishings for the many Anglo-Catholic churches then being built in the neo-Gothic style; the stained glass produced by the firm was remarkably fine in quality. Morris's genius for pattern design now became manifest. He soon began to produce his famous designs for wallpapers, which would be mentioned in the next prospectus. His designs for the textiles produced by the firm over the years, eventually including woven tapestries, carpets, and chintzes as well as embroidered hangings, are widely regarded as among the finest ever produced. The firm provided a focus for the development of one of Morris's chief talents, and he continued diligently at the work of the firm for the rest of his life.

Red House was the Morrises' home until 1865. Another daughter, Mary (May), was born there in 1862. It became the meeting place for his still-boisterous and fun-loving circle of friends, including Burne-Jones and his wife, Georgiana (Georgie), whom he had married in 1860. The Rossettis, married the same year, were also frequent companions until Lizzie's suicide in 1862. But the increasing work of the firm began to demand more of Morris's time; and after he contracted rheumatic fever in 1864, he was not able to make the daily journey to the firm's headquarters in London. In 1865 he finally brought himself to leave Red House and take up residence above the firm's location in Queen Square, Bloomsbury, where the family lived until 1872. At Queen Square Jane Morris's health began to fail, and their marriage began to deteriorate.

Amid the wreckage of his hopes for personal happiness, Morris resumed writing poetry. In 1867 he published a long narrative poem, *The Life and Death of Jason: A Poem,* which was well received by both the critics and the public. It had originally been planned as a shorter work, part of *The Earthly Paradise.* These two publications made Morris a famous poet, and nothing else he wrote equaled their popularity during his lifetime. *The Earthly Paradise,* the longest poem in the language, is a collection of twenty-four verse narratives drawn from classical and northern myth and folklore.

Cover, designed by Morris and Philip Webb, for Morris and Eiríkr Magnússon's 1870 translation of Icelandic sagas

Of all the stories in this complex and subtle work, not least poignant is that of Morris's own emotional anguish as his wife rejected him and turned to Rossetti. There has been much speculation about this situation. It is now clear that Morris knew of Jane's affair with Rossetti and was forced by his own principles to acquiesce in a situation that was extremely painful to him, doing what he could to suppress his own feelings and present a respectable facade to the world in order to shield the lovers and protect his children.

In 1871 Morris and Rossetti became joint tenants of Kelmscott Manor, a small Elizabethan manor house on the upper Thames where Jane and Rossetti could be together. Rossetti's mental and physical health were precarious during this time; addicted to chloralhydrate, he became paranoiac and attempted suicide in 1872. He finally gave up his share of the tenancy of Kelmscott Manor in 1874, much to Morris's relief, and, according to the diary of Wilfred Scawen Blunt, Jane's lover in the 1880s, she ended her affair with Rossetti in 1875, although the two remained close friends until his death in 1882. What little remained of the old friendship between Rossetti and Morris was over in 1875, when an acrimonious dispute over Morris's proposed reorganization of the firm was finally settled. As for Jane, Morris seems always to have treated her with the utmost consideration; and though Rossetti's passion for her had been too obvious to remain unnoticed by others, the Morrises continued to the end to maintain an appearance of domestic unity.

Despite what must have been painful associations, Morris came to love Kelmscott Manor above all other places. He maintained it as his country residence for the rest of his life, and he made it the setting for the culminating scenes of his utopian *News from Nowhere*. Scholars have suggested that the masquelike poem *Love is Enough; or, The Freeing of Pharamond: A Morality* (1873) expresses in allegorical form Morris's feelings at that time about Jane, Rossetti, and Kelmscott. Thus, though neither critics nor readers responded well to this intricate and difficult work when it was published, it has considerable autobiographical interest. Of some importance also for its autobiographical relevance is the unfinished realistic novel Morris attempted during this period. Like so many of his writings, it deals with a triangular love relationship. It has been published as *The Novel on Blue Paper* (1982).

In the late 1860s, at about the time of Jane's involvement with Rossetti, Burne-Jones also became involved in an extramarital affair. Morris and Georgiana Burne-Jones found what consolation they could in the deep friendship that developed between them during these difficult years. Morris presented several calligraphic manuscripts of his own making to her, including the beautifully illuminated *A Book of Verse* (1870), written especially for her. She seems to have become his model of ideal womanhood in his later writings, perhaps inspiring such fictional portraits as the character of Ellen in *News from Nowhere*. But he derived his chief consolation from work, whether writing, managing and designing for the firm, or eventually in public life. Indeed, it is probable that his personal disappointments were responsible for the extraordinary extent of his accomplishments during the last half of his life. Among these was his decision to set about learning the language and literature of Iceland.

As the northern tales of *The Earthly Paradise* demonstrate, Morris's early fascination with the literature and myth of the north had never waned. In 1868 he met Eiríkr Magnússon and began to read Icelandic; during the late 1860s, the 1870s, and the 1890s they published various translations from the Icelandic sagas. (In 1875 Morris also published his translation of Virgil's *Aeneid*.) The history of Iceland was of such compelling interest to Morris that he made two journeys there, in 1871 and 1873, with Magnússon and two other friends. Morris's work on the Volsunga saga led him to write his own epic poem on the subject, *The Story of Sigurd the Volsung and the Fall of the Niblungs* (1876). Though its brilliance was acknowledged by the critics and its author considered it his masterpiece, it was too arcane, too difficult, and too authentically northern to find favor with the reading public. It was his last major work of poetry.

During these years of ceaseless literary work Morris continued to manage the firm and care for his family. In 1872 the Morrises moved to Horrington House, near Turnham Green, a western suburb of London, where they lived until moving to Hammersmith in 1878. He named his Hammersmith home "Kelmscott House" in honor of Kelmscott Manor. In 1876 Morris suffered another personal tragedy when his elder daughter, Jenny, was stricken with epilepsy, from which she suffered for the rest of her life.

Nevertheless, despite his family troubles and the continuing financial worries attendant on his management of the firm, Morris was now ready to finish what he had started with the *Oxford and Cambridge Magazine* in reforming the world. Late in 1876 he began a new career as a public figure, speaking out against Benjamin Disraeli's foreign policy on Turkey and Russia. As an elected member of the committee of the Eastern Question Association, Morris gained practical political experience. He also acquired a permanent cynicism about the established political system when Disraeli ultimately triumphed. During the following year Morris took up the cause of historic preservation, protesting not only the demolition of architecturally important buildings but the deplorable "restorations" of the Victorian period, which were responsible for the virtual destruction of many medieval buildings. As one of the founders of the Society for the Preservation of Ancient Buildings, which he called "Anti-Scrape," Morris was drawn into several controversial issues. His political views became more and more radical as he became increasingly convinced that the capitalist system itself was his real foe. This was not really a new idea to Morris; in one way or another the capitalist system had always been his foe, and he had always been a reformer at heart. Even those works that in his lifetime were regarded as escapist literature, such as *The Earthly Paradise*, are now generally understood to have been concerned in fundamental ways with the pervasive materialism and greed of nineteenth-century Britain.

In 1879 Morris became an elected official in the National Liberal League, a wing of the Liberal

Party. In his thinking, however, he was already well on his way to socialism. In 1883 he joined a Marxist group, the Democratic Federation, which soon became the Social-Democratic Federation; began reading Karl Marx; and, fully committed to political activism, became a spokesman for socialism. His fame as a poet gave him considerable influence both within the movement and without; he was undeniably one of the most valuable assets of British socialism. The remaining years of his life were in large part devoted to the socialist cause – speaking, writing, demonstrating, and even handing out pamphlets on the street. These years were far from tranquil. Aside from the general public's unfavorable view of socialism, the movement was torn by factionalism. In 1885, because of his disagreement with the views and policies of its autocratic leader, H. M. Hyndman, Morris left the Social-Democratic Federation and helped to found as well as finance the Socialist League; he also supported *Commonweal*, which became an important socialist journal. He wrote prolifically for *Commonweal*, and his most important socialist writings appeared in its pages. Among these were the 1886 narrative poem, *The Pilgrims of Hope: A Poem in Thirteen Books*, autobiographically interesting because of its love-triangle plot; two works of short fiction later published together as *A Dream of John Ball and A King's Lesson*; and his utopian romance, *News from Nowhere*, considered by many readers and critics to be his masterpiece.

A Dream of John Ball is a parable from history written for Morris's fellow socialists in the form of a dream vision. The setting is medieval; his source was Froissart's *Chronicles* (1369–circa 1400). The first-person narrator is Morris, the dreamer, who finds himself in Kent during the Peasants' Rebellion of the fourteenth century. He listens to a sermon by John Ball, the revolutionary priest, who melds Christian doctrine with communist theory to incite his audience of peasants to rebellion, and a skirmish follows in which the revolutionaries are victorious over a group of soldiers. Following a celebration, Morris, who retains his nineteenth-century identity, spends the night in conversation with Ball and, it seems, becomes a character of whom Ball is dreaming. Because of his knowledge of subsequent events, Morris is able to predict the failure of Ball's attempt to bring about change. Nevertheless, the narrator advises, such hopeless causes must be undertaken in the certainty of ultimate success, as the "Fellowship of Men shall endure." *A Dream of John Ball* complements the later and more complex dream vision *News from Nowhere*, in which the narrator – again Morris himself – awakens to find himself in an En-

gland of the future, when it has become a socialist utopia.

Both works demonstrate Morris's acute awareness of historical change, which was evident in his earliest works. The use of the dream framework was always one of his favorite narrative devices and links these mature works to the *Oxford and Cambridge Magazine* tales. The narrative technique in these later works, however, is masterfully ironic; the dual consciousness of the narrator makes possible his superior knowledge and renders the events of *A Dream of John Ball* poignant, even while his self-parody makes the reader smile. Humor is more noticeably a part of *News from Nowhere* and makes its didacticism palatable. These works are among the few things Morris wrote that exhibit his sense of humor; and though they were written for socialists, their artistry has won for them a broader readership.

A King's Lesson, a much slighter work, was first published in *Commonweal* in 1886 as "An Old Story Retold." Morris's source was a short piece titled "The Golden Age of Hungary," published in the 1852 Christmas number of Charles Dickens's *Household Words*. Like the later *A Dream of John Ball*, which it anticipates in its use of medieval history for didactic purposes, *A King's Lesson* was intended as a parable for the readers of *Commonweal*. It has received virtually no attention from commentators, perhaps because its message is so plain that comment seems superfluous. The plot concerns a Solomon-like lesson that the king of Hungary, Matthias Corvinus, "the Alfred the Great of his time and people," teaches his courtiers. First the courtiers are made to labor in a vineyard to teach them the harshness of peasant life. But though the upper classes live by exploiting the peasants, the king and his captain conclude, they may safely continue to do so for many generations because, even though rebellion "*shall* be preached," none will heed except those who put to death "the setters forth of new things that are good for the world."

Despite incessant internal power struggles, by 1886 the socialist movement had begun to make a political impact and accordingly to bring upon itself the hostile attention of the government. Police began to arrest and attack socialist demonstrators; Morris was arrested several times and, on 13 November 1887, witnessed the violence of Bloody Sunday, when unarmed demonstrators in Trafalgar Square were attacked, some killed and many wounded, by soldiers and police.

The Socialist League, troubled with dissension, eventually came to be dominated by anarchists who in 1890 removed Morris as editor of *Common-*

Engraving by Morris's lifelong friend Edward Burne-Jones for an 1892 illustrated edition of Morris's 1888 socialist romance A Dream of John Ball

weal. Within a few months the Hammersmith Branch of the Socialist League became the Hammersmith Socialist Society under Morris's leadership. From this time he withdrew from the turbulent factionalism within the movement, but he continued to work for the cause until the end.

During these years of seemingly frenetic political activity Morris neglected none of his other activities and even took on new projects. Besides publishing his own translations of the *Odyssey* (1887) and *Beowulf* (1895), he continued to work with Magnússon on the saga translations. He continued to work for the Society for the Protection of Ancient Buildings as well as Morris and Company. Beginning in 1877 he had delivered a series of influential lectures on the decorative arts. The Ruskinian revolution in design and manufacture that Morris and the firm had promoted over the years seemed well under way in 1888 with the formation of the Arts and Crafts Exhibition Society, which he supported. Through the Arts and Crafts movement Morris had a profound influence on many important designers and architects, including Gustav Stickley and Frank Lloyd Wright. But Morris had one more reform to

undertake, that of printing. The Kelmscott Press, which he began in 1891 after considerable study, was the logical outgrowth of his lifelong interest in medieval manuscripts and printing and was given new immediacy in 1888 by the Arts and Crafts Exhibition. The standard of nineteenth-century printing was low and for many years had been a source of frustration to Morris, who believed that books, like everything else in daily use, should be beautiful. The Kelmscott Press attained the highest level of craftsmanship, and the revival of interest in fine printing by handpresses that it sparked was one of the most important aspects of the Arts and Crafts movement.

The Kelmscott Press published several of Morris's books, including the long prose romances of this period beginning with *The Story of the Glittering Plain Which Has Been Also Called the Land of Living Men or the Acre of the Undying* (1891). Morris in effect created a new genre with these romances, which would inspire such writers as J. R. R. Tolkien and C. S. Lewis. Like the shorter romances he had written for the *Oxford and Cambridge Magazine* in his youth, these later works have medieval or earlier settings and employ folktale patterns, especially the pattern of the quest. The heroes and heroines of the later romances are successful in their quests – winning love, regenerating their worlds, and inspiring the reader with hope. If it is valid to see in Morris's many writings reflections of the author's self, then Morris in these years had at last achieved the most elusive end of all quests, the serenity of self-integration. Whether he was ever satisfied with his accomplishments, it became clear during his last years that the world acknowledged his worth.

Following Tennyson's death in 1892, Morris was among those considered to fill the post of poet laureate and in fact was unofficially approached by a member of William Gladstone's cabinet. Morris's socialist principles made it impossible for him to accept the offer. Though he could not be thus officially distinguished, he had become famous, and many sought to meet him. The Sunday evening meetings of the Hammersmith Socialist Society at Kelmscott House were regularly attended by many admirers, some of them notable; Bernard Shaw and W. B. Yeats were among the younger writers Morris influenced during these last years.

By 1894, the year of his mother's death, Morris's own health was failing. He continued to write, to support the socialist cause, to work for Anti-Scrape, and to supervise the printing of the Kelmscott edition of the works of Geoffrey Chaucer, the masterpiece of the press. In 1896, following a trip to Norway, he became weak with various ailments, including diabetes and lung congestion. Morris died at Kelmscott House on 3 October, a reformer to the end – among his last words were "I want to get mumbo-jumbo out of the world." He was buried at Kelmscott, in the churchyard of the parish church of St. George, the scene of the climactic harvest festival in *News from Nowhere*.

Letters:

The Letters of William Morris to His Family and Friends, edited by Philip Henderson (London & New York: Longmans, Green, 1950);

The Collected Letters of William Morris, edited by Norman Kelvin, volume 1, 1848–1880 (Princeton: Princeton University Press, 1984); volume 2, part A, 1881–1884; volume 2, part B, 1885–1888 (Princeton: Princeton University Press, 1987).

Bibliographies:

H. Buxton Forman, *The Books of William Morris Described, with Some Account of His Doings in Literature and in the Allied Crafts* (London: Hollings, 1897; Chicago: Way & Williams, 1897);

Temple Scott (J. H. Isaacs), *A Bibliography of the Works of William Morris* (London: Bell, 1897);

Theodore G. Ehrsam, *Bibliographies of Twelve Victorian Authors* (New York: Wilson, 1936), pp. 162–187;

William E. Fredeman, "William Morris and His Circle: A Selective Bibliography of Publications," *Journals of the William Morris Society,* 1 (Summer 1964): 23–33; 2 (Spring 1966): 13–26;

Fredeman, *Pre-Raphaelitism: A Bibliocritical Study* (Cambridge, Mass.: Harvard University Press, 1965; London: Oxford University Press, 1965);

John J. Walsdorf, *William Morris in Private Press and Limited Editions: A Descriptive Bibliography of Books by and about William Morris, 1891–1981* (Phoenix: Oryx Press, 1983);

K. L. Goodwin, *A Preliminary Handlist of Manuscripts and Documents of William Morris* (London: William Morris Society, 1984);

Gary L. Aho, *William Morris: A Reference Guide* (Boston: G. K. Hall, 1985);

David Latham and Sheila Latham, *An Annotated Critical Bibliography of William Morris* (London: Harvester Wheatsheaf, 1991; New York: St. Martin's Press, 1991).

Biographies:

John W. Mackail, *The Life of William Morris,* 2 volumes (London & New York: Longmans, Green, 1899);

Margaret R. Grennan, *William Morris: Medievalist and Revolutionary* (New York: King's Crown Press, 1945);

Philip Henderson, *William Morris: His Life, Work and Friends,* second edition (Harmondsworth, U.K.: Penguin, 1973);

Jack Lindsay, *William Morris: His Life and Work* (London: Constable, 1975);

E. P. Thompson, *William Morris: Romantic to Revolutionary,* revised edition (London: Merlin Press, 1977; New York: Pantheon, 1977).

References:

J.-M. Baïssus, "Morris and the *Oxford and Cambridge Magazine,*" *Journal of the William Morris Society,* 5 (Winter 1982): 2–13;

Florence S. Boos, "Dislocation of Personal Identity in Narratives of William Morris," *Journal of Pre-Raphaelite Studies,* 1 (November 1980): 1–13;

Boos, "The Structure of Morris's Tales for the *Oxford and Cambridge Magazine,*" *Victorian Periodicals Review,* 20 (Spring 1987): 2–12;

Boos and Carole G. Silver, eds., *Socialism and the Literary Artistry of William Morris* (Columbia & London: University of Missouri Press, 1990);

Peter Faulkner, ed., *Jane Morris to Wilfrid Scawen Blunt: The Letters of Jane Morris to Wilfrid Scawen Blunt Together with Extracts from Blunt's Diaries* (Exeter: University of Exeter, 1986);

Faulkner, ed., *William Morris: The Critical Heritage* (London & Boston: Routledge & Kegan Paul, 1973);

Walter Kelly Gordon, "A Critical Selected Edition of William Morris's *Oxford and Cambridge Magazine* (1856)," dissertation, University of Pennsylvania, 1960;

Wendell V. Harris, *British Short Fiction in the Nineteenth Century: A Literary and Bibliographic Guide* (Detroit: Wayne State University Press, 1979);

John Hollow, "William Morris and the Judgment of God," *PMLA,* 86 (May 1971): 446–451;

R. Stahr Hosmon, "The *Germ* (1850) and *Oxford and Cambridge Magazine* (1856)," *Victorian Periodicals Newsletter,* 4 (April 1969): 36–47;

Charles H. Kegel, "An Undergraduate Magazine, 1856 Style," *Basic College Quarterly,* 2 (Winter 1956): 27–32;

Frederick Kirchhoff, "Morris' 'Childe Roland': The Deformed not Quite Transformed," *Pre-Raphaelite Review*, 1 (November 1977): 95–105;

Kirchhoff, *William Morris* (Boston: Twayne, 1979; London: Prior, 1979);

Kirchhoff, *William Morris: The Construction of a Male Self, 1856–1872* (Athens: Ohio University Press, 1990);

John Le Bourgeois, "The Love and Marriage of William Morris: A New Interpretation," *South Carolina Review*, 9 (April 1977): 43–55;

Roderick Marshall, *William Morris and His Earthly Paradises* (Tisbury, Wiltshire, U.K.: Compton Russell, 1979);

The Oxford and Cambridge Magazine (New York: AMS Press, 1972);

Silver, ed., *The Golden Chain: Essays on William Morris and Pre-Raphaelitism* (New York & London: William Morris Society, 1982);

Silver, *The Romance of William Morris* (Athens: Ohio University Press, 1982);

Hartley S. Spatt, "William Morris and the Uses of the Past," *Victorian Poetry*, 13 (Autumn–Winter 1975): 1–9;

Helen Timo, "A Church without God: William Morris's 'A Night in a Cathedral,'" *Journal of the William Morris Society*, 4 (Summer 1980): 24–31;

Timo, "A Not So Golden Age: The Genesis of Morris's 'A King's Lesson,'" *Journal of the William Morris Society*, 7 (Spring 1988): 16–18.

Papers:

The British Library in London holds the major collection of Morris's letters, manuscripts, and other papers, both literary and political. In England other important collections are at the Birmingham City Museum and Art Gallery; the Bodleian Library, Oxford University; the Fitzwilliam Museum, Cambridge University; the Victoria and Albert Museum Library, London; and the William Morris Gallery, Walthamstow. Repositories in the United States include the Beinecke Rare Book and Manuscript Library, Yale University; the Sanford and Helen Berger Collection in Carmel, California; the Harry Ransom Humanities Research Center of the University of Texas, Austin; the Henry E. Huntington Library, San Marino, California; the Pierpont Morgan Library, New York City; and the William R. Perkins Library, Duke University. The International Institute of Social History, Amsterdam, also holds a significant collection.

Neil Munro

(3 June 1864 – 22 December 1930)

J. Randolph Cox
Saint Olaf College

BOOKS: *The Lost Pibroch and Other Sheiling Stories* (Edinburgh: Blackwood, 1896);

John Splendid: The Tale of a Poor Gentleman and the Little Wars of Lorn (Edinburgh: Blackwood, 1898; New York: Dodd, Mead, 1898);

Gilian the Dreamer: His Fancy, His Love, and Adventure (London: Isbister, 1899); republished as *Gilian the Dreamer: His Youth, His Love, and Adventure* (New York: Dodd, Mead, 1899);

The Shoes of Fortune: How They Brought to Manhood, Love, Adventure and Content as Also into Divers Perils on Land and Sea in Foreign Parts and in an Alien Army Paul Greig of the Hazel Den in Scotland, One Time Purser of 'The Seven Sisters' Brigantine of Hull and Late Lieutenant in the Regiment D'Auvergne All as Writ by Him and Now for the First Time Set Forth (London: Isbister, 1901; New York: Dodd, Mead, 1901);

Doom Castle: A Romance (Edinburgh: Blackwood, 1901; New York: Doubleday, Page, 1901);

Children of Tempest: A Tale of the Outer Isles (Edinburgh & London: Blackwood, 1903);

Erchie, My Droll Friend, as Hugh Foulis (Edinburgh: Blackwood, 1904);

The Vital Spark and Her Queer Crew, as Hugh Foulis (Edinburgh: Blackwood, 1906);

The Clyde, River and Firth (London: Black, 1907);

The Daft Days (Edinburgh: Blackwood, 1907); republished as *Bud: A Novel* (New York: Harper, 1907);

Fancy Farm (Edinburgh & London: Blackwood, 1910);

In Highland Harbours with Para Handy, S.S. Vital Spark, as Hugh Foulis (Edinburgh: Blackwood, 1911);

Ayrshire Idylls (London: Black, 1912);

The New Road (Edinburgh: Blackwood, 1914);

Jimmy Swan, the Joy Traveller, as Hugh Foulis (Edinburgh & London: Blackwood, 1917);

Jaunty Jock and Other Stories (Edinburgh: Blackwood, 1918);

Neil Munro (Hulton Deutsch Collection)

Hurricane Jack of the Vital Spark, as Hugh Foulis (Edinburgh & London: Blackwood, 1923);

The History of the Royal Bank of Scotland, 1727–1927 (Edinburgh: Privately printed by R. & R. Clark, 1928);

The Bayley Balfour Memorial, Puck's Glen, Banmore, Argyll (Edinburgh: Privately printed, 1928);

The Poetry of Neil Munro (Edinburgh & London: Blackwood, 1931);

The Brave Days: A Chronicle from the North (Edinburgh: Porpoise Press, 1931);

The Looker-On (Edinburgh: Porpoise Press, 1933).

Collections: *Collected Novels and Stories of Neil Munro,*
10 volumes (Edinburgh: Blackwood, 1923);
Para Handy, and Other Tales, as Hugh Foulis (Edinburgh: Blackwood, 1931);
The Inveraray Edition, 9 volumes (Edinburgh: Blackwood, 1935);
Para Handy Tales (Edinburgh & London: Blackwood, 1955).

PLAY PRODUCTION: *Macpherson,* Glasgow, Royalty Theatre, 20 November 1909.

OTHER: Robert Burns, *Poems,* introduction by
Munro (London: Blackie, 1906);
Gaelic Society of Glasgow, *The Old Highlands: Being Papers Read Before the Gaelic Society of Glasgow, 1895–1906,* introduction by Munro (Glasgow: Sinclair, 1908);
William Henry Drummond, *The Poetical Works,* appreciation by Munro (New York: Putnam, 1912);
"Old Brand," in *The Queen's Gift Book, in Aid of Queen Mary's Convalescent Auxiliary Hospitals for Soldiers and Sailors Who Have Lost Their Limbs in the War* (London & New York: Hodder & Stoughton, 1918), pp. 132–136;
Fred A. Farrell, *The 51st Highland Division: War Sketches,* introduction by Munro (Edinburgh: Jack, 1920);
Leonard Merrick, *The Worldlings,* introduction by Munro (London: Hodder & Stoughton, 1920; New York: Dutton, 1920);
"The Oldest Air in the World," in *The Pipes of War: A Record of the Achievements of Pipers of Scottish and Overseas Regiments during the War, 1914–18,* by Sir Bruce Seton and John Grant (Glasgow: Maclehose, Jackson, 1920), pp. 246–254;
William Walcott, *The Arteries of Great Britain,* commentary by Munro (London & New York: Dickins, 1922);
Angus Robertson, *The Ogha Mor; or, The Tale-Man on His Elbow,* introduction by Munro (Glasgow & London: Gowans & Gray, 1924);
"The Pirate Ship," in *Blackie's Graded Story Readers* (London: Blackie, 1933), pp. 3–18.

Once one of the most popular Scottish fiction writers and widely considered to be the most likely to succeed to the position once held by Robert Louis Stevenson as a stylist and Sir Walter Scott as a historical novelist, it was for his humorous short fiction about Capt. Peter Macfarlane ("Para Handy") rather than his eight novels that Neil Munro seemed destined to be remembered at the time of his death. His nearly two hundred short stories, most collected in eight volumes, include historical adventure, Celtic legends, delineations of character, supernatural tales, contemporary humor, and topical sketches.

Novelist, short-story writer, journalist, and promoter of Scottish national subjects, Neil Munro was born on 3 June 1864 in Inveraray, Argyll, Scotland. His ancestors were shepherds and farmers who belonged to the Campbell clan. No biographical reference work names his parents, but Alan Bold's *Modern Scottish Literature* (1983) indicates he knew the name of his father although he never met the man. In a 10 March 1921 letter from Munro to Lynn Doyle there is more than a hint of tragedy in the story of his childhood. The extent of his formal education is not specified in any of the autobiographical columns and articles he wrote, but he was obviously an omnivorous reader. In an article collected in *The Brave Days: A Chronicle from the North* (1931) he describes some of the treasures he found in a combination post office and circulating library operated from a neighbor's home, and in an early novel, *Gilian the Dreamer: His Fancy, His Love, and Adventure* (1899), he uses the same situation in fictional terms. It is tempting to read his fiction closely to see just how much of the author may be found between the lines.

Munro left the parish school in Glen Aray at age twelve and worked for a time in the law office of the county sheriff's clerk before taking up journalism as a career. He never seems to have had any formal training for either the law or letters, but he taught himself much from the pages of Sir Isaac Pitman's *Reporter's Assistant* (first edition of many published in 1867). Nevertheless, he received the honorary degree of Doctor of Laws from the University of Glasgow in 1908. Thus reviewers of his *History of the Royal Bank of Scotland, 1727–1927* (1928) correctly referred to him as Doctor Munro, and even the copyright notice on the posthumously published omnibus collection of his Para Handy stories cites "the Executors of the late Dr. Neil Munro."

Munro's work in the law office included copying legal forms by hand. In *The Brave Days* he relates the story of a customer's request for a special inscription in a mysterious volume he owned. Not being able to read, this customer did not know this was the *Glasgow Foundry Catalog,* but Munro, at age fourteen or fifteen, obliged with a flowery title done in his best penmanship.

When Munro was seventeen he obtained a position on the *Scottish News,* a small, provincial paper, and began contributing poems and essays to the

Greenock Advertiser. Later he moved up to writing for the *Glasgow News,* then edited by Frederick Wicks, where he stayed until it ceased publication. During the 1880s he held a position with the *Falkirk Herald* for a brief time and contributed a "turnover" – a short, exciting story begun at the bottom right corner of the first page that continued on the next page, where the editorials appeared – to the London *Globe* once a week for three years, but for most of his career in journalism he was associated with the *Glasgow Evening News* as a chief reporter, assistant editor, art critic, dramatic critic, and literary critic, serving as its editor from 1919 to 1924. For many years he contributed material for two columns, "The Looker-On" on Mondays and "Views and Reviews" on Thursdays. He found journalism a ready road to gratifying his literary aspirations.

In 1893 Munro submitted a short story, "The Secret of the Heather Ale," to the *Speaker,* where it appeared in the May issue, following it up that year with "Red Hand" for W. E. Henley's *National Observer.* He submitted the next story he wrote to *Blackwood's Edinburgh Magazine,* where it was rejected; however, the editor asked to see more of his work, and "Shudderman Soldier" (published in October 1893) was the result. This began his long association with *Blackwood's* and the publishing firm of William Blackwood, both of which would publish most of his literary works, first in magazine serial form and then as books.

This relationship with *Blackwood's* resulted in enough stories along the same general theme to make up a collection of eleven stories, published in 1896 as *The Lost Pibroch and Other Sheiling Stories.* The blind piper, Paruig Dall, figures in three stories, "The Lost Pibroch," "Castle Dark," and "Red Hand." In the first he is able to play the legendary pibroch, the "tune of broken clans," which so touches the souls of the men of Half Town that they leave their families behind in search of the undefinable.

There are twists to the endings of some of the stories, as the true patrimony of one character is revealed or the heritage of a family resurfaces after skipping one generation. Some are not so much plotted stories as sketches or incidents. In "War" the effects of war – the preparation, the waiting at home for the departed, and the homecoming – are all shown from the perspective of those left behind. "The Fell Sergeant" shows a dying woman as she watches the preparations for her own funeral, and "The Secret of the Heather Ale" turns on the extent to which one clan will guard the secret from another.

Cover for the second book Munro wrote as Hugh Foulis, a 1906 collection of five stories about his most popular characters, Skipper Para Handy and his crew

The response to this collection was generally favorable, although some reviewers complained that the stories seemed to read like translations and that Munro relied too heavily on unfamiliar Gaelic terms that made a glossary in the back of the book necessary in the first printing. The themes of the eleven stories came from Celtic legends, thus classifying Munro from the start as a writer of the Celtic Twilight or even the Kailyard School and not as a realist. Some critics later found the dichotomy of Munro as journalist and "romanticist" to be detrimental to considering him as a serious writer. On the positive side, some considered the book to be fresh and original, full of atmosphere and the open air, demonstrating Munro's close observation and love of nature. For them the vividness of the setting gave reality to the characters.

Munro took a step from Celtic legend to the historical romance so closely associated with Scott with his first novel, *John Splendid: The Tale of a Poor Gentleman and the Little Wars of Lorn,* first serialized in *Blackwood's* (1897–1898) and then published as a book by Blackwood in 1898. Set in the mid seventeenth century in a period when the Marquess of Montrose's men were devastating the land, the novel is narrated by Elrigmore, who describes his friendship with M'Iver of the Barbreck – also known as Iain Aluinn, which is rendered as "John Splendid." Much of the picaresque plot is made up of a series of episodes that serve to display the complexity of the title character. The reviews were generally favorable, and many critics felt that Munro had the potential to become a great literary artist. Along with *The New Road* (1914), *John Splendid* is often cited as one of the author's best performances and proof of the validity of his claim to be a true disciple of Stevenson.

Munro's second novel, *Gilian the Dreamer,* was received both as a departure from and an advancement over *John Splendid.* Like the first novel, it is set in the past, but a past only a few decades removed from the time of its composition, the period following the Napoleonic Wars. It is the story of a boy growing to manhood for whom illusions are the most important part of his life. Later criticism has emphasized how much Munro critiques rural Scottish society as a stagnant world only imagination can truly bring to life.

In 1898 Munro contributed a series of descriptive sketches under the title "Hungry Ireland" to the *Glasgow News,* but they have never been collected in book form. At some point in the mid 1890s he resigned his position on the *Glasgow Evening News* and moved his family to a house in the country to devote his time to literature. He continued to contribute columns on a regular basis to the newspaper.

With his next novel, *The Shoes of Fortune* (1901), Munro came even closer to a parallel with Stevenson with a story reminiscent of *Kidnapped* (1886). His new hero and narrator, Paul Greig, begins as a law clerk, much like Munro himself, who returns home at the request of his father, kills a rival suitor for a woman's hand, and flees aboard a brigantine with a villainous captain. During his many adventures he becomes involved with Charles Edward Stuart and his attempt to gain the throne of England.

By the turn of the century many leading literary journals featured articles about Munro as writer as well as reviews of his work. He was portrayed as something of a literary dilettante, working when the mood was on him, since he continued to write for the newspapers. Quoted in the New York *Bookman* in 1900, he said he felt "journalism is a very wholesome thing, a fine tonic for a man who is writing literature. It prevents him from becoming morbid through being too much in the company of his own imagination."

Munro's next novel was *Doom Castle: A Romance* (1901), which again ran as a serial in *Blackwood's* (1900–1901) before being published in book form by Blackwood. Set in the days just after the Jacobite rebellion, the novel used many traditional Gothic elements, including a ruined castle, a mysterious baron, strange cries in the night, and a hero seeking to find and punish a spy who had betrayed the woman with whom he had been in love. It is an ironic portrait of romance in which Munro is able to criticize some of the traditions in romantic literature while using them.

Around 1902 Munro moved his family from Waterfoot, near Glasgow, to Gourock, overlooking the Firth of Clyde, where he alternated working in the dining room and in a hut built on the cliff behind the house. Little has been published about his family. His son, Hugh, who was born around 1893 and to whom he dedicated *John Splendid,* studied medicine at Glasgow University, joined the Argyll and Sutherland Highlanders in 1914, and was killed in action the following year. The introduction to *The Brave Days* also refers to Munro's daughters but does not give any information about them.

In 1903 Munro published his next novel, *Children of Tempest: A Tale of the Outer Isles,* which marked a return to the Celtic Twilight school in style, while the plot referred to specific events in Scottish history. Critics felt the story was lost in the style. The novel was not one of Munro's greater achievements and was the first of his novels not published in the United States.

In 1903 Munro joined a group of journalists for a trip to Canada, during which they journeyed by train from Quebec to Victoria and back. His unpublished journal of this trip is illustrated with newspaper clippings and photographs.

As though recognizing the limitations of the Celtic Twilight, Munro turned to a different form entirely for his next book. For some time he had continued his journalistic writing along with his literary work, perhaps as much for the remuneration it brought as for the chance to keep up his professional skills. In order to keep the two segments of his work separated he chose a pseudonym for the humorous sketches he contributed to the *Glasgow Evening News,* "Hugh Foulis." No origin for this

SPRING—A TYPICAL GLEN

AYRSHIRE
IDYLLS
BY·NEIL·MUNRO
ILLUSTRATED·BY
GEORGE·HOUSTON

ADAM AND CHARLES BLACK
SOHO SQUARE · LONDON · MCMXII

Frontispiece and title page for Munro's ten stories about life in the Lowlands

name appears to have been recorded, and some accounts suggest that the dual identity was an open secret. Munro published five books under the pseudonym during his lifetime.

The earliest title was *Erchie, My Droll Friend* (1904), a collection of twenty-nine sketches about Erchie Macpherson, waiter at Glasgow public dinners and beadle of St. Kentigern's Kirk. The dialogue is all in Scots but tempered so that it is easier to comprehend as it presents the Scot as a familiar comic figure. If the narrator, who does not use Scots, did not address him as "Erchie" and refer to his wife as "Jinnet," it could be suggested that their correct names are Archie and Janet Macpherson.

Erchie is a street philosopher with an opinion on everything, from the proper kind of Christmas card to send, to why dinner parties are not what they used to be, to why a Glasgow funeral is better than any other, to why the city is the only place in which to live. The stories are peopled with enough minor characters to fill in the backgrounds and give life to the otherwise slight situations. The structures of the stories are simple: the narrator encounters Erchie coming down the street and asks him for an

explanation of his present condition, or Erchie offers a monologue on what life might be like for Andrew Carnegie's little girl if he had one or what is behind the king's trip up the west coast of Scotland based on reports he has read in the papers. Some of the stories are badly dated, but others give glimpses of a universal homely philosophy of life, while the best involve such classic comic incidents as the time Jinnet was determined to take in lodgers or to arrange a tea party to celebrate the coming marriage of Duffy and Leezie, unknowingly inviting the bride's former suitor. The aftermath of such innocent beginnings makes up as much of the humor as the dialect.

The Erchie stories were immediately successful and popular, and Munro did not return to serious historical fiction again for a decade. With the creation of Peter Macfarlane ("Para Handy," meaning Peter, son of Sandy), skipper of the Clyde "puffer" *Vital Spark*, he enjoyed his greatest popular success. The eighty-one stories appeared periodically under the name "Hugh Foulis" in the *Evening News*. In 1906 Blackwood published twenty-five of them as *The Vital Spark and Her Queer Crew*.

Para Handy is described as a red-bearded man, short and heavyset, dressed in a blue pilot's jacket and trousers, a sailor's jersey, and a hard, round felt hat. He is fond of boasting of his experiences on sea and land but in particular of the qualities of his boat, a little coal-carrying tramp steamer. His crew is made up of three men: Dougie, the mate; Colin Turner, known usually as "the Tar"; and Macphail, the engineer. When he is telling someone else a story he punctuates it with the assertion that if only Dougie were there he would vouch for his truthfulness. He says it so often that he forgets once that Dougie *is* there and is actually the man being addressed.

In the first collection there is a pretense that these are stories being told to the narrator by Macfarlane himself, but this framing device is quickly dispensed with, which enables the reader to follow the events more closely. The captain is not above delaying delivery of a cargo in order to go ashore and sample the wares of the tavern, but he has a kind heart. In one tale he succeeds in showing young Alick that working on shipboard is not as romantic as the books say, thus calming the fears of the boy's parents. Para Handy idolizes one man, Hurricane Jack, who is fearless, handsome, learned in the ways of the sea, and named for the time he stole a sheep. The story behind the naming of Hurricane Jack becomes a sort of shaggy-dog story, as the explanation the narrator asks is put off every time by Para Handy's assuring him that he will get to that in time. He never does.

Munro introduces Erchie Macpherson into the stories when Hurricane Jack, engaged to Macpherson's niece Jean MacTaggert, sends Para Handy and Dougie to explain to Erchie why he was unable to accompany the lady to a ball, not knowing that Jack had already been to Jean's but was so inebriated she went with Mackay the policeman instead. The collection ends with an account of the captain's marriage to widow Mery Crawford, whom he has been courting for ages.

Munro went from a fictional use of the Clyde and its environs to a factual travel account in *The Clyde, River and Firth* (1907), which was illustrated with sixty-seven paintings by Mary Y. and J. Young Hunter. The same year Munro published a novel under his own name, *The Daft Days,* that took him firmly into the Kailyard School and Scottish popular culture. Serialized in *Blackwood's* in 1906 and 1907, it was the last of his novels to be published in the United States, where it appeared as *Bud: A Novel,* named for the little orphaned Chicago girl who comes to stay with her Scottish relatives. Set in

the contemporary world and bright and cheerful in tone, it may have been written with the export market in view, since it seems to interpret Scottish ways to the foreigner and there is scarcely a Gaelic phrase or Scots dialect word in the whole book. In recent years it has been forgotten.

Munro took a sabbatical from fiction for three years. His next novel, and perhaps the least successful, *Fancy Farm,* was not published until 1910, the same year it appeared as a serial in *Blackwood's.* The novel is a contemporary comedy in which the widowed, eccentric Sir Andrew Schaw sets out to find a second wife, whom he aspires first to train for the position, since he married his first wife by mistake – he had been courting a woman by telegraph, and his aunt brought home the wrong one.

In 1911 "Hugh Foulis" published another collection of twenty-six Para Handy stories, *In Highland Harbours with Para Handy, S.S. Vital Spark,* in which the framing device of Captain Macfarlane telling his story to a newspaperman is quickly dispensed with altogether. There are several variants of the formula established in *The Vital Spark* here. "The Tar" is replaced by his cousin, Davie Green, known as "Sunny Jim," who serves as cook and entertains the crew by playing the melodeon. The Tar returns as a gentleman yachtsman, and there is a lively discussion as to whether it is really the Tar at all. The constant reading by various members of the crew of "novelettes," with their tales of fraudulent claims to estates and fortunes, convinces them that this is a clever impersonator. Here the reader discovers the mate's full name is Dougald Campbell and sees just how Munro could on occasion use material from his newspaper columns to serve as background for his fiction. The episodes involving the Tarbert Fair in "The Fortune Teller" will be familiar to readers of *The Brave Days.*

The humor in this collection is as good as before. When the chronometer on board the *Vital Spark* is stolen, the crew gets a watchdog whose only faults are that he is deaf and that he does not recognize Para Handy in his Sunday clothes and will not let the captain on board his own ship. When Mary Macfarlane – spelled "Mery" as well in both dialogue and exposition – turns vegetarian, her husband is comforted by Sunny Jim's version of the old "stone soup" story and promptly stocks up on stones for his wife. Hurricane Jack comes into a small inheritance, which he promptly disposes of in fines for breaking every law he finds ridiculous, such as turning in a false alarm. Social historians may find the xenophobic attitudes toward Germans and toward German spies in this pre–World War I text of some interest. In a competition over which nation can build more dreadnoughts, the crew fears the Germans are ahead of the British. A foreigner selling onions is suspected of being a German spy and is imprisoned in the hold of the *Vital Spark*. A man is suspected of being German and not a Scot because he is sober.

The following year Munro published under his name a collection of ten short stories, *Ayrshire Idylls,* which must have been an experiment for him on several levels. Illustrated with twenty color plates of Ayrshire and twenty drawings by George Houston, it was published in an attractive format resembling his travel book on the Clyde. The themes of the stories, some of which are little more than sketches, are historical and feature Samuel Johnson (on a visit to Ayrshire in the company of James Boswell), Alexander Peden, and the Covenanters. Four of the stories feature Robert Burns in various aspects of his legend and personality, the best being an imaginative and near-poetic re-creation of the creative processes that led to the writing of Burns's most famous narrative poem, "Tam o' Shanter" (1791). Perhaps the most entertaining of the collection is "Magic Casements," in which two old childhood friends meet as grown men, one a writer and free spirit who plays the flute, the other a tradesman who had remained at home. The tradesman (and narrator) is entranced by the story of the vagabond who tries to entice them to follow him to strange lands, but the poet sees only a lunatic. The narrator concludes that his friend has been away from Scotland too long. Later critics have argued that in writing of the Lowlands in *Ayrshire Idylls* Munro's imagination was defeated and the stories never came alive.

Munro's last novel published under his own name was *The New Road,* considered by some critics to be his most serious work of historical fiction. Set in the period between the Jacobite rebellions of 1715 and 1745, the novel describes the disillusionment of its hero, young Aeneas Macmaster, and the changing society in Scotland represented by the laying of roads in the Highlands by Field Marshal George Wade. Compared to Stevenson's *Kidnapped* and *Catriona* (1893), the novel serves as a critique of false romance and false history.

In 1917 "Hugh Foulis" published a collection of thirty stories about a young commercial traveler for Campbell and Macdonald dry goods, *Jimmy Swan, the Joy Traveller.* While his stock may be only dry goods to most, James Swan is convinced he is bringing happiness to those he encounters and thus considers himself to be a salesman of joy. Others,

on hearing this declaration, consider him to be drunk. At fifty-five, he has a wealth of experience to share with all he meets and conveys a positive attitude toward life.

The stories are all variations on a common theme as Swan visits customers on his rounds, trying to bring cheer to the pious Mr. Jago, serving as matchmaker for Miss Cleghorn, or chairing an amateur concert in Birrelton to aid the Poor Coal Fund when someone protests that his recordings of Harry Lauder are better than the current performer. In all of these situations and many others Jimmy Swan proves himself adequate to the task. The stories have had their supporters for decades and have never remained out of print for long. They are suitable summer reading for any connoisseur of the humorous sketch and more polished than some of Munro's earlier, more serious short stories.

While not a prolific poet nor a significant one, Munro wrote many poems between 1897 and the 1920s that appeared in *Blackwood's,* the *Saturday Review of Literature,* and *Littell's Living Age.* In 1917 he planned to collect some of them as "Bag-pipe Ballads and Other Poems," but he never accomplished this goal. Shortly after Munro's death in 1930, John Buchan gathered his verse into a collection called *The Poetry of Neil Munro* (1931), in the preface of which he discusses Munro's mastery of language and the manner in which his prose utilizes poetic cadences and rhythms. Hugh MacDiarmid considered "John O'Lorn" a gem of its kind as a poem but believed that all the others read as though they were translations.

Jaunty Jock and Other Stories (1918) was the last short-story collection Munro published under his own name during his lifetime. The eleven stories are on themes similar to those in *The Lost Pibroch,* but there is more of the Celtic Twilight here than historical adventure. An old couple in "Young Pennymore," in an attempt to save their hanged son's body and to avenge his death at the hands of the Campbells, mistakenly kill the man who carries the papers that will exonerate their son. The humor of "A Return to Nature" seems designed to prove there is a thin line between barbarism and civilization when Andrew Macaulay, the factor of the captain of Kilree, learns his ancestral home is to be torn down and reverts to the old ways of the countryside. "The Brooch" is a story of the supernatural, while "The First-Foot" and "The Tudor Cup" employ the stereotype of the canny Scotsman. Red John in "The Tale of the Boon Companion" proves his loyalty to his friend, Alan, by providing escape for him and a maid, Ealasaid, at the expense of his own life. By this time Munro had mastered an easy and appropriate use of dialect, and the stories no longer seem like translations but like clean renderings of familiar legends.

In 1919 Munro became editor of the *Glasgow Evening News,* a position he held until 1924. As a result of his turning more completely to journalism and away from literature, the only book of his stories from this period is the final collection of thirty stories devoted to the exploits of Para Handy, *Hurricane Jack of the Vital Spark* (1923). For the first time the reader learns that Hurricane Jack's full name is John Maclachlan. The first story in the collection is another framed narrative as told by Para Handy to the anonymous newspaper reporter who was his audience in the first collection. Several stories belong in a group, where it is revealed just what part the crew of the *Vital Spark* played in protecting Scotland from German spies and helping to win World War I. Perhaps most representative of Munro at his imaginative best in this collection is "An Ocean Tragedy." Para Handy enjoys telling stories to anyone who will listen. Here he gets carried away and convinces himself that the *Vital Spark* had sunk in a storm. When he is shown the ship, whole and well, he concludes that once again things have been exaggerated in the report from Glasgow.

Another linked group of stories concerns Sunny Jim's desire to join the army, from which he is barred because he has a glass eye, something the rest of the crew had never noticed in the past five years. When engineer Dan Macphail — another example of Munro supplying a Christian name for a character many years after his first introduction — decides he does not want to enlist after all, Sunny Jim takes his papers and enters under an assumed name.

Apart from these topical stories, most are the same mixture as before, with examples of Scots humor and resourcefulness combining self-denigration and skillful anticlimaxes. The crew resorts to the skill of a local fortune-teller when Hurricane Jack is missing and spend their spare time learning about life as depicted in the Blue Bell novelettes so plentiful on local newsstands.

The Para Handy stories have been collected in an omnibus volume with the Erchie and Jimmy Swan stories, *Para Handy, and Other Tales* (1931), and by themselves as *Para Handy Tales* (1955), and they have seldom been out of print. In the 1960s they served as the basis for a BBC television series, *The Vital Spark.*

Munro's last substantial work was a bicentennial history of the Royal Bank of Scotland published in 1928. He had resigned from his regular duties on the *Glasgow Evening News* the year before to devote himself to this work. This handsome illustrated volume of more than four hundred pages was written from his study of the minute books kept by the Court of Directors and Court of Proprietors of the Royal Bank with the aid of a synopsis of important events provided by a member of the bank's staff.

According to his friend George Blake, a contemporary and friend of his son, Hugh, Munro wrote a series of "Random Reminiscences" under the name "Mr. Incognito" for the *Daily Record and Mail* of Glasgow during the last years of his life. Many of these were collected after his death in *The Brave Days,* which was followed by a similar collection, *The Looker-On* (1933), drawn from his many columns and features published over the years in the *Evening News.* Whether he had any other plans for spending his remaining years writing fiction is not certain. He died at his home in Craigendoran, Dunbarton, at age sixty-six on 22 December 1930. He is buried in Kilmalieu.

Neil Munro still has his readers but has received little genuine critical or bibliographical attention, and his name is missing from many standard reference works dealing with literary subjects. Histories of Scottish literature place him with Stevenson and John Buchan as writers for the popular press and discuss the historical novels *John Splendid, Doom Castle,* and *The New Road* seriously. His potential reputation as a major writer, however, was eclipsed by the popularity of the Para Handy stories.

In his best works he makes the old Highland live again with his descriptions of life in Inveraray. Despite a fine feeling for romance, he never broadened his scope with time, and his success as a humorist replaced his original literary ambitions. MacDiarmid considered him at best only a respectable craftsman but one of the six best short-story writers produced by Scotland. Munro reproduced some of the essentials of the Scottish character better than anyone. His most original work remains the Para Handy series, in which he wrote not of dandies, lords, and ladies but of riveters, deckhands, and dockside casuals.

As an individual Munro disliked pomposity and sham and treated journalism as a preposterous enterprise not to be taken seriously. In spite of his work as a journalist he seldom depicted his profession in his fiction, but in 1918 he contributed to *The Queen's Gift Book* a story, "Old Brand," about the experience of writing the obituary for the leading obituary writer of a newspaper. According to Blake, Munro was an "infinitely whimsical" man who enjoyed life and saw its humorous aspects. Angus MacVicar, a Scottish writer of thrillers, once wrote him for advice on becoming an author, and Buchan had fulsome praise for his major historical novels. So little attention has been paid to the details of his life that biographical sketches in standard reference books erroneously claim that he turned to writing novels of realism and contemporary life after writing historical fiction. Such novels of realism have now been forgotten. The truth is that he returned to writing historical fiction after a brief experiment with two novels of contemporary life. Whether or not they were more realistic than his other work is questionable; they still read smoothly and tell a good story, but it is for Para Handy that Munro really survives. Like other writers before him with aspirations in a chosen field, he found a lucrative sideline in which he created a minor masterpiece.

Bibliography:

W. R. Aitken, *Scottish Literature in English and Scots: A Guide to Information Sources* (Detroit: Gale, 1982).

References:

George Blake, Introduction to Munro's *The Brave Days: A Chronicle from the North* (Edinburgh: Porpoise Press, 1931);

Blake, Introduction to Munro's *The Looker-On* (Edinburgh: Porpoise Press, 1933);

Alan Bold, *Modern Scottish Literature* (London & New York: Longman, 1983);

Beth Dickson, "Foundations of the Modern Scottish Novel," in *The History of Scottish Literature,* volume 4, edited by Cairns Craig (Aberdeen: Aberdeen University Press, 1987), pp. 49–60;

Brodie Fraser, "The Art of Neil Munro," *Bookman* (London), 64 (July 1923): 205–206;

Francis Russell Hart, *The Scottish Novel: From Smollett to Spark* (Cambridge, Mass.: Harvard University Press, 1978);

William Harvie, "Mr. Neil Munro," *Westminster Review,* 174 (July 1910): 67–70;

Brownlie Hendry, "Neil Munro: The Gael in Literature," *Bookman* (London), 81 (December 1931): 168–169;

C. Keith, "Neil Munro, The Savage from Inveraray," *Queen's Quarterly,* 56 (Summer 1949): 202–213;

James MacArthur, "Neil Munro," *Bookman* (New York), 11 (April 1900): 122–124;

Hugh MacDiarmid, "Neil Munro," in his *Contemporary Scottish Studies: First Series* (London: Parsons, 1926), pp. 29–34;

D. S. Meldrum, "Neil Munro," *Bookman* (London), 48 (July 1915): 97–100;

Cameron Rogers, "Neil Munro," *Saturday Review of Literature,* 3 (16 July 1927): 971–972; revised as "MacCailen's Bard" in his *Oh Splendid Appetite* (New York: Day, 1932), pp. 68–84;

Gavin Wallace, "Compton Mackenzie and the Scottish Popular Novel," in *The History of Scottish Literature,* volume 4, edited by Craig (Aberdeen: Aberdeen University Press, 1987), pp. 243–257;

Roderick Watson, *The Literature of Scotland* (London: Macmillan, 1984);

Herbert Wernitz, *Neil Munro und die nationale Kulturbewegung im modernen Schottland* (Berlin: Junker & Dunnhaupt, 1937);

Kurt Wittig, *The Scottish Tradition in Literature* (Edinburgh: Oliver & Boyd, 1958).

Papers:

Munro's personal papers, primarily consisting of manuscripts of his novels and short stories, with some of his notebooks and journals as well as cuttings from newspaper articles by and about him, are in the National Library of Scotland. Small groups of letters are in other institutions. The National Library of Scotland *Catalogue of Manuscripts Acquired Since 1925* (Edinburgh: HMSO, 1938–) and the *Location Register of Twentieth Century English Literary Manuscripts and Letters* (London: British Library, 1988) list some of the sources for his papers.

Ouida
(Marie Louise de la Ramée)
(1 January 1839 – 25 January 1908)

Beverly F. Gibson
Troy State University

See also the Ouida entry in *DLB 18: Victorian Novelists After 1885.*

BOOKS: *Held in Bondage; or, Granville de Vigne: A Tale of the Day* (3 volumes, London: Tinsley, 1863; 2 volumes, Philadelphia: Lippincott, 1864); republished as *Granville de Vigne, or Held in Bondage: A Tale of the Day* (Philadelphia: Lippincott, 1866);

Strathmore (3 volumes, London: Chapman & Hall, 1865; 1 volume, Philadelphia: Lippincott, 1866);

Chandos (3 volumes, London: Chapman & Hall, 1866; 1 volume, Philadelphia: Lippincott, 1866);

Under Two Flags (3 volumes, London: Chapman & Hall, 1867; 1 volume, Philadelphia: Lippincott, 1867);

Idalia (3 volumes, London: Chapman & Hall, 1867; 1 volume, Philadelphia: Lippincott, 1867);

Randolph Gordon and Other Stories (Philadelphia: Lippincott, 1867);

Cecil Castlemaine's Gage, Lady Marabout's Troubles, and Other Stories (Philadelphia: Lippincott, 1867); expanded as *Cecil Castlemaine's Gage, and Other Novelettes* (London: Chapman & Hall, 1870);

Beatrice Boville and Other Stories (Philadelphia: Lippincott, 1868);

Tricotrin: The Story of a Waif and Stray (3 volumes, London: Chapman & Hall, 1869; 1 volume, Philadelphia: Lippincott, 1869);

Puck: His Vicissitudes, Adventures, Observations, Conclusions, Friendships, and Philosophies (3 volumes, London: Chapman & Hall, 1870; 1 volume, Philadelphia: Lippincott, 1871);

Folle-Farine (3 volumes, London: Chapman & Hall, 1871; 1 volume, Philadelphia: Lippincott, 1871);

A Dog of Flanders and Other Stories (London: Chapman & Hall, 1872); republished as *A Leaf in the*

Ouida (Marie Louise de la Ramée), photograph by Adolphe Beau

Storm, and Other Stories (Philadelphia: Lippincott, 1872; with original title, 1893);

Pascarel: Only a Story (3 volumes, London: Chapman & Hall, 1873; 1 volume, Philadelphia: Lippincott, 1873);

Two Little Wooden Shoes (London: Chapman & Hall, 1874; republished as *Bébée, or Two Little Wooden Shoes* (Philadelphia: Lippincott, 1874; with original title, 1897);

Signa (3 volumes, London: Chapman & Hall, 1875; 1 volume, Philadelphia: Lippincott, 1875);

In a Winter City (London: Chapman & Hall, 1876; Philadelphia: Lippincott, 1876);

Ariadnê: The Story of a Dream (3 volumes, London: Chapman & Hall, 1877; 1 volume, Philadelphia: Lippincott, 1877);

Friendship (3 volumes, London: Chatto & Windus, 1878; 1 volume, Philadelphia: Lippincott, 1878);

Little Grand and the Marchioness; or, Our Maltese Peerage and Other Stories (New York: Munro, 1878);

Moths (3 volumes, London: Chatto & Windus, 1880; 1 volume, Philadelphia: Lippincott, 1880);

Pipistrello and Other Stories (London: Chatto & Windus, 1880; New York: Munro, 1880);

A Village Commune (2 volumes, London: Chatto & Windus, 1881; 1 volume, Philadelphia: Lippincott, 1881);

In Maremma (3 volumes, London: Chatto & Windus, 1882; 1 volume, Philadelphia: Lippincott, 1882);

Bimbi: Stories for Children (London: Chatto & Windus, 1882; Philadelphia: Lippincott, 1882);

Frescoes, etc.: Dramatic Sketches (London: Chatto & Windus, 1883; Philadelphia: Lippincott, 1883);

Wanda, 3 volumes (London: Chatto & Windus, 1883); republished as *Wanda, Countess von Szalras,* 1 volume (Philadelphia: Lippincott, 1883);

Afternoon, and Other Sketches (New York: Munro, 1884);

Princess Napraxine (3 volumes, London: Chatto & Windus, 1884; 1 volume, Philadelphia: Lippincott, 1884);

Wisdom, Wit, and Pathos, edited by F. Sydney Morris (Philadelphia: Lippincott, 1884; London: Chatto & Windus, 1890);

A Rainy June (London: Maxwell, 1885; New York: Lovell, 1885);

Othmar (3 volumes, London: Chatto & Windus, 1885; 1 volume, Philadelphia: Lippincott, 1885);

Don Gesualdo (London: Routledge, 1886; New York: Munro, 1886);

A House Party (New York: Lovell, 1886; London: Hurst & Blackett, 1887);

Guilderoy (3 volumes, London: Chatto & Windus, 1889; 1 volume, Philadelphia: Lippincott, 1889);

Ruffino and Other Stories (London: Chatto & Windus, 1890; New York: United States Book Company, 1890);

Syrlin (3 volumes, London: Chatto & Windus, 1890; 1 volume, Philadelphia: Lippincott, 1890);

Santa Barbara and Other Stories (London: Chatto & Windus, 1891; New York: Lovell, 1891);

The Nürnberg Stove (Boston: Knight, 1892);

The Tower of Taddeo (3 volumes, London: Heinemann, 1892; 1 volume, New York: Hovendon, 1892);

Ouida's Works, 12 volumes (New York: Collier, 1892);

The New Priesthood: A Protest against Vivisection (London: E. W. Allen, 1893);

Two Offenders (London: Chatto & Windus, 1894; Philadelphia: Lippincott, 1894);

The Silver Christ and A Lemon Tree (London: Unwin, 1894; New York & London: Macmillan, 1894);

Toxin (London: Unwin, 1895; New York & London: Stokes, 1895);

Views and Opinions (London: Methuen, 1895);

Le Selve (London: Unwin, 1896); republished as *Muriella; or, Le Selve* (Boston: Page, 1897);

An Altruist (London: Unwin, 1897; London & New York: Neely, 1897);

The Massarenes (London: Sampson Low, Marston, 1897; New York: Fenno, 1897);

La Strega and Other Stories (London: Sampson Low, Marston, 1899; Philadelphia & New York: Biddle, 1899);

The Waters of Edera (New York: Fenno, 1899; London: Unwin, 1900);

Street Dust and Other Stories (Philadelphia & New York: Biddle, 1899; London: White, 1901);

Critical Studies (London: Unwin, 1900; New York: Cassell, 1900);

Two New Dog Stories and Another (London & Philadelphia: Biddle, 1900);

A Rainy Day, and Other Stories (London: Chatto & Windus, 1905);

Helianthus (London & New York: Macmillan, 1908);

Moufflou and Other Stories (Philadelphia: Lippincott, 1908).

SELECTED PERIODICAL PUBLICATIONS –
UNCOLLECTED: "Dashwood's Drag," *Bentley's Miscellany,* 45 (April 1859): 335–343; 45 (May 1859): 487–496;

"Carlyon's Vacation," *Bentley's Miscellany,* 45 (June 1859): 555–580;

"The Bar and the Bush," *Bentley's Miscellany,* 46 (August 1859): 115–133;

"Guy Villiers," *Bentley's Miscellany,* 47 (June 1860): 630–652;

"Fleur-de-lys, and the Two Viscounts," *Bentley's Miscellany,* 48 (September 1860): 227–256;

Villa Farinola in Scandicci, Italy, where Ouida lived for fourteen years

"A Coquette's Campaign," *Bentley's Miscellany,* 48 (October 1860): 407–440;

"Our Diamonds Reset," *Bentley's Miscellany,* 49 (November 1860): 523–550;

"The Stamp on the Paper," *Bentley's Miscellany,* 48 (December 1860): 622–650;

"Our Corps Friends and Foes," *Bentley's Miscellany,* 49 (January 1861): 72–83; 49 (February 1861): 183–192; 49 (March 1861): 308–321;

"La Chatelaine Sans Chateau," *Bentley's Miscellany,* 50 (September 1861): 221–239;

"Favette and Thargelie," *Bentley's Miscellany,* 51 (March 1862): 333–346;

"The Last Coquetry of Lady Caprice," *Bentley's Miscellany,* 51 (June 1862): 610–620; 52 (July 1862): 30–37;

"Obliteration of Florence," *National Review,* 16 (November 1890): 303–309;

"Poor Abel!," *Fortnightly Review,* old series 57, new series 51 (April 1893): 535–542;

"Birds and Their Persecutors," *Nineteenth Century,* 37 (January 1895): 45–56;

"Mr. Irving on the Art of Acting," *Nineteenth Century,* 37 (May 1895): 786–797;

"The Crispi Dictatorship," *Contemporary Review,* 68 (August 1895): 241–255;

"The Italian Awakening," *Fortnightly Review,* old series 65, new series 59 (April 1896): 541–546;

"A Highway Robber [The Tramway]," *Fortnightly Review,* old series 66, new series 60 (July 1896): 83–90;

"Italy (No. 1): Marquis di Rudini and Italian Politics," *Fortnightly Review,* old series 66, new series 60 (September 1896): 350–362;

"The Twentieth Italian Parliament," *Fortnightly Review,* old series 67, new series 61 (May 1897): 679–686;

"Felice Cavallotti," *Fortnightly Review,* old series 69, new series 63 (April 1898): 601–603;

"The Misgovernment of Italy," *Fortnightly Review,* old series 69, new series 63 (June 1898): 957–976;

"Canicide," *Fortnightly Review,* old series 70, new series 64 (October 1898): 581–586.

Sensational, romantic, sentimental, and eccentric as her self-coined name "Ouida" would indicate, Marie Louise de la Ramée must surely have envisioned for herself a more prominent position among nineteenth-century writers. Thirty years after her death Ouida had become merely one in a series of "Eccentric Englishwomen" described by

Rose Macaulay, who depicted the once-popular and wealthy author as "[a] fool; a grandiose and vanity-devoured egotist; a ridiculous writer; eccentric in (as Henry James put it) a common, little way." Although Ouida has been the subject of several biographies, one as recent as 1957, her works have not attracted serious critical attention. Indeed, anecdotes from her life survive more vividly than do characters, scenes, or even titles from her works. There are reports that in her young womanhood she entertained the dandified guardsmen who were so often her subjects at lavish dinners in the smoky atmosphere of which no other women were present; there she supposedly gained her material. Later comes the perhaps apocryphal story of Ouida dragging a romantic rival from her carriage and horse-whipping her in the streets of Florence. In her final years the impoverished and reclusive author once again served rich dinners – for her beloved dogs. From her self-romanticized childhood through her grandstanding early career in London and exotic exile in Italy to her fantastically debt-ridden last years surrounded by dogs, she composed her life in the same extravagant, reckless manner as she did her stories. Although never accorded serious critical attention in her own time, either – her second novel, *Strathmore* (1865), was burlesqued by Sir Francis Burnand in *Punch* as "Strapmore! A Romance by 'Weeder' " – she did attract a wide popular following, and her works earned her considerable wealth. Max Beerbohm noted in 1899 that "Ouida is not, and never was, an artist"; art may indeed conceal, he goes on to argue, the matter of the writer's work. It is in the subject matter of Ouida's work that her present critical significance may be found: her fiction contains, writ large, the sensationalism, romanticism, and sentimentalism that marked the popular literary scene of the late nineteenth century.

Maria Louise Ramé – "Ouida" was how, as a small child, she pronounced Louise – was born on 1 January 1839 in her widowed grandmother's small semidetached house in Bury St. Edmunds, Suffolk. She was the only child of Louis and Susan (Sutton) Ramé. Her mother, daughter of a Suffolk wine merchant, had married young to a plain, middle-aged Frenchman, who despite his unexceptional appearance and manner aroused interest and speculation in the quiet town, where he taught French to the local young ladies. His marriage certificate states that Ramé's father was a tailor and lists his own occupation as "gentleman"; his elusive nature and his increasingly frequent absences contributed to the rumors surrounding his background and occupa-

tion, leading his English relatives to believe that he was a Bonapartist agent. The effect of her father's intermittent company on Ouida's early years was apparently profound; from him she gained an appreciation of history, a fascination with politics, and a love of animals and nature. Perhaps the most significant gift he gave his young daughter was fuel for the imagination, which would produce a steady stream of stories and the income to support her grandmother, her mother, and herself. Her home life, despite her father's lack of tangible support, was happy, secure, and filled with loving family members. Although never physically attractive, Ouida developed a strong, secure personality and early engaged her imagination in making cutouts of knights and ladies, which she painted and used as puppets to act out stories for herself. As a child she read widely in both English and French and spoke and wrote the latter language with ease; later in life she would teach herself Italian. Her father encouraged her to read both Honoré de Balzac and Stendhal, and at age eleven she traveled, along with her mother, to visit him in France. These early Continental influences led to a predictable dissatisfaction with the quiet provincial life of Bury St. Edmunds, and at age eighteen she succeeded in convincing her grandmother and mother to leave the town for London. She harbored no sentimental attachment to her birthplace, which she never saw again. Forty-one years later, upon being informed in a courteous letter from Mr. G. Milner-Gibson-Cullum that a commemorative plaque had been placed at her birthplace, Ouida replied, "This tomfoolery in Suffolk annoys me very much. I identify myself with my father's French race and blood." Her attachment to, and increasing romanticization of, this Frenchness led her eventually to affix the "de la" and extra "e" to her paternal name.

When the female Ramé household established itself in London in 1857, Ouida set immediately to work. From her visits to Henley, Goodwood, and Ascot she derived a sense of the social set that would populate her stories and novels, and she began rapidly churning out stories. The family's neighbor and doctor, Francis Ainsworth, was impressed by her work and introduced her to his cousin, William Harrison Ainsworth, the popular author of historical novels and editor of *Bentley's Miscellany,* a conservative periodical devoted to popular entertainment. Ainsworth was impressed with the stories she sent him and accepted them immediately for publication. "Dashwood's Drag" was serialized in the April and May issues of *Bentley's Miscellany* in 1859, and every issue until July 1862 contained a story by Ouida.

During Ouida's years in London, where she lived until age thirty-two, her reputation as a popular author grew and solidified after her debut in *Bentley's Miscellany*. This productive period saw the publication of eight novels and three collections of stories. *Granville de Vigne*, serialized in Ainsworth's *New Monthly Magazine*, became her first novel. *Held in Bondage; or, Granville de Vigne: A Tale of the Day* (1863), was published in Britain, in the popular three-volume form, as were most of her works until the end of the century. This first novel contains all the elements that became Ouida's hallmarks: glamorous military life, adventure, lavish living, dramatic romantic entanglements, women with mysterious backgrounds and dangerous natures, and heroes of impossible sophistication, beauty, and courage. These qualities reached their zenith in the novels *Strathmore* and *Under Two Flags* (1867), the works on which her reputation now primarily rests.

The year 1867 saw also the publication of her first collection of stories, *Randolph Gordon and Other Stories*, followed the next year by *Beatrice Boville and Other Stories*; both gather works that had originally appeared in *Bentley's*. In addition to the title story, the first volume includes "How One Fire Lit Another," "The Marquis's Tactics," "Blue and Yellow," "Belles and Blackcock," "How I Was Tracked by Trappers," "Trente-et-un," and "The Donkeyshire Militia." The second volume contains, in addition to its title story, "A Line in the 'Daily,' " "Holly Wreaths and Rose Chains," "Silver Chimes and Golden Fetters," "Slander and Sillery," "Sir Galahad's Raid," " 'Redeemed,' " "Our Wager," and "Our Country Quarters." *Cecil Castlemaine's Gage, Lady Marabout's Troubles, and Other Stories* (1867), an American edition published in England with previously collected stories as *Cecil Castlemaine's Gage, and Other Novelettes* (1870), completed the republication of most of the *Bentley's* stories by including the title story plus "Lady Marabout's Troubles" and "The Beauty of Vicq d'Azyr," to which were added some new stories, most notably "Deadly Dash" and "Little Grand and the Marchioness."

All of these stories share the subjects, themes, and even narrative techniques of the early novels that had become Ouida's stock-in-trade, being what Wendell V. Harris calls "tales" – often running to twenty thousand words (in the cases of "Silver Chimes and Golden Fetters," for example) – rather than briefer "short stories." "Beatrice Boville" is representative of the early stories, with its setting in fashionable London club society; its distinguished, brilliant, multitalented hero, this time not a military man but a member of Parliament; and Beatrice, the "Pythoness" woman, who serves as both the center of romantic intrigue and foil. After Beatrice's insufficient concealment of her suspicious past brings the hero to the brink of professional, personal, and physical ruin, the "Pythoness" is "tamed" as "her great love for him vanquished all else" and she "threw her arms around him and sobbed like a child on his breast." Typical also is the first-person male narrator, who relates the story from close social proximity but relative emotional distance. The tone is one of almost decadent sophistication bordering upon ennui, relieved only in moments when lurid displays of emotion require more purple prose. These same qualities, plus military adventure and more exotic settings, appear in "Deadly Dash." The story's title is the name given to a fast-living, accomplished marksman remembered by the narrator during a slow day at Epsom. Deadly Dash finally pushes his luck and skill too far when he kills a Russian prince in a duel over the love of a café singer; he drops out of the service and disappears, but the narrator, as fate would have it, encounters him by chance in the midst of a skirmish in Virginia during the American Civil War. Captured by Union forces, Dash goes to his death, having taken the place of his love's husband in a "reprisal" conscription execution, saying to the narrator, "Tell her I died for her," about which the narrator observes, "We never knew him justly till he perished there."

The galloping pace of most of these stories creates a momentum that carries the reader along despite unengaged sympathies and often frank incredulity. This response to Ouida's work was not uncommon in her time; as G. K. Chesterton noted in his reader's report to Unwin on *The Waters of Edera* (1899), "age does not wither nor custom stale her infinite lack of variety," but he added that "though it is impossible not to smile at Ouida, it is equally impossible not to read her." Her popularity with readers may be attributed to this storytelling gift, but it may be equally attributable to her employment of the elements of sensation, a flourishing form from the 1860s onward. She appealed to a public devoted to the likes of Joseph Sheridan Le Fanu, Mary Elizabeth Braddon, and Mrs. Henry Wood, writers whose stories depicting sensational events, guilty secrets, lurid emotional revelations, and implausible happenings stirred a sublimated emotional chord in the Victorian public.

The success that the early novels and stories brought her enabled Ouida to begin living the lifestyle she had previously only observed and described. In 1866 she moved her mother and her dogs to more-fashionable apartments. One year later, upon the success of *Under Two Flags,* she moved her household into the new, extravagant Langham Hotel, a spot favored by the Prince of Wales. There she kept candles lit at all hours and flowers in abundance. At the Langham she lavishly entertained dashing guardsmen and such worthies as the explorer Richard Burton and authors George Alfred Lawrence, Edward George Earle Bulwer-Lytton, and Henry Wadsworth Longfellow. She dressed herself in gowns from Paris. By the last years of the 1860s, despite the pleasures of society that now came to her, she had become dissatisfied with London and turned her sights toward the Continent. In 1871 she and her mother traveled through Belgium and Germany, ending their trip in Italy, where they settled at the Hotel de l'Italy in Florence. In 1874 she secured the Villa Farinola, three miles south of Florence, and she remained there until forcibly removed fourteen years later.

During her residence in Florence from 1871 to 1888, Ouida produced fifteen more novels and six collections of stories. The first work composed there, based on her travels, was *A Dog of Flanders and Other Stories* (1872), the four stories of which had originally appeared in *Lippincott's Magazine.* The title story, inspired by her visit to Belgium, tells about a child who dreams of being a great painter and the child's dog, who shares with him a death from starvation and exposure. Each of the three other stories – "A Branch of Lilac," "A Provence Rose," and "A Leaf in the Storm" – concerns village life in France during the Franco-Prussian war. This collection appeared in the United States in the same year under the title *A Leaf in the Storm, and Other Stories.* The subjects and themes of these stories appear as well in the novel *Two Little Wooden Shoes* (1874), the story of a Belgian girl who, after being abandoned as a baby, is reared by a kindly old peasant, whose death leaves her at the mercy of the cruel world. The novels *In a Winter City* (1876), *Friendship* (1878), and *Moths* (1880) deal with Florentine high society, its intrigues and, increasingly, its corruptions, and are generally understood to be portraits of Ouida's own involvements, especially her unrequited passion for the Marchese Lotteria Lotharing della Stufa and her violent rivalry with his mistress, Mrs. Ross (Janet Duff Gordon). The six stories included in *Pipistrello and Other Stories* (1880) deal predominantly with the problems of Italian peasants, a theme she addressed at length in her next novel, *A Village Commune* (1881).

Portrait of Ouida by Alice Danyell (published in The Whitehall Review, *5 October 1878)*

The vivid detail and portrayal of strong feeling that had marked her earlier works remained essential qualities as Ouida's work developed, but her own experience seemed to remove from her work the idealization of the leisured life of the privileged classes. This was replaced by a rather sentimentalized view of the peasantry, whose lives in her work appear through a gauzy lens of romanticism, along with a generally condemnatory attitude toward modern bureaucracy and the money supporting it. Still, she never abandoned her adoration of the virtuous and valiant heroic man. She once gave an elaborate dinner party for Robert Bulwer-Lytton, Lord Lytton, former viceroy of India, and formed a lifelong attachment with another viceroy, George Nathaniel Curzon, Lord Curzon. The sensationalism of her early career mellowed into a fondness for adventure tinged with emotionalism and bald melodrama. In this regard her work bears some resemblance to the late-nineteenth-century romanticism of Stanley J. Weyman, Sir Arthur Thomas Quiller-Couch ("Q"), Sir Anthony Hope Hawkins, and Sir Arthur Conan Doyle, all of whom enjoyed considerable success in a period often seen as dominated by aestheticism and decadence.

Ouida brought to this romantic attitude a sentimentality manifested in an often stylized manner, a simple sense of psychology, and overt moralizing. Her affinity for this mode is most apparent in her works for children, which in their worldview, if not their subject matter, resemble works such as Robert Louis Stevenson's *Treasure Island* (1883) and J. M. Barrie's *Peter Pan* (1904). *Bimbi: Stories for Children* (1882) contains several stories written for a Florentine neighbor's grandson, among them a predecessor of Frances Hodgson Burnett's *Little Lord Fauntleroy* (1886) titled "The Little Earl" and the often reprinted "The Nürnberg Stove." The brief story "Lampblack" illustrates the ideology of these stories clearly: its central character is a tube of black paint, reviled by its fellows in the artist's studio because the master never makes use of him, never allows him to contribute to beauty in the world; finally, Lampblack is made into a "no trespassing" sign to keep poachers away from the master's birds, and at last he sees the beauty of the world and contributes to the beauties of nature. Other stories in this collection include "The Ambitious Rose-Tree," "Moufflon," "The Child of Urbino," "In the Apple-Country," "Findelkind," and "Meleagris Gallopavo." One explanation for the genesis of such stories lies in the romance writer's response to the growing popular taste for realism; although Ouida's works continued to sell, the days of the three-volume romantic novel were drawing to a close, and the emotionalism once suitable for adult fiction was now increasingly reserved for children's literature.

As the 1880s drew to a close Ouida began to feel the effects of her diminished sales. Unpaid bills mounted as her income fell increasingly short of supporting her extravagant lifestyle. Her publisher's response to her financial complaints was that she should write more, and so followed a rapid spate of light novels with Continental settings – *A Rainy June* (1885), *Othmar* (1885), *Don Gesualdo* (1886), and *A House Party* (1886). Her eccentricities – among them her refusal to kennel or muzzle her dogs even during a rabies scare and her belief that plants have souls and feelings and so should never be clipped or pruned – became enough of a nuisance to her Florentine neighbors to cause significant trouble. Finally she and her mother were evicted from the Villa Farinola and commenced a life of wandering about Italy.

During this period she continued to write and to bring in a modest income, first producing the

four stories of *Ruffino and Other Stories* (1890). "Ruffino" is a story of love between a Roman prince and a Russian aristocrat; "The Orchard" and "Trottolino" are stories of peasants battling suffering and corruption: and "The Bullfinch" is a fairy-tale-like story of an anthropomorphic bird. The volume did not sell well. She followed this effort with *Santa Barbara and Other Stories* in 1891. Of the six stories in this volume "The Stable Boy," the story of a boy's search for his dog, is illustrative in its sentimentally treated juvenile subject.

In 1893 Ouida's mother died. The grieving author, now impoverished, refused to part with the body until friends intervened, and her mother was buried in a pauper's grave in the Allori cemetery.

In 1894 Ouida produced two collections of stories, *Two Offenders* and *The Silver Christ and A Lemon Tree,* the former containing tales of political persecution and the latter three accounts of the virtuous Italian peasantry, but neither of these brought any financial relief. *Le Selve* (1896) was likewise poorly received. Its title story concerns a Russian working as steward on a Roman estate, where his attempts to deal fairly with peasants result in a misunderstanding that leads to their murdering him. Her next novel, *The Massarenes* (1897), a quasi-Jamesean story of European-American relationships, received rare critical approval and prompted a laudatory, although somewhat backhanded, review by Beerbohm. The final three collections of stories she submitted to her publishers – *La Strega and Other Stories* (1899), *Street Dust and Other Stories* (1899), and *Two New Dog Stories and Another* (1900) – repeat her all-too-familiar narrative subjects and themes: the simple nobility of peasant life, the virtue inherent in nature, and the emotional (and moral) superiority of dogs. Her publisher's belief that she had lost the power to write successful fiction was correct.

The strongest writing Ouida produced during this period was her nonfiction, much of which appeared in British political and news periodicals such as the *Fortnightly Review,* the *National Review,* and *The Nineteenth Century.* These observations on Italian and European politics and the state of literature were collected in *Views and Opinions* (1895) and *Critical Studies* (1900). They were the final flower of her earlier nonfiction work protesting vivesection, *The New Priesthood: A Protest against Vivisection* (1893), and her collection of sketches and essays on Italian life, *Frescoes, etc.: Dramatic Sketches* (1883). Between 1900 and her death in 1908 she produced one novel; three collections of stories, including reprints; and one nonfiction work. None of these brought her remotely near the level of her early popularity and power, and in the absence of these Ouida died of pneumonia on 25 January 1908 in Viareggio. She was buried in the English cemetery at Bagni di Lucca through the generosity of an anonymous admirer.

The final word on Ouida's abilities is summed up by Chesterton on *The Waters of Edera:* "This is, of course, a picturesque, animated, poetic, eloquent, and supremely nonsensical story: it is by Ouida. . . . In the gorgeous and symbolic colouring, intoxicating to the eyes, we forget the silliness of the subjects and the absurdity of the human anatomy." Her great strength as a writer lay in the energy of her narration, the vividness of her descriptions, and the strength of her emotions. Her great weakness was, as Beerbohm noted, that she was not an artist; she had practically no control over her technique and no interest in acquiring any. Still, she is notable to modern readers for the clarity with which she reveals the popular tastes of her time, which her often glaring crudity of method lays bare.

Biographies:

Elizabeth Lee, *Ouida: A Memoir* (London: Unwin, 1914);

Monica Stirling, *The Fine and the Wicked: The Life and Times of Ouida* (London: Gollancz, 1957; New York: Coward-McCann, 1958).

References:

Max Beerbohm, *More* (London: Lane, 1899);

Eileen Bigland, *Ouida: The Passionate Victorian* (London: Jarrolds, 1950; New York: Duell, Sloan & Pearce, 1951);

Yvonne ffrench, *Ouida: a Study in Ostentation* (London: Cobden-Sanderson, 1930; New York: Appleton-Century, 1938);

Wendell V. Harris, *British Short Fiction in the Nineteenth Century: A Literary and Bibliographic Guide* (Detroit: Wayne State University Press, 1979);

Rose Macauley, "Eccentric Englishwomen: Ouida," *Spectator* (7 May 1937): 855–856;

Natalie Schroeder, "Feminine Sensationalism, Eroticism, and Self-Assertion: M. E. Braddon and Ouida," *Tulsa Studies in Women's Literature,* 7 (Spring 1988): 87–103.

Walter Pater

(4 August 1839 – 30 July 1894)

Hayden Ward
West Virginia University

See also the Pater entry in *DLB 57: Victorian Prose Writers After 1867.*

BOOKS: *Studies in the History of the Renaissance* (London: Macmillan, 1873); revised as *The Renaissance: Studies in Art and Poetry* (London: Macmillan, 1877; New York: Macmillan, 1877; revised again, London & New York: Macmillan, 1888; revised again, London & New York: Macmillan, 1893);

Marius the Epicurean: His Sensations and Ideas (2 volumes, London: Macmillan, 1885; 1 volume, London & New York: Macmillan, 1885; revised, 2 volumes, London & New York: Macmillan, 1892);

Imaginary Portraits (London & New York: Macmillan, 1887; New York: Macmillan, 1899);

Appreciations, with an Essay on Style (London & New York: Macmillan, 1889);

Plato and Platonism: A Series of Lectures (London: Macmillan, 1893; London & New York: Macmillan, 1893);

An Imaginary Portrait (Oxford: Privately printed, 1894); republished as *The Child in the House: An Imaginary Portrait* (Boston: Copeland & Day, 1895);

Greek Studies: A Series of Essays (New York & London: Macmillan, 1895; London & New York: Macmillan, 1901);

Miscellaneous Studies: A Series of Essays (New York & London: Macmillan, 1895; London & New York: Macmillan, 1900);

Gaston de Latour: An Unfinished Romance (New York & London: Macmillan, 1896; London: Macmillan, 1902);

Essays from "The Guardian" (London: Privately printed, 1896; Portland, Maine: Mosher, 1897);

Uncollected Essays (Portland, Maine: Mosher, 1903);

Sketches and Reviews (New York: Boni & Liveright, 1919).

Walter Pater, circa 1889

Collections: Edition DeLuxe, 9 volumes (London & New York: Macmillan, 1900–1901);

New Library Edition, 10 volumes (London: Macmillan, 1910);

Imaginary Portraits by Walter Pater: A New Collection, edited by Eugene J. Brzenk (New York: Harper & Row, 1964).

Walter Pater called the short fictions he published between 1878 and 1893 "imaginary portraits." They are a distinctive blend of history, myth, and autobiography, the outgrowth of his study and writing in the 1860s and 1870s on the Italian and French Renaissance and the society and religion of ancient Greece. They point to his effort to create a literary form that would express the ways in which the values and rituals of earlier cultures are preserved and transmitted to a later time through the medium of a temperament decidedly like Pater's own. The imaginary portraits may be considered not so much conventional stories as complex, dramatized meditations on the process by which the modern personality is shaped by the interplay of historical forces – literary, artistic, philosophical – and individual memory. As the first British writer to treat this process, Pater links the revolutionary representations of selfhood characteristic of earlier nineteenth-century Romanticism with the analysis and reinterpretation of history central to the modernist literature of the early twentieth century.

The details of his early life are sketchy. Walter Horatio Pater was born on 4 August 1839 in Shadwell in east London, the second son of Richard and Maria Pater. His father, a surgeon, died when Walter was four, and the family moved to Enfield, a north London suburb, near the home of Maria's sister, Pater's favorite "Aunt Bessie." His older brother, William, left home at fifteen in 1851, and Pater remained at home with his mother and sisters, Clara and Hester. The family moved again in 1853, to Harbledown near Canterbury, where Pater attended the King's School as a day student. He seems to have had few friends and to have taken little significant part in school life. The psychological isolation of his adolescence, especially from authoritative men and close friends his own age, is significant for the central figures in his later quasi-autobiographical imaginary portraits.

Pater entered Queen's College, Oxford, in 1858 and that same year visited his sisters in Heidelberg, where they were studying under Aunt Bessie's supervision. There he developed the interest in German Romantic literature – G. W. F. Hegel, Friedrich von Schiller, Johann Gottlieb Fichte, and Johann Wolfgang von Goethe were among the authors he read – that served eventually as the basis of his appointment as a fellow at Brasenose College, Oxford. At Queen's he studied Greek under Benjamin Jowett, who later opposed his advancement among Oxford faculty, and read on his own such controversial contemporary French writers as Théophile Gautier, Charles Baudelaire, and Gustave Flaubert. Thus, by his graduation in 1862 Pater had already learned much about the litera-

tures of ancient Greece, eighteenth-century Germany, and nineteenth-century France.

By the late 1860s Pater was publishing in periodicals a series of essays on the art and literature of the Renaissance, treating such figures as the medieval theologian Peter Abelard, the artists Michelangelo and Leonardo da Vinci, and the eighteenth-century German archaeologist and aesthetician Johann Joachim Winckelmann. The essays were collected in 1873 as *Studies in the History of the Renaissance,* with a "Conclusion" culled from an 1868 essay on the poems of William Morris as exemplary of the art of the self-styled Pre-Raphaelite poets and painters (condemned in a virulent 1871 essay by Robert Buchanan as "the fleshly school"). The book, although favorably received by some critics, offended many of the staid authority figures of Oxford, although it delighted many of the undergraduates. It seemed irreligious and willfully sensual, urging younger readers to the skeptical enjoyment of the life of the senses and deprecating orthodox beliefs. The conclusion, with its injunction "to burn always with a hard, gem-like flame"; the provocative, erotic description of da Vinci's Mona Lisa; and the veiled treatment of Winckelmann's murder by a jilted male lover were especially marked for censure, and Pater was urged by Oxford authorities to withdraw the book from circulation. He did delete the offending conclusion from the second edition but restored it for the third. The scandal caused by *Studies in the History of the Renaissance* put Pater's academic standing in question.

During this period rumors circulated among the colleges that Pater was having an affair with a Balliol undergraduate, William M. Hardinge, who was eventually dismissed from the university, and Pater's personal conduct was subjected to further gossip and even closer scrutiny. The matter was handled quietly, but he never altogether recovered his good name with the Oxford authorities. Jowett, as Master of Balliol, later saw that he was denied appointment as Slade Professor of Fine Arts, an action possibly reflecting the earlier suppressed scandal. Pater was moved to caution and greater indirection in his future writings.

Although *Studies in the History of the Renaissance* met with moral disapproval in Oxford, Pater asserted in that book the theme central to all his subsequent work, that only in the physical world as fixed and perfected by the artist was the realization of the ideal or spiritual world possible. The implication, which many in his original audience understood as subversive of Christian doctrine, was that art was not merely an adjunct of church teaching in the promotion of religious feeling and belief but the principal medium by which religious sentiment was stimulated and faith expressed. Following the personal crisis the publication of the book caused him, he sought for other subjects, other terms, by which to dramatize the interrelation of aesthetic and religious activity.

His first impulse in the mid 1870s was to do so in a series of essays on major figures of English literature. Two essays from this period, on William Wordsworth and essayist Charles Lamb, especially demonstrate this intention. In 1878 he published in *Macmillan's Magazine* the first of his imaginary portraits, "The Child in the House," a thinly veiled autobiographical sketch depicting, like Wordsworth's *The Prelude* (1850), the growth of an aesthetic and moral sensibility. The "process of brain-building" that Pater describes throughout the story is a rendering of the Romantic concept of *Bildung*, psychological development, into the terms of Victorian middle-class domestic life. Pater is not a theorist of the novel or of short fiction, but his recurrent treatment in "The Child in the House" and the subsequent imaginary portraits of the way "sensations" become "ideas" may have influenced subsequent writers such as Henry James, Joseph Conrad, James Joyce, and Marcel Proust. Eugene Brzenk, editor of a collection of Pater's short fictions, observes a pattern common to them:

> They all create the same sort of childhood impression 'in that process of brainbuilding by which we are, each one of us, what we are' – early memories closely centered about the home; intense reactions to beauty and sorrow, the latter often connected with the death of a young person; a love of ritual and ceremony, not necessarily religious in nature; and a growing sense of the individual's isolation.

Critic Wendell Harris places Pater's imaginary portraits in a tradition of aesthetic fiction that begins with Dante Gabriel Rossetti's "Hand and Soul" (1850) and the early stories of Morris and extends through Robert Louis Stevenson, Pater, and Arthur Symons. Of Pater's fictions Harris observes that "each portrays a mind seeking to impose a particular pattern on experience.... In each portrait an artist attempts to achieve an ideal, an unusually sensitive person attempts to become like or live like a work of art, or the imagined return of a pagan god exemplifies the inhumanity ... which alone would make it possible to live simultaneously as artist and work of art."

In comparing "The Child in the House" and Pater's other fictions to the work of other writers of his time, one notes certain distinctive features. The first is a minimum of directly represented action: the stories are transcriptions of the central character's impressions of the world he encounters, or, in a few instances, of a narrator's impressions and evaluations of the central character's impressions. There is no plot in the usual sense but instead a succession of static scenes that the narrator describes the central character observing and translating into aesthetic and moral conceptions, with virtually no physical or verbal contact with the other characters involved. Pater's fictions are virtually without dialogue; they take place almost entirely within the mind of the central character. Yet they are not interior monologues or records of a stream of consciousness but a series of discrete yet linked statements defining attitudes or changes in attitude rather than a quasi-logical chain of sensuous observation and judgment that leads to action.

Finally, despite Pater's emphasis in "The Child in the House" and the later imaginary portraits on the crucial role of a sense of place in the formation of the central character's sensibility, a lack of definite place and time is characteristic, as though the particularities of setting had already been rendered into highly charged connotations removed from the denotative precision of vivid description. The reader's impression is of a sensuous world vivid in the mind of the narrator or central character but seen by the audience as through a mist, a realization blurred or dimmed as by a theater scrim. Similarly, the voice of memory, devoted to recording the accreting sensations of the protagonist, usually seems indefinitely nostalgic or even vague. Life is languorous and indeterminate in these works. These puzzling qualities of his fiction may owe more to the seriousness and astute grasp with which Pater addressed the physical sciences and philosophy of his time than they do to any commitment to the theories of well-made, realistic fiction then current.

In addition to "The Child in the House," Pater began another "English Portrait," probably in the early 1880s, called "An English Poet," which reflected his studies in the 1870s of Greek mythology, especially of the god Dionysus. The manuscript eventually appeared in the *Fortnightly Review* in 1931. The poet's Norman mother is visited on her remote farm by a "slim figure with delicate hands and golden hair." An avatar of Dionysus, his mysterious, brief presence suggests perhaps the ancient heritage, mingled with the Norman maternal home, to which the young poet must return from his childhood exile in the northern cold of Wordsworthian

Cumberland. Such trips of discovery and recovery, from north to south, are common in Pater's fictions, perhaps symbolizing his own efforts to reclaim Gallic, Italian, and ancient Greek culture as part of the English inheritance. In "An English Poet" he describes the search not only for an integrated life but for the literary form or language in which the poet can express his imaginative sense of the facts of his experience. The crucial role of art, most prominently writing, in the full and accurate realization of the inner life is a central subject in his work.

The verbalization of the inner life in relation to religion and philosophy occurs in Pater's longest fictional portrait, *Marius the Epicurean: His Sensations and Ideas* (1885). On 22 July 1883 Pater wrote to his friend Vernon Lee,

> I have hopes of completing one half of my present chief work – an Imaginary Portrait of a peculiar type of mind in the time of Marcus Aurelius – by the end of this Vacation. . . . I am wishing to get the whole completed, as I have visions of many smaller pieces of work the composition of which would be actually pleasanter to me. However, I regard this present matter as a sort of duty. For, you know, I think that there is a fourth sort of religious phase possible for the modern mind, over and above those presented in your late admirable paper in the Contemporary, the conditions of which phase it is the main object of my design to convey.

Possibly because it is a novel rather than a sketch, *Marius the Epicurean* is far more vividly and fully detailed in its representation of second-century Rome (as a historical analogue to late Victorian Britain) than are the London suburbs of "The Child in the House" and the Norman and Cumberland settings of "An English Poet." The country estate where Marius grows up, called White-Nights; the court of the Stoic emperor Marcus Aurelius; and the church community of Saint Cecilia, situated atop the catacombs where the dead of the faith lie, are rendered with impressive clarity and thoroughness. However, the line of philosophical argument or internal debate over the relative merits of the various systems of thought Marius encounters is both less clear and more complex than the moral and aesthetic ideas advanced in Pater's earlier short portraits. One reason for this increasing lack of intellectual clarity is that Pater's ideas have become more abstruse and elaborately qualified and are couched in a denser, more syntactically tortuous style, a writing strategy that he increasingly employed as his career continued, perhaps in an effort to avoid being firmly pinned down by controversialists and critics.

Pater in 1872, drawing by Simeon Solomon (Fondazione Horne, Florence)

Pater's fiction after *Marius the Epicurean* takes the form of an overlay of myth derived from his study of Dionysian myth in the 1870s. More evidently than in the novel and the earlier English portraits, his later protagonists are invested with the attributes of the Greek god. Often the attributes of Dionysus – his wild, improvisational, carnivalesque artistry and his sympathy with the growing things of the earth and with animals and children – are in conflict with Apollo, a god in many respects developed in Greek myth from the older Dionysus. Among Apollo's complex qualities are a nurturing of intellectual order through the playing of austerely rational music and the impulse to create religion and art of a complex symbolic kind – in short, a tendency toward abstract idealism and away from the representation of purely sensuous form. Dionysus is the god of erotic play, Apollo the god of mind who sublimates, controls, and shapes these erotic impulses into the forms of high art. In the imaginary portraits Pater composed in the 1880s and 1890s the complementary and antagonistic relationship of these two mythic powers is dramatized.

In 1883 Pater gave up tutoring, although he retained his Brasenose fellowship. In 1885 – at the time his nomination to succeed John Ruskin as Slade Professor of Fine Arts was turned aside – he and his sisters moved to London, where, according to Lee, who visited regularly, they entertained a "fashionable bohemian element" drawn perhaps by his literary reputation. Frank Harris in the second series of his *Contemporary Portraits* (1919) found the ambience less glamorous: "The house might have belonged to a grocer." Charles Holmes, later director of the National Gallery, noted Pater's military bearing and greater liveliness in London than in Oxford, obsrving that "he might have been a retired major in the Rifle Brigade. The Paters lived in London until 1893, when they returned to a house in Oxford, suggestively in the neighborhood of the Martyrs' Monument.

Despite the apparently sedate bourgeois circumstances of his London life, Pater wrote several of his most striking portraits during these years. Between October 1885 and May 1887 he published four of them in *Macmillan's Magazine,* an association he continued until 1892. On 24 May 1887 Macmillan published them as *Imaginary Portraits.* Significantly, Pater omitted "The Child in the House" from the collection, even though he had once referred to it, in a note preserved among his papers at Harvard University, as "the germinating, original, source, specimen of all my imaginative work." Possibly he felt that the mythic pattern of the four portraits from the mid 1880s imparted to them a thematic unity that the more directly autobiographical "Child in the House" did not share.

The first piece in *Imaginary Portraits,* "A Prince of Court Painters," originally published in October 1885, depicts the life of the French painter Jean-Antoine Watteau. The narrative is in the form of selected fragments from the fictional diary of the older sister of Jean-Baptiste Pater, a younger painter who studied with Watteau and whom Pater and his sisters liked to claim as an ancestor. From the point of view of this sister – who observes Watteau's promise even when he learns his craft as a boy in their northern French town of Valenciennes, noted as a center of provincial art – the story tells of his move to Paris to study. He quickly becomes celebrated for his "new manner" of painting the aristocratic life of the capital. However, the narrator becomes concerned at the evident fatigue and restlessness he exhibits, despite his great success, during his occasional visits to his native city. She discerns

his contempt for the superficial glamour of the world his art has so brilliantly captured; he feels like an alien in his maturity amid the persons and scenes his youthful aesthetic vision has enabled him to master:

> Methinks Antony Watteau reproduces that gallant world, those patched and powdered ladies and fine cavaliers, so much to its own satisfaction, partly because he despises it; if this be a possible condition of excellent artistic production. People talk of a new era now dawning upon the world of fraternity, liberty, humanity, of a novel sort of social freedom in which men's natural goodness of heart will blossom at a thousand points hitherto repressed, of wars disappearing from the world in an infinite, benevolent ease of life – yes! perhaps of infinite littleness also. And it is the outward manner of that, which, partly by anticipation, and through pure intellectual power, Antony Watteau has caught, together with a flattering something of his own, added thereto. Himself really of the old time – that serious old time which is passing away, the impress of which he carries in his physiognomy – he dignifies by what in him is neither more nor less than a profound melancholy, the essential insignificance of what he *wills* to touch in all that, transforming its mere pettiness into grace.

By echoing the "Liberté, Egalité, Fraternité" slogan of the French Revolution and the "novel sort of social freedom" an early eighteenth-century narrator might hope that such a revolution could bring, Pater imparts to Watteau the kind of visionary or prophetic power that the nineteenth century attributed to the Romantic poet. The other side of Watteau's character – his restless melancholy and his sense of displacement from his true home, provincial if not rural – is an expression of his exile. In the service of a modern idea he has lost the sensuous harmony with earth that Dionysus represents. He is a type of the divided nature of the artist as Pater's Victorian era came to conceive it. This alienation is figured in the tuberculosis that kills him, as it did John Keats and other Romantic artists. Watteau does not, as the poet did, travel south in search of an earthier, warmer climate but goes to England, "the native country of consumption," as Pater has the narrator call it. Eventually, although he returns to Valenciennes briefly, Watteau goes back to Paris and to his Apollonian art, only deepened now by a partially recovered religious sentiment that gives at least a measure of tranquility before death. However, the narrator closes by emphasizing not this slight recovery but the ultimately futile effort to regain the wholeness of being that his career destroyed: "He has been a sick man all his life. He was always a seeker after something in the world that is there in no satisfying measure, or not at all."

The second piece in *Imaginary Portraits,* originally published in *Macmillan's Magazine* for October 1886, is "Denys l'Auxerrois," which draws upon the belief, expressed in Heinrich Heine's monograph *Les Dieux en exil* (The Gods in Exile, 1853), that the ancient Greek deities are reincarnated in disguise during the Christian era, embodiments of the transmittal of myth from one culture to another. Although Pater's fiction is not explicit about whether or not Denys is a god, the gradual revelation of his Dionysian appearance, behavior, and influence make clear that he is at least a human avatar of Dionysus, come with liberating and disruptive force into the northern French city of Auxerre, which is dominated by the sedate Apollonian rituals of the medieval church.

The mythic mystery of Denys's story is heightened by Pater's narrator, a nineteenth-century tourist whose antiquarian enthusiasm is piqued by the discovery of "a large and brilliant fragment of stained glass" and "an entire set of tapestries," both of which depict citizens of the town under the spell of a strange music, dancing in the presence of an "oft-repeated figure," "a flaxen and flowery creature, . . . a suffering, tortured figure. With all the regular beauty of a pagan god, he has suffered after a manner of which we must suppose pagan gods incapable." With the aid of notes to help him interpret the stained glass and the tapestries, the narrator finds that "the story shaped itself at last." By the time Pater employed it, the device of the narrator as scholar/editor/detective was a well-established convention of Victorian fiction.

The narrator construes Denys as an inspirer of "the assertion of individual freedom" and "that new, free generous manner in art." Denys's effect on the cathedral town and its surrounding farms is carnivalesque, a spontaneous infusion of anarchic vitality, as in the quaint Easter ball game played within the cathedral, when Denys makes his first appearance, "leaping in among the timid children" and inspiring both boys and priests to play "almost like madmen." This effect becomes increasingly violent in the celebration of the harvest, at which Denys himself, now known as an eater of raw flesh, has his lip bloodied and is torn apart by the frenzied crowd, much as Dionysus was in some ancient rites dismembered, his remains scattered over the land to encourage bounty in the next year's crop.

Pater here uses his earlier study of the Dionysus myth to produce a kind of political parable in which the divine liberator or his human sur-

rogate becomes the sacrificial victim of the wild energies his influence brings out in a society controlled by usually benevolent authoritarianism. The parallel between the medieval town awakened to "a new birth of freedom" that issues in uncontrollable disorder and death and the revolutionary climate in Europe during the nineteenth century would have been evident to Pater's Victorian readers, who were preoccupied with both the ecstatic promise and the threat of anarchy in the contemporary world.

The third piece in *Imaginary Portraits,* "Sebastian van Storck," originally published in *Macmillan's Magazine* in March 1886, is more somber than "A Prince of Court Painters" and "Denys l'Auxerrois." The young Sebastian is so alienated from the prosperous, sensuously rich world of his seventeenth-century Dutch burgomaster father and the company of artists and middle-class merchant families that mingle convivially in the van Storck home that he seeks solitary refuge in an isolated tower to brood on the illusoriness of the rich, concrete images that the Dutch genre painters of the time have so vividly represented.

Sebastian is alienated not merely from the idea of home, as Pater's Watteau is, but from the art that idealizes that home. His "lonely thinking power" concentrates instead on the contemplation of vast, dehumanized, wintry countrysides and open seascapes. Pater makes telling use in this portrait of the ambiguous Dutch attitude toward the sea, both provider and potential destroyer. Sebastian associates this distant terrain and water with a desire, only half realized, for his own death and finds confirmation for his views, he believes, in the teachings of the Dutch philosopher Benedict de Spinoza and the Roman naturalist Pliny the Elder.

Sebastian's virtual solipsism leads him to reject one of the leading principles of Pater's own aesthetic humanism, "that golden art, surrounding us with an ideal world, beyond which the real world is discernible indeed, but etherealised by the medium through which it comes to one: all this, for most men so powerful a link to existence, only set him on the thought of escape . . . into a formless and nameless infinite world, quite evenly grey." Pater saves Sebastian from the sin of intellectual pride by making his morbid philosophy, his desire to die into thought, the consequence of "a vein of physical *phthisis*" or tuberculosis, his sensuous powers literally "consumed," like those of Watteau, by disease. So that his young thinker may have some respite from his aberrant Apollonianism, Pater has him die while saving a young child from drowning as the sea rushes through a ruptured dike, an act

IMAGINARY PORTRAITS

BY

WALTER PATER, M.A.

FELLOW OF BRASENOSE COLLEGE, OXFORD

LONDON
MACMILLAN AND CO.
AND NEW YORK
1887

Title page for a collection of short stories in which Pater combines history, myth, and autobiography

history is possibly the equivalent of or replacement for the traditional religious revelation of God's will.

In order to escape south, like the "English poet" of the earlier sketch, Duke Carl fakes his own death and leaves Rosenmold, only to be called back having barely glimpsed Italy from a distant mountaintop — Pater's possible allusion to the comparable fate of Moses, another light-bearing prophet. Ironically, Carl suffers a brutal death, trampled by the horses and cannon of an invading army. His Apollonian mission remains unfulfilled until Goethe and his generation reveal to Germany and the rest of Europe "the permanent reality of a poetic ideal in human life." An aesthetic rather than a political revolutionary, Carl dies before he can implement his visionary scheme in the practical affairs of his provincial world. This story reflects Pater's increasing emphasis on the violent end and failure of his idealistic heroes.

Although *Imaginary Portraits* was Pater's favorite among his books, the volume received a more subdued critical response than his earlier writings, perhaps because the style blurred even more than the heavily philosophical content of *Marius the Epicurean* the generic distinction between the personal essay and fiction. Oscar Wilde praised "Sebastian van Storck," possibly because it revealed the pathetic consequences of disdain for the sensuous power of art and the repression of desire. The distinguished American critic George Woodberry commended "A Prince of Court Painters" as being "highly finished." Another critic, Eleanor Price, thought the collection "the saddest book Mr. Pater has yet written" and singled out "Denys l'Auxerrois" as especially characteristic of "Mr. Pater's peculiar style." Almost none of the reviewers spoke positively of "Duke Carl of Rosenmold"; possibly because modern readers value Pater more as a cultural critic than as a story writer, its explicit and detailed exposition of a theory of the transmission of cultural values now gives it special interest, for modern critics among the four portraits. For the most part Pater's contemporaries seem not to have understood or to have ignored his pioneering experiment in mythopoeic representation of the forces of historical change, an experiment that in some degree makes him the precursor of such major modernist writers as Joyce, Virginia Woolf, William Butler Yeats, and E. M. Forster.

Following the May 1887 publication of *Imaginary Portraits,* despite the death of his older brother, William, Pater was at work on what, in a letter of March 1886 to William Stanley Withers, he identified as what would be the second volume of "a kind

prompted by a residual Dionysian instinct not wholly suppressed by a life of lonely meditation.

The final piece included in *Imaginary Portraits,* "Duke Carl of Rosenmold," originally published in *Macmillan's Magazine* in May 1887, presents a cultural hero of a less equivocal kind, a young German aristocrat who seeks to bring the benefits of the Enlightenment, the *Aufklärung,* to his sleepy little duchy. To this end Duke Carl attempts the recovery of Greek art and culture and its application to the conditions of late-eighteenth-century German life, a motive that resembles the aspirations of the English "Hellenists" of the Victorian era. Duke Carl explicitly associates this task with Apollo, revealer of "light." As in his other fictions, Pater creates in this imaginary portrait a Romantic parable of the historical consciousness of his own time. For Pater the autobiographically centered interpretation of

of trilogy," of which *Marius the Epicurean* had been the first. From June to October 1888 he published in *Macmillan's Magazine* five chapters of *Gaston de Latour,* set "in France, at the end of the 16th century." He brought out a sixth chapter in the August 1889 *Fortnightly Review* and then abandoned the work in 1891, leaving six chapters in manuscript. These manuscripts have been edited by Gerald C. Monsman for publication, along with the six initial chapters printed in book form by Charles Shadwell in 1896, in a complete text of the novel for publication in 1995.

The core of *Gaston de Latour* is the encounters the title character, a young Catholic, has with three prominent figures representing new currents of art and philosophy in a France beset with religious persecution and political turmoil: poet Pierre de Ronsard, leader of a school of poets called the Pléiade who are known especially for their amatory sonnets; the skeptical humanist philosopher Michel de Montaigne, best known for his *Essais* (Essays, 1580, 1588); and the peripatetic Italian Dominican orator Giordano Bruno, whose obscure teachings emphasized God as the unity of spirit and matter. Each encounter leads Gaston further along a path of estrangement from his early orthodox faith toward a formulation of provisional beliefs that recalls the intellectual epicureanism of Marius. In both *Gaston de Latour* and *Marius the Epicurean* Pater's treatment of the historical aesthetic, religious, and philosophical issues is plainly meant as analogous to the issues of the Victorian age.

In 1889 Pater published *Appreciations, with an Essay on Style,* a volume of his essays on English literature, and in 1893 he brought out the book version of the lectures he had delivered at Oxford, *Plato and Platonism.* In the interval between these two nonfictional works he published in periodicals three more imaginary portraits, which were not reprinted in his lifetime. They are his last works of short fiction and perhaps his most moving.

"Hippolytus Veiled," based on a tragedy by Euripides, tells about Hippolytus, the son of Antiope, queen of the Amazons, who, having married her Athenian conqueror, Theseus, is soon cast off and exiled with her infant to a remote rural region of Greece in favor of a new wife, Phaedra. As he grows to young manhood Hippolytus becomes the votary of Artemis, goddess of chastity. On a visit to Athens, Hippolytus is urged by Phaedra to worship Aphrodite, goddess of love, and when he refuses she falsely accuses him to Theseus of having tried to seduce her — Pater implies a comparison with the story in Genesis of Joseph and Potiphar's wife —

and Theseus, with the aid of the sea god Poseidon, has the boy killed when the horses pulling his chariot along the shore are spooked and drag him over the rough rocks. His grieving mother dies soon afterward.

In *Greek Studies: A Series of Essays* (1895) Pater defines the theme of his version of the myth as "progress triumphant through injustice." In an extended opening exposition he writes of the ways in which many charming and worthwhile customs and rituals of ancient rural life and religion survive in somnolent isolation until they are either assimilated or effaced by the influence of a centralizing urban civilization or empire, represented here by the ascendancy of Athens over the other *demes* (townships or districts) of ancient Attica. This process of conquest and failed assimilation leading to destruction is presented by the fate of Antiope, alienated from her Amazon women warriors by marriage to Theseus and later by the failed seduction and betrayal of Hippolytus by Phaedra. The story also implies a dialectical process at work in Greek history — and by implication in later Western history — that Pater outlines in the early lectures of *Plato and Platonism.*

The second of these late portraits, "Emerald Uthwart," occasioned by a nostalgic visit Pater made in 1891 to the King's School, Canterbury, was published in the *New Review* in June and July 1892. It depicts a boy from an old county family who, endowed with a "genius of submissiveness," absorbs completely, as with the quality of the diaphanous temperament Pater had outlined nearly thirty years earlier, the ethical and social influence of the public school he attends. Surrounded by the imposing medieval buildings and subjected to the ascetic training of school life, he becomes a model of honorable courage and disciplined intelligence and becomes, as the time demands, a soldier in the British army fighting against Napoleon. Inspired by a desire for valorous action, Emerald and his closest friend from school, James Stokes, engage in a rash military adventure against orders, are court-martialed, and are sentenced to execution by firing squad for desertion. Stokes dies but Emerald is spared, only to die at his family home some years later, after a period of disconsolate wandering, with a mysterious bullet removed from his body after death.

This strange tale of an unjustly punished military martyr, whose godlike English beauty, intelligence, and virtue of getting on well with all who know him in the world of stern discipline and mortal danger he chooses to enter, is a story of the sacrifice of youth in the service of a harsh nationalistic ideology. The portrait also recalls Pater's earlier representations of the suffering Dionysus as cultural icon and victim. Significantly, Pater's lecture "Lacedaemon" in *Plato and Platonism* describes with general approval the ascetic training of ancient Spartan youth in an analogous cause.

The last piece of Pater's fiction published in his lifetime was "Apollo in Picardy," which appeared in the November 1893 *Harper's New Monthly Magazine*. As in "Denys l'Auxerrois" he draws on Heine's *Les Dieux en exil* as background for the story of "Hyperborean Apollo," a wintry version of the god with qualities of Dionysus mixed into his nature who comes to northern France and disrupts the tranquil, enclosed world of a medieval monastery. Pater calls the figure "Brother Apollyon," after the "destroyer" angel mentioned in Revelation 9:11, to suggest the "devilish" side of this winter Apollo's vivifying influence, which enlivens and enlightens only to kill before vanishing.

The chief character of the story is Prior Saint-Jean, a monastic mathematician at work upon an abstruse treatise until his health breaks, when he is sent to a country grange to recuperate accompanied by Hyacinthus, a boyish monk. One night the prior discovers Apollyon sleeping in a barn; he resembles "old Adam fresh from his Maker's hand," and his presence makes the land around the grange seem like "a veritable paradise, still unspoiled." But like Adam, Apollyon will sin and thus turn the landscape once more into a fallen world. Pater subtly weaves together in this story elements of ancient Greek myth and the biblical myth of the fall from paradise to suggest the historical process by which the recovery of classical culture undermined the stability of medieval Christian learning and religious faith.

At first Brother Apollyon's influence is benign. Playing his wonderful music on a magical lyre or harp, he inspires the workmen laboring to construct a new barn for the grange. This barn built to music has its severe Gothic lines softened by the grace of classical architecture. The influence of Brother Apollyon, however, is also malign. Even as he makes flowers bloom mysteriously in winter, he also maims or kills the small animals that seek his protection. He destroys a Gothic pigeon house and mutilates the birds. Most notoriously, he crushes the head of young Hyacinthus by throwing a discus in one of the better-known elements from the myth that Pater uses in the story.

Central to the story is the god's impact on Prior Saint-Jean, who is distracted from his orderly mathematical labors and driven into an erratic, fragmented, sensuous creativity by Apollo's influence –

for instance, drawing images in the margins of his "crabbed" manuscript. When Apollyon vanishes suddenly after the death of Hyacinthus, Prior Saint-Jean is confined at the monastery where he has spent most of his life, suspected of the brutal murder and presumably mad with grief. He dies at his window, looking in the direction of the fatal grange for signs of hyacinths in the fields. Pater leaves the reader wondering if he is also looking, with ambiguous emotions, for the return of Brother Apollyon. In Prior Saint-Jean's bizarre fate Pater epitomizes in fictional form the downfall of medieval scholarship and asceticism and leaves indeterminate the consequences of its violent collision with the revived and potent force of ancient beliefs about the complex moral nature of humanity.

Pater died of a massive heart attack on 30 July 1894 in his Oxford home with his sisters at his side, as they would be in Holywell Cemetery after their own deaths in 1910 and 1928. The funeral was held on 2 August, during the university's summer vacation; the published eulogies were muted and constrained. Perhaps more than most Victorian authors Pater was subjected, as he probably would have wished, to the prevailing code of biographical reticence. The close study of his writings remained subordinated, until recent decades, to a sanitized reminiscence of his Oxford career and some efforts at evaluating his aesthetic and historical theories.

Most of the significant criticism treating Pater's various imaginary portraits focuses on an analysis of his use of Dionysian and Apollonian myth, a scheme first outlined in a 1961 article by R. T. Lonaghan and interpreted in considerable detail by Monsman in *Pater's Portraits: Mythic Pattern in the Fiction of Walter Pater* (1967). The fictions are also treated in Monsman's study of the "self-reflexive text" in *Walter Pater's Art of Autobiography* (1980). M. F. Moran cogently assesses a shift in emphasis in Pater studies, and in criticism more generally, in recent years:

Focus on Pater's mythography and transformations confirms his interest in a modern consciousness divided against itself: a theory of personality which Paterian scholars have deemed a 'commonplace in Modernist literature.' But more radically, the mythic fiction highlights a particular manifestation of this divided modern spirit located in critical practice itself. At the same time as the tales express a 'reading' of the modern cultural dilemma, their form and narrative strategies call into question traditional concepts of 'reading,' of the process of ascribing meaning, of the practice and nature of interpretation.

First page from the unfinished manuscript for "Tibalt the Albigense," one of Pater's "imaginary portraits" (Houghton Library, Harvard University)

Pater has gone from being a nearly forgotten minor Victorian writer to a critic and writer of experimental fictions and a major ancestral presence in modern literature and criticism.

Letters:
Letters of Walter Pater, edited by Lawrence Evans (Oxford: Oxford University Press, 1970).

Bibliographies:
Lawrence Evans, "Walter Pater," in *Victorian Prose: A Guide to Research,* edited by David J. DeLaura (New York: Modern Language Association, 1973), pp. 321–359;

Samuel Wright, *A Bibliography of the Writings of Walter H. Pater* (New York: Garland, 1975);

Franklin E. Court, ed., *Walter Pater: An Annotated Bibliography of Writings About Him* (De Kalb: Northern Illinois University Press, 1980).

Biographies:
A. C. Benson, *Walter Pater* (London & New York: Macmillan, 1906);

Thomas Wright, *The Life of Walter Pater,* 2 volumes (London: Everett, 1907; New York: Putnam, 1907);

Germain d'Hangest, *Walter Pater: L'homme et l'oeuvre,* 2 volumes (Paris: Didier, 1961);

Michael Levey, *The Case of Walter Pater* (London: Thames & Hudson, 1978);

R. H. Seiler, *Walter Pater: A Life Remembered* (Calgary: University of Calgary Press, 1987);

Denis Donoghue, *Walter Pater: Lover of Strange Souls* (New York: Knopf, 1995).

References:
Ed Bloch Jr., "Walter Pater's 'Diaphaneitè' and the Pattern of Reader Response in the Portrait Essay," *Texas Studies in Literature and Language,* 25 (Fall 1983): 427–447;

Harold Bloom, "The Crystal Man," Introduction to *Selected Writings of Walter Pater* (New York: New American Library, 1974), pp. vii–xxxi;

Laurel Brake, *Walter Pater* (Plymouth, U.K.: Northcote House, 1994);

Eugene J. Brzenk, "The Unique Fictional World of Walter Pater," *Nineteenth-Century Fiction,* 13 (December 1958): 217–226;

William E. Buckler, *Walter Pater: The Critic as Artist of Ideas* (New York: New York University Press, 1987);

John Coates, "Aspects of the Intellectual Context of Pater's *Imaginary Portraits," Yearbook of English Studies,* 15 (1985): 93–108;

John J. Conlon, *Walter Pater and the French Tradition* (Lewisburg, Pa.: Bucknell University Press, 1982);

Steven Connor, "Myth and Meta-myth in Max Müller and Walter Pater," in *The Sun Is King: Painting, Literature and Mythology in the Nineteenth Century,* edited by J. B. Bullen (Oxford: Clarendon, 1989), pp. 199–222;

Connor, "Myth as Multiplicity in Walter Pater's *Greek Studies* and 'Denys l'Auxerrois,'" *Review of English Studies,* new series 34 (February 1983): 28–42;

David J. DeLaura, *Hebrew and Hellene in Victorian England: Newman, Arnold, and Pater* (Austin: University of Texas Press, 1969);

Richard Dellamora, *Masculine Desire: The Sexual Politics of Victorian Aestheticism* (Chapel Hill: University of North Carolina Press, 1990), pp. 102–116;

Linda Dowling, *Language and Decadence in the Victorian Fin de Siècle* (Princeton: Princeton University Press, 1986);

Iain Fletcher, *Walter Pater* (London: Longmans, Green, 1959);

Wendell Harris, *British Short Fiction in the Nineteenth Century* (Detroit: Wayne State University Press, 1979);

John Smith Harrison, "Pater, Heine, and the Old Gods of Greece," *PMLA,* 39 (September 1924): 655–686;

Graham Hough, *The Last Romantics* (London: Duckworth, 1949), pp. 134–174;

Billie Andrew Inman, "Estrangement and Connection: Walter Pater, Benjamin Jowett, and William M. Hardinge," in *Pater in the 1990s,* edited by Brake and Ian Small (Greensboro, N.C.: ELT Press, 1991), pp. 1–20;

Inman, *Walter Pater's Reading, 1858–1873* (New York: Garland, 1981);

Inman, *Walter Pater's Reading, 1874–1877* (New York: Garland, 1990);

Wolfgang Iser, *Walter Pater: The Aesthetic Moment* (Cambridge: Cambridge University Press, 1987);

Frank Kermode, *Romantic Image* (London: Routledge & Kegan Paul, 1957; New York: Macmillan, 1957);

U. C. Knoepflmacher, *Religious Humanism and the Victorian Novel: George Eliot, Walter Pater, and Samuel Butler* (Princeton: Princeton University Press, 1965);

R. T. Lenaghan, "Pattern in Walter Pater's Fiction," *Studies in Philology,* 58 (January 1961): 69–91;

J. Hillis Miller, "Walter Pater: A Partial Portrait," *Daedalus,* 105 (Winter 1976): 97–113;

Gerald C. Monsman, "Pater Redivivus," in *The Victorian Experience: The Prose Writers,* edited by Richard A. Levine (Athens: Ohio University Press, 1982), pp. 203–239;

Monsman, "Pater's 'Child in the House' and the Renovation of the Self," *Texas Studies in Literature and Language,* 28 (Fall 1986): 281–295;

Monsman, *Pater's Portraits: Mythic Pattern in the Fiction of Walter Pater* (Baltimore: Johns Hopkins University Press, 1967);

Monsman, *Walter Pater* (Boston: Twayne, 1977);

Monsman, *Walter Pater's Art of Autobiography* (New Haven: Yale University Press, 1980);

M. F. Moran, "Pater's Mythic Fiction: Gods in a Gilded Age," in *Pater in the 1990s,* edited by Brake and Small (Greensboro, N.C.: ELT Press, 1991), pp. 169–188;

Daniel O'Hara, "The Temptations of the Scholar: Walter Pater's *Imaginary Portraits,*" in *De-structing the Novel: Essays in Applied Postmodern Hermeneutics,* edited by Leonard Orr (Troy, N.Y.: Whitston, 1982), pp. 65–111;

Robert Peters, "The Cult of the Returned Apollo: Walter Pater's *Renaissance* and *Imaginary Portraits,*" *Pre-Raphaelite Review,* 2 (November 1981): 53–69;

John R. Reed, "Decadent Style and the Short Story," *Victorians Institute Journal,* 11 (1983): 1–12;

R. H. Seiler, ed., *Walter Pater: The Critical Heritage* (London: Routledge & Kegan Paul, 1980);

William F. Shuter, "The Arrested Narrative of 'Emerald Uthwart,' " *Nineteenth-Century Literature,* 45 (June 1990): 1–25;

Shuter, "Walter Pater and the Academy's 'Dubious Name,' " *Victorians Institute Journal,* 18 (1988): 129–147;

Jane Spirit, "Nineteenth-Century Responses to Montaigne and Bruno: A Context for Pater," in *Pater in the 1990s,* edited by Brake and Small (Greensboro, N.C.: ELT Press, 1991), pp. 217–227;

Anthony Ward, *Walter Pater: The Idea in Nature* (London: Macgibbon & Kee, 1966);

René Wellek, "Walter Pater," in *A History of Modern Criticism, 1750–1950,* volume 3 (New Haven: Yale University Press, 1965), pp. 381–399;

Carolyn Williams, *Transfigured World: Walter Pater's Aesthetic Historicism* (Ithaca: Cornell University Press, 1989).

Papers:

The major collection of Pater manuscripts is in the Houghton Library at Harvard University. Most of the material is from the last years of Pater's life and includes several fragmentary "imaginary portraits" and a nearly complete essay on John Henry Newman. Harvard also has the manuscript of the 1880 version of Pater's essay on Samuel Taylor Coleridge. The manuscript of the published chapters of *Gaston de Latour* is in the Berg Collection of the New York Public Library, while the manuscripts for the unpublished chapters are at the library of the University of Arizona. The manuscript of Pater's essay on *Measure for Measure* is in the Folger Shakespeare Library, Washington, D.C., while that of "Diaphaneitè" is at the King's School, Canterbury. The manuscript of "Pascal," Pater's last, unfinished essay, is in Duke Humphrey's Library of the Bodleian Library, Oxford. Pater's letters to his principal publisher, Macmillan, are in the Macmillan Archive of the British Library.

Alice Perrin

(July 1867 – 13 February 1934)

Anne Colclough Little
Auburn University at Montgomery

BOOKS: *Into Temptation,* 2 volumes (London: White, 1894);

Late in Life, 2 volumes (London: Hurst & Blackett, 1896);

East of Suez (London: Treherne, 1901);

The Spell of the Jungle (London: Treherne, 1902; New York: Duffield, 1910);

The Stronger Claim (London: Eveleigh Nash, 1903; New York: Duffield, 1910);

The Waters of Destruction (London: Chatto & Windus, 1905);

Red Records (London: Chatto & Windus, 1906);

A Free Solitude (London: Chatto & Windus, 1907);

Idolatry (New York: Duffield, 1909; London: Chatto & Windus, 1909);

The Charm (New York: Fitzgerald, 1910; London: Methuen, 1910);

The Anglo-Indians (London: Methuen, 1912; New York: Duffield, 1913);

The Woman in the Bazaar (London: Cassell, 1914);

The Happy Hunting Ground (London: Methuen, 1914);

Separation (London: Cassell, 1917);

Tales That Are Told (London: Skeffington, 1917);

Star of India (London: Cassell, 1919);

The Vow of Silence (London: Cassell, 1920);

The Mound (London: Methuen, 1922);

Government House (London: Cassell, 1925);

Rough Passages (London: Cassell, 1926);

Other Sheep (London: Benn, 1932).

Alice Perrin's short stories and novels are appropriately designated Anglo-Indian fiction, both because of their content and her background. This term generally applies either to works about the English and Indians of British India or to works by men and women who had lived there, usually as sons, daughters, or wives of English officers, civil servants, or missionaries. Popularized by Rudyard Kipling, Anglo-Indian fiction was most prevalent during the late nineteenth and early twentieth centuries, and although E. M. Forster and George Or-

well are sometimes labeled Anglo-Indian, most writers associated with the subgenre are much less well known. Often grouped with Perrin are other approximate contemporaries of Kipling, including Flora Annie Steel, Maud Diver, B. M. Croker, F. E. F. Penny, and E. W. Savi. During their heyday Anglo-Indian writers were extremely popular because they offered readers a look at the previously unknown place referred to as "the gem of the Empire" and satisfied a market for romantic, sometimes supernatural stories set in exotic places. Especially during the period before colonialism was widely challenged, these works were also excellent vehicles for celebrating British imperialism and encouraging support for what Kipling called "the white man's burden." Perrin's novels and short stories are typical of Anglo-Indian fiction, with what can now be recognized as characteristic flaws of the subgenre as well as some felicitous exceptions that challenge the obscurity to which she has been consigned.

Few details are known about Perrin's life. She was born in India in July 1867, two years after Kipling, to Bertha Biederman Robinson and Maj. Gen. John Innes Robinson of the Bengal Cavalry. Following a tradition common among Anglo-Indian families and among her characters, her family had a long association with India, most notably through her grandfather, Sir George Abercrombie Robinson, who had been a director and chairman of the East India Company and was created baronet. She was one of five children, and two of her brothers eventually held the baronetcy, which was passed down from their uncle. Like the offspring of most British military officers and civilians serving in India, Perrin was educated in England, and, continuing the tradition, she returned to India in adulthood after her marriage on 24 May 1886. Her husband, Charles Perrin, member of the Institute of Civil Engineers, served in the Indian Public Works Department for around twenty-five years. Probably only two of Perrin's stories, "Caulfield's Crime" (1892) and "In the Next Room" (1893), and two of her novels, *Into Temptation* (1894) and *Late in Life* (1896), were published while she lived in India. Traveling with her husband as he performed his duties, however, gave her an intimate knowledge of India, its people, and the English overlords, each of which she would write about for the rest of her life.

All Perrin's short stories are set in India, England, or both, and all except four contain characters who live or have lived in India. Her stories about Indians examine their customs, beliefs, and superstitions, and many stories, those set in India and those set in England, include supernatural elements, primarily ghosts, although like many of her contemporaries she usually offers a rational explanation the reader may choose to believe. Like many female writers of her day, she frequently focuses on love, male-female relationships, or marital discord, perhaps because these topics were considered appropriate for female authors, perhaps because she knew these subjects well, or maybe simply because they sold well to a predominantly female audience. Her Anglo-Indian heroines are usually young and beautiful, and although they often flirt, they generally make the "correct" moral choices. Perrin's stories also frequently deal with loneliness, family separation, isolation, and – especially when her setting is India – deadly diseases, an oppressively hot climate, strange and often dangerous animals, and sometimes threatening people. Not all her menacing characters are Indian, however; the British can be equally so. She frequently examines the contrast between England and India, as Kipling often does. But despite her obvious chauvinism for British customs and people, her tendency to stereotype Indian characters (although not always negatively), and her celebration of the benevolence of imperialism, she almost always writes with sympathy for her characters, English and Indian, even those whose behavior is misguided.

Perrin's first two stories appeared in holiday issues of *Belgravia,* a London magazine that often featured love or adventure stories in exotic settings. The first tale, "Caulfield's Crime," concerns the murder of a fakir who had been scaring away the game that Caulfield, an Englishman, is trying to shoot. After his death the fakir is reincarnated as a jackal and torments Caulfield. When Caulfield dies from rabies, the narrator wants not to believe it was caused by the bite of the jackal. This story set in India has elements that characterize much of Perrin's work: the conflict between English and Indian characters, a supernatural occurrence, and punishment for the guilty. Especially representative are her realistic details, which create a strong sense

of place. Caulfield and the narrator, for instance, pitch their tents "in the scanty shade of some stunted dak jungle trees with thick dry bark, flat, shapeless leaves, that clattered together when stirred by the wind." The men hunt near a village where the "yellow mud walls were ruined and crumbling, and the inhabitants seemed scanty and poverty-stricken." Caulfield's decline and death come during the spring, with "its plague of insects and scorching winds" and dust storms that bring "a few tantalising drops of rain, or more often [left] the air thick with a copper-coloured haze." The setting creates an effective atmosphere in which to tell this story of murder, revenge, and reincarnation.

Perrin's second tale, "In the Next Room," is about an Englishwoman in India who is saved from murder by the voices of ghosts in the next room. Her husband attributes the voices to her indigestion. While some scenes are effective, the story as a whole lacks the mystery Perrin's setting evokes in "Caulfield's Crime" and is weakened by the husband's dismissal of the ghosts. Many ghost stories create ambiguity by providing a possible natural explanation for what appear to be supernatural occurrences, but here the explanation is too improbable. The impact of the supernatural is also diminished by the coincidental timing of the appearance of the ghosts.

Around the turn of the century Perrin and her husband returned to England, where he subsequently worked for the London Water Board and the Ministry of Health. Probably shortly after their return she published her third book and first story collection, *East of Suez* (1901), which includes her two early tales. The title of the book marks the setting and subtly establishes a tone with its allusion to Kipling's "Mandalay" (1892):

> Ship me somewhere east of Suez,
>   where the best is like the worst,
> Where there aren't no Ten Commandments
>   an' a man can raise a thirst.

Although Perrin's India is not the overtly lawless or immoral place that Kipling's poem suggests, her stories of ordinary human emotions – love, jealousy, anger, revenge, greed, fear, grief – are heightened by the exotic atmosphere of India and its people. The alien beauty of the landscape; the bizarre, sometimes frightening behavior of the Indians; the superstitions and supernatural occurrences that seem appropriate to the place – all combine to create an eerie strangeness in the volume.

Two of the fourteen stories in *East of Suez,* "The Belief of Bhagwan, Bearer" and "The White

EAST OF SUEZ

BY
A. PERRIN
AUTHOR OF
'INTO TEMPTATION,' 'LATE IN LIFE'

LONDON
ANTHONY TREHERNE & CO. LIMITED
3 AGAR STREET, CHARING CROSS
1901

*Title page for Perrin's first collection of short stories. The title is
an allusion to Rudyard Kipling's poem "Mandalay" (1892)*

Tiger," have Indians as central characters, but the other twelve focus primarily on Anglo-Indians, the most common themes being love or relations between the sexes. Typical of the love stories is "An Eastern Echo," set in a provincial Indian town during a Muslim festival. Meg Murray, engaged to army officer Henry Sinclair, sees and is strongly attracted to Police-Inspector Somerton, rumored to be the dissolute grandson of an earl. When the celebrants become unruly, Meg senses that Somerton is in danger and thoughtlessly runs into the smothering crowd. After Somerton rescues her she confesses she had feared for his safety. Although he shares the attraction, he nobly returns her to her fiancé without response. Her judgment recovered, Meg marries as expected, retiring with Henry to England, but she remains mystically bound to Somerton, crying out in her sleep at the moment of his death in India the shouted festival chant, "Hasan! Husain!"

Although weakened by stereotyped characters and a predictable plot, the story is interesting because of its strong sense of place. The setting of "An Eastern Echo" provides a suitably frenzied atmosphere in which the passionate meeting of Meg and Somerton can occur. The "crowded, stifling streets" of the small northern India town and the "glaring" road outside it are filled with "fanatical Mohammedans." Some are tearing "their clothes . . . and throwing themselves on the ground in fervor of sorrow" as others "[stride] along half-naked . . . shrieking with ardent zeal." Discovered in the context of this exotic scene, Somerton is associated in Meg's mind with excitement, passion, and even danger. Likewise, Henry represents the "calm tranquility" reflected in the English garden where Meg sits two years after having met Somerton. The contrast between the two settings mirrors the contrast between the romantic Somerton and the safe Sinclair. Perrin's sketches help the reader understand Meg's reaction when Somerton's death leaves her with "the vague suspicion of something forever missed and unattainable." The bond so suddenly formed between Meg and Somerton is made more believable by the vividly realized setting in which they meet.

As in "An Eastern Echo," the strangeness of many scenes in *East of Suez* is often created or enhanced by Indian characters who seem alien to the British mind. Often the Indians appear to be only part of the exotic setting, like the ubiquitous punkah coolies who operate the fans to keep the English cool. Sometimes, however, Indians have an important, even threatening role, like that of the fakir in "Caulfield's Crime" or the nursemaid who kills the child in her care out of revenge against the child's mother in "Chunia, Ayah." Sometimes, even when the Indian is the main character, Perrin stresses his or her bizarre behavior, as she does in "The White Tiger." Here a man uses his dead brother's body as bait for a killer tiger. East of Suez, Perrin reminds the reader, is a strange and sometimes dangerous place.

The best of the love stories and one of the best tales in *East of Suez* is "Beynon, of the Irrigation Department." Beynon, a bachelor engineer at an isolated Indian outpost, falls in love with the wife of his friend, then, disillusioned and despairing, falls or walks into the Ganges River and is eaten by alligators. Although retaining the obligatory moral resolution, Perrin achieves much more complexity of characterization and plot than she had in "An Eastern Echo." Beynon has a combination of eagerness, vulnerability, and moral rigidity that makes his tragic end entirely credible.

Psychological dangers occur in several stories in *East of Suez*. In "The Summoning of Arnold" a friend stays with a lonely man "because it was the kind of night in India when, if a man is not happy, he probably begins to wander about the compound with a revolver to shoot pariah dogs that bark and keep him awake, and sometimes, instead of a dead dog, it is the man who is found shot, through the roof of his mouth." The inclusion of the phrase "in India" implies that something about the place could trigger suicide, an idea that recurs in other stories.

The power of India to influence the mind comes through most vividly in the last story, another strong one called "The Biscobra." A young Bengal civilian named Krey arrives at his isolated outpost with Nell, his pregnant wife. A biscobra, a large, ugly lizard that inhabits their thatched roof, falls on Nell, frightening her into premature labor, and both she and her baby die. When Krey seeks a transfer to escape his grief, his loyal servant Beni stays to tend the graves. Later, near mental and physical collapse, Krey returns before leaving for England and finds Beni dying but frantic about who will care for the baby. Puzzled, Krey watches in horror as a biscobra emerges from a hole under the grave marker and drinks the milk Beni offers. In an insane rage, Krey kills the lizard, and Beni dies believing Krey murdered the soul of the child.

Although Perrin often shows the beauty of India, the bungalow in "The Biscobra" is an ominous place: "The thatched roof needed renewing, the walls seemed to be composed of mud and white ants, and nails driven into them disappeared and were no more seen. Wasps had made their dwellings in corners . . . and mysterious creatures ran to and fro with sharp, pattering feet over the loose discoloured ceiling cloths." For the naturally fearful Nell the surroundings induce such a precarious psychological state that the biscobra's fall triggers an extreme reaction. Even though bolder than his wife, Krey too is ultimately affected by the place. Already distraught over her death, he goes mad on seeing the lizard at his baby's grave.

Perrin's setting also helps to create an ambiguous ending. The reader may at first assume that Beni's grief or senility causes him to confuse the biscobra with the child, but since reincarnation is a common belief in India, Beni's final words raise the possibility that Krey may in fact have killed the soul of his own child. Because Beni is convincing in his belief, the supernatural element of the ending is not so easily dismissed.

With its strong sense of place, *East of Suez* is Perrin's best collection, both for the effect of individual stories and the cumulative impact of the volume. It was initially well received, benefiting in part from the popularity of Kipling's stories and the hunger of the reading public for accounts of India, and was successful enough to be reprinted in 1909. The collection was widely reviewed in such magazines as *Vanity Fair, Field, Truth, Sporting Times,* and *Outlook. The Scotsman* praised Perrin's "powers of perception and observation," while *Literary World* noted that she "writes as one who knows the East from personal knowledge, and she paints Indian scenes with photographic vividness and accuracy." The 23 October 1901 *Punch* stated that "for graphic description, sharp incisive sketches of character, and effective dramatic situation," her stories "are second only to the *Plain Tales,* by Rudyard Kipling; while two or three of them run even the best of Kipling's uncommonly close."

After leaving India, Perrin and her husband spent about twenty-two years in England, where she belonged to the Writers' Club and the Ladies' Imperial Club. Her 15 February 1934 obituary in the *Times* states that she was remembered as a "tall and handsome" woman "with an exuberant sense of humor and a gift of good conversation which made her the best of good company." She was respected, it says further, for her literary criticism and her encouragement of younger writers as well as her "high sense of duty" and a "courage which carried her through private sorrows of no ordinary kind." What those sorrows might have been, however, is left to the reader's imagination.

After *East of Suez* Perrin published at least fifteen more books while she lived in England: two additional collections of short stories, *Red Records* (1906) and *Tales That Are Told* (1917), and thirteen novels, including *The Anglo-Indians* (1912), one of her best known. All but two of the seventeen stories in *Red Records,* her seventh book, reflect her Indian experiences. The two exceptions, though, are love stories involving objects from other exotic places. In "The Sistrum" a rattle shaken at ritual human sacrifices in Africa brings together a man and woman in England. In "The Bead Necklace" a sailor sends the woman he loves a necklace strung on the sinews of an Englishman murdered in the South Seas. The necklace protects the woman from the drunken lecher whom her father wants her to marry and who by a remarkable coincidence had abandoned the Englishman to cannibals. Of course, the sailor makes his fortune and will get the woman.

In several stories in *Red Records* the action is divided between England and India, with a narrator in one place telling about events in the other or with a character moving from one place to another. Whenever India and England are both included, they contrast with each other as they had in "An Eastern Echo."

Like *East of Suez,* the title *Red Records* suggests an atmosphere for the collection, as it hints of journals written in blood or chronicles about death. In almost every story someone dies, often with bloodshed. A young officer is killed by a frightened mob of coolies in "Momai Walla Sahib." Two Christian missionaries, one Indian and one Eurasian, die from a culturally inbred fear of Kali in "The Powers of Darkness." A man kills his own mother to get revenge on his neighbor in "Justice."

Perrin enhances the atmosphere of the volume with the epigraph, a Hindu proverb: "In this world the strongest of all things is fate." Sometimes fate is simple chance, as in the weakest stories, where it keeps lovers apart or brings them together. For example, the casual wish for a rare souvenir precipitates one suitor's death and a confession of love from another in "The Musk Pod." The use of lilac cologne attracts the man to the wrong woman in "The Pupil." Unlike similarly formulaic stories in *East of Suez,* however, most of these in *Red Records* lack a strong sense of place to distinguish them.

In "Moore," the best of the tales relying on chance, Perrin achieves some complexity, as a series of random occurrences leads a missionary named Moore to lay to rest the ghost of a wastrel named Moore. The strongest stories in *Red Records* are the ones examining the more complex forces shaping events, also labeled fate, and these are frequently about Indian characters. Although Perrin's portraits are often marred by comments that stereotype Indians, her studies of their customs, superstitions, fears, and even prejudices against the sahibs usually demonstrate sympathy and close observation. For example, "Kismet" tells the moving story of a Hindu peasant who will not defend herself against a murder charge because she superstitiously believes punishment is her fate.

Another study of the interaction of superstition and fate is "The Evil Eye." Innes, an English subaltern ignorant of Hindustani and of Indian customs, treats a young peasant woman in a way she construes as a curse. Thinking she will contract leprosy, she takes a pilgrimage to the Ganges to be cleansed, cuts her foot, steps where a leper's sore had oozed, and in fact gets the disease. She then allows herself to be buried alive, believing she will thus protect her children from the curse.

In this story fate is again accomplished through chance and superstition, but Innes is also a factor. With his dismissal of the need to know the language and beliefs of the land that he is helping to occupy and with his casual disregard for the consequences of his ignorance, Innes precipitates the tragic sequence of events. After learning what had happened, his commander protects him by withholding the information and thus does not acknowledge Innes's responsibility, but Perrin makes clear the subaltern's failings at the beginning of the story. She falls short of explicitly declaring English complicity in the misfortunes of the Indians, but, surprisingly for an Anglo-Indian of her generation, she certainly raises the possibility.

In "The Rise of Ram Din" a careless order given by a drunken Englishman and obeyed by a literal-minded Indian servant causes another servant's death. Although ostensibly an exposé of the stupidity of the Indian, the story is subtly ironic, revealing that his "unquestioning obedience" was a ploy and that the Englishman's behavior contributed to the death.

The critic reviewing *Red Records* in *The Bookman* (June 1906) found the stories generally better than "the efforts of the rank-and-file of our women story-tellers" but thought the volume as a whole weaker than *East of Suez* because of the "feeblest" stories, "which might serve well enough in the lighter of the monthly magazines." However, the collection was reissued in 1928.

The ten stories of *Tales That Are Told,* Perrin's fifteenth book and third collection, are the usual assortment of love stories and stories of male-female relationships in conflict. A few tales are enlivened by her description, as in "The Palace of Snakes" with its "labyrinth of halls and chambers and holes and hovels." Other stories reveal the sense of humor attributed to Perrin. For example, a faithful spaniel comes back as a ghost to protect her master from a husband-seeking shrew. Overall, however, *Tales That Are Told* is weaker than *East of Suez* and *Red Records,* especially when Perrin abandons her Indian and Anglo-Indian characters, as brief summaries of two stories suggest. In "Buffalo" a London cat saves a servant girl and her mistress from a fire, thus acting as matchmaker between the girl and the mistress's brother; in "Thirty Acres" a bull in a small English village is an instrument of revenge that kills a neighbor. Although plots are generally not her strength, the stories in *Tales That Are Told* also often lack the mystery and complexity of her best tales. One important exception, "Gift of God," is actually a twenty-thousand-word novella examining mixed marriage, a theme Perrin had already studied in novels such as *The Stronger Claim* (1903), *The Charm* (1910), and *The Anglo-Indians*. "Gift of God" tells of a wealthy young Indian whose marriage to an Englishwoman triggers a murder plot and a cholera epidemic that kills him and most of his town. Here Perrin creates a full, convincing, and unpatronizing picture of Muslim culture, although she suggests that marriage outside one's race, culture, or class is doomed.

Another of Perrin's best stories appears in this weaker collection. "Mary Jones," a quiet, easily overlooked tale that ends the volume, is economical and evocative. Sayne, an Anglo-Indian doctor now back in England, examines an elderly woman who has been struck by a car. Although she is uninjured, the trauma affects her mind and, much to Sayne's surprise, she begins to speak in Hindustani, then dance and sing a song associated with Indian nautch girls, dancers who performed in rajah's palaces and wealthy homes. Just before the woman dies, her husband is aroused momentarily from his senile stupor and says almost intelligible words that seem to confirm the woman's origin. But before Sayne can question him, the old man relapses, leaving her past a mystery.

In a brief eleven pages Perrin reveals the complexity of the doctor's attitude toward the two cultures. The doctor had wanted to escape India, "where human beings, both dark and white, might be perfectly well in the morning and dead before the day was out; where he had seen natives die by hundreds in the twenty-four hours; where he had treated, continuously, such terrible maladies as plague, small-pox, leprosy, cholera." By contrast, England is kinder. All a doctor there had to deal with were "teething ailments, whooping-cough . . . and worn-out, bedridden peasants dying peacefully, readily, of old age," surrounded by friends. But every object Sayne sees reminds him of India. Even his first glimpse of Mary Jones, with her clumsy boots, wrinkled skin, and weathered hands, evokes "that land of eternal mysteries" that dominates his thoughts. His conscious mind rejects India, but his reactions reveal how much he values the land, its people, and its culture. With the ending of the story Perrin challenges the stereotypes with which the doctor had at first characterized the two countries. Mary Jones and her husband live the long, peaceful lives Sayne associates with England, but ironically the suddenness of Mary's death and the couple's isolation belie his original pleasant image. As in all Perrin's stories comparing the two, England and India are very different places, but again neither is

necessarily better than the other. In "Mary Jones," instead of telling about the country, Perrin shows it through the responses of Sayne. More than a decade and a half had passed since Perrin had lived in India, and the memories she relied on to create a strong sense of place in her best stories had dimmed. In "Mary Jones," however, she builds her story on the elusiveness of memory and the ambiguous feelings that come from looking back, thus succeeding by means of the very factors that weaken other stories in the collection.

The reviewer in *Punch* (5 December 1917) found most of the stories in *Tales That Are Told* "indifferent stuff," not up to Perrin's previous work. However, the collection was reissued two years after its initial release, again indicating that the book had been well received by the public.

Sometime in the mid 1920s Perrin and her husband moved to Tour de Peilz, Switzerland, making only occasional visits to England after that. She published only three books while in Switzerland: her last collection of stories, *Rough Passages* (1926), and her last two novels, *Government House* (1925) and *Other Sheep* (1932), which appeared the year after her husband's death on 2 May 1931 and two years before her own on 13 February 1934 in Vevey, Switzerland. Although *Rough Passages* is Perrin's weakest volume, some of the stories move in new if not better directions.

All except one of the ten stories in *Rough Passages* are about Anglo-Indians, usually living in India, and most of the plots involve conflict or intrigues with the opposite sex, with predictable didactic results. The flirtatious young woman in "The Gooseberry" and the careless young woman in "The Spell" learn almost too late that they love their older husbands. In "The Planter's Wife" the wife is finally rewarded for her loyalty to her invalid husband by having him die and leave her free to marry the man she loves. Misunderstanding separates the young lovers and coincidence reunites them in "The Tiger's Luck-Bone." Like many of Perrin's other love stories, these deal with faithfulness; the heroines, though sorely tempted, ultimately behave with honor. In this volume, however, attractions between the sexes have more overtly sexual overtones than those in earlier stories. For example, in "The Fakir in the Forest" the wife is attracted to a man she cannot resist, and she is kept faithful only by the intervention of a fakir who sends a tiger to kill her tempter. The man and the wife had met during her engagement, and the dialogue between them shows that their relationship had been passionate, perhaps even sexual. Both the language and the nature of the attraction mark a change from earlier stories in which love, not passion, is the focus.

In "The Brahminy Bull," one of the most interesting stories in *Rough Passages,* Avice Trent's tempter, Mr. Vassal, had been a bull in a past life as punishment for his "lower instincts." His beastly nature is apparent in his present body as well when he looks at Avice with a "curious red gleam" in his eyes or walks toward her "a big, loosely built figure slouching heavily." Although at first attracted to Mr. Vassal, Avice is frightened by his sensuality and marries the safer Captain Maxwell. In these stories Perrin may be reacting to the sexually freer climate of the modern period, but even though her characters now feel passion, they reject it, at least outside of marriage.

Another change apparent in *Rough Passages* is the more open inclusion of politics. Many earlier stories had depicted a benevolent, paternalistic relationship between English master and Indian servant that had affirmed a similar relationship between England and its empire. At times Perrin or her characters had noted the benefits of imperialism, but "For India" is her most overtly propagandistic story. The heroine goes to India "to investigate the wrongs of an oppressed people, that she might return and rouse the sympathies of the great English public." But on her visit she falls in love with a dedicated civil servant who refuses to put her ahead of his duty during a cholera epidemic. Although she angrily returns to England, she has been converted to his viewpoint: "She had expected to find a vast deal of misgovernment" by the British but finally had concluded "that there was no country better managed than India, none in which the administration did more for the masses of people." The political message of the story reflects the growing debate over the issue of imperialism in the years following World War I. The assumptions about the concept of empire that shaped most earlier Anglo-Indian works were under attack, and "For India" is Perrin's most direct response. More subtle than "For India," "Ann White" also supports the British colonial presence by drawing a parallel between the bloody Sepoy Rebellion, in which many Anglo-Indians were killed, and a contemporary conflict with the Indians.

Although popular in her time, Perrin's work has since received little attention. In *A Survey of Anglo-Indian Fiction* (1934) Bhupal Singh found some of the stories in *East of Suez* to be among her best, mentioned the 1928 version of *Red Records,* and

praised "the occult and the mysterious" stories of *Rough Passages* that resemble Kipling's. Benita Parry included *East of Suez* in her *Delusions and Discoveries: Studies on India in the British Imagination, 1880–1930* (1972) but saw little to praise. Grouping Perrin with Penny, Croker, Diver, and I. A. R. Wylie and labeling them "Romancers" or "lady novelists," Parry criticized Perrin for showing "India as a place of vast mysteries and immense horrors" and said the collection "suggests an obsession with sudden, violent death and sinister disasters." Antiquarian book dealers seldom stock Perrin's books. Isolated copies are closely guarded in special collections in libraries around the United States, valued more for their rarity than for their contents, and her name is scarcely mentioned in critical studies except for an occasional brief reference by scholars reexamining Anglo-Indian fiction or the works of forgotten women authors of her time. Even the studies that include Perrin often simply list her books or group her with other writers, sometimes to draw generalizations about the subgenre. Her work frequently does have the flaws frequently attributed to Anglo-Indian works, but she was sometimes able to create a realistic look at a certain time and place in history, and for these vignettes she deserves to be read. She was also on occasion able to achieve a more subtle blend of character, setting, and theme that transcends the other limitations of the subgenre, and for these stories she deserves to be studied.

References:

Allen J. Greenberger, *The British Image of India: A Study in the Literature of Imperialism, 1880–1960* (London, New York & Toronto: Oxford University Press, 1969);

Susanne Howe, *Novels of Empire* (New York: Columbia University Press, 1949);

Benita Parry, *Delusions and Discoveries: Studies on India in the British Imagination, 1880–1930* (Berkeley & Los Angeles: University of California Press, 1972);

Elaine Showalter, *A Literature of Their Own: British Women Novelists from Brontë to Lessing* (Princeton: Princeton University Press, 1977);

Bhupal Singh, *A Survey of Anglo-Indian Fiction* (London: Curzon Press / Totowa, N. J.: Rowman & Littlefield, 1934);

Rashna B. Singh, *The Imperishable Empire: A Study of British Fiction on India* (Washington, D.C.: Three Continents Press, 1988).

Charlotte Riddell

(30 September 1832 – 24 September 1906)

Susie Paul
Auburn University at Montgomery

BOOKS: *Zuriel's Grandchild,* as R. V. Sparling (London: Newby, 1856); republished as *Joy After Sorrow,* as Mrs. J. H. Riddell (London: Newby, 1873);

The Ruling Passion, 3 volumes, as Rainey Hawthorne (London: Bentley, 1857);

A Poor Fellow (New York: Dick & Fitzgerald, 1858); republished as *Poor Fellow!* (London: White, 1902);

The Rich Husband, 3 volumes, as the author of *The Ruling Passion* (London: Skeet, 1858; Philadelphia: Peterson, 1867?);

The Moors and the Fens, 3 volumes, as F. G. Trafford (London: Smith, Elder, 1858);

Too Much Alone, as F. G. Trafford, (3 volumes, London: Skeet, 1860; 1 volume, Boston: Burnham, 1866);

City and Suburb, 3 volumes, as F. G. Trafford (London: Skeet, 1861);

The World in the Church, 3 volumes, as F. G. Trafford (London: Skeet, 1862);

George Geith of Fen Court, as F. G. Trafford (3 volumes, London: Tinsley, 1865; 1 volume, Boston: Burnham / New York: Felt, 1865);

Maxwell Drewitt, as F. G. Trafford (3 volumes, London: Tinsley, 1865; 1 volume, New York: Harper, 1866);

Phemie Keller, as F. G. Trafford (3 volumes, London: Tinsley, 1866; 1 volume, New York: Harper, 1866);

The Race for Wealth (3 volumes, London: Tinsley, 1866; 1 volume, New York: Harper, 1866);

Far above Rubies (3 volumes, London: Tinsley, 1867; 1 volume, Philadelphia: Lippincott, 1867);

The Miseries of Christmas (London: Routledge, 1867);

My First Love (London: St. James's Christmas Box, 1869); republished with *My Last Love* (London: Hutchinson, 1891; New York: Lovell, 1891);

Austin Friars (3 volumes, London: Tinsley, 1870; 1 volume, New York: Scribner, Welford & Armstrong, 1875);

Long Ago (London: Arnold, 1870);

A Life's Assize (3 volumes, London: Tinsley, 1871; 1 volume, New York: Harper, 1871);

Charlotte Riddell, portrait by W. F. Thomas (from S. M. Ellis, Wilkie Collins, Le Fanu, and Others, 1931)

The Earl's Promise (3 volumes, London: Tinsley, 1873; 1 volume, New York: Scribners, 1890);

Home, Sweet Home, 3 volumes (London: Tinsley, 1873);

Fairy Water: A Christmas Story (London & New York: Routledge, 1873);

Mortomley's Estate, 3 volumes (London: Tinsley, 1874);

Frank Sinclair's Wife, and Other Stories, 3 volumes (London: Tinsley, 1874);

The Uninhabited House (London: Routledge, 1875); republished with *The Haunted River* (London & New York: Routledge, 1883);

Above Suspicion, 3 volumes (London: Tinsley, 1876; Boston: Estes & Lauriat, 1876?);

Her Mother's Darling (3 volumes, London: Tinsley, 1877; 1 volume, New York: Munro, 1880);

The Haunted River: A Christmas Story (London & New York: Routledge, 1877); republished with *The Uninhabited House* (London & New York: Routledge, 1883);

The Disappearance of Mr. Jeremiah Redworth (New York: Munro, 1878; London: Routledge, 1879);

The Mystery in Palace Gardens (3 volumes, London: Bentley, 1880; 1 volume, New York: Munro, 1881);

Alaric Spenceley; or, A High Ideal, 3 volumes (London: Skeet, 1881);

The Senior Partner (3 volumes, London: Bentley, 1881; 1 volume, New York: Harper, 1882);

Daisies and Buttercups (3 volumes, London: Bentley, 1882; 1 volume, New York: Harper, 1882);

The Prince of Wales's Garden Party and Other Stories (London: Chatto & Windus, 1882; New York: Munro, 1882);

A Struggle for Fame (3 volumes, London: Bentley, 1883; 1 volume, New York: Harper, 1883);

Susan Drummond (3 volumes, London: Bentley, 1884; 1 volume, New York: Harper, 1884);

Berna Boyle: A Love Story of the County Down (3 volumes, London: Bentley, 1884; 1 volume, New York: Munro, 1884);

Weird Stories (London: Hogg, 1884);

Mitre Court: A Tale of the Great City, 3 volumes (London: Bentley, 1885);

For Dick's Sake (London: Society for Promoting Christian Knowledge, 1886; New York & Boston: Crowell, 188?);

Miss Gascoine (London: Ward & Downey, 1887; New York: Appleton, 1887);

The Government Official, 3 volumes, anonymous (London: Bentley, 1887);

Idle Tales (London: Ward & Downey, 1888);

The Nun's Curse (3 volumes, London: Ward & Downey, 1888; 1 volume, New York: Munro, 1888);

Princess Sunshine and Other Stories (2 volumes, London: Ward & Downey, 1889; 1 volume, New York: Lovell, 1890);

A Mad Tour; or, A Journey Undertaken in an Insane Moment through Central Europe on Foot (London: Bentley, 1891; New York: Lovell, 1891);

The Head of the Firm (1 volume, New York: Lovell, 1891; 3 volumes, London: Heinemann, 1892);

The Rusty Sword; or, Thereby Hangs a Tale (London: Society for Promoting Christian Knowledge, 1893);

A Silent Tragedy (London: White, 1893);

The Banshee's Warning and Other Tales (London: Remington, 1894);

A Rich Man's Daughter (New York: International News, 1895; London: White, 1897);

Did He Deserve It? (London: Downey, 1897);

Handsome Phil, and Other Stories (London: White, 1899);

The Footfall of Fate (London: White, 1900).

Collection: *The Collected Ghost Stories of Mrs. J. H. Riddell,* edited by E. F. Bleiler (New York: Dover, 1977).

OTHER: "Couleur De Rose," *Novels, Tales, and Poetry by the Author of "Guy Livingstone"* (London: Routledge, 1868?);

"The Curate of Lowood; or, Every Man Has His Golden Chance," *Proverb Stories for Boys and Girls* (London: Office of London Society, 1882).

Charlotte Riddell was best known among her contemporaries as a novelist of the City, the financial center of London. As a short-story writer she was less well known, though she published seven collections. However, her recent reputation rests upon her abilities in this genre, in particular upon her talents as a writer of ghost stories; according to bibliographer and critic E. F. Bleiler she was "preeminent" among female authors of such stories in the Victorian period.

Charlotte Elizabeth Lawson Cowan was born on 30 September 1832 in Carrickfergus, a small town near Belfast, to an Irish father, James Cowan, high sheriff for County Antrim, and an English mother, Ellen Kilshaw. Bleiler describes her mother as a "beautiful, graceful, and accomplished English woman." Her father Bleiler calls in his introduction to *The Collected Ghost Stories of Mrs. J. H. Riddell* (1977) a "shadowy" figure; Riddell told Helen Black, "I never knew him at his best, for as far as my memory goes back he was always more or less a sufferer." Yet she also told Black, "From my father I think I got the few brains I possess." At his death, when Riddell was around twenty-one, she and her mother were left with limited means and forced to leave their home for Dundonald in the adjoining county of Down. Unable to survive even in a small village under such reduced circumstances, they decided to move to London, where Riddell might earn a living as a writer.

"I never remember the time when I did not compose," she told Black. She finished her first novel, never published, at fifteen. According to biographer S. M. Ellis, she arrived in London in January 1855 and endeavored to write; to care for her mother, who was ill with cancer; and to publish her work. In 1856, under the pseudonym R. V. Sparling, she published *Zuriel's Grandchild*. Her mother died, and in 1857 she married Joseph Hadley Riddell, a civil engineer. According to Ellis he supplied her with information about "company promoting, engineering and business ways" as well as life in the City, but he left her seriously in debt at his death in 1880. Though under no legal obligation to do so, she was determined to pay off these debts, crippling herself financially for the rest of her life. As Ellis maintains, "It was well for him and his wife that the latter continued her literary work assiduously after marriage, for otherwise the future would have held ruin for them both." Thus, like her contemporaries Mary Elizabeth Braddon, author of *Lady Audley's Secret* (1862), and Mrs. Oliphant, Riddell was the chief support for the household. Yet she spoke of her husband without rancor, describing him as "courageous and hopeful, gifted" despite his failed "long quest after fortune." They had no children.

The shape of Riddell's career as a short-fiction writer is hard to determine. As Ellis claimed, "there are probably many short stories hidden away and unidentified in the pages of forgotten magazines." According to Bleiler, Riddell wrote at least forty-one short stories, a figure he says is incomplete, for she published many of her stories anonymously. Thus, except for a handful of pieces, her career is best understood as found in her seven short-story volumes.

Beginning her career as a novelist in 1847, by the 1860s Riddell had established a reputation as a professional writer, though not without intense struggle. In her autobiographical novel *A Struggle for Fame* (1883) she writes of her young heroine, Glen Westly, "She was losing – she had lost – heart altogether. . . . From place to place she trudged valiantly, taking the familiar 'no' with stoical indifference." Yet Riddell came of age as a professional writer in London at a time when, as Elaine Showalter describes in *A Literature of Their Own: British Women Novelists from Brontë to Lessing* (1977), the literary market for women was opening up tremendously and when women were fully exploiting the business potential of the literary profession as editors, publishers, and printers. Two interrelated publishing phenomena of the 1860s contributed to such opportunities for Riddell and her generation of women writers. First was a proliferation of periodicals. In the 1860s there was an explosion of shilling magazines; several published Riddell's fiction, and in 1868 she became part owner and editor of one of them, *St. James's Magazine* (founded 1861). Popular in these magazines was the second phenomenon, the serialized novel later published in book form; often this was a "three-decker" and a "sensation" novel.

A reviewer for the *Spectator* wrote in 1883 in praise of Riddell's books, "they do not all turn upon the same subject and run in the same groove." She wrote novels and stories of four distinct kinds of settings – those of City life and the world of business; those set in her native Ireland; tales of domestic life, especially of courtship and marriage; and ghost stories. Such versatility, according to the *Spectator* reviewer, set her apart from those writers, "especially of the feminine gender," who "content themselves far too much" with depicting "over and over" characters in the kind of society where "everybody drinks five o'clock tea, dines at eight, plays lawn tennis, shops at Marshall and Snelgrove's, and goes out of town at the end of the season." Her characters were not wholly consumed by the "love-and-twaddle business" but rather were men and women who could be "heartily in love, and yet go about their daily work like rational beings, . . . like real people." Unifying her diverse fiction is the persistent exploration of the effects of change, sometimes traumatic, on the lives of real people of every sort, especially as it tests character and relationships and as it affects their places in a society where boundaries between classes are disintegrating. In her fiction as in her life, money is always an issue.

During the 1860s Riddell published nine novels, primarily under the pseudonym F. G. Trafford, including *George Geith of Fen Court* (1865), upon which her reputation would primarily rest during her lifetime. Though its hero is an accountant, this three-volume work also possesses qualities of the sensation novel: George Geith, honest and industrious in business, broods over an unsavory past and lives with a terrible secret, which comes to be his and his beloved's ruin. The novel thus anticipates much of Riddell's short fiction; whether the story is primarily domestic or supernatural, there is typically a haunting – a specter from the past, a moral transgression that abides as guilt and visits as ruin, or a real ghost. Bleiler dates only two stories to this first decade of her professional career: "Hertford O'Donnell's Warning," published in *London Society* (Christmas 1867), and "A Strange Christmas Game," published in *Broadway Annual* (Christmas 1868). Hertford O'Donnell's story involves moral regeneration on Christmas Eve because of a dream and the visitation of a banshee, after the pattern of Charles Dickens's *A Christmas Carol* (1843).

Having left Ireland after his and his beloved's families refuse to allow their marriage, O'Donnell comes to London. A handsome, charming, but godless man and a gifted surgeon, he pursues wealth and social status. The moaning call of the banshee precedes a visit to the hospital, where he recognizes a child he has dreamed of saving from drowning. When the severely injured child, who turns out to be his illegitimate son, requires his surgical skill, O'Donnell faints. The child dies, but the surgeon is reunited with the child's mother, a woman he loved deeply and abandoned. Like so many of Riddell's protagonists, O'Donnell is a young man struggling to make his way in London and an outsider – in this case because he has left behind his aristocratic and typically profligate family and Ireland. Flawed from the start, he succumbs to the call of the city to get and spend. Also characteristic is her consideration of O'Donnell's Irishness as well as her brief but sharply drawn satiric treatment of the pretentious pickle heiress he marries before the banshee calls.

Though this is an early story, it reveals Riddell's talents as a ghost-story writer as well. Bleiler notes that the ideas in her ghost stories were not novel; demanding little suspension of disbelief, reality is breached only once, and the ghost, or banshee in this case, obtrudes in a realistically detailed setting. O'Donnell and his adopted world are richly drawn. While Riddell typically uses the ghost story, as she does here, as a means for exploring a moral problem, this story has a psychological resonance that some of her other stories lack. O'Donnell is saved from his own cold rationality and selfishness by the visitation of dream and banshee and by the death of his young son, but he is also a man who has left the Ireland he loved "to the core of his heart," his family, and the woman he wanted to marry. The banshee's wail and the "familiar" boy whom he cannot save call to the denied Irish self and resurrect it along with the morally redeemed O'Donnell.

Like most writers who supplied periodicals with short fiction during the Victorian era, Riddell did not write stories of the modern kind, with their relentless economy, unity, effaced narrators, and dramatic presentation. While this story is tighter than some, there is a leisurely exploration of O'Donnell's character as the story opens, a digression on the history of the banshee in Ireland, and an awkward paragraph recapitulating O'Donnell's and

his fiancée's complicated past, by way of tying up loose ends, at the story's close. Digressive and intrusive commentary in all of Riddell's fiction, more extreme in her three-volume novels, irked her critics. Her complaint in "Hertford O'Donnell's Warning" that Gerrard Street, Soho, "was not then an utterly shady and forgotten locality" is a brief but typical example of the kind of comment that riled critics. "Why cannot Mrs. Riddell be satisfied," asks the reviewer in the 23 January 1886 *Spectator,* "with giving us an interesting and well-written novel, without cramming down our throats . . . absolutely irrelevant antiquarian disquisitions, and abuse alike of the fiends who pull down, and the demons who restore old buildings?"

In the 1870s Riddell moved her household five times – the first few times to escape the urbanization of once-rural suburbs, but in 1875 to Addleston in Surrey to cut expenses. She was at this time an established author, having received eight hundred pounds from Tinsley for *George Geith of Fen Court,* which Ellis calls an "exceedingly liberal" offer for that period. The novel was so popular that in 1877, twelve years after its publication, it was dramatized by Wybert Reeve, and the play was revived in 1883 at the Crystal Palace. She was established enough in the profession to be of significant help to young writers such as Harry Furniss, who went on to become a successful cartoonist, offering him letters of introduction and advice. Despite such success, the financial disaster her husband created meant she had to continue to work hard.

Riddell's forays into the Christmas annual market were confined almost entirely to the 1870s, when she published, in addition to seven novels and a short-story collection, five long stories, each as a Routledge's Christmas Annual; four of these are supernatural tales. According to Bleiler, in the Victorian era the ghost story was strongly linked to Christmas, especially to the Christmas annual, a "book of entertainments" including thrilling stories as well as puzzles, jokes, stunts, and games. Each of Riddell's stories was long enough and sufficiently entertaining to stand alone as the Christmas offering for that year. Though these works are generally categorized as novels or novellas, they are much shorter than Riddell's many three-volume works and are extended versions of the kinds of ghost story she had tried earlier. Wendell V. Harris might call them tales, both because they follow what he describes in *British Short Fiction in the Nineteenth Century: A Literary and Bibliographic Guide* (1979) as the Gothic tradition and because, while they "have cohesion" as befits a suspenseful and thus successful thriller, they also tell readers "more about certain matters, even about the central character, than we need to know. . . . [P]lot, technique, character, and scenic picturesqueness vie with one another in interest." For example, in Riddell's earliest Christmas annual, *Fairy Water: A Christmas Story* (1873), the narrator, H. Stafford Trevor, is described well beyond the need to establish his credibility as a witness to the story's supernatural occurrences. Riddell also develops a romantic subplot that includes circumstances allowing her to demonstrate the injustice of certain inheritance laws.

Riddell's long ghost stories feature houses haunted by ghosts who seek to reveal their murderers and characters, male and female, who are tested within the confines of these houses and successfully cope. The hero of *The Uninhabited House* (1875) solves the mystery of River Hall for the solicitors who employ him as a clerk, daring to stay in a house no one else has inhabited for long because it is so raucously haunted. Poor half sisters rent a decaying house on the Thames in Surrey and deal not only with poverty and a haunting but with a swindling, lecherous landlord in *The Haunted River: A Christmas Story* (1877). Her last long ghost tale, *The Disappearance of Mr. Jeremiah Redworth* (1878), also features a female protagonist, Miss Gower, who is able to solve the mystery of the disappearance and subsequent haunting and who also expresses rage, as opposed to the stoic resignation of some of Riddell's female characters, at her lover's betrayal.

Also from this period is a three-volume collection, *Frank Sinclair's Wife, and Other Stories* (1874), the title story of which is a domestic tale. Belle Sinclair is spoiled and selfish when she marries and is a rather extreme example of many of the women Riddell creates who spend and waste, failing to appreciate the difficulty of earning a living, as their husbands do out in the world of work. As one of Riddell's realistic domestic tales, "Frank Sinclair's Wife" suffers from technical problems Harris sees everywhere in stories of the era. There is too little space for the creation of a full-scale fictional world. In this tale, moreover, she relies heavily on summary and does not curb commentary; thus "Frank Sinclair's Wife" is diffuse and weak compared to her ghost tales of the same era. Yet it explores a timely issue, as Belle and Frank exchange roles for a time: "People may object to the institution of women's rights, . . . but there can be no question that an open sore is better than one falsely healed." Riddell was a proud professional woman, but the conclusion of "Frank Sinclair's Wife" – Belle destroys Frank's business, and one of

the children falls ill in her absence and dies – suggests a largely orthodox view of women's roles. Also significant is her unsentimental portrayal of the difficult individual adjustments a marriage requires if it is to succeed. Finally, Riddell's understanding of businessmen and their world, unusual for a woman of her day, is displayed. She once told an interviewer for the *Pall Mall Gazette* (18 February 1890), "I fancy I must have a certain sympathy with City men, their lives and hopes and struggles." She claimed to "understand men well," finding "them easier to describe than women."

Between 1880 and 1890, besides twelve novels, Riddell published four collections of stories: *The Prince of Wales's Garden Party and Other Stories* (1882), *Weird Stories* (1884), *Idle Tales* (1888), and *Princess Sunshine and Other Stories* (1889). Among these and among all her works of short fiction, *Weird Stories* is preeminent. Consisting of six supernatural stories, it is, according to Bleiler in *The Penguin Encyclopedia of Horror and the Supernatural* (1986), one of the "basic books of nineteenth-century supernaturalism," with old themes "revivified with new approaches" in some and new ideas serving as the bases for the plot in others. Most of Riddell's supernatural short fiction first appeared in periodicals, often anonymously; the stories gathered in this volume most likely were written in the previous decade. At least one tale – "The Old House in Vauxhall Walk," because the hero undergoes a change of heart on Christmas Eve – may have been written for the Christmas annual market, which did not extend much beyond the 1880s. Its hero is a young man, disowned by his father as a "coward, simpleton, and hypocrite," who finds himself "Houseless – homeless – hopeless!" A former family servant allows him to stay in a house he is leaving, haunted by the restless spirit of a murdered, once-miserly hag. Eventually the young man solves the mystery of the murder, lays the ghost to rest, recovers a fortune, and is reconciled with his father. "Open Door" is a shorter version of *The Uninhabited House* and also features a young man striving for success. Narrating his own story, he complains about his job trapped behind a desk in a clerk's position. He and the other workers are always "chaffing each other, playing practical jokes, telling stupid stories, scamping our work," and "looking at the clock." His employer, he says, sees him as full of "airs," indifferent, and insolent. The challenge of a haunted house is just what he needs. Besides being converted into a believer in ghosts, which he as a rash young man had dismissed as impossible, he is converted to a new maturity, granted the manage-

Cover for Riddell's 1877 Christmas story, which constitutes the entire issue of Routledge's Christmas Annual

ment of a farm and thus a steady income, and permitted to marry his beloved Patty, all because he lays the ghost behind the open door to rest.

Three more of the six stories involve haunted houses. "Nut Bush Farm," which Bleiler describes as "almost the High Victorian ghost story par excellence," is about a weary and sickly Londoner who comes to the country for some peace but finds he must deal with a ghost. "Walnut-Street House" tells of Mr. Stainton, who returns from Australia, where he has made his fortune, to reclaim his ancestral home, now haunted by a pathetically thin and ragged child. Stainton's sympathies are aroused and his roughness softened as he solves the mystery of the child ghost's restlessness, for which he too is rewarded with a bride. In "Old Mrs. Jones," the final and longest of the stories, Dick Tippens, who owns and drives his own cab, is of a different social class from many of Riddell's heroes in *Weird Stories,* yet like them he is struggling to succeed. The house he leases for his family is grander than any in which

they have ever lived before, as befits his increasing prosperity, but it is haunted by another of Riddell's hags, the witchlike Zillah, wife of Dr. Jones. Both disappeared one Christmas Eve, but the horrible and exotic Zillah, her throat scarred with red, terrorizes the Tippenses and their boarders and visits Dick's clear-eyed and practical cousin Anne Jane in her dreams. This "incarnation" of the "ideal sewing-maid in a good family" leads the authorities to Dr. Jones, living in a nearby mansion with his wife's embalmed body locked in a box in his laboratory. In most of Riddell's stories, those who bring a crime to light are rewarded, but the Tippenses are brought close to ruin. Because of the haunting they have been unable to keep the rooms let, necessary if they are to pay for this grand house. In the end, however, they are released when the house burns.

This tale is flawed by a long discourse on problems in coming up in the world financially, in particular the tendency to want more and to give up economizing. Despite the digression, because the Tippenses are culpable in this way, the story within their story of Dr. and Mrs. Jones – the doctor a spendthrift, Mrs. Jones an ugly, miserly woman he married for her money – parallels the framing tale in a way unusual for Riddell's ghost stories. It is almost as if the Tippenses are haunted by their own flaws, albeit in extreme form, and punished, though they work hard, for being a little too optimistic and too comfortable in their new prosperity – a state Riddell knew from hard and recent experience never to be taken for granted. Also powerful here is the final image of the story, the ghost of Mrs. Jones, an ugly woman betrayed by the handsome, clever, and younger man, "standing in the parapet in the fiercest of the fire" she had set, "wringing" her hands, her grey hair "streaming," an image of rage and agony.

Two of Riddell's realistic domestic tales of the 1880s surely reflect her anxieties about money following her husband's death in 1880: "The Misses Popkin" from *Idle Tales* and "Princess Sunshine" from the same volume. At the heart of each of these stories is an orphaned young woman dependent upon relatives. These girls come fresh and a little wild into rather staid households. Riddell created many such strong and spirited girls in her fiction – Kitty Popkin has Riddell's own gray eyes – though she tempers them with sacrifice and tames them in marriage. Both Kitty and Joan, the "princess sunshine," are future heiresses whose predicted source of fortune fails. The families of adult sisters upon whom these girls depend are in turn each financially dependent upon brothers. In "Princess Sunshine" this brother is an anonymous hack writer sending out reams of manuscripts from his office on Fleet Street in order to support his family. The stories end happily but certainly reflect Riddell's preoccupation with finances. "Princess Sunshine" fills one and a half volumes; "The Misses Popkin" is briefer but still a long story. Each greatly depends upon summary; in contrast, the stories in *Weird Stories* abound in dramatic presentation and realistic detail. They are also peopled with unforgettable minor characters, such as the beer-guzzling, quarrelsome, and assertive Miss Gostock of "Nut Bush Farm" or Mickey, the swindling man-of-all-work whose point of view "was the nearest tap." A reviewer writing for the *Spectator* in 1883 dismissed Riddell's *Weird Stories* as "manufactured," yet among more-recent specialists in supernatural fiction this volume is considered a landmark.

In 1883 Riddell took a young friend of the family, twenty-three-year-old Arthur Hamilton Norway, into her home at South Lambeth Road. According to Ellis he had come to London to take up an appointment in the secretariat of the post office. He remained with her for three years, moving with her away from the city and back to the countryside to Middlesex, where she lived in a house called the Cottage until 1892. During this time he traveled with her to Germany and also to Ireland in 1885.

Riddell traveled in Ireland again for a final time in 1889, and Irish influences are important in the two volumes of short fiction she published between 1890 and her death in 1906. *The Banshee's Warning and Other Tales* (1894) has as its title story a retitled "Hertford O'Donnell's Warning." In 1899 she published *Handsome Phil, and Other Stories* a collection of eight stories set almost entirely in Ireland and including two Irish supernatural tales. They do not treat her lost homeland in a facile or sentimental way.

The two ghost stories are hardly ghost stories at all. "Conn Kilrea," about an Irish private in the British Light Bays, is a tale primarily of a young man's agonizing introspection triggered by the visitation of an ancient relative's ghost, traditionally presaging the death of someone in the family. Strangely, the ghost's appearance is never dramatized; only Conn's reaction to seeing it is reported, through his horrified expression and pale countenance. Such a shift in technique may reflect an effort to focus on what goes on inside Conn Kilrea's mind, the specter becoming a portent and reminder only he can see and thus a personal demon. Likewise, in "Diarmid Chittock's Story" it is unclear whether all the clatter that leads Mr. Danson and

his friends to the body beneath the house is ghost, wind, or sea. The true ghost is Diarmid Chittock wasting away from guilt, having murdered in a fit of passion the father of Oona Rosterne, the woman he wished to marry. No banshee haunts this Irish estate, but Oona's singing is so "rare" she casts a spell of "utter silence" over her audience. Hearing that Danson has uncovered his crime, Chittock poisons himself; thus the ghost is laid to rest. Like "Conn Kilrea," this story approaches the psychological thriller.

While in "Diarmid Chittock's Story" Mr. Danson reveals his prejudice against the Irish by misjudging Chittock's servant Gorey, in "Handsome Phil," the longest story in the collection, the prejudice is on the other side. Philip Keegan, the ne'er-do-well Irish groom, is glad to leave his English employer: "No hateful Englishmen prying around and interfering with things they know nothing about." Though Riddell does not lay the blame for Phil's weak character on his Irishness, she does make him the most radically political character in this story. He has taught his assistant, who looks up to him and upon whom he foists all his work, an old ballad termed "seditious" in its sentiments by the Master, who "had his own . . . notions about Tenant Rights, Church Patronage, the Export Duty on Whiskey – specially Bushmills, . . . but Rebel he was not." This is not a strong story, though it and one other in the volume have a politically sharper edge than her earlier Irish stories. "In Deadly Peril" is the story of a renowned Irish surgeon who risks his life to save the severely wounded servant of an Irish landlord whose tenants have rebelled with violence. What is so admirable about the surgeon, besides his courage in saving a man's life, is his cool rationality, his refusal to succumb to political feeling and prejudice.

"Out in the Cold," a weak story constructed almost entirely of summary, is poignant when its autobiographical elements are considered. In 1892 Riddell was diagnosed with cancer, the disease that had killed her mother. Her work was then increasingly out of fashion. According to Ellis, she wrote her friend Victoria Matthews on 16 April 1889, "I have never hit the popular taste, being behind the age instead of abreast of it." She was also poor, the first author to receive financial support from the Society of Authors. Like Riddell, Miss Saridge of "Out in the Cold" lives, unbeknownst to her neighbors, in poverty and is virtually starving to death. Most significant, she is a writer, in secret, but her stories do not appeal to popular tastes. An old friend finally recognizes her work as that of Miss Saridge, her girlhood soul mate, and rushes to the rescue. Miss Saridge is revived and warmed by the renewed friendship but dies anyway, having overexerted herself one night with "purposeless scrawls such as a young child might have scribbled." Riddell's narrator comments that women of that time vaguely in the past were "regarded with doubtful eyes" if they wrote, "as, indeed, they are regarded by several even to the present time." Yet for Miss Saridge it was "a labor of delight." The narrator adds, "Literature has its compensations as well as its trials, and she rarely had time to brood over sorrows which might well have broken an idle woman's heart."

Riddell died on 24 September 1906. Although she was still writing and publishing until within four years of her death, she became increasingly poorer as her health failed and as she was paid increasingly less for her work. She succeeded at last in paying off her husband's debt, but in 1893 she was financially desperate enough to ask for help from a Miss Matthews, to whom, according to Ellis, she wrote that she "hesitated about writing" and that "after my request was posted I longed to recall it." Also in that year, however, Black included Riddell in *Notable Women Authors of the Day* as the "famous author of 'George Geith of Fen Court.'" The popularity of this one novel presumedly explains why Showalter identifies Riddell as a "sensation novelist," grouping her with Braddon, Ouida, Amelia Edwards, Florence Marryat, and Mrs. Henry Wood. Bleiler, who has written the most seriously and recently about Riddell, considers her, in contrast to the sensation novelists, primarily concerned with "the inevitability of ultimate morality," regarding the more sensational and especially the sentimental elements of her works as concessions to popular tastes. The unevenness of her nonsupernatural fiction is evident in her realistic short fiction as well.

As a writer of supernatural fiction, however, she is noteworthy. In an era when, as Julia Briggs writes in *Night Visitors: The Rise and Fall of the English Ghost Story* (1977), women practitioners of ghost-story writing proliferated, Riddell's supernatural fiction was outstanding in several ways. According to Bleiler, "She had a knack of evoking the supernatural out of very convincing domestic or social backgrounds." Reflecting the dominant literary fashion of her time, she is essentially a realist. "Realism of thing, place, and time is Riddell's greatest virtue as a writer of uncanny stories in which the supernatural is set in such a solid matrix of realism that it can be overlooked until she wishes the reader

to feel its power," writes James L. Campbell Sr. The ghost story rises out of the Gothic tradition, but Riddell uses the form not so much to shock or thrill but to explore, writes Bleiler in *A Treasury of Victorian Ghost Stories* (1981), "a moral problem and as a means for stating the evanescence of human life and the permanence of eternal values."

Interview:

Helen Black, "Mrs. Riddell," *Notable Women Authors of The Day* (Glasgow: Bryce, 1893), pp. 11–25.

Bibliographies:

S. M. Ellis, "Mrs. J. H. Riddell: The Novelist of the City and Middlesex," in his *Wilkie Collins, Le Fanu, and Others* (London: Constable, 1931), pp. 323–335;

E. F. Bleiler, "Bibliography of Mrs. Riddell," in *The Collected Ghost Stories of Mrs. J. H. Riddell,* edited by Bleiler (New York: Dover, 1977), pp. 342–345.

References:

E. F. Bleiler, "Mrs. J. H. Riddell," in *The Penguin Encyclopedia of Horror and the Supernatural,* edited by Jack Sullivan (New York: Viking, 1986), pp. 353–355;

Bleiler, "Mrs. J. H. Riddell," in *A Treasury of Victorian Ghost Stories,* edited by Bleiler (New York: Scribners, 1981), p. 164;

Bleiler, "Mrs. Riddell, Mid-Victorian Ghosts, and Christmas Annuals," in *The Collected Ghost Stories of Mrs. J. H. Riddell,* edited by Bleiler (New York: Dover, 1977), pp. v–xxvi;

Julia Briggs, *Night Visitors: The Rise and Fall of the English Ghost Story* (London: Faber & Faber, 1977);

James L. Campbell Sr., "Mrs. J. H. Riddell," in *Supernatural Fiction Writers,* 2 volumes, edited by Bleiler (New York: Scribners, 1985), I: 269–277;

S. M. Ellis, "Mrs. J. H. Riddell: The Novelist of the City and Middlesex," in his *Wilkie Collins, Le Fanu, and Others* (London: Constable, 1931), pp. 267–335;

Wendell V. Harris, *British Short Fiction in the Nineteenth Century: A Literary and Bibliographic Guide* (Detroit: Wayne State University Press, 1979);

Elaine Showalter, *A Literature of Their Own: British Women Novelists from Brontë to Lessing* (Princeton: Princeton University Press, 1977).

Frederick William Rolfe
(Baron Corvo)
(22 July 1860 – 23 October 1913)

Jeffrey D. Parker

See also the Rolfe entry in *DLB 34: British Novelists, 1890–1929: Traditionalists.*

BOOKS: *Tarcissus: The Boy Martyr of Rome* (Essex: Boardman, 1880);

Stories Toto Told Me (London & New York: John Lane, 1898);

The Attack on St. Winefride's Well; or, Holywell Gone Mad, anonymous (N.p., 1898?);

In His Own Image (London & New York: John Lane, 1901);

Chronicles of the House of Borgia (London: Richards / New York: Dutton, 1901); republished as *A History of the Borgias* (New York: Modern Library, 1931);

Hadrian the Seventh: A Romance (London: Chatto & Windus, 1904; New York: Knopf, 1925);

Don Tarquinio: A Kataleptic Phantasmatic Romance (London: Chatto & Windus, 1905);

Don Renato: An Ideal Content Historical Romance (London: Griffiths, 1909);

The Weird of the Wanderer: Being the Papyrus Records of Some Incidents in One of the Previous Lives of Mr. Nicholas Crabbe, by Rolfe and Harry Pirie-Gordon as Prospero and Caliban (London: Rider, 1912);

The Bull against the Enemy of the Anglican Race (London: Privately printed, 1929);

The Desire and Pursuit of the Whole: A Romance of Modern Venice (London, Toronto, Melbourne & Sydney: Cassell, 1934; New York: New Directions, 1953);

Hubert's Arthur: Being Certain Curious Documents Found among the Literary Remains of Mr. N.C., by Rolfe and Pirie-Gordon as Prospero and Caliban (London, Toronto, Melbourne & Sydney: Cassell, 1935);

Three Tales of Venice (Thames Ditton, U.K.: Corvine Press, 1950);

Amico di Sandro: A Fragment of a Novel (Harrow, U.K.: Privately printed, 1951);

Frederick William Rolfe, circa 1887–1888 (photograph by William Wort)

The Cardinal Prefect of Propaganda and Other Stories (London: Vane, 1957);

Nicholas Crabbe; or, The One and the Many: A Romance (London: Chatto & Windus, 1958);

The Armed Hands and Other Stories and Pieces, edited by Cecil Woolf (London: Woolf, 1972);

Collected Poems, edited by Woolf (London: Woolf, 1972).

OTHER: *The Rubaiyat of Umar Khaiyam,* translated by Corvo (London & New York: John Lane, 1903);

Owen Thomas, *Agricultural and Pastoral Prospects of South Africa,* ghostwritten by Corvo (London: Constable, 1904);

The Songs of Meleager, translated by Rolfe (London: The First Edition Club, 1937).

SELECTED PERIODICAL PUBLICATION – UNCOLLECTED: "The Solitary Soul," anonymous, *Holywell Record* (November 1896): 1–7.

Since he had no formal education past fourteen, it is likely that Frederick William Rolfe would have fallen into oblivion if not for the interest in his personal eccentricities that has largely precluded any convincing appraisal of his literary merits. Commentaries on his fiction are typically marginal, as in the frequently quoted remark by Stuart Gilbert in his *James Joyce's Ulysses* (1952) that Corvo's hero Nicholas Crabbe in *The Desire and Pursuit of the Whole: A Romance of Modern Venice* (1934) "had a good deal in common with Stephen Dedalus." Commentaries on Rolfe's personality, which has attracted far more detailed and enthusiastic discussion, are perhaps best summed up in A. J. A. Symons's *The Quest for Corvo: An Experiment in Biography* (1934; revised, 1955), where he characterizes encounters with Rolfe as "minor experiments in demonology."

Rolfe was born on 22 July 1860 in Cheapside, London, to Ellen Elizabeth Pilcher and James Rolfe, who was eleven years her senior. The Rolfe family had been moderately successful as manufacturers of pianofortes since 1784, but the family business in the hands of John Rolfe had deteriorated from being a manufacturer of pianos to a piano manufacturer's agent by the time of Rolfe's birth. In 1874, at age fourteen, Rolfe left North London Collegiate School in Camden Town as a result of awakening religious zeal and his difficult adolescence, a period he later described as the most awful period in the life of a boy. Little of his life before he began writing is known.

Rolfe's full name was Frederick William Serafino Austin Lewis Mary Rolfe, a name that was never affixed to any of his published books and pamphlets or his many contributions to various periodicals. He preferred to conceal himself behind different names and poses, what he referred to as "trade names," including Frederick Austin, Fr. Rolfe, A. W. Riter, Al Siddik, Franz Wilhelm V. Bracht, Frederick of Venice, Uriele de Ricardi, V.

Bonhorst, May Chester, Vincenza Duchess of Deira, Ifor Williams, and the name most frequently associated with Rolfe, Baron Corvo.

Three of Rolfe's early works of short fiction are on the theme of premature burial. Perhaps the most interesting is "An Unforgettable Experience," published by Jerome K. Jerome in the 21 April 1894 issue of *To-Day.* In typical "Corvine" fashion, Rolfe sent the story to Jerome typewritten in blue italics on Japanese silk copying paper. In this story a woman in a workhouse who is pronounced dead of a fever by a workhouse doctor is sent home with her dead child for burial. Since her burial is to take place in a Protestant cemetery, a priest, Father Serafico, reads the service over her open coffin in her slum rooms. He hesitates momentarily because when he looks at the woman he cannot believe she is actually dead. The narrator, who calls himself Baron Corvo, is involved in several frantic attempts to revive her. He is finally successful, and she can be seen any day at early mass at Father Serafico's church.

This story is similar thematically to Rolfe's later "How I Was Buried Alive" and "The Solitary Soul" (1896), but it reveals scenes he likely witnessed while living with socialist Henry Hyde Champion, who founded three socialist journals. It is also possible that this story was drawn from events early in 1892, when Rolfe stayed at the house of the Fathers of Charity in Ely Place, London. The description in "An Unforgettable Experience" of a slum dwelling where old and young live together in crowded acceptance of suffering – the woman in her coffin with her dead infant at her side, her other children writhing on a dirty bed "like maggots in cheese" – reflects the poverty and tragic circumstances of the urban poor. But Rolfe's interest is more with the priest than with the poor, and he was no socialist, even though he spent most of his life in poverty as an outcast. In fact, after reading Edward Carpenter's *Towards Democracy* (1883–1902) Rolfe drafted a reply titled "Towards Aristocracy." Nonetheless, "An Unforgettable Experience" is unique among his short fiction as his only attempt to portray such an environment.

Rolfe was capable of transforming his experiences, frequently those from his Holywell days, to mythic proportions, but his imagination could also produce stories designed to offend and expose those he felt had slighted him. Under the pen name of A. W. Riter he published "The Saint, the Priest, the Nowt, the Devil" in the *Holywell Record* on 31 August 1897. This story is drawn from his sense of having been swindled by a Catholic priest, Father Beauclerk, who agreed to provide lodgings for Rolfe and attempt to find him commissions. In exchange, he was to paint banners for the church using art supplies provided by Beauclerk. Rolfe eventually learned of the priest selling one of his designs and demanded the extravagant sum of £1,000 from the priest for the banners he had painted. The priest refused, and as part of Rolfe's revenge he composed a story portraying his own version of these events and the priest's responsibilities to him. The story is fascinating as a work of fiction and because it is an early example of Rolfe's lifelong practice of retelling perceived slights and attacks on him from his own subjective perspective. Rolfe continued his onslaughts against Father Beauclerk in *Hadrian the Seventh: A Romance* (1904), where he is portrayed as Blackcote and as Father Saint Albans, who is described as looking like "a flat female with chlorosis." Rolfe did not limit himself to attacks on Beauclerk in fiction, and he was removed from his position in November 1898, due partly to Rolfe's having written letters directly to his superior general in Rome.

Insights into the imaginative workings of Rolfe's mind can be gleaned from comparing descriptions of him from one who knew him intimately during his Holywell days, John Holden, with Rolfe's description of himself as the "nowt" in his fictional account. Holden describes Rolfe as being of below average height, having a monklike appearance and faded hair, wearing extremely powerful glasses, and being very shabbily dressed. His face was inscrutable, and the servants were terrified of him. He also had an insatiable appetite for gossip and was concerned with any bit of information concerning any individual living in the town. Holden also recounts how he learned what Rolfe's comment that knowledge was power really meant when Rolfe, after assuming the editorship of the *Holywell Record,* used this information to reveal in the pages of the paper secrets told to him in confidence.

Rolfe's self-portrait as the "nowt" reveals a quite different figure from the one described by Holden. Rolfe's version is of one who worked like a slave and spoke to few, proud and yet reserved but able to hold a roomful attentive when he spoke. Because of his delicacy of manners, his speech, and his habits, he was stamped as a gentleman, a person of culture and consideration. In the story he renamed Holywell Sewer's End and characterized Beauclerk's brand of religion as "consisting of eternal principles modified to suit temporal requirements."

The "nowt" asks only for an honorarium, which he will contribute to the church. After a series of events the "nowt" is paid and does in fact donate his money to charity. However, in real life Rolfe asked for £1,000 and offered to give a percentage to charity. Father Beauclerk was forced to hire a solicitor to extricate himself from the unreasonable claim and continual harassment, and Rolfe accepted the solicitor's first offer of fifty pounds and donated nothing to charity. His vindictive nature in this story does reveal a rather humorous side, but it is checked by its relationship to actual events. Rolfe's humor also presents itself clearly in an early pamphlet he probably published in 1898, again from his Holywell experiences, *The Attack on St. Winefride's Well; or, Holywell Gone Mad.* This anonymously written pamphlet contradicts fictional allegations that claim Saint Winefried's Shrine had fallen into the hands of a bottling company.

The name Baron Corvo, with its pretense to nobility, drew the indignant wrath of an anonymous author in a three-part exposé motivated by Rolfe's pseudoreminiscence "How I Was Buried Alive," published in *The World Wide* (November 1898). Demonstrating as much familiarity with Rolfe's early years as any biography before or since, the series — first published in the Aberdeen *Daily Free Press* and *Evening Gazette* in November 1898 and republished soon after in *The Catholic Times and Catholic Opinion* — details Rolfe's early years as an undermaster at Grantham School, where he converted to Roman Catholicism; his years of starvation in London; and his appointment as master at a school for outcast boys at Oban. The attack included the circumstances leading to the baron's "title," which was evidently bestowed on him by a Roman Catholic English lady with the Italian title Duchess Carolina Sforza. The duchess agreed to finance Rolfe at a rate stated variously by him of £150 to £300 per year. Even though her generosity ended after two years, he continued to lay claim to the title she awarded him.

Although the article was anonymously published, Symons attributes a substantial portion of the exposé to the authority of writer Sir Shane Leslie, a friend of Rolfe's. Rolfe at first suspected it was the work of Dom Hunter Blair, a Benedictine who composed endless articles for various Catholic periodicals, but by 1903 he was convinced that it was the work of Father Patrick Green, whom he had ridiculed at Scots College when both were students there. Rolfe's revenge was to describe Green in *Hadrian the Seventh* as "the blubber lipped gorger who mopped up gravey with a crum wedge and gulched

Photograph by Rolfe of Toto, the inspiration for Rolfe's Toto stories, in Rome, 1890

the sop." Regardless of the authorship, the series of attacks is notable because the majority of the information is essentially true and therefore provides useful but brief coverage of Rolfe's most productive years as a writer of short fiction.

The attack focuses on Rolfe's pretense to nobility in light of his unfortunate experiences since 1886. In addition to his failed attempts at the priesthood and his expulsion from Oscott and Scots College in 1890 for not having a vocation, the anonymous author also points out that Rolfe was considered a general nuisance at Scots. In 1892 Rolfe applied with G. W. Wilson and Company photographers. Although he requested to be hired as an apprentice, he was at first told there was no work for him. Finally the owners relented, and he was hired as a helper. In this capacity he came and went as he pleased without regard to work or schedules. The firm released him, but he refused to be fired and kept returning to work each day until he was threatened by the police with removal. His response was to write a letter to the owners acknowledging that it might be a bad time to ask, but he wanted to know whether "one would be allowed to invest a small sum, say 1000 pounds, in your business, and to secure a permanent and congenial appointment suited

to my capacities." He had no money, but he was not finished with the affair. He went to a legal firm in Aberdeen and got them to write to the photography company a claim of about three hundred pounds for the retention, he claimed, of certain property of his and for breach of contract. Wilson pointed out to the firm the kind of man Rolfe was, and they immediately dropped the suit. The 1898 attack further documented Rolfe's experiments in underwater photography when he unsuccessfully attempted to obtain funding from the Royal Navy and the *London Illustrated News*.

The motivation for these articles, "How I Was Buried Alive," is one of the few short pieces by Rolfe to receive serious critical discussion. It is the story of how Baron Corvo, a member of an Italian noble family, falls into a catalepsy after a lizard jumps onto his arm. It begins with his expulsion from the seminary into the streets of Rome on a Saturday night in May 1890 because he has no vocation. An Italian family takes him to their villa, San Giorgio, to recuperate from the trauma of his eviction. The description Rolfe renders of the villa romanticizes the setting and the surrounding countryside, transforming it into a place of mythic significance. The villa stands on the top of a rock amid hills, with an old garden whose paths wind down to the edge of cliffs. At least once a week mass is held in the garden.

In *New Quests for Corvo* (1965) Vivian Godfrey White equates this setting with the lake and religious house belonging to Monsalvat, the Mount of the Holy Grail, a place of mystical initiation. She also notes that to be buried alive, the experience Corvo endures in the story, and to be raised again is a symbol of initiation. The question is whether the narrative reveals a true initiation or what White refers to as an initiation deferred. Also important to this story is the symbolism of the reptile that frightens Corvo into his trance. This fictional event was probably drawn from an actual experience related to Symons by Holden. Holden described how, after returning from mass, Rolfe saw a toad under the kitchen table, which frightened him to the extent he screamed, turned white as chalk, and stood motionless except for the twitching of his mouth. Holden pushed him onto a chair, where he remained for more than an hour. After Rolfe recovered enough to walk, Holden put him on his bed, where he remained until eleven the next morning. When he finally awoke, Rolfe claimed to remember nothing after first seeing the toad. In "How I was Buried Alive" Corvo explains that the occurrence he narrates in the story was the third such event in his life.

White notes that this is the third occurrence or trial and that it takes place on Saint Michael's Day at the Villa San Giorgio. Therefore, Corvo endures his trial under the patronage of two great dragon slayers of the church, Saint Michael and Saint George. In this instance the dragon is merely a toad, but it causes dread and yet attraction. White claims that the reptile is symbolic of sexual virility — feared, hated, and secretly worshiped. Although White's Freudian interpretation may appear a bit fanciful, it is convincingly enriched by biographical evidence concerning Rolfe's eccentricities during his years at Holywell. Holden recounted how Rolfe often made derogatory remarks about women, quoting from early Christian writers and adding comments such as "there's no more loathsome sight in nature than a pregnant woman" or "the worst of a woman is that she expects you to make love to her." At the same time, Rolfe retained a more personal interest in women and on a monthly basis would journey to Rhyl or Manchester in hopes of "a chance romance of the street." After these excursions he would return and recount specific details to Holden and frequently ask if Holden thought he was impotent.

Corvo's third encounter with the reptile in "How I Was Buried Alive" begins with a newfound courage gained by thinking, after seeing a lizard on the wall of the terrace, that he can sweep it away with a butterfly net. This attempt is revealing because a net is used for capturing rather than removing. The result is that the lizard crawls up the sleeve of his jacket, causing him to rip off his clothes and fall into another trance state that ends in his being pronounced dead. Corvo awakens after his funeral; he has been placed in a coffin with the lid nailed down in the burial vault of the chapel. He survives by kicking the lid off the coffin and returning to the world of the living. Rolfe continued to allude during his lifetime to his feeling that he had been buried alive in poverty, obscurity, and friendlessness. This theme also prevails in his longer works, such as *The Desire and Pursuit of the Whole*. This novel, described by Rolfe as a modern novel about friendship and literary life, begins with the autobiographical protagonist "buried" and chronicles his attempts to free himself from his "crab shell."

No insights into Rolfe's intentions as a writer of short fiction can be gathered from a list of magazines he deemed appropriate for his contributions since he was looking for monetary rewards rather than a serious literary reputation. In January 1891 he clipped a listing of names of magazines, their editors, and their rates of payments; from this list he circled *Blackwood's, Cassell's, Cornhill Magazine, Good*

Words, Temple Bar, and the *Strand.* While he was searching for magazines to publish his essays and short fiction he was writing his first drafts of the novel *Don Renato: An Ideal Content Historical Romance* (1909). The magazine best suited for his stories proved to be *The Yellow Book,* which began publishing his stories in October 1895.

The Yellow Book was published at the Bodley Head by John Lane, with Henry Harland serving as literary editor and Aubrey Beardsley as editor for contributions in visual art. The editors of *The Yellow Book* published only thirteen volumes from April 1894 to April 1897. Its list of contributors is impressive: in addition to such major writers as Henry James and W. B. Yeats, contributors included virtually all of the "sad men of the nineties," including Arthur Symons, Ernest Dowson, Lionel Johnson, Hubert Crackanthorpe, John Davidson, Kenneth Grahame, Theodore Wratislaw, and Max Beerbohm. The first two tales, "About San Pietro and San Paolo" and "About the Lilies of San Luigi," under the general heading of "Stories Toto Told Me" and signed "Baron Corvo," appeared in the October 1895 issue of *The Yellow Book.* These were the first of six stories by Rolfe appearing in *The Yellow Book* between October 1895 and October 1896. These were revised and eventually published in a single volume *Stories Toto Told Me* (1898). At the suggestion of John Lane, these six and his story "About What Is Due to Repentance," first published in the *Butterfly* in August 1899, were combined with two dozen others and republished in 1901 as *In His Own Image.*

The editors and publisher of *The Yellow Book* frequently encouraged new writers and artists and published their work even when it had been rejected by virtually every other publisher. In addition to providing an avenue for publication for artists of similar temperaments and aesthetic sensibilities, the contributors bonded together in mutual support and encouragement, but there is nothing to indicate that Rolfe had any continued contact with any of these writers or that he noticed them with even a passing interest. Even though the list of contributors to *The Yellow Book* was impressive, the magazine was not without its detractors. Criticism of the quarterly and its contributors was expressed succinctly in the February 1895 issue of *Harper's.* The editor, arguing against the claims of originality by *The Yellow Book,* suggested, "Yellow literature is not new. There have always been diseased people seeking notoriety by reason of their maladies."

In her *A Study in Yellow: The Yellow Book and Its Contributors* (1960) Katherine Lynn Mix suggests,

"In a literary decade which teemed with 'queer uns' Baron Corvo was pre-eminent." She claims her comments are directed more toward Rolfe's personality than to his contributions to *The Yellow Book,* which offer little if any hint of his eccentricities. Her comments are interesting, but they also lead her to the surprisingly naive characterization of *Stories Toto Told Me* as Italian folktales. These stories have folkloric elements, but they rely more on the fantastic and homoerotic than on any system of shared beliefs and cultural values that could be vaguely described as Italian. Symons describes these stories as folklore legends of Catholic saints and of their human motives and characteristics in a language of archaism and broken English.

Biographer Miriam J. Benkovitz notes that the pieces in *Stories Toto Told Me* have the summer of 1890 as their origin – a time Rolfe spent wandering in the Alban mountains. She also argues that these stories reveal actual events taken from his life, and thus most of the first six stories were likely completed before he went to stay with Champion in Aberdeen in 1893. Biographer Donald Weeks suggests that Rolfe's first Toto story was written in June 1891.

The narrator of these tales is Toto Maidalchini, whom Rolfe describes as the beautiful leader of a group of boys with whom he spent the summer. This group of boys serves him without question out of adoration. Benkovitz suggests that, taken together, the stories constitute an ideal of friendship, "long desired and long pursued, with himself at the heart." Toto is variously described as an example of unquestioning faith, an uneducated peasant, and the triumph of oral tradition over literature. Rolfe also expressed the opinion that it was undeniable that "the very funniest of tales in all the world should be those which concern holy persons and holy things." Benkovitz claims a more serious side to the stories, noting that in Toto one finds a combination of all the complex tendencies in Rolfe's personality, including his hostilities and his fidelity to a benign and humble Christianity based on spontaneous charity.

However, when Toto is described as "a slim faun in the forest" or is said to have "undulated deliciously," another aspect of Rolfe's personality surfaces, calling to mind the contents of his Venice letters and his penchant for photographing young boys in the nude. The homoerotic tendencies in Rolfe's writing were evident early in his life and are apparent in his "Ballad of Boys Bathing," published in the April 1890 *Art Review.* At this time he was writing his Toto stories and nearing the end of his probationary period as a candidate for the priesthood at Scots College. Weeks provides a brief description of this recently documented phenomenon in British literature, characterizing it as an outpouring of homosexual expression evidenced in the later half of the nineteenth century, and cites Brian Reade's *Sexual Heretics* (1970) as his authority in identifying the perceived compatibility between these interests and Catholicism. The tradition mentioned by Reade has much in common with Rolfe's own tendencies. According to Reade, Roman Catholicism viewed homosexual feelings as mental events leading to celibacy and dedication to the monastery. If, however, these feelings led to physical acts, they were considered venial sins. Rolfe seems to have struggled between these two concepts for most of his life.

Rolfe's links to this tradition can be clearly identified in some of his novels, in *The Venice Letters: A Selection* (1966 [i.e., 1967]), and in many of the selections from *Stories Toto Told Me.* "About Beata Beatrice and the Mamma of San Pietro" serves as an example. In this story the reader is reminded of Toto's physical attractiveness and the fact that he is the leader of a whole group of boys whose task it is to wait on the narrator of the tale, who is simply referred to as "the Baron." Toto has fallen in love with a young girl and is afraid of how his master will react. He disguises the young girl as a young boy to make her appear more presentable and more useful to his master. When Toto's master first sees the girl he notes with great satisfaction that "this girl of his would pass anywhere for a very pretty boy, with just the plump roundness of the Florentine Appollino, and no more." The Baron seems to give his approval but later confides to the reader, "Besides, I have reason to know, oh jolly well, the futility of interfering between the male animal and his mate." Toto, who had been earlier described as a figure like Benvenuto Cellini's Perseus, with the young girl has fallen from an idealized form in the eyes of a man Toto describes as a saint from heaven to the level of mating animals. Rolfe's initial attraction and eventual revulsion toward feminine beauty frequently takes the shape of a young girl concealing her identity in boys' clothing and is especially found in his novel *The Desire and Pursuit of the Whole.*

In "About Beata Beatrice and the Mamma of San Pietro," Rolfe avoids any exploration of the love between Toto and San Pietro by cleverly changing the direction of the narrative, with the narrator asking Toto what sort of mamma the Madonna had given to San Pietro. This tale is one of the strangest of the collection. Because of her

First page from the 1891 manuscript for Rolfe's first Toto story (from Donald Weeks, Corvo, *1971)*

evil-doings, especially her lack of charity, the mamma of San Pietro is condemned to hell, but she is offered an escape by her guardian angel if she had done just one good deed in her life. Her one good deed was to toss an onion top to an old beggar woman who was starving. The angel is commanded to hold an onion top over the boiling stew of hell so that San Pietro's mamma can grasp it when she boils up to the top. She grabs hold, and the others, seeing her escape, grab on to her clothing to free themselves. The angel rises higher and higher, carrying a long line of tortured souls clinging to San Pietro's mamma, who is angered by this because she is "a nasty selfish and cantankerous woman." Finally, she grabs the onion top by her teeth to free her hands so that she can beat those who are clinging to her. She fights so violently that she bites through the onion top and tumbles back into the flames of hell. Toto, noting what seems to him the moral of the story, states, "So you see, sir, that it is sure to be to your own advantage if you are kind to other people and let them have their own way, so long as they don's interfere with you." In the final line in the story the narrator says, "I chuckled at Toto's moral reflections."

Not all of the *Stories Toto Told Me* are free from Rolfe's vindictive attacks on people and institutions he felt had wronged him. In "About the Heresy of Fra Serafico" he begins his tale with a description of one of Toto's brothers, Nicola, who was going to be a priest. There is no light in his eyes, and he is gaunt, awkward, and the absolute opposite of Toto. The narrator declares his absolute respect for the priesthood but wonders why priests always slink along by the wall, "expressing by the cringing obsequiousness of their carriage that they would take it as a favour for some one to kick them." This kind of attack and many others stemmed from Rolfe's exclusion from the priesthood, his continuing battle with Father Beauclerk, and his general pleasure in attacking Catholicism – in, for example, "Jelly-Fish Catholics," published in the 22 June 1897 *Holywell Record*.

Rolfe's reputation as a writer of short fiction rests on *Stories Toto Told Me*. They reveal his talents at their most imaginative, humorous, and vindictive. After these tales were written, he devoted his talents to writing and rewriting novels, many of which were posthumously published because of legal entanglements and his desire to prevent his creditors from reaping any financial reward from them. He also worked on editorials and such typical projects as "Reviews of Unwritten Books" and tried to survive in the face of outright destitution.

It is indeed amazing that Rolfe could have endured the period during which he negotiated with John Lane for the publication of his stories. In one of his early letters to Lane he begged for a position on Lane's staff as a reader or editor, claiming, "All I want is to be picked out of this hole where I am buried." Even though for the first six of his "Stories Toto Told Me" Rolfe received praise as one of the most original writers for *The Yellow Book,* at the time Lane was planning to republish them in a Bodley Booklet, Rolfe wrote back in May 1898 at the news, asking Lane to consider "a naked little thing, sitting at the bottom of a mud-hole, with pen, ink, paper, copying-book, & diurnal in one hand, and Mr. Lane's onion-top in the other." But Lane, unlike the mother of San Pietro's rescuer, was not to be Rolfe's guardian angel. After filling Rolfe with hope by providing him with names of other publishers who might be interested in his work, he promised to discuss arrangements for publishing *Stories Toto Told Me.* Rolfe's expectations were deflated the next morning when Lane offered him twenty pounds for his new stories. Rolfe left Lane's office with ten pounds, with the rest due on publication of the book. This led him to Grant Richards, who commissioned him to write the history that became *Chronicles of the House of Borgia,* published by Richards in 1901. For this project Rolfe earned fifty pounds. Also in 1901 Rolfe published his short story "The Cardinal Prefect of Propaganda" in the 22 June issue of *The Candid Friend.* This story was written after the beginning of his quarrel with Father Beauclerk in 1897, and Rolfe's intention was to show the form that his retaliation would take for the wrongs he said Beauclerk had done him. This short story netted Rolfe thirty shillings. He never received a single penny for his best-known work, *Hadrian the Seventh,* or for *Don Tarquinio: A Kataleptic Phantasmatic Romance,* published in 1905 by Chatto and Windus.

Disappointed by repeated failures and weakened by disease, Rolfe died in Venice on 23 October 1913. The last years of his life were much like the years between 1890 and 1901, his most productive as a writer of short fiction. What he left behind for his readers is difficult to assess because of a lack of serious critical interest in his work by his contemporaries, compounded by the difficulty in obtaining his work today. His critical reputation lies somewhere between the myth surrounding "Baron Corvo," which has attracted a cult following since the publication of Symons's *The Quest for Corvo,* and Rolfe as an innovative experimenter with language, capable of both highly sensual and provocative de-

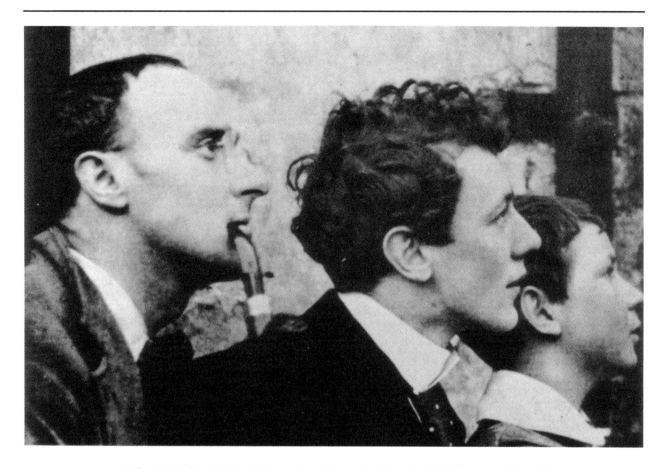

Rolfe with his friends John Holden and Leo Schwarz in Holywell, 1896 (photograph by Rolfe)

scriptions rivaling the work of any contributor to *The Yellow Book* or of any other writer of the 1890s. But Rolfe can become tiresome in his tirades against thinly disguised fictional characters drawn from his personal experience, apparent in his short fiction and in the novel on which his reputation most likely will rest, *Hadrian the Seventh.*

At his best Rolfe was an innovator who expanded the limits of autobiographical fiction and historical romance by using the genre to air his grievances in a context he highly romanticized and in a language of his own invention. Even his excessive use of pen names had a particular purpose, even if he claimed at times that they represented various personalities. For example, he used the name of Vincenza Duchess of Deira when publishing his simulated translations in the *Holywell Record* to conceal the fact that he was virtually the sole contributor to the paper for almost the entire year.

These translations also reflect Rolfe's continuing experimentation with narrative perspective, a practice he began as early as 1882, when he wrote the diary of a beetle for schoolboys. He described his experiments as attempts to write in someone else's skin, relying on the narrator to tell his story and thereby expose his own character. Benkovitz points out that the Toto stories are not told by Toto but by a narrator who describes Toto and repeats what the boy says. The practical result is to provide a framing device for the narrative, but this sometimes opens a gap between what Toto considers significant elements of the tale and the narrator's approval of Toto's perception of them. This method also appears in Rolfe's novel *Don Renato.*

Rolfe's novels and short stories are more the object of pursuit by rare-book collectors than serious readers, and his life has generated far more attention than any of his works of fiction. Possibly with no other writer is the line between the life and work so thinly drawn. His fiction displays many of the characteristics of the decadent movement, especially of the kind found in *The Yellow Book,* and his life also displays these values. In November 1893 Arthur Symons defined decadence in *Harper's* as a literary movement, but his description perfectly fits both Rolfe's life and art: "decadence: an intense self-consciousness, a restless curiosity in research, and over-subtilizing refinement, a spiritual and moral perversity."

Letters:

Letters to Grant Richards (Hurst, U.K.: Peacocks Press, 1951);

Letters to C. H. C. Pirie-Gordon, edited by Cecil Woolf (London: Vane, 1959);

Letters to Leonard Moore, edited by Woolf and Bertram W. Korn (London: Vane, 1960);

The Letters of Baron Corvo to Kenneth Grahame (Hurst, U.K.: Peacocks Press, 1962);

Letters to R. M. Dawkins, edited by Woolf (London: Vane, 1962);

"Without Prejudice": One Hundred Letters from Frederick William Rolfe, "Baron Corvo," to John Lane, edited by Woolf (N.p.: Privately printed for Allen Lane, 1963);

The Venice Letters: A Selection, edited by Woolf (London: Privately printed, 1966 [i.e., 1967]).

Bibliography:

Cecil Woolf, *A Bibliography of Frederick Rolfe, Baron Corvo,* revised edition (London: Hart-Davis, 1972).

Biographies:

A. J. A. Symons, *The Quest for Corvo: An Experiment in Biography,* revised edition (London: Cassell, 1955; East Lansing: Michigan State University Press, 1955);

Donald Weeks, *Corvo* (London: M. Joseph, 1971);

Miriam J. Benkovitz, *Frederick Rolfe, Baron Corvo: A Biography* (New York: Putnam, 1977).

References:

Katherine Lynn Mix, *A Study in Yellow: The Yellow Book and Its Contributors* (Lawrence: University Press of Kansas, 1960);

Cecil Woolf and Brocard Sewell, eds., *New Quests for Corvo* (London: Icon, 1965).

Papers:

Many of Rolfe's letters and portions of his manuscripts are in the hands of private collectors. His "Venice letters," written to Masson Fox between October 1909 and August 1910, are located at the Harry Ransom Humanities Research Center, University of Texas at Austin. Other important collections of letters and manuscripts are housed at the Berg Collection, New York Public Library; the Bodleian Library, Oxford University; the British Museum, London; the Houghton Library at Harvard University; and the Z. Smith Reynolds Library at Wake Forest University.

Olive Schreiner
(24 March 1855 – 11 December 1920)

Gerald Monsman
University of Arizona

See also the Schreiner entry in *DLB 18: Victorian Novelists After 1885.*

BOOKS: *The Story of an African Farm,* as Ralph Iron (2 volumes, London: Chapman & Hall, 1883; 1 volume, Boston: Little, Brown, 1883);

Dreams (London: Unwin, 1890; Boston: Roberts, 1891); republished as *So Here Then Are Dreams* (East Aurora, N.Y.: Roycroft, 1901);

Dream Life and Real Life: A Little African Story, as Ralph Iron (London: Unwin, 1893; Boston: Roberts, 1893);

The Political Situation, by Schreiner and S. C. Cronwright-Schreiner (London: Unwin, 1896);

Trooper Peter Halket of Mashonaland (London: Unwin, 1897; Boston: Roberts, 1897);

An English-South African's View of the Situation: Words in Season (London: Hodder & Stoughton, 1899);

A Letter on the Jew (Cape Town: Privately printed by Hyman Liberman, 1906);

Closer Union: A Letter on the South African Union and the Principles of Government (London: Fifield, 1909);

Woman and Labour (London: Unwin, 1911; New York: Stokes, 1911);

Dreams, and Dream Life and Real Life (London: Unwin, 1912);

Thoughts on South Africa (London: Unwin, 1923; New York: Stokes, 1923);

Stories, Dreams and Allegories, edited by S. C. Cronwright-Schreiner (London: Unwin, 1923; New York: Stokes, 1923; enlarged edition, 1924);

From Man to Man; or, Perhaps Only . . . (London: Unwin, 1926; New York & London: Harper, 1927);

Undine (New York & London: Harper, 1928; London: Benn, 1929).

OTHER: "The Salvation of a Ministry," in *The Life of Olive Schreiner,* by S. C. Cronwright-Schreiner (London: Unwin, 1924), pp. 202–205.

Olive Schreiner (Courtesy of the Lilly Library, Indiana University)

SELECTED PERIODICAL PUBLICATIONS –
UNCOLLECTED: "The Dawn of Civilisation," *The Nation and the Athenaeum,* 26 (March 1921): 912–914;

"Diamond Fields: Only a Story of Course," *English in Africa,* 1 (March 1974): 3–29.

Though better known for *The Story of an African Farm* (1883), a vivid description of provincial, stolid Boer (Afrikaner) society, Olive Schreiner also was the author of many shorter works of fiction.

Both *Dreams* (1890) and *Dream Life and Real Life: A Little African Story* (1893) were published during her life; and *Stories, Dreams and Allegories* (1923), edited by her husband, appeared after her death in 1920, as did two other novels. These three slim collections contained eight short stories (two intended for children) and twenty-six dreams and allegories. Schreiner's novels and sometimes even her discursive prose also enclosed allegories or stories that interpreted or enhanced the surrounding narrative or argument, such as the allegory, separately printed in *Dreams,* of "The Hunter" (later 1870s or 1880) in *The Story of an African Farm* or "The Child's Day" (1888) in the posthumous *From Man to Man; or, Perhaps Only ...* (1926).

The first significant native writer of South Africa, Schreiner criticized the narrowly patriarchal and racial underpinnings of nineteenth-century Anglo-African society. As discussed in Gerald Monsman's "Olive Schreiner's Allegorical Vision" (1992), her most significant legacy was a concern with personal relationships, manners, and values that lifted British colonial fiction from the mediocrity of hunters' tales, native uprisings, and hairbreadth escapes to a tough-minded depiction of the political character of colonialism, the clash between indigenous ways of life, and the march of capitalistic development. Hardly less significant were her brief allegories – surreal and fuguelike word paintings that only just fell short of poetry. Her preoccupation with dreams and illusion belonged to the zeitgeist that produced Sigmund Freud's probing of archetypal myths and Vincent van Gogh's hallucinatory landscapes. Not surprisingly, she used the surreal and allegorical as devices to reflect the intensely private anguish of the outsider, including her own as a colonial woman writer. Schreiner's aspirations for an ideal land and society have stood for a century at the fountainhead of much Third World and Commonwealth literature, influencing later fiction writers such as William Plomer, Isak Dinesen, Virginia Woolf, Alan Paton, Doris Lessing, and Nadine Gordimer.

Named after three siblings who died in infancy, Olive Emilie Albertina Schreiner was born on 24 March 1855 in the mud-floored Wittenberg mission station near the border of Basutoland in South Africa's Cape Colony, the ninth of twelve children. She once remarked in the February 1889 *Book Buyer,* "I was many years old before I saw a town." Her gentle, unworldly father, Gottlob Schreiner, was a German-born, British-trained missionary who had gone to Africa in 1838 under the auspices of the London Missionary Society, which

two years later sent David Livingstone to the South African field. The defensive and narrow morality of her mother, Rebecca Lyndall Schreiner, an English parson's daughter, inculcated in the young Olive a corrosive sense of moral inadequacy, a reactive free-thinking, and a sense of racial apartheid: "I started in life," she remarked in her posthumously published *Thoughts on South Africa* (1923), with "insular prejudice and racial pride. . . . Later on, my feeling for the Boer changed, as did later yet, my feeling towards the native races." Without formal schooling, she precociously began the reading from which her novels and stories would come, including works by Edward Gibbon, John Locke, Charles Darwin, Herbert Spencer, John Ruskin, Thomas Carlyle, J. S. Mill, Michel de Montaigne, Johann Wolfgang von Goethe, and Friedrich von Schiller. As she noted in *Thoughts on South Africa,* "The solitary white child, who grows up in the mission house ... may discover ... that from the old book-shelf with its score of volumes read and reread and long pored over, and from the mail-bag arriving once a month, ... it had learnt most of what London and Paris had to teach it."

After her father lost his post in 1865 for violating the society's trading prohibition – indicative, perhaps, of the inevitable frontier connection between religious proselytizing and commercial applications – the family disintegrated financially. For some years Olive was shunted back and forth among the households of friends and relatives, including a stint living in a tent with her older brother and sister, Theo and Ettie, at the recently discovered New Rush (renamed Kimberley in 1873) diamond fields. This nomadic lifestyle, followed by a succession of posts as an overworked governess on the remote Afrikaner farms of the Karoo, the Cape Colony's hauntingly bleak desert plain, confirmed her ideas about the social, sexual (she had a brief affair in her teens), and educational difficulties of women.

Schreiner had noticed early that the social message of the Bible was not part of the overt behavioral or cultural activity within the colony or empire. As artist and social crusader she embodied the same devoted earnestness as her missionary parents, but by espousing the Sermon on the Mount, to which her society merely paid lip service, she situated herself in a subversive or antagonistic position vis-à-vis dominant social politics. Her solution to a transformation of the master-servant, male-female, empire-colony hierarchy was not a role reversal in which the disempowered seize control but a radical role dissolution, equality through love. Her insight is that society cannot have just one "story" but must listen to many stories, told by the voices of children, women, and, by extension, the land and its native inhabitants. Her stories and allegories often were set in the desert or in the hills and tablelands of her childhood, less occasionally in the degrading sensuality of the London of her adult years, described in *From Man to Man* as a city occluded by rain and blankness. Idealized as the inexhaustible source of renewal, the land prevails over patriarchal oppression as well as the commercial squalor of the diamond mines and urban milieus of despair.

The young Schreiner's essential Africa had been, as she says in *Thoughts on South Africa,* "the land of Livingstone . . . where the smoke of the mighty falls goes up, whose roar is heard twenty-five miles off; of hippopotami playing in the water, and of elephants and lions, and white rhinoceroses. . . . In that land there were no Sunday afternoons and no boredom; you could do as you liked. The very names Zambesi and Limpopo drew us, with the lure of the unknown." This utopian peaceable kingdom dominates the fantasies or experiences of Schreiner's fictional children. Political bloodshed, as described in *Trooper Peter Halket of Mashonaland* (1897), may contaminate this land but never entirely destroys Schreiner's belief in its revitalizing power.

Schreiner said in her dedication to *Dream Life and Real Life* that the title narrative was "one of the first I ever made." Probably begun in childhood, it was completed about 1879 at the Lelie Kloof farm, South Africa, and first appeared in print in 1881 in *The New College Magazine.* The orphan child Jannita dreams of a loving father, an ideal inverted by the reality of her cruel master, a Boer farmer whose goats she tends. The interplay between "dream life" and "real life" begins in the moonlight when Jannita seeks to realize her dream of a loving father by fleeing to freedom. In the light of the nearly full moon, the harsh landscape is beautiful; if her fear of the valley of the shadow of death is momentarily present, so also is a sheltering aloe under which she sleeps. When morning comes, the love of the absent father and her freedom in the moonlight are given expression in Jannita's natural surroundings, especially "the rock that took care of her."

But if dream has lent waking reality its colors, reality also chills the dream when once again in sleep not only the image of the loving father returns but also a sinister premonition of death in the willows and river shadows. Overhearing plans by a Hottentot, a Bushman, and a navvy, a trio of embittered scoundrels, for an attack upon the Boer,

Cover for Schreiner's 1890 collection, featuring the first of her allegorical stories

the little shepherd sacrifices herself when she runs to warn him of the danger. Literally a shepherd, she figuratively becomes the sacrificial lamb. Like the angora goats, her hair is silky, and the knife that kills the goat kills her. Ironically, even the Boer supposes jackals must be at his sheep when he hears Jannita's cries. Her death illustrates a vision of forgiveness and love that is not yet wholly translated from dream into reality. Although the symbolic pastoralism of Psalm 23 or the Sermon on the Mount pervades Jannita's dream-infused sense of the landscape, the ideal of the father as shepherd is cruelly mocked by the stick and whip of the Boer and by the murderous knife of the three men. The light of the now-full moon, shining enigmatically on the child's grave, is either a fragile promise or an ironic denial that at some future time the horror of patriarchal and colonial violence may be transformed.

Schreiner sailed from South Africa to England in 1881, originally in the hope of gaining a medical education. However, her chronic asthma and her depressive tendencies, overtreated with powerful, addictive drugs, soon turned her from the altruistic ideal of practical healer to the role of maverick social reformer by means of fiction and polemical works. She also wrote several children's stories that reflected her psychological preoccupations with neglect, rejection, and an almost impossibly utopian level of noble action and affection.

"The Adventures of Master Towser" (1882), an almost grotesque literalization of Schreiner's youthful sense of being the underdog, is an account of a small, outcast mongrel's quest for love. Towser dances and is kicked, goes to live with a pretty lady, but loses her affection to a lapdog (an experience that anticipates Schreiner's romantic life) and rescues a boy who then beats him. In a story of wish fulfillment, "The Wax Doll and the Stepmother" (written around 1882), the doll, an artificial person, is more real to the children of the story than their brittle stepmother, unloving and hence unreal, until Nina's offer of her beloved doll wins the stepmother's love. The child's gift restores affectionate relationships to their proper sphere, real love from a real mother. Nina's situation echoes that of George MacDonald's Sophie in "The Gifts of the Child Christ" (1882), whose innocent ways also melt the heart of her stepmother. Schreiner had been reading MacDonald's books and attended a lecture by him in October 1882.

When "almost a child," Schreiner said in the February 1889 *Book Buyer,* she had started her best-known fictional work; by 1881 she largely had completed *The Story of an African Farm,* published in London under the pseudonym Ralph Iron to instant acclaim. Its story-within-a-story allegory "The Hunter," undoubtedly begun during the later 1870s and surely completed by 1880, appears in the novel's exact center and serves as an interpretive key to the book. Although not unusual in Victorian or Edwardian texts, the structural interpolations or miniature narratives in Schreiner's work were conceived by her as separable from their contextualizing plots. Such an attitude may be more typical of a writer for whom ideas and argument are more significant than an art-for-art's-sake ideal. Of Schreiner's allegories, only "The Lost Joy," which she said in a 24 February 1890 letter to Havelock Ellis was the first she ever wrote, and Undine's parables for Diogenes in Schreiner's posthumously published novel *Undine* (1928) preceded or were contemporaneous with the figure of the Hunter, an everyman questing for the White Bird of Truth.

The Hunter glimpses in the water the reflection of this mystical bird and pursues this vision throughout his lifetime, dying on the steps of a great mountain still hoping to see it again. One large feather drifts down to touch his hand before he dies, proof of its transcendental reality beyond temporal and spatial limits. The style of this allegory is indebted to a variety of sources: to biblical parables and to Schreiner's favorite book of the Bible, Revelation, and to such childhood models as William Adams's *Sacred Allegories* (1856) or John Bunyan's *Pilgrim's Progress* (1678, 1684). In the broadest sense this is an allegory of the relationship of the infinite to the finite, but as an allegory in the novel *of* the novel it suggests that the work of art is never limited to one interpretation but has "a thousand meanings, and suggests a thousand more." This idea is startlingly evident on the novel's last page, when the male protagonist, Waldo, the enthralled auditor of "The Hunter," dies; the farmyard chickens climb on his body, transposing and seemingly ironizing the allegory's images of quest, mountain, and vast bird of truth.

Having ventured on large philosophical issues and declared, according to Sarah Gertrude Millin, "the rights of women and the doubt of God" in *The Story of an African Farm,* Schreiner was sought out by writers such as George Moore and Arthur Symons. Social radicals such as Havelock Ellis, the pioneering sexologist, and Eleanor Marx, daughter of Karl Marx, included her in their circle of friends. Attempting to define the role of women in a capitalist economy, Schreiner extended the ideas of Mary Wollstonecraft and John Stuart Mill to create one of the earliest expressions of the then-new feminism under the rubric of the Woman Question, which anticipated and inspired early-twentieth-century feminism.

Though Schreiner tried to break away from the period's rigid sexual stereotypes, she did not find personal happiness. With Ellis she shared an intellectual sympathy but never physically consummated her love; a destructive relationship with a sadist and humiliating rejections by several other men contrasted with her utopian belief in the mutual evolution of sexual love between men and women. On more than one occasion she remarked in her letters on her sense of agonized symbolic oneness with prostitutes, old and young. Although she interpreted the subjugation or conflict of races and sexes as an economic imbalance of power, part of the struggle between capital and labor, she stopped short of a Marxist socialism. As she remarked in a 2 May 1884 letter to Ellis, "I haven't faith in anything that promises to raise us by purely material means." Rather, the vitality of her encounter with developing feminist and socialist thought was the product of her personal missionary mysticism, which sought the spiritual regeneration of herself and her world in visionary moments. Yet as Lessing deplores in an introduction to *The Story of an African Farm,* Schreiner "always seemed to be in flight – away from people and towards some place where at last she could feel well."

Leaving England in distress when it became evident that Karl Pearson, a mathematician with whom she was emotionally involved, was impatient to end their relationship, Schreiner traveled to France, Switzerland, and Italy. Renunciation and martyrdom, compassion and forgiveness, the struggle for love and the thirst for social reform – all seem to have come together to move Schreiner to produce her best allegories in the 1880s.

In Italy Schreiner wrote, polished, or drafted several allegories. She likely had begun "Three Dreams in a Desert" a few years earlier, and "The Sunlight Lay Across My Bed" (completed in 1889) was started sometime after this period, but at Alasso she composed in their entirety several other allegorical pieces, the most significant of which is "In a Ruined Chapel" (1887). Although she often uses *allegory* as synonymous with *story,* there is a distinction between the two in her work: her local-color fiction presents the details of the desert and its settlers as a subject interesting in itself, whereas her allegories, though also more often than not set in the desert, take the form of an extended metaphor in which a moral or spiritual significance stands behind the surface events. The relationship between her stories and allegories may be reflected in the distinction she draws in a 7 August 1884 letter to Ellis between her "plain" and "ribbed" style, dispassionate description in contrast to emotional painting of thought: "I *think* I generally write descriptions in the plain and philosophise or paint thought in the ribbed. (You know in knitting there are two stitches, one makes a plain surface and the other makes ribs. Ribbed knitting goes up and down, up and down.)" In such painterly prose she could express, as she wrote in an August 1888 letter to Mrs. J. H. Philpot, her "deepest personal feelings" as well as "the passion of abstract ideas . . . and . . . humanity, not merely this man or that."

Much as "The Hunter" was related to *The Story of an African Farm,* so "Three Dreams in a Desert" (begun in the early to mid 1880s) had been extracted for publication in *Dreams* from an earlier, destroyed version of *Woman and Labour* (1911), where, she writes, she "had in each chapter one or more allegories; because while it is easy clearly to express abstract thoughts in argumentative prose, whatever

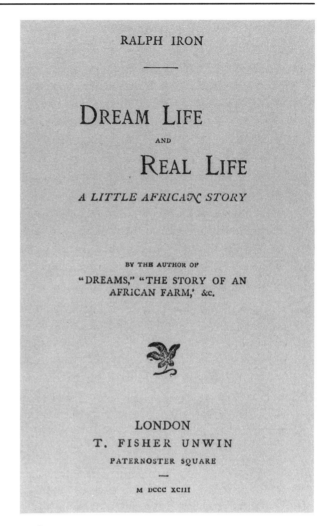

RALPH IRON

DREAM LIFE

AND

REAL LIFE

A LITTLE AFRICAN STORY

BY THE AUTHOR OF
"DREAMS," "THE STORY OF AN
AFRICAN FARM,' &c.

LONDON
T. FISHER UNWIN
PATERNOSTER SQUARE

M DCCC XCIII

Title page for Schreiner's third book, three allegorical stories about the nature of women

emotion those thoughts awaken I have not felt myself able adequately to express except in the other form." The threatening multiplicity of bodily distortions throughout Schreiner's work – often women's bodies dismembered, shackled, or crushed – is distilled here into the narrator's dream of two monumental and ancient figures, a prostrate female struggling to rise and a standing male fettered to her. The next dream is of Woman seeking the land of Freedom and proceeding down the banks of Labor through the river of Suffering in a garment of Truth. Reason insists that Passion, a cupid figure, be left to fly across by himself. In the final dream the narrator says she saw a heaven where brave men and woman walk "hand in hand" and where "the women also hold each other's hands." Schreiner's allegory is saved from pseudointellectual sentimentality if one recognizes that its rhetorical devices and literary tropes satisfied profoundly felt needs seldom met fully in women who were the products of a psychosexual patriarchy. In "Three Dreams in a Desert" the sketchy but intensely visual framing scene of desert heat, mimosa, and ants in the red sand combine with abstractions so simplified as to snag every free-floating anxiety or aspiration desiring articulation. Because each reader could find here the secrets of his or her heart ostensibly shared, as Waldo imagined in "The Hunter," these formulas of sorrow were open to appropriation by varying interpretive communities, notably though not exclusively the British suffragettes.

The narrator of "In a Ruined Chapel" has a vision of an enemy he cannot forgive, but God empowers an angel "to unclothe a human soul," and the man recognizes himself in his enemy. The angel then further strips this soul of its spatial and temporal qualities, and the narrator sees God. The "ruined" aspect of the chapel under the blue sky suggests the replacement of historical faith with a landscape and sky of vitality; the dream vision is the mystical means whereby the broken fresco of the mutely suffering crucified Christ is transformed into hope.

Another, just slightly less interesting allegory, "The Artist's Secret" (1887), describes the mysterious rubicund glow of a painter's color that after death seems explained by an obscure wound above his heart, suggesting that art is created by the "blood" of suffering. Finally, in "I Thought I Stood" (1887) a woman stands at the gate of Heaven accusing men of hurting women. She is refused admittance because she does not see her own guilt. In a parody of housewifery, the tidy angels must wash her bloody footprints from the floors. She returns, chastened, with a prostitute whom she has embraced; together they are sent as human, yet more than angelic, missionaries of compassion to selfish men and women. The paradox presented by these and Schreiner's other allegories is that, though the divine infinite dwells within each, mortal defects are not yet swallowed up in spiritual victory – but neither is spiritual reality wholly crushed by suffering and time. Hope for some unification of "real life" and "dream life" lies in reifying the allegorical correspondences between them.

"The Child's Day," written in 1888, combines the regional color of an African farm with the profounder themes generated by little Rebekah's experiences of reproach, affection, and, according to critic Margaret Fairley, "the mysteries of birth and death." Conceived in a flash of inspiration at Alasso, this allegorical story was first published posthumously as the "prelude" to From Man to Man.

Schreiner's recasting of the central episode from MacDonald's "The Gifts of the Child Christ," it is an indirectly autobiographical and highly symbolic account of a day in which Rebekah's mother delivers twins, one living and one stillborn. The child accidentally discovers her stillborn sibling and intends to adopt it as her own plaything. The farm is an Eden, complete with a snake; and its orchard and tree support fantasies in which Rebekah, on an island of her own, is both a counterpart to Queen Victoria and an ideal mother for an imaginary child that has replaced the doll-like sibling the adults deny her. The snake, as the apocalyptic manifestation of the knowledge of good and evil, strips her of illusions; Rebekah suddenly understands the meaning of the funeral procession for her dead sister and also, significantly, the purpose of human sexuality. The "day" of the child is now no longer merely a twelve-hour period in which she must fend for herself owing to her parents' inattention; it is the duration between birth and death in which mortality mocks every fantasy of power and freedom. Though originally she had refused to kiss the other baby in her mother's arms, Rebekah in the final scene is found asleep, protectively intertwined with the living sister. By opening herself to the uncertainties of time by sharing the surviving sibling with her mother and by giving up her utopian island for an emotional investment in her living sister, Rebekah has dreams that are constructively related to actual circumstance.

On 11 April 1889 Schreiner wrote to Ellis, "I'm writing a most grizzly Dream about blood, blood, blood. At least I'm enlarging it. I'll be so glad to get back to my novel." The allegory undergoing expansion was "The Sunlight Lay Across My Bed." She asserted in a 6 November 1890 letter to Ellis that her novel From Man to Man was conceived as an "objective" or more neutrally omniscient version of this allegory. It is a vision of the world as a hell, its beauty poisoned at the core by selfishness. Adapting to humanity's self-destroying sinfulness the image of the winepress of God's wrath from Revelation 14:20 and combining this with the episode of Belshazzar's feast from Daniel 5, Schreiner writes a diminutive Divine Comedy, principally an Inferno and a Paradiso, with God as her Virgil. Equally, however, it is a socialist allegory, in the style of William Morris, of capitalism feeding on the blood of the workers.

In Hell the privileged few drink the blood of their fellows. It is suggested that the ruins of a banquet hall on seven hills represent Rome and its bygone empire. Even the downtrodden beg for a small libation of their own gore. Ascending next to Heaven, the narrator climbs, like the Hunter, through three levels. On the first level she sees heterosexual and same-sex couples. Their light is intensified on the next level by men and women gathered together mining gems to produce a single crown of light. On the highest level is an androgynous figure of redeemed humanity creating the music of the spheres. (Notably, Schreiner switches from the pronoun *it* to *he*.) She awakens in her attic room to a world of men and women, a quavering barrel organ, and, across her bed, "a long yellow streak of pale London sunlight." Her hope is in the transformation of this pallid reality away from the intoxication of blood and toward the higher light.

Though the oracular and moralistic is devalued by modern realist standards, Schreiner's allegories received an enthusiastic reception when they were collected and published in *Dreams* in 1890. Her publisher, T. Fisher Unwin, later observed that many regarded the volume as her greatest literary work. The success of *Dreams* owed much to the volume's compatibility with Platonic myth (Schreiner relished Benjamin Jowett's 1871 translation of Plato's works), with Swedenborgian and German Romanticism, and with British Romanticism from William Blake and Carlyle to the visionary art of the Pre-Raphaelites and the lyricism of W. B. Yeats. Her friend Symons, reviewing the volume, also implicitly connected her allegorical "poems in prose" with the French Symbolists' mystical correspondences and visionary ideals.

Symons comes close to acknowledging that what preeminently colors these pieces is their precarious message of hope nearly canceled out by a quiet desperation:

> they are ... expressions of sympathy with man who cannot find truth, who will not seek beauty, who has wandered away from good. Some of them are consecrated, in a yet more special sense, to the cause of woman: the 'Three Dreams in a Desert,' for instance, and 'I Thought I Stood.' The message of the book is a word of hope – ascetic, unrestful hope, born painfully of the brave, acquiescent despair of the earlier book, but still hope.

Indeed, the allegorical pattern of movement from the figurative to the literal furnished a transforming paradigm for relationships of dominance and subservience, which explains why Schreiner was so enthralled by the genre. The freedom of correspondence between a higher, universal signification and confining surface events provided her feminist, progressive sensibilities with a recuperative analogue

S. C. Cronwright-Schreiner at Krantz Plaats house, 1892

or alternative configuration for the patriarchal and colonial suppression of the "thousand meanings" of women's, children's, or natives' lives. This is also why she remarked to Symons in 1889 that her allegories were "the very essence of art: all art is a symbol, and these are pure symbol themselves."

Schreiner's increasingly active role in South African and English politics ultimately led her to break publicly with the government of Cecil Rhodes and, as some felt, to betray her heritage by siding with the Afrikaners in the Boer War. Already in "The Salvation of a Ministry" (written in 1891), which was first published in her husband's 1924 biography of her, she had composed a political allegory satirizing Rhodes's support of the so-called Strop Bill, legislation permitting the lashing of servants. Here her idealized scenes of female intimacy are supplanted by a strong sense of feminist anger at males who club together. Heaven is a parliament presided over by a ludicrous God with all the limitations of a benevolent colonial governor. Notably without omniscience, he has a tendency to excuse nearly every failing on the part of Rhodes's all-male cabinet. Though salvation is by grace, not merit, Schreiner's allegory disparages a theology that merely reflects an established colonial order. Having been made "too great" to fit in Hell, Rhodes must be placed in the front row of Heaven at God's feet.

In "The Woman's Rose" (1891), a literary tone poem of longing for sisterly solidarity against fickle and aggressive frontier males, a mildewed acacia given to the narrator by a virile suitor is thrown out of her box of souvenirs, though its damp materiality lingers in "a faint, strong smell." However, the perfume of the carefully kept white rose presented to the narrator by her ostensible rival is now entirely a memory, yet for the narrator its fragrance remains timelessly fresh, indicating some future feminist spring. One interpretation is that only when women abandon their ingrained competition for men and practice mutual charity will there be any healthy relationship between the sexes as well. But when one considers that the man's not-quite-white flowers are now only a polluting gummy smell, he is as unattractively portrayed as the effeminate Gregory Rose in *The Story of an African Farm,* who dresses as a woman to earn the heroine's acceptance, or as the virile Frank in *From Man to Man,* who, betraying his wife by sexually preferring a native servant, is superseded in his wife's autoerotic fantasies when she casts herself as the male that holds and comforts her double.

The direct dramatization of bisexual emotional attachments in Schreiner's latter-day romance of the rose, drawn from her experience, offers a powerful clue to the causes for the pain of her entanglements with men and to how she recast their rejections into a preference for what she felt to be the nobler bonds of sisterhood. "I Thought I Stood" already had embodied much of this sentiment, adroitly masking a fear or resentment of men that she claimed belonged not to her but to "those infernal gatherings of women" by positing a feminist guilt and forgiveness that turns women exclusively toward white roses of inconceivable purity.

In "On the Banks of a Full River," written circa 1889–1892 and posthumously published in *Stories, Dreams and Allegories* (1923) with several pages missing, Schreiner dramatizes how social conventions force women into the hypocrisy of acting by flattery and manipulation because they cannot be as open as men in their emotional expressions. On the banks of a storm-swollen river an older woman tells a sixteen-year-old colonial girl how she renounced a passion and refused to falsify her emo-

tional life. The engorged watercourse recalls the "angry and red" river in "Dream Life and Real Life," either suggesting an emotional fullness that produces the heroines' headlong, self-destructive torrent of courage and action or, more likely, epitomizing society's impassable conventions that block any emotional connection between different sexes or among members of the same sex. The bare hovel in which the women shelter may be an image of a house, and their lives, without heterosexual love.

Schreiner clearly believed that male-female relationships, though successful in relatively simple cultures, such as that of the Boers, were subject to increasing emotional distortions as they came under the influence of complex cultural preconditions, particularly in developed metropolitan centers. In " 'The Policy in Favour of Protection — .' *Was it Right? – Was it Wrong?* " (1892) a female author deals with the issue of possessiveness and sexual competition – which is no less complex than the analogous economic issue of free trade and protectionism, the title suggests – in a manner that reflects Schreiner's 21 December 1884 comment to Ellis: "I made up my mind three years ago never to let a man care for me whom another woman thought she had any claim to." The story turns around a younger woman asking the authoress to give up the man they both love; ironically, the man then marries an even younger, wealthier woman. Schreiner is rumored to have said that her story was a reflection of her relationship with Ellis, though this triangle pattern also corresponds to imaginative myths from the time of her earliest completed novel, *Undine,* in which she had adapted Hans Christian Andersen's "The Little Mermaid" as the background for the dreamed-about male who marries another, more conventional woman.

In 1892, three years after her return to her native land, Schreiner met a ruggedly virile South African ostrich farmer, Samuel Cron Cronwright. In a photograph from that year published in his biography of Schreiner, he sits in pith helmet, feet widely planted, holding on his thighs an immense hybrid wildcat. He may have proposed to her; not long after, Schreiner seemingly impulsively fled back to England. Leaving Africa, she sent him "The Buddhist Priest's Wife," a clue to her views on sex and marriage. The story's title suggests the protagonist's desire for Buddhism's integration of wisdom and compassion and intimates that her marital ideals are anything but conventionally Victorian. Schreiner had described in a letter to W. T. Stead the story's theme in July 1890: "A woman scientific in tendency and habits of thought but intensely emotional

Schreiner with one of her African servants (William Plomer Collection)

loves a brilliant politician; she is going away where she will never see him again, she invites him to see her the last night, and they discuss love, the ideal of marriage, prostitution, and the evils of celibacy." In a 13 September 1892 letter she added that "the substance of it is that which I have lived all these years to know, and suffered all that I have suffered." The woman's disappearance and the male's belated realization of his love for her may be how Schreiner visualized her breakup with Karl Pearson when she began the story in 1890, rationalizing that the power imbalances in Victorian monogamy precluded a highly cultivated spiritual love. For Schreiner in 1893, however, Cronwright's letters prevailed; she soon returned to the Cape to marry him, though she apparently strained the engagement by confessing to what may have been a sexual transgression while in England.

Also while in England, she arranged for the publication of *Dream Life and Real Life,* containing her early story of that title and also "A Woman's

Rose" and "The Policy in Favour of Protection." The common theme in each of the three stories – about a child who sacrifices her life for a cruel master, a nubile adolescent who bestows a smile and white rose upon her social rival, and a professional woman who renounces her suitor for the sake of a younger woman's infatuation – is the female's altruistically protective nature, her noble subordination of self-interest. The implicit subtheme here and elsewhere in Schreiner's fiction is the aggressive or callously indifferent male paragon or the unavailable father, throughout all of her fiction a figure of remote preoccupation or absence by premature death. In each instance the womanly gesture is made without any expectation of compensating benefit; it has an entirely instinctive spontaneity of motivation beyond conventional gender roles.

The settings and protagonists of the stories seem intentionally arranged to form a progression in terms of woman's chronological age and social context – from a rural child to the frontier village adolescent and finally to the urban woman. The continuity of charitable acts, supporting even the undeserving, suggests that Schreiner understands altruism as a defining moral trait or special virtue of the female character under a variety of circumstances. Unwin remarked in 1924 that though short, the volume had been reprinted continually, selling thirty thousand copies.

When Schreiner married Cronwright in 1894, they combined surnames to become the Cronwright-Schreiners. Her much-desired child lived only for a few hours, dying on 1 May 1895; but refusing to abandon it as she herself perhaps had felt abandoned, she carried it in a little white coffin when she moved. As a writer she had employed her earlier years on works of imagination. In her later years, however, especially as her brother, Will, grew prominent in politics, capping his career as prime minister of the Cape Colony in 1898, her interests markedly shifted from fiction to polemical writings. Her novel *Trooper Peter Halket of Mashonaland* and her short story "Eighteen-Ninety-Nine" (1904) carried her fiction writing in more political directions.

The story celebrates a fierce Boer loyalty to family, folk, and land, to a pioneer way of life, and to a young man's mission to defend his land and family freedom against the capitalistic greed of the English. In "Eighteen-Ninety-Nine" all of Afrikaner history is distilled in the lifetime experiences of the "woman," whose memories extend from the massacre of her family on the Great Trek of the Boers in the 1830s to the recurrent deaths of her husband, sons, and grandson Jan.

The first two parts of the story are the contexts for the birth and death of Jan respectively, the grandmother's memories filling in most of part 1 in the form of flashbacks. Jan's death in the Boer War in 1899 is a crucial moment of transition between two centuries, between preindustrial Boer states and the emergent capitalistic state, and more broadly between human death and a far-off rebirth of political freedom. The epigraph from 1 Corinthians 15:36 pinpoints the crux of this story: Jan's martyrdom — he is repeatedly shot and stabbed in combat — is necessary for any final political or economic emancipation of the land. Thus Jan, whose hair is "as yellow as the tassels that hang from the head of ripening mealies," is figuratively reincarnated in the mealie seeds sown by mother and grandmother that lie in the earth and "rot there, seemingly, to die," until the rain and the sun cause them to sprout and "lift their feathery plumes and hang out their pointed leaves and silken tassels." Schreiner's style here has biblical simplicity of narration, dis-

tilled into the most basic essentials of place, object, and act, that infuses a sense of the sacred and the ritualistic into daily life.

Schreiner's thematic development seems to have gone from a nearly defeatist self-sacrifice in "Dream Life" to a qualifiedly optimistic self-sufficiency in "The Child's Day" and finally to an affirmation of nature's infinite power of renewal, albeit lugubriously portrayed in "Eighteen-Ninety-Nine." After the Boer War the rights of native Africans loomed larger for Schreiner; the Boers, she remarked in a letter to her husband dated 9 May 1906, "are more than able to take care of themselves. But the Natives are always with me." At times writing polemically about race or gender conflict, not fictionally dramatizing lives deformed by it, she may not have risen much above mere pamphleteering, though the influence of her *Woman and Labour* on contemporary British feminists was extraordinary.

From 1913 until 1920 she again lived principally in England, separated by World War I from her husband, but her previous support of the Boers, her views on race relations, and her developing pacifist opinions and opposition to involvement in World War I increasingly alienated her British reading public. Much of her marriage had been spent separated from her husband, but she always pretended to herself that theirs was an idyllic union. When she was reunited in London with her husband in 1920, she had aged so much he barely recognized her when she opened the door. Returning to South Africa without him just after he had sold his business and come to England, she died three months later at Wynberg, Cape Town, on 11 December 1920, at age sixty-five. The autopsy revealed blocked coronary arteries and lungs enlarged by emphysema.

In the decades following her death, preoccupation with Schreiner's controversial, even flamboyant, personality resulted in many biographical studies, but not until a century after *The Story of an African Farm* did objections over her limited literary production yield to a more precise appreciation of her adroit use of the symbolic fable, of the spiritual quest, and of social and political satire to illuminate the failures of colonialism. A growing interest in women writers, provocative approaches that combine reader-response criticism with feminist psychology, and a growing multiculturalism in English-language societies — including recent unanticipated political changes within South Africa itself — have elevated Schreiner to a position among the most seminal transitional figures between high Victorianism and modernism or between the empire and its postcolonial demise. Increasingly sophisticated literary criticism of her contributions to fictional form and theme, particularly her sociological contexts, and a scholarly edition of her work will contribute to her growing reputation.

Letters:

The Letters of Olive Schreiner 1876–1920, edited by S. C. Cronwright-Schreiner (London: Unwin, 1924; Boston: Little, Brown, 1924);

Olive Schreiner: Letters – Volume 1, 1871–1899, edited by Richard Rive (Oxford: Oxford University Press, 1988);

My Other Self: The Letters of Olive Schreiner and Havelock Ellis, 1884–1920, edited by Yaffa Draznin (New York: Peter Lang, 1992).

Bibliographies:

Evelyn Verster, *Olive Emilie Albertina Schreiner (1855–1920): Bibliography* (Cape Town: University of Cape Town, School of Librarianship, 1946);

Roslyn Davis, *Olive Schreiner (1920–1971)* (Johannesburg: University of Witwatersrand, Department of Bibliography, Librarianship and Typography, 1972);

Ridley Beeton, *Olive Schreiner, A Short Guide to Her Writings* (Cape Town: Timmins, 1974).

Biographies:

S. C. Cronwright-Schreiner, *The Life of Olive Schreiner* (London: Unwin, 1924);

Vera Buchanan-Gould, *Not Without Honour: The Life and Writings of Olive Schreiner* (London: Hutchinson, 1948);

D. L. Hobman, *Olive Schreiner: Her Friends and Times* (London: Watts, 1955);

Johannes Meintjes, *Olive Schreiner: Portrait of a South African Woman* (Johannesburg: Keartland, 1965);

Ruth First and Ann Scott, *Olive Schreiner* (London: Deutsch, 1980; New York: Schocken, 1980).

References:

Joyce Berkman, *The Healing Imagination of Olive Schreiner: Beyond South African Colonialism* (Amherst: University of Massachusetts Press, 1989);

Cherry Clayton, ed., *Olive Schreiner* (Johannesburg: McGraw-Hill, 1983);

Margaret Fairley, "The Novels of Olive Schreiner," *Dalhousie Review,* 9 (1929): 168–180;

Gerald Monsman, "Olive Schreiner: A Child on the Farm," in *International Literature in English: Essays on the Major Writers,* edited by Robert L. Ross (New York & London: Garland, 1991), pp. 5–19;

Monsman, *Olive Schreiner: Landscape and Power* (New Brunswick, N. J.: Rutgers University Press, 1991);

Monsman, "Olive Schreiner's Allegorical Vision," *Victorian Review,* 18 (1992): 49–62;

Claudia Roth Pierpont, "A Critic at Large: A Woman's Place (Olive Schreiner)," *New Yorker,* 67 (27 January 1992): 69–83;

Malvern Smith and Don Maclennan, eds., *Olive Schreiner and After: Essays on South African Literature in Honour of Guy Butler* (Cape Town: Philip, 1983).

Papers:

Collections of Schreiner's papers and correspondence are held at the Harry Ransom Humanities Research Center, University of Texas at Austin; the Archives Division, Sheffield City Libraries, Sheffield, England; the University College Library, London; Cullen Library, Department of Historical Papers, University of Witwatersrand, Johannesburg; Cory Library, Thomas Pringle Collection for English in Africa, Rhodes University, Grahamstown, South Africa; Cradock Public Library, Cradock, South Africa; Albany Museum, 1820 Settlers Memorial Division, Grahamstown, South Africa; Rhodes House Library, Oxford; J. W. Jagger Library, African and Special Collections, University of Cape Town, Rondebosch, South Africa; Africana (Strange) Library, Johannesburg Public Library; and Special Collections, South African Public Library, Cape Town.

William Sharp
(Fiona Macleod)

(12 September 1855 – 5 December 1905)

Thomas L. Cooksey
Armstrong State College

BOOKS: *Dante Gabriel Rossetti: A Record and a Study* (London: Macmillan, 1882);

The Human Inheritance, The New Hope, Motherhood (London: Stock, 1882);

Earth's Voices: Transcripts from Nature, Sospitra, and Other Poems (London: Stock, 1884);

Euphrenia; or, The Test of Love: A Poem (London: Kegan Paul, Trench, 1884);

Life of Percy Bysshe Shelley (London: Scott, 1887);

Romantic Ballads and Poems of Phantasy (London: Scott, 1888);

The Sport of Chance, 3 volumes (London: Hurst & Blackett, 1888);

Life and Writings of Heinrich Heine (London & New York: Scott, 1888); republished as *Life of Heinrich Heine* (London: Scott / New York: Whittaker, 1888);

The Children of To-morrow: A Romance (London: Chatto & Windus, 1889; New York: Lovell, 1890);

Life and Writings of Robert Browning (London & New York: Scott, 1890); republished as *Life of Robert Browning* (London: Scott, 1890);

Sospiri di Roma (Rome: Privately printed, 1891);

A Fellowe and His Wife, by Sharp and Blanche Willis Howard (Boston & New York: Houghton Mifflin, 1892);

Flower o' the Vine: Romantic Ballads and Sospiri di Roma (New York: Webster, 1892);

The Life and Letters of Joseph Severn (London: Sampson Low, Marston, 1892; New York: Scribners, 1892);

Pharais: A Romance of the Isles, as Fiona Macleod (Derby: Harpur & Murray, 1894; Chicago: Stone & Kimball, 1895);

Vistas (Chicago: Stone & Kimball, 1894; Derby: Frank Murray at the Moray Press, 1894);

Fair Women in Painting and Poetry (London: Seeley, 1894; New York: Macmillan, 1894; revised and enlarged edition, London: Seeley, 1907);

William Sharp (Fiona Macleod) (Courtesy of the Lilly Library, Indiana University)

The Gypsy Christ, and Other Tales (Chicago: Stone & Kimball, 1895); enlarged as *Madge o' the Pool, The Gipsy Christ and Other Tales* (London: Constable, 1896);

The Mountain Lovers, as Fiona Macleod (London: John Lane, 1895; Boston: Roberts, 1895);

The Sin-Eater and Other Tales, as Fiona Macleod (Edinburgh: Geddes, 1895; Chicago: Stone & Kimball, 1895);

The Washer of the Ford and Other Legendary Moralities,
as Fiona Macleod (Edinburgh: Geddes, 1895;
Chicago: Stone & Kimball, 1896);

Ecce Puella and Other Prose Imaginings (London: Elkin
Mathews, 1895);

*From the Hills of Dream: Mountain Songs and Island
Runes,* as Fiona Macleod (Edinburgh: Geddes,
1896); revised and enlarged as *From the Hills of
Dream: Threnodies, Songs and Other Poems* (Port-
land, Maine: Mosher, 1901; London:
Heinemann, 1907);

Green Fire: A Romance, as Fiona Macleod (New York:
Harper, 1896; London: Constable, 1896);

Wives in Exile: A Comedy in Romance (Boston & New
York: Lamson, Wolffe, 1896; London: Richards, 1898);

Spiritual Tales, as Fiona Macleod (Edinburgh: Geddes, 1897);

Barbaric Tales, as Fiona Macleod (Edinburgh: Geddes, 1897);

Tragic Romances, as Fiona Macleod (Edinburgh: Geddes, 1897);

*The Laughter of Peterkin: A Retelling of Old Tales of the
Celtic Wonderworld,* as Fiona Macleod (London:
Constable, 1897); republished as *The Laughter
of Peterkin: A Retelling of Old Tales of the Celtic
Underworld* (London: Heinemann, 1927);

The Dominion of Dreams, as Fiona Macleod (London:
Constable, 1899; New York: Stokes, 1900);

Silence Farm (London: Richards, 1899);

*The Divine Adventure; Iona; by Sundown Shores: Studies
in Spiritual History,* as Fiona Macleod (London:
Chapman & Hall, 1900; New York: Duffield,
1910);

Progress of Art in the Century (Philadelphia: Linscott,
1902; London & Edinburgh: Chambers,
1903);

Literary Geography (London: Pall Mall, 1904; New
York: Scribners, 1904); enlarged as *Literary
Geography and Travel-Sketches* (London:
Heinemann, 1912; New York: Duffield,
1912);

*The Winged Destiny: Studies in the Spiritual History of the
Gael,* as Fiona Macleod (London: Chapman &
Hall, 1904; New York: Duffield, 1911);

The Immortal Hour: A Drama in Two Acts (Portland,
Maine: Mosher, 1907; London: Foulis,
1908);

The Works of Fiona Macleod, 7 volumes, edited by
Elizabeth Sharp (London: Heinemann, 1910–
1912);

At the Turn of the Year: Essays and Nature Thoughts (Edinburgh & London: Foulis, 1913).

OTHER: *The Poetical Works of Walter Scott,* selected,
with a critical essay, by Sharp (London & New
York: Scott, 1885);

The Sonnets of This Century, selected, with a critical introduction, by Sharp (London: Scott, 1886;
New York: Whittaker, 1887);

*For a Song's Sake and Other Stories by Philip Bourke Mar-
ston,* selected, with an introduction, by Sharp
(London: Scott, 1887);

American Sonnets, selected by Sharp (London: Scott /
New York: Gage, 1889);

Great Odes: English and American, selected, with an introduction, by Sharp (London: Scott, 1890);

Matthew Arnold, *The Strayed Reveller, Empedocles on
Etna, and Other Poems,* selected, with a critical
introduction, by Sharp (London: Scott, 1896);

Algernon Charles Swinburne, *Atlanta in Calydon and
Lyrical Poems,* selected, with an introduction,
by Sharp (Leipzig: Tauchnitz, 1901);

The Essays of Sainte-Beuve, edited, with a critical
memoir, by Sharp (London: Gibbings / Philadelphia: Lippincott, 1901);

The Songs, Poems, and Sonnets of William Shakespeare,
edited, with a critical introduction, by Sharp
(London & Newcastle-on-Tyne: Scott, 1902);

*Dramatic Sonnets, Poems and Ballads: Selections from the
poems of Eugene Lee-Hamilton,* introduction by
Sharp (London & Newcastle-on-Tyne: Scott,
1903).

SELECTED PERIODICAL PUBLICATIONS –
UNCOLLECTED: "A Note on Climate and Art,"
Modern Thought, 3 (June 1881): 153–155;

"Dust and Fog," *Good Words,* 24 (October 1883):
721–723;

"Some Personal Reminiscences of Walter Pater,"
Atlantic Monthly, 74 (December 1884): 801–
814;

"Some Reminiscences of Christina Rossetti," *Atlantic Monthly,* 75 (June 1895): 736–749;

"Sir Edward Burne-Jones," *Atlantic Monthly,* 82 (September 1898): 375–383;

"Mr. George Meredith," *Good Words,* 40 (July
1899): 477–482;

"Garden of the Sun," *Century,* 71 (March 1906):
663–681; 72 (May 1906): 37–54.

William Sharp impressed many people with
his robust and masculine features, his genial charm,
and his bluff manner. Writing in 1912, his wife,
Elizabeth Sharp, recalled that "he was a Viking in
build, a Scandinavian in cast of mind, a Celt in
heart and spirit." Arthur Waugh, father of novelist
Evelyn Waugh, described Sharp in the 14 August

1936 *Spectator* as "Olympian" in stature, with a "bright complexion, full head of hair, and well-kempt beard." Waugh added that "his manner was a mixture of suavity and aggression, and he knew (no man better) how to overcome the hesitation of editors." In marked contrast William Butler Yeats, his former friend, grew to "hate his red British face of flaccid contentment," as he once wrote in a letter. Thus, it was extremely surprising when it was revealed in 1906, a year after Sharp's death, that since 1894 he had written and published extensively under the pseudonym Fiona Macleod, "the Celtic siren," the veritable high priestess and chief creator of Celtic Twilight literature in Scotland. Sharp had even gone so far as to have his sister Mary copy his Macleod manuscripts and correspondence so that his handwriting might not betray his true identity. At the end of an era that had seen women such as the Brontë sisters and George Eliot publish under men's names, Sharp represented an anomaly.

Flourishing at the end of the nineteenth century, Sharp was a productive poet, editor, art critic, and literary journalist, churning out a continuous stream of biographies, reviews, and critical introductions as well as volumes of poetry and potboilers. As a young man he made the acquaintance of Dante Gabriel Rossetti, George Meredith, and the remnants of the Pre-Raphaelite circle. Later he counted among his friends Arthur Symons, Walter Pater, Oscar Wilde, Robert Louis Stevenson, and Yeats. It is on his work as Fiona Macleod, however, that Sharp's enduring reputation rests. From 1894 until his early death Sharp as Macleod produced novels, plays, poems, essays, and short stories centered around Celtic legends, folklore, and mythology and concerned with a spiritual transcendence through a mystical identity with Celtic and Gaelic roots.

Sharp was born in Paisley, near Glasgow, Scotland, on 12 September 1855, the oldest of eight children born to Katherine Brook Sharp and David Galbraeth Sharp. The Sharps were a prosperous middle-class family, and his father was a partner in an old and well-established mercantile house. Little is known about William's childhood or his siblings. He claimed facetiously that the three greatest influences on him were the wind, woods, and sea. He received his early formal education at the Glasgow Academy. More significantly, he learned stories and Gaelic songs from his Highland nurse, Barbara. After an attack of typhoid fever at age sixteen, he was sent to the western Highlands to convalesce, spending much of the year sailing the lochs and fjords. Here he made the acquaintance of an old

fisherman named Seumas Macleod, who added to his stock of Celtic lore. Many of the Fiona Macleod stories are thinly disguised autobiography, presented in the narrative frame of a tale or legend recounted to the young Fiona while sailing with Pàdruig Macrae and Ivor McLean, two old fishermen wise in the mysteries of the Gael.

Sharp's father envisioned his eldest son entering the family business. William therefore enrolled at Glasgow University. He was restless, however, and, according to his wife's memoir, in the summer of 1873, at age eighteen, he "took to the heather" for three months, joining a band of Gypsies in the West Country. Eventually apprehended in his truancy, he agreed to return to the university and also to apprentice for the law. An unexceptional scholar, he left the university without taking a degree, though not without extensive reading in literature, folklore, and mythology. The sudden death of his father in August 1876 precipitated a breakdown in his own health, and the following month he was sent to Australia to recover his strength and to begin a career in banking. While he enjoyed the opportunity of touring the bush country, he returned to London in 1878 via the South Seas, taking up a position in the London branch of the Melbourne Bank. He was dismissed from this position in 1881 because, as he is quoted in his wife's memoir, "I had not heard the cuckoo that season, so I resolved to forget business for the day." By this time Sharp had begun to enter literary circles and saw a career for himself in literature.

As early as 1879 Sharp had begun to contribute poems, reviews, and articles to various papers and periodicals such as *Good Words* and the *Examiner*. Also at this time his friend Noel Paton introduced him to Rossetti. Admitted to Rossetti's circle, he soon came to know Meredith, Pater, Algernon Charles Swinburne, William Morris, Robert Browning, and the painters William Bell Scott, Ford Madox Brown, and William Holman Hunt – in short, the leading literary and artistic figures of the day. Rossetti proved to be a sympathetic friend, encouraging the younger man with his writing.

In 1882 Sharp published his first volume of poetry, *The Human Inheritance, The New Hope, Motherhood,* a work that showed the influence of both Rossetti's sonnet sequence "The House of Life" (completed in 1881) and Meredith's *Modern Love* (1862). After Rossetti's death in the same year, Sharp published a biography, *Dante Gabriel Rossetti: A Record and a Study,* his first major work as a critic and the start of a hectic career as an editor and literary journalist. He was soon hired by Eric Gill to

produce biographies of Percy Bysshe Shelley (1887), Heinrich Heine (1888), and Browning (1890) for the Great Writers series and by Ernst Rhys to become an editor of the Canterbury Poets series, producing collections of the poems of Sir Walter Scott (1885), Matthew Arnold (1896), William Shakespeare (1902), and Eugene Lee-Hamilton (1903), among others. He also became a contributing staff member of the *Glasgow Herald* and *Art Journal.* Amid the crush of literary hackwork Sharp continued to produce poetry, including the volumes *Earth's Voices: Transcripts from Nature, Sospitra, and Other Poems* (1884) and *Romantic Ballads and Poems of Phantasy* (1888).

Sharp also produced his first two novels, *The Sport of Chance,* a Victorian triple-decker first serialized in 1887 then published as a book in 1888, and *The Children of To-morrow: A Romance* (1889), a sort of reconfiguration of Browning's "Andrea del Sarto" (1855) synthesized with a mixture of Heine's cosmopolitanism and Olive Schreiner's feminism. Sharp's most important work of fiction under his own name, *Children of To-morrow* examines the social and sexual mores of a younger generation of avantgarde artists as a gauge of the spiritual state of the age. He is particularly interested in their search for an ideal nationalism, a cosmopolitan spirit contrary to what he took as the stultifying atmosphere of late-Victorian propriety. In a foreshadowing of his aspirations for Celtic nationalism, Sharp equates nationalism and cosmopolitanism, a seemingly paradoxical nationalism of the spirit, a worldview that informed art and metaphor rather than politics or petty tribalism.

Despite his busy career, Sharp managed to enjoy a personal life as well. In 1882–1883 he made a lengthy excursion to Italy, which helped to develop his perspective on modern British society. Returning to London, he married his first cousin Elizabeth Sharp the following year. As his success started to grow, he continued his various travels. In 1887 American critic Edmund Clarence Stedman, interested in Sharp's poetry, began a correspondence that culminated in an invitation for Sharp to visit the United States, which the Sharps did in the summer of 1889. The visit was a great success, and America became for Sharp a "fortunate Eden." Through Stedman, Sharp was introduced to William Dean Howells and various publishers interested in his work. Sharp also became seriously interested in American literature, especially the work of Walt Whitman. The immediate product of this interest was a series of articles on American literature and the edited volumes *American Sonnets* (1889) and

The Sin-Eater
And other Tales
By FIONA MACLEOD
Author of "Pharais" and
"The Mountain Lovers"

PATRICK GEDDES & COLLEAGUES
THE LAWNMARKET, EDINBURGH
STONE & KIMBALL, CHICAGO

Title page for the American edition of one of Sharp's pseudonymous story collections

Great Odes: English and American (1890). The Sharps cut many of their ties in London after the American trip and made a long trip to the Continent (1890–1891), settling first in Rome and later Stuttgart.

This second trip to Italy marked a watershed in Sharp's artistic development. Continuing his editorial and critical efforts, he completed a book on John Keats and Joseph Severn, published in 1892 as *The Life and Letters of Joseph Severn.* The more important accomplishment of the trip, however, was a new volume of poems, *Sospiri di Roma* (1891), inspired by the free verse of Whitman and William Ernest Henley. In his exploration of natural sensuality and sexuality Sharp anticipates D. H. Lawrence's *Birds, Beasts and Flowers* (1923). The theme of naked sexuality led Sharp to examine the role of masks and personae in relation to the self. He began to contemplate a duality between inner self and personae, or even divisions within the self. Looking toward the works of Luigi Pirandello, Sharp's views on masks would also exercise an influence on Wilde.

Responding to the criticism of *Sospiri di Roma*, Sharp published the *Pagan Review* (September 1892), a journal bearing the motto "Sic transit gloria Grundi" (So pass the glories of [Mrs.] Grundy), with the aim of satirizing conventional morality. In the one issue published, Sharp was the only contributor, producing articles under seven different pseudonyms. The literary ruse allowed him to explore "the sexual morale" of the day as well as take critics to task. It also suggested to him the possibilities of pseudonymous composition.

With the composition of *Sospiri di Roma* Sharp achieved a level of artistic maturity that called for a more serious and sustained level of work than he had thus far achieved. His friend George Cotterell recommended a Celtic romance. Having reached a momentary lull in his various efforts, Sharp meditated on various possibilities. Elizabeth Sharp later recalled their stay at Phenice Croft, a cottage in Sussex where they spent summers from 1882 to 1894: "Once again, he saw visions and dreamed dreams; the psychic subjective side of his dual nature predominated. He was in an acutely creative condition; and, moreover he was passing from one phase of literary work to another, deeper, more intimate, more permanent." Out of this creative ferment emerged Fiona Macleod.

Drawing on his stock of Celtic folklore, Sharp composed a story titled "The Last Fantasy of James Achanna," submitting it to *Scott's Observer* in 1893. Though he rejected the story, the editor was encouraging. (Sharp later published a reworked version of it as "The Archer" in *The Dominion of Dreams* in 1899.) Undeterred, Sharp began work on a novel, which he submitted under the name Fiona Macleod, ostensibly a cousin and talented protégé. The examples of Thomas Chatterton's Roweley and perhaps more significantly James Macpherson's Ossian offered a ready precedent for such an action. This novel, *Pharais: A Romance of the Isles,* was published in 1894. "I can write out of my heart in a way I could not do as William Sharp," he later explained to a friend; "indeed I could not do so if I were the woman Fiona Macleod is supposed to be, unless veiled in scrupulous anonymity." Whether the mask of Fiona Macleod freed some inner self in Sharp or simply gave him a convenient literary license, the strategy worked, and *Pharais,* the Gaelic word for paradise, was an immediate success. It was quickly followed by two more Fiona Macleod novels, *The Mountain Lovers* (1895) and *Green Fire: A Romance* (1896). Evoking a Highland setting, each novel is about motherhood, childbirth, and death. Sharp's heroines, and indeed Fiona Macleod herself, represent what biographer Flavia Alaya terms "an idealization of humanity, through the mother idea." In this regard Sharp is part of a "feminist counter-revolution" that saw women as a sort of natural earth mother and laid the groundwork for figures such as James Joyce's Molly Bloom, Lawrence's assorted heroines, and Robert Graves's White Goddess.

While Sharp was writing and publishing his novels and poetry, he was also composing short stories, some of which appeared in various periodicals. In 1895 he published two collections of the stories he considered worth preserving. The first was *The Gypsy Christ, and Other Tales,* followed shortly by *Ecce Puella and Other Prose Imaginings.* Sharp planned the appearance of these volumes to be concurrent with that of two volumes of Fiona Macleod stories, *The Sin-Eater and Other Tales* (1895) and *The Washer of the Ford and Other Legendary Moralities* (1895), to reinforce the impression of separate identities. *Madge o' the Pool, The Gipsy Christ and Other Tales,* the 1896 expansion of his first collection, brought together four stories, including the two title pieces plus "The Coward: An Episode of the Franco-Arab War" and "The Lady in Hosea." Of these, only "Madge o' the Pool" retains some interest. Jumping between melodrama and naturalism, the story shows the strong influence of Charles Dickens's *Our Mutual Friend* (1864), and its heroine, like Dickens's Lizzie Hexam, inhabits a nether realm along London's Thames waterfront. Despite a series of hardships, including the death of her river policeman lover, the stillbirth of the child by her lover, and her own eventual drowning, Madge remains noble-minded, a "naturally innocent soul." The importance of the story is in Sharp's naturalistic concern for the shaping role of the urban environment, especially as it anticipates his later preoccupation with the spiritual nourishment of the western Highlands. Madge is the inevitable product of her world, a symbol of the atmosphere that creates her. Sharp's story was among a chorus of neo-Romantic works, such as James Thomson's poem *The City of Dreadful Night* (1880) or John Ruskin's essay *The Storm-Cloud of the Nineteenth Century* (1884), despairing at what they took to be the spiritual poverty of the modern urban environment.

Ecce Puella and Other Prose Imaginings collected six pieces: "Ecce Puella," "Fragments from the Last Journals of Piero di Cosimo," "The Birth, Death, and Resurrection of a Tear," "The Sister of Compassion," "The Hill-Wind," and "Love in a Mist." Drawing on the narrative technique developed by Browning and Pater, especially in Pater's *Imaginary*

Portraits (1887), "Fragments from the Last Journals of Piero di Cosimo" was first published in *Art Review* (June 1890), where some readers took it as an authentic document. In the story Sharp dramatizes episodes from the life of the Renaissance painter as he paints the portrait of a pregnant woman and contemplates the "terrible brutality of motherhood." Greatly admired by Pater, the story underlines Sharp's sympathy with women and points to the theme of pregnancy and childbirth recurrent in many of the Fiona Macleod stories.

"The Lady in Hosea," from the first collection, and "The Birth, Death, and Resurrection of a Tear," from the second, are also of interest. Originally written at about the same time as *Children of To-morrow* and glancing back to Meredith, they show Sharp continuing his exploration of unhappy relationships between men and women in contemporary society. The first story is about a wife who is unfaithful to her husband and disillusioned by her lover. She finally returns to the forgiving husband, who is an embodiment of the cosmopolitan spirit. While much of the story is trite, the characterization is, according to Alaya, "bold and sensitive" and shows psychological complexity. In the second story, narrated from a first-person point of view that approaches stream of consciousness, a husband finds himself alienated by the coldness of his wife. He eventually learns from a tear shed at a critical moment that she truly loves him and that her chilly deportment was a defense mechanism to mask feelings society had taught her not to express.

The Fiona Macleod stories and novels appeared at an opportune time, quickly taken up by a surge of interest in Gaelic and Celtic culture, known variously as the Celtic Renaissance and the Celtic Twilight, among literary circles in Scotland and Ireland. Sharp soon became the literary adviser to the influential "Evergreen" group formed in Edinburgh by Patrick Geddes, J. Arthur Thompson, and others. This led to various publishing ventures, including a journal called the *Evergreen* (1895–1896) and the Celtic Library series. While Sharp encouraged the inclusion of different foreign authors whom he judged to be sympathetic to the spirit if not substance of Scottish cosmopolitanism, including Anatole France, Hamlin Garland, and Giovanni Verga, Fiona Macleod was the chief contributor, publishing two volumes of short stories with Geddes, *The Sin-Eater and Other Tales* and *The Washer of the Ford and Other Legendary Moralities.* Sharp subsequently rearranged, supplemented, and reissued them as *Spiritual Tales, Barbaric Tales,* and *Tragic Romances* (all 1897) and *The Dominion of Dreams.* He also

published *From the Hills of Dream: Mountain Songs and Island Runes* (1896), a volume of poems and closet dramas, including the much-admired but never performed *The Immortal Hour* and *The House of Usna.* The posthumous seven-volume *Works of Fiona Macleod* (1910–1912), edited by Elizabeth Sharp following her husband's instructions, includes fifty-six short stories.

The Fiona Macleod stories tend to fall into one of two broad narrative categories: either realistic accounts of fantasy or pure fantasy tales. In the former, Fiona Macleod acts as a sort of ethnographer, recording the tales and anecdotes of her various Highland informants. The naturalistic accounts of magic occurrences by fishermen and peasants create a narrative distance that allows the reader to accept the tale either at face value or as the product of the informants' superstitious imaginations. In the other type of narrative Macleod retells Celtic tales or legends from a third-person point of view.

Typical of the first type are stories such as "The Ninth Wave" and "The Judgment o' God," both from *The Sin-Eater and Other Tales.* In "The Judgment o' God" Macleod is sailing with her fishermen friends Ivor and Pàdriug. At the sight of a seal Pàdriug stands up and recites a long Gaelic curse. When Macleod asks about this sudden outburst, he explains that in Celtic lore seals are incarnations of damned souls and then tells the story of Murdoch, a shepherd who lived on an isolated island. Overcome by the "gloom," a sort of existential state of despair, Murdoch goes insane and eventually disappears. To the locals it is evident that he has become a seal and returned to the sea.

A similar theme underlies another story in *The Sin-Eater and Other Tales,* "The Dàn-nan-Ròn," one of a cycle of six tales about the seven sons of Robert Achanna and subsequently collected under the title *Under the Dark Star* in *Works of Fiona Macleod.* To keep their cousin Anne Gillespie from leaving their desolate island, Gloom Achanna, the seventh son and the most sinister of the brothers, plots to murder Anne's lover, Mànus MacCodrum. Suspicious because of Gloom's constant piping of the "dàn-nan-ròn," a magic chant to the spirit of the seal, MacCodrum is able to escape, supposedly killing Gloom and another Achanna brother. Thinking they are safe, Anne and MacCodrum marry, but after a year MacCodrum suddenly starts to hear the dàn-nan-ròn being played in the night. Driven insane, he runs among the seals on the reef, where they savagely tear him to pieces. The story ends on an ambiguous note. Has Gloom Achanna come back from the dead to cast a magic spell on

ECCE PUELLA

AND OTHER PROSE IMAGININGS

BY

WILLIAM SHARP

LONDON
ELKIN MATHEWS, VIGO STREET
MDCCCXCVI

*Title page for an 1896 printing of one of the two collections
Sharp published under his own name in 1895 (Courtesy
of the Lilly Library, Indiana University)*

MacCodrum, awakening the spirit of the seal and the draw of the sea within him, or has MacCodrum simply gone mad? In Sharp's spiritual vision the boundary between magic and psychology is not rigid.

The second type of story represents a retelling of fairy stories, Celtic sagas, or the exploits of ancient Viking and Highland chieftains. Some, such as "St. Bride of the Isles," "The Fisher of Men," and "The Last Supper," all collected in *The Washer of the Ford,* translate Christian moralities into the Celtic mythical idiom, underlining Sharp's belief that Roman Catholicism and Celtic paganism shared common spiritual roots in an ancient nature religion. In "The Washer of the Ford," for instance, the blind pagan harper Torcall Dall encounters an old woman washing shrouds at the ford of a river. Learning that the woman is Mary Magdalen, Torcall Dall is invited to pass through the river to a new life: " 'Take your harp,' Mary said, 'and go in unto the Ford. But, lo, now I clothe you with a white shroud. And if you fear the drowning flood, follow the bells that were your tears; and if the dark affright you, follow the song of the prayer that came out of your heart.' " Sometimes the syncretism becomes bizarre. In "St. Bride of the Isles" young Bride, or Bridget, passes through the Druidic Fountain of Young in Dun-I to Bethlehem, where she cares for the infant Christ, earning the epithet "Muime Chriosd," "The Foster-Mother of Christ."

Sharp considered "The Harping of Cravetheen," included in *The Sin-Eater and Other Tales,* among the best of his "barbaric tales." The Irish chieftain Conairy Mòr wishes to marry his ward, Eilidh, to his retainer Art Mac Art Mòr. Eilidh, however, loves Cormac Conlingas and is pregnant by him. Angry with Eilidh and Cormac but also angry with Art Mac Art Mòr for his insults to Eilidh, Conairy marries her to an old harper named Cravetheen. After Eilidh gives birth to her son, Cravetheen goes into a trance and draws the spirit out of the infant's body by harping "elfin-music": "Sure, it is a hard thing for the naked spirit to steal away from its warm home of the flesh, with the blood coming and going forever like a mother's hand, warm and soft. But to the playing of Cravetheen and the Green Harper there was no denying." When Cormac comes for Eilidh, they are put under a spell by Cravetheen's "wild harping" and then consumed in a burning hut. "All there died in the flame," the narrator explains. "That was the end of Eilidh, that was so fair. She laughed the pain away, and died. And Cormac smiled, and as the flame leaped on his breast he muttered, *'Ah, hot heart of Eilidh! – heart to me – move to me!'* And he died." The story exemplifies a favorite theme of Sharp's, the linkage of sexual consummation with death and spiritual transfiguration. He subsequently reincarnated his star-crossed lovers in the stories "Silk o' the Kine" in *The Sin-Eater and Other Tales* and "Ula and Urla" in *The Washer of the Ford,* suggesting that all such true lovers embody the same spirit.

Perhaps the best-known and best-crafted of the Fiona Macleod stories is "The Sin-Eater." As with many of the tales, it creates a narrative ambiguity between fantasy and naturalism. The reports of magical or unnatural happenings are only presented through the subsequent accounts of the locals. In a formula that Sharp uses repeatedly, the story begins with a lone figure walking along a desolate landscape. This man, Neil Ross, encounters an old woman and after much talk is invited to her cottage for shelter, where she tries to convince him to be a sin-eater. According to ancient custom, if a person eats and drinks over a corpse he will absorb the sins of that corpse. If a disinterested stranger does this, the absorbed sins can be washed away in the sea, unless the sin-eater holds some grudge against the dead man, whereupon the sins will stick. Ross relents and agrees to relieve the troubled soul of the recently departed Adam Blair. Ross, secretly hating Blair, hopes to damn Blair's soul by the act. Soon after performing the ritual and cursing Adam Blair and his family, Ross begins to hear voices and supposes that he is haunted by Blair's sins. Raving, he starts to wander naked around the island, calling himself Judas. In the end, after much suffering, he lashes himself to a cross made of wreckage and throws himself into the sea, disappearing "down the back-sweep of a drowning big wave," never to be seen again.

At one level the story examines the primitive customs and superstitions of the Highlanders. At another it explores the psychology of consuming hatred and obsession. At the same time, Sharp uses his material to suggest a spiritual allegory. Ross is a sort of Everyman who takes on the heavy burden of the sins of Old Adam (Blair), a theme linked in Celtic folklore to a legendary encounter between Saint Brendan and Judas. On all of its levels, as well as its careful and sustained construction of setting, "The Sin-Eater" remains one of Sharp's most memorable efforts.

Many of the Macleod stories have little or no plot, and what plot there is serves primarily as a convenient vehicle for recounting anecdotes of Celtic lore. Other tales are really conventional romantic melodramas put into exotic dress. The primitive setting and folk context serve to give what are often otherwise formulaic stories and clichéd dialogue an air of profundity. Waugh, who claimed to have seen through the Macleod disguise, thought that Sharp was using his pseudonym to pass off his "less saleable productions." Yeats, who apparently did not see through the disguise, was both more sympathetic and insightful. Reviewing *From the Hills of Dream* for the London *Bookman* (December 1896), he observed, "Miss Macleod is always best when she writes under a Gaelic and legendary and mythical influence. Emotions which seem vague or extravagant when expressed under the influence of modern literature, cease to be vague and extravagant when associated with ancient legend and mythology, for legend and mythology were born out of man's longing for the mysterious and the infinite." Sharp is more concerned with creating myth than plot, with evoking the atmosphere of the Celtic netherworld than telling a story. Often the stories

are more prose poems than narrative fiction, comparable in places to those of St.-John Perse (Alexis Saint-Léger Léger).

In a similar fashion, the figures who inhabit Macleod's Highlands are more a part of the atmosphere than well-rounded or psychologically complex characters. Macleod's Highland fishermen, shepherds, and peasant farmers, like William Wordsworth's Michael, the old Cumberland beggar, or the leech gatherer, represent primal beings, closer to the rhythms of nature and what Sharp understood to be the spiritual foundation of reality and as such inseparable from it. Despite their hardships and despite the intensity and violence of their passions, they are for Sharp uncorrupted by the alienating forces of the city. In "The Anointed Man," a story in *The Sin-Eater and Other Tales,* the narrator, Macleod, breaks into convulsive sobbing, overcome by the oppressiveness of the blighted landscape. Comforting his friend, the hero of the story, Alasdair Achanna, says, "Whenever my eyes fell upon those waste and desolate spots, they seemed to me passing fair, radiant with lovely light." Elaborating in terms that could be lifted from William Blake and Wordsworth, he adds that "in the places they call slums, and among the smoke of factories, and the grime of destitution, I could see all that other men saw, only as vanishing shadows. What I saw was lovely, beautiful with strange glory, and the faces of men and women were sweet and pure, and their souls were white."

Reviewing *The Dominion of Dreams* in the July 1899 *Bookman,* Yeats observed that "other writers are busy with the way men and women act in sorrow or in joy, but Miss Macleod has re-discovered the act of myth-making, and gives a visible shape to joys and sorrows, and makes them seem realities and men and women illusions." Sharp's characters and setting become one, the product of style and atmosphere.

After five years of feverish production, Sharp's initial inspiration for Fiona Macleod began to wane. While he continued to rework his poems, plays, and stories, he also began to shift his Fiona Macleod efforts to critical and philosophical essays, publishing under her name *The Divine Adventure; Iona; By Sundown Shores: Studies in Spiritual History* in 1900, and *The Winged Destiny: Studies in the Spiritual History of the Gael* in 1904. At the same time, he continued to produce essays and fiction under his own name, including the novel *Silence Farm* (1899) and the volumes *Progress of Art in the Century* (1902) and *Literary Geography* (1904), among others.

Sharp was overworked and always of delicate constitution, and his health began to deteriorate seriously after 1896, requiring frequent trips to warmer climates. Toward the end of his life Sharp and his wife spent most of their time in Sicily, especially in the village of Taormina as the guests of Alexander Hood, Duke of Brontë. Active to the end, Sharp died in Hood's villa on 5 December 1905 at age fifty. In a romantic gesture that Sharp would have appreciated, he was buried near the base of Mount Etna, his grave marked by an epitaph he had composed for himself: "Farewell to the known and exhausted, / Welcome the unknown and illimitable."

In evaluating William Sharp (Fiona Macleod), it is important to put him and his work into larger cultural and historical contexts. His desire to return to Celtic material is part of a wider neo-Romanticism at the end of the nineteenth century, a transition between the cultures of Victorian realism and modernism. Like writers such as Ernest Dowson, Lafcadio Hearn, Maurice Maeterlinck, and Gabriele D'Annunzio, Sharp as Macleod prefigures the sense of alienation, sexual crisis, and spiritual exhaustion that marks much of modernism. In this he anticipates Joyce, Lawrence, T. S. Eliot, and the later work of Yeats. At the same time, his mysticism, symbolism, and obsession for the visionary look back to the Romanticism of Wordsworth and Blake. Perhaps the best summation of Sharp's work and his place in literary history comes from his description of Taormina, which appeared in his last essay, "Garden of the Sun" (1906), which was published in the *Century*. Using terms reminiscent of those he used to describe the Celtic Highlands, he characterized it as a place "where, in the dim, impenetrable past, a mysterious race worshipped a mysterious goddess of the sea whose very name has passed from the memory of man." It had, he explained, "a spirit, a presence, a Past that is the Present, a Pres-

ent that is the Past." Such words apply equally to Sharp and his greatest work of fiction, Fiona Macleod.

Biographies:
Elizabeth A. Sharp, *William Sharp (Fiona Macleod): A Memoir,* 2 volumes (London: Heinemann, 1912);
Flavia Alaya, *William Sharp — "Fiona Macleod": 1855–1905* (Cambridge, Mass.: Harvard University Press, 1970).

References:
Graham Hough, *The Last Romantics* (New York: Barnes & Noble, 1961);
Georgiana Goddard King, "Fiona Macleod," *Modern Language Notes,* 37 (June 1918): 352–356;
Christine Lahey-Dolega, "Some Brief Observations on the Life and Work of William Sharp (Fiona Macleod)," *Forum,* 21 (1980): 18–26;
Chris Morgan, "Fiona Macleod: 1855–1905," in *Supernatural Fiction Writers: Fantasy and Horror,* 2 volumes, edited by E. F. Bleiler (New York: Scribners, 1985), I: 369–374;
Isobel Murray, "*Children of To-morrow*: A Sharp Inspiration for *Dorian Gray,*" *Durham University Journal,* 80 (December 1987): 69–76;
William Butler Yeats, *First Reviews and Articles: 1886–1896,* volume 1 of *Uncollected Prose of W. B. Yeats,* edited by John P. Frayne (New York: Columbia University Press, 1970);
Yeats, *Reviews, Articles and Other Miscellaneous Prose,* volume 2 of *Uncollected Prose of W. B. Yeats,* edited by Frayne and C. Johnson (New York: Columbia University Press, 1976).

Papers:
The bulk of Sharp's letters and manuscripts are in the National Library of Scotland, Edinburgh.

Flora Annie Steel

(2 April 1847 – 12 April 1929)

Julie English Early
University of Alabama in Huntsville

BOOKS: *Wide-Awake Stories: A Collection of Tales Told by Little Children between Sunset and Sunrise, in the Punjab and Kashmir,* by Steel and R. C. Temple (Bombay: Education Society, 1884); republished as *Tales of the Punjab Told by the People,* illustrated by J. Lockwood Kipling (London & New York: Macmillan, 1894);

The Complete Indian Housekeeper and Cook: Giving the Duties of Mistress and Servants, the General Management of the House, and Practical Recipes for Cooking in All Its Branches, by Steel and Grace Gardiner (Edinburgh: Murray, 1888; revised editions, London: Heinemann, 1899, 1902, 1904, 1909, 1921);

From the Five Rivers (London: Heinemann, 1893; New York: Appleton, 1893);

Miss Stuart's Legacy (3 volumes, London & New York: Macmillan, 1893; 1 volume, New York & London: Macmillan, 1893);

The Flower of Forgiveness (2 volumes, London: Macmillan, 1894; 1 volume, New York & London: Macmillan, 1894);

The Potter's Thumb (3 volumes, London: Heinemann, 1894; 1 volume, New York: Harper, 1894);

Music Hath Charms (New York & London: Macmillan, 1895);

Red Rowans (New York & London: Macmillan, 1895);

The Swimmers (New York & London: Macmillan, 1895);

On the Face of the Waters (London: Heinemann, 1897 [i.e., 1896]; Rahway, N.J.: Mershon, 1896);

The Gift of the Gods (New York: Chartres, 1897; London: Heinemann, 1911);

In the Permanent Way and Other Stories (London: Heinemann, 1898 [i.e., 1897]; New York & London: Macmillan, 1897);

In the Tideway (London: Constable, 1897; New York: Macmillan, 1897);

The Modern Marriage Market, by Steel, Marie Corelli, Lady Jeune, and Susan, Countess of Malmsbury (London: Hutchinson, 1898; Philadelphia: Lippincott, 1900);

The Hosts of the Lord (New York: Macmillan, 1899; London: Heinemann, 1900);

Voices in the Night: A Chromatic Fantasia (London: Heinemann, 1900; New York & London: Macmillan, 1900);

In the Guardianship of God (London: Heinemann, 1903; New York & London: Macmillan, 1903);

The Flatterer for Gain (London: Daily Mail, 1904);

Salt Duty (London: Heinemann, 1904);

A Book of Mortals: Being a Record of the Good Deeds and Good Qualities of What Humanity Is Pleased to Call the Lower Animals (London: Heinemann, 1905; New York: Macmillan, 1906);

India, text by Steel, paintings by Mortimer Menpes (London: Black, 1905); republished as *Socio-Religious History of India* (Delhi: B. R., 1984);

A Sovereign Remedy (London: Heinemann, 1906; New York: Trow, 1906);

India through the Ages: A Popular and Picturesque History of Hindustan (London: Routledge / New York: Dutton, 1908);

A Prince of Dreamers (London: Heinemann, 1908; New York: Doubleday, Page, 1909);

King-Errant (London: Heinemann, 1912; New York: Stokes, 1912);

The Adventures of Akbar, illustrated by Byam Shaw (London: Heinemann, 1913; New York: Stokes, 1913);

The Mercy of the Lord (London: Heinemann, 1914; New York: Doran, 1914);

Dramatic History of India; Twenty Playlets (Bombay: Cooper, 1917);

Marmaduke (London: Heinemann, 1917; New York: Stokes, 1917);

Mistress of Men (London: John Lane, 1917; New York: Stokes, 1917);

English Fairy Tales, illustrated by Arthur Rackham (London & New York: Macmillan, 1918);

Flora Annie Steel

Tales of the Tides, and Other Stories (London: Heinemann, 1923);

A Tale of Indian Heroes: Being the Stories of the Mâhâbhârata and the Râmâyana (London: Hutchinson, 1923; New York: Stokes, 1923);

The Law of the Threshold (London: Heinemann, 1924; New York: Macmillan, 1924);

The Builder (London: John Lane, 1928; New York: Stokes, 1928);

The Curse of Eve (London: John Lane, 1929);

The Garden of Fidelity: Being the Autobiography of Flora Annie Steel, 1847–1929 (London: Macmillan, 1929).

Collection: *Indian Scene: Collected Short Stories of Flora Annie Steel* (London: Arnold, 1933; Freeport, N.Y.: Books for Libraries Press, 1971).

At the end of the nineteenth century Flora Annie Steel's short stories and novels of Indian and Anglo-Indian life established her reputation as Rud-

yard Kipling's only serious rival. The comparison with Kipling reflected the stature accorded her work but also established the criteria for criticism. Especially in her short stories, Steel focused not on Anglo-Indian life but on rural Indian life, the contrasts between Eastern and Western conduct and philosophy, and on Indian women. In a 1907 survey of Anglo-Indian fiction Edward Farley Oaten noted in particular that "the tales display a very accurate knowledge of native habits and ways of thought." In her novels she represented Anglo-Indian as well as her Indian interests, prompting Sir Alfred Lyall in his October 1899 *Edinburgh Review* essay to observe somewhat regretfully of *On the Face of the Waters* (1896), her novel of the 1857 mutiny, "Here at any rate is a book which is not open to the remark that the Anglo-Indian novelist usually leaves the natives in the background.... Mrs. Steel's canvas is crowded with Indian figures ... so abundantly demonstrated as occasionally to bewilder the inexperienced reader." The 11 December 1897 *Spectator* review of *In the Permanent Way and Other Stories* (1897) noted, not entirely favorably, an "appreciation of the oriental standpoint, both ethical and religious," and even suspected a partiality to eastern modes of thought. With Kipling as the reviewers' point of reference, much of the response to Steel struggled to define gender differences, often allying them to gendered conceptions of the masculine West and the feminized East.

If gender and the proper view of empire were often inextricable issues for contemporary reviewers, they equally ground the limited modern attention to Steel's work. While contemporary reviewers detected too high a regard for Indian culture and philosophy, modern feminists find in Steel a woman who subscribed to women's rights and supported the suffrage movement in England but who, as a loyalist to the empire, reinscribed racism and classism in an Indian career — no matter how energetic — that failed to challenge patriarchal and imperialist assumptions. In Oaten's view "the greatest novelist, in the strictest sense of the word, of whom Anglo-Indian literature can boast" and identified in the 17 April 1929 *Times* obituary photograph caption as "The Great Novelist of India," Steel perhaps will not receive a broader modern assessment of her work until a fuller sample of her thirty-two published volumes is brought back into print.

Flora Annie Webster and Henry William Steel, a civil engineer on leave from the Indian Civil Service (ICS), married on 31 December 1867 in Scotland; within twenty-four hours they were on board a ship to India to begin a twenty-two-year stay. Both colonial life and government service were familiar through her family background: her mother, Isabella MacCallum Webster, was heiress to Jamaican property, and her father, George Webster, was a Scottish parliamentary agent in London and then the sheriff-clerk of Forfarshire in Scotland. Flora Annie Webster, born on 2 April 1847 at Sudbury Park, Harrow, was one of eleven children. Within ten years, after financial reverses, the family moved to a country house in Scotland and spent summer holidays with relatives in the West Highlands — settings that permitted a somewhat boisterous and inventive childhood and that encouraged her perception of a wild, primitive energy in the Scottish landscape and history that she later mined in short stories and novels set there. Except for six months at a school in Brussels, she was educated at home, largely by having been given free reign of her parents' substantial and eclectic library. She had come to know Henry Steel when they were children

in Harrow — Steel's father was a housemaster at the school and vicar of a nearby parish — and the connection was kept up as her brothers attended Harrow and later Cambridge, with some of them, like Steel, entering the ICS.

In *The Garden of Fidelity: Being the Autobiography of Flora Annie Steel, 1847–1929* (1929) Steel reflects on her long and successful marriage but frankly wonders why she and Henry Steel had married: she had not loved him; they had had no courtship; and he had even proposed by letter because he was too afraid of her in person. Despite a companionable and successful, if passionless, marriage, Steel insisted that she had never in her life been in love, and she continued to find sexual passion a curious but apparently compelling phenomenon to be scrutinized in the lives of men and women, both British and Indian.

Known primarily for her fiction set in India, Steel did not fully begin her writing career until after her return to England on her husband's retirement in 1889. In the thirty-eight years between April 1891 — when she published her first short story, "Lal," in *Macmillan's Magazine* — and her death in April 1929, she published five volumes of Indian short stories: *From the Five Rivers* (1893), *The Flower of Forgiveness* (1894), *In the Permanent Way and Other Stories, In the Guardianship of God* (1903), and *The Mercy of the Lord* (1914). She also published one volume of stories set in Scotland, *Tales of the Tides, and Other Stories* (1923); the novella *In the Tideway* (1897), included in this collection, had previously been published separately. In addition, at least four stories — *Music Hath Charms* (1895), *The Swimmers* (1895), *The Flatterer for Gain* (1904), and *Salt Duty* (1904) — were published individually before they appeared in collections. Steel also wrote six novels of Indian and Anglo-Indian life, including her best-known work, *On the Face of the Waters*; a series of four historical/biographical novels on the Mogul dynasty; four nonfiction works on India; five novels, contemporary and historical, set in the British Isles; four children's books on English or Indian subjects, along with various educational materials for use in Indian schools; a book on animals; and her autobiography.

When Steel began writing stories she found a regular outlet for her work in *Macmillan's Magazine*. Between 1891 and 1897 she contributed twenty stories; in 1893 her first novel, *Miss Stuart's Legacy,* also ran serially. Despite the enthusiasm of the magazine's editor, Mowbray Morris, she did not necessarily receive favored treatment with the magazine's parent publishing house. Macmillan,

Kipling's publisher, published only some of her early work. The firm rejected her novel of the mutiny, *On the Face of the Waters,* outright, much to its later regret. Thus, even while she maintained relations with Macmillan, Steel was also placing material with the new firm of William Heinemann, who brought out her first volume of short stories, *From the Five Rivers,* a collection of new material. Heinemann overlapped with Macmillan, with each publishing volumes that included various stories that had appeared in *Macmillan's Magazine.* After the impressive success of *On the Face of the Waters* — 46,000 copies were sold in the first three years — Steel continued to publish the majority of her work with Heinemann, much of which remained in print with strong sales until shortly after her death.

During her twenty-two years in India, Steel's unusual curiosity about the country and its people led her to experiences that would provide material, incidents, and observations that she would later develop in her fiction. In India she immersed herself in a range of activities unimaginable to the majority of memsahibs who wished to know nothing of the Indians whom the ICS governed. There were few immediate restraints on her in the Steels' many remote postings, primarily in the Lahore district (they moved fifteen times in sixteen years, with only a few longer tenures), and she rarely had the society of other government wives. She instead involved herself in her husband's duties, even accompanying him on his tours of the district. Adept at languages, she learned different vernaculars and encouraged Punjab villagers to tell her folktales, which she collected and published in India as *Wide-Awake Stories: A Collection of Tales Told by Little Children between Sunset and Sunrise, in the Punjab and Kashmir* (1884). Steel intended the volume for children but also agreed to include scholarly notes and analyses by folklorist R. C. Temple. Ten years later, with her literary reputation established, the volume was retitled *Tales of the Punjab Told by the People* and published in England, remaining in print into the 1990s. Some of the tales also continue to appear individually as texts for children's picture books.

A year before her departure from India, Steel made a more immediately significant mark in the Anglo-Indian community with the publication of *The Complete Indian Housekeeper and Cook: Giving the Duties of Mistress and Servants, the General Management of the House, and Practical Recipes for Cooking in All Its Branches* (1888), cowritten with Grace Gardiner. Steel wrote from twenty years of experience in varied Indian stations and dedicated this specialized version of "Mrs. Beeton's" (a standard nineteenth-century housekeeping manual) to its audience, "The English Girls to whom Fate may assign the Task of being House-Mothers in our Eastern Empire." Intended as a thorough and practical manual, the book was periodically updated through ten editions over the next thirty years.

Excerpts from this guide appear frequently in modern assessments of Steel's career to illustrate her decidedly imperial politics. The "Indian household," Steel and Gardiner write, "can no more be governed peacefully without dignity and prestige than the Indian Empire," and she instructs the memsahib to view the Indian servant as "a child in everything save age." Firmly reiterating the precepts of colonial administration, *The Complete Indian Housekeeper and Cook* takes as its keynote efficiency — a quality that Steel, however, found notably lacking in a bureaucratic administration whose officials were too often steeped in ignorance and prejudice. Even while pointing to some British superstitions about Indians, however, the book upheld the boundaries of class and the imperial mission — all with the aim of enabling the Anglo-Indian woman to fulfill her domestic duty with dispatch.

Steel, disagreeing with her coauthor, also recommended sending one's children back to England. Steel's first child had died at birth in 1869; her daughter, Mabel, born in 1870, was raised in England. According to the book, memsahibs, with efficient households and reduced family responsibilities, should then avoid idle social life and romantic intrigues to attend to useful service to the empire. As a model, Steel sought greater opportunities for her own talents not by challenging the colonial hierarchy but by attempting to redefine the niche in the hierarchy that she might occupy.

Energetic and industrious, Steel was also unapologetically opinionated and autocratic. Convinced that the British bureaucracy was shortsighted and inefficient, she involved herself in local affairs to a degree that often made her a nuisance to the ICS. In remote stations she took the initiative to provide medical care to women and children, instituted schools for women, or intervened in what she felt were the inadequate methods of existing missionary schools. After twelve years of ad hoc action Steel was offered a semiofficial position in education as Inspectress of Schools for a region covering fourteen thousand square miles, stretching from Peshawar to Delhi. She embraced the duties of officialdom enthusiastically but frequently found herself in conflict with official policy; at the same time, while she prided herself on being sensitive to Indian points of view, not all of her reforms were popular in the communities she supervised.

Steel's scuffles with authorities and her unbending regard for her own notion of standards in the schools appear not to have prevented her from establishing relations with her students that allowed her to learn a great deal about their lives. Indeed, her knowledge of various types of Indian households and of women's lives singularly distinguishes her vision of India from Kipling's. Her stories about women offer particularized and sympathetic renderings of women's lives. Unlike most of the missionaries, Steel did not believe that Indian women were thoroughly degraded or enslaved, nor did she argue against the Hindu system of arranged marriages, which she felt often resulted in happier marriages than those inspired by romantic impetuosity.

In her stories of domestic life Steel accepts the idea that woman's primary duty is to bear a son and acknowledges the hierarchy of power among women in the family; many of her stories focus on women's responses to childlessness and the relationships of wives and their mothers-in-law or widows living with them. The childless wife responds to her circumstances in varied ways. If she is respected by her husband – as is the protagonist of "Uma Himavutee," collected in *In the Permanent Way* – she lives peaceably with the other wife, or she may – as in "A Sorrowful Hour," also in *In the Permanent Way* – be anxious that the new wife's child will not love her and place her faith in spells that will help her to conceive her own. She may value the honor of the family, like the wife in "Footsteps of a Dog" in *The Mercy of the Lord,* who goes into seclusion with her widowed sister-in-law so that it will appear that she, not the sister-in-law, is carrying her husband's baby, thus insuring the child's legitimacy.

In some instances the women of a household who are badly treated may be justified in taking their revenge. "In the House of a Coppersmith," collected in *The Flower of Forgiveness,* concerns a man who betrays his childless wife by secretly courting his brother's widow, then betrays the widow by contracting a second marriage. The widow helps the wife to poison him by cooking in the pot in which they have used tamarind to clean the ornaments for his wedding ceremony. In "Gunesh Chund," included in *From the Five Rivers,* Steel explores not only a husband's grief at having to take a second wife when he loves his first but also the ferocious love of his mother, as she insists that he marry again to have a son.

While some of Steel's stories depict the sorrow of the child widow prohibited from remarrying, others represent what Western observers often failed to understand, the sanctity of widowhood in Indian

Flora Annie Webster, 1867

culture. Stories in which Indian characters attempt to apply Western ideas of reform to Indian conditions inevitably end in tragedy; in "On the Second Story," collected in *In the Permanent Way,* Ramanund, a descendant of Brahman priests and a student of the writings of John Stuart Mill, attempts to apply Christian tradition to Hindu principles. His efforts to marry a young widow result in her death and his loss of faith in reform. The young lover of "Amor Vincit Omnia," also in *In the Permanent Way,* becomes consumed by ideas of love and romance taken from novels that put extraordinary demands on his child-marriage and cause him to lose his scholarship and finally his life. Steel consistently represents the strength of character and dignity of women in a system of marriage inconceivable for many Western women. To a public convinced of a deplorable sensuality in Indian art and a corresponding eroticism of Indian women, Steel depicted women of modesty, duty, and devotion "to the immortality of their race," as she wrote in *The Modern Marriage Market* (1898), who embodied, she felt, a type of womanly beauty inadequately appreciated in the West.

Certainly issues of sexuality and the most propitious grounds for marriage are questions threading through her fiction set both in India and England. The development of decided views drawn, she argued, from having lived in two cultures prompted her to enter the debate on the appropriate grounds for marriage by contributing an article to an 1897 series in the *Lady's Realm* initiated by Marie Corelli's claim for the sanction of love and passion over the market values of position and property. Steel rejected both, arguing against the self-serving demand for personal happiness to promote her understanding of the "Eastern view" – that "marriage is not a purely personal matter. . . ; it is a duty to the race." In the "rational happiness" of duty and social responsibility "lingers the great truth – so unpalatable to our Western individualism – that man and woman stand related, not to each other, but to the immortality of their race."

Like many moderate family-centered feminists, Steel joined the Eugenics Education Society, whose principles appeared to offer a powerful social role to women as mothers and whose scientific claims appeared to offer protection to Englishwomen from the marital threats of alcoholism and venereal disease. As one strain of the interests of the New Women of the 1890s, these concerns later appear in Steel's collection of English and Scottish short stories *Tales of the Tides, and Other Stories*, particularly in the novella *In the Tideway* and in the stories "Fatherhood" and "Ammophila Arsenoctonous," which respectively take up hereditary alcoholism, venereal disease, and the concern for racial stock.

Steel's autobiography reflects a woman who readily voiced her opinions, both in contemporary debate and in her fiction, on social concerns as well as a wide range of issues involving government management. After a few years' experience in rural India, she seized the opportunity offered by an editor's illness to write leaders for a Lahore paper, *Public Opinion*, in which she denounced policies that encouraged money lenders to foreclose on peasants. "At the Great Durbar," collected in *In the Permanent Way*, depicts the unresponsiveness of a government that will not hear, as she believed the Moguls would have done, the petition of farmer Nanuk Singh for a reduction of the revenue he owes. During a time of widespread famine the government instead proceeds to mount extravagant Durbar festivities. The plight of the Indian farmer frequently figures in her stories of rural Indian life and forms a backdrop to representations of the varied problems and ways of life in her Indian novels.

Stories such as "Suttu" and the ballad "Shurfu the Zaildar" in *From the Five Rivers*, "Lal" and "Harvest" in *The Flower of Forgiveness*, and "A Bit of Land" in *In the Permanent Way* reflect the vagaries of the land in rural life: the periodic threat of famine, the capricious course of Punjab rivers that alternately enrich or destroy fields, the intervention of a bureaucracy that often seems equally capricious with its technologies to control irrigation, and disputes over land rights and the increasing powerlessness of the farmer to seek redress.

Steel's first published story, "Lal," begins with a district officer on horseback surveying from the bank of the Indus the shifts in the river's course from the previous year, "for year after year, armed by the majesty of law and bucklered by foot-rules and maps, the Government of India, in the person of one of its officers, came gravely and altered the proportion of land and water on the surface of the globe, while the river gurgled and dimpled as if it were laughing in its sleeve." As the river submerges wheat fields, the villagers sow trial crops of vetch on muddy banks that may well disappear by harvest time, but the surveyor nonetheless marks them on the revenue map, "for Governments ignore chance." Far more attuned to chance than the surveyor with his "ruthless iron chain" is the elusive Lal, "a straight-walking, a labourful man" who appears in the story only in the tales that the villagers tell of him. His fields are worked with tools and sown with seed lent him by the village, and he only harvests what is left after the pigs, squirrels, and parrots have fed from it. When the government agent asks how Lal will pay his revenue for the year, the villagers laugh at the notion. Whether Lal, as the villagers claim in the following year, has died, or indeed whether he has existed at all, the government agent can never know. Like the river, Lal remains "an unknown quantity" and represents a relationship to nature and to the community that eludes a government committed to boundaries and measurable exchanges.

A character similarly outside the British administrative understanding is the romanticized cattle rustler "Shurfu the Zaildar," whose freewheeling adventures live on in legends even as his type disappears. Shurfu complains to the collector-sahib that "your reign has been death to all sport. / E'en a cattle-thief thinks like a banker, and scarcely gives honour a thought." Shurfu is amusedly tolerant of the pet projects of each in the rapid succession of administrators: "Not a hobby his district sahib's ridden, but Shurfu has ridden it too." From Shurfu's perspective a faintly absurd British administration is not particularly difficult for him to manage.

Like many wives in unofficial service to the empire, Steel supported the imperial mission, but her respect and sympathy for Indian culture also led her to register a sense of loss at some aspects of its transformation. In her novels she balanced political conservatism with her philosophical misgivings, yet her novels reflect and perhaps suffer from the conflict of the two positions. Some reviewers of her novels complained not only about the preponderance of Indian characters but about dense multiple plotlines that may have conveyed the confusion of India but tended to strain the reader. Often dominated by social and political ideas palatable to English readers, the novels offer obligatory noble, brave, and upstanding Anglo-Indian characters who are nonetheless rather pallid figures, perhaps well-suited to a stolid bureaucracy but less compelling than either the Indian characters or the Anglo-Indians capable of independent action.

Even with reviewers' reservations that her Indian novels contained more of India than a British reader might wish, they were consistently well-received. Steel achieved her greatest fame for *On the Face of the Waters.* Her aim in the novel, as she indicated in the preface, was that "the two races might forget and forgive" the acts of 1857. In an attempt to represent events from both sides, she had extensively researched historical records. Her sources, however, were predominantly British, and as Daya Patwardhan has pointed out, her understanding was inevitably thwarted by her failure to perceive the fundamental commitment to throw off foreign rule; she saw only a military uprising provoked largely by palace intrigue.

In her short stories Steel is freed from the impulse appearing in her novels to represent the full range and complexity of Indian and Anglo-Indian life. In particular, her stories of rural life and of women's lives have a slow pace ritualizing the rhythms of the lives she depicts and permitting careful description of the specificity and subtlety of landscape and setting. Her concentration on simple lives lived in relation to the land or to the domestic politics of custom in marriage, childlessness, widowhood, and death may at times reach for pathos, yet these stories also maintain a precise focus on event and character within the structure of rural Indian

Illustration by J. Lockwood Kipling for Steel's Tales of the Punjab Told by the People *(1894), in which she retells Indian folktales*

life on its own terms. Her first four volumes of Indian stories tend to be freer of moralizing implications or statements about Britain's political agenda than either her novels or her last volume of Indian stories.

Steel's last collection of Indian short stories, *The Mercy of the Lord,* includes stories that reiterate many of her previous subjects but also reflects a troubled consideration of gains and losses in a contemporary India twenty-five years removed from her residence there. Several of the stories, such as "The Mercy of the Lord," "The Wisdom of Our Lord Ganesh," "The Son of a King," and "The Birth of Fire," recapitulate and further develop the suggestive challenge that first appeared in "Lal": the mysterious elusiveness of Indian philosophy, conduct, and belief to the surety of the materialist Western mind. Yet even the mysticism that had fascinated Steel in much of her earlier work here appears oddly nostalgic, even as a strange survival – just as the stories of another Indian survival, the faithful servant, vacillate between admiring the selfless devotion of this anachronism and, as in *Salt Duty,* using the character nearly to parody the values of the colonial system that produced him.

The poorly used widow also reappears. "An Appreciated Rupee" is the story of an impoverished widow who takes courage from the representation of the queen stamped on the rupee hung around her neck to demand that English officials see that she get her widow's portion from the relatives who would withhold it. She is successful, but the story ends, "It happened years ago, but the story is worth telling today, when women can no longer sing 'God Save the Queen.' "

The calm and justice that Steel represents in the "old" India contrast with her strident approach to events in the "new" India, in which, for example, she indiscriminately identifies Indian patriots as terrorists in "A Maiden's Prayer" and "Silver Speech and Golden Silence." The desire for national independence, especially among the educated, is rarely foregrounded but appears instead as a threatening and persistent backdrop, particularly in stories applauding the dignity of older Eastern ways. In "The Gift of Battle" two lifelong enemies, "the best representatives of Hindu and Mahomedan feeling in the district," are made honorary magistrates and find that "their innate sense of justice, fostered by the fact that they had both been brought up in the India of the past, that they represented its laws, its morals, its maxims, made their judgments identical." Together these feudal representatives order the whipping not only of disruptive students "singing patriotic songs and doing wanton mischief " but of the teachers who have failed to control them. When the district government intervenes to ask for their retirement, these men of principle, dismayed by a deteriorating world, choose a path of honor and die by one another's swords.

In the final story of the collection, "The Slave of the Court," the mysterious past joins the present when an ancient man descended from those who had served princes approaches a chief of security to inquire if he has engaged tasters for a state dinner. The officer laughs at "other days other manners," explaining that "we have to look after bombs, not poisons, nowadays." The man, however, mutters that "the wickedness of men's hearts is ever the same, Huzoor." At the dinner, one tray of koftahs being served to the crowned head is upset; a dog fed the only retrieved morsel dies. The story ends with the officer placing flowers on the grave of the ances-

tor of the ancient servant of the court, who may have mysteriously compensated for the absence of a taster.

Throughout her career Steel failed to understand the Indian desire for independence or to perceive virtues in democracy. Despite her support of the British presence in India, she accommodated her respect for Indian culture by revering the golden age of the Indian princes, not for the splendors that many Anglo-Indians admired but for what she regarded as principled and just autocratic rule. In her autobiography she recounts an incident that she reworked in *The Hosts of the Lord* (1899). An elaborate tent city was being erected on a Lahore plain for the visit of the Prince of Wales. She imagines it to be only a pale approximation of the royal Mogul camps, which must have stretched for miles. At the camp's center now is a flagstaff flying the British flag, "yet those with seeing eyes can but regret that it replaces the big, shining lantern which in old time proclaimed far and near that here was the Lamp of Justice, ready to produce Light out of Darkness by the wise councils of the King."

As an Anglo-Indian within the structure of British rule in India, Steel adopted an imperious voice of bustling management and reform. In her fiction, however, this confidence is anxiously undermined in the mood and temper of her reflections on Indian life. Even while she remained oblivious to British responsibility for many of the conditions she sympathetically observed, she had, as Patwardhan points out, a keen eye for identifying the problems that modern India would confront. With curiosity and sympathy, she nonetheless remained somewhat coolly at a remove, becoming impassioned only about her own issues, such as her disagreements with government; often admiring but never identifying with the people she wrote about, she never challenged what she saw as a fit hierarchical order.

In a substantial body of work Steel articulated full support for the British imperial mission while she presented, in the view of many of her contemporary readers, an unorthodox view of Indian life. Her line of vision differed in important ways from Kipling's, yet she also enjoyed great popularity with the English public. A full-length critical biography would do much to ground further study.

Bibliography:

Brijen K. Gupta, *India in English Fiction: An Annotated Bibliography* (Metuchen, N. J.: Scarecrow Press, 1973).

Biography:
Violet Powell, *Flora Annie Steel: Novelist of India* (London: Heinemann, 1981).

References:
Pat Barr, *The Memsahibs: The Women of Victorian India* (London: Secker & Warburg, 1976);
Maud Diver, *The Englishwoman in India* (Edinburgh & London: Blackwood, 1909);
Allen J. Greenberger, "Englishwomen in India," *British History Illustrated,* 4 (1978): 42–51;
Rosemary Hennessy and Rajeswari Mohan, "The Construction of Woman in Three Popular Texts of Empire: Towards a Critique of Materialist Feminism," *Textual Practice,* 3 (Winter 1989): 323–359;
Edward Farley Oaten, *A Sketch of Anglo-Indian Literature; The Le Bas Prize Essay for 1907* (London: Kegan Paul, Trench, Trübner, 1908);
Daya Patwardhan, *A Star of India: Flora Annie Steel, Her Works and Times* (Bombay: A. V. Grika Prakashan, 1963);
Nancy Paxton, "Feminism Under the Raj: Complicity and Resistance in the Writings of Flora Annie Steel and Annie Besant," *Women's Studies International Forum,* 13, no. 4 (1990): 333–346;
Rebecca Saunders, "Gender, Colonialism, and Exile: Flora Annie Steel and Sara Jeannette Duncan in India," in *Women's Writing in Exile,* edited by Mary Lynn Broe and Angela Ingram (Chapel Hill: University of North Carolina Press, 1989), pp. 303–324;
Jenny Sharpe, "The Rise of Memsahibs in an Age of Empire: *On the Face of the Waters,*" in her *Allegories of Empire: The Figure of Woman in the Colonial Text* (Minneapolis: University of Minnesota Press, 1993), pp. 85–110;
Bhupal Singh, *A Survey of Anglo-Indian Fiction* (London: Oxford University Press, 1934).

Papers:

Steel's papers have not been collected. Apart from scattered letters included in collected papers of her many correspondents, the largest grouping is in the Harry Ransom Humanities Research Center, the University of Texas at Austin. Their Robert Lee Wolff Collection of Victorian Fiction includes approximately 320 pieces of correspondence to her agent, to and from the Authors' Syndicate, and to Beatrice Harraden, as well as the manuscript of "In the Permanent Way." In England some of her correspondence to Macmillan is included in the Macmillan Archive at the British Library. A few readers' reports from Heinemann are held by the R.I.B. Library of Reed Book Services, Rushden, Northhants, agents for William Heinemann.

Robert Louis Stevenson

(13 November 1850 – 3 December 1894)

William F. Naufftus
Winthrop University

See also the Stevenson entries in *DLB 18: Victorian Novelists After 1885, DLB 57: Victorian Prose Writers After 1867,* and *DLB 141: British Children's Writers, 1880–1914.*

BOOKS: *An Appeal to the Clergy of the Church of Scotland, with a Note for the Laity* (Edinburgh & London: Blackwood, 1875);

An Inland Voyage (London: Kegan Paul, 1878; Boston: Roberts, 1883);

Travels with a Donkey in the Cévennes (London: Kegan Paul, 1879 [i.e. 1878]; Boston: Roberts, 1879);

Edinburgh: Picturesque Notes (London: Seeley, Jackson & Halliday, 1879; New York: Macmillan, 1889);

Virginibus Puerisque and Other Papers (London: Kegan Paul, 1881; New York: Collier, 1881);

Familiar Studies of Men and Books (London: Chatto & Windus, 1882; New York: Dodd, Mead, 1887);

New Arabian Nights (2 volumes, London: Chatto & Windus, 1882; 1 volume, New York: Holt, 1882);

The Story of a Lie (London: Hayley & Jackson, 1882); republished as *The Story of a Lie and Other Tales* (Boston: Turner, 1904);

The Silverado Squatters: Sketches from a Californian Mountain (London: Chatto & Windus, 1883; New York: Munro, 1884);

Treasure Island (London, Paris, & New York: Cassell, 1883; Boston: Roberts, 1884);

A Child's Garden of Verses (London: Longmans, Green, 1885; New York: Scribners, 1885);

More New Arabian Nights: The Dynamiter, by Stevenson and Fanny Van de Grift Stevenson (London: Longmans, Green, 1885; New York: Holt, 1885);

Prince Otto: A Romance (London: Chatto & Windus, 1885; New York: Roberts, 1886);

Robert Louis Stevenson

Strange Case of Dr. Jekyll and Mr. Hyde (London: Longmans, Green, 1886; New York: Scribners, 1886);

Kidnapped (London: Cassell, 1886; New York: Scribners, 1886);

Some College Memories (Edinburgh: University Union Committee, 1886; New York: Mansfield & Wessels, 1899);

The Merry Men and Other Tales and Fables (London: Chatto & Windus, 1887; New York: Harper, 1887);

Underwoods (London: Chatto & Windus, 1887; New York: Scribners, 1887);

Memories and Portraits (London: Chatto & Windus, 1887; New York: Scribners, 1887);

Memoir of Fleeming Jenkin (New York: Scribners, 1887; London & New York: Longmans, Green, 1887);

The Misadventures of John Nicholson: A Christmas Story (New York: Munro, 1887);

The Black Arrow: A Tale of the Two Roses (London, Paris, New York & Melbourne: Cassell, 1888; New York: Scribners, 1888);

The Master of Ballantrae: A Winter's Tale (London, Paris, New York & Melbourne: Cassell, 1889; New York: Collier, 1889);

The Wrong Box, by Stevenson and Lloyd Osbourne (London: Longmans, Green, 1889; New York: Scribners, 1889);

Ballads (London: Chatto & Windus, 1890; New York: Scribners, 1890);

Father Damien: An Open Letter to the Reverend Dr. Hyde of Honolulu (London: Chatto & Windus, 1890; Portland, Maine: Mosher, 1897);

Across the Plains, with Other Memories and Essays (London: Chatto & Windus, 1892; New York: Scribners, 1892);

A Footnote to History: Eight Years of Trouble in Samoa (London, Paris & Melbourne: Cassell, 1892; New York: Scribners, 1892);

Three Plays: Deacon Brodie, Beau Austin, Admiral Guinea, by Stevenson and W. E. Henley (London: Nutt, 1892; New York: Scribners, 1892);

The Wrecker, by Stevenson and Osbourne (London, Paris & Melbourne: Cassell, 1892; New York: Scribners, 1892);

Island Nights' Entertainments: Consisting of The Beach of Falesá, The Bottle Imp, The Isle of Voices (London, Paris & Melbourne: Cassell, 1893; New York: Scribners, 1893);

Catriona: A Sequel to "Kidnapped" (London, Paris & Melbourne: Cassell, 1893); republished as *David Balfour* (New York: Scribners, 1893);

The Ebb-Tide: A Trio and a Quartette, by Stevenson and Osbourne (Chicago: Stone & Kimball, 1894; London: Heinemann, 1894);

The Body Snatcher (New York: Merriam, 1895);

The Amateur Immigrant from the Clyde to Sandy Hook (Chicago: Stone & Kimball, 1895);

The Strange Case of Dr. Jekyll and Mr. Hyde, with Other Fables (London & Bombay: Longmans, Green, 1896);

Weir of Hermiston: An Unfinished Romance (London: Chatto & Windus, 1896; New York: Scribners, 1896);

A Mountain Town in France: A Fragment (New York & London: John Lane, 1896);

Songs of Travel and Other Verses (London: Chatto & Windus, 1896);

In the South Seas (New York: Scribners, 1896; London: Chatto & Windus, 1900);

St. Ives: Being the Adventures of a French Prisoner in England, completed by Arthur Quiller-Couch (New York: Scribners, 1897; London: Heinemann, 1898);

The Morality of the Profession of Letters (Gouverneur, N.Y: Brothers of the Book, 1899);

A Stevenson Medley, edited by S. Colvin (London: Chatto & Windus, 1899);

Essays and Criticisms (Boston: Turner, 1903);

Prayers Written at Vailima, with an Introduction by Mrs. Stevenson (New York: Scribners, 1904; London: Chatto & Windus, 1905);

Essays of Travel (London: Chatto & Windus, 1905);

Essays in the Art of Writing (London: Chatto & Windus, 1905);

Essays, edited by W. L. Phelps (New York: Scribners, 1906);

Lay Morals and Other Papers (London: Chatto & Windus, 1911; New York: Scribners, 1911);

Records of a Family of Engineers (London: Chatto & Windus, 1912);

The Waif Woman (London: Chatto & Windus, 1916);

On the Choice of a Profession (London: Chatto & Windus, 1916);

Poems Hitherto Unpublished, edited by G. S. Hellman, 2 volumes (Boston: Bibliophile Society, 1916);

New Poems and Variant Readings (London: Chatto & Windus, 1918);

Diogenes in London (San Francisco: Edwin and Robert Grabhorn for John Howell, 1920);

Diogenes at the Savile Club (Chicago: Frank M. Morris, printed by Edwin and Robert Grabhorn for David G. Joyce, 1921);

Poems Hitherto Unpublished, edited by Hellman and W. P. Trent (Boston: Bibliophile Society, 1921);

Robert Louis Stevenson: Hitherto Unpublished Prose Writings, edited by H. H. Harper (Boston: Bibliophile Society, 1921);

When the Devil Was Well, edited by Trent (Boston: Bibliophile Society, 1921);

Confessions of a Unionist: An Unpublished Talk on Things Current, Written in 1888, edited by F. V. Livingston (Cambridge, Mass.: Privately printed, 1921);

The Best Thing in Edinburgh: An Address to the Speculative Society of Edinburgh in March 1873, edited by K. D. Osbourne (San Francisco: Howell, 1923);

Selected Essays, edited by H. G. Rawlinson (London: Oxford University Press, 1923);

The Castaways of Soledad: A Manuscript by Stevenson Hitherto Unpublished, edited by Hellman (Buffalo, N.Y.: Privately printed, 1928);

Monmouth: A Tragedy, edited by C. Vale (New York: Rudge, 1928);

The Charity Bazaar (Westport, Conn.: Georgian Press, 1929);

The Essays of Robert Louis Stevenson, edited by M. Elwin (London: Macdonald, 1950);

Salute to RLS, edited by F. Holland (Edinburgh: Cousland, 1950);

Tales and Essays, edited by G. B. Stern (London: Falcon, 1950);

Silverado Journal, edited by John E. Jordan (San Francisco: Book Club of California, 1954);

An Old Song and the Edifying Letters of the Rutherford Family, edited by Roger Swearingen (Hamden, Conn.: Archon & Wilfion Books, 1982);

Robert Louis Stevenson: The Scottish Stories and Essays, edited by Kenneth Gelder (Edinburgh: University of Edinburgh Press, 1989);

Tales from the Prince of Storytellers, edited by Barry Menikoff (Evanston, Ill.: Northwestern University Press, 1993).

Collections: *The Works of R. L. Stevenson,* Edinburgh Edition, 28 volumes, edited by Sidney Colvin (London: Chatto & Windus, 1894–1898);

The Works of Robert Louis Stevenson, Vailima Edition, 26 volumes, edited by Lloyd Osbourne and Fanny Van de Grift Stevenson (London: Heinemann, 1922–1923; New York: Scribners, 1922–1923);

The Works of Robert Louis Stevenson, Tusitala Edition, 35 volumes (London: Heinemann, 1924);

The Works of Robert Louis Stevenson, South Seas Edition, 32 volumes (New York: Scribners, 1925);

Robert Louis Stevenson: The Complete Shorter Fiction, edited by Peter Stoneley (London: Robinson, 1991; New York: Carroll & Graf, 1991);

Robert Louis Stevenson: The Complete Short Stories, Centenary Edition, 2 volumes, edited by Ian Bell (New York: Holt, 1993).

PLAY PRODUCTIONS: *Deacon Brodie; or, The Double Life,* Bradford, Pullan's Theater of Varieties, 28 December 1882;

Beau Austin, London, Theatre Royal, Haymarket, 17 November 1890;

Admiral Guinea, London, Avenue Theatre, 29 November 1897;

Macaire, London, Strand Theatre, 4 November 1900.

SELECTED PERIODICAL PUBLICATION –

UNCOLLECTED: "The Enchantress," edited by David D. Mann and Susan Garlond Mann, *Georgia Review,* 43 (Fall 1989): 550–568.

At the time of his death in Samoa in 1894, Robert Louis Stevenson was regarded by many critics and a large reading public as the most important writer in the English-speaking world. "Surely another age will wonder over this curiosity of letters," wrote Sir Arthur Quiller-Couch at the time, "that for five years the needle of literary endeavor in Great Britain has quivered toward a little island in the South Pacific, as to its magnetic pole." Critics as demanding as Henry James and Gerard Manley Hopkins agreed on Stevenson's importance, a fact difficult to imagine today when his critical stature is so much more modest. While Stevenson's short fiction is an important part of his achievement, his output was fairly small because he spent most of his brief life working in other literary genres. Beginning primarily as an essayist and travel writer, he soon moved on to short fiction, but after the publication of *Treasure Island* in 1883, the novel was his preferred form. He also wrote memorable poetry and forgettable plays, but it was short fiction – *Strange Case of Dr. Jekyll and Mr. Hyde* (1886) – that first gained him a large adult readership, and short fiction was a form he practiced to a certain extent throughout his life.

If one takes approximately fifty thousand words as a limit, Stevenson produced approximately thirty short stories and novellas himself; collaborated with his wife on a volume of short stories; coauthored a novella with his stepson, Lloyd Osbourne; and authored twenty very short narratives he called fables. His short fiction varies enormously in length, technique, and theme; it also appeared before the public in several different contexts. Stevenson published three volumes of collected short stories by himself besides the one with his wife. Most of his stories were published in periodicals before being collected, and several stories published in periodicals were left out of the various collections. One of his best, "The Tale of Todd Lapraik," is told by one character to another in Stevenson's last completed full-length novel, *Catriona: A Sequel to "Kidnapped"* (1893).

Except for *The Strange Case of Dr. Jekyll and Mr. Hyde,* this short fiction is no longer the most popular or the most critically admired part of Stevenson's work, but it has an extremely important role in the development of British short fiction. The modern short story developed on the Continent and in the United States far sooner than in Britain. While many nineteenth-century British writers wrote short fiction, it was generally what Wendell V. Harris has called "sophisticated tales," rather loosely constructed miniature novels rather than "true short stories" with their characteristic unity of effect. Stevenson and Rudyard Kipling share the distinction of domesticating the true short story in England, and Stevenson's first short stories preceded Kipling's by ten years. Thus, while short fiction was often a secondary interest for Stevenson, initially being overshadowed by nonfiction and later by the novel, he is appropriately regarded as the originator of the British short story in something recognizably like its modern form. One recent critic, Barry Menikoff, has argued in his introduction to *Tales from the Prince of Storytellers* (1993) that Stevenson accomplished this by combining the formal rigor of the French *conte* as practiced by Théophile Gautier and Prosper Mérimée with the moral earnestness of the American short story as practiced by Nathaniel Hawthorne, with the result that Stevenson "created, in effect, the 'moral art story,' or the art story with a moral."

Stevenson's early life was in some respects extremely conducive to his later eminence as a writer of fiction. He was born on 13 November 1850 in Edinburgh to Thomas Stevenson and Margaret Balfour Stevenson. His father was a distinguished engineer who specialized in the design of lighthouses and other coastal works, and his mother was the daughter of a clergyman. Both parents are usually described by biographers as rather grim Scots Calvinists, and it is certainly true that Robert Louis Stevenson had more than his share of generational conflict with his father, who hoped that his son would share both his orthodox Presbyterian worldview and his choice of engineering as a profession. While these parental hopes were to be disappointed, Thomas Stevenson's love of evening storytelling was inherited by his son, and even the paternal Calvinism can be seen as a central ingredient in many of Stevenson's stories, most notably *The Strange Case of Dr. Jekyll and Mr. Hyde.* The younger Stevenson's extremely delicate health both discouraged his parents from having more children and made them more indulgent of their one child than they might otherwise have been. One form this indulgence

Cover for the first volume of Stevenson's two-volume collection of stories based on The Arabian Nights' Entertainments *(Special Collections, Thomas Cooper Library, University of South Carolina)*

took was that, despite the most painful and bitter disagreements with their son on theological and moral questions, the parents gave him the financial support that freed him for generally impecunious literary work. This parental support allowed Stevenson to write what he pleased when he pleased and as little as he pleased until he finally developed a voice and form that would both suit him and provide a satisfactory income.

Because of his poor health Stevenson began his formal schooling late and frequently moved from one school to another. He eventually entered the University of Edinburgh to study engineering but later shifted to law after convincing his father in 1871 to let him train for a career as something other than a lighthouse engineer; Louis, as he was usually called, wanted to be a writer, and his father was willing to accept the law as a respectable and practical compromise. During his years of school and university Louis developed bohemian habits and friendships and frequently spent his evenings in company that his parents, had they known of it, would not have approved. This secret life and the equally secret religious skepticism that developed at the same time presumably helped Stevenson later to produce sympathetic pictures of Dr. Jekyll and other characters who led double lives or had bohemian habits and also led him to produce many novels and stories involving conflicts between fathers and sons. His light-hearted attitude toward his prospects as a lawyer and his consequent dependence on parental largesse also presumably had a role in his creation of a large number of young men in his fiction who are expensively and impractically educated and who find, shortly after completing their studies, that they are completely incapable of supporting themselves.

In May 1872 Stevenson joined an Edinburgh law firm and began studying for the Scottish Bar examination, passing the preliminary test in November. Shortly thereafter, he confessed his religious doubts to his parents, beginning a long period of family warfare that included the risk of disinheritance. For several months the three lived uncomfortably together, either arguing about religious matters or waiting grimly for the eruption of the next argument. Louis was released from this tense situation by an invitation to spend time with English relatives at the rectory in Cockfield, Suffolk, where he promptly fell in love with a thirty-four-year-old woman named Frances Sitwell, unhappily married and staying at the rectory to avoid her husband, the Reverend Albert Sitwell. In an apparently platonic manner, she helped Louis get over much of his awkwardness around ladies and also introduced him to another of her admirers, Sidney Colvin, Slade Professor of Fine Arts at Cambridge, ultimately her second husband and more immediately Stevenson's first contact with the literary world of London. Through Colvin's good offices he met and befriended other literary figures, including Edmund Gosse, Leslie Stephen, William Ernest Henley, and George Meredith. Stevenson also began to publish essays in Stephen's *Cornhill Magazine* and elsewhere, and starting in 1873 he began spending a large share of his time in France – both in Paris and at various artists' colonies such as Barbizon and Grez-sur-Loing in the forest of Fontainebleau, often accompanied by his cousin Bob Stevenson.

Here Stevenson met another older, unhappily married woman living apart from her husband, an American named Fanny Vandegrift Osbourne. She had left her very difficult husband, Sam Osbourne, in California and had come to France with her children to study art. She and Louis fell in love and

rather imprudently decided to marry as soon as Fanny could return to California and obtain a divorce. This love affair, which began in 1876 or 1877, ended only with Stevenson's death in 1894 and had a considerable influence on his writing. Fanny and her children were often the first audiences and critics of a Stevenson story, listening in the evening to the draft of the day's work and generally offering suggestions, some of which at least were accepted. She coauthored one volume of short fiction with her husband, while her son, Lloyd, ultimately coauthored three books with Stevenson; her daughter, Belle, eventually became her stepfather's amanuensis, transcribing his last, fragmentary novels from dictation. After 1894 all three of the Osbournes became, in various ways, keepers of the Stevenson legend, influencing posthumous publications, collected editions, and authorized biographies and producing memoirs and reminiscences of their own. Among them they did a great deal to create the misleadingly saintly image of Stevenson that emerged in the years before World War I and contributed to the anti-Stevenson reaction that began around 1914 and has not quite ended yet.

Between 1873 and 1876 Stevenson wrote book reviews, literary and historical essays, and once-admired familiar essays of moral uplift such as "Ordered South," first published in *Macmillan's Magazine* in 1874. His first full-length book, *An Inland Voyage* (1878), grew out of a canoe trip he took through Belgium and northern France in 1876 with his friend Sir Walter Simpson. But 1877 marks Stevenson's first publication of short fiction, and three stories written that year – "An Old Song," "A Lodging for the Night," and "Will o' the Mill" – are interesting examples of the different kinds of short fiction he would produce throughout his career.

"An Old Song," Stevenson's first short story, appeared anonymously in *London* (February–March 1877) and was attributed to him by Roger Swearingen in 1980. While not a particularly successful effort, it introduces themes that were to play an important role in Stevenson's later fiction. In its forty-year time frame and its bulk – over fifteen thousand words in twelve chapters – it suggests the earlier English tradition of the sophisticated tale rather than the modern short story. It begins with Lt. Col. John Falconer, who distresses his parents by joining the army and leading a wild life before suddenly becoming a devoutly strict Presbyterian at a revival meeting. After his conversion he enjoys "the delights of what we may call Black Happiness," the pleasure that comes from any misery undertaken for the sake of conscience. Black Happiness eventually requires the colonel to return to his un-congenial estate at Grangehead and undertake the upbringing of his two nephews, John and Malcolm. John, who is three weeks older than his cousin, is to be the colonel's heir and shares both his name and aggressive personality. Malcolm is shy at his first meeting with his uncle and develops into an adolescent who exhibits both "a winning way" and "petty selfishness."

The narrative then skips ahead to John's eighteenth birthday, when he discovers to his horror that his intended, Mary Rowland, actually loves Malcolm, who also loves her. Suffering the Black Happiness of enjoying martyrdom, John gets drunk, quarrels with the colonel, is disinherited, and goes off to London, where he becomes a hack journalist. When John is "well on in his thirties," the vicissitudes of the newspaper business drive him back to Grangehead, where Malcolm initially welcomes the prodigal but ultimately banishes him again when he declares his old love for Mary.

During their final interview the two cousins both "by some electric sympathy" look simultaneously in the mirror: "John's face was deformed with hatred, and in an instant Malcolm's was stricken with the scarcely less hideous image of fear," with the result that "they looked like a couple of lost spirits." They grapple, Malcolm hits his head but soon recovers, and John bids farewell and walks out into the rain. The story concludes, "It rained without intermission, and the roads in that part of the country were hardly passable for travellers on foot." The reader is never told John's fate on the impassable roads, but the tale nevertheless has a garrulous mid-Victorian narrator. While he is unwilling to tell the contents of a letter the colonel has written on his deathbed, he is quite anxious to deliver comic judgments on Mary's literary pretensions and little essays on such tangential topics as the effect of nocturnal railway whistles on "wakeful youth." Creating an appropriate narrative voice was a frequent problem for Stevenson, and paired opposites such as John and Malcolm also reappear frequently in his later work – most obviously in *The Strange Case of Dr. Jekyll and Mr. Hyde* and *The Master of Ballantrae: A Winter's Tale* (1889), where a strong, wild elder brother abandons an estate and a bride but later comes back to reclaim them from a softer, more amiable younger brother, leading to a conflict that only ends with the death of both. In fact, the material of "An Old Song" was better suited to a novel than to a short story: there is simply too much ground to be covered here for Stevenson to get it all into either the word length he has chosen

or anything like the conventions of the modern short story.

Stevenson's real career as a short-story writer began with his next story. "A Lodging for the Night" was begun right after the completion of "An Old Song" during the summer of 1877 and published in *Temple Bar* in October. It begins with a beautiful description of a bitterly cold medieval Paris night, reminiscent of John Keats's "The Eve of St. Agnes." Just as Keats's Porfiro must find shelter from the cold in a castle full of enemies, Stevenson's hero, the medieval French poet François Villon, must find a similar lodging in a city where he has already alienated practically everybody who knows him. He must leave his original lodging, a thieves' den, because he needs to distance himself from the murder that has just been committed there. The contrast between the deathly cold of the Paris night and the dangerous heat of a thieves' den is quite reminiscent of Keats's poem. "The snow fell over Paris with rigorous, relentless persistence. . . . High up overhead the snow settled among the tracery of the Cathedral towers. Many a niche was drifted full; many a statue wore a long white bonnet on its grotesque or sainted head." But in the small house in the cemetery of Saint John "a great pile of living embers diffused a strong and ruddy glow from the arched chimney." The twenty-four-year-old Villon is working on a poem while his companions play a game of chance that ends in an argument in which one kills another. After the survivors scatter, Villon walks through Paris, and "choosing a street at random," he hears the watch coming and hides in a porch, where he finds the frozen corpse of a prostitute. When he tries to pocket the two small coins he finds "in her stocking," he discovers that his purse has been stolen. Since Villon cannot now pay for a night's lodging, he looks for a house where he can break in, stay the night, and "issue, on the morrow, with an armful of valuable plate."

At this point Villon sees an impressive house with a light in the window and is admitted by a courteous old knight, who introduces himself as the Sire de Brisetout and goes to fetch him dinner while Villon estimates the value of the old gentleman's plate. These two ill-assorted companions then spend the rest of the night debating morality and theology, with Villon arguing that the knight's chivalric warfare is basically indistinguishable from the violence of robbers and Brisetout, who "yearned to convert the young man to a better way of thinking," advocating knightly virtues and Christian piety. During this debate Villon shows "inimitable insolence," while the old man shows a certain intellectual slowness and inflexibility. Ultimately the morning arrives, and the elderly knight, by now feeling himself disgraced by having harbored such a guest, escorts the poet to the door. Villon gives "many thanks for the cold mutton" and goes out into the "chill, uncomfortable" street thinking, "A very dull old gentleman. . . . I wonder what his goblets may be worth."

Standard histories of the English short story by T. O. Beachcroft and Walter Allen recognize the historical importance of "A Lodging for the Night." Allen, for example, says that "the change to the specifically modern short story in English writing "can be dated fairly precisely" to October 1877, when "A Lodging for the Night" was first published. On the other hand, Harold Orel's substantial chapter on Stevenson in *The Victorian Short Story: Development and Triumph of a Literary Genre* (1986) never even mentions this story, and the story is not frequently anthologized. In fact, its historical significance is greater than its artistic merit. The debate between the bohemian young Villon and the elderly, respectable, and orthodox knight presumably reflects Stevenson's own moral and theological arguments with his father, but the discussion is not particularly original; and after the evocative and exciting opening of the story, there is a certain sense of anticlimax as Villon walks off in the cold Paris morning. The merely verbal and theoretical confrontation between poet and knight seems tame and insipid after the violence in the thieves' den. Stevenson has not managed to embody his moral message in the narrative and consequently resorts to explicit sermonizing.

The third story written in 1877, "Will o' the Mill," is entirely dominated by this sermonizing impulse. It is an exercise in parable that narrates the life of Will, from his adoption in childhood by the miller to his meeting with Death in hale old age, creating a time frame even longer than the forty years of "An Old Song." Practically nothing happens in Will's long life because he has determined that it is better to desire than to have. Thus, he looks out from his mountain home at the distant plain, longing for its cities but never actually going to visit them. Similarly, he loves the parson's daughter Margery but decides that they will be happier contemplating each other from a distance, so she marries someone else. As he gets older, the reader is told, rather improbably, that "his fame was heard of in the cities of the plain; and young men . . . spoke together in cafes of Will o' the Mill and his rough philosophy." The rough philosopher is eventually confronted one night by a youthful traveler who in-

troduces himself as Death and invites Will to join him in his carriage for a final ride. This story bears a certain resemblance to Hawthorne's more allegorical works such as "The Great Stone Face," and it has had its admirers. Given the lack of action, however, the narrative seems intolerably prolix at nine thousand words; furthermore, the characters are stick figures, and (most fatally in this kind of story) the ideas are not sufficiently interesting to sustain the reader's attention. Much later in Samoa, Stevenson shocked an admirer by describing Will's philosophy as "cat's meat."

"Will o' the Mill" was published in the *Cornhill Magazine* in January 1878; and while it is Stevenson's longest conventional "fable," he worked periodically throughout his life on a series of shorter fables, which were eventually edited and published after his death by his widow and Sidney Colvin. In June 1874 Stevenson had reviewed Edward Robert Bulwer Lytton's *Fables in Song* in the *Fortnightly Review* and had spoken favorably about the possibilities of the genre. In a letter to Colvin during the summer of 1874 he remarked in passing that "I have done no more to my *Fables,*" indicating that several (Colvin thought five) had already been written by that time. By the winter of 1887–1888 he had written enough of them to talk to a representative of Longmans, Green, about a book of fables, a contract for which was signed on 31 May 1888. The book finally appeared posthumously in 1896 after periodical publication in *Longmans Magazine* (August and September 1895) and *McClure's Magazine* (February 1896). The complete volume contains twenty fables varying widely in length, from exactly twenty-eight words in "The Tadpole and the Frog" to approximately twenty-five hundred in "The Touchstone." As Orel says, they are "unfinished experiments in story-telling," but he grants their significance in illustrating "the running battle between Stevenson's allowing the imagination free rein and his concern that he might not be serious enough to deserve the attentive respect of his audience." The fables attempt to present a message, sometimes with almost no story line. While their brevity may make them more palatable to most readers than "Will o' the Mill," together they represent one pole of the Stevensonian conflict. Adventure stories such as *Treasure Island* or *Kidnapped* (1886) represent the other, while most of the short fiction – most successfully *The Strange Case of Dr. Jekyll and Mr. Hyde* – attempts to combine an engaging story with a worthwhile message.

In the summer of 1878 Fanny returned to the United States to obtain either a divorce from, or a reconciliation with, her husband, while Stevenson remained in France. In September he undertook a walking tour in the Cévennes mountains in southern France; in December his *Edinburgh: Picturesque Notes* was published; and in May 1879 *Travels with a Donkey in the Cévennes* appeared, giving a generally comic view of his September walking tour. From October 1878 through at least January 1879 he worked with Henley on *Deacon Brodie; or, The Double Life,* the first and most interesting of the four plays they would eventually coauthor. The double life referred to in the subtitle is the historical William Brodie's combination of respectable daytime life as Edinburgh cabinetmaker and town councillor and nocturnal life as leader of a gang of burglars, leading ultimately to his apprehension and execution in 1788. As all commentators have noted, this story looks forward to the double life of Dr. Henry Jekyll as Mr. Edward Hyde. The rest of 1879 included work on several short stories and a larger number of essays, until in August a telegram from Fanny led him to depart immediately for the United States on the S.S. *Devonia* without telling his parents or bothering to collect adequate funds for the voyage. During this voyage he completed "The Story of a Lie," which he had begun in Scotland in May. It was published in the *New Quarterly Magazine* in October. Nobody has ever admired this story very much, but it is biographically interesting. Its protagonist, Dick Naseby, is a wellborn young man who quarrels bitterly with his stern but loving father because Dick decides to marry Miss Van Tromp, a young lady of modest means whose father, a bohemian and parasitic old artist, is the most vivid character in the story. Dick obviously resembles Stevenson, and Fanny resembles Miss Van Tromp in her economic status, her dubious respectability, and even her Dutch maiden name.

Stevenson, of course, was risking a final break with his father because of this trip, so it was appropriate that he sailed second-class, familiarizing himself for the first time with the rigors of life without money. To make matters worse, his health was precarious on the Atlantic crossing, during his brief stay in New York, on his railroad trip across the continent, and during the four months he spent in Monterrey (through December 1879) and the five months he spent in San Francisco and Oakland before he and Fanny were finally able to marry on 19 May 1880. The Atlantic crossing is described in *The Amateur Immigrant from the Clyde to Sandy Hook* (1895), the railway journey to California in *Across the Plains, with Other Memories and Essays* (1892), and the new couple's eccentric honeymoon at an abandoned sil-

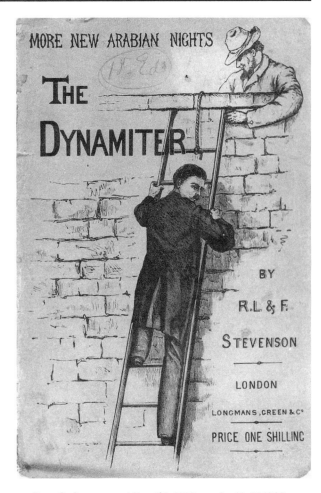

Cover for Stevenson and his wife's 1885 sequel to his 1882 New Arabian Nights *(Special Collections, Thomas Cooper Library, University of South Carolina)*

ver mine on Mount Saint Helena in *The Silverado Squatters: Sketches from a Californian Mountain* (1883). The grim tone of the first two books is a striking contrast to the insouciance of *An Inland Voyage* and *Travels with a Donkey in the Cévennes* and is the major reason for their delayed publication, but the honeymoon narrative shows Stevenson recapturing some of his old good spirits.

By midsummer his health was much better, so he and his bride traveled back to New York and sailed for Liverpool, first-class this time, on the *City of Chester* for a fateful encounter with the older Stevensons. His parents were pleasantly surprised by their new daughter-in-law, so a complete reconciliation was effected, after which the newlyweds went to Switzerland so that Stevenson could enroll at the famous new tuberculosis sanatorium at Davos, later the scene of Thomas Mann's *Der Zauberberg* (1924; translated as *The Magic Mountain,* 1927).

In April 1881 the essay collection *Virginibus Puerisque and Other Papers* became Stevenson's fifth published book, and during the summer of 1881 he and his family stayed in several Scottish holiday spots, including the cottage at Braemar where he began *Treasure Island* as a present for his stepson, Lloyd. By October they were all back in Davos, where Stevenson befriended John Addington Symonds. In March 1882 *Familiar Studies of Men and Books* was published, and by April it was decided that Stevenson's health problems were not due to tuberculosis, so the family left Davos for another summer in Scotland, to be followed by a series of residences in the south of France. In July 1882 Stevenson's first short-story collection, *New Arabian Nights,* was published in two volumes by Chatto and Windus. It included "A Lodging for the Night" and ten other stories, all of which had been published in periodicals and seven of which were linked together by an Arabian editor and the character Prince Florizel of Bohemia.

These seven stories had been begun in the spring of 1878 when Stevenson was living at Burford Bridge Inn in Surrey and completed the following summer at Le Monastier in southern France, just before he set off on the journey in the Cévennes with Modestine the donkey. They were published serially in *London* from June to October 1878 as "Latter-Day Arabian Nights: The Suicide Club, The Rajah's Diamond," and they made up the first volume of *New Arabian Nights.*

Prince Florizel with "his confidant and Master of the Horse Colonel Geraldine" wanders through Paris, London, and presumably other capital cities outside his own realm in search of diversions, adventures, and wrongs to be righted. His lavish and frequently aimless way of life, oddly combined with occasional displays of heroism and an underlying firm moral purpose, make him an interesting embodiment of both the decadent and counterdecadent impulses of the era. Decadence is, however, the more obvious influence in the first story, "The Young Man with the Cream Tarts." Here the prince, wearing false whiskers, and the colonel, disguised as a seedy journalist, are driven by inclement weather into an oyster bar near Leicester Square, where they observe a young man going about the room offering free cream tarts to anybody who will accept one. The prince discovers that the young man, having run through his inheritance, is squandering all his remaining money except the forty pounds he will need for "entry money" to a secret organization called the Suicide Club. The prince and the colonel, claiming to be down on their luck,

accompany him to the club, where they take an oath of obedience to club rules and then join the other club members, who are drinking champagne and toasting the memories "of notable suicides of the past." At the end of the evening the president deals cards to the members; the member who draws the ace of spades is to be killed by the one who draws the ace of clubs, with the president providing an inventive method for the crime. This evening a Mr. Malthus draws the ace of spades, and the young man of the cream tarts is horrified to learn that he is to be the murderer rather than the victim.

The next day the newspapers report the accidental death of the respectable Mr. Malthus, and Prince Florizel, pitying the young man who is now a murderer, swears vengeance on the president. Over Colonel Geraldine's protest, the following night the prince returns to the club, where he draws the victim's ace of spades and then, realizing he is bound by his oath to obey club rules, is overwhelmed by remorse at having "gambled away his future and that of a brave and loyal country." On leaving the club, however, he is "unceremoniously thrust into a carriage," not by assassins but by a "celebrated detective" and his agents hired by Colonel Geraldine to save the prince from his quixotic determination to honor his membership oath. Florizel is "overjoyed to yield to friendly violence" and returns to his London residence, where "in his official robes and covered with all the orders of Bohemia" he passes judgment on the members of the club, who have been kidnapped and are now brought before him. He offers to pay the debts of those who have been driven to seek death because of poverty; he recommends repentance to those driven by remorse; and he sends the president to Paris under the guard of Colonel Geraldine's younger brother. The story ends with a note from "my Arabian author" informing the reader that the young man of the cream tarts "is now a comfortable householder in Wigmore Street, Cavendish Square," presumably because of Prince Florizel's munificence, and inviting the reader to read the next tale, "The Story of the Physician and the Saratoga Trunk."

This second story and the third, "The Adventure of the Hansom Cab," complete "The Suicide Club," taking the story to Paris, where the president murders Colonel Geraldine's brother and escapes, and back to London, where the prince finally kills the president in a nocturnal fencing match. Both stories begin, like the first, with rather aimless young men who are arbitrarily drawn into the secret struggle of good and evil. In the first, a young

American in Paris gets involved by peering through a hole in the wall of his hotel room at the glamorous Madame Zephyrine and ends up being framed for the murder of young Geraldine. In the second, Lt. Brackenbury Rich, recently returned from "the lesser hill wars" in India, ultimately becomes Prince Florizel's second in the duel with the president after being recruited by a cabdriver who has been offered a reward for finding any single gentlemen of military bearing in evening dress.

The first three stories of "The Rajah's Diamond" also center on aimless young men who are drawn into unexpected adventures, this time centered on a fabulous jewel rather than a secret organization. This jewel belongs to Gen. Sir Thomas Vandeleur; it is "the sixth known diamond in the world" and was obtained from the Rajah of Kashgar for "some service the nature of which had been often whispered and repeatedly denied." The young man in the first tale, "The Story of the Bandbox," is Harry Hartley, who runs errands for the glamorous Lady Vandeleur and believes himself to be in love with her. The "Story of the Young Man in Holy Orders" focuses on the Reverend Simon Rolles, who had "distinguished himself in the Moral Sciences" at Oxford; when, however, he finds the rajah's diamond, he is inspired "with very low ideas of university training," realizing that, "with learning enough to be a Bishop, . . . I positively do not know how to dispose of a stolen diamond" and become rich. In "The Story of the House with the Green Blinds" an unworldly Scottish bank clerk named Francis Scrymgeour comes into possession of the diamond and finds himself pursued through the streets of Paris by General Vandeleur's terrifying brother, John, the former dictator of Paraguay.

Prince Florizel appears briefly in the second story, where he advises Simon Rolles to read Emile Gaboriau's detective novels, and in the third, where he happens to be seated in the Cafe Americain when Francis Scrymgeour runs in there during his flight. The concluding tale, "The Adventure of Prince Florizel and the Detective," consists largely of a conversation on a bridge over the Seine between Prince Florizel and the detective who has just arrested him, on John Vandeleur's warrant, for the theft of the rajah's diamond. The prince recounts the story of the diamond's nefarious influence, throws the jewel into the middle of the river, and – having thus disposed of the evidence of his "guilt" – suggests that the detective's silence will be rewarded. The collection then ends with the information that the Vandeleurs amused the residents of Paris by "vast diving operations on the River Seine" (in the wrong location) and that the prince "now keeps a cigarstore in Rupert Street" as a result of "a recent revolution that hurled him from the throne of Bohemia, in consequence of his continual absence and edifying neglect of public business."

Some of the characters in this collection could have wandered in from the plays or fictions of Oscar Wilde; others would have been at home in the romantic Ruritania of Anthony Hope's *The Prisoner of Zenda* (1894), though none of those works had yet been written. The character of Florizel presumably owes something to Harun al-Rashid, who went about disguised among his people, but a closer parallel may be Sherlock Holmes, who would be created by Stevenson's admirer Arthur Conan Doyle several years later. Florizel tells the officer who arrests him that "rightly looked upon, a Prince and a detective serve in the same corps. We are both combatants against crime; only mine is the more lucrative and yours the more dangerous rank." His omniscience and "bohemianism" are both reminiscent of Holmes, as are his love of disguises and his sudden transformations from languid observer to stern moralist or vengeful instrument of justice. Even his enthusiasm for tobacco and for Gaboriau's detective novels are links; but if the president of the Suicide Club resembles Professor Moriarty, Colonel Geraldine is an unsatisfactory Watson, disappearing altogether in "The Rajah's Diamond."

Clearly Stevenson was experimenting with this fiction, working out his intentions as he went along. The point of view, characterization, and tone of "The Rajah's Diamond" are much more consistent than those of "The Suicide Club." In the former collection Prince Florizel seems to be a different character from one page to the next, lurching from guilty realization of his folly in joining the Suicide Club and being bound by its oath to insouciant acceptance of Geraldine's strong-arm tactics in saving him from himself and then on to the vengeful minister of justice – who nevertheless feels obligated to kill the president in a duel rather than break the club oath by turning him over to the police. But all the talk about gentlemen's honor in "The Suicide Club" disappears in "The Rajah's Diamond," the Arabian endnotes function fitfully, and the conclusion of the second series with Florizel installed in his Rupert Street cigar store suggests that Stevenson did not take the whole project too seriously. In their concern with crime, however, these stories anticipate some of Stevenson's most popular tales, so perhaps it is not surprising that Prince Florizel was resurrected several years later in *More New Arabian Nights: The Dynamiter* (1885).

The second volume of *New Arabian Nights* consists of "A Lodging for the Night" and three other stories: "The Sire de Maletroit's Door," "Providence and the Guitar," and "The Pavilion on the Links." The first of these shares with "A Lodging for the Night" a fifteenth-century French setting and the time frame of a single night. Its protagonist, Denis de Beaulieu, a French knight during the Hundred Years' War, is overtaken by darkness in a town full of English soldiers and, hiding in the porch of a mansion to escape a patrol, finds the door unlocked and enters, to find himself caught in a trap set for someone else. The elderly Sire de Maletroit, knowing that his niece Blanche has an assignation with a lover, has filled his house with armed men and now, believing Denis is the lover, offers him the choice of marrying the niece or dying in the morning. Denis believes that chivalry forbids him from forcing himself on Blanche, while she assumes that he would be dishonored by a union with a woman who has loved another. By morning, however, they have fallen in love and are embracing when Maletroit enters chuckling and bids "his new nephew a good morning." The contrast between the cynical old man and the chivalrous young one in this story reverses the situation in "A Lodging for the Night," and if the earlier story questioned the knightly code, this one certainly affirms it. "The Sire de Maletroit's Door" lacks the wonderful opening of "A Lodging for the Night," but it achieves greater unity, with everything building toward the final decision for matrimony in the last lines of the story.

"Providence and the Guitar," written in October and November and originally published in *London* in November 1878, deals with Leon Berthelini and his wife, Elvira, two traveling musicians who are locked out of their hotel and threatened with arrest in a small French town. Like François Villon and Denis de Beaulieu, they are seeking a lodging for the night in a hostile world, but they have the advantage of inhabiting a comic universe. In the company of Stubbs, a penniless Cambridge undergraduate on a walking tour, they wander around in the dark until they come upon a house where a painter and his wife are loudly quarreling over his refusal to accept a clerkship of £150 per year because he wants to devote himself to art. The rest of the night is then passed in a debate on the relative merits of reliable incomes versus artistic fulfillment, until Berthelini's singing of a love song brings about a reconciliation between the host and hostess. As dawn comes up, Stubbs departs, thinking that the two couples are "all mad — but wonderfully de-

cent." This story gives a far more realistic side of Stevensonian bohemia than the world of Prince Florizel. Like the two medieval French stories, it takes place in a single night, but it lacks their unity. It is long and is divided into six numbered chapters; the initial comic-ironic tone is eventually abandoned; and the conclusion seems abrupt and anticlimactic. The concluding debate, like the one between Villon and the Sire de Brisetout, seems tacked on to a potentially more interesting adventure.

But the next story, "The Pavilion on the Links," has plenty of adventure. At twenty thousand words, it looks forward to such novels as *Treasure Island* and *Kidnapped* and also to such later short fiction as "The Beach of Falesá" in its evocative handling of atmosphere, exciting pacing of narrative plot, and use of first-person narrative. The narrator, Frank Cassilis, is at the time of the action a wandering misanthrope, "gypsying" over England and Scotland with a horse and cart, and one September camping out in the sea woods at Graden Easter, the estate of R. Northmour, Esq., the long-estranged friend of his youth. This estate is located on the Scottish North Sea coast and includes an abandoned two-story pavilion on the links (the beach), where one night Frank sees a mysterious light. From here the story proceeds to the nocturnal landing of a party from a yacht, evidence of an additional person lurking in the sea wood, and a desperate siege of the pavilion by Carbonari, members of a secret Italian revolutionary society. Northmour has fallen in love with a young woman named Clara Huddlestone and has been hiding her and her father, a corrupt and cowardly old banker who has speculated with Carbonari funds and lost them. Cassilis joins Northmour in defending the pavilion, but the situation is made more desperate still by the two men's rivalry for Clara's affections. Finally, with the pavilion in flames and bullets flying, Mr. Huddlestone rises above the selfish cowardice that has so far characterized his behavior and walks out the front door, where he is promptly shot dead. At this point the Carbonari turn out to be "gentlemen and soldiers" and disappear without hurting anyone else, leaving Northmour and Cassilis to fight over Clara. When the sinister, Byronic Northmour finally gets Cassilis in his power, however, he surprises everyone by quietly returning his yacht and later makes a good end, being "killed fighting under the colours of Garibaldi for the liberation of the Tyrol."

There is much of *Treasure Island* in this story, which was Stevenson's longest adventure narrative to date and his first use of first-person narrative. The isolated and mystified narrator and menacing clues and hints in the early chapters of the two works are similar; the Carbonari are initially as sinister and exotic as pirates; and the besieged pavilion on the links looks forward to the besieged stockade on Treasure Island. Another parallel is the improbable happy ending, in which professed villains turn out to be rather good people after all. Northmour surely differs from Long John Silver, but he is the first of a long line of mixed hero-villains in Stevenson's fiction, including Long John, Henry Jekyll, Alan Breck Stuart in *Kidnapped,* Richard III in *The Black Arrow: A Tale of the Two Roses* (1888), and the Master of Ballantrae.

Reviews of *New Arabian Nights* were generally enthusiastic. George Saintsbury, writing in the *Pall Mall Gazette,* praised the author's "excellent faculty of description," his "fertility of extravagant incident," and his "humour in the construction of character." On the other hand, he complained of "the introduction of irrelevant details" and argued that several stories are "hastily and inartistically wound up." The *Saturday Review* similarly thought that the stories "lack finish and care" and regretted "the curiously ill-judged burlesque ending" of volume one, with Prince Florizel reduced to a tobacconist, "pulling down the whole fabric of splendour and knightly valour which he has raised for our delight." But this is a basically positive review: it compares Stevenson to Alexandre Dumas *père,* thinks "nothing could be more exciting than 'The Pavilion on the Links,' " and believes that all the stories have "a touch of genius." The *Spectator* claimed that Stevenson is actually better than Dumas because he has a sense of humor and found the stories "perfect in form and finish" and "a fresh departure in romance-writing." Only the *Westminster Review* was entirely negative, complaining about everything from "a certain haziness of expression" to "the morbid tone which more or less runs through all the stories," concluding, "they much too nearly resemble glorified and mundane 'Penny Dreadfuls.' "

The period from the middle of 1882 to August 1887 was an unusually calm one for Stevenson and his family. From September 1882 to the summer of 1884 they lived in the south of France. The climate and his new domestic situation were both agreeable, and his writing progressed impressively, focusing for the first time on long fictional narratives including *Treasure Island, The Black Arrow,* and *Prince Otto: A Romance* (1885). But his health remained precarious, and in the summer of 1884 concern about a local outbreak of cholera persuaded the Stevensons

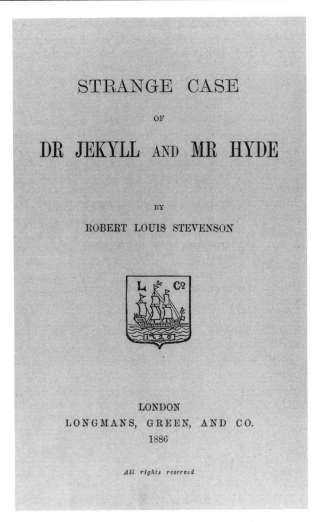

Title page for Stevenson's best-known novella (Special Collections, Thomas Cooper Library, University of South Carolina)

to move to Bournemouth, a resort city on the south coast of England, where in April 1885 his father bought them an attractive house with an ocean view as a belated wedding present. Fanny and her mother-in-law filled the house with antiques, and Stevenson was, at thirty-five, for the first time in something like normal upper-middle-class circumstances: a married householder with a family about him and a certain level of professional recognition. For the first time he could welcome friends beneath his own comfortable roof with a wife by his side, and prominent among these friends were Henley and James. *Deacon Brodie,* Stevenson's and Henley's first play, had been performed with some success in several British theaters, culminating in a short London run at the Prince's Theater in July 1884, just before the Stevensons' return from France. In the fall of 1884 and the winter of 1885 the two men worked on several other plays – *Admiral Guinea,*

Beau Austin, and *Macaire* – all of which were privately printed by Henley as a step toward eventual performance, though no theater director could be persuaded to produce any of them until the 1890s, and they were not successful then. The acquaintance with James had begun because in December 1884 Stevenson had published in *Longman's Magazine* "A Humble Remonstrance," a critical essay that championed fictional romance by disagreeing with James's classic essay "The Art of Fiction," published in the same magazine three months earlier. The argument was handled in such an amiable manner that it led to a correspondence, which continued through the end of Stevenson's life, and to frequent visits by James to Skerryvore, the name the Stevensons gave their Bournemouth house.

These were the years when Stevenson first became a popular and financially successful author. *Treasure Island* appeared late in 1883. No novels were published in 1885, but the short story "The Body Snatcher" came out that December in the Christmas issue of *Pall Mall Magazine,* and 1885 saw three books published: *A Child's Garden of Verses* in March, *More New Arabian Nights: The Dynamiter* in April, and the novel *Prince Otto* in November. The year 1886 marks Stevenson's final establishment as a popular writer, since in January *Strange Case of Dr. Jekyll and Mr. Hyde* was published in London by Longmans, Green, and in New York by Scribners; then in July Cassell and Scribners published British and American editions of the extremely popular novel *Kidnapped.*

"The Body Snatcher," the first of the new short fictions, had been written in the summer of 1881, shortly before *Treasure Island,* but its author never liked it, considering it "horrid" and only publishing it because he owed a story to the *Pall Mall Gazette* and did not have anything else available. He insisted on having his fee reduced from forty to thirty pounds because of the story's low merit and never reprinted it in any collection of his short fiction. The story is actually fairly effective but also rather gruesome and not particularly original. It begins in the parlor of a public house in a small English town, where four men, including the narrator and an "old drunken Scotsman" named Fettes, gather every night to pass the time. "One dark winter night" a wealthy member of Parliament is taken sick on the road and is brought to the public house, where an eminent London physician, Dr. Wolfe Macfarlane, is called in to attend him. Fettes recognizes Macfarlane as the companion of his youth and reveals that many years ago they had both been what might now be called lab assistants in the anat-

omy classes of the University of Edinburgh medical school. There they habitually bought cadavers from suspicious characters who were almost certainly murderers selling the bodies of their victims. They also stole bodies from graves, and one dark and stormy night they dug up a body that terrified them because it was not what they were expecting. The two grave robbers are more surprised by the conclusion than the reader is, and the gothic machinery is fairly shopworn, but the double life of Macfarlane, a respected London physician with a secret criminal past, obviously looks forward to that other London physician, Dr. Henry Jekyll.

More New Arabian Nights: The Dynamiter is a collection of interrelated stories written collaboratively by Stevenson and his wife and published as a volume without prior serialization in periodicals. The book begins in London, "The Baghdad of the West," with a "Prologue of the Cigar Divan," in which Prince Florizel welcomes three impecunious young gentlemen – Challoner, Somerset, and Desborough – to his cigar store on Rupert Street. There they all realize, like many young men in Stevenson's fiction, that their gentlemanly educations have prepared them for no gainful employment. "The fact is," says Desborough, "that I am waiting for something to turn up." In the newspaper they spot an advertisement of a £200 reward for "information on the whereabouts of a man observed the previous day near Green Park wearing a sealskin coat," and given this impetus they decide to become detectives.

The rest of the book consists of the three narratives of their separate but coincidentally interrelated adventures, plus four tales told to them by characters they meet during the course of these adventures. Only one of these latter tales-within-tales, "Zero's Tale of the Explosive Bomb," is attributed solely to Stevenson by Swearingen. Two other tales-within-tales, "The Destroying Angel" and "The Fair Cuban," Swearingen attributes solely to Fanny, while he believes everything else to be a collaborative effort. "The Destroying Angel" interestingly anticipates the Mormon subplot of Doyle's *A Study in Scarlet* (1888), not published until three years later, and the whole book anticipates the interest in anarchist bomb threats by Joseph Conrad, H. G. Wells, and G. K. Chesterton a few years later. Zero, Stevenson's philosophical terrorist, bears a certain resemblance to later literary anarchists and nihilists and to the earlier president of the Suicide Club, but his immediate cause is Irish independence, and the subtitle of the book, *The Dynamiter,* cashed in on current outrage over Fenian bombings. After many adventures, coincidences, and embedded tales, Zero finally blows himself up by mistake in a London railroad station. The book then concludes with an "Epilogue of the Cigar Divan," in which the three young men return to tell Prince Florizel their adventures. One of them, Desborough, has married the beautiful (and now penitent) young woman who has figured in all of the adventures as Zero's assistant and as the narrator of "The Destroying Angel" and "The Fair Cuban."

Surprisingly, in view of her insistence on the importance of allegory in her husband's writing, Fanny's two stories are simple damsel-in-distress romances, while the stories to which he contributed show considerable comic elements and far more philosophical debate about the morality of terrorism, with Zero making extreme claims and contradicting himself at every turn. The epilogue includes a long lecture from Prince Florizel to the new Mrs. Desborough on the evils of her former life, which had endangered women and children, and a reconciliation of the young woman with her mother, who had been Somerset's aristocratic landlady. The Arabian narrator makes only one perfunctory appearance in a footnote to the prologue. The debates about terrorist ethics sound a bit like the arguments between François Villon and the Sire de Brisetout in "A Lodging for the Night," and Prince Florizel is at best a questionable structural device.

A much more successful work of short fiction is the novella *The Strange Case of Dr. Jekyll and Mr. Hyde,* but its success has led to oft-lamented distortions in its many adaptations for stage and screen. Stevenson himself was already complaining about this process in 1887 when Thomas Sullivan's stage adaptation was playing to packed houses in England and the United States. Since that time Elaine Showalter has counted more than seventy adaptations for film and television, including major film versions starring John Barrymore (1920), Fredric March (1932), and Spencer Tracy (1941). Almost everyone seems to have heard of the story, and many have viewed it, but relatively few have read it. As with such other nineteenth-century fictions as Mary Shelley's *Frankenstein* (1818) and Bram Stoker's *Dracula* (1897), this has led to widespread misconceptions about the novel's message and even its plot – in part because all the major film productions include romantic interests conspicuously absent from Stevenson's novella.

As Stevenson wrote the story, there are at least four narrative voices, all representing middle-aged professional men. Most of the story is told by an omniscient narrator who focuses on the doings

and thoughts of Dr. Jekyll's friend and attorney, Gabriel John Utterson. Utterson's friend, the "well-known man about town" Richard Enfield, provides the second narrative voice, as he tells Utterson about the night when, returning home at three o'clock one morning, he saw "a little man" named Hyde trample on a young girl and then placate the hostile crowd that gathers by unlocking a nearby door and returning with ten pounds in gold and a check for ninety pounds signed by a man who is "the pink of proprieties, celebrated too."

Enfield assumes that the celebrated man is being blackmailed, and since Utterson has recently been asked by Dr. Henry Jekyll to draw up a will leaving his entire estate to Mr. Edward Hyde, he knows that it is Jekyll who has signed the check and becomes worried that Hyde may kill his benefactor in order to inherit this considerable estate. When Hyde is identified the following October as the murderer of Sir Danvers Carew, M.P., Utterson confronts Jekyll with the question of whether or not he is hiding the murderer, and Jekyll shows him a letter from Hyde expressing regret for his actions and saying that he has gone where he is safe. Later that night Utterson compares this letter with a note from Jekyll and, realizing that the handwriting is essentially the same, concludes only that Jekyll has forged Hyde's letter. The following January he is entrusted with another letter by Jekyll's former friend Dr. Lanyon, marked "not to be opened until the death or disappearance of Dr. Henry Jekyll." Then, one evening in March, Utterson is summoned to Dr. Jekyll's house by the butler, who believes that Hyde has murdered his benefactor and is hiding in the doctor's laboratory. Utterson and the butler break down the door to find that Hyde has just taken poison and is in his death throes, strangely dressed in Jekyll's clothes, which are too big for him. Searching for the corpse of Dr. Jekyll, Utterson and the butler find only a sealed envelope containing a narrative of Dr. Jekyll's secret life.

"Dr. Lanyon's Narrative" and "Dr. Jekyll's Final Statement of the Case" then constitute the last two chapters of the story, adding the final two narrative voices. Lanyon describes how, following the instructions in a letter from Jekyll, he helped Hyde get chemicals from Jekyll's laboratory and then received the shock of his life when the chemicals transformed Hyde into Jekyll. Jekyll's own statement of the case is more like the story familiar to filmgoers, relating the discovery of the drug that turns the repressed, middle-aged Jekyll into the younger, spontaneous Hyde and how the process of turning into Hyde became progressively easier – fi-

Stevenson (center) surrounded by family and servants at Vailima in Tahiti. He is flanked by his stepson, Lloyd Osbourne, and his wife, Fanny.

nally requiring no drug at all – while the process of turning back into Jekyll became progressively harder, finally becoming impossible in the last days of Jekyll/Hyde's life.

When Stevenson first read his manuscript to Fanny and Lloyd, she objected that it had failed to develop its allegorical potential, being – as Lloyd later remembered her words – "merely a story – a magnificent bit of sensationalism – when it should have been a masterpiece." Stevenson then burned the original manuscript and rewrote the story in its present form, presumably making it less a shilling shocker and more a philosophical inquiry into the dual nature of humanity. Publication was delayed until January 1886 to avoid competition with the previous month's Christmas stories, and reviewers were uniformly enthusiastic. An unsigned review in the London *Times* on 25 January complimented Stevenson for being "far deeper" than Edgar Allan Poe and equaling the moral vision of George Eliot but

"with no formal preaching." In the 9 January issue of the *Saturday Review* Andrew Lang had already made the comparison with Poe and saw evidence of Stevenson's skill in creating "a wild tragedy" out of the unpromising lives of "successful middle-aged professional men" living "in the most ordinary and respectable quarters of London." James Ashcroft Noble, writing in the 23 January issue of the *Academy,* thought the book's "impressiveness as a parable" was "equal to its fascination as a work of art" and declared it "worthy of Hawthorne." By 6 February *Punch* was running a parody about Dr. Trekyl and Mr. Hidanseek, and by April the *Contemporary Review* was suggesting that Stevenson's little book might even be better than Hawthorne's *The Marble Faun* because "the parable is deeper, and, we would venture to add, truer." Within six months 40,000 copies were sold in England, and American readers were equally receptive, buying an estimated 250,000 copies by 1900.

In *The French Lieutenant's Woman* (1969) John Fowles's narrator says that "the fact that every Victorian had two minds . . . makes the best guidebook to the age very possibly *Dr. Jekyll and Mr. Hyde*. Behind its latterday Gothick lies a very profound and epoch-revealing truth." It is, at least, Stevenson's most thoroughly analyzed work, with the "allegory" of Jekyll/Hyde's split personality being interpreted in many ways. Hyde can represent the underclass, the repressed id, or some other political or psychological force, depending on the critic's governing assumptions. Recently Elaine Showalter in *Sexual Anarchy: Gender and Culture at the Fin de Siècle* (1990) has seen the book as "a fable of fin-de-siècle homosexual panic, the discovery and resistance of the homosexual self." In this reading Utterson and Enfield fear that Hyde is the proletarian homosexual lover of the wealthy Jekyll, and everyone's visceral loathing of Hyde reflects late-Victorian fear of homosexuality itself. Critics have also made much of the fact that all the men in the story are bachelors and that there are no women characters, a feature first noted in contemporary reviews and interestingly revised by Valerie Martin in her popular and critically admired novel *Mary Reilly* (1991), which retells the story from the point of view of a character not mentioned by Stevenson, Jekyll's maid and romantic admirer, Mary Reilly.

The year 1887 brought many changes for Stevenson. Books continued to be published: *The Merry Men and Other Tales and Fables,* short fiction, in February; *Underwoods,* poetry; and *Memories and Portraits,* an essay collection, later in the year. In May, Thomas Stevenson died, leaving his son three thousand pounds and closing a relationship that had always been intense and frequently difficult. Stevenson's health was so bad during the three weeks he spent in Edinburgh that he could not attend his father's funeral, and in August he closed up Skerryvore and took Fanny, Lloyd, Belle, and his mother to the United States on the cattle ship *Ludgate Hill,* which arrived in New York on 7 September. They passed the autumn and winter in spartan conditions in a small cabin on Saranac Lake in the Adirondacks, where Stevenson was treated again for tuberculosis, this time by the celebrated Dr. E. L. Trudeau. During the extremely cold winter Stevenson continued to write prolifically: a series of essays for *Scribner's Magazine;* the novel *The Wrong Box* (1889), the first of his collaborations with Lloyd; and the initial work on *The Master of Ballantrae.* However, Trudeau decided, as had the physicians at Davos, that Stevenson did not have tuberculosis, so in April – after a violent epistolary quarrel with

Henley, who had slighted one of Fanny's literary efforts – Stevenson left for New York City, where he briefly met with Mark Twain. He then traveled by train to California, where Fanny had gone ahead to look for a rental yacht suitable for an extended cruise in the Pacific.

Although it includes several of his most successful stories, *The Merry Men and Other Tales and Fables* has less unity than Stevenson's other collections of short fiction. Two generally admired stories, "The Merry Men" and "Thrawn Janet," deal with superstitions in eighteenth-century Scotland. The rest are set in continental Europe: the impressive "Markheim" and the early fable "Will o' the Mill" in unspecified Germanic locations; "Olalla" in Spain (apparently during the Napoleonic Wars); and "The Treasure of Franchard" in modern France. The tone of the collection is similarly diverse, ranging from the placidity of "Will o the Mill" and the comic irony of "The Treasure of Franchard" to the gothicism of "Thrawn Janet" and "Olalla."

The title story of this collection, written in 1881 and originally published in the *Cornhill Magazine* in June and July 1882, deals with the familiar theme of buried treasure and with the conflict between rational and superstitious attitudes. The setting is the Hebrides, and the "Merry Men" of the title are a group of loud and dangerous coastal breakers that make a noise like laughter. The protagonist and narrator, Charles Darnaway, has long heard and doubted local stories about a sunken galleon from the Spanish Armada, but his historical research at the University of Edinburgh has uncovered evidence that a galleon may indeed lie submerged near the island farm where he lives with his uncle Gordon and his cousin Mary Ellen. Gordon, on the other hand, is preoccupied with the more recent sinking of another ship and with a bogle who has haunted him ever since. The plot is complicated and a bit contrived; it concludes with storms, another shipwreck, and the drowning of the finally deranged Gordon Darnaway. Stevenson wrote to Colvin in July 1881 saying that he liked this tale "above all my other attempts at story-telling" and predicting that he would have future success by working in the same direction. That direction – eighteenth-century adventure stories with first-person narrators and shipboard dangers – led him both to *Treasure Island* and *Kidnapped,* but Fanny later claimed that her husband was not finally satisfied with "The Merry Men," regarding it as an overall failure despite its success in conveying the terror of the sea.

"Thrawn Janet," written in June 1881 in Scotland and published in the October 1881 issue of the

Cornhill Magazine, consists of a brief, neutral introduction in English and then the tale itself, told in Scots by a superstitious narrator – an unnamed member of the parish of Balweary, where for fifty years the Reverend Murdoch Soulis has been minister of the kirk and an object of terror to all the local people. The title character is Janet M'Clour, the old housekeeper of the manse, who is widely suspected of being the devil's familiar. These suspicions are based on her youthful indiscretions with a dragoon, her not having received communion for thirty years, and her habit of wandering around mumbling to herself at night. The story could easily have become an attack on rural superstition and the paranoid persecution of eccentric old women, and this is in fact the view taken by Mr. Soulis when he first comes to Balweary, "fu' o' book-learnin' an' grand at the exposition, but, as was natural in sae young a man, wi' nae leevin experience in religion." At the recommendation of the local laird and despite the warnings of his parishioners, he hires Janet as his housekeeper, but on the terrible night of 17 August 1712, amid thunder and rain, Mr. Soulis sees sights that convince him she is a witch – a discovery that turns him into the "bleak faced old man, dreadful to his hearers" that he is when the story is narrated. This tale seems to owe a good deal to Hawthorne, but it lacks the studied ambiguity of, for example, "Young Goodman Brown" (1835).

"Markheim," the other well-known story in the volume, is more reminiscent of Poe or Fyodor Dostoyevsky. Similar to Raskolnikov in Dostoyevsky's *Crime and Punishment* (1866), Markheim begins his story by murdering a pawnbroker and ends by confessing his crime and surrendering himself to the police. Like the protagonist of Poe's "The Tell-Tale Heart" (1843), his murder confession is caused by a supernatural or hallucinatory experience presumably caused by a guilty conscience. After committing the murder on a rainy Christmas day, Markheim is confronted by a figure who prophesies for him a life of increasing depravity and offers to assist him in another murder. When Markheim, in horror, rejects such help and goes to give himself up, "the features of the visitor began to undergo a wonderful and lovely change," brightening and then fading, mirroring Markheim's redemption and suggesting that the apparition was his alter ego rather than Satan.

The even more gothic "Olalla" was originally published in the Christmas 1885 issue of *Court and Society Review* and is narrated by its protagonist, a British soldier who has been wounded while fighting for Spain and is sent to recuperate in a "residencia" in the mountains, where a once-great family in reduced circumstances is willing to take him as a paying lodger. The family consists of a young woman named Olalla; her brother, Felipe; and their mother. Felipe is a Pan-like primitive, full of animal grace and apparent innocence, who suddenly shows his hidden brutality by catching a squirrel and torturing it. Felipe's mother, who combines "an expression of almost imbecile goodhumour" with "a perfectness of feature and a quiet nobility of attitude," similarly reveals herself by a sudden act to be some sort of vampire. Olalla herself is beautiful, intelligent, and devout, but, like Poe's Roderick Usher, she belongs to a doomed house and dares not produce a new generation. She and the narrator are in love, but she eventually persuades him to leave. Seeing her "leaning on the crucifix," he concludes "that pleasure is not an end but an accident; that pain is the choice of the magnanimous."

"The Treasure of Franchard" strikes a very different note. It was begun in Scotland, finished in France, where it takes place, and originally published in *Longman's Magazine* in April 1883. It is an old-fashioned long tale of approximately twenty thousand words and divided into eight chapters, covering several months in the lives of Dr. Desprez; his wife, Anastasie; and Jean-Marie, a young boy who has been an acrobat and a thief before becoming the doctor's stableboy, disciple, and eventual foster son. The story is set in the forest of Fontainebleau, where the doctor philosophizes, works daily and ineffectually on his *Comparative Pharmacopia, or Historical Dictionary of All Medicines,* and one day, in the gorges of Franchard, discovers a treasure consisting of monastery plate and a "very heavy" casket looted and hidden during the Hundred Years' War. The story treats the doctor with gentle irony throughout. He imagines himself to be a model of Gallic rationalism but is in fact logically inconsistent and is more or less crazed by the thought of his newfound wealth. On the other hand, he is contrasted favorably with his brother-in-law, Casimir, a pragmatic, cynical businessman. Anastasie has her brother's common sense and her husband's benevolence, and Jean-Marie actually becomes the hero of the story since he "steals" the treasure, which he sees is destroying Desprez's happiness, and returns it at the end of the story when an earthquake and unfortunate stock-market fluctuations have reduced the doctor to poverty, making the Franchard treasure a necessity rather than a luxury. The story reflects Stevenson's abiding interest in buried treasure; it also shows his affection for what he saw as the French character and for the forest of Fontaine-bleau, where he had spent happy days and fallen in love with Fanny.

Stevenson had ambivalent views about this volume as a whole, and reviews, as with most of his short fiction, were also mixed. The *Athenaeum* admired "Mr. Stevenson's precise attention to style" and basically liked "The Treasure of Franchard" but dismissed "Markheim" as "a horrible study of a murderer's mind" and condemned the conclusion of "The Merry Men": "The story, indeed, seems to collapse, and the reader almost feels that he has been interested only to be made a fool of." Altogether, the reviewer believes that "it may be a matter for serious doubt whether any of the six tales . . . will live even twenty years." R. H. Hutton, writing in the *Spectator,* disliked "Thrawn Janet" and "Will o' the Mill" but thought "Markheim" worthy of Hawthorne, "The Merry Men" a match for Sir Walter Scott, and "The Treasure of Franchard" the best of all. An entirely laudatory review came from the *Nation,* which proclaimed – in words that sound odd today – that "for grip of the vitals of humanity he is George Eliot's successor and only peer."

"The Misadventures of John Nicholson," another of Stevenson's uncollected short fictions, was written at Skerryvore and published in Cassell's Christmas annual *Yuletide* in December 1887 when its author was at Saranac Lake. While it has a certain autobiographical interest and repeats themes that recur throughout Stevenson's work, its author told James that it was "silly" – a judgment many readers will share. John Nicholson, like the young Stevenson, lives in Edinburgh with a stern father who refuses him an allowance and whom he disobeys by frequenting questionable establishments with morally dubious companions. One of these companions persuades him to commit certain imprudent acts, which result in his losing four hundred pounds that had been entrusted to him for deposit in the bank. Unable to bear his father's recriminations, he leaves for California, "borrowing" the funds he finds in his father's unlocked desk. Ten years later, having prospered in speculations on the San Francisco stock exchange but never having written home, John suddenly decides to return to Edinburgh to repay his "loan" and bring about reconciliation with his father. By a malign coincidence, this decision is made when he has again been entrusted with a large sum of money for deposit in a bank, and in his haste he leaves these funds with an unreliable friend. By the time he returns to Edinburgh, John is wanted for embezzlement by the police in San Francisco and manages to add suspicion

of murder to his difficulties before all is finally explained and ends happily.

The last six years of Stevenson's life were spent, far from Edinburgh austerities, on various islands in the Pacific Ocean or sailing about among them on several long cruises. When he and his family rented the ninety-five-foot racing yacht *Casco* in June 1888, their intention had been simply to take a cruise that would enable them to see an interesting new part of the world, to try the effect of sea air on Stevenson's precarious health, and ultimately to return to Europe. The sea air did not do a great deal for his health, but the islands did. As he wrote to Colvin, "the sea is a horrible place, stupifying to the mind and poisonous to the temper . . . but you are amply repaid when you sight an island, and drop anchor in a new world." The first islands sighted were the Marquesas, the wildest part of Polynesia and the setting for Herman Melville's *Typee* (1846) and *Omoo* (1847). One month after leaving San Francisco the passengers could stop reading Edward Gibbon out loud to each other and take stock of a bewilderingly alien world where the natives could speak no European language and had only recently given up the open practice of cannibalism. After some initial nervousness, Stevenson soon began traveling in the interior and loving everything he saw, writing to Colvin, "I did not dream there were such places or such races." He also began to share the islands' athletic way of life, swimming or riding horses for hours each day and gaining strength. The generosity and politeness of the Marquesans made a very favorable impression on the whole Stevenson family, and on one of these islands Stevenson heard the legend that later provided the basis for his story "The Isle of Voices."

After the Marquesas, the *Casco* sailed to Tahiti and then to Hawaii. The stay in Tahiti was prolonged because of repairs required by the yacht and because Stevenson's health took an alarming turn when he contracted a potentially fatal head cold. He recuperated in a remote Tahitian village, where he and his family ran out of money and were generously supported by Princess Moe, the former queen of Raiateia. As his convalescence progressed Stevenson resumed the athletic life he had developed in the Marquesas and completed most of the work remaining on *The Master of Ballantrae.* On Christmas 1888 the *Casco* sailed for Honolulu, where it arrived one month later after a difficult passage. The next five months were spent in a rambling house at Waikiki, where he finally finished *The Master of Ballantrae,* which had already begun serial publication in *Scribner's Magazine,* and worked on revising

Cover for Stevenson's 1893 collection, which includes "The Beach of Falesá," "The Bottle Imp," and "The Isle of Voices"

Lloyd's draft of *The Wrong Box.* Stevenson also got to know King Kalakaua of Hawaii and wrote a pamphlet defending the leper missionary Father Damien from a published attack by a local Presbyterian minister. But none of the Stevensons much liked the Westernized towns of the Pacific; they had been distressed by the "half and halfness" of the Tahitian capital of Papeete and now found Honolulu too American for their tastes. They were consequently delighted to rent the *Equator,* a smaller and less luxurious yacht than the *Casco,* and set off for the South Seas in June 1889; this time Stevenson never returned.

During the voyage of the *Equator* Stevenson and Lloyd began writing their second collaboration, *The Wrecker* (1892), a novel of modern crime and adventure on the Pacific, ending in a fight around a wrecked ship on Midway Island. The *Equator* vis-

ited the Gilbert Islands in Micronesia, where Stevenson became involved in a potentially dangerous situation involving a drunken celebration of the Fourth of July and the king's consequent imposition of a taboo on alcohol. Stevenson was assailed by rock-throwing natives and was sufficiently worried to have his pistols sent ashore, where he was living with the local missionary. This episode may have suggested some of the material in the South Seas story "The Beach of Falesá." On another of the Gilbert Islands, another king allowed Stevenson to stay in a house that he surrounded by a taboo line that could be crossed only by those natives who were assigned as servants to the Europeans. The Stevensons stayed here for two months, during which the *Equator* was off trading among the islands, and the stores had run dangerously low before the ship finally returned. By December 1889 the party finally reached Samoa, which was to be Stevenson's home for most of the five years that remained of his life. Here he was persuaded by Harry Moors, a resident American entrepreneur, to buy more than three hundred acres of jungle land in the highlands of the island of Upolu, three miles from the modern capital of Apia and six hundred feet above sea level. The original idea seems to have been to turn this "bush" into a commercially viable cacao plantation, but instead this estate of Vailima (Samoan for "five streams") became Stevenson's romantic but very expensive tropical approximation of a Scottish Highland castle.

At the time, however, Samoa was just another stop on a cruise. In February 1890 the *Equator* arrived at Sydney, where Stevenson was sick again, and in April the Stevensons resumed their travels, this time on the steamer *Janet Nichol,* for a four-month cruise that took them back to the Gilberts but also to thirty-five other islands they had not seen before. After returning to Sydney for August and September, they went back to Samoa and took up temporary residence in a small cottage on their Vailima estate. In these temporary quarters they were visited by Henry Adams, who, in a letter dated 21 October 1890 to Anne Cabot Mills Lodge, described "a very dirty wood cabin with a still dirtier man and woman in it, in the middle of several hundred burned tree-stumps." Adams found Stevenson's appearance very peculiar, his mind second-rate, and his way of life appalling; but when the "big house" at Vailima, with its fifty-foot great hall, was completed and filled with the furniture from Thomas Stevenson's Edinburgh house, their way of life was considerably more elegant. Here Stevenson did his best to create a modern feudal estate. He rose at 5:30, had breakfast at 6:00, and then either began writing or joined his kinsmen and Samoan retainers in clearing the land. These retainers ultimately numbered more than twenty and wore as a uniform the Samoan lavalava woven in the Royal Stuart tartan. They were chosen for strength, good looks, and social polish and were all subjected to a code of obedience to Stevenson as laird. At Vailima Stevenson received delegations from Samoan villages and officiated in the rituals of hospitality appropriate to a chief. To the British reading public this all seemed heroic and romantic compared with the world of the London bookmen and also fit in well with the ethos of the New Imperialism, which was then reaching its zenith.

Stevenson's years in the South Pacific resulted in many letters to friends in Europe and the United States; a new travel book, *In the South Seas* (1896); two novels coauthored with Lloyd, *The Wrong Box* and *The Wrecker;* two completed novels, *The Master of Ballantrae* and *Catriona;* two novels left incomplete at his death: *Weir of Hermiston: An Unfinished Romance* (1896) and *St. Ives: Being the Adventures of a French Prisoner in England* (1897); and several works of short fiction. Of these, two long stories – "The Beach at Falesá" and "The Ebb-Tide" (1893), coauthored with Lloyd – deal with Europeans in the South Pacific, while two much shorter stories, "The Bottle Imp" (1891) and "The Isle of Voices" (1893), both deal with superstitions or the supernatural in Hawaii.

Stevenson thought "The Beach of Falesá" the most important of the lot because, as he told Colvin in a letter on 28 September 1891, "It is the first realistic South Sea story. . . . You will know more of the South Seas after you have read my little tale than if you had read a library." Kipling's *Plain Tales from the Hills* (1888) and H. Rider Haggard's *King Solomon's Mines* (1886) had created a vogue for fiction about the New Imperialism in India and Africa, but no one had yet begun to write similar stories about the Pacific. This story is the first of an impressive line of short stories about the South Seas beginning with those of Jack London, who chose to stay in the house occupied by Stevenson while in the Marquesas, and continuing through W. Somerset Maugham – who like Stevenson sets stories in Samoa and Hawaii and mentions Stevenson's grave in "The Pool" – and James A. Michener's *Tales of the South Pacific* (1946). It also looks forward to several short and long fictions by Joseph Conrad, whose chosen geographical focus was, however, the Malay Archipelago.

"The Beach of Falesá" is set on the fictional Polynesian island of Falesá; the "beach" of the title is the white men who live on the beach and buy copra from the interior. The protagonist and narrator, John Wiltshire, arrives in Falesá "sick for white neighbors" after four years on an island near the equator where he had been the only European. Wiltshire's racial attitudes have occasioned a good deal of comment from critics, so it might be helpful to know that in his lexicon "a Negro is counted a white man, and so is a Chinese! A strange idea, but common in the islands." It is the culture of the islands that he detests and, of course, the race that maintains that culture – particularly "getting tabooed" and the loneliness of being an outsider in a unified society. His racism is thus directed only against Polynesians, whom he calls Kanakas, and he looks benevolently on black, yellow, or white men who like him are outsiders in the Polynesian world. Stevenson himself took a much more favorable view of Polynesians, both those he met in travels from Hawaii to Tahiti and those he lived among in Samoa, and he presumably includes Wiltshire's prejudices in the interest of the realism which he claimed for the story.

A rival trader named Case welcomes Wiltshire to Falesá by arranging a bogus marriage with a beautiful young island woman named Uma. Initially focused entirely on her physical charms, Wiltshire is ultimately appalled by the wedding ceremony, with "the odd volume of a novel" masquerading as a prayer book and a certificate saying that Uma "is illegally married to Mr. John Wiltshire for one night, and Mr. John Wiltshire is at liberty to send her to hell next morning." Uma, being illiterate, clearly treasures this certificate, and her happiness leads her new husband to pity and eventually to love her. The whole marriage, however, has been a trick on Wiltshire because Uma is considered taboo, and his being married to her prevents the natives from trading with him. It now also appears that Case has killed one of Wiltshire's predecessors and scared off the other; furthermore, he has convinced everyone that he is in league with the devils that inhabit an abandoned section of the island. Wiltshire's investigations reveal that the "devils" are simply aeolian harps and luminous paint that Case has used to create "supernatural" sounds and sights, and the story then reaches its climax in a nocturnal gunfight between the two white men in this deserted area of jungle, with Case killed and his various dishonest dealings brought to light. The conclusion finds Wiltshire and Uma on another island, where she has put on weight and he wonders confusedly what to do with his daughters: "They're only half-castes, of course; . . . and there's nobody thinks less of half-castes than I do; but they're mine, and about all I've got. I can't reconcile my mind to their taking up with Kanakas, and I'd like to know where I'm to find the whites."

This story was initially found unwholesome by Clarence Shorter, the editor of the *Illustrated London News,* who insisted on various revisions before finally publishing it in the July and August 1892 issues of his magazine. For example, he changed the phrase "one night" in the wedding certificate to "one week" and toned down several examples of profanity. This bowdlerized text was then used when the story was collected in *Island Nights' Entertainment; Consisting of the Beach of Falesá, The Bottle Imp, The Isle of Voices* (1893) and frequently reprinted later. The original text is now available, and the whole textual question has now been impressively discussed in Menikoff's *Robert Louis Stevenson and "The Beach of Falesá": A Study in Victorian Publishing with the Original Text* (1984). The story has moreover suffered from comparisons made by David Daiches and Peter Gilmour with Conrad's "Heart of Darkness" (1899). Both stories involve white imperialists in tropical environments that provide temptations not normally encountered in Europe, and both stories are told by unreliable, obtuse, racist narrators who go on dangerous voyages into the jungle and manage to return safely. Stevenson's story, for all its South Pacific realism, seems superficial in vision and amateurish in technique compared to Conrad's masterpiece, as does much of the rest of Conrad's own fiction. But of course Conrad's story had not been written yet and may actually owe a certain debt to Stevenson's well-known earlier story.

The two stories dealing with Polynesian superstitions drew on Stevenson's long-standing interest in stories of the supernatural, but they are not "crawlers" like "Thrawn Janet" or "The Body Snatcher," in part because the Polynesian stories both end happily. "The Bottle Imp" was apparently written sometime in 1889, perhaps in Hawaii, and originally published in the New York *Herald* from February to March 1891. Its source is not Polynesian but German – Stevenson found it in a melodrama, *The Bottle Imp,* written by Richard Brinsley Peele from German folk sources and first performed in 1828 – but it was adapted for a Polynesian audience by setting most of it on Hawaii and Tahiti and by making the major characters Hawaiian. The story deals with a magic bottle: "the glass of it was white like milk, with changing rainbow colors in the grain. Withinsides something obscurely moved, like

a shadow and a fire." Whoever owns the bottle can have almost all his wishes granted, but the bottle cannot prolong life, and if the owner should die still in possession of the bottle, he must burn in hell forever. The two conditions for selling the bottle are that the sale price must be lower than the purchase price and that all of this information must be fully explained to the buyer.

The story begins when a Hawaiian named Keawe buys the bottle for fifty dollars in San Francisco; gains wealth, a great house, and a beautiful wife; and then sells the bottle at a loss. But when he contracts leprosy, he has to buy the bottle back again to gain a cure; and since this time the purchase price was only two cents, he goes through great difficulties in trying to sell it even at a loss since the next owner will have to buy it for one cent and will presumably be stuck with it. Eventually Keawe manages to unload it on a drunken sailor in Tahiti, and he lives happily ever after with his wife, Kokua. With Stevenson's help, an Anglican missionary in Apia translated this story into Samoan, with the result that literal-minded Samoan visitors to Vailima often asked, somewhat nervously, to see the bottle. They also dubbed Stevenson "Tusitala" (storyteller), a name later given to one of the four collected editions of his works, but this was the only one of his stories that they actually knew.

"The Isle of Voices" is more legitimately a Polynesian tale, since it was apparently based on a legend that Stevenson had heard from the French consul in the Marquesas. It was written at Vailima in 1892 and published in four weekly installments in the *National Observer* in February 1893. It is set on the Hawaiian island of Molokai, where Father Damien had worked with lepers, and deals with the conflict between Keola, a young man who is "an idle dog," and his father-in-law, Kalamake, a sorcerer. After discovering the secret of his father-in-law's magic, Keola tries to blackmail the old man into getting him a concertina. This rather frivolous demand causes the sorcerer to assume enormous size, take Keola to the middle of the ocean, and leave him there. After various adventures Keola swims ashore on the Isle of Voices, where he falls among cannibals who fatten him up for a future feast, but he solves all of his problems when he realizes that the voices of the island are those of invisible sorcerers, including Kalamake, who come here to work magic. Keola tricks the cannibals into fighting with the wizards, and while all of his enemies are fully engaged he escapes from the island, leaving his terrible father-in-law trapped there.

In 1893 these three stories were collected as *Island Nights' Entertainments* and published in April to generally favorable reviews. The reviewer for *Black and White* praised the book's verisimilitude: "As you read you become (I swear) sun-burned and weather-beaten." He particularly admires the "altogether delightful" Uma because "Mr. Stevenson is not usually fortunate with his female characters" but finds that the other two stories "leave one comparatively cold." Lionel Johnson's review in *Academy* argues that Stevenson's combination of human sympathy and mastery of prose style have enabled him to capture the Pacific as memorably as Joseph Addison captured Queen Anne's London. The public agreed, and this collection sold far more copies than *The Merry Men*.

While immersed in Polynesian lore and surroundings, Stevenson had not forgotten Britain, where most of his late novels are set. One short story from this period is at least as intensely Scottish as "The Isle of Voices" is Polynesian. "Black Andie's Tale of Tod Lapraik" is told to David Balfour in *Catriona* by Black Andie Dale, one of the Highland kidnappers who have imprisoned him on a small rocky island called the Bass. Like "Thrawn Janet" and "The Body Snatcher," this story is prefaced by a realistic description of a possibly superstitious primary narrator; in this case David gives an English description of Andie, who then narrates the main story in Scots, the same linguistic dichotomy that Stevenson had employed in "Thrawn Janet." Andie has heard most of the story from his father, Tom Dale, though he was present himself as a small boy at the climax. The story's main events take place in 1706, when Tom is employed as keeper of the Bass, a job for which his primary competitor had been Tod Lapraik, a man who professed piety but sometimes went into mysterious trances from which it was difficult to awaken him. During these trances it is suspected that Tod's spirit takes various forms and travels about doing evil. One such form, seen dancing maniacally on top of the Bass, is shot with a silver bullet; at that very moment, back on the mainland, Tod Lapraik falls down dead in the middle of one of his trances, and an autopsy discovers a silver bullet. Like "Thrawn Janet" and "The Body Snatcher," this story can be read as a tale of demon possession or a story of Scottish superstition, though its placement approximately in the middle of a realistic historical novel makes it a very different reading experience. Emma Letley, in her *Oxford World Classics* edition of *Kidnapped and Catriona,* compares it to Scott's "Wandering Willie's Tale," also a tale of the supernatural told in Scots by a possibly unreliable narrator in the middle of a realistic historical novel, in this case *Redgauntlet* (1824). The fact that Stevenson was working almost simultaneously on Polynesian and Scottish short stories parallels the fact that he wrote longer fictions set in both locations during these years and that the whole Vailima enterprise was itself an odd combination of Polynesia and the Scottish Highlands.

"The Ebb-Tide" resembles a Conrad story in that part of it takes place on a difficult sailing trip across the Pacific. The first section, "A Trio," begins "on the beach" at Tahiti, where three disreputable Anglo-Saxons have been brought by their vices to wonder about the source of their next meal. Robert Herrick has studied at Oxford but has been thrown into the world by his father's bankruptcy. He has drifted through a series of unsuccessful clerkships in the United States and finally changed his name and spent his last dollar on a ticket to Tahiti, with only a tattered volume of Virgil as a link to his past. John Davis is a disguised American former ship captain whose ship had sunk with the loss of six lives when he was drunk; Huish, the third man, is a "vulgar and bad hearted Cockney clerk" who has managed to alienate almost everyone on Tahiti, "for he was wholly vile." These three unpromising characters get a chance to redeem themselves when the schooner *Farallone,* bound for Sydney, sails into Papeete after losing the captain and all officers to smallpox. In desperation, the American consul offers the ship to Davis, who signs on his two friends as officers and promptly sails off for Peru to sell the cargo, champagne, on the black market. The journey fails because Davis stays drunk on the champagne, and most of the cargo turns out to be bottled water. (The ship's original voyage had apparently been a scheme of insurance fraud.)

In "A Quartette," the novella's second section, the *Farallone* comes across an uncharted island presided over by an aristocratic muscular Christian named Attwater — six feet, four inches tall, with "an eye that bid you beware of the man's devastating anger." Attwater and his Polynesian retainers are operating a pearl fishery whose sole contact with the outside world is the schooner *Trinity Hall,* named after Attwater's old Cambridge college and currently absent on a trip to Sydney. Davis and Huish soon decide to kill Attwater and seize his property; Attwater kills Huish instead and gives Davis and Herrick a chance to repent and redeem themselves, which is where the story ends. Stevenson originally planned to continue the narrative but was persuaded that it already worked as a novella and brought it out in a slim volume in 1894. The character of Attwater is surely the most interesting

An illustration for "The Bottle Imp" in Island
Nights' Entertainments

aspect of the story. He is a harsh but just, devout, and benevolent imperialist with superhuman strength, impeccable manners, and considerable common sense. Far more than John Wiltshire, he presented the kind of image that many of the readers of the 1890s wanted to have of their empire builders. Like the heroes of Conrad's *Lord Jim* (1900) and *Victory* (1915), he is a wellborn European who rules over an isolated group of natives in the East. Like various British imperialists in Maugham's stories or later pulp fiction, he dresses formally for dinner in the wilds. He has real, historical counterparts – Gen. Charles "Chinese" Gordon and Sir James Brooke, the "White Rajah" of Sarawak, have been suggested. Except for his orthodox theology and physical strength, he may have been much like the image that Stevenson had of himself among his uniformed Polynesian retainers on Vailima.

Reviewers, however, were not particularly positive. The *Saturday Review* granted that most pages "clearly reveal the creative genius and literary craftsmanship of Mr. Stevenson" but complained

that "the final scene falls somewhat flat" and "the story is by no means a model of design nor a good example of the art of cumulative construction." Writing in the *Star,* Richard Le Gallienne criticized the "air of unreality" created by the characters, especially "the insufferable, impossible Attwater" and the "literary daintiness" of Herrick, with his tattered volume of Virgil. The reviewer for the *Speaker* expressed "woeful disappointment to have to descend" to *The Ebb-Tide* after "the inimitable distinction of style and tone" of *Catriona*. But Le Gallienne admitted that the book included "as thrilling a piece of narrative as Mr. Stevenson has written," and the *Speaker* granted the strength of the story while lamenting "the unutterably loathesome material" of which it was constructed. The most favorable review came from Israel Zangwill, a distinguished writer of realistic short stories about the Jewish neighborhoods of London. Writing in the New York *Critic* on 24 November 1894, he hailed "this little masterpiece" about "the romance of the modern." Lamenting only the book's exotic South Seas setting, he concludes, "It will be an eternal pity if a writer like Stevenson passes away without having once applied his marvellous gifts of vision and sympathy to the reproduction and transfiguration of every-day human life, if he is content to play perpetually with wrecks and treasures and islands, and to be remembered as an exquisite artist in the abnormal."

Stevenson's death nine days after this review appeared guaranteed, however, that this was how he would be remembered. After many years of extremely precarious health he seemed finally to have found the right climate and way of life in Samoa, so his sudden death caught everyone by surprise on 3 December 1894, shortly after his forty-fourth birthday. He had spent the day, apparently in fine health, working on *Weir of Hermiston* but began to complain of head pains in the late afternoon and died of a cerebral hemorrhage several hours later. His romantic burial, with Samoan retainers hacking a trail through the jungle and hauling the casket draped in the Union Jack to the top of Mount Vaea, completed the romantic image Zangwill regretted, and this image remained intact – carefully guarded by his mother, his widow, and her children – for about a quarter century. Previously unpublished works were posthumously published, and the first collected edition, Colvin's Edinburgh Edition in twenty-eight volumes, was completed by 1898. The two-volume hagiographic "official" biography, *The Life of Robert Louis Stevenson* by Stevenson's cousin Graham Balfour, appeared in 1901, and Stevenson shrines were established at Vailima and elsewhere.

Among the posthumous publications which began to appear almost immediately after Stevenson's death and have continued crop up for almost a century were a substantial number of short fictions. In addition to the twenty *Fables* which Colvin published in 1896, seven pieces of Stevenson's short fiction have appeared since his death, including juvenilia and fragments. "The Plague Cellar," for example, may have been written when Stevenson was thirteen: it deals, in precocious but adolescent fashion, with a fanatical seventeenth-century Covenanter, a legendary curse, a secret chamber, and a possibly unreliable narrator. When Stevenson learned in Samoa that a cousin in Edinburgh had found this boyish manuscript, he wrote that he "would rather perish unmourned than allow" it "to appear . . . under any pretense." It was, however, published in 1989 in Kenneth Gelder's *Robert Louis Stevenson: The Scottish Stories and Essays*. Three fragmentary short fictions also eventually appeared in print. "Edifying Letters of the Rutherford Family" is an epistolary work mirroring Stevenson's reli-

gious conflict with his father. The senior Rutherford is presented with remarkable sympathy and the story seems promising, but it ends part of the way into the fourth letter, perhaps because Stevenson did not know what to do with the conflict once he had outlined it. This story and "An Old Song" were edited for publication in 1882 by Roger Swearingen. "Diogenes in London" and "Diogenes at the Savile Club" are very slight satires on detectives and the London literary scene. They were presumably written in the early 1880s and intended as chapters in a larger work but were first published individually in 1920 and 1921.

Three more substantial works of posthumously published short fiction are "The Waif Woman," "When the Devil Was Well," and "The Enchantress." "The Waif Woman" was written in Samoa and intended by Stevenson for inclusion in *Island Nights' Entertainments* but first published in *Scribner's Magazine* in December 1914. Its medieval Icelandic setting qualified it for a book about islands but would have been anomalous in a volume otherwise dealing entirely with modern Polynesia. The story is a morality tale about greed and the wiles by which a willful wife gets her weak husband to violate his conscience, with disastrous results for all concerned. "When the Devil Was Well" was written in 1875 and is a romantic love story set in the Italian Renaissance. In its historical setting, conflict between chivalry and cynicism, swordplay, hair's-breadth escapes, and happy ending, this early tale resembles "The Sire de Maletroit's Door" or *The Black Arrow*. It was first published by the Bibliophile Society in 1921. The most recent addition to Stevenson's posthumous short fiction (and perhaps the last) is "The Enchantress," first published in the *Georgia Review* in 1989. According to Osbourne, Stevenson wrote the story while aboard ship in the Pacific, presumably in 1888 or 1889, but its mood is that of the Arabian Nights stories of several years earlier. A desperate young man who has just gambled away his last funds at a French casino approaches a beautiful young heiress for a loan and is invited to marry her instead. The young woman has her lawyers draw up a marriage settlement giving her husband only a modest allowance, mysteriously leads him to Edinburgh for the wedding ceremony, and then immediately disappears. In a final scene, her lawyer explains to the groom that, by the terms of her father's will, the young lady only gained control of her fortune when she married and that Scotland was chosen for the wedding because "it's quiet, . . . and then there are great facilities for divorce." These last three stories, while not likely to substantially improve Stevenson's reputation as a short-story writer, at least bear comparison with many that he published in his own lifetime.

The veneration which followed Stevenson's death was not, of course, permanent. In 1914 Frank Swinnerton's *R. L. Stevenson: A Critical Study* began the process of reducing Stevenson's literary stature, and biographical works by J. A. Steuart (1924) and George Hellman (1925) undermined his image as a secular saint by digging up, often on slim evidence, scandals from his bohemian youth. The experience of World War I did even more to convince many people that Stevensonian romanticism was either silly or dangerous, though such romanticism continued to be popular with the general reading public, as evinced by the continued sales of his books; the popularity in the interwar years of such Stevensonian writers as Doyle, Quiller-Couch, John Buchan, and Neil Munro; and the vigorous defense of his work by G. K. Chesterton (1927). However, Stevenson has been almost excluded from the academic canon, despite significant and generally positive biographies by J. C. Furnas (1951), James Pope Hennessy (1974), Jenni Calder (1980), Ian Bell (1993), and Frank McLynn (1993) and admiring critical studies, particularly those by Daiches (1947), Robert Kiely (1965), Edwin M. Eigner (1966), and Menikoff (1984). While no short story by Stevenson is currently included in such standard works as the *Norton Anthology of English Literature,* the 1990s have seen "complete" editions of his short fiction by Peter Stoneley (1991) and Bell (1993) and Menikoff's selection *Tales from the Prince of Storytellers,* with a substantial introduction making high claims for Stevenson's achievement. The 1994 centennial of Stevenson's death inspired more attention to his work and continued his return to a status more nearly like the one he enjoyed one hundred years before.

Letters:

Vailima Letters: Being Correspondence Addressed by Robert Louis Stevenson to Sidney Colvin, November 1890–October 1894 (1 volume, London: Methuen, 1895; 2 volumes, New York: Scribners, 1902);

The Letters of Robert Louis Stevenson to His Family and Friends, 2 volumes, edited by Sidney Colvin (London: Methuen, 1899; New York: Scribners, 1899);

RLS: Stevenson's Letters to Charles Baxter, edited by De Lancy Ferguson and Marshall Waingrow (New Haven, Conn.: Yale University Press, 1956);

The Letters of Robert Louis Stevenson, 8 volumes projected, edited by Bradford A. Booth and Ernest Mehew (New Haven, Conn.: Yale University Press, 1994–   ).

Bibliographies:

J. H. Slater, *Robert Louis Stevenson: A Bibliography of His Complete Works* (London: Bell, 1914);

W. F. Prideaux, *A Bibliography of the Works of Robert Louis Stevenson,* revised edition, edited and supplemented by Mrs. Luther S. Livingston (London: Hollings, 1918);

George L. McKay, *A Stevenson Library: Catalogue of a Collection of Writings by and about Robert Louis Stevenson Formed by Edwin J. Beinecke,* 6 volumes (New Haven, Conn.: Yale University Press, 1951–1964);

Roger Swearingen, *The Prose Writings of Robert Louis Stevenson: A Guide* (Hamden, Conn.: Archon, 1980).

Biographies:

Graham Balfour, *The Life of Robert Louis Stevenson,* 2 volumes (London: Methuen, 1901);

John A. Steuart, *Robert Louis Stevenson: A Critical Biography,* 2 volumes (Boston: Little, Brown, 1924);

George S. Hellman, *The True Stevenson: A Study in Clarification* (Boston: Little, Brown, 1925);

Janet Adam Smith, *Robert Louis Stevenson* (London: Duckworth, 1937);

J. C. Furnas, *Voyage to Windward: The Life of Robert Louis Stevenson* (New York: Sloane, 1951);

James Pope Hennessy, *Robert Louis Stevenson* (London: Cape, 1974; New York: Simon & Schuster, 1975);

Jenni Calder, *RLS: A Life Study* (London: Hamilton, 1980);

Ian Bell, *Dreams of Exile: Robert Louis Stevenson — A Biography* (New York: Holt, 1993);

Frank McLynn, *Robert Louis Stevenson: A Biography* (New York: Random House, 1993).

References:

Walter Allen, *The Short Story in English* (New York: Oxford University Press, 1981);

Jenni Calder, ed., *Stevenson and Victorian Scotland* (Edinburgh: University of Edinburgh Press, 1981);

G. K. Chesterton, *Robert Louis Stevenson* (London: Hodder & Stoughton, 1927; New York: Dodd, Mead, 1928);

David Daiches, *Robert Louis Stevenson* (Norfolk, Conn.: New Directions, 1947);

Daiches, *Robert Louis Stevenson and His World* (London: Thames & Hudson, 1973);

Edwin M. Eigner, *Robert Louis Stevenson and the Romantic Tradition* (Princeton: Princeton University Press, 1966);

Harry M. Geduld, ed., *The Definitive Dr. Jekyll and Mr. Hyde Companion* (New York: Garland, 1983);

Wendell V. Harris, *British Short Fiction in the Nineteenth Century* (Detroit: Wayne State University Press, 1979);

Robert Kiely, *Robert Louis Stevenson and the Fiction of Adventure* (Cambridge, Mass.: Harvard University Press, 1965);

Emma Letley, Introduction and Notes to Stevenson's *Kidnapped and Catriona* (Oxford: Oxford University Press);

Paul Maixner, ed., *Robert Louis Stevenson: The Critical Heritage* (London: Routledge & Kegan Paul, 1981);

Barry Menikoff, Introduction, *Tales from the Prince of Storytellers* (Evanston, Ill.: Northwestern University Press, 1993);

Menikoff, *Robert Louis Stevenson and "The Beach of Falesá": A Study in Victorian Publishing with the Original Text* (Stanford, Cal.: Stanford University Press, 1984);

Andrew Noble, *Robert Louis Stevenson* (Totowa, N.J.: Barnes & Noble, 1983);

Harold Orel, *The Victorian Short Story: Development and Triumph of a Literary Genre* (Cambridge: Cambridge University Press, 1986);

Irving S. Saposnik, *Robert Louis Stevenson* (New York: Twayne, 1974);

Elaine Showalter, *Sexual Anarchy: Gender and Culture at the Fin de Siècle* (New York: Viking Penguin, 1990);

Frank Swinnerton, *R. L. Stevenson: A Critical Study* (London: Martin Secker, 1914);

William Veeder and Gordon Hirsch, eds., *Dr. Jekyll and Mr. Hyde after One Hundred Years* (Chicago: University of Chicago Press, 1988).

Papers:

The most important collection of Stevenson manuscripts is in the Beinecke Rare Book and Manuscript Library at Yale University. Additional important collections of Stevenson's papers are located at the Harry Elkins Widener Memorial Library at Harvard University; the Firestone Library at Princeton University; the Henry E. Huntington Library in San Marino, California; and the Pierpont Morgan Library in New York.

Edward Thomas

(3 March 1878 – 9 April 1917)

Bruce G. Nims

University of South Carolina at Lancaster

See also the Thomas entries in *DLB 19: British Poets, 1880–1914* and *DLB 98: Modern British Essayists: First Series.*

BOOKS: *The Woodland Life* (Edinburgh & London: Blackwood, 1897);

Horae Solitariae (London: Duckworth, 1902; New York: Dutton, 1902);

Oxford (London: Black, 1903);

Rose Acre Papers (London: Brown Langham, 1904);

Beautiful Wales (London: Black, 1905);

The Heart of England (London: Dent, 1906; London: Dent / New York: Dutton, 1906);

Richard Jefferies, His Life and Work (London: Hutchinson, 1909; Boston: Little, Brown, 1909);

The South Country (London: Dent, 1909; London: Dent / New York: Dutton, 1932);

Windsor Castle (London: Blackie, 1910; Boston: Estes, 1910);

Rest and Unrest (London: Duckworth, 1910; New York: Dutton, 1910);

Feminine Influence on the Poets (London: Secker, 1910; New York: John Lane, 1911);

The Isle of Wight (London: Blackie, 1911);

Light and Twilight (London: Duckworth, 1911);

Maurice Maeterlinck (London: Methuen, 1911; New York: Dodd, Mead, 1911);

Celtic Stories (Oxford: Clarendon Press, 1911; Oxford & New York: Clarendon Press, 1913);

The Tenth Muse (London: Secker, 1911);

Algernon Charles Swinburne, A Critical Study (London: Secker, 1912; New York: Kennerley, 1912);

George Borrow, The Man and His Books (London: Chapman & Hall, 1912; New York: Dutton, 1912);

Lafcadio Hearn (London: Constable, 1912; Boston & New York: Houghton Mifflin, 1912);

Norse Tales (Oxford: Clarendon Press, 1912);

The Icknield Way (London: Constable, 1913; New York: Dutton, 1913);

The Country (London: Batsford, 1913);

Edward Thomas, circa 1917 (photograph by E. O. Hoppé)

The Happy-Go-Lucky Morgans (London: Duckworth, 1913);

Walter Pater, A Critical Study (London: Secker, 1913; New York: Kennerley, 1913);

In Pursuit of Spring (London, Edinburgh, Dublin & New York: Nelson, 1914);

Four-and-Twenty Blackbirds (London: Duckworth, 1915);

The Life of The Duke of Marlborough (London: Chapman & Hall, 1915; New York: Brentano's, n.d.);

Keats (London: Jack, 1916; London: Jack / New
   York: Dodge, 1916);
Six Poems, as Edward Eastaway (Flansham, U.K.:
   Pear Tree Press, 1916);
A Literary Pilgrim in England (London: Methuen,
   1917; New York: Dodd, Mead, 1917);
Poems by Edward Thomas ("Edward Eastaway") (Lon-
   don: Selwyn & Blount, 1917; New York: Holt,
   1917);
Last Poems (London: Selwyn & Blount, 1918);
Collected Poems (London: Selwyn & Blount, 1920;
   New York: Seltzer, 1921; enlarged edition,
   London: Ingpen & Grant, 1928);
Cloud Castle and Other Papers (London: Duckworth,
   1922; New York: Dutton, 1923?);
Two Poems (London: Ingpen & Grant, 1927);
The Last Sheaf, Essays by Edward Thomas (London:
   Cape, 1928);
*The Childhood of Edward Thomas: A Fragment of Autobi-
   ography* (London: Faber & Faber, 1938);
The Friend of the Blackbird (Flansham, Sussex: Pear
   Tree Press, 1938);
The Prose of Edward Thomas, edited by Roland Gant
   (London: Falcon Press, 1948);
The Poems of Edward Thomas, edited by R. George
   Thomas (Oxford: Clarendon Press, 1978;
   New York: Oxford University Press, 1978);
The Fear of Death (Edinburgh: Tragara Press, 1982);
A Sportsman's Tale (Edinburgh: Tragara Press,
   1983);
The Pilgrim and Other Tales, edited, with an introduc-
   tion, by R. George Thomas (London: Dent /
   Rutland, Vt.: Tuttle, 1991).

OTHER: Richard Jefferies, *The Hills and the Vale,* introduction by Thomas (London: Duckworth,
   1909);
This England: An Anthology from Her Writers, edited by
   Thomas (London: Oxford University Press,
   1915).

The literary career of Edward Thomas was an
unusual one in that he did not work in the genre for
which he is now most noted – poetry – until he had
put in eighteen years writing pastoral essays, criticism, biographies, travel books, collections of short
fiction, and a novel. He devoted only two years to
poetry – the last years of his life before his death in
the trenches of France. Yet, thanks to the later advocacy of influential critics such as F. R. Leavis, his
poems have overshadowed his other work. Certainly his poetry was the best literary work of his
short life, but his short prose fiction does have
value in chronicling the development of the imagi-

nation that came to fruition in his poetry. In addition several of his best stories powerfully interfuse
reality with dreams and visions and offer poignant
psychological insight.

Philip Edward Thomas was born in London
on 3 March 1878, the eldest of the six sons of Philip
Henry Thomas and Mary Elizabeth Townsend
Thomas, both natives of Wales. Though born and
raised in England, Thomas strongly identified with
his Welsh heritage, visiting Wales often and finding
inspiration for many of his essays in its landscape,
culture, and folkways.

A staff clerk at the Board of Trade, Philip
Henry Thomas had raised himself through his own
efforts. He was active in all manner of social and
philanthropic causes, a high-minded and aggressive
example of the rising middle class that the British
bureaucracy had nurtured to carry out the mundane tasks of administering the empire. The elder
Thomas conveyed a strong sense of social idealism
to his son, but they were much different in temperament, with the father having little patience with
Edward's more sensitive and introspective nature.
Philip Thomas saw his son as too contemplative
and impractical; the son saw his father as simplistic
and overbearing. This conflict lasted all Edward
Thomas's life.

Despite his poor relations with his father,
Thomas's youth and education were not without
some recompense. By means of his own energy and
curiosity, as well as trips to the English and Welsh
countryside, he developed the profound appreciation of nature that informs so much of his prose. He
settled early on his vocation as a writer; writing
suited his solitary outlook and gave him a sense of
control that he seemed to lack in ordinary life. He
also had the good fortune to find a mentor in critic
and journalist James Ashcroft Noble, to whom he
was introduced in 1894 by a Unitarian minister
sympathetic to the young man's literary gifts. Noble
encouraged Thomas to draw on his love of nature
and outdoor rambles to produce essays based on
immediate experience. Noble's support no doubt
provided Thomas with a mature alternative to his
father. Philip Thomas insisted that his son attend
St. Paul's, a public school in Hammersmith for
which he was not entirely prepared, and that he
study for civil-service examinations, for which he
had no inclination.

By the time he was eighteen years old, Edward
Thomas was already a published writer, making
some eighty pounds a year. In addition to Noble,
Thomas was much influenced by the nature writer
and noted eccentric Richard Jefferies, author of

Thomas at age twenty (Collection of Myfanwy Thomas)

works such as *The Amateur Poacher* (1879) and *After London* (1885). Jefferies's writings not only conveyed an almost mystical appreciation of nature, they also offered a sense of bucolic freedom to a young man chafing under the autocratic rule of his father. Another important influence was Thomas's friendship with the Wiltshire gamekeeper David "Dad" Uzzell. Uzzell was the prototype of the unfettered "natural man" who lived by his wits and survived unscathed throughout a sometimes brutal life by means of his intuitive harmony with natural forces. By 1897 Thomas's first book, *The Woodland Life,* had been published (with the aid of Noble), and Thomas had irrevocably begun his professional literary life.

Literary encouragement was not all that James Ashcroft Noble gave to Edward Thomas. There was also his second daughter, Helen Noble. Her account of their courtship in her autobiographical novel *World Without End* (1931) captures vividly an image of the two young lovers as turn-of-the-century "flower children" too idealistic to allow

their pure love to be confined within a middle-class institution like marriage. By 1899, however, Helen was pregnant with their first child, and they married on 20 June. In the meantime Thomas had been accepted at Oxford as a noncollegiate student and had won a scholarship in history. In June 1900 he received a second-class honors degree in history, and with a family to support he started on a trying life as a reviewer and commissioned writer.

The life of the young Thomas family was neither financially nor emotionally stable. Thomas was determined to avoid the grind of a daily office job that would not only repress his creativity but also prove his father right after all. The overwork and financial stress brought on by a heavy load of literary piecework exacerbated the tendency toward profound depression to which Thomas had been subject since his teenage years. His second collection of essays, *Horae Solitariae,* was published in 1902 – the year in which his emotional and financial problems came to a crisis with the birth of a second child. The situation was somewhat alleviated by his elevation to regular reviewer for the *Daily Chronicle* (London) and by a commission to write the text for an illustrated book about Oxford, on which Thomas worked away from home.

By 1903 Thomas was able to move his family to the country near Bearsted in Kent and actually to live the country life he wrote about so fervently. In 1904 he published another collection of pastoral essays, *Rose Acre Papers.* The market for this kind of back-to-nature writing had been created by a reaction against the excesses of the Industrial Revolution: pollution, rural depopulation, the exploitation of the laboring classes, and the all-too-familiar urban slums that resulted. In these writings Thomas was very much of his time, clearly influenced by such men as Jefferies, Walter Pater, and William Morris. Thomas's style was self-consciously artful and atmospheric, celebrating natural details, personalities, and experiences without providing enough information for the reader to gain a sense of the actual location Thomas was writing about. It was escapist literature, but the escape was guided by Paterian rules of good style and a philosophic Platonism that offered a better life through elevated ideas. Thus, it did not really matter if Thomas's readers could not identify the actual places in his essays; he, and others like him, were offering an ideal of nature as a replacement for the religion that seemed less and less relevant to the progressive minds of the era. This format also gave Thomas the opportunity to indulge in verbal portraits of lively rural personalities and in flights of fancy that evolved into the prose fiction he was writing by the end of the decade.

Over the next few years Thomas gradually earned a small literary reputation and made friends in the worlds of writing and publishing. Among them were Gordon Bottomley, Arthur Ransome, Edward Garnett, and poet W. H. Davies. He also wrote two more nature books, *Beautiful Wales* (1905) and *The Heart of England* (1906). He felt that his style and insight were maturing and that his works could be vehicles for conveying not only a vicarious appreciation of nature for a chair-bound reader but also an original transcendent vision. He believed that his pastoral subjects, particularly people like "Dad" Uzzell, were in touch with a mythic substratum of reality more profound and true than the false sophistication of the commercial and industrial world that seemed so materially triumphant. Thomas even put his sympathy for myth to good commercial use late in his career. During 1911 and 1912 Thomas published *Celtic Stories* and *Norse Tales* respectively, two collections drawn from standard sources, arranged by Thomas, and updated by him into a modern style accessible to a student audience. In both collections, however, Thomas challenged young readers by not turning the myths into romantic fables. He kept the clipped, matter-of-fact style of the originals intact and made no attempt to simplify the complex interrelationships among characters or to soften the darker philosophical implications. This complexity is particularly true in the *Norse Tales,* from which a student could obtain enough understanding of the essentially pessimistic Norse mythology to grasp the story behind, for instance, Richard Wagner's Ring operas. Critics have never noticed either of these collections as being of any particular literary merit, but *Celtic Stories* was actually a small commercial success, thanks to a bulk order of two thousand copies from Australian educational authorities.

Although he continued to receive support and encouragement from his small coterie of discriminating readers throughout the first decade of the twentieth century, Thomas's literary career remained in the doldrums. After an abortive stint as an assistant secretary to the Royal Commission on Ancient Monuments in Wales and Monmouthshire (November 1908–October 1909), he returned to commissioned work but with a new determination to write more creatively. Neither his biography of Richard Jefferies (1909), for which he had high hopes, nor his account of travels in Wales, *The South Country* (1909), had attracted any significant notice, and Thomas began to focus on fiction. He had always believed that his digressions into personality and philosophy had been the strongest features of his nature books, and he decided to try his hand at compiling a set of these "essays" into a volume.

The first fruit of these efforts was *Rest and Unrest* (1910). Thomas received genuine satisfaction from this work and was encouraged and supported in it by his friend Edward Garnett, who was a publisher's reader for the house of Duckworth, which published *Rest and Unrest* and its successor, *Light and Twilight* (1911). Despite their author's enthusiasm and Garnett's friendly support, these collections attracted little notice from the critics and even less from the reading public. The marketability of these works may have suffered from the fact that Thomas's work in this vein was hard to classify. He was known as a nature writer and critic, but these collections did not fall into either category. In fact, while several of the "essays" in *Rest and Unrest* and *Light and Twilight* are clearly identifiable as short stories, others are not very different from the portraits and digressions he had inserted into his earlier nature works.

The ultimate subject behind these works is Thomas's own troubled and (at least in his own mind) oppressed personality. This fact did not go unnoticed by some of Thomas's contemporaries. In December 1913 W. H. Hudson wrote to Edward Garnett about Thomas's novel *The Happy-Go-Lucky Morgans* (1913):

> Thomas is essentially a poet, one would say of a Celtic kind. . . . I should say that in his nature books and fiction he leaves all that is best in him unexpressed. . . . I believe that if Thomas had the courage or the opportunity to follow his own genius he could do better things than these. You noticed probably in reading the book that every person described in it . . . are [*sic*] one and all just Edward Thomas. A poet trying to write prose fiction often does this.

Thomas enjoyed a period of psychological stability while writing the stories in *Rest and Unrest* and *Light and Twilight.* As a person who felt himself victimized, Thomas may have found writing compelling portraits of victims to be therapeutic. For example, the stories "The First of Spring" and "Sunday Afternoon" in *Rest and Unrest* are vivid accounts of domestic oppression.

In "The First of Spring" Alice Lacking, a sensitive invalid, reflects on her unfulfilled potential, reminiscing about a childhood talent lost and unrecognized by her family – much like Thomas's own gifts. Deprived of her creativity and her fertility, Alice hopes to adopt the unwanted child of a

Helen Noble, Thomas's future wife, in 1899 (Collection of Myfanwy Thomas)

servant's relative, but her hopes are dashed before she can express them when she learns that the child has suffered brain damage in a fall. The final scene with her father is a vivid picture of the discontinuity between her inner feelings and the smug indifference of the world around her:

> "I think, Alice," said Colonel Lacking that evening, "you had better have a sea voyage. We will take one together, I think. Yes. This English spring is too much for us when we are no longer young. You're looking a fright." "It's not the spring, father, it's myself." "Where shall it be?" he continued, looking at a map of the world.

"Sunday Afternoon" lays bare the process by which tyrannical parents can crush the spirit and independence of their children. Mrs. Wilkins, having driven one daughter to suicide and the other three into dependent spinsterhood, has taken in the daughter of the suicide. Thomas provides a pathetic rendering of how the grandmother's well-meaning but brutally relentless program of discipline and self-improvement leaves the little girl, Cathie, miserable and bewildered. Mrs. Wilkins is probably a composite of Thomas's father and Mrs. Noble, his mother-in-law, who self-righteously drove Helen Noble from her home over her romance with Thomas. The real value in life for Alice Lacking and Cathie lies in their inner worlds of imagination, dream, and fantasy. Unfortunately, these dreams

and fantasies offer no means of reconciliation with others more conventional, and it is clear that both characters can only withdraw further from any successful engagement with the world – a powerful alienation that Thomas himself must have experienced during his periods of intense depression.

Not all of Thomas's victims are so hopeless, however. In "Mothers and Sons" in *Rest and Unrest* he paints a portrait of an entire Welsh town victimized by mining and industrialization: the scenery destroyed, the river polluted, the village suburbanized and decadent. Ostensibly visiting a poet there, the narrator, Mr. Phillips, discovers that he enjoys the company of the poet's mother, Mrs. Morgan, much more. She is a hardened survivor with a rustic stoicism that, to Phillips, contrasts favorably with the false aestheticism of her son. Phillips accompanies her to a friend's house, where the unaffected Welsh spirit seems to belie the grime and exploitation. In contrast to many of Thomas's stories, where clarity is reserved for inner reflection and what little dialogue there is shuffles woodenly across the page, Mrs. Morgan comes alive in vigorous and straightforward speech:

> We old ones didn't exactly look to be happy in this world except on New Year's Eve and the like, yet it came about that we were happy, too, beyond our deserts, I daresay. I have seen changes in my time, and wages have gone up and food gone down, and glad I was when the loaf came cheap and we could afford to fat three pigs and sell one, but, bless you, it isn't by wages and food that we are made happy. They were good things, and I hope they will stay and wages be higher and food be as good as it is cheap, but there's something else, though what it is I'm not going to try to say; that's for the poets, Willy.

Light and Twilight includes two of Thomas's most disturbing portraits of his own psychological weakness, "Hawthornden" and "The Attempt." At various times in his life Thomas consulted specialists about his self-destructive depressions. He even tried modifying his diet, becoming a vegetarian, but nothing worked.

"Hawthornden" is the portrait of a man grown self-conscious in the extreme. Nothing in reality lives up to his intellectual expectations. His romantic attraction to country life seems no more than idle affectation; he constantly finds fault with his wife and family; he is too prickly and critical to enjoy the companionship of others. He lusts for the freedom of open spaces, but he is always home for tea. In fact, his punctuality for tea begins to pain him more than anything else. Finally, he dies from overexertion while out walking, and the fact of his death is proven by nothing more than his unpunctual absence from tea. This unappealing character is almost certainly a wicked self-caricature drawn from how Thomas saw himself inwardly – alienated, bitter, and yearning for the death that will free him from his perverse and petty obsessions.

"The Attempt" is another and even more painful examination of Thomas's suicidal tendencies. In this story Morgan Traheron makes rather elaborate inner preparations for his suicide. He has only one cartridge for his pistol, thus to prove his confidence and resolve to whoever might find his body. He tries to hide himself so that he will not be discovered until after a decent interval and not by his wife; he points the gun to different parts of his body, considering the maximum of efficiency and propriety in the act. At the crucial moment, though, he thinks someone may be watching, and he tosses the gun aside. He slinks home and asks his wife for tea. The irony here is palpable: a man is drawn to suicide by his sense of fastidiousness and embarrassment; yet he is too fastidious and embarrassed to carry it out. Thomas's comments on this story in an undated letter to Garnett are testimony to how closely Thomas identified with the events in the story:

> You will see from the start that his chances of pulling the trigger were small. Perhaps he is more morbid and self-conscious than you thought, and thus perhaps the last part of p. 4 will no longer seem "intolerably affected," especially as these considerations do not – as I point out – really weigh with him in his decision. You are unjust in your view of what you call "literary" phrases that "smell of the lamp." Such phrases however bad come to me without thinking or seeking. It is your "simple and direct" phrases that I have to seek for. I think you might accept my objectionable gracefulness now as no offence of mine. About the first pages I cannot decide, but was inclined to think that they should stand as they – & even their "leisureliness" – help to suggest the man who is going to make a fool of himself once more.

The words "Perhaps he is more morbid and self-conscious than you thought" give Thomas away here, as does the phrase "the man who is going to make a fool of himself once more." "The Attempt" is an example of naked and unflattering psychological honesty, but the subjective anguish that Thomas struggles to convey conflicts too much with the "simple and direct" prose that Garnett is urging him to write. "The Attempt" is another clear confirmation of Hudson's observation that Thomas was "a poet trying to write prose fiction," an observation with which Robert Frost agreed after he and

Thomas became friends in 1914, and a judgment with which Thomas, fortunately for English poetry, ultimately concurred.

That many of Thomas's poems are improvements on earlier prose passages has been extensively documented by critics such as William Cooke and R. George Thomas. Probably the most exact correspondence between prose and poetry can be found in the "Streatley to East Hendred" chapter of *The Icknield Way* (1913) – one of Thomas's last nature books – and Thomas's 1916 poem "Rain." In "Streatley to East Hendred" Thomas stays in an inn in East Hendred while rain gushes down outside. The weather leads him into a meditative digression (that goes on for about three pages) concerning rain as a "majestic and terrible thing." In "Rain" this three-page meditation is condensed into eighteen lines of well-crafted blank verse. The poem honestly asserts that Thomas's love of the rain is symbolic of his love of death, an insight he only hinted at in the prose passage. Both the prose passage and the poem include the line "Blessed are the dead that the rain rains upon," but the line ends the prose passage. In the poem Thomas ends the line with a colon and develops eleven more lines, revealing almost ruthlessly how these "words I used to love" express his inescapable loneliness in the face of death.

Two stories published in limited editions during the 1980s, *The Fear of Death* (1982) and *A Sportsman's Tale* (1983), show Thomas using his prose style to good effect in documenting powerful visionary experiences that reflect the increasing honesty with which he was coming to express his darker impulses. Both stories offer powerful images of alienation from nature and confrontation with death, two themes that Thomas developed with striking force in his poetry several years later.

"A Sportsman's Tale," collected in *The Pilgrim and Other Tales* (1991), is probably the earlier of the two stories, though its date of composition is uncertain. In this story the narrator, John Hughes, is reunited with an old friend who has returned from South Africa. After reflecting on childhood experiences together, they agree to go hunting the next morning. While on the hunt, the friend, an excellent and confident marksman, regrets having shot a rabbit, recalling that his hunting mentor had told him that certain animals were "forbidden" and that there was a limit to man's dominion over nature. After lunch Hughes falls asleep and has a vision in which he journeys under the earth to the abode of Pan, where the god is worshiped by the spirits of all the animals, living and extinct. Few humans are admitted because of the way that they have been alienated from the god:

*Thomas in December 1916 as a second lieutenant in the Royal
Garrison Artillery (Collection of Myfanwy Thomas)*

Men were the god's dream, and they in turn dreamed
him, but they were an error, and became a nightmare,
and their creator fled down to the underworld to escape
from them. They cut themselves off from their kind,
from the rest of the animals. They never wearied of
persecuting those others of whom many disappeared
from the earth and were safe only in the pastures under
the world.

In Hughes's vision humans become clouds,
flowers, and winds when they die, "so their hot spirits are calmed and cooled and humbled and taught
to forget." At the end of the twentieth century, this
passage reads not as a pastoral effusion but as a prophetic ecological parable. This sense of the mystery
and the mythic character of nature, offering an
order and wisdom with which humans have lost
touch, appears very clearly in Thomas's early poem
"March." He asks, "What did the thrushes know?" —
and follows with how their song seems to fend off

the night. But he returns to the thought fourteen
lines later: "Something they knew — I also, while they
sang / And after." Thomas never really knows, in
anything other than an intuitive sense, what the
thrushes "know." He can only merge with the passion of their voices for a while as a sympathetic and
spiritually favored listener. To Thomas there is an
inscrutable mystery in nature that can be appreciated only by one who tries to harmonize with nature rather than manipulate it. "A Sportsman's
Tale" makes an explicit myth of that mystery,
which Thomas evoked in more condensed form in
his poetry.

In "The Fear of Death," first published in the
5 October 1912 issue of *The Nation,* the narrator —
again rather transparently Thomas himself — enjoys
a beautiful summer day that he describes in his best
pastoral manner. The mood is then broken, not by
subjective morbidity, but by an objective presence,

The Spirit of the Fear of Death. Believing that this spirit wishes to claim one of his children, the narrator tries desperately to alter the outcome:

> He was trying to save her. He was dreaming that he could destroy the order of Nature by a unique miracle. He was conscious of being alone and against an awful power. Because such a triumph had never fallen to a man before, it seemed certain now that it would be his, that he was to make death pass by without touching this one victim. He had a feeling of exultation approaching. He called silently for the enemy to come up swiftly to the encounter. And it was granted. The Spirit of the Fear of Death stood before him, mighty and dark. His eyes were closed and could not see it. It was as a tree suddenly apprehended half a pace ahead in the dark night. He was waiting in the calmness of power for the conflict. He waited – how long he could never know. When he opened his eyes the child was at his knee; she had taken his hand and was leading him into the garden to see the snapdragons.

Here the vision provides Thomas the necessary objectivity to make his prose "simply and directly" describe a dreamlike state with powerful spiritual and psychological overtones, prefiguring Thomas's frankness in facing the fact of death in poems such as "What Will They Do" and "Lights Out." In "What Will They Do" Thomas imagines how little his death will affect others: "they will do without me as the rain / Can do without the flowers and the grass / That profit by it and must perish without." In "Lights Out" Thomas asserts, "There is not any book / Or face of dearest look / That I would not turn from now / To go into the unknown / I must enter and leave, alone, / I know not how." In these poems death takes form in powerful, totally direct imagery, without a hint of the romantic "presence" evoked in "The Fear of Death." Yet "The Fear of Death" seems an important document for understanding Thomas's transition from prose writer to poet. The story dispenses with the morbid affectation that infects "The Attempt"; instead Thomas is documenting a growth in inner strength with both personal and literary implications. In "The Fear of Death" death is no longer an abstract escape; it becomes a powerful reality to confront as a brute, imposing fact. His clear and understated description of this intensely heightened experience with death anticipates the realistic, focused treatment of impending death he would be able to produce later in such poems as "What Will They Do" and "Lights Out." These poems were written as Thomas was on the verge of leaving for France, having enlisted in July 1915 for military service in World War I. England was not so desperate as to be forcing men nearly forty with wives and children into the frontline trenches. Thomas volunteered, knowing the probable consequence, and was killed by a stray shell while serving as an artillery lieutenant during the Arras offensive.

Edward Thomas's short prose fiction was largely confined to the years 1909 to 1913. Its quality was uneven, and to the modern reader many of his pieces seem more like essays or journalism than short stories. He had no talent for variety and distinctness in characterization, tending to put different names on the same basic set of characters modeled on himself and his close circle of family and friends. Some of the tendency to overwrite that is so prevalent in his nature writing also bleeds over into the style of his short fiction, making many of his characters and situations literally overwrought. Too many years of hackwork in which he was bound by publishers' demands for word count took their toll.

Despite his significant shortcomings, Thomas's short fiction has many positive qualities. He was a writer of broad and democratic sympathies in a class-bound society, and his sincere love for his culture and environment, tempered by some occasionally harsh realism, previews the sensibility that would make him a fine poet in the last two years of his life. Although he could be accused of self-absorption, his stories are always candid about troubled states of mind. In many ways he seems almost "existential" in his portrayals of an unflattering subjectivity. In some stories he also shows a gift for portraying vision and parable that displays considerable powers of imagination. Although his short prose fiction was largely ignored in his lifetime and will certainly always be seen by critics as secondary to his poetry, some of his best stories have been republished in recent years and may yet find an audience. In his introduction to *The Pilgrim and Other Tales* R. George Thomas sums up the strengths of Edward Thomas's short fiction as follows:

> Edward Thomas's best prose accords readily with the plangent concerns of the later twentieth-century reader. Always aware of his own roots, he inevitably describes his characters within their total environment.... For him, despite his many bouts of acute depression, the essential quality of successful living was not based on cultivated eccentricity or slavish conformity, but on alert acceptance of things as they are.... he chose to write about the simple, the unaffected, the artless, and the independently free people he encountered.... Wales, like Cornwall and Wiltshire, became a potent evocative symbol in all his writing for the things that endure.

Letters:

Letters from Edward Thomas to Gordon Bottomley, edited by R. George Thomas (London, New York & Toronto: Oxford University Press, 1968);

A Selection of Letters to Edward Garnett (Edinburgh: Tragara Press, 1981);

Letters to America, 1914–1917 (Edinburgh: Tragara Press, 1989).

Biographies:

Helen Thomas, *As It Was* (London: Heinemann, 1926);

Helen Thomas, *World Without End* (London: Heinemann, 1931);

Robert B. Eckert, *Edward Thomas: A Biography and Bibliography* (London: Dent, 1937);

Eleanor Farjeon, *Edward Thomas: The Last Four Years* (London: Oxford University Press, 1958);

William Cooke, *Edward Thomas: A Critical Biography, 1878–1917* (London: Faber & Faber, 1970);

Helen Thomas, *Time & Again: Memoirs and Letters* (Manchester: Carcanet, 1978);

Myfanwy Thomas, *One of These Fine Days: Memoirs* (Manchester: Carcanet New Press with Mid Northumberland Arts Group, 1982);

R. George Thomas, *Edward Thomas: A Portrait* (Oxford: Clarendon Press, 1985; New York: Oxford University Press, 1985).

References:

H. Coombes, *Edward Thomas* (London: Chatto & Windus, 1956);

Michael Kirkham, ed., *The Imagination of Edward Thomas* (Cambridge & New York: Cambridge University Press, 1986);

Jan Marsh, *Edward Thomas: A Poet for His Country* (New York: Harper & Row, 1978);

Stan Smith, *Edward Thomas* (London & Boston: Faber & Faber, 1986).

Papers:

The Harry Ransom Humanities Research Center, University of Texas at Austin, has letters from Edward Thomas to Edward Garnett. The Berg Collection at the New York Public Library has correspondence with Gordon Bottomley as well as manuscripts for poems and uncompleted prose works. The Dartmouth College Library has letters to Robert Frost and manuscripts for poems sent to Frost. The Lockwood Memorial Library, State University of New York at Buffalo, has letters to Harold Munro and Holbrook Jackson. The University College Library, Cardiff, Wales, has nature notebooks, manuscripts, and family letters. Other manuscripts are located at the Bodleian Library and Lincoln College, Oxford; the British Library; and the National Library of Wales, Aberystwyth.

John Watson
(Ian Maclaren)
(3 November 1850 – 6 May 1907)

Jep C. Jonson
University of South Carolina

BOOKS: *A Year in the Fields* (Edinburgh: D. Douglas, 1888);

Beside the Bonnie Brier Bush, as Ian Maclaren (London: Hodder & Stoughton, 1894; New York: Dodd, Mead, 1894); republished in part as *A Doctor of the Old School* (New York: Dodd, Mead, 1895; London: Hodder & Stoughton, 1895);

The Days of Auld Lang Syne, as Maclaren (London: Hodder & Stoughton, 1895; New York: Dodd, Mead, 1895);

Order of Service for Young People (London: Hodder & Stoughton, 1895);

The Upper Room (London; Hodder & Stoughton, 1896; New York: Dodd, Mead, 1895);

Kate Carnegie, as Maclaren (New York: Dodd, Mead, 1896); also published as *Kate Carnegie and those Ministers* (London: Hodder & Stoughton, 1896); republished in part as *Rabbi Saunderson* (London: Hodder & Stoughton, 1898; New York: Dodd, Mead, 1898);

The Cure of Souls (New York: Dodd, Mead, 1896; London: Hodder & Stoughton, 1896);

The Mind of the Master (London: Hodder & Stoughton, 1896; New York: Dodd, Mead, 1896);

The Ian Maclaren Yearbook (London: Hodder & Stoughton, 1897; New York: Dodd, Mead, 1897);

The Potter's Wheel (London: Hodder & Stoughton, 1897; New York: Dodd, Mead, 1897);

Afterwards and Other Stories, as Maclaren (London: Hodder & Stoughton, 1898; New York: Dodd, Mead, 1898);

Companions of the Sorrowful Way (London: Hodder & Stoughton, 1898; New York: Dodd, Mead, 1898);

The Golden Morning; or The Bible Illustrated and Explained, by Watson, Rev. H. M. Wharton, and J. William Buel (Philadelphia: American Bible House, 1899); also published as *Home and*

John Watson

School of the Bible; or, the Scriptures Illuminated (Chicago: C. F. Bexley, 1899);

The Light of the World, or the Bible Illuminated and Explained, Watson, Wharton, and Buel (Philadelphia: Winston, 1899); also published as *The Story of the Bible* (Chicago: Imperial Publishing, 1899);

Church Folks; Being Practical Studies in Congregational Life, as Maclaren (New York: Doubleday, Page, 1900; London: Hodder & Stoughton, 1900);

The Doctrines of Grace (New York: McClure, Phillips, 1900; London: Hodder & Stoughton, 1900);

Young Barbarians, as Maclaren (New York: Dodd, Mead, 1901; London: Hodder & Stoughton, 1901);

The Life of the Master (New York: McClure, Phillips, 1901; London: Hodder & Stoughton, 1901);

His Majesty Baby and Some Common People, as Maclaren (London: Hodder & Stoughton, 1902); republished as *Our Neighbors* (New York: Dodd, Mead, 1903);

The Homely Virtues (New York: Dodd, Mead, 1902; London: Hodder & Stoughton, 1903);

The Inspiration of our Faith, and other Sermons (London: Hodder & Stoughton, 1905; New York: A. C. Armstrong, 1905);

St. Jude's, as Maclaren (Philadelphia: Sunday School Times, 1907; London: Religious Tract Society, 1907);

God's Message to the Human Soul (London: Hodder & Stoughton, 1907; New York: Revell, 1907);

The Scot of the Eighteenth Century: His Religion and his Life (New York: A. C. Armstrong, 1907; London: Hodder & Stoughton, 1907);

Graham of Claverhouse, as Maclaren (New York: Cupples & Leon, 1907; London: John Murray, 1908);

Respectable Sins (London: Hodder & Stoughton, 1909);

From a Northern Window: Papers, Critical, Historical, and Imaginative (London: Nisbet, 1911);

Books and Bookmen, as Maclaren (New York: Hodder & Stoughton/George H. Doran, 1912; London: Nisbet, 1912);

Children of the Resurrection (London: Nisbet, 1912; New York: Dodd, Mead, 1912);

Illustrated Bible Stories for Young and Old, by Watson and Buel (London: Syndicate Publishing, 1913).

John Watson, a Presbyterian minister who published his short stories under the pseudonym Ian Maclaren, occupies a peculiar position in Scottish literary history. Along with J. M. Barrie and S. R. Crockett, he was a member of what came to be known derisively as the Kailyard School of late Victorian Scottish fiction. Enormously popular in Britain and America during the last two decades of the nineteenth century, these writers presented idylls of a vanishing rural Scottish peasantry, which was being eradicated by industrialization and by the intrusion of agrarian capitalism into an essentially feudal society. A twentieth-century reaction against sentimentality made the Kailyarders a stock object of ridicule; yet, ironically, this tradition of condemnation has rescued Watson and his short stories from the obscurity that otherwise would have been theirs. In the latter part of the twentieth century, as the ideological basis of the Scottish Renaissance itself is coming under the microscope, some Scottish critics have begun to reassess the Kailyard writers on their own merits.

Watson, the only child of John Watson and his wife, Isabella Maclaren, was born on 3 November 1850 at Manningtree, Essex. His father was a tax collector with the Inland Revenue Service, eventually becoming receiver-general of taxes for Scotland. When Watson was four his family moved to Perth, where Watson attended the local grammar school. Eight years later they went to live in Stirling, where he attended Stirling High School. By his own admission, Watson was an indifferent scholar. According to his biographer, William Robertson Nicoll, "His father once threw a book at his head, and remarked with much frankness that 'of all the stupid blockheads he stood alone.' " He was also a frail, introspective child. Because of his poor health, his doctor recommended that Watson spend time in the country, so throughout his youth he frequently spent summers on his uncles' farms in the Perthshire Highlands. His experience of farm life provided the sources for many of the characters and incidents in his short stories.

In 1866, at sixteen years of age, Watson matriculated at Edinburgh University. In Edinburgh, Watson again proved an unremarkable scholar. Well into his final year at university, Watson had not formed any plans for an occupation. It was his father's decision that he should become a clergyman, Watson himself having neither the intention nor the desire to do so. His father quite simply presented him with two alternatives: the Church or the Bar, and clearly indicated that the Bar would disappoint both father and mother. In 1870, after graduating with an M.A. from the university, Watson entered New College, Edinburgh, the theological college of the Scottish Free Church.

At New College Watson was exposed to many of the liberalizing influences that were then moderating the orthodox Calvinism of the Free Church. Darwinism, the Higher Criticism, and neo-Hegelianism were all having a profound influence on Scottish theology, and Watson's reading included works by John Ruskin, Ralph Waldo Emerson, and

KATE CARNEGIE

BY

IAN MACLAREN

NEW YORK
DODD, MEAD AND COMPANY
1896

Frontispiece and title page for the first American edition of the third book Watson set in the fictional parish of Drumtochty, closely modeled on his first parish, Logiealmond in Perthshire (Thomas Cooper Library, University of South Carolina)

Matthew Arnold as well as the expected diet of theological writings. Watson was known less as a diligent student than as a brilliant talker and a boon companion, who continued to develop his boyhood talents as a raconteur and a mimic. As one of his New College classmates remarked, "No one could approach him . . . in his power of hitting off good-humouredly the peculiarities of his classmates, or, be it said with bated breath, of his class professor. Many a New College student is best remembered by some of us to-day through a phrase or story of Watson's." Watson concluded his studies at New College with a semester of study at Tübingen during summer 1874, characteristically deriving more social than theological benefit from his exposure to the university there.

On returning to Edinburgh in the autumn Watson, having been licensed to preach by his presbytery, spent three months as a "probationer," as-sisting at an evangelical Free Church in Edinburgh, where he was theologically at odds with minister and elders. These three months, an exceptionally short time to be a probationer, were such an unhappy time for Watson that he very nearly gave up the ministry to practice law. He was no doubt relieved to accept an appointment to the Logiealmond parish in Perthshire late that year. Any laxity he showed as a scholar did not reappear in his life as a pastor; he worked diligently to develop his talents as a preacher, to the extent of fasting and wearing a hair shirt to improve his self-discipline.

Although he was genuinely happy at Logiealmond, in 1877 he accepted a call to Free Saint Matthew's Church in Glasgow. There he met Jane Burnie Ferguson, the daughter of a prominent Glasgow businessman and a niece of the Irish poet Sir Samuel Ferguson. They were married on 6 June 1878 and eventually had four sons. Watson was popular but not contented in Glasgow, and in 1880 he accepted the call to Sefton Park Church in Liverpool. He built Sefton Park into one of the most influential churches in the city, including two mayors and four lord mayors in his congregation. He was also active in civic affairs, playing an instrumental part in the founding of the University of Liverpool. Before he ventured on a literary career, Watson developed a considerable renown as a preacher. Matthew Arnold heard him preach at Sefton Park on the day he died (15 April 1888) and said that he had rarely been so affected by any preacher.

After nearly fifteen years at Sefton Park Watson began his literary career quite by accident. In 1893 William Robertson Nicoll, who made a specialty of discovering Kailyard writers, had asked Watson to write religious articles for the *Expositor,* a journal he edited. When Watson then visited Nicoll in London, Nicoll was "so struck with the racy stories and character-sketches" that Watson told, he asked him to write them up as articles for the *British Weekly,* a Nonconformist literary newspaper, which Nicoll also edited. "How We Carried the News to Whinnie Knowe," published in the *British Weekly* on 2 November 1893, proved an immediate success. It was included along with three other sketches in the first section of *Beside the Bonnie Brier Bush,* which was published in October 1894.

In 1895 Watson quickly followed up on the success of *Beside the Bonnie Brier Bush* with the publication of *The Days of Auld Lang Syne,* stories republished in part from *Blackwood's Edinburgh Magazine* and other journals. Nicoll considered that Watson's first two books were "in reality one, and should go together." Indeed they are both set in the fictional parish of Drumtochty, and both present the same group of colorful, rural characters. Concentrating less on the life of the church and more on the everyday life of Scottish peasant farmers than the first collection, *The Days of Auld Lang Syne* presents Drumtochty in weekday clothes rather than the Sunday finery of *Beside the Bonnie Brier Bush.*

Watson modeled the parish of Drumtochty on the Logiealmond parish. The stories are not impelled by plot. They are either character sketches or human fables exemplifying a moral or religious theme. Watson's characterization is both individualistic and communal. His Scots are all idiosyncratic, but their characters develop through juxtaposition with each other. Because of the emphasis on community, much of the character development is achieved through dialogue. Domsie's earnestness is a foil for Drumsheugh's apparent miserliness;

Marget Howe's belief in divine love is a foil for Kirsty Stewart's belief in divine judgment.

In these stories the recurring tension between rigid Calvinism and the theology of salvation through divine love and mercy presents a conflict that was very active in the Victorian Scottish church and was represented in microcosm in Watson's boyhood home. His father was a Free Churchman of Evangelistic and Calvinist leanings, while his mother was a Moderate who would have been happy to see him enter the Established Church. Watson himself preferred his mother's liberal, humanist theology to his father's orthodoxy. The attempt to reconcile the disparate theologies of the Scottish Church is a constant theme in all Watson's fiction, as indeed it was in his practice of the ministry.

The "Domsie" section, which opens *Beside the Bonnie Brier Bush,* concerns the local schoolmaster, or "dominie," and his attempts to send George Howe, a promising but poor local scholar, to Edinburgh University. Domsie extorts the money from Drumsheugh, a notoriously tightfisted farmer, and George sweeps up all the honors to be had at Edinburgh. George, the "lad o' pairts" modeled on Watson's boyhood friend William Durham, returns to Drumtochty with a double first in mathematics and classics. He is obviously dying, and in the last two stories of the section he and his mother take solace in their love for one another and for God. George's faith brings Domsie back to the faith he had abandoned as a young man. "A Scholar's Funeral," which concludes the opening section, explains that "Drumtochty never acquitted itself with credit at a marriage . . . but the parish had a genius for funerals," showing the combination of pathos and humor that characterizes Watson's Kailyardism: "Drumtochty gave itself to a 'beerial' with chastened satisfaction, partly because it lay near to the sorrow of things, and partly because there was no speculation in it. 'Ye can hae little rael pleesure in a meriege,' explained our gravedigger, in whom the serious side had been perhaps abnormally developed, 'for ye never ken hoo it will end; but there's nae risk about a "beerial." ' "

The second section, "A Highland Mystic," centers on Donald Menzies, a full-blooded Celt subject to strange transports, prophetic visions, and incomprehensible utterances. The inhabitants of Drumtochty try to help Donald through a spiritual crisis, assistance made problematic by their inability to understand its precise nature. Donald triumphs in his dark night of the soul, winning his battle against Satan through the recognition of salvation through mercy – a conspicuous victory not only over Satan but over Calvinist theology. Donald exemplifies Watson's view of the Celts as born mystics – a trait he believed he had partially inherited from his Highland ancestry.

The third section comprises only one story, "His Mother's Sermon," in which a bright young Free Church minister prepares to deliver his first sermon. The minister, who is later identified as John Carmichael and who is in many respects Watson's self-parody, was planning an elaborate theological sermon – appropriate to the holder of "the MacWhammel scholarship" – in which he would present a "trenchant criticism of old-fashioned views." But his old aunt convinces him that such a sermon will not minister to the needs of rural folk and reminds him of his promise to his mother, now five years dead, that in his first sermon he would "speak a gude word for Jesus Christ." The young minister agonizes over this conflict but finally burns his elaborately argued sermon and spends all Saturday praying for a new subject. His aunt watches as the memory of his mother softens the didacticism of the young minister, and when he preaches on the love of Christ, he himself has been transformed by love. Donald Menzies, the Highland mystic, is transported "into the third heaven," and when Marget Howe meets the young minister after the service, she remarks tearfully, "My only son wes preparin' for the ministry, but God wanted him nearly a year syne. When ye preached the Evangel o' Jesus the day I heard his voice, and I loved you. Ye hev nae mither on earth, I hear, and I hae nae son, and I wantit tae say that if ye ever wish tae speak tae ony woman as ye wud tae yir mither, come tae Whinnie Knowe, an' I'll coont it ane of the Lord's consolations."

"The Transformation of Lachlan Campbell" presents the conversion of a strict, Old Testament Calvinist into a New Testament Moderate. Lachlan Campbell, "The Grand Inquisitor" of the local church session, all but disowns his daughter for running away from home, going so far as to strike her name from the family Bible. The experience of losing his daughter, however, eventually softens Campbell's Calvinist heart, and he becomes one of Drumtochty's leading proponents of divine as well as human love.

"The Cunning Speech of Drumtochty," a humorous sketch about the contrast between Drumtochty speech and that of "visitors" from the south, is an apology for the apparent dourness of Scottish character and a celebration of the subtlety of rural wit. Its main character is Jamie Soutar, who

Cover for the first British edition of the six stories about an idiosyncratic Calvinist minister that Watson first published as part of Kate Carnegie

habitually takes the measure of "English veesitors" without their suspecting it. "A Wise Woman" is the story of Elspeth Macfadyen, the local authority on sermons, and her prowess at remembering all the "heads" and "points" of any preacher on a single hearing. She is defeated for the first time by a visiting Highland minister, whose sermon is so mystical it defies any logical categorization.

"A Doctor of the Old School" recounts the history of the local medical doctor, William MacLure, and his extraordinary efforts to preserve his patients from death. Drumsheugh, the miserly farmer who sent George Howe to university, reappears and donates a hundred guineas to bring a specialist to the Glen, thus saving Annie Mitchell's life. The doctor himself wearies and dies from overwork, and farmers and ploughmen from miles around brave an impenetrable blizzard to attend his funeral.

"A Triumph of Diplomacy" opens *The Days of Auld Lang Syne* with a description of the negotiation of leases between the local farmers and the laird's "factor," with Hillocks wringing a series of concessions from the factor and reporting "his achievement to the kirkyard next Sabbath in the tone of one who could now look forward to a life of grinding poverty." In "For Conscience Sake" a new factor, whom the laird brings from England, tries to drive Burnbrae from his tenancy for not attending the Established Church. While the laird is away in Europe, the factor orders Burnbrae from his farm, and not even the protests of Dr. Davidson, the Established Church minister, can dissuade the factor from the eviction. Burnbrae's farm implements have been auctioned, and Burnbrae and his wife are moving to a new house, when Dr. Davidson's letter brings the laird back to Drumtochty. The factor is dismissed; Burnbrae is reinstated; and all Drumtochty — both Established Church and Free — return Burnbrae's auctioned possessions, refusing any compensation.

The three stories of "Drumsheugh's Love Story" tell of the secret love Drumsheugh has been harboring for Marget Howe. His notoriety as a miser in fact screens the anonymous donations he has been making to Marget's family. In "Past Redemption," Posty, the local postman, dies saving a young girl from a flood. Speculation about Posty's salvation troubles Drumtochty, for Posty was a noted imbiber, and John Carmichael survives a test of his theology by declaring that saving the child's life will ensure Posty's salvation. "Jamie" takes up another familiar theme in Watson's work — faithfulness in love. Notorious as a cynical bachelor throughout Drumtochty, Jamie Soutar is asked on his death bed what set him against marriage. Soutar confesses that he was never against marriage but remained a bachelor in honor of his love for a dead fiancée. "A Servant Lass" presents another recurring theme — that of the world outside the glen as a hostile world, full of false religion and traps for the young. Lily Grant goes into service in London, and is taken ill. With no one to care for her, she is bounced from her mistress's house to a public hospital, before a Scottish doctor takes her to his own home so that she might die among friends. Jamie Soutar visits her just as she is dying and takes her body back to Drumtochty, transporting her in state because of the largess of the doctor and Lily's minister.

Both Watson's first two books were immediate popular successes. *Beside the Bonnie Brier Bush* sold more than 100,000 copies in its first year, eventually selling more than 250,000 copies in Britain and nearly half a million in the United States. Watson wasted no time capitalizing on this success, republishing the Doctor MacLure stories from *Beside the Bonnie Brier Bush* under the title *A Doctor of the Old School* (1895). *The Days of Auld Lang Syne* continued Watson's success, with a first British printing of 30,000 copies, Edinburgh alone accounting for 5,000 copies in advance orders.

The critical attention given to *Beside the Bonnie Brier Bush*, although expressing some reservations about Watson's sentimentality and the accuracy of his portrayal of Scotland, was generally warm. Nicoll's effusions — he claimed, "I have not been able to trace a single unfavourable review" — are exaggerated but substantially true; contemporary critical reception lagged only slightly behind popular acclaim. Much of the positive response came from journals that specialized in publishing popular and religious literature. These periodicals included *The Bookman* and the *British Weekly* — both with strong ties to Nicoll and his publishers, Hodder and Stoughton — which were predictably laudatory. Neutral publications, such as the *Athenaeum* and the *Critic*, offered qualified approval. They found the book a good example of its genre but noted the limitations of regional fiction as well as the sentimentality and preponderance of religious themes.

The elements of Watson's fiction that stimulated gentle criticism in many critics provoked, however, a full broadside from J. H. Millar, who coined the epithet *Kailyard* in his 1895 article "The Literature of the Kailyard." The term quickly adhered to all writers of sentimental fiction in Scottish dialect, defining them as a literary "school," and came to be used both by supporters and detractors of the Kailyard writers. According to Millar's attack, the Kailyard writers portray an unrealistic, sentimentalized version of Scottish character, which is calculated to sell to the English by reinforcing their patronizing attitudes toward the Scots. The Kailyard story, in Millar's estimation, does nothing but add to the "curious superstitions the Southron breast has long nourished with regard to Scotland." He regards Watson's sentimentality as particularly offensive, claiming "that Mr. Maclaren has a diseased craving for the pathetic. He is never really happy save when he is wringing your heart, and a plenteous distillation of plum-tree gum from the eyes would, we suspect, be his dearest reward."

Millar's acerbic comments undoubtedly affected the critical reception of *The Days of Auld Lang Syne*. Beginning with this book, Watson's reviewers tend to divide into two camps: pro- and anti-

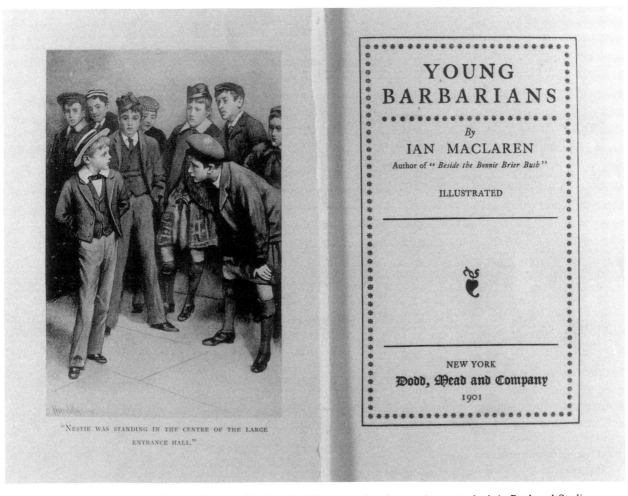

"NESTIE WAS STANDING IN THE CENTRE OF THE LARGE
ENTRANCE HALL."

YOUNG
BARBARIANS

By
IAN MACLAREN
Author of " Beside the Bonnie Brier Bush "

ILLUSTRATED

NEW YORK
Dodd, Mead and Company
1901

Frontispiece and title page for the collection of boys' stories Watson based on his experiences at schools in Perth and Sterling

Kailyard. Among the most virulent of the anti-Kailyarders was T. W. H. Crosland, a London journalist and avid detester of almost all things Scottish, who brutally satirized the Kailyard writers in *The Unspeakable Scot* (1902). His savage lampoons of Kailyard excesses have enough truth in them to bite hard, but he is not too particular about facts. He is ruthless in his treatment of the "For Conscience Sake" section of *The Days of Auld Lang Syne,* claiming that the story of an English factor trying to evict tenants over a question of church is entirely improbable and that "Dr. Maclaren cannot make us believe that a Scotchman would part freely and without price with anything that he had once bought." In making a visit to Logiealmond to prepare illustrations for Watson's books, however, American artist Frederick C. Gordon found that Watson had drawn the story from actual accounts of Tory landlords attempting to force Nonconformist tenants off the land.

After *The Days of Auld Lang Syne* the pro-Kailyard reviewers became increasingly defensive about charges of sentimentality and lack of realism, arguing that sentiment places Maclaren in a distinguished literary tradition, including Jean-Jacques Rousseau and Samuel Richardson, and that Watson's picture of an "ideal" Scotland is not unfaithful to the truth simply because it leaves out all that is sordid. Watson himself seemed sensitive to the assertions that he was being unfaithful to Scottish character. In an interview granted to James Ashcroft Noble, he defended his typological view of character, claiming that in his works "the people are simply individualisations of types that are familiar to every minister – or, for the matter of that, to every layman – in any Highland parish." He claimed, however, that he would abandon his Drumtochty setting after *The Days of Auld Land Syne* because he would have "exhausted all the available types, and to go on would be to make bricks without straw," adding "I should like to write a story dealing with the darker side of Scottish life – and there is a darker side that I have not yet touched, but that is a big task and a difficult one." William Power has argued that the commercial success of the Kailyarders with a large middle-class audience – combined with the defining power of Millar's epithet – created Kailyard fiction as an inviolable literary convention. The demands of the audience for "more of the same" prevented the Kailyard writers from diversifying.

Kate Carnegie (1896) continued the Drumtochty setting and the preponderance of "wholesome" themes. Although Nicoll commissioned it as a novel, the plotting and characterization show little development from that in Watson's previous two books. The separate chapters are more closely related than before, but each story is still a vignette, a static tableau; and plot develops only through juxtaposition of these tableaux. The setting is still Drumtochty, but the focus of attention is no longer the native peasants. The main characters are Gen. Jack Carnegie and his daughter, Kate, the last of the Carnegies, who return to Tochty Lodge to administer what remains of a dwindled ancestral estate. The Free Church minister, John Carmichael, is immediately smitten with Kate, and the plot shows the vicissitudes and doubts leading up to their realization – on the last page – that each is in love with the other. The significant subplot of the book involves Rabbi Saunderson, the idiosyncratic Calvinist minister of Kilbogle, and the charges of heresy he brings against Carmichael, his protégé and best-loved pupil.

Contemporary critics thought *Kate Carnegie* a failure as a novel, generally because of the failures in plot and character development. The pro-Kailyard reviewers maintained that in spite of its overall failure, it did include some of Watson's best writing, notably in the character of Rabbi Saunderson. The love story is conventionally sentimental. In trying to expand beyond the depiction of Scottish peasants, Watson fell back on stock representations of British imperialism, such as the Indian general and his daughter. His talent for individualizing detail rescues his broad Scots characters from the dullness of stereotype, but Kate and her father, who lack this detail, are flat and uninteresting. The conflict between Rabbi Saunderson and John Carmichael, and even more so the conflict within Rabbi

Saunderson's own conscience, is more convincing and much the best part of the book. As he had done earlier with *A Doctor of the Old School,* Watson collected the six Rabbi Saunderson stories and published them as a separate volume, *Rabbi Saunderson* (1898).

In October 1896 Watson made the first of three American lecture tours, organized by the American impresario Maj. J. B. Pond. The tour began at Yale University, where Watson delivered the Lyman Beecher lectures on preaching and was awarded an honorary Doctor of Divinity degree. The Yale lectures were published as *The Cure of Souls* (1896). The tour was a resounding success, earning Watson more than $35,000. Because of his duties in Liverpool, Watson declined Pond's offer of an additional $24,000 to extend the tour.

After his return to Liverpool, the marked increase in demands for his sermons and lectures, in addition to his pastoral duties, curtailed his literary output; as a result his publications in 1897 were *The Potter's Wheel,* a religious work published under his own name, and the *Ian Maclaren Yearbook,* a collection of previous writings organized as daily readings.

Afterwards and Other Stories (1898) marks Watson's partial departure from the Kailyard. It is a collection of stories set variously in London, the French Riviera, Glasgow, and Liverpool as well as back in Drumtochty. In "Afterwards" Edward Trevor, a London lawyer aspiring to Parliament, realizes only after the death of the shy, unsophisticated, and unfashionable wife whom he regarded as a political liability, that she was a liability only with the superficially sophisticated parasites of London's smart set. Alerted by telegraph, he tries to return from the Riviera before she dies, but in vain. The cards of condolence – which arrive from all strata of society – confirm her saintly charity and convict him of the shallowness of his own ambitions. At the heart of the story is the same distrust of urban slickness that makes Drumtochty an idyllic community. "The Minister of St. Bede's" continues the theme of city versus country, as Henry Rutherford, a rural Highland minister, takes a position at a fashionable church in the West End of Glasgow, "a kirk which contained many rich people and thought not a little of itself." A church elder tries to dissuade Rutherford from marrying the daughter of a Highland crofter, significantly named Magdalen Macdonald, and when Rutherford will not be dissuaded, the elder secretly persuades Magdalen to break their engagement so as not to impede Rutherford's career. They both remain faithful to their love, and some twenty years later they are reunited.

A theme that runs throughout the collection is the discovery of unexpected charity. Government employees, such as Mr. Perkins in "A Government Official" and the collector of "The Collector's Inconsistency," are seemingly passionless functionaries whose devotion to law and routine conceals hidden philanthropy. Samuel Dodson, the miserly Liverpool millionaire of "The Right Hand of Samuel Dodson," undergoes a change of heart and sends anonymous donations to deserving people in need, all under the signature of "Zaccheus." All these stories of hidden charity exemplify Watson's belief in the triumph of love and fit within the contemporary theological conflict between Moderate and Calvinist Presbyterianism. As he moved away from the rural setting of Drumtochty, Watson tried to show the same sense of community operating beneath the apparent self-centeredness of city life. As in *Kate Carnegie,* he tended to be out of his depth in depicting middle-class character. Neither his aspiring M.P. nor his Liverpool industrialist is convincing enough to evoke real sympathy, but the depictions of oddity in his government employees, and in other sketches involving struggling ministers, combine humor and pathos in a more engaging way.

In 1899 Watson made his second American tour, also organized by Major Pond and lasting from 19 February until 10 May. After his return home, work for the church occupied his time, notably establishing Westminister College, Cambridge, as the Presbyterian Theological College. As a result his literary output again declined. Watson spent the year of 1900 as Moderator of the Presbyterian Church in England, an exhausting job that may have permanently damaged his health and contributed to his early death. During this year he published *Church Folks; Being Practical Studies in Congregational Life* (1900) as Ian Maclaren and *The Doctrines of Grace* (1900) under his own name. He also worked on *The Life of the Master* (1901) and *Young Barbarians* (1901). *Young Barbarians* is a collection of stories for boys, based on Watson's own experience at school in Perth and Stirling. The only other work of fiction Watson was to publish in his lifetime was *His Majesty Baby and Some Common People* (1902), based in part on his experiences of America. He retired from Sefton Park Church and the ministry in 1905, pleading ill health, but he kept up a vigorous schedule of lectures and sermons. In 1906 he was appointed president of the National Free Church Council and was nominated to the principalship of Westminster College, Cambridge. On 30 January 1907 he began his third American tour, lecturing along the east coast until March, before striking out

west through Canada and Montana in April. When he arrived in Mount Pleasant, Iowa, on 23 April for a series of lectures at Iowa Wesleyan University, he was already ill, and a doctor diagnosed him as having acute tonsillitis and "quinsy with complications." The infection spread; he fell into a coma on 5 May and died the following day.

His son Frederick edited and published the works he had in hand at the time of his death. *St. Jude's,* a collection of stories set primarily in Liverpool, and *Graham of Claverhouse,* a historical novel along the lines of Walter Scott, were both published later that year. *Books and Bookmen* (1912) is a collection of Watson's essays on literature. In addition, four volumes of religious writings were published between 1909 and 1913.

At the time of Watson's death, the Kailyard's popularity had already started to decline, but it was still possible in 1935 for William Power to regard the three main Kailyarders as "first rate literary craftsmen" and to claim that Watson "had a delicate touch of pathos and humour that ranks him with the best of homely idyllists in any country." As Scottish life became increasingly industrial and urban, however, nostalgic idylls of a bucolic past became less and less relevant to most Scots. *Kailyard* became a term of opprobrium. Critics of the 1950s and 1960s, progeny of Hugh MacDiarmid's Scottish Renaissance, tended to follow George Blake in condemning the Kailyard for its sentimentality, for its refusal to face Scottish urban squalor and the deracination of the provinces, and for its "queer sort of toadying to the old traditions of Toryism, in which the 'lower classes' are the honest, feckless, delightful friends of their superiors in education and financial resources."

There were dissenting voices. In 1962 Scottish poet Edwin Morgan argued that such vehement denunciation of the Kailyard was a distortion and that there is "an important place for sentiment and pathos in any literature." He also argued that it was time for a limited reappraisal of the Kailyard, "if only because some deep-rooted human feelings are involved in the phenomenon, and it may be possible to study what it has to offer, while continuing to reject its falsifications." A reassessment began in the late 1970s, with more sympathetic reviews of the Kailyard by Ian Carter, Eric Anderson, Francis Russell Hart, and Christopher Harvie. Except for Carter, these critics hold a higher view than their immediate predecessors of the Kailyarders' literary craftsmanship. The salient feature of the Kailyard reassessment is the view that both Kailyard and anti-Kailyard represent different manifestations of the same debate within Scottish literary culture, as Hart describes it, "poles . . . of the same field." The recognition that both Kailyard and anti-Kailyard are ideological as much as literary stances has led some critics, such as Thomas Knowles, to consider the Kailyard in its sociological context, to ask again some old questions: How accurately did the Kailyard depict rural Scotland? What does the Kailyard phenomenon say about late-Victorian perceptions of Scotland, and to what extent is the anti-Kailyard vehemence also an attempt to "falsify" Scotland? Although Kailyard fiction will never be confused with great literature, it is now becoming possible to appreciate its modest, but real, literary merits and to see what the phenomenon can say, not only about the late-Victorian reading public but also about the twentieth-century critical establishment that so vehemently denounced Ian Maclaren and the Kailyard School.

Biography:
William Robertson Nicoll, *"Ian Maclaren": Life of the Rev. John Watson, D.D.* (London: Hodder & Stoughton, 1908; New York: Dodd, Mead, 1908).

References:
Eric Anderson, "The Kailyard Revisited," in *Nineteenth Century Scottish Fiction,* edited by Ian Campbell (Manchester: Carcanet, 1979), pp. 130–147;
George Blake, *Barrie and the Kailyard School* (New York: Roy, 1951);
Campbell, *Kailyard* (Edinburgh: Ramsay Head Press, 1981);
Ian Carter, "Kailyard: The Literature of Decline in Nineteenth Century Scotland," *Scottish Journal of Sociology,* 1 (November 1976): 1–13;

T. W. H. Crosland, *The Unspeakable Scot* (London: Richards, 1902; New York: Putnam, 1902), pp. 76–91;
Frederick C. Gordon, "A Visit to Drumtochty," *Bookman* (New York), 4 (December 1896): 358–359;
Francis Russell Hart, *The Scottish Novel from Smollett to Spark* (Cambridge, Mass.: Harvard University Press, 1978);
Christopher Harvie, "Behind the Bonnie Brier Bush: 'The Kailyard' Revisited," *Proteus,* 3 (June 1978): 55–70;
Thomas D. Knowles, *Ideology, Art and Commerce: Aspects of Literary Sociology in the Late Victorian Scottish Kailyard* (Göteborg: Acta Universitatis Gothoburgensis, 1983);
J. H. Millar, *A Literary History of Scotland* (New York: Scribners, 1903), pp. 511, 655–661, 680–682;
Millar, "The Literature of the Kailyard," *New Review,* 12 (1895): 384–394;
Edwin Morgan, "The Beatnik in the Kailyaird," in his *Essays* (Cheadle Hulme, Cheshire: Carcanet, 1974), pp. 166–176;
William Robertson Nicoll, "London Letter: Ian Maclaren," *Bookman* (New York), 2 (December 1895): 311–314;
James Ashcroft Noble, "Ian Maclaren at Home," *Bookman* (New York), 1 (March 1895): 93–96;
Maj. J. B. Pond, *Eccentricities of Genius: Memories of Famous Men and Women of the Platform and Stage* (New York: Dillingham, 1900), pp. 404–451;
William Power, *Literature and Oatmeal: What Literature has Meant to Scotland* (London: Routledge, 1935), pp. 160–164.

H. G. Wells

(21 September 1866 – 13 August 1946)

Kevin J. H. Dettmar
Clemson University

See also the Wells entries in *DLB 34: British Novelists, 1890–1929: Traditionalists* and *DLB 70: British Mystery Writers, 1860–1919.*

BOOKS: *Text-Book of Biology,* 2 volumes (London: Clive, 1893; volume 1 revised, 1894);

Honours Physiography, by Wells and R. A. Gregory (London: Hughes, 1893);

Select Conversations with an Uncle, Now Extinct, and Two Other Reminiscences (London: John Lane, 1895; New York: Merriam, 1895);

The Time Machine: An Invention (London: Heinemann, 1895; New York: Holt, 1895);

The Wonderful Visit (London: Dent, 1895; New York: Macmillan, 1895);

The Stolen Bacillus, and Other Incidents (London: Methuen, 1895);

The Island of Doctor Moreau (London: Heinemann, 1896; New York: Stone & Kimball, 1896);

The Wheels of Chance: A Holiday Adventure (London: Dent, 1896); republished as *The Wheels of Chance: A Bicycling Idyll* (New York: Macmillan, 1896);

The Plattner Story, and Others (London: Methuen, 1897);

The Invisible Man: A Grotesque Romance (London: Pearson, 1897; enlarged edition, New York: Arnold, 1897; London: Pearson, 1900);

Thirty Strange Stories (New York: Arnold, 1897);

Certain Personal Matters: A Collection of Material, Mainly Autobiographical (London: Lawrence & Bullen, 1897);

The War of the Worlds (London: Heinemann, 1898; New York & London: Harper, 1898);

When the Sleeper Wakes: A Story of the Years to Come (London & New York: Harper, 1899); revised as *The Sleeper Awakes* (London: Nelson, 1910);

Tales of Space and Time (London & New York: Harper, 1899; New York: Doubleday, McClure, 1899);

A Cure for Love (New York: Scott, 1899);

H. G. Wells arriving in New York City, 1934

Love and Mr. Lewisham (London & New York: Harper, 1900);

The First Men in the Moon (London: Newnes, 1901; Indianapolis: Bowen-Merrill, 1901);

Anticipations of the Reaction of Mechanical and Scientific Progress upon Human Life and Thought (London: Chapman & Hall, 1901; New York & London: Harper, 1902);

The Discovery of the Future: A Discourse Delivered to the Royal Institution on January 24, 1902 (London: Unwin, 1902; New York: Huebsch, 1913);

375

The Sea Lady: A Tissue of Moonshine (London: Methuen, 1902); republished as *The Sea Lady* (New York: Appleton, 1902);

Mankind in the Making (London: Chapman & Hall, 1903; New York: Scribners, 1904);

Twelve Stories and a Dream (London: Macmillan, 1903; New York: Scribners, 1905);

The Food of the Gods, and How It Came to Earth (London: Macmillan, 1904; New York: Scribners, 1904);

A Modern Utopia (London: Chapman & Hall, 1905; New York: Scribners, 1905);

Kipps: The Story of a Simple Soul (London: Macmillan, 1905; New York: Scribners, 1905);

In the Days of the Comet (London: Macmillan, 1906; New York: Century, 1906);

The Future in America: A Search after Realities (London: Chapman & Hall, 1906; New York & London: Harper, 1906);

Faults of the Fabian (London: Fabian Society, 1906);

Reconstruction of the Fabian Society (London: Privately printed, 1906);

Socialism and the Family (London: Fifield, 1906; Boston: Ball, 1906);

The So-Called Science of Sociology (London: Macmillan, 1907);

This Misery of Boots (London: Fabian Society, 1907; Boston: Ball, 1908);

Will Socialism Destroy the Home? (London: Independent Labour Party, 1907);

New Worlds for Old (London: Constable, 1908; New York: Macmillan, 1908);

The War in the Air, and Particularly How Mr. Bert Smallways Fared While It Lasted (London: Bell, 1908; New York: Macmillan, 1908);

First and Last Things: A Confession of Faith and Rule of Life (London: Constable, 1908; New York & London: Putnam, 1908; revised and enlarged edition, London, New York, Melbourne & Toronto: Cassell, 1917);

Tono-Bungay (New York: Duffield, 1908; London: Macmillan, 1909);

Ann Veronica: A Modern Love Story (London: Unwin, 1909; New York & London: Harper, 1909);

The History of Mr. Polly (London, Edinburgh, Dublin, New York, Leipzig & Paris: Nelson, 1910; New York: Duffield, 1910);

The New Machiavelli (New York: Duffield, 1910; London: John Lane, 1911);

Floor Games (London: Palmer, 1911; Boston: Small, Maynard, 1912);

The Country of the Blind, and Other Stories (London, Edinburgh, Dublin, Leeds, New York, Leipzig & Paris: Nelson, 1911); revised as *The Country of the Blind* (London, 1939);

The Door in the Wall and Other Stories (New York & London: Kennerly, 1911; London: Richards, 1915);

The Great State: Essays in Construction, by Wells and others (London: Harper, 1912); republished as *Socialism and the Great State* (New York: Harper, 1914);

The Labour Unrest (London: Daily Mail, 1912);

Marriage (London: Macmillan, 1912; New York: Duffield, 1912);

War and Common Sense (London: Daily Mail, 1913);

Liberalism and Its Party: What Are the Liberals to Do? (London: Good, 1913);

Little Wars: A Game for Boys from Twelve Years of Age to One Hundred and Fifty and for That More Intelligent Sort of Girls Who Like Boys' Games (London: Palmer, 1913; Boston: Small, Maynard, 1913; revised, London & Toronto: Dent, 1931);

The Passionate Friends (London: Macmillan, 1913; New York & London: Harper, 1913);

An Englishman Looks at the World: Being a Series of Unrestrained Remarks upon Contemporary Matters (London, New York, Toronto & Melbourne: Cassell, 1914); republished as *Social Forces in England and America* (New York & London: Harper, 1914);

The World Set Free: A Story of Mankind (London: Macmillan, 1914; New York: Dutton, 1914);

The Wife of Sir Isaac Harman (London & New York: Macmillan, 1914);

The War that Will End War (London: Palmer, 1914; New York: Duffield, 1914);

The Peace of the World (London: Daily Chronicle, 1915);

Boon, the Mind of the Race, the Wild Asses of the Devil, and the Last Trump, Being a First Selection from the Literary Remains of George Boon, Appropriate to the Times (London: Unwin, 1915; New York: Doran, 1915);

Bealby: A Holiday (London: Methuen, 1915; New York: Macmillan, 1915);

The Research Magnificent (London & New York: Macmillan, 1915);

What Is Coming? A Forecast of Things after the War (London, New York, Toronto & Melbourne: Cassell, 1916); republished as *What Is Coming? A European Forecast* (New York: Macmillan, 1916);

Mr. Britling Sees It Through (London, New York, Toronto & Melbourne: Cassell, 1916; New York: Macmillan, 1916);

The Elements of Reconstruction: A Series of Articles Contributed in July and August 1916 to the Times (London: Nisbet, 1916);

War and the Future: Italy, France, and Britain at War (London, New York, Toronto & Melbourne: Cassell, 1917); republished as *Italy, France, and Britain at War* (New York: Macmillan, 1917);

God the Invisible King (London, New York, Toronto & Melbourne: Cassell, 1917; New York: Macmillan, 1917);

A Reasonable Man's Peace (London: Daily News, 1917);

The Soul of a Bishop: A Novel (with Just a Little Love in It) about Conscience and Religion and the Real Troubles of Life (London, New York, Toronto & Melbourne: Cassell, 1917; New York: Macmillan, 1917);

In the Fourth Year: Anticipations of a World Peace (London: Chatto & Windus, 1918; New York: Macmillan, 1918);

Joan and Peter: The Story of an Education (London, New York, Toronto & Melbourne: Cassell, 1918; New York: Macmillan, 1918);

British Nationalism and the League of Nations (London: League of Nations Union, 1918);

The Undying Fire: A Contemporary Novel (London, New York, Toronto & Melbourne: Cassell, 1919; New York: Macmillan, 1919);

The Idea of a League of Nations, by Wells and others (London: Oxford University Press, 1919; Boston: Atlantic Monthly Press, 1919);

The Way to a League of Nations, by Wells and others (London: Oxford University Press, 1919);

History Is One (New York: Ginn, 1919);

The Outline of History, Being a Plain History of Life and Mankind (24 parts, London: Newnes, 1919–1920; 1 volume, London: Newnes, 1920; 2 volumes, New York: Macmillan, 1921);

Frank Swinnerton, Personal Sketches: Together With Notes and Comments on the Novels of Frank Swinnerton, by Wells, Arnold Bennett, and G. M. Overton (New York: Doran, 1920);

Russia in the Shadows (London: Hodder & Stoughton, 1920; New York: Doran, 1921);

The Salvaging of Civilisation (London, New York, Toronto & Melbourne: Cassell, 1921; New York: Macmillan, 1921);

The New Teaching of History: With a Reply to Some Recent Criticisms of The Outline of History (London, New York, Toronto & Melbourne: Cassell, 1921);

Washington and the Hope of Peace (London, Glasgow, Melbourne & Auckland: Collins, 1922); republished as *Washington and the Riddle of Peace* (New York: Macmillan, 1922);

What H. G. Wells Thinks about "The Mind in the Making" (New York & London: Harper, 1922);

The Secret Places of the Heart (London, New York, Toronto & Melbourne: Cassell, 1922; New York: Macmillan, 1922);

The World, Its Debts, and the Rich Men: A Speech (London: Finer, 1922);

University of London Election: An Electoral Letter (London: Finer, 1922);

A Short History of the World (London, New York, Toronto & Melbourne: Cassell, 1922; New York: Macmillan, 1922);

Men Like Gods (London, New York, Toronto & Melbourne: Cassell, 1923; New York: Macmillan, 1923);

Socialism and the Scientific Motive (London: Cooperative Printing Society, 1923);

To the Electors of London University General Election, 1923, from H. G. Wells, B.Sc., London (London: Craig, 1923);

The Labour Ideal of Education (London: Craig, 1923);

The Story of a Great Schoolmaster: Being a Plain Account of the Life and Ideas of Sanderson of Oundle (London: Chatto & Windus, 1924; New York: Macmillan, 1924);

The Dream: A Novel (London: Cape, 1924; New York: Macmillan, 1924);

A Year of Prophesying (London: Unwin, 1924; New York: Macmillan, 1925);

Christina Alberta's Father (London: Cape, 1925; New York: Macmillan, 1925);

A Forecast of the World's Affairs (New York & London: Encyclopaedia Britannica, 1925);

The World of William Clissold: A Novel at a New Angle (3 volumes, London: Benn, 1926; 2 volumes, New York: Doran, 1926);

Mr. Belloc Objects to The Outline of History (London: Watts, 1926; New York: Doran, 1926);

Democracy under Revision: A Lecture Delivered at the Sorbonne, March 15th, 1927 (London: Leonard & Virginia Woolf, 1927; New York: Doran, 1927);

Meanwhile: The Picture of a Lady (London: Benn, 1927; New York: Doran, 1927);

Experiments on Animals: Views For and Against, by Wells and George Bernard Shaw (London: British Union for the Abolition of Vivisection, 1927);

Playing at Peace (London: National Council for the Prevention of War, 1927);

The Short Stories of H. G. Wells (London: Benn, 1927; Garden City, N.Y.: Doubleday, Doran, 1929);

Wells circa 1895, when he published his first short novel, The Time Machine

republished as *The Complete Short Stories* (London: Benn, 1966);

Wells's Social Anticipations, edited by H. W. Laidler (New York, 1927);

The Way the World Is Going: Guesses and Forecasts of the Years Ahead (London: Benn, 1928; Garden City, N.Y.: Doubleday, Doran, 1929);

The Open Conspiracy: Blue Prints for a World Revolution (London: Gollancz, 1928; Garden City, N.Y.: Doubleday, Doran, 1928; revised, London: Leonard & Virginia Woolf, 1930); revised again as *What Are We to Do With Our Lives?* (London: Heinemann, 1931; Garden City, N.Y.: Doubleday, Doran, 1931);

Mr. Blettsworthy on Rampole Island (London: Benn, 1928; Garden City, N.Y.: Doubleday, Doran, 1928);

The King Who Was a King: The Book of a Film (London: Benn, 1929); republished as *The King Who Was King: An Unconventional Novel* (Garden City, N.Y.: Doubleday, Doran, 1929);

The Common Sense of World Peace: An Address Delivered to the Reichstag at Berlin, on Monday, April 15th,

1929 (London: Leonard & Virginia Woolf, 1929);

The Adventures of Tommy (London: Harrap, 1929; New York: Stokes, 1929);

Imperialism and the Open Conspiracy (London: Faber & Faber, 1929);

The Science of Life: A Summary of Contemporary Knowledge about Life and Its Possibilities, by Wells, Julian Huxley, and G. P. Wells (31 parts, London: Amalgamated Press, 1929–1930; 3 volumes, London: Amalgamated Press, 1930; 4 volumes, Garden City, N.Y.: Doubleday, Doran, 1931);

The Autocracy of Mr. Parham: His Remarkable Adventures in This Changing World (London: Heinemann, 1930; Garden City, N.Y.: Doubleday, Doran, 1930);

Points of View: A Series of Broadcast Addresses, by Wells and others (London: Allen & Unwin, 1930);

The Way to World Peace (London: Benn, 1930);

The Problem of the Troublesome Collaborator: An Account of Certain Difficulties in an Attempt to Produce a Work in Collaboration and of the Intervention of the Society of Authors Therein (Woking, U.K.: Privately printed, 1930);

Settlement of the Trouble between Mr. Thring and Mr. Wells: A Footnote to The Problem of the Troublesome Collaborator (Woking, U.K.: Privately printed, 1930);

Divorce as I See It, by Wells and others (London: Douglas, 1930);

The Work, Wealth and Happiness of Mankind (2 volumes, Garden City, N.Y.: Doubleday, Doran, 1931; 1 volume, London: Heinemann, 1932);

The New Russia: Eight Talks Broadcast, by Wells and others (London: Faber & Faber, 1931);

After Democracy: Addresses and Papers on the Present World Situation (London: Watts, 1932);

The Bulpington of Blup: Adventures, Poses, Stresses, Conflicts, and Disasters in a Contemporary Brain (London: Hutchinson, 1932; New York: Macmillan, 1933);

What Should be Done – Now: A Memorandum on the World Situation (New York: Day, 1932);

The Shape of Things to Come: The Ultimate Revolution (London: Hutchinson, 1933; New York: Macmillan, 1933);

Experiment in Autobiography: Discoveries and Conclusions of a Very Ordinary Brain (Since 1866), 2 volumes (London: Gollancz & Cresset, 1934; New York: Macmillan, 1934);

Stalin-Wells Talk: The Verbatim Record and a Discussion by G. Bernard Shaw, H. G. Wells, J. M. Keynes,

Ernst Toller and Others (London: New Statesman & Nation, 1934);

The New America: The New World (London: Cresset,
1935; New York: Macmillan, 1935);

*Things to Come: A Film Story Based on the Material Con-
tained in His History of the Future, "The Shape of
Things to Come"* (London: Cresset, 1935; New
York: Macmillan, 1935);

The Anatomy of Frustration: A Modern Synthesis (London: Cresset, 1936; New York: Macmillan,
1936);

The Croquet Player: A Story (London: Chatto &
Windus, 1936; New York: Viking, 1937);

*The Idea of a World Encyclopedia: A Lecture Delivered at
the Royal Institution, November 20th, 1936* (London: Leonard & Virginia Woolf, 1936);

*Man Who Could Work Miracles: A Film Story Based on
the Material Contained in His Short Story* (London: Cresset, 1936; New York: Macmillan,
1936);

Star Begotten: A Biological Fantasia (London: Chatto &
Windus, 1937; New York: Viking, 1937);

The Informative Content of Education (London: British
Association, 1937);

Brynhild (London: Methuen, 1937); republished as
Brynhild; or, The Show of Things (New York:
Scribners, 1937);

The Camford Visitation (London: Methuen, 1937);

The Brothers: A Story (London: Chatto & Windus,
1938; New York: Viking, 1938);

World Brain (London: Methuen, 1938; Garden City,
N.Y: Doubleday, Doran, 1938);

Apropos of Dolores (London: Cape, 1938; New York:
Scribners, 1938);

The Holy Terror (London: Joseph, 1939; New York:
Simon & Schuster, 1939);

Travels of a Republican in Search of Hot Water
(Harmondsworth, U.K.: Penguin, 1939);

*The Fate of Homo Sapiens: An Unemotional Statement of
the Things That Are Happening to Him Now and of
the Immediate Possibilities Confronting Him* (Lon-
don: Secker & Warburg, 1939); republished as
*The Fate of Man: An Unemotional Statement of the
Things That Are Happening to Him Now and of the
Immediate Possibilities Confronting Him* (New
York: Alliance/Longmans, Green, 1939);

*The New World Order, Whether It Is Attainable, How It
Can Be Attained, and What Sort of World a World
at Peace Will Have to Be* (London: Secker &
Warburg, 1940; New York: Knopf, 1940);

The Rights of Man; or, What Are We Fighting For?
(Harmondsworth, U.K. & New York: Penguin, 1940);

Babes in the Darkling Wood (London: Secker & Warburg, 1940; New York: Alliance, 1940);

*The Common Sense of War and Peace: World Revolution or
War Unending?* (Harmondsworth, U.K. & New
York: Penguin, 1940);

All Aboard for Ararat (London: Secker & Warburg,
1940; New York: Alliance, 1941);

Two Hemispheres or One World? (N.p., 1940);

*Guide to the New World: A Handbook of Constructive
World Revolution* (London: Gollancz, 1941);

You Can't Be Too Careful: A Sample of Life 1901–1951
(London: Secker & Warburg, 1941; New
York: Putnam, 1942);

*The Outlook for Homo Sapiens: An Amalgamation and
Modernization of Two Books, The Fate of Homo Sapiens and The New World Order, Published Sever-
ally in 1939 and 1940* (London: Secker & Warburg, 1942);

*Modern Russian and English Revolutionaries: A Frank Ex-
change of Ideas between Commander Leu Uspensky,
Soviet Writer, and H. G. Wells* (London: Privately printed, 1942);

Science and the World-Mind (London: New Europe,
1942);

*Phoenix: A Summary of the Inescapable Conditions of
World Reorganisation* (London: Secker & Warburg, 1942; Girard, Kans.: Haldeman-Julius,
1942);

*A Thesis on the Quality of Illusion in the Continuity of Indi-
vidual Life of the Higher Metazoa, with Particular
Reference to the Species Homo Sapiens* (London:
Privately printed, 1942);

*The Conquest of Time, by H. G. Wells: Written to Replace
His First and Last Things* (London: Watts,
1942);

The New Rights of Man (Girard, Kans.: Haldeman-
Julius, 1942);

Crux Ansata: An Indictment of the Roman Catholic Church
(Harmondsworth, U.K. & New York: Pen-
guin, 1943; New York: Agora, 1944);

The Mosley Outrage (London: Daily Worker, 1943);

*'42 to '44: A Contemporary Memoir upon Human Behav-
iour during the Crisis of the World Revolution* (London: Secker & Warburg, 1944);

Reshaping Man's Heritage: Biology in the Service of Man,
by Wells, J. S. Huxley, and J. B. S. Haldane
(London: Allen & Unwin, 1944);

The Happy Turning: A Dream of Life (London & Toronto: Heinemann, 1945);

Mind at the End of Its Tether (London: Heinemann,
1945);

*Mind at the End of Its Tether and The Happy Turning: A
Dream of Life* (New York: Didier, 1946);

The Desert Daisy, edited by Gordon N. Ray (Urbana, Ill.: Beta Phi Mu, 1957);

Hoopdriver's Holiday, edited by Michael Timko (West Lafayette, Ind.: Purdue University Press, 1964);

H. G. Wells, Journalism, and Prophecy, 1893–1946: An Anthology, edited by W. Warren Wagar (Boston: Houghton Mifflin, 1964);

The Wealth of Mr. Waddy: A Novel, edited by Harris Wilson (Carbondale: Southern Illinois University Press, 1969; London: Feffer & Simmons, 1969);

Early Writings in Science and Science Fiction, edited by Robert M. Philmus and David Y. Hughes (Berkeley, Los Angeles & London: University of California Press, 1975);

H. G. Wells's Literary Criticism, edited by Patrick Parrinder and Philmus (Brighton, U.K.: Harvester, 1980; Totowa, N.J.: Barnes & Noble, 1980);

H. G. Wells in Love, edited by G. P. Wells (London & Boston: Faber & Faber, 1984).

Collections: *The Scientific Romances* (London: Gollancz, 1933);

Stories of Men and Women (London: Hutchinson, 1933);

The Man with a Nose and Other Uncollected Short Stories of H. G. Wells, edited by J. R. Hammond (London: Athlone, 1984).

Editions: *The Works of H. G. Wells,* Atlantic Edition, 28 volumes, revised by Wells (London: Unwin, 1924; New York: Macmillan, 1924);

The Works of H. G. Wells, Essex Edition, 24 volumes (London: Benn, 1926–1927).

OTHER: Amy Catherine Wells, *The Book of Catherine Wells,* edited, with an introduction, by H. G. Wells (London: Chatto & Windus, 1928; Garden City, N.Y.: Doubleday, Doran, 1928).

Herbert George Wells was one of the most prolific and most popular writers of short fiction of his era and of the twentieth century. Some of his longer fictions, such as *The Time Machine: An Invention* (1895) and *The War of the Worlds* (1898), have formed the basis of well-known radio and screen productions; one or two tales nearly always find their way into anthologies of the modern short story and science fiction. Over the years the tastes of the reading public have changed, however, and his work has not always fared well; also, reading deeply in the stories is not always as rewarding as reading selectively, for themes and characters, too often repeated, begin to sound stale on successive encounters. Nevertheless, H. G. Wells remains one of the most important innovators in the history of short fiction.

Wells's career as a writer of short fiction is remarkable both for its fecundity and its brevity. His 1927 *The Short Stories of H. G. Wells* (republished as *The Complete Short Stories,* though not in fact complete) runs to 1,028 pages. But though Wells continued to write both fiction and nonfiction prolifically until his death in 1946, an essentially complete edition of the stories could have been compiled by 1910. He published one novella and four collections of short stories between 1895 and 1903; after that he continued to publish new collections of short stories, but they were primarily made up of work that had already appeared in the four original collections. Aside from apprentice work, Wells wrote eighty-one stories; of these, fully sixty-eight were written by 1903, and all but seven by 1910. Such a situation might seem to bode ill for the quality of the stories. Wells's stories are the products of his youth, but for this very reason they are the portion of his life's work that will be longest remembered. Much of Wells's late writing, most critics agree, is seriously marred by self-righteous preaching; the short stories, written earlier, are largely spared this infelicity, though hints of the bombast to come are just visible to the discerning eye. The best explore the inner world of the imagination, exploiting Wells's unbounded capacity for fantastic invention and the creation of logically derived possible worlds.

Wells was born on 21 September 1866 in the working-class community of Bromley, Kent, to Joseph and Sarah Wells. His parents were not well-to-do; his father, though in his past an outstanding cricketer, had become an unsuccessful small shopkeeper. When her husband's health prevented him from working after 1879, Sarah – who had been a lady's maid before her marriage – went back into service with her old mistress, becoming head housekeeper at Up Park, Sussex, one of the better-known country houses of England and the model for Bladesover in Wells's novel *Tono-Bungay* (1908). From 1879 to 1882 Wells himself served a series of completely uncongenial apprenticeships with a chemist and two drapers. Though he later made good use of his experiences in the drapers' shops in his novels *Kipps: The Story of a Simple Soul* (1905) and *The History of Mr. Polly* (1910), these were, as he put it in his *Experiment in Autobiography: Discoveries and Conclusions of a Very Ordinary Brain (Since 1866)* (1934), "the most miserable years of my life."

Finally, at age sixteen, a new life began when he convinced his mother to allow him to enroll as a student at the Midhurst Grammar School. He did so well at his studies that two years later, in 1884, he was awarded a scholarship to the Normal School of Science in South Kensington. Here, from 1884 to 1887, Wells studied the natural sciences and came under the influence of the great post-Darwinian evolutionist T. H. Huxley. He also began to write for publication in the student magazine, *The Science School Journal,* which he also edited. In addition to editorial prose, his student writings included several short stories. "A Tale of the Twentieth Century" (May 1887) deals with a high-velocity locomotive in 1999 that explodes, killing its passengers and making them martyrs to scientific progress. "The Devotee of Art" (November–December 1888) concerns a painter who ignores his wife to pursue his art, and "Walcote" (December 1888–January 1889) is a murder story with supernatural overtones. All of these stories suggest themes that recur in Wells's later work, but his most important student story is "The Chronic Argonauts" (April–June 1888), the first version of *The Time Machine.*

Wells also drew on his student days for "A Slip under the Microscope" (1896), one of his better short stories. "The year I spent in Huxley's class," Wells wrote in *Experiment in Autobiography,* "was beyond all question, the most educational year of my life." However, "A Slip under the Microscope," published in the avant-garde magazine *The Yellow Book,* suggests something of the doubts and anxieties of Wells's student days. William Hill, the story's protagonist, is torn between the claims of Darwinian/Huxleyan evolution on the one hand – which, as he hears during a lecture, declares that "from ovum to ovum is the goal of the higher vertebrata" – and on the other hand the claims of the aesthetic life, as articulated by artists such as William Morris. Responding to the "depressing peroration" of the biology lecturer, Hill replies, "That is our goal, perhaps – I admit it, as far as science goes. . . . But there are things beyond science."

One of those "things beyond science," as the story shows, is the love of a woman; at untoward moments Hill finds "his attention wandering from the fate of the mesoblastic somites or the probable meaning of the blastopore, to the thought of the girl with the brown eyes who sat at the table before him." Wells himself had fallen in love with his cousin Isabel Mary Wells in 1887, when he moved into a spare room her parents made available to him during his student years, and his infatuation with her nearly ruined him as a student. "Proximity and isolation," Wells said in his autobiography, "forced upon us the role of lovers, very innocent lovers."

Hill still does extremely well in his studies, but on his next exam he commits the sin alluded to in the story's title: while examining a slide, he unpremeditatedly moves it slightly, so that he gains an unfair advantage and is able to identify the specimen easily. He comes out on top in the examination, but though his dishonesty is not observed, he is haunted by the memory of its. Though his teachers insist that human life is merely the survival of the fittest – in this view cheating, if it helps one to come out on top, is wholly justified – Hill himself cannot help but feel that his victory is tainted. Finally, he confesses to the professor, who insists that Hill must be failed on the exam and as a result dismissed from the school. Even the school officials, it would seem, cannot carry their deterministic philosophy out to its logical conclusion.

Wells also left the Normal School without a degree because he needed to earn some money before completing his studies and getting married. He began with a disastrous teaching experience in Wales, where his health broke down, and he was forced to resign after a few months. He moved in with his mother at Up Park to convalesce from tuberculosis and kidney trouble. For a while he appeared to be in serious danger, but he recovered and was able to take another teaching job in 1888 at Henley House School near London. After receiving his B.Sci. degree in 1890, he began teaching for the University Correspondence College, and in 1891 he and Isabel were married. By this time he was becoming established as a journalist and working on his first two books under the auspices of the University Correspondence College: *Honours Physiography* (1893), with R. A. Gregory, and the two-volume *Text-Book of Biology* (1893).

About this time the tempestuous pattern that was to characterize Wells's romantic relationships began to develop. After only a few weeks of marriage Wells seduced one of Isabel's friends; as biographers Norman and Jeanne MacKenzie succinctly put it, "Infidelity became a symbol of freedom" for Wells. By the end of 1893 he had left Isabel and had moved in with one of his students from the University Correspondence College, Amy Catherine Robbins, whom Wells later christened "Jane." In 1895 Wells and Isabel were divorced, and on 27 October 1895 he and Amy Robbins were married.

During the time between his separation and divorce Wells returned to writing short fiction, this time in the *Pall Mall Budget.* In *Experiment in Autobiography* Wells later recalled its editor, Lewis Hind, suggesting "the idea of utilizing my special knowledge of science in the expanded weekly, in a series

Amy Catherine Robbins, who became Wells's second wife in 1895

of short stories to be called 'single sitting' stories. I was to have five guineas for each story." The first of these scientific stories was "The Stolen Bacillus" (published on 21 June 1894). Despite its foreboding title, it is a delightful lark, a sort of shaggy-dog story foisted off on both the reader and the story's antagonist. Like other Wells stories, it features a protagonist with a generic, scientific name: "the Bacteriologist." His foe is an anarchist and something of a social and physical degenerate. Convinced that it is full of deadly cholera bacteria, the anarchist steals a test tube from the Bacteriologist's laboratory, intending to poison the water supply of the entire city of London. But the Bacteriologist, it turns out, has lied to him about the contents of the test tube; like the anarchist, the Bacteriologist has tried to inflate his own importance by claiming that he held deadly cholera germs in his hand when in fact the test tube contained only a primate virus. When the anarchist is thwarted in his plans to contaminate the city's water, he drinks the "deadly" vial himself, hoping to become the agent of disaster. But the worst that will happen, according to the Bacteriologist, is that he may break out in a rash of blue spots.

Wells published nineteen short stories in 1894 and another fourteen the following year. One of the most interesting stories from the second year is "The Remarkable Case of Davidson's Eyes," published in the 21 March 1895 issue of the *Pall Mall Budget*. The narrator, Bellows, is at work in the lab-

oratory next door to Davidson's in the Harlow Technical College when he hears two loud crashes. When Bellows rushes over to see what is the matter, he is greeted by the spectacle of Davidson laughing maniacally and responding to objects and sights that are not present in his immediate environment. Davidson's eyes are wide open, and he is perfectly conscious, but of an altogether different place. In the course of one of his experiments he has smashed an electrometer and been blinded by a bright flash. Standing in his laboratory, Davidson believes himself to be standing on a beach and watching a ship.

After conversing with Bellows, Davidson is reluctantly convinced that he is indeed standing in his laboratory in England, but the visual hallucination persists. Finally, after three weeks of living exiled in his "phantasmal world," Davidson gradually begins to recover normal vision. As he regains normal vision, however, he starts to long for the vision of the beach that has been his home the past three weeks. Nevertheless, Davidson lets the vision go, marries Bellows's sister, and goes on to lead a regular life. Two years after his cure, however, Davidson chances to meet a man named Atkins, a former crew member of H.M.S. *Fulmar* – the ship that Davidson, when shown a picture, recognizes as the very ship of his "phantasmal world." Davidson's eyes had evidently been focused not on some imaginary scene but on a different slice of the real world – a phenomenon Bellows dubs "vision at a distance." The story closes with Bellows adducing, somewhat skeptically, the explanation put forward by his colleague Wade – an argument Bellows claims not to be able to understand, involving as it does "the Fourth Dimension, and a dissertation on theoretical kinds of space."

A similar scientific concept lies at the center of Wells's best-known story, *The Time Machine,* serialized in William Ernest Henley's *New Review* beginning in March 1895 and published as a book the following July. Ford Madox Ford later described the success Wells found with *The Time Machine:* "It did not take us long to recognize that here was Genius. . . . Fairy tales are a prime necessity of the world, and 'he and Science were going to provide us with a perfectly new brand.' And he did. And all Great London lay prostrate at his feet."

Part of Wells's genius in these stories of space and time is his controlled use of realistic setting and detail. The MacKenzies describe the strategy of *The Time Machine* and stories like it this way: "He heard of some new concept or invention. He next set the novel theory in a conventional background. Then, having made the incredible acceptable by his attention to detail, his imagination was free to make what fantasies he pleased out of the resulting conflict." Like Sir Arthur Conan Doyle's genius Sherlock Holmes, Wells's hero the Time Traveller is introduced in the congenial warmth of a sitting room, with a fire burning brightly and a group of men engaged in after-dinner conversation.

The Time Traveller develops for his guests a theory that the influence of Albert Einstein has made almost a commonplace today – that time is a fourth dimension. "Clearly . . . any real body," the Time Traveller explains to his auditors, "must have Length, Breadth, Thickness, and – Duration." The Time Traveller and his after-dinner companions discuss the vagaries of the time-space continuum for six pages, but Wells rescues the story from tedium by describing a working model of the Time Machine itself precisely but selectively in terms of materials and objects that would be familiar to his readers: "a glittering metallic framework, scarcely larger than a small clock, and very delicately made. There was ivory in it, and some transparent crystalline substance." In an unmanned trial the model works, and when the Time Traveller mounts the Time Machine itself, he is indeed transported far into the future.

The Time Traveller's vision of the future is strongly influenced by Wells's own views on evolution – another reason the story was so popular with its 1895 audience. Wells's views on the descent of humanity were not orthodoxly Darwinian but colored by the speculations of his teacher Huxley, who believed that, logically, evolution could as easily result in the decline of humankind as in its continual improvement. The world that the Time Traveller finds in A.D. 802,701 has long since passed its zenith and is in the process of precipitous decline. As a result of evolution humankind has become polarized into two distinct species. The Time Traveller first meets one of the Eloi, the highly refined, effete earth dwellers: "He struck me as being a very beautiful and graceful creature, but indescribably frail. His flushed face reminded me of the more beautiful kind of consumptive." Wells's conception of the Eloi seems influenced by contemporary concerns about decadence, flaunted by writers such as Walter Pater and Oscar Wilde. The explanation for this deterioration turns out to be surprisingly simple. "Diseases had been stamped out," the Time Traveller reports; additionally, "there were no signs of struggle, neither social nor economical struggle." For this life of ease, "what we should call the weak are as well equipped as the strong, are indeed no longer weak."

The Time Traveller meets a woman, one of the Eloi named Weena; together they encounter the other species of human beings, the Morlocks. In *Experiment in Autobiography* Wells suggests, "The future depicted in *The Time Machine* was a mere fantasy based upon the idea of the human species developing about divergent lines." The relegation of the Morlocks to subterranean territory is, according to Wells, the logical outcome of the increasing disparity during the nineteenth century between the haves and the have-nots. The split between the Eloi and the Morlocks replicates in some ways the difference between the Houyhnhnms and Yahoos in Jonathan Swift's *Gulliver's Travels* (1726), and like the Yahoos, the Morlocks are physically repulsive, being "just the half-bleached colour of the worms and things one sees preserved in spirit in a zoological museum." The Morlocks and Eloi exist in a kind of perpetual civil war; the Morlocks are forced to stay below ground during the day, but at night they surface and wreak havoc among the Eloi. The Morlocks, as the Time Traveller quickly discovers, are afraid of light and fire; but the Eloi, in their degenerate state, have lost the art of kindling flame.

The Time Traveller spends little more than a week with Weena and the Eloi; at his sojourn's end, however, rather than returning to 1895, he elects to continue on into the future to discover how the evolutionary pageant he has observed would play out. As he moves further into the future, the forms of life on earth grow less and less developed; eventually, "more than thirty million years hence," traces of life are no longer visible on the earth. Having seen the earth to its essential end, the Time Traveller returns home, tells his story to a largely unbelieving audience, and finally mounts his craft again. As the story closes, he has been gone for three years.

No piece of fiction, of whatever length, from the last decade of the nineteenth century presents a richer source of contemporary intellectual history. In its attitudes toward Marxism, communism, social degeneration, scientific knowledge, and even its proto-Einsteinian understanding of the continuity between space and time, *The Time Machine* is both profoundly a product of its time and, perhaps more interestingly, predictive of the future. It began drawing favorable comments in the *Review of Reviews* when it was still being serialized, and reviewers were uniformly enthusiastic when it appeared as a book the following July. The initial unsigned notice in the *Review of Reviews* labeled Wells "a man of genius" and concluded that "he has an imagination as gruesome as that of Poe," the first of many comparisons with the American author. Another un-signed review, in the *Daily Chronicle* for 27 July 1895, repeats the comparison with Edgar Allan Poe and adds a comparison with Robert Louis Stevenson's *The Strange Case of Dr. Jekyll and Mr. Hyde* (1886). Israel Zangwill spent much of his column in the September 1895 *Pall Mall Magazine* arguing with Wells's theory of time as the fourth dimension and the philosophical consequences of time travel, but he also judges the book "a brilliant little romance," and the Eloi and Morlocks "a fine imaginative creation worthy of Swift."

Later in 1895 Wells published his first short-story collection, *The Stolen Bacillus, and Other Incidents.* Including the title story and "The Strange Case of Davidson's Eyes," there are fifteen stories in this volume. One of the most interesting is "The Flowering of the Strange Orchid," originally published in the 2 August 1894 issue of the *Pall Mall Budget.* This is another scientific story; the protagonist, Winter-Wedderburn, is a botanist who hopes to gain immortality from the cultivation of orchids, since new varieties are commonly named for their discoverers. As the story opens, he attends an orchid auction and comes home with a mysterious bulb among his other purchases. All that Winter-Wedderburn knows for certain is that it is the last bulb that a collector named Batten procured before his death in the jungle. Batten was found in a swamp with "every drop of blood . . . taken out of him by the jungle-leeches."

Since Winter-Wedderburn believes this plant may be his ticket to immortality, he nurtures it painstakingly. When at last the orchid blooms it fills the air of the greenhouse with a "rich, intensely sweet scent, that overpowered every other." Winter-Wedderburn is overcome by the aroma, and when he does not return to the house for his 4:30 tea, his cousin finds him imprisoned in the aerial rootlets of the orchid, which are slowly draining the blood from his unconscious body. She manages to free him from the plant's grip, and he recovers; the orchid, however, declines and dies. Such, Wells seems to suggest, is the nature of obsession, scientific or otherwise; too frequently the relationship of master and servant suffers a reversal, and the scientist becomes thrall to the object of his study.

The mythopoeic "The Lord of the Dynamos," which critic Roslynn D. Haynes calls one of Wells's "almost perfect short stories," has an even clearer moral. Like Joseph Conrad's "Heart of Darkness" (1902), Wells's story is about the clash of the traditional and modern worlds. A representative of the ancient world, Azuma-zi, "out of the mysterious

East," arrives in England and encounters the industrial world in the form of a dynamo. Sensing the immense power the dynamo wields, Azuma-zi makes it the object of his veneration. Eventually he decides that Holroyd, his brutal British foreman, must be sacrificed to the Lord of Dynamos and wrestles him into the live coils of the machine, where he is killed instantly. Soon after, Azuma-zi decides to offer another human sacrifice to the machine. This time, however, he does not win the wrestling match, and at the prospect of having his earlier murder uncovered, Azuma-zi rushes headlong for the dynamo and electrocutes himself. Thus ends the worship, as the narrator calls it, of "the Dynamo Deity" – "perhaps the most short-lived of all religions. Yet withal it could at least boast a Martyrdom and a Human Sacrifice."

Actually, worship of the machine is one of the most enduring forms of worship in modern history. Holroyd, though he does not literally worship the dynamo, does deliver a "theological lecture" on the machine: " 'Look at that,' said Holroyd; 'where's your 'eathen idol to match 'im? . . . Kill a hundred men. Twelve per cent. on the ordinary shares,' said Holroyd, 'and that's something like a Gord.' " Like a vast and impersonal god, it carries on in power, despite the death of two human beings in its coils; the only sign to the outside world that anything is amiss is the momentary disruption in rail service they experience. It is possible that Henry Adams's well-known chapter in *The Education of Henry Adams* (1907) called "The Virgin and the Dynamo" owes something to the metaphor Wells originates here.

The Stolen Bacillus, and Other Incidents is not entirely concerned with science and technology. "The Temptation of Harringay," originally published in *St. James Gazette* (9 February 1895), is one of the most interesting of Wells's many stories that deal with the dilemma of the artist. R. M. Harringay is, as the story opens, an extremely competent painter, but he wants to be great. Quite suddenly his wish appears to have been granted. He has just completed a portrait of an organ grinder, but it does not wholly please him. As he continues to contemplate and touch up the painting, Harringay imagines that the expression on the face changes of its own accord. Harringay's attempts to touch up the portrait become a struggle not with his own vision but with the painting itself; finally the painting declares its independence in an overt gesture: "*The diabolified Italian before him shut both his eyes, pursed his mouth, and wiped the colour off his face with his hand.*"

The figure in the painting quickly reveals himself both as a devil and as a figure of the self-doubt

*The first page of the magazine publication of Wells's short story
about a man who dreams of the end of the world*

felt by all artists, telling Harringay, "you haven't an idea what your picture ought to look like." As the conversation develops, the painting begins to reproach Harringay particularly for his overly intellectual approach to art, arguing that this is the source of his paralysis; but what appears, dramatically, to be preventing Harringay from pursuing his gift is not his knowledge but rather the self-consciousness represented in and given voice by the painting itself.

Harringay attempts to paint out the Italian devil in the canvas with red paint and thus silence his internal censor. Painter and painting struggle, and as Harringay gains the upper hand the painting is ready to make a deal. But Harringay has found his lost nerve and is not interested in the devil's pact: "Rubbish. . . . Do you think I want to go to perdition simply for the pleasure of painting a good picture." The devil ups the ante to two, three, four, and finally five masterpieces in exchange for his life,

but Harringay, having fetched a large tin of enamel and a large brush, proceeds to paint *his* masterpiece out of existence. The story thus presents an allegory of the struggle involved in all true artistic creation; in order to keep painting, Harringay must obliterate his one true masterpiece, for its genuine greatness gives the lie to the stale expressions and gestures of his other works. Thus, as the story concludes, Harringay "never has produced a masterpiece, and in the opinion of his intimate friends probably never will."

Despite the success of *The Time Machine,* this collection earned Wells only a twenty-pound advance from his publisher and was not widely reviewed. The *Bookman* of London and *The Athenaeum* noticed it favorably but briefly. Frank Harris's *Saturday Review,* however, gave it a more substantial discussion, mentioning the author's "remarkable deftness in the employment of scientific resources" and declaring that "the tales in this volume remind one not infrequently of Mr. Rudyard Kipling" – very high praise in 1895. On the other hand, Arthur Waugh, the father of Evelyn Waugh and an important reviewer, in his "London Letter" for the New York *Critic* on 21 March 1896 was presumably thinking of this volume when he suggested that Wells should give up short stories and concentrate on longer works: "Mr. H. G. Wells, the author of 'The Time Machine,' is, I am told, about to give up the writing of short stories. . . . His judgment may have helped him here, for he is certainly best when he has a wide canvas."

During the mid 1890s Wells and Jane changed residences frequently as their financial situation improved, finally buying their first house in 1896 in Worcester Park. These years brought new literary friendships for Wells – with George Gissing, whom he first met in 1896, and with Arnold Bennett, with whom he began to correspond in 1897. By this time Wells had become a very prolific writer, publishing between 1895 and 1897 – in addition to his short fiction – six books, including two popular science-fiction novels, *The Island of Dr. Moreau* (1896) and *The Invisible Man: A Grotesque Romance* (1897).

In 1897 Wells also published his second short-story collection, *The Plattner Story, and Others,* which like *The Stolen Bacillus, and Other Incidents* contained fifteen stories, including "A Slip under the Microscope." "Pollock and the Porroh Man," originally published in the *New Budget* (23 May 1895), continues Wells's fascination, seen in "The Lord of Dynamos," with the encounter between the "civilized" and "savage" mind. Its drama consists almost entirely in the struggle between the two title characters: an Englishman named Pollock, on business on the west coast of Africa, and a sort of witch doctor of the Mendi people called the Porroh Man. Pollock witnesses the murder of a native woman at the Porroh Man's hands; he instinctively fires at him and wounds him in the hand. Using British standards of right conduct, Pollock sees himself as justified in attempting to prevent or avenge the young woman's murder; but, significantly, no one else, including his British superior Waterhouse, believes that Pollock has acted appropriately. Part of the story's fascination is owing to Wells's canny decision never to define precisely one of the story's central concepts, "Porroh." It seems to be a species of native witchcraft, perhaps akin to voodoo, but it is never explained, and the repeated references to "Porroh" cumulatively create a sense of undefined menace that haunts both the readers and Pollock. He is sent home in disgrace; when he reaches the port of Sulyma, on his way back to England, the

local white trader runs through a short list of the signs that the Porroh is in effect, and Pollock recognizes every one: bad dreams, snakes, pains in the bones. Pollock even has the Porroh Man murdered, but when he gets back to England he continues to be haunted day and night. Finally, on Christmas morning, when his sense of touch betrays him as well, Pollock realizes he cannot go on and takes his life. First published in 1895, several years before Conrad's "Heart of Darkness," it is tempting to read Wells's story as an allegory of the imperialist guilt that was building in the collective psyche of the British people during the last years of Victoria's reign.

While "Pollock and the Porroh Man" bears a strong political and social message, "The Sad Story of a Dramatic Critic," originally published in the *New Budget* (15 August 1895), is simply an entertaining literary fable. When he wrote this story Wells was acting as dramatic critic for the *Pall Mall Gazette.* The parallels between his situation as dramatic critic and Egbert Craddock Cummins's situation in the story are too pronounced to be ignored. In their biography the MacKenzies describe the story of Wells's appointment. Early in 1895 he was summoned to the office of Harry Cust, the editor. "When he arrived, Cust put two tickets into his hand and informed him that, from the following night, he had become a theatre critic. Wells protested that his experience was limited to Gilbert and Sullivan, the Crystal Palace annual pantomime and two plays. 'Exactly what I want,' Cust drily replied." This incident, only thinly veiled, is the opening of "The Sad Story of a Dramatic Critic," with "Barnaby, the editor of the *Fiery Cross*" standing in for Cust and Egbert Cummins for Wells.

Starting from this frankly autobiographical basis, Wells takes the story in an altogether original and delightful direction. Cummins is overwhelmed by his first experience of the theater; as he returns to his rooms that evening, he finds the stylized and exaggerated speech and gestures of the stage actors taking over his otherwise timid self. He decides, half joking, that he has been stricken with the rare disease "Stage-Walkitis"; acting was too much for his delicate and high-strung system. As Cummins grows more and more affected, his fiancée grows less and less interested in his suit. " 'Egbert,' she said, 'you are not yourself.' 'Ah!' Involuntarily I clutched my diaphragm and averted my head (as is the way with them.) 'There!' she said. *'What do you mean?'* I said, whispering in vocal italics." Cummins subsequently loses her and begins, fatally, to associate with actors. He is left in the desperate situation,

as the story draws to a close, that no one in "the ordinary life" will take him seriously. He grows de-
spondent and concludes that he must "abandon the
struggle altogether" and take to the stage. In "The
Sad Story of a Dramatic Critic" Wells cleverly
holds the mirror up to contemporary dramatic fashion in a comic mode; indeed, the story will stand as
a savagely funny criticism of the 1890s English
stage long after the reviews he wrote for the *Pall
Mall Gazette* are forgotten.

"Under the Knife," which marks a return to
scientific themes, was first published in January
1896 in the *New Review*. The story is the first-person
narrative of an unmarried, unnamed middle-aged
man. He is suffering from an unnamed medical condition having something to do with his liver, which
requires surgery. The first quarter of the story is
given over to the narrator's thoughts as he considers the possibility of his death under the knife. He is
sobered by the realization that few if any would
miss him, but so dead does he feel already, before
undergoing surgery, that he says, "I could not pity
myself, nor feel sorry for my friends, nor conceive
of them as grieving for me." This dullness of affect
the narrator suspects may be an anticipation of actual corporeal death. The surgeon and his assistant
arrive, and the narrator breathes in the chloroform
and is rendered unconscious. He, however, is certain that he is not unconscious but dead.

The narrator flies out of his body and above
London, like Peter Pan, and describes his pan-
oramic view of the city and environs. Haynes calls
the "magnificent sweep of the . . . narrator's dream
experiences . . . the most original of the dreams in
Wells's fiction." As he flies farther and farther from
earth, the things of earth recede from consciousness: "I saw things with a serene self-forgetfulness,
even as if I were God." At a great distance from the
earth, from London, from his body, however, the
narrator is summoned back to the world of matter;
a huge cloud appears as a huge, clenched, shadowy
hand, which then metamorphoses into the real hand
of the surgeon poised above the narrator's liver. Before he knows he is still alive in surgery, the narrator hears "a voice, which seemed to run to the utter-
most parts of space," which declares, "There will be
no more pain." The voice is not that of God, however, but that of the surgeon (though the confusion
is surely not accidental). The narrator has survived
the surgery, which is pronounced a success. Given
the psychic journey the patient has taken under the
anesthetic, there is reason to believe at the story's
end that he may have been restored to emotional
health by the surgical procedure as well.

"The Red Room," published in March 1896 in
the *Idler,* is a psychologically motivated ghost story
similar to Henry James's famous *The Turn of the
Screw* (1898). Its first-person narrator has decided to
take up a challenge, unvoiced within the story itself,
to spend a night alone in the infamous red room of
Lorraine Castle. To a reader of gothic fiction the
initial scenic and character descriptions would be
enough to argue against the vigil; the night is dark
and lonely, and the residents of the castle, according to the narrator, are grotesque. The room itself,
when the narrator enters it, is largely unremarkable.
The only significant way in which it is out of the ordinary, apparently, is that it has "two big mirrors,"
and there are unpleasant echoes. In its physical
characteristics the red room puts a modern reader
in mind of the Marabar Caves of E. M. Forster's *A
Passage to India* (1924). In that novel the caves mock-
ingly send back all sensory data sent out to them, so
that they function like psychic amplifiers, bombard-
ing their occupant with the contents of her own
mind.

This, in effect, is what Lorraine Castle's red
room accomplishes. The room and its attendant legends create a heightened awareness in even a skeptical investigator such as the narrator, thus creating
ghosts of the most ordinary sort of epiphenomena.
Waking in the morning, bruised and bandaged, the
narrator slowly recovers his memory of the previous night and proceeds to tell a cautionary tale to
the castle's caretakers. What haunts the room, he
says, is "the worst of all the things that haunt poor
mortal man, and that is, in all its nakedness – *Fear!*"
Such fear, Wells suggests, is perhaps the last and
most tenacious vestige of a prescientific, premodern
age.

"The Plattner Story," the title story of the collection, was first published in April 1896 in the *New
Review*. The reason for its priority in Wells's estimation is not easy to guess. Like "The Remarkable
Case of Davidson's Eyes," it traces the strange
physical changes that befall a scientist after an explosion during a laboratory experiment; also like
that story and *The Time Machine,* it investigates
travel in the fourth dimension. Finally, like "Under
the Knife," it describes its protagonist's journey outside of space and time – a journey that, however,
fantastic, begins to sound a bit too familiar.

In "The Sea-Raiders," originally published in
the *Weekly Sun Literary Supplement* on 6 December
1896, Wells takes a fantastic creature worthy of his
otherworldly stories and locates it in the present.
The sea raiders of the title, *Haploteuthis Ferox,* are apparently members of the class Cephalopoda, which

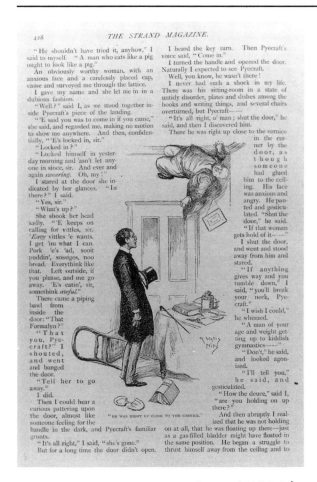

A page from the 1903 magazine publication of Wells's "The Truth about Pyecroft," a story in which a man takes a mysterious "recipe" to lose weight

includes the cuttlefish, squid, and octopus; beyond this conjecture, however, Wells is teasingly vague about the exact appearance of these creatures. Some of the incidentals of the beast – for example, its Latin name and the location of previous sightings – are quite specific. But in real, visual terms, especially at the story's opening, the narrator is suggestively vague, since menace described becomes less menacing. The beast becomes vivid and real through "the extraordinary affair at Sidmouth," which the story narrates. The hero of the story is a retired tea dealer named Fison spending time at the seaside town of Sidmouth. Walking on the shore, he catches sight of a pinkish object floating in the seaweeds, which turns out on closer inspection to be "the partially devoured body of a human being, but whether man or woman he was unable to say." Fison quickly discovers that he is surrounded by the monsters who have killed the person that floats before him. After several attacks, Fison finally escapes, and the sea raiders swim out to sea.

The sea raiders seem to resemble the giant sea creatures in Jules Verne's *Vingt Mille Lieues sous les mers* (1870; translated as *Twenty Thousand Leagues under the Sea,* 1873) – primordial creatures that seem to tap into an irrational fear in modern readers. The narrator, in closing, bids them good riddance in terms that invite psychological interpretation, hoping that they have now "returned for good, to the sunless depths of the middle seas, out of which they have so strangely and so mysteriously arisen." Here the sea creatures seem to symbolize the primeval inhabitants of the psyche; as Sigmund Freud predicts, these repressed, primordial beings return, breaking through the surface of the conscious mind and terrorizing modern citizens.

The Plattner Story, and Others was more widely and enthusiastically reviewed than *The Stolen Bacillus, and Other Incidents* had been. An unsigned review in the *Athenaeum* expressed relief that Wells had "happily given up the exaggerated horrors of *The Island of Dr. Moreau* for stories quite in his best vein." This review noted that "precision in the unessential and vagueness in the essential are really the basis of Mr. Wells's art, and they convey admirably the just amount of conviction." Similarly, the *Daily Chronicle* said that "he tells us just as much as enables us to persuade ourselves that we understand all about it, and when once he has gotten us to that comfortable state of mind we are prepared to believe anything."

Some reviewers, unlike the reviewer for the *Athenaeum,* seemed to think these stories were too gruesome. Thus the *Review of Reviews* said that they "compel you to realize horrible possibilities, and to look nightmares in the whites of their eyes." When later in 1897 Wells's first American collection of short stories, essentially combining the contents of the two British volumes, was published as *Thirty Strange Stories* (1897), the reviewer for *The New York Times* regretted that "Mr. Wells, as a general thing, revels in the awful and is very fond of the ghastly" but pointed out that the stories "are not invariably as grim and shocking as might be expected. There is real fun in some of them."

The year 1898 was a difficult one for Wells, as several years of overwork resulted in a serious breakdown of his health, with the problem, as in 1887, variously diagnosed as tuberculosis and kidney trouble. He was now in a position to take some time off from writing, and he and Jane spent much of the year in different seaside resorts on the Kentish coast. Here he met and befriended both Henry James and Joseph Conrad, who lived nearby; he also went to Italy with Gissing, the first of his many trips abroad. This year also saw the publication of Wells's widely known novel *The War of the Worlds,* a story of the invasion of Earth by Martians who are finally defeated only by their lack of resistance to Earth's diseases.

In 1899 Wells's third collection of short fiction, *Tales of Space and Time,* appeared. It shows a continued interest in Mars. In "The Crystal Egg" an antique dealer discovers that an egg in his shop enables him to see scenes on the red planet — and presumably allows the Martians to see into his antique shop. "The Star" is a more serious story, and although Martians figure in it only peripherally, it is as apocalyptic as *The War of the Worlds.* It was originally published in the Christmas 1897 issue of *Graphic,* and the story's Christmas, and Christian, symbolism is not accidental; neither, perhaps, is the fact that the story was published at the end of the nineteenth century. The story begins on "the first day of the new year," when irregularities in the orbit of Neptune first suggest to scientists that something is amiss in the solar system. Within a few days the cause has become apparent: "A vast mass of matter it was, bulky, heavy, rushing without warning out of the black mystery of the sky into the radiance of the sun." The heavenly body is on a collision course with Neptune, and it occurs in due time. The newpapers announce the imminent planetary collision, and scientists as well as the public at large wait with interest to witness the destruction of that planet.

Though it is hit, the planet is not destroyed. Instead, Neptune and the satellite combine and begin to fall toward the sun. The computations of a master mathematician show that the new star will not only fall into the sun but will apparently collide with the Earth on its way. As days pass, the star grows larger every night, then larger by the hour; on Earth temperatures rise; tides rise; and volcanoes erupt. The apocalypse seems near, but at the last minute Earth is given a miraculous reprieve. The collision is avoided, but the Earth has been devastated, since earthquakes, floods, volcanoes, and tidal waves have pummeled the land. There are also permanent changes: "everywhere the days were hotter than of yore, and the sun larger, and the moon, shrunk to a third of its former size, took now fourscore days between its new and new."

Despite these cataclysmic changes, Wells chooses in the end not to emphasize difference but stasis, for the story concludes with the viewpoint of Martian astronomers. " 'Considering the mass and temperature of the missile that was flung through our solar system into the sun,' one wrote, 'it is as-tonishing what a little damage the earth, which it missed so narrowly, has sustained.' " Planetary collision, when the planet was Neptune, was nothing more than light entertainment for the residents of Earth, and the near devastation of the Earth at the story's end seems minor to the Martians.

A matched pair of stories that Wells referred to as "two series of linked incidents," originally published in 1897, make for an interesting study in opposites. The two stories, clearly intended by Wells as complementary, are "A Story of the Stone Age," published in the *Idler,* and "A Story of the Days to Come," which appeared in the *Pall Mall Magazine.* They present striking contrasts in both their chronological settings and their literary merits. "A Story of the Days to Come," as might be expected, spurs on Wells's imagination to heights only rarely seen in the stories; "A Story of the Stone Age," on the other hand, is a sort of Paleolithic dime novel recounting the adventures and exploits, fifty thousand years ago, of the improbably named Ugh-lomi and "his woman," Eudena. In some of the scenic and character description Wells's knowledge of archaeology in particular and the world of science in general stands him in good stead. However, once the primitive-sounding names and uncivilized setting are stripped away, the story is really the worst sort of melodrama.

The far more substantial and interesting "A Story of the Days to Come" takes place sometime early in the twenty-second century, when the state of British civilization bears interesting similarities to the world described in George Orwell's *Nineteen Eighty-Four* (1949). The story focuses early on the fortunes of Morris, or Mwres, as it comes to be spelled and pronounced in the twenty-second century, who works at an appropriately futuristic occupation as an official of "the Wind Vane and Waterfall Trust." Several of Wells's visions for the future were remarkably prescient; for instance, he liked in later life to take credit for having invented the military tank in his 1903 story "The Land Ironclads." In "A Story of the Days to Come" he predicts a shift from a print-based to an audiovisually based culture. Another great change in the world of the story is the far greater reliance upon the skills of the hypnotist, whose role is "impressing things upon the memory, effacing unpleasant ideas, controlling and overcoming instinctive but undesirable impulses," paralleling the role assumed by brainwashing in Orwell's novel.

Mwres has consulted a hypnotist in the hope that he might persuade his daughter, Elizabeth, not to marry Denton, the young man with whom she has become infatuated. Uncharacteristically for their time, Elizabeth and Denton believe that love can conquer all obstacles, and when they marry, they face a terrible ordeal: "To marry and be very poor in the cities of that time was – for any one who had lived pleasantly – a very dreadful thing. . . . In the twenty-second century . . . the growth of the city storey above storey, and the coalescence of buildings had led to a vast series of sumptuous hotels in the upper storeys and halls of the city fabric; the industrial population dwelt beneath in the tremendous ground-floor basement, so to speak, of the place."

Denton and Elizabeth work at menial jobs for minimal wages, eking out a bloodless and increasingly loveless existence. As Denton descends to the subhuman level of his coworkers, he has increasingly little in common with his bowed but unbroken wife, but they are able to stay together until the story's end, when Wells self-consciously connects the story to the earlier "A Story of the Stone Age," locating his twenty-second-century couple on grounds "that had once been the squatting-place of the children of Uya," Ugh-lomi's archenemy. The story's closing dialogue mirrors, in an even more dispassionate and pessimistic tone, the close of "The Star": "Whether we die or live, we are in the making. . . . As time goes on – *perhaps* – men will be wiser. . . . Wiser. . . . Will they ever understand?"

The fifth and last story in the volume, "The Man Who Could Work Miracles," strikes an entirely different note, dealing with a little clerk named Fotheringay who is much given to debates in the bar of the local public house, the Long Dragon. One evening, in the middle of asserting the impossibility of miracles, he begins to work them. Beginning with small miracles, such as turning a lamp upside down, he moves on to bigger things – miraculously transporting a meddling police constable to San Francisco, then helping the Congregational minister miraculously to reform all the drunkards in the neighborhood. Finally the minister, impatient to reform all the village's problems before sunrise, asks Fotheringay to make time stop by stopping the rotation of the Earth. Suddenly Wells brings in a scientific perspective and puts Fotheringay and the minister in the middle of all the calamities that would actually occur on the surface of the planet if it suddenly stopped its rotation. Since Fotheringay still has his miraculous powers, however, he is able to undo the damage by wishing everything back the way it was before – giving up his powers and suddenly finding himself back in the Long Dragon in the middle of his debate just before his first miracle.

This comic version of his own apocalyptic tendencies was the one Wells short story that was made into a movie during his lifetime; it was directed by Lothar Mendes and starred Roland Young as Fotheringay. Wells did not write the screenplay, which differed substantially from the original story, but he did play a role in the production, which was favorably received when it appeared in 1936.

The critical reception of *Tales of Space and Time,* however, was far less favorable than that accorded Wells's earlier volumes of short fiction. The *Academy* was reasonably positive, saying, "All of these tales are good: clearly and courageously thought out, fitted together expertly, straightforward and unhesitating; but . . . they mark no important advance in Mr. Wells's career." The *Bookman* of London thought that "The Star" was a "masterpiece of dramatic progression," but the *Spectator* missed "the delightful vein of humor and humanity" seen in Wells's 1896 bicycling tale *The Wheels of Chance: A Holiday Adventure.* On 4 March 1900, a few months after the publication of *Tales of Space and Time,* the *Bookman* of New York wrote dismissively of Wells's science fiction in general: "Even the best of his marvel stories were but nine days wonders, demanding an immense amount of attention for the moment and then forgotten."

In 1900 Wells was far from finished as a writer, but he had already finished most of the short stories he would ever write, and he clearly saw the need to branch out from science fiction. That year he published *Love and Mr. Lewisham,* his first successful realistic novel, which deals with the conflicts between academic ambition and sexual desires in a protagonist much like Wells during his undergraduate years and early teaching career. Also, in December 1900 Wells and Jane moved into Spade House, their impressive new country house on the Kentish coast. Jane continued to serve as amanuensis for Wells in addition to caring for their two sons, George Philip ("Gip"), born on 17 July 1901, and Frank Richard, born on 31 October 1903. Wells continued to be a prolific writer, continuing to produce science fiction such as *The First Men in the Moon* (1901) but in other books beginning to set himself up as a prophetic figure. Thus in *Anticipations of the Reactions of Mechanical and Scientific Progress upon Human Life and Thought* (1901) and *The Discovery of the Future: A Discourse Delivered to the Royal Institution on January 24, 1902* (1902) he both predicted the future course of certain historical trends and recommended the best ways to cope with the challenges of the future. Wells was now taken far more seriously than in the past. At Spade House he became an enthusiastic host for weekend parties with well-known guests, and in these years he began his relationship with the Fabian Society.

In 1903 Wells brought out his last entirely original collection of short fiction, *Twelve Stories and a Dream.* The thirteen stories in this volume, while certainly competent, do not break much new ground; many are characteristic forms of science fiction. In "The Valley of the Spiders" a party of medieval knights is attacked by giant spiders reminiscent of the Sea Raiders, and in "Filmer" an aeronautical inventor becomes a martyr to science, a theme dealt with before in "A Tale of the Twentieth Century" and "The Argonauts of the Air" (1895). The most original science fiction in the volume is probably "The New Accelerator," which concerns the invention of a central nervous system stimulant – an "accelerator" – by a scientist named Professor Gibberne. Gibberne has been searching for "an all-around nervous stimulant to bring languid people up to the stresses of these pushful days." Instead, he concocts "something to revolutionise human life": a drug that would both speed up the nervous system and increase the body's central energy supplies, thus allowing its user to function at two or three times the ordinary pace. Gibberne is at story's end preparing a commercial version for the market, washing his hands of the moral implications of his new technology and allowing free-market and democratic forces to decide its fate. Clearly Wells foresaw the increasingly complex medical, moral, and ethical dilemmas that biotechnological innovations such as the New Accelerator would force on society and realized as well that entrepreneurs would be more than willing to skirt those issues in order to make money.

Two stories dealing with contact between Europeans and the non-Western world deserve mention for their comic treatment of themes that were decidedly grim in "The Lord of the Dynamos" and "Pollock and the Porroh Man." In "Jimmy Goggles the God," originally published in the December 1898 *Graphic,* a sailor diving for sunken treasure in the South Pacific wades ashore to find that his diving gear has convinced the islanders that he is a sea god. The rest of his first-person narrative concerns the comic trials of pretending to be a god while encased in a bulky diving suit and helmet in tropical heat. "The Truth about Pyecroft," originally published in *The Strand Magazine* (April 1903), concerns the efforts of Pyecroft, "the fattest clubman in London," to lose weight by taking a mysterious Indian "recipe," which he hopes will succeed where Western science has failed. The Indian recipe indeed re-

moves all of Pyecroft's weight but unfortunately does nothing to reduce his fat, so he finds himself floating against the ceiling of his study and is only able to resume normal life by wearing lead underclothing. As Patrick Brantlinger points out, this story is a comic version of a frequent theme in late-Victorian and Edwardian fiction – the sinister curse brought home from the empire to England.

The dream in the title of this collection refers to "A Dream of Armageddon," originally published in *Black and White* (1901), a perfectly appropriate choice to close the volume – and not simply because an apocalypse makes for a memorable ending. It is a strikingly personal story, though the personal material is lightly disguised. In it Wells seems to meditate on the course his own life and art had taken by 1901 and to insist that if he had it to do all over again, he would not change a thing. The bulk of the story is a dream that is recounted by a rather tiresome old man in a railway carriage. He is something of an Ancient Mariner figure, who bears the burden of a terrible story he must tell. The dream is set sometime in the future, though how far its dreamer cannot tell. It was an especially vivid dream, and most vivid of all its images is the face of a girl – what Peter Kemp calls "the spectre of the disruptive lady." "I have lived three-and-fifty years in this world," the old man confides. "I have had mother, sisters, friends, wife and daughters – all their faces, the play of their faces, I know. But the face of this girl – it is much more real to me."

It is almost impossible to read "A Dream of Armageddon" without making reference to Wells's own biography – his penchant for extramarital affairs was legendary, or infamous, even in his own time. In the dream the dreamer, whose name is Cooper, effectively renounces his political career for his mistress; Wells in effect had done the same thing at various times, since each new scandal made publishing contracts more difficult to secure and alienated larger and larger segments of the reading public. But as the dream progresses, an even larger sacrifice will be required of Cooper: not only will he be asked to leave his work for his mistress, but he will feel compelled to leave both behind in order to try to prevent oncoming war. Though encouraged by his mistress as well as by his party, Cooper still refuses to return to his home to help prevent the war. He has become a private man, he says – words that would have resonated deeply for Wells. "I might have gone back, I think, and saved the world," Cooper tells his fellow passenger on the train, but he chooses to stay with his mistress and is

J. M. Barrie and Wells playing croquet

defiant in his refusal to reconsider the course he has chosen: "Even now, I do not repent; I made my choice, and I will hold on to the end." Here, as clearly as anywhere in Wells's writing, one hears the voice of the author through the page.

Twelve Stories and a Dream had mixed reviews, suggesting that the charm of novelty, which had once been so strong for Wells's science fiction, was wearing off. *The Independent* concluded that none of these stories "equal the best of his former tales, but there are some that are quite amusing and some that are quite gruesome." *Outlook,* on the other hand, decided that "in at least half of these stories Mr. Wells is seen at his best." *The New York Times* praised the "varied entertainment which Mr. Wells offers" and ended by saying that "he has never offered any better." The *Review of Reviews* expressed relief that in this volume of short stories, unlike in his recent nonfiction, Wells "has but rarely any prophetic or scientific axe to grind" and concluded, with decid-

edly limited praise, "*Twelve Stories and a Dream* will not lower Mr. Wells's reputation as an imaginative writer, which his previous volumes probably did."

When this volume was published in 1903, Wells still had forty-three years to live and most of his books still to write, but he would write little more short fiction. Between 1903 and the publication of his next short-story collection, *The Country of the Blind, and Other Stories,* in 1911, Wells published only seven short stories. He remained, however, a prolific writer in other genres, producing eighteen books in this same period, most of them intensely political and argumentative. Also in this period, he developed into an important realistic novelist with *Kipps, Tono-Bungay, Ann Veronica: A Modern Love Story* (1909), and *The History of Mr. Polly.*

Highlights of Wells's public life between 1903 and 1911 included his speaking and writing on behalf of the Fabian Society; friendships and quarrels with Fabian leaders such as Beatrice and Sidney

Webb and George Bernard Shaw; and his resignation from the society in 1906. Another important public event was his 1906 tour of the United States, which included a meeting with Theodore Roosevelt at the White House and resulted in a book, *The Future in America: A Search after Realities* (1906). Wells's private life was marked by serious liaisons with Rosamund Bland and Amber Reeves, with Reeves bearing him a child, Anne Jane, in 1909. In 1909 Wells and Jane sold Spade House and moved back to London, moving again in 1911 to Easton Glebe, a house they constructed on the estate of Wells's friend the countess of Warwick.

The Country of the Blind, and Other Stories collected twenty-nine stories, almost all of which had already appeared in periodicals and one of his previous volumes of short stories. These were, Wells said in his introduction, all the short stories for which he cared to be remembered, and the publication of this selection indicates that he thought he was finished with the genre. In addition to stories from earlier collections, this volume included several tales written since 1903, two of which are among the best Wells ever wrote.

The title story, "The Country of the Blind," is in one respect another story about a seer without honor. At least one critic, Kinley E. Roby, considers it "Wells's finest achievement as a writer of short fiction"; Arnold Bennett, in his 1909 review of *Tono-Bungay,* called it "one of the radiant gems of contemporary literature." In the midst of the Ecuadoran Andes, the story says, lies nestled a valley completely cut off from all contact with the outside, "civilized" world – the Country of the Blind. Isolated as it is from the outside world, the people of the valley, as Wells would have known, comprise a very restricted gene pool; and when catastrophic illness strikes the valley's residents, it leaves them blind. The Old Testament language of paradise, fall, and the desire for redemption is strong both in this story and in "The Door in the Wall," the other important new story in the book.

Nunez, a mountaineer from near Quito, stumbles and falls into the valley, landing unharmed. Little by little, he realizes that everyone else in the valley is blind, and he cannot help but think of the possibilities the situation suggests, remembering constantly the old saw, "In the Country of the Blind the One-eyed Man is King." Logically, this should make Nunez king here, but in the Country of the Blind vision makes no sense; the visual sensations of which Nunez speaks have no correlation to the blind inhabitants' experience of the world, and Nunez is therefore treated as almost a madman.

Eventually he falls in love with Medina-sarote, the beautiful daughter of his master, and as their intimacy grows, Nunez desires to speak to her of sight, but such talk makes her uncomfortable. Her father will not consent to their marriage because he fears that Nunez is "an idiot." As a result, Nunez decides to make the ultimate sacrifice: he consents to have his eyes removed by the blind surgeons. As the hour approaches, however, he raises his eyes and sees "the morning like an angel in golden armour, marching down the steeps." Entranced by the gift of vision, Nunez walks out of his hut, out of the village, and out of the Country of the Blind altogether, never to return.

Having in greater degree a gift that exists among others – being able to see better, for instance, in the land of the sighted – is a blessing; but in the land of the blind, to see at all so completely falls outside the prevailing worldview that it can only lead to ostracism. J. R. Hammond calls this story "a parable of intolerance." In Roby's reading, the story is essentially "a pessimistic restatement of Plato's Allegory of the Cave. . . . Like the prisoners of the cave, the blind have made the remote valley a symbol of estrangement."

"The Door in the Wall," originally published in the *Daily Chronicle* (14 July 1906), is surely one of Wells's most poignant stories. In a review of *The Short Stories of H. G. Wells* in 1928, T. E. Lawrence called the story "a very lovely thing, [which] seems rather by itself – like a gloss on an E. M. Forster fragment." The story concerns a man, Lionel Wallace, whose life passes him by altogether too quickly. As a young boy of five, Lionel wanders off from his home and discovers a green door, set into a white wall, which he is sure will open for him. When he tries the door, he is let into a beautiful garden: "In the instant of coming into it one was exquisitely glad – as only in rare moments, and when one is young and joyful one can be glad in this world." The modern reader is put in mind of C. S. Lewis's *The Chronicles of Narnia* (1950–1956), in which the children discover a magical world through a passageway in their uncle's wardrobe, and of Frances Hodgson Burnett's *The Secret Garden* (1911), in which an orphan girl discovers a world of beauty – a secret garden – behind a "door in the wall." Lionel leaves the garden that first day fully intending to return – but he never does. Life gets busier and more complicated; on those very rare instances when he chances to pass the door again, though it seems not always to be in the same place – on his way to Oxford, rushing back to Parliament to cast a crucial vote – he does not have time to stop.

The story is told by Wallace's friend, for, as he sits down to write it, Wallace is dead, never having found his way back to the garden. Hammond calls it "a fantasia on a characteristically Wellsian theme – that of the man who believes he has found a way of escape from the commonplace world of everyday into a *different* life, a life of paradisal enchantment." As in "The Country of the Blind," the allegory is quite evident here. But for the man who wrote the story in 1906, the forty-year-old Wells, who had found more success than happiness and more notoriety than success, the story would have resonated at a very deep level.

In 1911 an American publisher brought out *The Door in the Wall and Other Stories,* an expensive illustrated collection of some of the stories included in *The Country of the Blind, and Other Stories*; a British edition was published in 1915. Neither collection was reviewed very widely, presumably since neither offered much that was new and because Wells was now identified in the public mind with realistic novels and prophetic nonfiction. *The New York Times* had positive things to say about most of the stories in *The Door in the Wall and Other Stories* but undercut its praise by saying that Wells's excursions into dreamland "have not quite the authentic thrill and atmosphere belonging to the dream stories of the men who have done the great things in that kind." The reviewer concludes by saying that the illustrations are "works of great beauty, and the volume would be a desirable possession for them alone."

Between 1911 and 1927 Wells wrote only four narratives that could be called short stories, two of them chapters in *Boon, the Mind of the Race, the Wild Asses of the Devil, and the Last Trump, Being a First Selection from the Literary Remains of George Boon, Appropriate to the Times* (1915), which included his rather cruel parody of his former friend Henry James. Wells continued, however, to churn out novels and nonfiction, including his very successful wartime novel *Mr. Britling Sees It Through* (1916) and his phenomenally popular *The Outline of History, Being a Plain History of Life and Mankind* (1920). In public life he worked for the Ministry of Information during World War I, supported the League of Nations, and traveled to Russia in 1914 and 1920. By 1922 Wells had joined the Labour Party and ran as its candidate for Parliament at different times, all unsuccessfully. His romantic attachments in these years included a long affair with Rebecca West, lasting from 1913 to 1923 and resulting in the birth of a son, Anthony West.

By 1927 Wells had decided that his 1911 collections were not the way he wanted to leave his short fiction, after all, so that year he brought out his *Short Stories of H. G. Wells,* which included sixty-one stories: *The Time Machine,* the forty-eight stories from *The Stolen Bacillus, and Other Incidents; The Plattner Story, and Others; Tales of Space and Time;* and *Twelve Stories and a Dream,* and twelve other stories. Five of these twelve had been included in *The Country of the Blind, and Other Stories;* three, including one chapter from *Boon,* had been written since 1911; and four, including "The Land Ironclads," had been published in periodicals before 1911 but not reprinted in any of Wells's previous collections. Aside from the *Boon* chapter, the new stories were "The Grisly Folk" – more an essay than a story, about hypothetical battles between *Homo sapiens* and Neanderthals – and "The Pearl of Love," a parable about a north Indian prince who builds a beautiful tomb for his beloved dead princess but eventually forgets her as he falls in love with the tomb itself.

The Collected Short Stories was much more widely and favorably reviewed than the two collections of 1911. Wells was by this time a literary institution, and so rich a collection of his early work called for measured estimates of his achievement. Writing in the *Spectator,* T. E. Lawrence was initially impressed that the publishers were charging so little (7s. 6d.) for so big a book (1,150 pages) and wondered how they did it. "It is nearly as difficult," he continues, "to see how Mr. Wells did it." So many short stories, along with so much other writing, seems impressive to Lawrence, and he goes on to argue that the defining quality of the work is "the standpoint of the student of biology," which produced both the science fiction and Wells's impressive "concern for the mass of human nature." The reviewer for the *Literary Digest* found himself "regretting Mr. Wells's abandonment of this earlier form for his later preachments. In it he had practically no rivals." Less effusively, the *Times Literary Supplement* called him the first to make "a finished art of the scientific fairy story," but *The Nation* was full of praise. "One peruses this collection of his shorter tales," its reviewer announces, "with a feeling of unqualified admiration. He is so obviously the master in the field of the bizarre and the extraordinary that it seems unnecessary to point out that where Jules Verne is merely ingenious, Mr. Wells is imaginative, and so on." But triumphing over Jules Verne is not the highest literary achievement, and the reviewer for *New York Post* struck perhaps the unkindest blow of all: "It seems to us that as a writer of short stories H. G. Wells is primarily a writer for boys. Boys are supposed to be notoriously uninterested in the human equation; all they want a writer to tell them is what happened next. Mr. Wells is forever telling us what happened next. He is our very own Jules Verne."

In 1927 Jane Wells died, and Wells sold Easton Glebe. He continued to travel, lecture, argue, and write. Always interested in new technologies, in 1928 he began giving broadcast talks on the BBC, and in the mid 1930s he was seriously involved in moviemaking, both with *The Man Who Could Work Miracles* and the even more successful *Things to Come* (1936), produced by Sir Alexander Korda. In 1934 Wells interviewed Joseph Stalin in Moscow, and in 1940 he remained at his London home in Hanover Terrace during the Blitz. In 1943, at age seventy-seven, Wells completed a D.Sc. thesis and was awarded the degree by London University. He apparently never fully recovered from an illness he contracted in 1942; his last years were relatively quiet ones. He died in his sleep on 13 August 1946.

As just one part of a vastly productive and varied writing career, the short stories of H. G. Wells nevertheless deserve a place of special distinction. Nowhere else in his writings was his extraordinary gift of imagination more freely indulged; and perhaps more important the further Wells's career advanced, the more his short stories largely stayed free of the wooden ideological strain that so seriously stains most of Wells's later writing. Having learned the art and craft of the short story as a young man, it would seem, Wells continued to write in that genre without the bad habits that crept into much of his other writing. As a result, the short stories comprise a pleasant avenue into the very heart of Wells's genius and his importance as a writer of fiction. Like the protagonist of the late story "The Door in the Wall," Wells was for a time able to regain access to the imaginative terrain and artistic freedom of his youth; but as his career gained in importance, he no longer had time for the simpler world to which the short story led, and as he left the writing of short fiction behind, Wells equally turned his back on what was most valuable in his writing.

Letters:

Henry James and H. G. Wells: A Record of Their Friendship, Their Debate on the Art of Fiction and Their Quarrel, edited by Leon Edel and Gordon N. Ray (Urbana: University of Illinois Press, 1958; London: Hart-Davis, 1958);

Arnold Bennett and H. G. Wells: A Record of a Personal and Literary Friendship, edited by Harris Wilson (Urbana: University of Illinois Press, 1960; London: Hart-Davis, 1960);

George Gissing and H. G. Wells: Their Friendship and Correspondence, edited by Royal A. Gettmann (Urbana: University of Illinois Press, 1961; London: Hart-Davis, 1961).

Bibliographies:

Fred A. Chappell, *Bibliography of H. G. Wells* (Chicago: Covici-McGee, 1924);

Geoffrey H. Wells, *The Works of H. G. Wells, 1887–1925: A Bibliography, Dictionary and Subject-Index* (London: Routledge, 1926);

H. G. Wells Society, *H. G. Wells: A Comprehensive Bibliography* (London: H. G. Wells Society, 1972);

J. R. Hammond, *Herbert George Wells: An Annotated Bibliography of His Works* (New York & London: Garland, 1977);

William Scheick and J. Randolph Cox, *H. G. Wells: A Reference Guide* (Boston: G. K. Hall, 1988).

Biographies:

Geoffrey West, *H. G. Wells: A Sketch for a Portrait* (London: Howe, 1930);

Vincent Brome, *H. G. Wells: A Biography* (London & New York: Longmans, Green, 1951);

Lovat Dickson, *H. G. Wells: His Turbulent Life and Times* (London: Macmillan, 1969; New York: Atheneum, 1969);

Norman and Jeanne MacKenzie, *The Time Traveller: The Life of H. G. Wells* (London: Weidenfeld & Nicolson, 1973); republished as *H. G. Wells: A Biography* (New York: Simon & Schuster, 1973);

Gordon N. Ray, *H. G. Wells and Rebecca West* (New Haven: Yale University Press, 1974; London: Macmillan, 1974);

Frank Wells, *H. G. Wells: A Pictorial Biography* (London: Jupiter, 1977);

J. R. Hammond, ed., *H. G. Wells: Interviews and Recollections* (London: Macmillan, 1980);

Anthony West, *H. G. Wells: Aspects of a Life* (London: Hutchinson, 1984; New York: Random House, 1984);

David C. Smith, *H. G. Wells: Desperately Mortal* (New Haven & London: Yale University Press, 1986).

References:

Brian Ash, *Who's Who in H. G. Wells* (London: Hamilton, 1979);

John Batchelor, *H. G. Wells* (Cambridge: Cambridge University Press, 1985);

Montgomery Belgion, *H. G. Wells* (London & New York: Longmans, Green, 1953);

Bernard Bergonzi, *The Early H. G. Wells: A Study of the Scientific Romances* (Manchester: Manchester University Press, 1961; Toronto: University of Toronto Press, 1961);

Bergonzi, ed., *H. G. Wells: A Collection of Critical Essays* (Englewood Cliffs, N.J.: Prentice-Hall, 1976);

Richard Hauer Costa, *H. G. Wells,* revised edition (Boston: Twayne, 1985);

J. R. Hammond, *H. G. Wells and Rebecca West* (New York: Saint Martin's Press, 1991);

Hammond, *H. G. Wells and the Modern Novel* (New York: Saint Martin's Press, 1988);

Hammond, *H. G. Wells and the Short Story* (New York: Saint Martin's Press, 1992);

Hammond, *An H. G. Wells Companion: A Guide to the Novels, Romances and Short Stories* (London: Macmillan, 1979; New York: Barnes & Noble, 1979);

Roslynn D. Haynes, *H. G. Wells: Discoverer of the Future* (New York and London: New York University Press, 1980);

Mark R. Hillegas, *The Future as Nightmare: H. G. Wells and the Anti-Utopians* (New York: Oxford University Press, 1967);

John Huntington, *The Logic of Fantasy: H. G. Wells and Science Fiction* (New York: Columbia University Press, 1982);

David Lodge, "Assessing H. G. Wells," in his *The Novelist at the Crossroads* (London: Routledge & Kegan Paul, 1971), pp. 205–220;

Frank McConnell, *The Science Fiction of H. G. Wells* (New York & Oxford: Oxford University Press, 1981);

Brian Murray, *H. G. Wells* (New York: Continuum, 1990);

Patrick Parrinder, *H. G. Wells* (Edinburgh: Oliver & Boyd, 1970; New York: Putnam, 1977);

Parrinder, ed., *H. G. Wells: The Critical Heritage* (London & Boston: Routledge & Kegan Paul, 1972);

Parrinder and Christopher Rolfe, eds., *H. G. Wells under Revision: Proceedings of the International H. G. Wells Symposium* (Selinsgrove, Pa.: Susquehanna University Press, 1990);

W. Warren Wagar, *H. G. Wells and the World State* (New Haven: Yale University Press, 1961).

Papers:
The Wells Archive is housed in the Rare Book Room, University of Illinois Library, Urbana-Champaign.

Stanley J. Weyman

(7 August 1855 – 10 April 1928)

James R. Simmons Jr.
University of South Carolina

See also the Weyman entry in *DLB 141: British Children's Writers, 1880–1914.*

BOOKS: *The House of the Wolf* (London & New York: Longmans, Green, 1890);

The King's Stratagem and Other Stories (New York: A. E. Cluett, 1891);

The New Rector (2 volumes, London: Smith, Elder, 1891; 1 volume, New York: American News Company, 1891);

The Story of Francis Cludde (London: Cassell, 1891; New York: Cassell, 1891);

A Gentleman of France, Being the Memoirs of Gaston de Bonne, Sieur de Marsac, 3 volumes (London & New York: Longmans, Green, 1893);

A Little Wizard (New York: Fenno, 1893);

The Man in Black (London: Cassell, 1894; New York: Cassell, 1894);

My Lady Rotha (London: Innes, 1894; New York: Longmans, Green, 1894);

Under the Red Robe (2 volumes, London: Methuen, 1894; 1 volume, New York: Longmans, Green, 1894);

From the Memoirs of a Minister of France (London: Cassell, 1895; New York: Longmans, Green, 1895);

The Red Cockade: A Novel of the French Revolution (London: Longmans, Green, 1895; New York: Harper, 1896);

The Snowball (New York: Merriman, 1895);

For the Cause (Chicago: Sergel, 1897);

Shrewsbury: A Romance of the Time of William and Mary (New York: Longmans, Green, 1897; London: Longmans, Green, 1898);

The Castle Inn (London: Smith, Elder, 1898; New York: Longmans, Green, 1898);

When Love Calls (Boston: Brown, 1899);

Sophia (London & New York: Longmans, Green, 1900; New York: Longmans, Green, 1900);

Count Hannibal (London: Smith, Elder, 1901; New York: Longmans, Green, 1901);

Stanley J. Weyman (Hulton Deutsch Collection)

In Kings' Byways (London: Smith, Elder, 1902; New York: Longmans, Green, 1902);

The Long Night (London: Longmans, Green, 1903; New York: McClure, 1903);

The Abbess of Vlaye (London & New York: Longmans, Green, 1904; New York: Longmans, Green, 1904);

Starvecrow Farm (London: Hutchinson, 1905; New York: Longmans, Green, 1905);

Chippinge (London: Smith, Elder, 1906); republished as *Chippinge Borough* (New York: McClure, Phillips, 1906);

Laid Up in Lavender (London: Smith, Elder, 1907; New York: Longmans, Green, 1907);

The Wild Geese (London: Hodder & Stoughton, 1908; New York: Doubleday, Page, 1909);

The Great House (London: John Murray, 1919; New York: Longmans, Green, 1919);

Ovington's Bank (London: John Murray, 1922; New York: Longmans, Green, 1922);

The Traveller in the Fur Cloak (London: Hutchinson, 1924; New York: Longmans, Green, 1924);

Queen's Folly (London: John Murray, 1925; New York: Longmans, Green, 1925);

The Lively Peggy (London: John Murray, 1928; New York: Longmans, Green, 1928).

Collections: *The Works of Stanley J. Weyman*, Author's Complete Edition, 21 volumes (London: Smith, Elder, 1911);

Historical Romances (New York: Longmans, Green, 1921);

The Works of Stanley J. Weyman, Thin Paper Edition, 24 volumes (London: John Murray, 1922–1929).

Historical fiction of the late nineteenth century was characteristically romance of the cloak-and-sword school, and perhaps no author's work typified this form as well as the stories and novels of Stanley J. Weyman, called "the prince of romantic novelists" by *The Cornhill Magazine*. Weyman's work was widely read not only in England and the United States, but also in countries such as France and Russia. A throwback to simpler times, his swashbuckling adventure stories offered readers an escape from the uncertainties of a society that was becoming increasingly complicated as it entered the twentieth century. Along with writers such as Robert Louis Stevenson, Arthur Conan Doyle, Rider Haggard, Rudyard Kipling, John Buchan, and Joseph Conrad, Weyman contributed to the general vogue of adventure fiction during the years 1880–1914, but unlike them, he is now relatively unknown. Although his renown failed to outlive the decline in the popularity of the historical romance that began during World War I, his contemporaries considered him one of the most important literary figures of their day.

Born at Ludlow, England, on 7 August 1855, Stanley John Weyman was the second son of Thomas Weyman, a solicitor, and Mary Maria Black Weyman. He was educated at Ludlow Grammar School and at Shrewsbury School before going on to Christ Church College, Oxford, where he acquired a B.A. with second-class honors in modern history in 1877. He was called to the bar in 1881, but his early career as a barrister seems to have

been wholly unsuccessful. He showed little literary acumen at this time, and his early writings consist mainly of a few vignettes of contemporary life, some of which were published in *Chambers's Journal*. As his legal career stagnated, Weyman's financial difficulties forced him to turn to other sources of income, and he began to consider writing fiction as a vocation.

Weyman's first published short story, "The Deanery Ball," appeared in *The Cornhill Magazine* in 1883. This story, like many of his published stories over the next ten years, is closely patterned on the work of Weyman's favorite author, Anthony Trollope. Like Trollope, Weyman wrote about episodes of daily English life, often set in a parsonage or a deanery. As a reviewer for *The Illustrated London News* later remarked of one of Weyman's tales, "If he did not know that Anthony Trollope was no more, a reader . . . might well suppose that he was reading Trollope, and during that novelist's best period." Weyman's stories — straightforward, slice-of-life narratives with some humor — were not popular with his contemporaries. In the changing literary scene of the late nineteenth century, this genre seemed passé, and Weyman showed little promise of future literary fame.

At about this same time, however, Weyman read Henry White's *Massacre of St. Bartholomew* (1868) and found the subject for the fiction that would make him famous. He was initially reluctant to experiment with writing historical romances but finally decided to attempt one after *Cornhill* editor James Payn encouraged him to write a novel. Payn's encouragement — coupled with Weyman's pressing financial needs and the public's indifference to his imitations of Trollope — led him to begin his first historical novel, *The House of the Wolf* (1890).

In 1885, before this novel was completed, Weyman was traveling in the south of France when he was arrested on suspicion of being a British spy. The British ambassador to France was forced to intervene. The British press protested Weyman's arrest and subsequent detention, and the matter was discussed in Parliament. By the time the incident was resolved and the charges were dropped, Weyman had gained a great deal of publicity, which helped to create a reputation for him as a man who was knowledgeable about matters of international intrigue. Considering that many of his stories concern covert operations, clandestine liaisons, and international machinations, the incident may well have contributed to his success as a writer of romantic adventures.

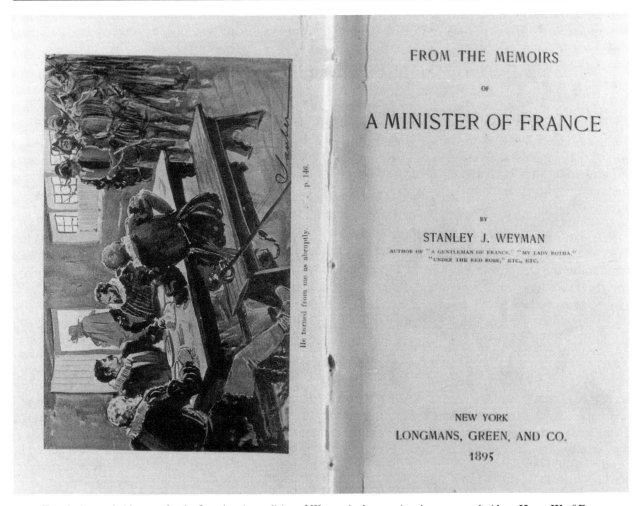

Frontispiece and title page for the first American edition of Weyman's short stories about a trusted aide to Henry IV of France

The House of the Wolf, which ran serially in *The English Illustrated Magazine* from October 1888 through March 1889, was more successful than his earlier writings. The novel is set during the Saint Bartholomew's Massacre in Paris, where in 1572, on the eve of Saint Bartholomew's Day, three thousand French Protestants, or Huguenots, were put to death on the authority of their Catholic ruler, Charles IX, supposedly on the advice of his mother, Catherine de Médicis, as well as the Pope and Philip II of Spain. Although the book was well received, Weyman did not completely stop writing Trollopean fiction. For the next few years he wrote tales of daily English life as well as historical romances.

The book publication of *The House of the Wolf* in 1890 brought Weyman immediate recognition in the United States as well as in England. His earlier short fiction, which had largely gone unnoticed, became increasingly in demand – particularly in the United States, where American readers had only

limited access to the British periodicals that published his stories. *The King's Stratagem and Other Stories* (1891), published only in the United States, took advantage of this new market for Weyman's fiction.

All six stories in *The King's Stratagem and Other Stories* had been published in England a few years earlier, and only the title story is a historical romance. Like many of Weyman's tales that followed it, "The King's Stratagem" takes place in the time of the French Huguenot King Henry of Navarre. During the war with the Catholic Holy League that preceded his ascension to the throne of France in 1589 – while Henry's forces are meeting under a flag of truce with those of Catherine de Médicis – one of Henry's men, Vicomte de Lanthenon, governor of Lusigny, loses a wager with the governor of Creance, a captain in Catherine's forces. Believing that his word of honor is stronger than his loyalty to Henry, the vicomte promises that he will repay his debt by leaving a gate in Lusigny open and unguarded so that the captain and his men may enter and capture the town. Henry learns of the treasonous plan, but rather than execute his subordinate, he forgives him and devises a means by which the vicomte may honor his word while doing little harm to the Huguenot cause. The captain and his men enter through the open gate, meet with almost no organized resistance, and claim the city for their own. Suddenly a rider arrives from Creance, informing the captain that his own city has been taken by Lanthenon and five hundred men, who overpowered the greatly understrength garrison. Thus the captain becomes not a hero but a fool, and Lanthenon, thanks to Henry, is in possession of a much greater stronghold than he had before. *The King's Stratagem and Other Stories* was reprinted several times in the United States before the end of the nineteenth century.

Weyman's next novel, *The New Rector* (1891), met with good reviews. Another work in imitation of Trollope, it sold poorly in Great Britain but was popular with readers in the United States. Weyman's historical romance novel *A Gentleman of France,* published in 1893, gave the British public more of what they wanted, and it secured Weyman's place among the preeminent literary figures of the day. Robert Louis Stevenson was among the chief admirers of this work, and soon Weyman found himself favorably compared to writers such as Alexandre Dumas, Arthur Conan Doyle, and Stevenson himself.

Weyman never completely abandoned narratives of everyday life. For the rest of his life he occasionally produced a work in the genre he loved best, but after *The Man in Black* was published in 1894, every one of the twelve major works that he published over the next ten years was cloak-and-sword fiction. The string began with two more historical romances, *My Lady Rotha* (1894) and one of Weyman's most popular novels, *Under the Red Robe* (1894). These two books were followed by *From the Memoirs of a Minister of France* (1895), Weyman's first collection of short stories to be published on both sides of the Atlantic.

Described as a sequel to Weyman's 1893 novel *A Gentleman of France, From the Memoirs of a Minister of France* comprises twelve short stories that had appeared in consecutive issues of *The English Illustrated Magazine* from October 1894 through September 1895. In each of the stories Minister Rosny, a character in *A Gentleman of France,* relates his experiences as an aide and friend to Henry IV of France, formerly Henry of Navarre. Narrated in retrospect after Henry IV has died, the historically accurate stories cover in chronological order the entire period of the king's reign over Navarre (1572–1589) and all of France (1589–1610). They deal with matters of diplomacy, espionage, and international intrigue, as well as events as mundane as Henry's romantic liaisons.

In "The Tennis Balls," set in 1599, Rosny tells the story of a Spanish refugee named Diego, a first-rate tennis player who plans to assassinate Henry by poisoning some bandages in the king's chambers at the tennis courts. Rosny, who has suspected Diego of being a spy, inspects the premises and deduces the plan. During a tennis game he has one of his aides "accidentally" scratch Diego. As a bandage is applied, Rosny says that the dressing has come from the king's box and sees Diego blanch. Realizing that his suspicions have been confirmed, Rosny warns Diego that if he removes the dressing he will have him broken on the wheel. Noticeably shaken, Diego continues to play the match until he collapses. He later dies, a victim of his own perfidy.

"The Lost Cipher" presents another example of treachery against Henry IV, this time by a member of his own inner circle. Returning from a diplomatic mission to England in 1601, Rosny has his secret codebook stolen through the machinations of the courtesan Madame Verneuil, Henry's former lover, who claims that Henry has entrusted her with the codebook to prove his love. Rosny discovers that an aide to the king must have taken the book and sold it to the courtesan. When the king confronts the thief, he admits his crime and commits suicide before he can be punished. In both these stories Rosny functions as a detective, resolving problematic situations by using his powers of ratiocination – much like Edgar Allan Poe's Auguste Dupin or Doyle's Sherlock Holmes. Yet in other stories Weyman characterizes Rosny as obtuse, prone to error, and guilty of gross exaggeration as well.

In 1895 Weyman also published another full-length historical romance, *The Red Cockade,* and in the United States his short story "The Snowball" appeared in a gift-book edition. Also narrated by Rosny, "The Snowball" begins as a tale of ratiocination and intrigue and develops into a lesson on the danger of suspecting plots against the king at every turn. On a winter day in 1602 a snowball is thrown into Rosny's carriage, and he finds in it a bit of paper on which someone has written "Beware of Nicholas." Immediately suspecting that Simon Nicholas, Henry's secretary, is plotting to assassinate the king, Rosny soon discovers that the message was sent by Nicholas's wife. When Rosny and the king confront her, she reveals – to the king's great amusement – that she thought she was throwing the snowball into the carriage of Monsieur Hallot, the husband of Nicholas's mistress.

In 1895 Weyman married Charlotte Panting. They were to have no children, but by all accounts it was a happy marriage. That same year Weyman's novel *Under the Red Robe* was adapted for the London stage. The production ran for 253 performances, from October 1896 through June 1897. Although other Weyman novels were adapted for the stage, the dramatic version of *Under the Red Robe* was by far the most popular.

In 1897 Weyman published another historical romance novel, *Shrewsbury,* and an American publisher brought out another collection of his short stories, *For the Cause,* five stories that had previously appeared in British magazines. Four are early Trollopean stories that Weyman had published in *The Cornhill Magazine* in 1883 and 1884, while the title story is a historical romance that appeared in *The English Illustrated Magazine* in 1889. Employing the classic disguised-sovereign motif used so successfully in Stevenson's *Prince Otto* (1885), "For the Cause" may have been resurrected to capitalize on the popularity of another such novel, Anthony Hope's recent best-seller *The Prisoner of Zenda* (1895).

Weyman's story – which the *New York World* called "the most powerful thing Mr. Weyman has ever written" – is set in the year 1589, shortly before Henry of Navarre became Henry IV of France. As in "The King's Stratagem," Weyman focuses on Henry's sense of honor and justice. As the story opens, a disguised Henry meets a dazed young man, Felix Portail, who reports that his father has been lynched by an angry mob because of his adherence to Henry's cause. Although the young man professes loyalty to no political faction, he is afraid that the mob will come for him. Later Felix discovers Henry's identity and overhears him planning strategy with his men, and Henry must decide if this youth of uncertain allegiance can be trusted to keep silent about what he knows or if he must be killed. Henry chooses the first option and lets Felix go, winning the young man's loyalty from that day forward.

Shrewsbury, set in the time of William and Mary, and *The Castle Inn* (1898), set in England in 1760, are the first of Weyman's historical novels to be set in a time and place other than the days of Henry IV in France. His next novel, *Sophia* (1900), is also set in eighteenth-century England. Between these books an American publisher brought out *When Love Calls* (1899), another collection of short

Stanley J. Weyman (Hulton Deutsch Collection)

works by Weyman. Unusual because it includes none of Weyman's cloak-and-sword stories, the book comprises three stories that may be described as the standard romantic fluff popular at the time and "Along the Garonne," a travel narrative of the sort that Weyman often contributed to *The English Illustrated Magazine.* The titles of these articles – "Mule-Back in Morocco," "Through the Pyrenees in December," and "Spanish Facts and English Fancies" – suggest the extent of his travels. "Along the Garonne" describes a journey in France that ends at the birthplace of Henry IV, yet another indication of Weyman's fascination with that king.

For his next novel, *Count Hannibal* (1901), Weyman returned to the time of Henry IV. This novel was followed by *In Kings' Byways* (1902), a collection of twelve short historical romances published in both Britain and the United States. Some of the stories were previously uncollected, while others – "The Snowball," "For the Cause," and "The King's Stratagem" – had appeared in book form only in the United States. *In Kings' Byways* received good reviews, and the stories in this collection are indeed the finest examples of his short historical fiction.

A reviewer for the *Buffalo Commercial* called "Flore," the first story in the collection, "marvelously intense in plot, and its execution, with a play of action and incident and thrilling situation that is incessant." Set in France in 1643, "Flore" is the story of Prosper, who was clerk to the insidious Bishop of Beauvais until he made an error in writing a speech that the bishop read to a congregation. Prosper is being transported to prison when he makes his escape and falls in with some men who appear to have kidnapped the queen's dog, Flore. One of these strangers forces Prosper to take the dog to the bishop, who rehires his clerk and returns the dog to curry favor with the queen. The delighted queen showers praise on the exultant bishop, but then the bishop's rival, Cardinal Mazarin, enters the room and points out that the dog looks like Flore but does not seem as intelligent. After the dog fails to perform tricks that Flore should know, the queen accuses the bishop of having had a hand in the mischief and banishes him. Meanwhile Prosper has realized that one of the kidnappers was Mazarin in disguise and concludes that the whole scheme was intended to discredit the bishop. The real Flore is soon returned to the queen, while Prosper – rewarded with one hundred crowns, a new job, and a new home – lives the rest of his life in ease, keeping Mazarin's secret until his death.

In Kings' Byways was Weyman's last collection of short historical fiction. It was followed by two more novels set in France at the time of Henry IV: *The Long Night* (1903) and *The Abbess of Vlaye* (1904). These works were his last book-length excursions into that time and place, even though the public still seemed interested in his treatments of Henry of Navarre's France. In fact, a stage adaptation of his *A Gentleman of France* opened in London on 4 June 1904.

Regardless of what the public wanted, by late 1904 Weyman seemed ready to move on to new subjects. *Starvecrow Farm* (1905) and *Chippinge* (1906), Weyman's personal favorite of his novels, both take place in nineteenth-century England. His next volume of short stories, *Laid Up in Lavender* (1907), is primarily early works from *The Cornhill Magazine* and *The English Illustrated Magazine*. Two stories had previously been collected in American volumes – "King Pepin and Sweet Clive" in *For the Cause* and "The Body-Birds of Court" in *The King's Stratagem* – but had their first British book publication in *Laid Up in Lavender*. None of the twelve stories is a historical romance.

"Family Portraits," first published in *The English Illustrated Magazine* in 1888, is a story of mystery and intrigue with a disguised protagonist. After years of captivity by American Indians, a man returns to his English home, his identity obscured by long unkempt hair, a long scar on his bearded face, and an American accent. The stranger finds that he is presumed dead and that his father, Lord Wetherby, is believed to have died intestate. By law the title and all the contents of the house have been inherited by the stranger's second cousin, who has stripped the house of its furnishings and is about to trick his cousin's "widow" out of the house by leasing it from the nearly penniless woman on disadvantageous terms. Identifying himself as a law clerk sent to draw up the lease, the stranger tells his cousin that he once prepared a will for the late lord and shows him a secret safe, which indeed contains a will in which the late lord leaves his son's wife a great deal of money. The new Lord Wetherby offers the man one hundred pounds if he will not mention the will until the next day. The stranger agrees, but when the wife reads the lease she recognizes her husband's writing and runs to his waiting arms, shouting that it is her long-lost husband. Reclaiming the husband's title and property, the happy couple banish the greedy cousin to well-deserved obscurity.

Weyman's next novel, *The Wild Geese* (1908), was the last book he published for more than a decade. Weyman, who was in his early fifties, had simply decided to stop writing. After nearly a quarter of a century of earning a living by his pen, he returned to the practice of law. He did continue his historical studies, and he spent time at his favorite hobbies, riding and cycling. Yet during his self-imposed exile from the literary world, he remained to some degree in the public eye.

One indication of Weyman's continued renown as a writer was the inclusion of one of his stories in *The Lock and Key Library* (1910), a ten-volume set that professed to include the greatest mystery and detective stories ever written. Other authors with stories in these volumes include Fyodor Dostoyevsky, Alexandre Dumas, Anton Chekhov, Honoré de Balzac, Voltaire, William Makepeace Thackeray, Edgar Allan Poe, Washington Irving, Charles Dickens, Nathaniel Hawthorne, Ambrose Bierce, Laurence Sterne, Thomas De Quincey, and Guy de Maupassant – in short, some of the greatest writers of all time. Weyman's story was included in the volume devoted to modern English stories with works by only five other writers: Rudyard Kipling, Arthur Conan Doyle, Wilkie Collins, Egerton Castle, and Robert Louis Stevenson.

Weyman's contribution to the collection was "The Fowl in the Pot," from the 1902 collection *In Kings' Byways*. Set in Henry of Navarre's France, the story is narrated once again by Rosny and describes another case in which Rosny's perception of reality is clouded by his zeal to protect his king. Told of an alleged assassination plot against himself and Henry, Rosny takes the king to observe the plotters, a man and his wife who discuss poisoning "Henry" and "Rosny" because they have become old and hateful. After the enraged king has the conspirators arrested, however, he is amused to discover that the couple has been talking about their old dogs, which they are going to kill because they are diseased. Rosny has been the butt of an elaborate joke. The story is more humorous than mysterious, and its inclusion in *The Lock and Key Library* probably owes more to Weyman's literary reputation at that time than to its merits as a mystery story.

During Weyman's sabbatical from writing his name was also kept in the public eye by adaptations of his works for stage and screen. A stage adaptation of *Count Hannibal,* which opened in Bristol in 1909, hit the London stage in 1910 and ran for 153 performances. In 1915 *Under the Red Robe* became the first of Weyman's works to be adapted as a motion picture.

In 1919 Weyman ended his break from writing with *The Great House.* This novel was followed by *Ovington's Bank* (1922), *The Traveller in the Fur Cloak* (1924), *Queen's Folly* (1925), and *The Lively Peggy,* the novel he had just completed before he died in 1928. All these novels are set in early-nineteenth-century England. No longer concerned with writing the sort of fiction the public wanted, Weyman returned to the subject that suited him.

In the late twentieth century Weyman is relatively unknown, his books regarded primarily as adventure stories for young boys. Weyman's work was still somewhat popular in the 1930s and 1940s,

when radio dramas were based on some of his early novels, and a sound-motion-picture version of *Under the Red Robe* was produced in 1937. Since World War II there have been occasional editions of his novels that target an adolescent male audience, but most of Weyman's books have been out of print for decades. In his own time, however, his fiction was highly regarded. Even the often acerbic Oscar Wilde admired Weyman's tales, writing in *De Profundis* (1905) that every library should include works by "Stevenson . . . Thackeray . . . Jane Austen . . . Stanley Weyman." One of the best assessments of Weyman's work comes from a memorial article written by Leonard Huxley in 1928:

> Stanley Weyman will long be remembered as a writer for the gallantry of his best romantic tales and the visions of the life-forces which animate the finest English stories. These stories will live, for they are swift and stirring, their substance rich and true, their atmosphere healthy, the historical characters strongly drawn from authentic sources. . . . Romance is but rarely wedded to such sincerity of purpose and sanity of outlook.

For thousands of his contemporaries Weyman was the preeminent figure in the genre of historical romance writing.

References:
Helen Muriel Hughes, "Changes in the Historical Romance, 1890s to the 1980s: The Development of the Genre from Stanley J. Weyman to Georgette Heyer and Her Successors," dissertation, University of Bradford, 1988;

Leonard Huxley, "In Memoriam: Stanley J. Weyman," *Cornhill Magazine,* series 3, 64 (June 1928): 752–755.

Papers:
The only substantial holding of Weyman's papers is in the De Coursey Fales Collection at the New York Public Library.

Oscar Wilde

(16 October 1854 – 30 November 1900)

Debra C. Boyd
Winthrop University

See also the Wilde entries in *DLB 10: Modern British Dramatists, 1900–1945; DLB 19: British Poets, 1880–1914; DLB 34: Traditionalists British Novelists, 1890–1929; DLB 57: Victorian Prose Writers After 1867;* and *DLB 141: British Children's Writers, 1880–1914.*

BOOKS: *Newdigate Prize Poem: Ravenna, Recited in the Theatre, Oxford, 26 June 1878* (Oxford: Shrimpton, 1878);

Vera; or, The Nihilists: A Drama in Four Acts (London: Privately printed, 1880);

Poems (London: Bogue, 1881; Boston: Roberts, 1881);

The Duchess of Padua: A Tragedy of the XVI Century, Written in Paris in the XIX Century (New York: Privately printed, 1883);

The Happy Prince and Other Tales (London: Nutt, 1888; Boston: Roberts, 1888);

The Picture of Dorian Gray (London, New York & Melbourne: Ward, Lock, 1891);

Intentions (London: Osgood, McIlvaine, 1891; New York: Dodd, Mead, 1891);

Lord Arthur Savile's Crime & Other Stories (London: Osgood, McIlvaine, 1891; New York: Dodd, Mead, 1891);

A House of Pomegranates (London: Osgood, McIlvaine, 1891; New York: Dodd, Mead, 1892);

Salomé: Drame en un acte (Paris: Librairie de l'Art Indépendant / London: Elkin Mathews & John Lane, Bodley Head, 1893); republished as *Salomé: A Tragedy in One Act,* translated by Alfred Douglas (London: Elkin Mathews & John Lane / Boston: Copeland & Day, 1894);

Lady Windermere's Fan: A Play about a Good Woman (London: Elkin Mathews & John Lane, Bodley Head, 1893);

Phrases and Philosophies for the Use of the Young (London: Privately printed, 1894 [i.e., 1902]);

The Sphinx (London: Elkin Mathews & John Lane, Bodley Head / Boston: Copeland & Day, 1894);

Oscar Wilde in 1885 (Hulton Deutsch Collection)

A Woman of No Importance (London: John Lane, Bodley Head, 1894);

The Soul of Man (London: Privately printed, 1895); republished as *The Soul of Man Under Socialism* (London: Privately printed, 1904);

The Ballad of Reading Gaol, as C.3.3. (London: Smithers, 1898);

The Importance of Being Earnest: A Trivial Comedy for Serious People (London: Smithers, 1899);

An Ideal Husband (London: Smithers, 1899);

Essays, Criticisms, and Reviews (London: Privately printed, 1901);

The Portrait of Mr. W. H. (Portland, Maine: Mosher, 1901; London: Privately printed, 1904);

The Harlot's House (London: Mathurin Press [i.e., Smithers], 1904);

De Profundis (London: Methuen, 1905; New York & London: Putnam, 1905);

Poems in Prose (Paris: Privately printed, 1905);

Impressions of America, edited by Stuart Mason (Sunderland, U.K.: Keystone Press, 1906);

Decorative Art in America (New York: Brentano's, 1906);

A Florentine Tragedy (Boston: Luce, 1908);

The Suppressed Portion of "De Profundis" (New York: Reynolds, 1913);

To M. B. J., edited by Mason (C. S. Millard) (London: Privately printed, 1920);

For Love of the King: A Burmese Masque (London: Methuen, 1922);

Teleny; or the Reverse of the Medal (Paris: Olympia Press, 1958);

The Literary Criticism of Oscar Wilde, edited by Stanley Weintraub (Lincoln: University of Nebraska Press, 1968);

The Artist as Critic: Critical Writings of Oscar Wilde, edited by Richard Ellmann (New York: Random House, 1969).

Editions and Collections: *First Collected Edition of the Works of Oscar Wilde,* edited by Robert Ross (volumes 1–11, 13–14, London: Methuen, 1908; Boston: Luce, 1910; volume 12, Paris: Carrington, 1908);

Second Collected Edition of the Works of Oscar Wilde, edited by Ross (volumes 1–12, London: Methuen, 1909; volume 13, Paris: Carrington, 1910; volume 14, London: John Lane, 1912);

The Complete Works of Oscar Wilde, edited by Vyvyan Holland (London: Collins, 1948);

Essays of Oscar Wilde, edited by Hesketh Pearson (London: Methuen, 1950);

Oscar Wilde: Complete Shorter Fiction, edited by Murray (Oxford: Oxford University Press, 1979);

Oscar Wilde's Oxford Notebooks: A Portrait of Mind in the Making, edited by Philip E. Smith II and Michael Helfand (New York: Oxford University Press, 1989);

Oscar Wilde, edited by Murray (Oxford: Oxford University Press, 1989);

Aristotle at Afternoon Tea: The Rare Oscar Wilde, edited by John Wyse Jackson (London: Fourth Estate, 1991);

Oscar Wilde: Plays, Prose Writings, and Poems, introduction by Terry Eagleton (London: David Campbell, 1991).

PLAY PRODUCTIONS: *Vera; or, the Nihilists,* New York, Union Square Theatre, 20 August 1883;

Guido Ferranti: A Tragedy of the XVI Century, New York, Broadway Theatre, 26 January 1891;

Lady Windermere's Fan, London, St. James's Theatre, 20 February 1892;

A Woman of No Importance, London, Haymarket Theatre, 19 April 1893;

An Ideal Husband, London, Haymarket Theatre, 3 January 1895;

The Importance of Being Earnest, London, St. James's Theatre, 14 February 1895;

Salomé, Paris, Théâtre de l'Oeuvre, 11 February 1896; London, Bijou, 10 May 1905;

A Florentine Tragedy, by Wilde, with opening scene by T. Sturge Moore, London, King's Hall, 10 June 1906.

Oscar Wilde's literary reputation rests primarily on his later plays and his only novel, *The Picture of Dorian Gray* (1891). Although he published only fourteen short stories and six prose poems, a meager number compared to many fiction writers of his time, the quality of his short fiction is consistently impressive. Because he wrote mostly fairy tales, critics have given his short fiction only passing glances; yet Wilde's short fiction complements and informs much of his other work, especially his plays and criticism. His stories work out his critical theories and test the social norms so popular in his plays. That he found fiction a natural form for him is not surprising, for as he told André Gide, "They [critics] believe all thoughts are born naked. . . . They don't understand that I can not think otherwise than in stories."

Born in Dublin on 16 October 1854, Oscar Fingal O'Flahertie Wills Wilde was the second child of Dr. William Robert Wills Wilde, a well-known eye and ear surgeon, and Jane Francesca Elgee Wilde, a poet and Irish nationalist. No doubt his parents provided incentive for Wilde to distinguish himself, for they were part of Dublin's vibrant cultural and social circles during Oscar's youth. Director of the 1851 medical census of Ireland (for which he was knighted), author of standard medical texts including *Practical Observations on Aural Surgery and the Nature of Diseases of the Ear* (1853), and Surgeon Oculist in Ordinary to Queen Victoria, Dr. William Wilde developed a flourishing medical practice as well as a reputation as an author, writing more than twenty books on Irish ethnology, archaeology, and folklore. Lady Jane Wilde served as the stronger parental and literary influence. Using Speranza as her pseudonym, Lady Wilde established herself as an Irish patriot, a vocal advocate for nationalism and for women's rights. During the mid

Wilde during his sophomore year at Trinity College, Dublin (William Andrews Clark Memorial Library, University of California, Los Angeles)

and late 1840s she wrote verses and essays advocating liberation and translated into English a host of works, including her 1849 translation of Wilhelm Meinhold's *Sidonia the Sorceress* (1847). According to Isobel Murray, Oscar Wilde called this work part of his "favourite romantic reading when a boy," and echoes of it may be found throughout his fiction.

Wilde's formal education began at the Portora Royal School in Enniskillen. In his last two years there (1869–1871), his talent in classical studies won him one of three Royal School entrance scholarships to Trinity College, Dublin. At Trinity, Wilde continued his study of the classics, focusing on Greek texts as he came under the influence of his tutor, the Rev. John P. Mahaffy, and eventually won the Berkeley Gold Medal for Greek and a Foundation Scholarship. In 1874 Wilde won one of two scholarships in classics awarded by Magdalen College, Oxford.

In his four years at Oxford, Wilde cultivated his personal, philosophical, and literary tastes, developing his ideas about the role of the artist and the individual. John Ruskin, Slade Professor of Art at Oxford, and Walter Pater, fellow of Brasenose College, most clearly influenced Wilde during his Oxford years; and the ideas of both men – especially of Pater's influential *Studies in the History of the Renaissance* (1873) – remained a continuing force in Wilde's career. In *De Profundis* (written in 1897) Wilde labeled Pater's book as one "which has had such a strange influence over my life." While Pater provided the impetus for Wilde's nascent aestheticism and modernism and his initiation into the religion of beauty, Ruskin's social and ethical concerns, including the relation between art and morality, nurtured young Wilde's ideals. Although volumes have been written on Wilde's deliberate cultivation of his flamboyant personality at Oxford (his blue china collection remains a popular topic), the young man also took his studies seriously enough to earn Firsts in Classical Moderations (Mods) in 1876 and in Greats in 1878 and to win the Newdigate Prize for Poetry with *Ravenna* (1878). Soon after receiving his B.A. from Oxford on 28 November 1878, Wilde decided to stake his chances on London, where he spent the next year living on a small patrimony and searching for suitable work when he was unable to secure a position at Oxford.

Taking rooms with Frank Miles at 13 Salisbury Street and later on Tite Street, Wilde began to construct his public image, one based on his developing attraction to aestheticism and Benjamin Disraeli's dandyism, and to develop his literary and critical reputation. His first play, *Vera; or, The Nihilists,* which examines political issues in Russia, was privately published in the fall of 1880. The December 1881 production planned for London was canceled because of the assassination of Czar Alexander II (who was the brother-in-law of the Princess of Wales). Wilde's next literary effort was a book of sixty-one poems, thirty of which had already appeared in magazines. Printed at Wilde's expense by David Bogue (a small publishing firm), *Poems* appeared in June 1881 in England and in October 1881 in the United States. Filled with vivid impressions of places and people, the poems reveal Wilde's growing belief in the importance of aesthetic intensity, the need to experience life fully and to reject the stultifying conventions of society.

Although his book of poems received little attention when it first appeared, it contributed to Wilde's controversial image, as did his taste for extravagant clothes and celebrities – including Lillie

Langtry and Sarah Bernhardt – and his pronouncements on aesthetic ideals in his art reviews. As his reputation grew, he soon became a popular topic of caricatures, including one in W. S. Gilbert and Arthur Sullivan's comic opera *Patience* (1881). Yet even public ridicule became an occasion for profit when producer Richard D'Oyly Carte hired Wilde in 1882 for an American lecture series intended to drum up business for *Patience,* which had opened in New York in September 1881. Personally and professionally rewarding for Wilde, this ten-month lecture tour of the United States and Canada made him the spokesman for the Aesthetic movement, articulating the dichotomy between art and reality and promoting the varied forms of aestheticism practiced by John Ruskin, William Morris, Dante Gabriel Rossetti, Pater, and James McNeill Whistler. While in America Wilde also secured a commitment from Marie Prescott to stage *Vera* and persuaded Hamilton Griffin and actress Mary Anderson to undertake a production of his play in progress, *The Duchess of Padua* (1883).

Returning to London in January 1883, Wilde took the profits from his lecture series and went to Paris to finish *The Duchess of Padua* and to work on poems such as "The Sphinx." Although his main exploits involved conquering the social scene and meeting the literati of Paris, he did finish the play, which was rejected in its final form by Griffin and Anderson. It was finally staged in January 1891 at the Broadway Theatre, New York, under a new title, *Guido Ferranti.* Set in sixteenth-century Italy, the revenge tragedy found a supportive audience but lasted for only twenty-one performances in New York. Wilde's *Vera* met an equally disappointing fate: opening night was 20 August 1883 at the Union Square Theatre in New York, and the closing performance was one week later. Needing funds to support his lifestyle, Wilde returned home to begin another lecture tour – this one in England, Ireland, and Scotland – on "The House Beautiful" and "Impressions of America."

During his tour he became reacquainted with Constance Lloyd, whom he had met in London in 1881; they were engaged on 25 November 1883 and married on 29 May 1884. Having recklessly spent most of their money on the renovation of their Tite Street house, Wilde had to find a steadier source of income than that from his literary works. He began to write reviews regularly for the *Pall Mall Gazette* and other periodicals, and he continued lecturing. Becoming for a time a devoted husband, Wilde worked hard to support his wife and sons, Cyril (born in 1885) and Vyvyan (born in 1886). He also

began working in earnest on his creative writing. For the next three years Wilde refined his critical talents and aesthetic philosophy. In 1887 he became editor of *The Lady's World,* immediately changing its name to *The Woman's World.* Hoping to make the magazine "the recognised organ for the expression of women's opinions on all subjects of literature, art, and modern life," Wilde solicited articles from prominent women and raised the intellectual level of the magazine; but growing weary of the daily grind and finding a market for his own creative work, he relinquished the editorship in 1889.

The years between 1887 and 1895 marked the most intensely productive period in Wilde's life, and his works ranged from collections of short stories to his best-known plays. As Murray asserts, it is not surprising that Wilde's first clear successes were short stories, for his work with periodicals of the time had made him acutely aware of the reading public's tastes. Although he claimed never to have written only for the public, he worked in traditional and popular short-fiction forms – such as the ghost story and fairy tales – and transformed them into delicate lessons in aesthetic and decadent theories. As Wendell Harris notes, Wilde characteristically used fantasy and paradox in his short fiction. Indeed, Wilde employed the fantastic in almost every story and created situations that are filled with irony and often resolved in paradoxical fashion. Although Wilde's fiction supports philosophical views advocated in his criticism (art as superior to nature, the seminal position of beauty, the significant collaboration between aestheticism and personality), these themes are most often raised in narratives that explore suffering, sacrifice, or the relationship between innocence and experience, good and evil. In addition, critics often note the epigrammatic quality of Wilde's fiction (and his works in general), a feature that some scholars have dismissed as superficial. In light of Wilde's aesthetic theories about beauty and personality, however, his style is well suited to convey his ideas. In fact, the tight structure and dramatic quality of his stories anticipate those aspects of the modern short story.

Four stories published in popular magazines during 1887 improved Wilde's literary fortunes. *The Court and Society Review* published "The Canterville Ghost" in its 23 February and 2 March issues and "Lord Arthur Savile's Crime" in its May issues. "Lady Alroy" (later retitled "The Sphinx without a Secret") appeared in the 25 May number of *The Court and Society Review,* and "The Model Millionaire" appeared in the 22 June issue of *The World.* These stories were later collected in *Lord Arthur*

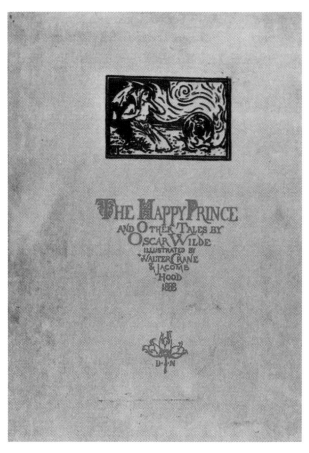

Cover for Wilde's collection of fairy tales written for his sons

Savile's Crime & Other Stories (1891). "The Sphinx without a Secret" and "The Model Millionaire" are brief examinations of the significant decisions individuals make, of how human behavior is often inexplicable. Set in Paris, "The Sphinx without a Secret" recounts the experience of Lord Gerald Murchison, who reluctantly tells the narrator of his ill-fated love for the mysterious Lady Alroy. In "The Model Millionaire" Hughie Erskine, a good-looking but impoverished young man, gives a sovereign to a man he thinks is a beggar but who turns out to be a "millionaire model" posing for Hughie's artist friend. These stories, which have received little critical attention, reveal Wilde's interest in social codes, an interest that he explored in comic ways in the other stories in this collection and in his later plays.

The title story and "The Canterville Ghost" are considered the best works in the collection. "Lord Arthur Savile's Crime" uses what Murray calls "through-the-looking-glass logic" to examine one man's interpretation of duty. Such an approach clearly looks forward to the witty but absurdist repartee in *The Importance of Being Earnest* (1899). Opening in the salon of Lady Windermere, the

story follows Lord Arthur, who has become engaged to the lovely Sybil Merton and is told by a palm reader that he will commit a murder. Repulsed by the thought of such a deed, Arthur decides, however, that "he had no right to marry until he had committed the murder." In parodic passages of melodramatic prose, Lord Arthur comically fulfills his "fate," as Wilde examines Victorian society and its obsession with convention.

Written during the heyday of the ghost story, "The Canterville Ghost" juxtaposes Victorian England and nineteenth-century America, poking fun at both cultures and mocking with good humor both the willingness and unwillingness to believe in ghosts. When the practical Otis family from the United States moves into Canterville Chase, an English castle haunted by the ghost of Sir Simon de Canterville, they pit their pragmatism against the dramatic appearances of Sir Simon. Removing reappearing blood stains from the sitting room floor with "Pinkerton's Champion Stain Remover and Paragon Detergent" is only one of the many sensible responses the Otises have to the machinations of the ghost. Sir Simon, on the other hand, envisions his ghostly occupation as a series of dramatic roles to be played and pulls out his theatrical bag of tricks, performing such characters as "Black Isaac, or the Huntsman of Hogley Woods" to frighten the family. The ghost's sense of decorum and duty is matched and overcome by the impertinence and ingenuity of the young Otis boys. The ghost weakens; and the story shifts dramatically when young Virginia Otis, a thoughtful fifteen-year-old, encounters the ghost, learns of his sordid past, and discovers that she must lay to rest his spirit. Her willingness to help Sir Simon leads to her enlightenment, although she tells her family only that the ghost has let her see "what Life is and what Death signifies, and why Love is stronger than both." Wilde's use of the ghost story to examine the moral issue of forgiveness is commonplace for its time, as seen in the works of Joseph Sheridan Le Fanu, Amelia Edwards, and Charlotte Riddell; however, his treatment of Virginia's initiation into maturity and the well-timed humor he employs raise the quality of the story above what is typically found in Christmas annuals of the time. Long after its publication, the story continued to find favor with the public, for it was adapted as a stage play in 1936 and 1963, as a movie in 1944, and as a television program in 1975.

When *Lord Arthur Savile's Crime & Other Stories* appeared, critical response was mixed. William Sharp, who wrote fiction under the pseudonym of Fiona Macleod, stated in the 5 September 1891 issue of the *Academy* that Wilde's stories would "not add to their author's reputation," citing the work of Robert Louis Stevenson as superior to Wilde's. In *United Ireland* (26 September 1891), William Butler Yeats expressed his disappointment, describing individual stories as either "amusing enough" or "quite unworthy of more than a passing interest." Modern critics have been much kinder; for example, Wendell Harris calls "Lord Arthur Savile's Crime" and "The Canterville Ghost" "Wildean tours de force," and Isobel Murray notes Wilde's skillful mockery of Victorian melodrama and the "hackneyed, conventional ghost-story setting."

The Happy Prince and Other Tales, Wilde's most successful collection of short fiction (illustrated by Walter Crane and Jacomb Hood), appeared in May 1888 to universal acclaim. Wilde described the fairy tale as a form that allows discussion of modern problems but "aims at delicacy and imaginative treatment . . . it is a reaction against the purely imitative character of modern art." The title story focuses on sacrifice and reward. A golden, jeweled statue of the late Happy Prince overlooks the city he ruled, a city filled with misery he never saw because he lived a sheltered, indulgent life. Saddened by the surrounding poverty and decay, the statue asks a swallow that lights on it to help alleviate the people's suffering by removing the jewels and gold-leaf from its body and giving them to the poor people in the city. In its examination of the relationship between beauty and sacrifice, the story echoes a theme of Alfred Tennyson's "The Palace of Art" (1832), for the statue and swallow achieve spiritual beauty through sacrifice and love for others.

"The Nightingale and the Rose" and "The Selfish Giant" reiterate this theme of beauty and sacrifice. The nightingale hears the lament of a young student for the woman he loves, a woman who will dance with him only if he gives her a red rose. Moved by the student's love, the bird gives its life to create the beautiful red rose for the student's benefit, only to have the rose (and the student) rejected by the woman in favor of "real jewels." In a letter to Thomas Hutchinson, Wilde stated that the "nightingale is the true lover. . . . She, at least, is Romance, and the Student and the girl are, like most of us, unworthy of Romance . . . but I like to fancy that there may be many meanings in the tale, for in writing it I did not start with an idea and clothe it in form, but began with a form and strove to make it beautiful enough to have many secrets and many answers."

The best-known story of sacrifice, that of Jesus Christ, serves as the basis for "The Selfish Giant."

Finding children in his garden and refusing to share its beauty, a giant frightens them away and builds a wall to keep them out. Winter descends on the garden and remains for more than a year. Finally, awakening to the smell of blossoms and the sound of birds in his garden, the giant discovers that the children have returned, bringing the spring with them. Suddenly realizing his selfishness, the giant welcomes them to his land and helps one tiny child climb a tree, which blossoms as the child sits in it. The giant now understands that the children are the beauty of his garden and invites them to visit whenever they wish. For years children come to play with the giant but not the tiny child whom the giant loved best. One day the child returns, his hands and feet marked by nail holes, and tells the giant, "You let me play once in your garden, to-day you shall come with me to my garden, which is Paradise." The next day the other children find the giant dead in his garden.

The two remaining stories in the collection – "The Remarkable Rocket" and "The Devoted Friend" – explore pride and selfishness. In the first, a pompous rocket from a fireworks display creates his own fiction, as he constructs a "reality" to suit his inflated vision of himself, a view that the narrator consistently undercuts. The setting for "The Devoted Friend" is a pond, where the linnet tells the story of Hans the gardener and Hugh the miller to the egotistical water rat, the duck, and her ducklings. Filled with irony, the story chronicles Hans's generous nature and deeds and relates how, in the name of friendship, he gives everything he owns to the miller and dies while getting the doctor for the miller's sick son.

One thousand copies of *The Happy Prince and Other Tales* sold in the first six months. Sales were helped by favorable reviews. An unsigned review in *The Athenaeum* is typical of the general response to Wilde's work: "The gift of writing fairy tales is rare, and Mr. Oscar Wilde shows that he possesses it in a rare degree. . . . [The tales] are not unworthy to compare with Hans Andersen, and it is not easy to give higher praise than this." In her recent discussion of these stories, Isobel Murray notes the influence of Hans Christian Andersen's "The Angel," "A Rose from the Grave of Homer," and "The Darning Needle"; however Wilde's stories never fall into the sentimentality of Andersen's and often mock the conventions used by Andersen. Wilde was thrilled with Pater's response to the collection in a letter to Wilde dated 12 June 1888: "it would be ungrateful not to send a line to tell you how delightful I have found him [the Happy Prince] and his companions.

Illustration by Walter Crane for Wilde's story "The Selfish Giant" in
The Happy Prince and Other Tales *(1888)*

I hardly know whether to admire more the wise wit of 'The Wonderful [Remarkable] Rocket' or the beauty and tenderness of 'The Selfish Giant': the latter certainly is perfect in its kind." As Wilde noted, the stories in this collection are "meant partly for children, and partly for those who have kept the childlike faculties of wonder and joy, and who find in simplicity a subtle strangeness." Illustrated editions can still be found in most bookstores, and "The Selfish Giant," "The Happy Prince," and "The Remarkable Rocket" were adapted as movies in 1971, 1973, and 1975, respectively.

Buoyed by his success, Wilde tried a more ambitious project for his next foray into fiction. Influenced by Pater's *Imaginary Portraits,* "The Portrait of Mr. W. H." (*Blackwood's Edinburgh Magazine,* July 1889) examines the theory that the W. H. in the dedication to William Shakespeare's sonnets was a young man named Willie Hughes, who, according to the story, was an actor in Shakespeare's company. George Erskine tells the narrator about Cyril Graham, who believed this theory and committed suicide after Erskine discovered that a portrait of Mr. W. H. was forged to persuade Erskine that the theory was valid. Erskine, in turn, plants the seed of belief in the narrator, who spends weeks attempting to prove the theory and becomes temporarily con-

vinced of its truth. Yet, as Erskine tells the narrator, "a thing is not necessarily true because a man dies for it." With its historical basis but fictional framework, the story has always posed problems for Wilde's readers, for it is both fiction and criticism, showing the limitations of historical criticism. In fact, critic Donald Lawler calls the work an example of critical deconstruction. Many of Wilde's contemporaries read the story in the context of its author's life, seeing the relationship between Shakespeare and Willie Hughes as suggesting Wilde's homosexuality, the part of his own life that, since 1886, had become increasingly important to him.

When the first version of Wilde's only novel – *The Picture of Dorian Gray* – appeared on 20 June 1890, in the July issue of *Lippincott's Monthly Magazine,* the suspicion aroused by "The Portrait of Mr. W. H." exploded in a firestorm of criticism. The novel follows the life of Dorian Gray, a young man who remains forever young, while a portrait of him ages and is physically affected by Dorian's spiritual degeneration. Although the novel never explicitly mentions homosexuality, initial public reaction to Dorian Gray's moral decay was hostile; and Wilde wrote many letters replying to charges that the novel is "incurably silly" (Samuel Jeyes, *St. James's Gazette,* 24 June 1890) and flawed by "effeminate frivolity . . . and garish vulgarity" (*Daily Chronicle,* 30 June 1890). Answering with restraint and decorum, Wilde asserted, once again, that "the sphere of art and the sphere of ethics are absolutely distinct and separate." In addition, he placed on the perceivers all responsibility for the evil perceived in the novel, for he argued that "there is a terrible moral in *Dorian Gray* – a moral which the prurient will not be able to find in it, but which will be revealed to all whose minds are healthy." Indeed, Wilde stated that the too-obvious moral was the only artistic flaw in the work and promised to correct that problem when the work appeared in book form. Yet the addition of six chapters and a theoretical preface in the book version, published in April 1891, only increased speculation about the work's meaning. Not all criticism was negative, and such publications as the *Christian Leader* and the *Scots Observer* carried reviews that lauded Wilde's attempt to demonstrate the perils of decadence. Pater's November 1891 essay in *The Bookman* focused on the beauty and artistry of *Dorian Gray,* favorably comparing Wilde to Edgar Allan Poe. In *The Picture of Dorian Gray,* the techniques used and themes explored in "Lord Arthur Savile's Crime" and "The Portrait of Mr. W. H." are developed in greater detail and with more confidence.

Wilde continued his exploration of the dark nature of humanity with his next collection of fairy tales, *A House of Pomegranates* (published in November 1891). The philosophical twin to *The Happy Prince, A House of Pomegranates* extends the consideration of suffering and loss but focuses more intently – except in "The Birthday of the Infanta" – on a series of awakenings by characters whose beauty or power has either blinded or sheltered them. "The Fisherman and his Soul" and "The Star-Child" appeared for the first time in this collection, while the other two stories had been published earlier: "The Young King" in the 1888 Christmas number of *The Lady's Pictorial* and "The Birthday of the Infanta" in *Paris Illustre* (in French and English) on 30 March 1889.

As Isobel Murray notes, "The Young King" serves as a bridge between *The Happy Prince* and *A House of Pomegranates*. The young king, who has been raised as a goatherd, is preparing for his coronation, when he learns – through a series of dreams – about the pain resulting from the creation of beautiful items for the ceremony. Rejecting an ornate robe, scepter, and crown, he puts on his rustic clothes, takes up a shepherd's staff, and wears a crown of wild briars. Mocked and threatened with death by the populace, the young king goes to the cathedral, where the bishop refuses to crown him without the trappings of kingship. While he prays before the image of Christ, the young king is suddenly and mystically arrayed in sunshine, which "wove round him a tissued robe that was fairer than the robe that had been fashioned for his pleasure. The dead staff blossomed, and bare lilies that were whiter than pearls. The dry thorn blossomed, and bare roses that were redder than rubies." For this young monarch, enlightenment comes before death and serves as a catalyst for change in his material existence.

A Faustian tale in which a fisherman gives up his soul in order to have the mermaid he idolizes, "The Fisherman and His Soul" examines the relationship between beauty and goodness and probes the result of actions taken without reference to conscience, themes similar to those explored in *The Picture of Dorian Gray*. Indeed, "The Birthday of the Infanta" and "The Star-Child" also raise the central questions about conscience and beauty found in the novel and in Wilde's play *Salomé* (1893). The young Infanta treats those around her with cruelty and disrespect. Her dwarf, who is physically ugly but does not know it, is kind and generous but dies of a broken heart when he finally sees his grotesque shape. The story ends with the Infanta petulantly pro-

claiming, "For the future let those who come to play with me have no hearts." The Star-Child's intense physical beauty is paradoxically matched by the depth and viciousness of his cruelty. Eventually his exterior matches his misshapen character, and he must learn kindness and compassion before his physical beauty can return.

A House of Pomegranates was not as exuberantly praised as *The Happy Prince and Other Tales*. Expecting simple fairy tales for children, adult readers were disturbed by the conditional morality of the stories and the elaborate, aesthetic descriptions. Wilde replied to his critics by stating, in a December 1891 letter to the *Pall Mall Gazette*, "in building this *House of Pomegranates* I had about as much intention of pleasing the British child as I had of pleasing the British public. . . . No artist recognises any standard of beauty but that which is suggested by his own temperament."

Although Wilde's next collection of stories, *Poems in Prose*, did not appear until 1905, two of these six stories had been published separately in magazines in 1893; and all had appeared together in the July 1894 issue of *The Fortnightly Review*. To Wilde's friends and acquaintances, they were also well known as part of his verbal repertoire. According to Isobel Murray, these works – which are considered prose poems rather than stories or tales because of their brevity, symbolic nature, and lack of character development – reveal the influence of French writers such as Charles-Pierre Baudelaire. "The Disciple" and "The House of Judgement," which had been published in *The Spirit Lamp* (in June 1893 and February 1893, respectively) and "The Artist," "The Doer of Good," "The Master," and "The Teacher of Wisdom" are short, impressionistic parables that violate expectations at almost every turn. For example, in "The Master" Joseph of Arimathea, finding a man crying after the death of Christ, tries to console the mourner, only to hear the young man exclaim, "It is not for Him that I am weeping, but for myself." As the man explains, he too has performed miracles but has not been crucified. As Murray and others have noted, the use of Christ as the central, though unnamed, figure in most of these stories shows Wilde's growing preoccupation with Christian myth, a focus that culminated in his equating himself with Christ in *De Profundis*, the well-known letter Wilde wrote to Lord Alfred Douglas in 1897. Known as Bosie, Douglas had met Wilde in 1891, and from their meeting until Wilde's imprisonment on charges of sodomy in 1895, they remained almost constant companions. The youngest son of John Sholto Douglas,

Constance and Cyril Wilde (William Andrews Clark Memorial Library, University of California, Los Angeles)

Marquess of Queensberry, Lord Alfred Douglas captured Wilde's fancy and his love. Sadly, their relationship led to Wilde's incarceration and ruin.

In addition to the fiction that circulated between 1887 and 1895, Wilde published a variety of other works. His well-known essay on social justice, "The Soul of Man under Socialism," appeared in the February 1891 number of *The Fortnightly Review* and was published separately as *The Soul of Man* in 1895. Also in 1891 *Intentions,* a collection of critical essays, provided an additional look at Wilde's critical perspectives. Essays such as "The Decay of Lying," "The Truth of Masks," and "The Critic as Artist" emphasize theories that Wilde practiced in his fiction and drama: that life imitates art, that the imagination is man's foremost faculty, and that criticism is an art form that depends on the personality of the critic. Wilde also wrote poetry during this 1885–1895 period, and poems such as "The Harlot's House" (1885), "Canzonet" (1888), "Symphony in Yellow" (1889), "In the Forest" (1889), and *The Sphinx* (1894) reveal Wilde's continuing interest in poetic forms and provide stylistic commentary on the poetic qualities of his fiction.

The most critically acclaimed works of this period, however, are Wilde's plays, especially his so-

cial comedies. With the 20 February 1892 premiere of *Lady Windermere's Fan* at St. James's Theatre, Wilde launched a short but remarkable career as a dramatist. Moving next to tragedy, he composed *Salomé* while in Paris in 1892. The play, written in French, was scheduled to star Sarah Bernhardt, but the Lord Chamberlain's office refused to issue a license for it because of a centuries-old ban prohibiting biblical characters on the English stage. The play was published in 1893 and eventually reached the stage in Paris in 1896; critics hailed it as a great triumph for Wilde. During 1892 he also wrote *A Woman of No Importance,* which opened at the Haymarket Theatre on 19 April 1893 to critical and public acclaim. In addition, he developed *A Florentine Tragedy,* produced in 1906, nearly six years after his death, and worked on "La Sainte Courtisane" (a play fragment). He began writing *An Ideal Husband* during 1893 and *The Importance of Being Earnest* during 1894 and saw both plays performed in 1895. With the exception of *The Importance of Being Earnest,* Wilde's comedies are populated with characters who have committed some injustice or social faux pas and seek to provide reparation or to receive forgiveness, much like the characters in many of his fairy tales. In *The Importance of Being Earnest,* however, the characters operate from a social code that glorifies the dandy, which lauds individual style over morality. The comedy of *The Importance of Being Earnest* stems from its consistent mockery of Victorian social norms, its deliberate adherence to Wilde's concepts of taste and temperament. All of Wilde's plays staged in this period were successful, with *Lady Windermere's Fan* and *The Importance of Being Earnest* garnering the most praise.

By 1895 Wilde had reached the pinnacle of his career and life; the dénouement was both swift and tragic. Bosie Douglas's father, the marquess of Queensberry, was determined to separate his son from Wilde. In February 1895, after months of harassing Wilde, Queensberry left his card with an insulting message for Wilde at the Albemarle Club: "To Oscar Wilde posing Somdomite [*sic*]." Wilde lodged an accusation of slander against Queensberry, and the case opened on 3 April 1895. Wilde's "feasting with panthers," as he called his homosexual forays, returned to haunt him as Queensberry's attorney provided evidence of Wilde's involvement with young men. Although Wilde held his own on the first day of the trial, by the third day his lawyer sought to end it, and Queensberry was found not guilty. Required to pay court costs, Wilde did not have the funds and was later declared bankrupt. His possessions (including manuscripts) were auctioned to cover his debts. Rather than fleeing to Europe after the trial, as most people expected him to do, Wilde went to the Cadogan Hotel to await his arrest on charges of offenses to minors, charges clearly established during the Queensberry trial. Estranged from Bosie Douglas by this time, Wilde faced his first trial alone, and it ended in a hung jury; in the second trial he was convicted and sentenced to two years of hard labor.

While in jail Wilde wrote *De Profundis,* a long letter that details his relationship with Douglas and explores Wilde's and Douglas's flaws, while also analyzing Wilde's philosophy of suffering. When released from Reading Gaol in May 1897, Wilde gave the letter to Robert Ross, his literary executor, requesting that a copy be sent to Douglas, who later claimed that he never received it. Ross published an expurgated version in 1905. A fuller version – with names included – appeared in 1949, and a complete version was published in Rupert Hart-Davis's edition of *The Letters of Oscar Wilde* (1962). Except for several letters on prison reform, Wilde's poem *The Ballad of Reading Gaol* (1898) was his last work to be published in his lifetime.

Wilde left prison and almost immediately departed for France, taking the name Sebastian Melmoth, a dramatic personal allusion to the central figure of the popular Faustian novel *Melmoth the Wanderer* (1820) by Charles Maturin, Wilde's great granduncle. Wilde's wife, Constance, died in 1898; and Wilde never again saw his sons, who had taken the surname of Holland. Reconciled with Bosie Douglas, Wilde died from encephalitic meningitis in Paris on 30 November 1900. On his deathbed he converted to Catholicism, a religion he had flirted with all his life. Initially buried in Bagneux graveyard, his remains were later moved to Père Lachaise Cemetery in Paris.

From Wilde's death until the late 1940s, critics generally focused on his biography, choosing to discuss the man rather than his writings, perhaps because Wilde himself had so emphasized the relationship between the personality of the writer and his works. Although several critical works (such as Edouard Roditi's *Oscar Wilde* (1947) and St. John Ervine's *Oscar Wilde: A Present Time Appraisal* (1951) appeared in the 1940s and 1950s, Ian Small correctly asserts that until the 1960s Wilde was relegated to being a minor figure in the Victorian pantheon of writers, one admired mainly for *The Importance of Being Earnest* or considered a representative of Aestheticism or the Decadent movement. In the last thirty years, however, Wilde's critical reputation has taken a dramatic upswing. Additional bio-

Wilde and Lord Alfred Douglas in 1894

graphical and textual materials have been made available, including Rupert Hart-Davis's editions of Wilde's letters, Richard Ellmann's biography of Wilde, and Philip E. Smith II and Michael Helfand's edition of Wilde's Oxford notebooks. These materials have allowed critics a better view of Wilde's own sense of his works and the degree to which he affected his contemporaries. In addition, poststructuralist criticism and gay studies have provided scholars with varied theoretical frameworks from which to examine Wilde's works: for example, Jonathan Dollimore, Richard Dellamora, and Eve Kosofsky Sedgwick have placed Wilde in the forefront of writers who examine the sexual and political dimensions of art. Although such work bodes well for Wilde's status as a major literary figure, his shorter fiction has largely been ignored in these discussions, which favor his plays, his criticism, or *The Picture of Dorian Gray.* Wilde's short fiction has recently been examined by critics such as Isobel Murray, Horst Schroeder, Lydia Wilburn, and Linda Dowling, and their analyses have helped to enhance Wilde's critical reputation. Yet more attention must be paid to his short fiction. In this age of literary theory, few writers can articulate as clearly as Wilde did the theoretical bases for their works and then actually practice what they preach. Wilde's stories show that he was able to merge theory and practice, creating works of art that stand up well to critical scrutiny.

Letters:

The Letters of Oscar Wilde, edited by Rupert Hart-Davis (New York: Harcourt, Brace & World, 1962);

Selected Letters of Oscar Wilde, edited by Hart-Davis (Oxford: Oxford University Press, 1979);

More Letters of Oscar Wilde, edited by Hart-Davis (New York: Vanguard, 1985).

Bibliographies:

Stuart Mason (Christopher Millard), *Bibliography of Oscar Wilde* (London: Laurie, 1914);

Donald L. Lawler, "Oscar Wilde in the *New Cambridge Bibliography of English Literature,*" *Papers of the Bibliographical Society of America,* 67 (1973): 172–188;

Ian Fletcher and John Stokes, "Oscar Wilde," in *Anglo-Irish Literature: A Review of Research,* edited by Richard Finneran (New York: Modern Language Association, 1976), pp. 48–137;

E. H. Mikhail, *Oscar Wilde; An Annotated Bibliography of Criticism* (London: Macmillan, 1978; Totowa, N.J.: Rowman & Littlefield, 1978);

Fletcher and Stokes, "Oscar Wilde," in *Recent Research on Anglo-Irish Writers,* edited by Finneran (New York: Modern Language Association, 1983), pp. 21–47;

Ian Small, *Oscar Wilde Revalued: An Essay on New Materials and Methods of Research* (Greensboro, N.C.: ELT Press, 1993);

Thomas A. Mikolyzk, *Oscar Wilde: An Annotated Bibliography* (Westport, Conn.: Greenwood Press, 1993).

Biographies:

Robert H. Sherard, *The Life of Oscar Wilde* (London: Laurie, 1906; New York: Kennerley, 1907);

Arthur Symons, *A Study of Oscar Wilde* (London: Sawyer, 1930);

Hesketh Pearson, *The Life of Oscar Wilde* (London: Methuen, 1946); republished as *Oscar Wilde: His Life and Wit* (New York: Harper, 1946);

Vyvyan Holland, *Son of Oscar Wilde* (London: Hart-Davis, 1954; New York: Dutton, 1954);

Lewis Broad, *The Friendships and Follies of Oscar Wilde* (London: Hutchinson, 1954; New York: Crowell, 1955);

Holland, *Oscar Wilde: A Pictorial Biography* (London: Thames & Hudson, 1960);

Phillippe Jullian, *Oscar Wilde,* translated by Violet Wyndham (London: Constable, 1969);

Rupert Croft-Cooke, *The Unrecorded Life of Oscar Wilde* (London & New York: Allen, 1972);

H. Montgomery Hyde, *Oscar Wilde: A Biography* (New York: Farrar, Straus & Giroux, 1975);

Sheridan Morley, *Oscar Wilde: An Illustrated Biography* (London: Weidenfeld & Nicolson, 1976);

Louis Kronenberger, *Oscar Wilde* (Boston: Little, Brown, 1976);

Richard Ellmann, *Oscar Wilde* (London: Hamilton, 1987; New York: Knopf, 1988);

Horst Schroeder, *Additions and Corrections to Richard Ellmann's "Oscar Wilde"* (Braunschweig, Germany: Privately printed, 1989).

References:

Bruce Bashford, "Hermeneutics in Oscar Wilde's 'The Portrait of Mr. W. H.,' " *Papers on Language and Literature,* 24 (Fall 1988): 412–422;

Karl Beckson, ed., *Oscar Wilde: The Critical Heritage* (New York: Barnes & Noble, 1970);

Joyce Bentley, *The Importance of Being Constance* (London: Hale, 1983);

J. E. Chamberlin, *Ripe Was the Drowsy Hour: The Age of Oscar Wilde* (New York: Seabury, 1977);

Barbara Charlesworth, *Dark Passages: Decadent Consciousness in Victorian Literature* (Madison: University of Wisconsin Press, 1965);

Philip Cohen, *The Moral Vision of Oscar Wilde* (Rutherford, N.J.: Fairleigh Dickinson University Press, 1976);

William A. Cohen, "Willie and Wilde: Reading 'The Portrait of Mr. W. H.,' " *South Atlantic Quarterly,* 88 (Winter 1989): 219–245;

Jean M. Ellis D'Allessandro, *Hues of Mutability: The Waning Vision in Oscar Wilde's Narrative* (Florence: University of Florence, 1983);

Richard Dellamora, *Masculine Desire: The Sexual Politics of Victorian Aestheticism* (Chapel Hill: University of North Carolina Press, 1990);

Jonathan Dollimore, "Different Desires: Subjectivity and Transgression in Wilde and Gide," *Textual Practice,* 1 (Spring 1987): 48–67;

Dollimore, *Sexual Dissidence: Augustine to Wilde, Freud to Foucault* (Oxford: Clarendon Press, 1991);

Linda Dowling, "Imposture and Absence in Wilde's 'Portrait of Mr. W. H.,' " *Victorian Newsletter,* 58 (Fall 1980): 26–29;

Richard Ellmann, ed., *Oscar Wilde: A Collection of Critical Essays* (Englewood Cliffs, N.J.: Prentice-Hall, 1969);

Ian Fletcher and Malcolm Bradbury, eds., *Decadence and the 1890s* (London: Arnold, 1979);

Regenia A. Gagnier, *Idylls of the Marketplace: Oscar Wilde and the Victorian Public* (Stanford: Stanford University Press, 1986);

Jonathan Goodman, *The Oscar Wilde File* (London: Allison, 1989);

Wendell Harris, *British Short Fiction in the Nineteenth Century* (Detroit: Wayne State University Press, 1979);

John Herdman, *The Double in Nineteenth-Century Fiction* (London: Macmillan, 1990);

H. Montgomery Hyde, ed., *The Trials of Oscar Wilde* (London: Hodge, 1948); republished as *The Three Trials of Oscar Wilde* (New York: University Books, 1956); enlarged as *Famous Trials, seventh series: Oscar Wilde* (Baltimore: Penguin, 1963);

Gerhard Joseph, "Framing Wilde," *Victorian Newsletter,* 72 (Fall 1987): 61–63;

Michael C. Kotzin, " 'The Selfish Giant' as Literary Fairy Tale," *Studies in Short Fiction,* 16 (Fall 1979): 301–309;

Robert K. Martin, "Oscar Wilde and the Fairy Tale: 'The Happy Prince' as Self-Dramatization," *Studies in Short Fiction,* 16 (Winter 1979): 74–77;

Stuart Mason (Christopher Millard), ed., *Oscar Wilde: Art and Morality, A Defence of "The Picture of Dorian Gray"* (London: Jacobs, 1907);

E. H. Mikhail, *Oscar Wilde: Interviews and Recollections,* 2 volumes (London: Macmillan, 1979);

Robert Keith Miller, *Oscar Wilde* (New York: Ungar, 1982);

Isobel Murray, Introduction to *Oscar Wilde: Complete Shorter Fiction,* edited by Murray (Oxford: Oxford University Press, 1979), pp. 1–18;

Christopher S. Nassaar, *Into the Demon Universe: A Literary Exploration of Oscar Wilde* (New Haven: Yale University Press, 1974);

Lewis J. Poteet, "Romantic Aesthetics in Oscar Wilde's 'Mr. W. H.,' " *Studies in Short Fiction,* 7 (Summer 1970): 458–464;

John Allen Quintus, "The Moral Prerogative in Oscar Wilde: A Look at the Fairy Tales," *Virginia Quarterly Review,* 53 (Autumn 1977): 708–717;

Arthur Ransome, *Oscar Wilde: A Critical Study* (London: Secker, 1912);

Edouard Roditi, *Oscar Wilde* (Norfolk, Conn.: New Directions, 1947);

Epifanio San Juan Jr., *The Art of Oscar Wilde* (Princeton: Princeton University Press, 1967);

Gary Schmidgall, *The Stranger Wilde: Interpreting Oscar* (New York: Dutton, 1994);

Horst Schroeder, "Oscar Wilde, The Canterville Ghost," *Literatur in Wissenschaft und Unterricht,* 10 (1977): 21–30;

Eve Kosofsky Sedgwick, *Between Men: English Literature and Male Homosocial Desire* (New York: Columbia University Press, 1986);

Sedgwick, *The Epistemology of the Closet* (London: Harvester-Wheatsheaf, 1991);

Lydia Reineck Wilburn, "Oscar Wilde's 'The Canterville Ghost': The Power of an Audience," *Papers on Language and Literature,* 23 (Winter 1987): 41–55;

Frances Winwar, *Oscar Wilde and the Yellow Nineties* (New York: Harper, 1940).

Papers:

The William Andrews Clark Memorial Library, University of California, Los Angeles, has the most extensive collection of Wilde's papers. Additional collections are held by the New York Public Library, the Pierpont Morgan Library; the Beinecke Library, Yale University; the British Library; the Harry Ransom Humanities Research Center, University of Texas at Austin; the Houghton Library, Harvard University; the University of Edinburgh Library; the Rosenbach Museum, Philadelphia; and Magdalen College, Oxford University.

William Butler Yeats

(13 June 1865 – 28 January 1939)

William H. O'Donnell
University of Memphis

See also the Yeats entries in *DLB 10: Modern British Dramatists, 1900–1945; DLB 19: British Poets, 1880–1914;* and *DLB 98: Modern British Essayists, First Series.*

BOOKS: *Mosada: A Dramatic Poem* (Dublin: Printed by Sealy, Bryers & Walker, 1886);

The Wanderings of Oisin and Other Poems (London: Kegan Paul, Trench, 1889);

John Sherman and Dhoya, as Ganconagh (London: Unwin, 1891; New York: Cassell, 1891);

The Countess Kathleen and Various Legends and Lyrics (London: Unwin, 1892; Boston: Roberts / London: Unwin, 1892);

The Celtic Twilight (London: Lawrence & Bullen, 1893; New York & London: Macmillan, 1894; revised and enlarged edition, London: Bullen, 1902; New York: Macmillan, 1902);

The Land of Heart's Desire (London: Unwin, 1894; Chicago: Stone & Kimball, 1894; revised edition, Portland, Maine: Mosher, 1903);

Poems (London: Unwin, 1895; London: Unwin / Boston: Copeland & Day, 1895; revised edition, London: Unwin, 1899; revised again, 1901, 1912, 1927);

The Secret Rose (London: Lawrence & Bullen, 1897; New York: Dodd, Mead / London: Lawrence & Bullen, 1897);

The Tables of the Law; The Adoration of the Magi (London: Privately printed, 1897; London: Elkin Mathews, 1904);

The Wind Among the Reeds (London: Elkin Mathews, 1899; New York & London: John Lane, 1902);

The Shadowy Waters (London: Hodder & Stoughton, 1900; New York: Dodd, Mead, 1901);

Is the Order of R. R. & A. C. [Rosae Rubeae et Aureae Crucis] To Remain a Magical Order? (N.p., 1901);

Cathleen ni Hoolihan (London: Bullen, 1902);

Where There Is Nothing (New York: John Lane, 1902; London: Bullen, 1903);

Ideas of Good and Evil (London: Bullen, 1903; New York: Macmillan, 1903);

William Butler Yeats

In the Seven Woods: Being Poems Chiefly of the Irish Heroic Age (Dundrum: Dun Emer Press, 1903; New York & London: Macmillan, 1903);

The Hour-Glass: A Morality (London: Heinemann, 1903);

The Hour-Glass and Other Plays (New York & London: Macmillan, 1904); republished as *The Hour-Glass, Cathleen ni Houlihan, The Pot of Broth* (London: Bullen, 1904);

The King's Threshold (New York: Privately printed, 1904);

The King's Threshold and On Baile's Strand (London: Bullen, 1904);

Stories of Red Hanrahan (Dundrum: Dun Emer Press, 1905);

Poems, 1899-1905 (London: Bullen / Dublin: Maunsel, 1906);

The Poetical Works of William B. Yeats, 2 volumes (New York & London: Macmillan, 1906, 1907; revised, 1912);

Deirdre (London: Bullen / Dublin: Maunsel, 1907);

Discoveries; A Volume of Essays (Dundrum: Dun Emer Press, 1907);

The Unicorn from the Stars and Other Plays, by Yeats and Lady Gregory (New York: Macmillan, 1908);

The Golden Helmet (New York: John Quinn, 1908);

The Collected Works in Verse and Prose of William Butler Yeats, 8 volumes (Stratford-on-Avon: Shakespeare Head Press, 1908);

Poems: Second Series (London & Stratford-on-Avon: Bullen, 1909);

The Green Helmet and Other Poems (Dundrum: Cuala Press, 1910; New York: Paget, 1911; enlarged edition, London: Macmillan, 1912);

Synge and the Ireland of His Time (Dundrum: Cuala Press, 1911);

The Countess Cathleen, revised edition (London: Unwin, 1912);

The Cutting of An Agate (New York: Macmillan, 1912; enlarged edition, London: Macmillan, 1919);

Stories of Red Hanrahan, The Secret Rose, Rosa Alchemica (London & Stratford-upon-Avon: Bullen, 1913; New York: Macmillan, 1914);

A Selection from the Love Poetry of William Butler Yeats (Dundrum: Cuala Press, 1913);

Poems Written in Discouragement 1912-1913 (Dumdrum: Cuala Press, 1913);

Responsibilities: Poems and a Play (Dundrum: Cuala Press, 1914);

Reveries over Childhood and Youth (Dundrum: Cuala Press, 1915; New York: Macmillan, 1916; London: Macmillan, 1916);

Responsibilities and Other Poems (London: Macmillan, 1916; New York: Macmillan, 1916);

The Wild Swans at Coole (Dundrum: Cuala Press, 1917; enlarged edition, London: Macmillan, 1919; New York: Macmillan, 1919);

Per Amica Silentia Lunae (London: Macmillan, 1918; New York: Macmillan, 1918);

Two Plays for Dancers (Dundrum: Cuala Press, 1919);

Michael Robartes and the Dancer (Dundrum: Cuala Press, 1920 [i.e., 1921]);

Four Plays for Dancers (London: Macmillan, 1921; New York: Macmillan, 1921);

Four Years (Dundrum: Cuala Press, 1921);

The Trembling of the Veil (London: Laurie, 1922);

Later Poems (London: Macmillan, 1922; New York: Macmillan, 1924);

Plays in Prose and Verse Written for an Irish Theatre, by Yeats and Lady Gregory (London: Macmillan, 1922; New York: Macmillan, 1924);

The Player Queen (London: Macmillan, 1922);

Plays and Controversies (London: Macmillan, 1923; New York: Macmillan, 1924);

Essays (London: Macmillan, 1924; New York: Macmillan, 1924);

The Cat and the Moon (Dublin: Cuala Press, 1924);

The Bounty of Sweden (Dublin: Cuala Press, 1925);

Early Poems and Stories (London: Macmillan, 1925; New York: Macmillan, 1925);

A Vision: An Explanation of Life Founded upon the Writings of Giraldus and upon Certain Doctrines Attributed to Kusta Ben Luka (London: Laurie, 1925; substantially revised as *A Vision* (London: Macmillan, 1937; New York: Macmillan, 1938);

Estrangement: Being Some Fifty Thoughts from a Diary Kept by William Butler Yeats in the Year Nineteen Hundred and Nine (Dublin: Cuala Press, 1926);

Autobiographies: Reveries Over Childhood and Youth and The Trembling of the Veil (London: Macmillan, 1926; New York: Macmillan, 1927);

October Blast (Dublin: Cuala Press, 1927);

Stories of Red Hanrahan and The Secret Rose (London: Macmillan, 1927);

The Tower (London: Macmillan, 1928; New York: Macmillan, 1928);

Sophocles' King Oedipus: A Version for the Modern Stage by W. B. Yeats (London: Macmillan, 1928; New York: Macmillan, 1928);

The Death of Synge, and Other Passages from an Old Diary (Dublin: Cuala Press, 1928);

A Packet for Ezra Pound (Dublin: Cuala Press, 1929);

The Winding Stair (New York: Fountain Press, 1929; enlarged edition, London: Macmillan, 1933; New York: Macmillan, 1933);

Stories of Michael Robartes and His Friends: An Extract from a Record Made by His Pupils; and a Play in Prose (Dublin: Cuala Press, 1931);

Words for Music Perhaps and Other Poems (Dublin: Cuala Press, 1932);

The Winding Stair and Other Poems (London: Macmillan, 1933; New York: Macmillan, 1933);

The Collected Poems (New York: Macmillan, 1933; London: Macmillan, 1933);

Letters to the New Island, edited by Horace Reynolds (Cambridge, Mass.: Harvard University Press, 1934; London: Oxford University Press, 1970);

The Words Upon the Window Pane (Dublin: Cuala Press, 1934);

Wheels and Butterflies (London: Macmillan, 1934; New York: Macmillan, 1935);

The Collected Plays (London: Macmillan, 1934; New York: Macmillan, 1935);

The King of the Great Clock Tower (Dublin: Cuala Press, 1934; New York: Macmillan, 1935);

A Full Moon in March (London: Macmillan, 1935);

Dramatis Personæ (Dublin: Cuala Press, 1935);

Poems (Dublin: Cuala Press, 1935);

Dramatis Personae 1896–1902, Estrangement, The Death of Synge, The Bounty of Sweden (New York: Macmillan, 1936; London: Macmillan, 1936);

Nine One-Act Plays (London: Macmillan, 1937);

Essays, 1931 to 1936 (Dublin: Cuala Press, 1937);

The Herne's Egg: A Stage Play (London: Macmillan, 1938);

The Herne's Egg and Other Plays (New York: Macmillan, 1938);

New Poems (Dublin: Cuala Press, 1938);

The Autobiography of William Butler Yeats, Consisting of Reveries Over Childhood and Youth, The Trembling of the Veil and Dramatis Personae (New York: Macmillan, 1938); revised, with *Estrangement, The Death of Synge,* and *The Bounty of Sweden,* as *Autobiographies* (London: Macmillan, 1955);

Last Poems and Two Plays (Dublin: Cuala Press, 1939);

On the Boiler (Dublin: Cuala Press, 1939);

Last Poems and Plays (London: Macmillan, 1940; New York: Macmillan, 1940);

If I Were Four-and-Twenty (Dublin: Cuala Press, 1940);

The Poems of W. B. Yeats, Definitive Edition, 2 volumes (London: Macmillan, 1949);

The Collected Plays of W. B. Yeats (London: Macmillan, 1952; New York: Macmillan, 1953);

The Variorum Edition of the Poems of W. B. Yeats, edited by Peter Allt and Russell K. Alspach (New York: Macmillan, 1957);

Mythologies (London & New York: Macmillan, 1959);

Senate Speeches, edited by Donald R. Pearce (Bloomington: Indiana University Press, 1960);

Essays and Introductions (London & New York: Macmillan, 1961);

Explorations (London: Macmillan, 1962; New York: Macmillan, 1963);

The Variorum Edition of the Plays of W. B. Yeats, edited by Russell K. Alspach, assisted by Catherine C. Alspach (London & New York: Macmillan, 1966);

Uncollected Prose, edited by John P. Frayne and Colton Johnson, 2 volumes (New York: Columbia University Press, 1970, 1976);

Memoirs: Autobiography, first draft, transcribed and edited by Denis Donoghue (London & New York: Macmillan, 1972);

The Speckled Bird, edited by William O'Donnell (Dublin: Cuala Press, 1974); annotated edition with variant versions (Toronto: McClelland & Stewart, 1976 [i.e., 1977]); additional section published as "Newly Identified Chapters for the 1897–98 Version of *The Speckled Bird:* 'The Lilies of the Lord,' " *Yeats Annual,* 7 (1990): 145–175;

Poems: A New Edition, revised edition, edited by Richard J. Finneran (London & New York: Macmillan, 1989);

Yeats's Poems, edited by A. Norman Jeffares (London: Macmillan, 1989);

The Works of W. B. Yeats, 14 volumes (London & New York: Macmillan, 1989–);

The Secret Rose: Stories by W. B. Yeats – A Variorum Edition, revised edition, edited by Phillip L. Marcus, Warwick Gould, and Michael J. Sidnell (London: Macmillan, 1992).

OTHER: *The Oxford Book of Modern Verse, 1892–1935,* edited, with an introduction, by Yeats (Oxford: Clarendon Press, 1936).

PLAY PRODUCTIONS: *The Land of Heart's Desire,* London, Avenue Theatre, 29 March 1894;

The Countess Cathleen, Dublin, Antient Concert Rooms, 8 May 1899;

Diarmuid and Grania, by Yeats and George Moore, Dublin, Gaiety Theatre, 21 October 1901;

Cathleen ni Houlihan, Dublin, St. Teresa's Hall, 2 April 1902;

The Pot of Broth, Dublin, Antient Concert Rooms, 30 October 1902;

The Hour-Glass, Dublin, Molesworth Hall, 14 March 1903; revised version, Dublin, Abbey Theatre, 21 November 1912;

The King's Threshold, Dublin, Molesworth Hall, 8 October 1903; revised version, Dublin, Abbey Theatre, 13 October 1913;

The Shadowy Waters, Dublin, Molesworth Hall, 14 January 1904;

Where There Is Nothing, London, Royal Court Theatre, 26 June 1904; revised as *The Unicorn from the Stars,* by Yeats and Lady Gregory, Dublin, Abbey Theatre, 21 November 1907;

On Baile's Strand, Dublin, Abbey Theatre, 27 December 1904;

Deirdre, Dublin, Abbey Theatre, 24 November 1906;

The Golden Helmet, Dublin, Abbey Theatre, 19 March 1908;

The Green Helmet, Dublin, Abbey Theatre, 10 February 1910;

At the Hawk's Well, London, privately performed, 2 April 1916; Dublin, Abbey Theatre, 25 July 1933;

The Player Queen, London, King's Hall, 25 May 1919;

The Only Jealousy of Emer, Amsterdam, Hollandsche Shouwburg, produced in English, 2 April 1922; Dublin, Abbey Theatre, 9 May 1926;

The Cat and the Moon, Dublin, Abbey Theatre, 9 May 1926;

Sophocles' King Oedipus, Dublin, Abbey Theatre, 7 December 1926;

Sophocles' Oedipus at Colonus, Dublin, Abbey Theatre, 12 September 1927;

Fighting the Waves, Dublin, Abbey Theatre, 13 August 1929;

The Words Upon the Window-Pane, Dublin, Abbey Theatre, 17 November 1930;

The Dreaming of the Bones, Dublin, Abbey Theatre, 6 December 1931;

The Resurrection, Dublin, Abbey Theatre, 30 July 1934;

The King of the Great Clock Tower, Dublin, Abbey Theatre, 30 July 1934;

Purgatory, Dublin, Abbey Theatre, 10 August 1938.

Yeats at the time he wrote most of his short fiction

William Butler Yeats, who won the Nobel Prize for Literature in 1923, is widely regarded as the best poet to write in English during the twentieth century. Yet from 1887 to 1905, the first third of his long career, he published twenty-three short stories and one short novel, and he left a second novel unfinished. Yeats always regarded himself primarily as a poet, however, and during the eighteen years he wrote fiction he also published a book of poems every three or four years. A few of Yeats's stories deserve attention on their own merits, but even his less accomplished stories remain interesting because they reflect his growing fascination with Irish folklore and with the occult during the 1890s. Yeats's work as a prose fiction writer also testifies to the vogue that short stories enjoyed during that decade.

Yeats was born in Dublin on 13 June 1865, but his family moved to London in 1867 when his father, John Butler Yeats (1839–1922), a brilliant conversationalist, abandoned his prospects of a career in law and enrolled as an art student. His wife, the quiet daughter of a prosperous Sligo businessman,

was dismayed at that decision, and she was right to worry, for as a portrait painter John Butler Yeats never earned more than a modest income. William Butler Yeats had two older sisters and a younger brother, Jack B. Yeats, who was to become an important Irish painter. William Butler Yeats attended school in London until 1881, when his family moved back to Dublin, where he finished high school with an undistinguished record and no hope of passing the entrance examination for Trinity College, Dublin, from which his father and grandfather had graduated. In 1884 Yeats enrolled in the Dublin Metropolitan School of Art but showed much less talent in drawing than in literature. He first published a poem in 1885, at the same time that he was beginning to develop his long-sustained interests in the occult and in Irish nationalism. Yeats studied theosophy with his friend George Russell (Æ), who became a poet, mystic, painter, agricultural cooperative organizer, and journal editor, and the two men formed the Dublin Hermetic Society and invited an Indian guru to Dublin to instruct them. The other powerful influence on Yeats during those years was Irish nationalism, an influence nourished through his friendship with John O'Leary, a widely known patriot and an enthusiast for Irish literature. Yeats became part of a circle of young Irish writers who, with O'Leary's encouragement, adopted native subject matter for their writing.

Yeats was twenty-one years old when he and his family moved back to London at the end of 1886. London offered better opportunities for a literary career, but the practical matter of his paltry finances made him wait almost another decade before he could afford his own lodgings. In London Yeats continued his instruction in theosophy, and then, in 1890, his strong interest in the occult led him to join the Hermetic Order of the Golden Dawn, a secret society that practiced ritual magic. Yeats was fascinated by the possibility, however remote and mysterious, that a mortal might be able to gain access to supernatural wisdom and to have a magically extended lifetime. From the 1890s and for the rest of his life, Yeats was convinced that the mind is capable of reaching beyond limits accepted by science and rationalism.

Yeats's prose fiction writing began in 1887 with "Dhoya," a short story based on folklore from County Sligo, where Yeats spent summers with his grandparents and where, in ancient times, the story is set. The title character is a sullen, silent giant whom a fairy chooses to join in the mortal world, but Dhoya eventually loses her in a chess game with a figure who comes to reclaim her. The story, which was published in December 1887, has little merit, and Yeats's father then suggested that he try writing a popular novel. By the end of 1888 Yeats had completed a short novel, *John Sherman,* but it and "Dhoya" then had to wait until November 1891 before they appeared together as a volume in the Pseudonym Library series published in London by T. Fisher Unwin and in the "Unknown Library" series published in New York by Cassell. Before publication of *John Sherman and Dhoya* Yeats wrote no more fiction, but his interest revived when the volume appeared. Despite having been required by the series to publish it pseudonymously, he had high hopes for the book and worked hard to have his friends review it. He selected the pseudonym "Ganconagh" (Irish for "love talker"), a variety of leprechaun, to emphasize the Irishness of both the short story and the novel, and in July 1891, Yeats asked a writer friend, Katharine Tynan, "Do what you can for it – for success with stories would solve many problems for me and I write them easily."

John Sherman was an isolated experiment in realistic writing by Yeats and his only published work of long fiction. The novel opens in a contemporary Irish town modeled on Sligo and develops an elaborate antithesis between the title character, a young man with strong loyalties to pastoral Ireland, and

his contemporary William Howard, a comically oversophisticated Anglican cleric in London. Sherman leaves Ireland for London, where he unenthusiastically begins a career in business and becomes infatuated with Margaret Leland, a beautiful but absurdly shallow London girl. Only after they have become engaged does he realize that his true love is his childhood sweetheart in Ireland. By managing to have William Howard "steal" Margaret Leland's affections, John Sherman frees himself to return to Ireland, where he then proposes to his sweetheart. Some of the best moments in *John Sherman* are in the humorous caricatures of William Howard and Margaret Leland.

The principal theme of the novel is that placing too much attention on hope for the future or on memory of the past can hinder the discovery of one's own role in the present. That theme is developed through the character antithesis of John Sherman and William Howard, first discussed by Richard Ellmann in *Yeats: The Man and the Masks* (1979). The novel makes extensive use of autobiographical material and echoes Yeats's affection for Sligo – as expressed in his well-known poem "The Lake Isle of Innisfree," which he wrote only a few weeks after finishing the novel. Yet readers should not forget Yeats's insistence on a clear differentiation between a writer's "artistic" and "daily" selves and on the necessity of a complex relationship between those two perspectives. Yeats faulted Irish novelist George Moore's "slice of life" realism, commenting in a diary in 1913 that Moore could never have become a great writer because "that antithesis which I see in all artists between the artistic and the daily self was in his case too crude and simple and the daily part too powerful."

Publication of *John Sherman and Dhoya* in November 1891 had an important impact on Yeats's career during the 1890s. The book went through two subsequent London editions in 1891 and 1892, and it earned royalties of about thirty pounds, unlike Yeats's collection of poetry *The Wanderings of Oisin and Other Poems,* which had not paid its way in 1889. Yeats chose to include *John Sherman,* with only superficial revisions, in the collected edition of his works in 1908, despite his comment in 1907 that "very careful verbal revision" of it was necessary. His failure to undertake those revisions can be attributed to the fast pace at which the volumes of the 1908 collected edition were published but perhaps also to his recognition of just how much work would have been needed. Yeats's exclusion of the novel from his next collected edition in 1925 underscores his 1904 opinion that *John Sherman* was "written when I was very young and knew no better."

The commercial success of *John Sherman and Dhoya,* even though small, was augmented through William E. Henley's invitation to Yeats in November 1891 to submit "stories like 'Dhoya' " to his magazine, the *National Observer.* Henley was himself a poet, and the fashion for short stories enhanced by lyrical tonalities was evident in the work of five of Yeats's fellow members of the Rhymers' Club, a group of talented young poets who met regularly in London during the early 1890s: John Gray, John Davidson, Richard LeGallienne, Lionel Johnson, and Ernest Dowson, as well as Yeats, all published short stories in the early 1890s.

Yeats was soon at work writing short fiction that would fill the *National Observer's* expected three or four columns for a story. Between November 1892 and September 1894 Yeats published ten stories, eight of which appeared in the *National Observer,* and all ten satisfied Henley's length restriction. Part of the appeal of Yeats's prose fiction lay in its "Irishness" − a quality that English readers found interesting. Yeats's adoption of Irish subject matter thus proved useful to him, as he had also edited a variety of Irish anthologies, including the best known of these, *The Celtic Twilight* (1893, enlarged 1902). That last collection of Irish prose folklore gave its title in the mid and late 1890s to a literary fashion for prose fiction and poetry that was often luxuriantly mannered and always consciously Celtic, including that of Scots such as "Fiona Macleod," pseudonym of William Sharp. Henley, himself a Scot, was fired by new owners of the *National Observer* in April 1894 and was not able to find a post as editor of the *New Review* until the end of that year. The *National Observer* published two of Yeats's stories after Henley's departure, but those perhaps had already been accepted by Henley. Forced to look elsewhere for a market, Yeats succeeded in placing one story with the *Speaker,* whose editor, Barry O'Brien, was a friend. At the same time an eye doctor told Yeats to do much less reading. That was distressing news for someone whose meager income came mostly from writing book reviews, but it made fiction writing even more attractive. For almost six months from October 1894 Yeats was a guest of an uncle in Sligo while he wrote new stories and revised old ones for a planned book, *The Secret Rose,* which did not appear until April 1897. From September 1894 until September 1895, however, none of his stories was published, and he was thus forced to maintain his reviewing duties. Then from September 1895 until the publication of his collection *The Secret Rose* in April 1897, Yeats sold eleven stories.

"The Devil's Book," published in the *National Observer* on 26 November 1892, is the first of several stories dealing with the character Red Hanrahan (called Owen O'Sullivan the Red in the earliest versions of Yeats's stories). This story was reprinted only once, in *The Secret Rose,* where it was retitled "The Book of the Great Dhoul and Hanrahan the Red." Yeats in part modeled this romantic, wandering hero on Owen Roe (Red) Sullivan, an eighteenth-century Gaelic poet from southern Ireland whose passion for women had earned him a denunciation from the pulpit and who had earned his living variously as a teacher in illegal Gaelic "hedge schools," as a potato digger, and, for a while, as a sailor in the Royal Navy. Owen Roe Sullivan's poems had personified Ireland as a woman (Kathleen-ni-Houlihan) whom young men are called to serve. He had also written an invective against old age, and he had died of a wound following a brawl with the servants of a Colonel Cronin, whom he had satirized. Yeats ensured his character's integrity by mixing his imaginative conception of Owen Roe Sullivan with that of another Irish poet, Timothy O'Sullivan the Gaelic, a profligate who later turned pious. These links with historical figures disappeared when Yeats changed his character's name to Red Hanrahan in *The Secret Rose* collection published in 1897, and in 1905 Yeats remarked, "Red Hanrahan is an imaginary name − I saw it over a shop in a Galway village − but there were many poets like him in the eighteenth century in Ireland."

Yeats's other stories about the character Red Hanrahan include "The Twisting of the Rope" (published in the *National Observer* on 24 December 1892), "Hanrahan and Cathleen, the Daughter of Holihan" (published as "Kathleen-ny-Hoolihan" in the *National Observer* on 4 August 1894), "Red Hanrahan's Curse" (published as "The Curse of O'Sullivan the Red upon Old Age" in the *National Observer* on 29 September 1894), "Hanrahan's Vision" (published as "The Vision of O'Sullivan the Red" in the *New Review* in April 1896), "The Death of Hanrahan" (published as "The Death of O'Sullivan the Red" in the *New Review* in December 1896), and "Red Hanrahan" (published in the *Independent Review* in December 1903). Probably during the summer of 1903 the last of these was written in collaboration with Lady Augusta Gregory, Yeats's friend and supporter, when Yeats heavily revised the Hanrahan stories during his residence at her home, Coole Park, in southeastern County Galway. "Red Hanrahan" adopted the local "Kiltartanese" speech patterns, which Yeats admiringly described as "a musical caressing English" marked by idioms

Cover for Yeats's 1897 collection of short stories (Special Collections, Thomas Cooper Library, University of South Carolina)

of the country people "who think in Irish." Lady Gregory used it with considerable success in her plays written for the Abbey Theatre in Dublin, a theatrical enterprise of which she and Yeats were founders.

"The Crucifixion of the Outcast," published as "A Crucifixion" in the *National Observer* on 24 March 1894, is among Yeats's best stories. Its hero is a medieval Irish gleeman, a poet-singer, who alone resists Irish Christianity's suppression of the culture's pagan heroic ideals and taunts the monks who eventually crucify him: "O cowardly and tyrannous race of monks, persecutors of the bard and the gleeman, haters of life and joy! O race that does not draw the sword and tell the truth! O race that melts the bones of the people with cowardice and with deceit!" Yeats took the first part of the story from an eleventh-century Irish poem but then darkened the ending of his story by not allowing the gleeman to escape crucifixion. The extreme cruelty

of the gleeman's execution brings no credit to Irish medieval Christianity, and the gleeman wins the reader's admiration, as does the legendary Irish hero Oisin in Yeats's long poem "The Wanderings of Oisin" (1889). Oisin throws away his rosary, rejecting Christianity and rejoining his pagan former comrades, legendary Irish warriors, "be they in flames or at feast," as he laments:

> We sang the loves and angers without sleep,
> And all the exultant labours of the strong.
> But now the lying clerics murder song
> With barren words and flatteries of the weak.

"The Wisdom of the King," published in the *New Review* in September 1895, presents an ancient Irish king who in his youth is transformed into a supernatural creature, acquires immortal wisdom, and ceases to be subject to mortal laws. Although he is at first unaware of his difference from ordinary mortals, a difference signaled by feathers that begin to grow in his hair, he attempts unsuccessfully to combine the roles of immortal dreamer and mortal doer. As soon as he discovers his condition, however, he leaves the mortal world and assumes the wisdom of the gods. He explains: "Law was made by man for the welfare of man, but wisdom the gods have made, and no man shall live by its light, for it and the hail and the rain and the thunder follow a way that is deadly to mortal things." Allen R. Grossman has found the story emblematic of the world's resistance to "the wisdom of the Messianic poet-king," although the story explicitly differentiates the king from the "men of verse." Yeats trimmed so much explanatory material in his revisions of 1914 and 1925 that the narrative was left very spare and sometimes difficult to understand, but all of the published versions are available in the variorum edition.

One story that Yeats dropped from his canon after 1897 – "The Binding of the Hair," published in the *Savoy* in January 1896 – has considerable interest because Yeats reused its basic plot in his play *The King of the Great Clock Tower* (1934). In the story the love of an Irish bard, Aodh, for the queen Dectira is tragically fulfilled when, after Aodh is killed in battle, his severed head sings to the queen the poem that Yeats titled "He Gives His Beloved Certain Rhymes" when it was republished apart from the story in *A Selection from the Love Poetry of William Butler Yeats* (1913).

"Where There is Nothing, There is God," published in the *Sketch* on 21 October 1896, is based on the story of Saint Angus and set in eighth-century Ireland. Its title announces its theme. The heavy cuts that Yeats made for an edition in 1914 seriously weaken the text as printed in *Mythologies* (1959), but earlier versions use irony effectively to indict clerical pride and materialism. Yeats planned to republish the earlier version in a collected edition for which he saw proofs in 1932, but that multivolume project was never published.

Yeats collected seventeen of his stories in *The Secret Rose,* published in April 1897 by Lawrence and Bullen in London and in New York by Dodd, Mead. The elaborate cover designs by Althea Gyles use Rosicrucian, Cabalistic, and Irish symbolism to emphasize the links of many of the stories with, as Yeats claimed in the preface, "the war of spiritual with natural order." Seven full-page illustrations by Yeats's father are not particularly successful, but the book showed sufficient promise to encourage publisher A. H. Bullen to agree, in December 1896, to pay modest advance royalties to Yeats for an unwritten novel. Seven years later, however, at least four hundred copies of *The Secret Rose* collection remained unsold, and Yeats had not finished writing the promised novel.

The best of the stories in *The Secret Rose* and Yeats's best work of fiction is "Rosa Alchemica," which was probably written in 1895 and was first published in the April 1896 issue of the *Savoy.* That fashionable, avant-garde magazine gave him a much larger audience than he had had for his stories in the *National Observer,* whose circulation just before Henley's dismissal in 1893 had numbered only a few hundred. Yeats's friend George Russell (Æ) wrote to him on 3 April 1897 with high praise for this story, calling it "a most wonderful piece of prose" in which the thoughts and words "are so rich they seem the gathering in the temple of the mind of thousands of pilgrim rays returning and leaving there their many experiences." He went on to say that if a book were filled with stories as good as "Rosa Alchemica," that book would be "one of the greatest things in literature." "Rosa Alchemica" is linked to two other stories not collected in *The Secret Rose:* "The Tables of the Law," first published in the November 1896 issue of the *Savoy,* and "The Adoration of the Magi," which may also have been destined for the *Savoy,* if the magazine had not ceased publication. All three stories share the same narrator, have an interlocking chronological sequence, and, unlike any of the other *Secret Rose* stories, have a contemporary setting. The unnamed narrator of "Rosa Alchemica" tells of his failed initiation into a mysterious Order of the Alchemical Rose. He lacks the complete dedication traditionally required of occultists, who must willingly abandon the mortal world in order to gain supernatural wisdom and fabled immortality. In Yeats's story the initiatory textbook of the Order of the Alchemical Rose defines alchemy as "the gradual distillation of the contents of the soul" toward the goal of being "ready to put off the mortal and put on the immortal." Thus, the traditional task of the alchemist to transmute lead into gold can be a metaphor for the purification of his soul from its earthly dross. The narrator doubts that anyone has achieved that goal, and although he is deeply fascinated by the prospect of initiation, he maintains his allegiance to the physical world. The narrator does not move beyond the limited commitment that Yeats himself made to a belief in magic in 1901 – when he wrote, in an essay titled "Magic," "I believe in the practice and philosophy of what we have agreed to call magic, in what I must call the evocation of spirits, though I do not know what they are, in the power of creating magical illusions, in the visions of truth in the depths of the mind when the eyes are closed."

In "Rosa Alchemica" the narrator finally decides that the initiatory ritual dance is sensual rather than spiritual, and he refuses its demand of ecstasy. Spiritual alchemy, Paterian aestheticism, and orthodox Christianity are each represented through a complex manipulation of perspective, and each is endorsed, at least temporarily or for dramatic purposes. The narrator tells the story in retrospect, after ten years of Christian orthodoxy, but he presents Christianity unfavorably by his hollow shows of religiosity and his links with the ignorant bigotry of a mob of peasants who storm the small building used by the Order of the Alchemical Rose on the west coast of Ireland. The mysterious fictional character Michael Robartes, who leads the narrator to the initiation and who appears in other works by Yeats, is affiliated with the spiritual multitude "who govern this world and time" and who are diametrically opposed to the "bustle and noise of the multitude in this world and in time."

The next of these tales of magic, "The Tables of the Law," also focuses on a failed attempt to achieve supernatural wisdom without totally abandoning the world. The story has two sections, separated by the ten years within which the action described in "Rosa Alchemica" occurs. The narrator and Michael Robartes have been school friends of Owen Aherne, the central character in "The Tables of the Law," which describes Aherne's attempt to found a mystical order that combines Christianity with magic. Aherne cites as his prototype Joachim de Flora, a twelfth-century Italian theologian who had advocated the right to transcend ordinary morality in a life of contemplation directed toward spiritual ecstasy, while still maintaining his personal sanctity and complete loyalty to the Catholic Church. After Aherne's plans fail, however, he renounces as "boundless wickedness" and "terrible danger" Joachim's combination of orthodoxy and quasi-heretical freedom to search for a superior spiritual world.

The third of these tales, "The Adoration of the Magi," does not match the achievement of "Rosa Alchemica" or even of "The Tables of the Law," which James Joyce mentioned favorably in *Stephen Hero* (1944), the posthumously published, partial first draft of *A Portrait of the Artist as a Young Man* (1916). In "The Adoration of the Magi" the narrator from "Rosa Alchemica" and "The Tables of the Law" recounts how three elderly Irishmen travel to Paris in search of secret wisdom from a dying woman who, as a supernatural voice announces, will assist the Immortals in overthrowing the present age and replacing it with a new, antithetical era. This story is an early presentation of the historical schema on which Yeats elaborated more than twenty years later in his book *A Vision* (1925) and in poems such as "The Second Coming" (1920). In Yeats's system of history, the Greek or pagan era had lasted from 2000 B.C. to A.D. 1, when it was supplanted by the Christian era, which would last two thousand years. Then, as alluded to in "The Adoration of the Magi," the Christian era would be replaced by a new civilization with pagan values diametrically opposed to those of the Christian era.

In June 1897 Lawrence and Bullen published "The Tables of the Law" and "The Adoration of the Magi" in a slim volume advertised in their catalogs, even though the title page identifies it as "privately printed." Yeats's preface announces, "These stories were originally intended to follow 'Rosa Alchemica' in *The Secret Rose*." If the publisher had been worried that the heterodoxy of these last two stories might diminish the popularity of the others, he need not have been. While ignoring "Rosa Alchemica," reviewers focused almost exclusively on the Irishness of the stories in *The Secret Rose. The Tables of the Law; The Adoration of the Magi* was republished in 1904 (with a preface that alluded to James Joyce) and in 1914. The two stories were collected, along with the *Secret Rose* stories, in the *Collected Works* of 1908 and in subsequent editions.

In December 1896 Yeats's prose fiction career reached a high point with a contract and advance royalties of £105 for a novel, *The Speckled Bird,* which he planned to write during the next six months. He worked on it intermittently for some

seven years, producing four versions of more than seven hundred pages in manuscript and typescript. Its problems demonstrate Yeats's difficulty in writing long narrative, and the novel never reached the level of polish that would have been necessary for publication. Nevertheless, he kept the large stack of pages, which appeared in a scholarly edition in 1977.

The materials of the novel are heavily autobiographical. Michael Hearne, the young hero, spends his childhood with his father, John, on a small, isolated estate that in the earliest sketch of the novel was in the Aran Islands – but which in all later drafts is near Kinvarra, on Galway Bay. The father has studied art in Paris and London before retiring to the West of Ireland, where he raises his son on classical languages, Lady Charlotte Guest's 1838–1849 translation of Welsh heroic tales from *The Mabinogion,* and art. Michael is told that orthodox religions are unsatisfactory for not allowing everything that an artist admires to be a part of religious art. He learns Irish fairy lore from peasant children, sees mystical visions, and falls in love with a strangely beautiful girl to whom he unsuccessfully proposes. She resembles in many ways the beautiful Maud Gonne, who was an Irish nationalist of independent means and shared some of Yeats's interests in the supernatural. Yeats sought her love for many years, with little or no success.

In the novel this young woman eventually becomes a Catholic and shocks Michael by announcing that she has married a Captain Peters. When her marriage proves unhappy, she torments Michael by trying to establish an intimate but platonic relationship with him. Michael leaves for London, intending to found a mystical order that will initiate young artists and provide them with a common basis for symbolism adapted from the Grail legends. He seeks the assistance of an occult magus named Maclagan, who fictionally embodies many of the less attractive traits of Macgregor Mathers, the leader of the Hermetic Order of the Golden Dawn when Yeats had joined it in 1890. Michael's idealistic hopes for artistic decorations and carefully developed ritual prove disastrously incompatible with the shoddy conventionality of London occultists, and he drifts into an affair with a woman who resembles Olivia Shakespear, a London novelist with whom Yeats had an affair in 1896.

By 1905 Yeats had turned from prose fiction. Drama increasingly occupied his attention, and his weak eyesight precluded laborious revision of a novel. His poetic style also altered radically in the first decades of the twentieth century, abandoning the luxuriant richness and musicality that readers had enjoyed in his earlier poetry – as well as in his prose. Yeats married late, but happily, at age fifty-two and moved permanently to Ireland, where he raised a family of two children. His wife and he spent hundreds of hours using spiritualistic techniques, "automatic writing" and "automatic speech," to compile materials from which Yeats composed the idiosyncratic theories of history and personality that he published in *A Vision.* For the first edition of that book Yeats wrote an extravagant introduction that hid the spiritualistic origins of the book.

Then in 1930 he briefly returned to prose fiction with one bizarrely comic story, "Stories of Michael Robartes and His Friends," inspired by the extravagant introductory matter of the 1925 *A Vision.* In 1931 Yeats published this brief, vigorous, and often bawdy comedy in a slim volume from the Cuala Press, operated by one of his sisters. He revised the story in 1936 for its publication in the front matter of the second edition of *A Vision* (1937), where it provides an amusing counterweight to the complex doctrines of that book.

Yeats consistently regarded his prose fiction as artistically subordinate to his poetry and drama, but he also believed that earning money by writing stories and novels was artistically preferable to reviewing and journalism. The best of his stories, "Rosa Alchemica" and "The Crucifixion of the Outcast," have literary merit in addition to the more generalized interest of all his prose fiction, which provides reflections on subjects that he also treated in poetry and, to some extent, in his plays.

Letters:

Letters on Poetry from W. B. Yeats to Dorothy Wellesley (London, New York & Toronto: Oxford University Press, 1940);

J. B. Yeats: Letters to His Son W. B. Yeats and Others, 1869–1922, edited by Joseph Hone (London: Faber & Faber, 1944; New York: Dutton, 1946);

Some Letters from W. B. Yeats to John O'Leary and His Sister, edited by Allan Wade (New York: New York Public Library, 1953);

W. B. Yeats and T. Sturge Moore: Their Correspondence, 1901–1937, edited by Ursala Bridge (London: Routledge & Kegan Paul, 1953);

Letters to Katharine Tynan, edited by Roger McHugh (Dublin: Clonmore & Reynolds / London: Burns, Oates & Washbourne, 1953; New York: McMullen, 1953);

The Letters of W. B. Yeats, edited by Wade (London: Hart-Davis, 1954; New York: Macmillan, 1955);

Georgiana Hyde-Lees, who married Yeats in 1917

Ah, Sweet Dancer: W. B. Yeats and Margot Ruddock – A Correspondence, edited by McHugh (London & New York: Macmillan, 1970);

The Correspondence of Robert Bridges and W. B. Yeats, edited by Richard J. Finneran (London: Macmillan, 1977);

Theatre Business: The Correspondence of the First Abbey Theatre Directors – William Butler Yeats, Lady Gregory and J. M. Synge, edited by Ann Saddlemyer (Gerrards Cross, U.K.: Colin Smythe, 1982; University Park: Pennsylvania State University Press, 1982);

The Collected Letters of W. B. Yeats, volume 1: 1865–1895, edited by John Kelly and Eric Domville (Oxford: Clarendon Press / New York: Oxford University Press, 1986); volume 3: 1901–1904, edited by Ronald Schuchard (Oxford: Clarendon Press / New York: Oxford University Press, 1994).

Interviews:

W. B. Yeats: Interviews and Recollections, edited by E. H. Mikhail, 2 volumes (London: Macmillan, 1976; New York: Barnes & Noble, 1977).

Bibliographies:

A. J. A. Symons, *A Bibliography of the First Editions of Books by William Butler Yeats* (London: First Edition Club, 1924);

Allen Wade, *A Bibliography of the Writings of W. B. Yeats,* third edition, revised and edited by Russell K. Alspach (London: Hart-Davis, 1968);

Jochum, "Annual Bibliography of Yeats Criticism," *Yeats: An Annual of Critical and Textual Studies,* 1– (1983–);

Warwick Gould, *Yeats Annual,* 3– (1985–);

K. P. S. Jochum, *W. B. Yeats: A Classified Bibliography of Criticism,* second edition (Urbana: University of Illinois Press, 1990).

Biographies:

Joseph M. Hone, *W. B. Yeats, 1865–1939,* second edition (London & New York: Macmillan, 1962);

A. Norman Jeffares, *W. B. Yeats: Man and Poet,* second edition (New York: Barnes & Noble, 1966);

Micheál Mac Liammóir and Eavan Boland, *W. B. Yeats and His World* (London: Thames & Hudson, 1971; New York: Viking, 1972);

Frank Touhy, *Yeats* (New York: Macmillan, 1976);

Richard Ellmann, *Yeats: The Man and the Masks,* third edition (Oxford: Oxford University Press, 1979; New York: Norton, 1979);

Augustine Martin, *W. B. Yeats,* second edition (Gerrards Cross, U.K.: Colin Smythe, 1990).

References:

Joseph Adams, *Yeats and the Masks of Syntax* (New York: Columbia University Press, 1984);

Douglas Archibald, *Yeats* (Syracuse, N.Y.: Syracuse University Press, 1983);

Harold Bloom, *Yeats* (New York: Oxford University Press, 1970);

Curtis B. Bradford, *Yeats at Work* (Carbondale: Southern Illinois University Press, 1965);

Raymond Cowell, *W. B. Yeats* (London: Evans, 1969; New York: Arno, 1970);

Elizabeth Cullingford, *Yeats, Ireland and Fascism* (London: Macmillan, 1981; New York: New York University Press, 1981);

Denis Donoghue, *William Butler Yeats* (London: Fontana, 1971; New York: Viking, 1971);

Richard Ellmann, *The Identity of Yeats,* second edition (New York: Oxford University Press, 1964);

Edward Engelberg, *The Vast Design: Patterns in W. B. Yeats's Aesthetic* (Toronto: University of Toronto Press, 1964);

Richard J. Finneran, *The Prose Fiction of W. B. Yeats: The Search for 'Those Simple Forms'* (Dublin: Dolmen Press, 1973);

Brian Finney, *The Inner I: British Literary Autobiography of the Twentieth Century* (London: Faber & Faber, 1985);

Ian Fletcher, *W. B. Yeats and His Contemporaries* (Brighton: Harvester Press, 1987; New York: St. Martin's Press, 1987);

John Wilson Foster, *Fictions of the Irish Literary Revival: A Changeling Art* (Syracuse, N.Y.: Syracuse University Press, 1987);

Joann Gardner, *Yeats and the Rhymers' Club: A Nineties' Perspective* (New York: Peter Lang, 1988);

George M. Harper, ed., *Yeats and the Occult* (Toronto: Macmillan, 1975);

Elizabeth Bergmann Loizeaux, *Yeats and the Visual Arts* (New Brunswick, N. J. & London: Rutgers University Press, 1986);

David Lynch, *Yeats: The Poetics of the Self* (Chicago: University of Chicago Press, 1979);

Edward Malins, *A Preface to Yeats* (New York: Scribners, 1974);

Phillip L. Marcus, *Yeats and Artistic Power* (New York: New York University Press, 1992);

Marcus, *Yeats and the Beginning of the Irish Renaissance* (Ithaca, N.Y.: Cornell University Press, 1970);

Virginia Moore, *The Unicorn: William Butler Yeats's Search for Reality* (New York: Macmillan, 1974);

William M. Murphy, *The Yeats Family and the Pollexfens of Sligo* (Dublin: Dolmen Press, 1971);

Shirley C. Neuman, *Some One Myth: Yeats's Autobiographical Prose* (Mountrath, Ireland: Dolmen Press, 1982);

William H. O'Donnell, *A Guide to the Prose Fiction of W. B. Yeats* (Ann Arbor, Mich.: UMI Research Press, 1983);

Daniel T. O'Hara, *Tragic Knowledge: Yeats's Autobiography and Hermeneutics* (New York: Columbia University Press, 1981);

James Olney, ed., *Autobiography: Essays Theoretical and Critical* (Princeton: Princeton University Press, 1980);

Leonard Orr, ed., *Yeats and Postmodernism* (Syracuse, N.Y.: Syracuse University Press, 1991);

John Pilling, *Autobiography and Imagination: Studies in Self-Scrutiny* (London: Routledge & Kegan Paul, 1981);

Balachandra Rajan, *W. B. Yeats: A Critical Introduction,* second edition (London: Hutchinson, 1969);

Joseph Ronsley, *Yeats's Autobiography: Life as Symbolic Pattern* (Cambridge, Mass.: Harvard University Press, 1968);

Stan Smith, *W. B. Yeats: A Critical Introduction* (Savage, Md.: Barnes & Noble, 1990);

John Unterecker, *A Reader's Guide to William Butler Yeats* (New York: Noonday Press, 1959);

Thomas R. Whitaker, *Swan and Shadow: Yeats's Dialogue with History,* second edition (Gerrards Cross, U.K.: Colin Smythe, 1989; Washington, D.C.: Catholic University of America Press, 1989);

David G. Wright, *Yeats's Myth of Self: The Autobiographical Prose* (Dublin: Gill & Macmillan, 1987; Totowa, N. J.: Barnes & Noble, 1987);

Yeats Studies: An International Journal, 1 (1971), special issue on Yeats's prose and the 1890s.

Papers:

The National Library of Ireland in Dublin houses the largest collection of Yeats papers. Copies of its papers are at the State University of New York at Stony Brook. Other collections are housed in the Berg Collection of the New York Public Library and at the Harry Ransom Humanities Research Center at the University of Texas at Austin, the British Library, Boston College, Emory University, Yale University, Cornell University, Harvard University, the University of Chicago, and the Huntington Library in San Marino, California.

Books for Further Reading

Allen, Walter. *The Short Story in English.* New York: Oxford University Press, 1981.

Altick, Richard D. *The English Common Reader: A Social History of the Mass Reading Public, 1800–1900.* Chicago: University of Chicago Press, 1957.

Beachcroft, Thomas Owen. *The Modest Art: A Survey of the Short Story in English.* London: Oxford University Press, 1968.

Beckson, Karl. *London in the 1890's: A Cultural History.* New York: Norton, 1992.

Bleiler, E. F., ed. *Supernatural Fiction Writers.* 2 volumes. New York: Scribners, 1985.

Brantlinger, Patrick. *Rule of Darkness: British Literature and Imperialism, 1830–1914.* Ithaca: Cornell University Press, 1988.

Briggs, Julia. *Night Visitors: The Rise and Fall of the English Ghost Story.* London: Faber, 1977.

Cannadine, David. *The Decline and Fall of the British Aristocracy.* New Haven: Yale University Press, 1990.

Cevasco, G. A., ed. *The 1890's: An Encyclopedia of British Literature, Art, and Culture.* New York: Garland, 1993.

Cross, Nigel. *The Common Writer: Life on Nineteenth-Century Grub Street.* Cambridge: Cambridge University Press, 1985.

Ely, Cecil DeGrotte. *The Road to Armageddon: The Martial Spirit In English Popular Literature, 1870–1914.* Durham, N.C.: Duke University Press, 1988.

Flora, Joseph, ed. *The English Short Story, 1880–1945: A Critical History.* Boston: Twayne, 1985.

Girouard, Mark. *Return to Camelot: Chivalry and the English Gentleman.* New Haven: Yale University Press, 1981.

Gross, John. *The Rise and Fall of the Man of Letters: Aspects of English Literary Life Since 1800.* London: Weidenfeld & Nicolson, 1969.

Hanson, Clare. *Short Stories and Short Fictions, 1800–1980.* London: Macmillan, 1985.

Harris, Wendell V. *British Short Fiction in the Nineteenth Century: A Literary and Bibliographic Guide.* Detroit: Wayne State University Press, 1979.

Hewitt, Douglas. *English Fiction of the Early Modern Period, 1890–1940.* London: Longmans, 1988.

Hobsbawm, Eric J. *The Age of Empire, 1875–1914.* New York: Random House, 1987.

Hough, Graham. *The Last Romantics.* London: Duckworth, 1947.

Hunter, Jefferson. *Edwardian Fiction.* Cambridge, Mass.: Harvard University Press, 1982.

Hynes, Samuel. *The Edwardian Turn of Mind.* Princeton: Princeton University Press, 1968.

Jackson, Holbrook. *The Eighteen Nineties: A Review of Art and Ideas at the Close of the Nineteenth Century.* New York: Kennerley, 1914.

Lohafer, Susan, and Jo Ellyn Clarey, eds. *Short Story Theory at a Crossroads.* Baton Rouge: Louisiana State University Press, 1989.

May, Charles, ed. *Short Story Theory.* Athens: Ohio University Press, 1976.

Morris, James. *Pax Britannica: The Climax of an Empire.* New York: Harcourt, Brace, 1968.

Orel, Harold. *The Victorian Short Story: Development and Triumph of a Literary Genre.* Cambridge: Cambridge University Press, 1986.

Penzoldt, Peter. *The Supernatural in Literature.* New York: Humanities Press, 1965.

Pittock, Murray. *Spectrum of Decadence: The Literature of the 1890's.* New York: Routledge, 1993.

Rose, Jonathan. *The Edwardian Temperament, 1895–1919.* Athens: Ohio University Press, 1986.

Sandison, Alan. *The Wheel of Empire.* New York: St. Martin's Press, 1967.

Sharpe, Jenny. *Allegories of Empire: The Figure of Woman in the Colonial Text.* Minneapolis: University of Minnesota Press, 1993.

Showalter, Elaine. *Sexual Anarchy: Gender and Culture at the Fin de Siècle.* New York: Viking Penguin, 1990.

Stanford, Derek. *Short Stories of the 'Nineties: A Biographical Anthology.* London: Baker, 1968.

Stokes, John, ed. *Fin De Siècle, Fin Du Globe: Fears and Fantasies of the Late Nineteenth Century.* New York: St. Martin's Press, 1992.

Sullivan, Jack. *Elegant Nightmares: The English Ghost Story from Le Fanu to Blackwood.* Athens: Ohio University Press, 1978.

Sutherland, John. *The Stanford Companion to Victorian Fiction.* Stanford, Cal.: Stanford University Press, 1989.

Thornton, A. P. *The Imperial Idea and Its Enemies: A Study in British Power.* London: Macmillan, 1959.

White, Robert B. Jr. *The English Literary Journal to 1900: A Guide to Information Sources.* Detroit: Gale Research, 1977.

Wolff, Michael, ed. *The Victorian Periodical Press: Samplings and Soundings.* Leicester, U.K.: Leicester University Press, 1982.

Contributors

William Atkinson .... *Appalachian State University*
Debra C. Boyd.. *Winthrop University*
Monika Brown .... *Pembroke State University*
Siobhan Craft Brownson....................................... *University of South Carolina*
Janet Galligani Casey... *College of the Holy Cross*
Thomas L. Cooksey .... *Armstrong State College*
J. Randolph Cox... *Saint Olaf College*
Kevin J. H. Dettmar... *Clemson University*
Julie English Early..................................... *University of Alabama in Huntsville*
Adrian Eckersley .... *Birkbeck College, London University*
Beverly F. Gibson... *Troy State University*
Donald Gray... *Indiana University*
Michael S. Helfand... *University of Pittsburgh*
John R. Holmes .... *Franciscan University of Steubenville*
Audrey F. Horton................................... *University of Miami School of Medicine*
George M. Johnson .... *University College of the Cariboo*
Jep C. Jonson... *University of South Carolina*
Anne Colclough Little .... *Auburn University at Montgomery*
Carolyn Mathews.......................... *University of North Carolina at Greensboro*
Gerald Monsman.. *University of Arizona*
Anne-Elizabeth Murdy .... *University of Chicago*
William F. Naufftus .... *Winthrop University*
Bruce G. Nims .... *University of South Carolina at Lancaster*
Charlotte H. Oberg... *University of Richmond*
William H. O'Donnell... *University of Memphis*
Jeffrey D. Parker... *Greensboro, North Carolina*
Susie Paul... *Auburn University at Montgomery*
Patricia Roberts .... *University of Missouri at Columbia*
Cannon Schmitt... *Grinnell College*
James R. Simmons Jr. .... *University of South Carolina*
Jane Bowman Smith... *Winthrop University*
Max Keith Sutton .... *University of Kansas*
Hayden Ward .... *West Virginia University*
P. T. Whelan... *Francis Marion University*

Cumulative Index

Dictionary of Literary Biography, Volumes 1-156
Dictionary of Literary Biography Yearbook, 1980-1994
Dictionary of Literary Biography Documentary Series, Volumes 1-12

Cumulative Index

DLB before number: *Dictionary of Literary Biography,* Volumes 1-156
Y before number: *Dictionary of Literary Biography Yearbook,* 1980-1994
DS before number: *Dictionary of Literary Biography Documentary Series,* Volumes 1-12

A

F

G

M

Preface to *The Disguis'd Prince* (1733), by
  Eliza Haywood [excerpt] DLB-39

Preface to *The Farther Adventures of Robinson
  Crusoe* (1719), by Daniel Defoe . . DLB-39

Preface to the First Edition of *Pamela* (1740), by
  Samuel Richardson DLB-39

Preface to the First Edition of *The Castle of
  Otranto* (1764), by
  Horace Walpole DLB-39

Preface to *The History of Romances* (1715), by
  Pierre Daniel Huet [excerpts] DLB-39

Preface to *The Life of Charlotta du Pont* (1723),
  by Penelope Aubin DLB-39

Preface to *The Old English Baron* (1778), by
  Clara Reeve DLB-39

Preface to the Second Edition of *The Castle of
  Otranto* (1765), by Horace
  Walpole DLB-39

Preface to *The Secret History, of Queen Zarah,
  and the Zarazians* (1705), by Delariviere
  Manley DLB-39

Preface to the Third Edition of *Clarissa* (1751),
  by Samuel Richardson
  [excerpt] DLB-39

Preface to *The Works of Mrs. Davys* (1725), by
  Mary Davys DLB-39

Preface to Volume 1 of *Clarissa* (1747), by
  Samuel Richardson DLB-39

Preface to Volume 3 of *Clarissa* (1748), by
  Samuel Richardson DLB-39

Préfontaine, Yves 1937- DLB-53

Prelutsky, Jack 1940- DLB-61

Premisses, by Michael Hamburger . . DLB-66

Prentice, George D. 1802-1870 . . . . . DLB-43

Prentice-Hall DLB-46

Prescott, William Hickling
  1796-1859 . . . . DLB-1, 30, 59

The Present State of the English Novel (1892),
  by George Saintsbury DLB-18

Prešeren, Francè 1800-1849 . . . . . . DLB-147

Preston, Thomas 1537-1598 . . . . DLB-62

Price, Reynolds 1933- DLB-2

Price, Richard 1949- Y-81

Priest, Christopher 1943- DLB-14

Priestley, J. B. 1894-1984
  . . . . DLB-10, 34, 77, 100, 139; Y-84

Prime, Benjamin Young 1733-1791 . . DLB-31

Primrose, Diana
  floruit circa 1630 . . . . DLB-126

Prince, F. T. 1912- DLB-20

Prince, Thomas 1687-1758 . . . . . DLB-24, 140

The Principles of Success in Literature (1865), by
  George Henry Lewes [excerpt] . . DLB-57

Prior, Matthew 1664-1721 . . . . DLB-95

Pritchard, William H. 1932- DLB-111

Pritchett, V. S. 1900- DLB-15, 139

Procter, Adelaide Anne 1825-1864 . . . DLB-32

Procter, Bryan Waller
  1787-1874 . . . . DLB-96, 144

The Profession of Authorship:
  Scribblers for Bread Y-89

The Progress of Romance (1785), by Clara Reeve
  [excerpt] DLB-39

Prokopovich, Feofan 1681?-1736 . . . DLB-150

Prokosch, Frederic 1906-1989 . . . . . . DLB-48

The Proletarian Novel DLB-9

Propper, Dan 1937- DLB-16

The Prospect of Peace (1778), by
  Joel Barlow DLB-37

Proud, Robert 1728-1813 . . . . DLB-30

Proust, Marcel 1871-1922 . . . . DLB-65

Prynne, J. H. 1936- DLB-40

Przybyszewski, Stanislaw
  1868-1927 . . . . DLB-66

Pseudo-Dionysius the Areopagite floruit
  circa 500 . . . . DLB-115

The Public Lending Right in America
  Statement by Sen. Charles McC.
  Mathias, Jr. PLR and the Meaning
  of Literary Property Statements on
  PLR by American Writers Y-83

The Public Lending Right in the United Kingdom Public Lending Right: The First Year
  in the United Kingdom Y-83

The Publication of English
  Renaissance Plays DLB-62

Publications and Social Movements
  [Transcendentalism] DLB-1

Publishers and Agents: The Columbia
  Connection Y-87

A Publisher's Archives: G. P. Putnam . . .Y-92

Publishing Fiction at LSU Press Y-87

Pückler-Muskau, Hermann von
  1785-1871 . . . . DLB-133

Pugh, Edwin William 1874-1930 . . . DLB-135

Pugin, A. Welby 1812-1852 . . . . DLB-55

Puig, Manuel 1932-1990 . . . . DLB-113

Pulitzer, Joseph 1847-1911 . . . . DLB-23

Pulitzer, Joseph, Jr. 1885-1955 . . . . . DLB-29

Pulitzer Prizes for the Novel,
  1917-1945 . . . . DLB-9

Pulliam, Eugene 1889-1975 . . . . DLB-127

Purchas, Samuel 1577?-1626 . . . . . . DLB-151

Purdy, Al 1918- DLB-88

Purdy, James 1923- DLB-2

Purdy, Ken W. 1913-1972 . . . . . . DLB-137

Pusey, Edward Bouverie
  1800-1882 . . . . .DLB-55

Putnam, George Palmer
  1814-1872 . . . . DLB-3, 79

Putnam, Samuel 1892-1950 . . . . .DLB-4

G. P. Putnam's Sons [U.S.] DLB-49

G. P. Putnam's Sons [U.K.] DLB-106

Puzo, Mario 1920- DLB-6

Pyle, Ernie 1900-1945 . . . . .DLB-29

Pyle, Howard 1853-1911 . . . . .DLB-42

Pym, Barbara 1913-1980 . . . . . . DLB-14; Y-87

Pynchon, Thomas 1937- DLB-2

Pyramid Books DLB-46

Pyrnelle, Louise-Clarke 1850-1907 . . .DLB-42

Q

Quad, M. (see Lewis, Charles B.)

Quarles, Francis 1592-1644 . . . . . . .DLB-126

The Quarterly Review
  1809-1967 . . . . .DLB-110

Quasimodo, Salvatore 1901-1968 . . .DLB-114

Queen, Ellery (see Dannay, Frederic, and
  Manfred B. Lee)

The Queen City Publishing House . . .DLB-49

Queneau, Raymond 1903-1976 . . . . . .DLB-72

Quennell, Sir Peter 1905-1993 . . . . .DLB-155

Quesnel, Joseph 1746-1809 . . . . .DLB-99

The Question of American Copyright
  in the Nineteenth Century
  Headnote
  Preface, by George Haven Putnam
  The Evolution of Copyright, by Brander
    Matthews
  Summary of Copyright Legislation in
    the United States, by R. R. Bowker
  Analysis of the Provisions of the
    Copyright Law of 1891, by
    George Haven Putnam
  The Contest for International Copyright,
    by George Haven Putnam
  Cheap Books and Good Books,
    by Brander Matthews DLB-49

Quiller-Couch, Sir Arthur Thomas
  1863-1944 . . . . DLB-135, 153

Quin, Ann 1936-1973 . . . . .DLB-14

Quincy, Samuel, of Georgia ?-? DLB-31

Quincy, Samuel, of Massachusetts
  1734-1789 . . . . .DLB-31

Quinn, Anthony 1915- DLB-122

A Symposium on *The Columbia History of
the Novel* Y-92

Synge, John Millington
1871-1909 . . . . DLB-10, 19

Synge Summer School: J. M. Synge and the
Irish Theater, Rathdrum, County Wiclow,
Ireland Y-93

Syrett, Netta 1865-1943 . . . . DLB-135

T

Taban lo Liyong 1939?- DLB-125

Taché, Joseph-Charles 1820-1894 . . . DLB-99

Tafolla, Carmen 1951- DLB-82

Taggard, Genevieve 1894-1948 . . . . . DLB-45

Tagger, Theodor (see Bruckner, Ferdinand)

Tait, J. Selwin, and Sons DLB-49

Tait's Edinburgh Magazine
1832-1861 . . . . DLB-110

The Takarazaka Revue Company Y-91

Tallent, Elizabeth 1954- DLB-130

Talvj 1797-1870 . . . . DLB-59, 133

Taradash, Daniel 1913- DLB-44

Tarbell, Ida M. 1857-1944 . . . . DLB-47

Tardivel, Jules-Paul 1851-1905 . . . . . . DLB-99

Targan, Barry 1932- DLB-130

Tarkington, Booth 1869-1946 . . . DLB-9, 102

Tashlin, Frank 1913-1972 . . . . DLB-44

Tate, Allen 1899-1979 . . . . DLB-4, 45, 63

Tate, James 1943- DLB-5

Tate, Nahum circa 1652-1715 . . . . . . DLB-80

Tatian circa 830 . . . . DLB-148

Tavčar, Ivan 1851-1923 . . . . DLB-147

Taylor, Bayard 1825-1878 . . . . .DLB-3

Taylor, Bert Leston 1866-1921 . . . . . DLB-25

Taylor, Charles H. 1846-1921 . . . . . . DLB-25

Taylor, Edward circa 1642-1729 . . . . DLB-24

Taylor, Elizabeth 1912-1975 . . . . . . DLB-139

Taylor, Henry 1942- DLB-5

Taylor, Sir Henry 1800-1886 . . . . . . DLB-32

Taylor, Jeremy circa 1613-1667 . . . . DLB-151

Taylor, John
1577 or 1578 - 1653 . . . . DLB-121

Taylor, Mildred D. ?- DLB-52

Taylor, Peter 1917-1994 . . . . Y-81, Y-94

Taylor, William, and Company DLB-49

Taylor-Made Shakespeare? Or Is
"Shall I Die?" the Long-Lost Text
of Bottom's Dream? Y-85

Teasdale, Sara 1884-1933 . . . . DLB-45

The Tea-Table (1725), by Eliza Haywood
[excerpt] DLB-39

Telles, Lygia Fagundes 1924- DLB-113

Temple, Sir William 1628-1699 . . . . DLB-101

Tenn, William 1919- DLB-8

Tennant, Emma 1937- DLB-14

Tenney, Tabitha Gilman
1762-1837 . . . . DLB-37

Tennyson, Alfred 1809-1892 . . . . DLB-32

Tennyson, Frederick 1807-1898 . . . . . DLB-32

Terhune, Albert Payson 1872-1942 . . . DLB-9

Terry, Megan 1932- DLB-7

Terson, Peter 1932- DLB-13

Tesich, Steve 1943- Y-83

Tessa, Delio 1886-1939 . . . . DLB-114

Testori, Giovanni 1923-1993 . . . . . . DLB-128

Tey, Josephine 1896?-1952 . . . . DLB-77

Thacher, James 1754-1844 . . . . DLB-37

Thackeray, William Makepeace
1811-1863 . . . . DLB-21, 55

Thames and Hudson Limited DLB-112

Thanet, Octave (see French, Alice)

The Theater in Shakespeare's
Time DLB-62

The Theatre Guild DLB-7

Thegan and the Astronomer
flourished circa 850 . . . . DLB-148

Thelwall, John 1764-1834 . . . . DLB-93

Theodulf circa 760-circa 821 . . . . . . DLB-148

Theriault, Yves 1915-1983 . . . . DLB-88

Thério, Adrien 1925- DLB-53

Theroux, Paul 1941- DLB-2

Thibaudeau, Colleen 1925- DLB-88

Thielen, Benedict 1903-1965 . . . . . . DLB-102

Thiong'o Ngugi wa (see Ngugi wa Thiong'o)

Third-Generation Minor Poets of the
Seventeenth Century DLB-131

Thoma, Ludwig 1867-1921 . . . . DLB-66

Thoma, Richard 1902- DLB-4

Thomas, Audrey 1935- DLB-60

Thomas, D. M. 1935- DLB-40

Thomas, Dylan
1914-1953 . . . . .DLB-13, 20, 139

Thomas, Edward
1878-1917 . . . . DLB-19, 98, 156

Thomas, Gwyn 1913-1981 . . . . .DLB-15

Thomas, Isaiah 1750-1831 . . . . . . DLB-43, 73

Thomas, Isaiah [publishing house] . . .DLB-49

Thomas, John 1900-1932 . . . . .DLB-4

Thomas, Joyce Carol 1938- DLB-33

Thomas, Lorenzo 1944- DLB-41

Thomas, R. S. 1915- DLB-27

Thomasîn von Zerclære
circa 1186-circa 1259 . . . . .DLB-138

Thompson, David 1770-1857 . . . . . . .DLB-99

Thompson, Dorothy 1893-1961 . . . . .DLB-29

Thompson, Francis 1859-1907 . . . . . .DLB-19

Thompson, George Selden (see Selden, George)

Thompson, John 1938-1976 . . . . .DLB-60

Thompson, John R. 1823-1873 . . . DLB-3, 73

Thompson, Lawrance 1906-1973 . . . .DLB-103

Thompson, Maurice
1844-1901 . . . . DLB-71, 74

Thompson, Ruth Plumly
1891-1976 . . . . .DLB-22

Thompson, Thomas Phillips
1843-1933 . . . . .DLB-99

Thompson, William Tappan
1812-1882 . . . . DLB-3, 11

Thomson, Edward William
1849-1924 . . . . .DLB-92

Thomson, James 1700-1748 . . . . .DLB-95

Thomson, James 1834-1882 . . . . .DLB-35

Thomson, Mortimer 1831-1875 . . . . .DLB-11

Thoreau, Henry David 1817-1862 . . . . .DLB-1

Thorpe, Thomas Bangs
1815-1878 . . . . DLB-3, 11

Thoughts on Poetry and Its Varieties (1833),
by John Stuart Mill DLB-32

Thrale, Hester Lynch (see Piozzi, Hester
Lynch [Thrale])

Thümmel, Moritz August von
1738-1817 . . . . .DLB-97

Thurber, James
1894-1961 . . . . DLB-4, 11, 22, 102

Thurman, Wallace 1902-1934 . . . . . . .DLB-51

Thwaite, Anthony 1930- DLB-40

Thwaites, Reuben Gold
1853-1913 . . . . .DLB-47

Ticknor, George
1791-1871 . . . . DLB-1, 59, 140

Ticknor and Fields DLB-49

Cumulative Index

ISBN 0-8103-5717-8

90000

9 780810 357174

Documentary Series